A Renaissance
Court

A Renaissance Court

Milan under Galeazzo Maria Sforza

Gregory Lubkin

University of California Press
Berkeley / Los Angeles / London

University of California Press
Berkeley and Los Angeles, California

University of California Press
London, England

Copyright © 1994 by
The Regents of the University of California

Library of Congress Cataloging-in-Publication Data
Lubkin, Gregory.
    A Renaissance court: Milan under Galeazzo Maria Sforza /
Gregory Lubkin
        p.   cm.
    Includes bibliographical references and index.
    ISBN 0–520–08146–3 (cloth)
    1. Milan (Italy)—History—To 1535.   2. Galeazzo Maria
Sforza, Duke of Milan, 1444–1476.   3. Milan (Italy)—Court
and courtiers.   4. Renaissance—Italy—Milan.   I. Title.
DG657.87.L83   1994
945′.05—dc20
                                                    93–17529
                                                    CIP

Printed in the United States of America

1 2 3 4 5 6 7 8 9

*This book is dedicated to
my parents,
James and Marianne Lubkin,
and to my late grandfather,
Walther Buchholz,
who opened the way to history for me*

Contents

Preface

This study is the fruit of an accidental obsession. I began graduate school in 1975 with some curiosity about a simple and obvious question: Why did princely courts become so important in later medieval and Renaissance Europe? The classic guide to proper behavior for "a gentleman that lives in courts of princes,"[1] Baldassare Castiglione's *Book of the Courtier,* appeared in this period, creating a model for centuries to follow. By 1700, every European prince worthy of the name had a splendid court or was scrambling to develop one. Those princes emulated the most brilliant manifestation in Western culture of the prince-in-court, Louis XIV of France at Versailles.[2]

In the opening pages of his masterpiece, Castiglione bemoaned the difficulty of choosing ideal forms from among "so many varieties of customs that are used in the courts of Christendom."[3] Notwithstanding the fame of his work, we know little about those customs or the lived reality of his courtly universe. What were courts like in the generations before he established the canons of courtiership? Who came to court, and how and why did they come? What were their occupations and recreations at court? How did they relate to one another and to the prince? How did princes relate to one another through their courts? Where did music, art, and literature fit amid the business of state, and where did all of these matters fit amid the routines of everyday life? Above all, what made the court such a compelling institution in the Renaissance era?

Defining a Princely Court

"I am in time and I speak of time," said [Saint] Augustine, "I do not know what time is." Similarly, I can say that I am in the court and I speak of the court; I do not know—God knows—what the court is. I do know that the court is not time; it is like time, though, changeable and various, space-bound and wandering, "never continuing in one state." When I leave it, I know it thoroughly; when I come back to it, I find little or nothing that I left there. . . . The court is the same, but its members have changed. Perhaps I shall not stray from the truth if I describe the court as Porphyry defines "genus" and call it a multitude of things all standing in a certain relation to one principle [principal]. Certainly we courtiers are a multitude, and a numberless one, and all striving to please one individual. But today we are one multitude; tomorrow we shall be another. The court is not changed, though, it is always the same. . . . If Boethius is right in saying that fortune "is constant only in its changing," then we can truthfully say the same of the court.[4]

After eight hundred years, Walter Map's witty and learned words still ring true. Historians have agreed far more about what happens in a princely court than about what a princely court is. One Italian historian wrote in the late 1970s, "As the following of a prince, the court does not possess a true shape of its own, while as a place in which various forces coalesced, it gives way to an analysis of those forces, figuring only as their site, perhaps the most appropriate."[5]

The royal court of England in which Map lived was one of the great courts in medieval Europe; its protean quality was characteristic of the period. That Angevin court developed from its Anglo-Norman predecessor, which a historian has described in the following terms:

In its strictly feudal aspect, the Curia Regis was the Court to which the King's tenants owed suit and service. . . . But the name "Curia Regis" means more than this. It may mean those great assemblies of the nation, on the three great feast-days of the Church—Easter, Pentecost, and Christmas—"when the king wore his crown." It also meant an assembly of the great men of the kingdom, "congregatis in aula primoribus regni." It was also applied to a meeting for business of the king's household or personal attendants.[6]

Another historian writing on the same topic commented on the occasions when the court reached its fullest extent.

In connection with the three great feasts of the Church, the chroniclers so frequently record that the king "tenuit curiam suam [held his court]" that the phrase is almost technical. The reference is primarily no doubt to an unusual gathering at the social court of the king at which frequently there was great display.

On these feast days the court was attended not only by the king and his magnates but also

by a crowd of persons of lesser rank, clergy of minor dignities, monks and clerks, rear vassals, minor vassals, and officials of all grades. These persons at-

tended upon their lords [and] added to their dignity and consideration. . . .
There is some evidence that . . . the king desired such attendance to increase the
pomp and display of the court.[7]

England was not the only polity in which the princely court was understood to be such a flexible institution. In Renaissance Milan, the ducal secretary Giovanni Simonetta wrote to Duke Galeazzo Maria Sforza about a "little
notebook that I had had made, of the order of the court." Galeazzo had requested an updated transcription of the notebook, and Giovanni reminded
him "that said little notebook, as [Your Lordship] knows, was not made to
keep track in this way of the names of those [persons] of the court, because it
would be necessary to redo it every month, as the persons are changed."[8]

Writing in the 1970s on Renaissance Italy, Lauro Martines asserted that
"at its strictest, a court was the space and personnel around a prince, as he
made laws, received ambassadors, dispatched letters, gave commands, decided cases, made appointments, took his meals, entertained, and proceeded
through the streets."[9] In the seventeenth century, Cesare Ripa defined the
court of his own era in simpler terms, as "a company of well-bred men in
the service of a distinguished superior."[10] A twentieth-century sociologist,
Norbert Elias, saw the court of early modern France as "nothing other than
the vastly extended house and household of the French kings and their dependents, with all the people belonging to it."[11]

The mutability of the peripatetic medieval court evolved into the self-
conscious rigidity of eighteenth-century Versailles, about which Emmanuel
Leroy Ladurie said, "The court does not possess power. But it is in the bosom
of the Court that one can best act on the levers of power; in addition to the
ministers, the members of the great families of mandarin-bureaucrats . . . are
in the Court and marry their children there. Weddings are made ceaselessly;
people encounter one another, socially and otherwise. There is an interpene-
tration and mutual familiarity between the two milieux: bureaucracy and aristocracy."[12] What is often called "the centralization of power" has been widely
viewed as a fundamental dynamic of the court. As Elias put it, the court in
France characterized a society that "concentrates an extraordinary degree of
power in the hands of a single person."[13] In Italy, Martines wrote, "power ra-
diated from the prince . . . [who] was the animating force of the courtly establishment."[14] The meaning of "power" is not so obvious as its confident use by
historians might suggest, but it certainly reflects the enormous range of activities and resources that a prince's authority could affect.

The most extended definition of the princely court in Europe has come
from Sergio Bertelli. In his coffee table book on Italian Renaissance courts,
he produced a potpourri of generalities, drawing heavily from the work of
other historians and anthropologists: "The court . . . may be seen as a microcosm of the state, and as carrying out all the chief business of the state. . . .
The court is . . . the ruler's actual, physical home, where he lives with those

who serve and guard him."[15] Bertelli recognized that a princely court was more than merely a princely residence or center of government: "The theory of the ruler's sacrality set the court yet further apart." He saw that court as a "sacred precinct," "a closed world."[16]

Although studies of princely courts have experienced a resurgence since the mid-1970s, no scholar has produced a precise and comprehensive definition of a princely court.[17] Indeed, an English historian writing in the early 1980s concluded pessimistically, "We must give up hope of defining the 'court' with any precision."[18] Such intellectual despair is unnecessary. The basic meaning of "court" is quite straightforward, and its application to the princely context is not mysterious.

The etymological origins of "court" or *corte,* denote an enclosed or bounded space.[19] The Indo-European root of "court" also appears today in the English word *garden* and the Russian *grad* (city). The sense of this root is evident in various uses of the word "court": architectural courts or court-yards, sports courts (tennis, squash, etc.), and even legal courts. All of these examples take their identity from their enclosed character. None of these enclosed spaces is impermeable or inaccessible, though; being enclosed does not mean being sealed. Persons and objects can pass into and out of a court through designated points of entry and exit. The space can be filled or emptied as appropriate, and the population can change completely from one day to the next without changing the nature or purpose of the space itself. One could use a tennis court or a courtroom for activities other than tennis or legal proceedings, but those activities would generally appear inappropriate.

In the case of a law court, the use of the term "court" extends beyond the physical space. The judge is generally referred to as "the Court," reflecting an institutional identity embodied in a single person. That person sits at the center of the proceedings, while others act at greater or lesser distances from the central point. Each law court also has an institutional identity in terms of its rulings, which may stand long after the individual judges who delivered them have been forgotten.

Similarly, each historical princely court had an institutional identity that distinguished it. The following definition and explication of such a court is the fruit of many years of research, discussion, and reflection. A princely court was the space (physical, social, and ritual), at the center of a princely dominion, in which the ruler customarily lived, worked, and played. That space was essentially inseparable from the persons, objects, and events that formed the substance of the court, although those persons, objects, and events were constantly changing. The purpose of the court was to contain the prince's person and power and to provide a context in which he or she could interact effectively with the rest of the universe. To facilitate that interaction, the prince's agents established and supervised the boundaries, entry points, structures, and activities of the court. The agents' actions were subject to the prince's ultimate authority, but all persons at court acted according to their own understanding of their own interests.

Such self-conscious princely courts did not develop automatically or "organically" around all rulers. Like gardens or cities, they had to be created and maintained with some deliberate effort if they were to remain distinct entities. Princely courts arose only in historical situations with certain social, cultural, and political configurations, but this study is not the place for an extended discussion of such a broad subject.

Why Milan?

It would be very satisfying to make a comparative study of courts in late medieval and Renaissance Europe. When I began this study as a seminar paper in graduate school, I had hoped to make such a comparison between two contemporaneous dukes: Galeazzo Maria Sforza of Milan (1466–1476) and Charles the Bold of Burgundy (1467–1477). Unfortunately, the groundwork had yet to be done; there was no secondary literature that treated either of these courts fully, and secondary literature for Milan in English was very sparse indeed.[20] The first step was to study a single court in some depth, to learn how one could approach this complex subject without either losing touch with the evidence or becoming lost in it.[21]

The duchy of Milan was one of Renaissance Italy's five major powers and the peninsula's wealthiest princely state. It was also located in a strategic position, at the crossroads for economic, cultural, and political activity originating on both sides of the Alps. The capital city itself was one of the largest in Christendom, with a distinguished history. Francesco Sforza, who assumed the ducal throne in 1450, was Jakob Burckhardt's premier example of social mobility in Renaissance Italy.[22]

Because this dominion had always enjoyed close ties to French and German princes as well as the Italian states, it was a promising place to begin asking that nagging question about the importance of the princely court. In the fourteenth century, the Visconti had married into virtually every ruling family in Europe, and in the 1490s, the court of Ludovico Sforza ("il Moro") stood out as one of the truly brilliant products of the High Renaissance.[23]

Since the Visconti archives had been largely destroyed in 1447, it was necessary to work in the Sforza era, which is very richly documented. This study focused initially on the reign of Galeazzo Maria Sforza for practical reasons, because it was neither so controversial nor so lengthy as those of his father, Francesco, son, GianGaleazzo, and brother, Ludovico. In particular, Ludovico's court has been renowned as the Golden Age of Milan, the home of Leonardo and Bramante, a major landmark in the history of the Renaissance. Galeazzo's reign seemed to offer a better opportunity to view a representative Renaissance court in action. It came as a surprise to discover how much information survived from that short-lived court and how important it was.

My investigation of Galeazzo's court was an inquiry without preconceptions. The fifth duke of Milan has been remembered mainly for his dramatic death and some personal excesses that were played up by Machiavelli and other contemporary historians. It took years of research to discover the full dimensions of Galeazzo's fascinating story. The court over which he presided is interesting also for the thousands of men, women, and children who participated in it during the duke's ten-year reign. They had their own stories, and the interactions between them provide vital material for understanding why the court became so important in Renaissance Europe.

Sources

Until quite recently, only two English-speaking historians had devoted their main research focus to Milan: Vincent Ilardi in the United States and Daniel Bueno de Mesquita in Britain. Both have contributed fundamentally to the field, especially in the areas of political, diplomatic, and administrative history. Ilardi has provided a particularly valuable service by making Milanese archival material more widely available. Recently, scholars have begun probing the interplay of politics and the arts in Renaissance Milan: Gary Ianziti has worked on humanist historiography, Diana Robin has written on Francesco Filelfo, and Evelyn Samuels Welch has assembled much useful information related to painting and architecture. Nevertheless, important gaps still remain to be filled. Among other things, no general history of Sforza Milan and its rulers has appeared in English since Cecilia Ady published one in 1907.[24]

Italian-language scholarship on the duchy of Milan has flourished in recent years, especially under the aegis of Giorgio Chittolini. His own work has focused on regional political issues, and he has coordinated extensive work by others on related topics. Riccardo Fubini has contributed exhaustive research on political and diplomatic history. Many other scholars have also generated articles and essays on various aspects of the Sforza dominion; the greatest contribution has come from Caterina Santoro, the *doyenne* of Milanese administrative history. Several general histories have been produced since World War II; the most comprehensive is the multivolume *Storia di Milano* published by the Fondazione Treccani degli Alfieri.[25]

This study has been written largely from collections in the Archivio di Stato di Milan, supplemented by crucial documents in other Milanese repositories. The Sforza archives in Milan are remarkably extensive, preserving much of the material so diligently gathered by the dukes' Privy Chancery

(*Cancelleria Segreta*). In addition, substantial collections of notarial, family, and institutional archives provide sources on other aspects of Milanese life. For the reign of Galeazzo Maria Sforza alone, the Archivio di Stato, Milan, holds millions of pages of administrative documents, personal letters, diplomatic correspondence, formal documents and notarial briefs, records from religious houses and local governments, and more.[26] Further material can be found in the Archivio Civico of Milan, the Biblioteca Ambrosiana, and other local archives and libraries.[27] For a complete study of the court and everyone involved in it, one would need to investigate every municipal and family archive in Lombardy, Liguria, and Canton Ticino as well as a host of other locations in Italy and elsewhere.

Some of the most revealing information on the Sforza court comes from letters that ambassadors sent to their principals, especially in Mantua, Florence, and Ferrara. These envoys could dare to put on paper facts and opinions that would have been far too dangerous to preserve within the duke's own dominion. It is fortunate that some of these colorful letters have survived, for Galeazzo's court had neither a Castiglione to express contemporary values nor a St.-Simon to describe events and personalities. The most interesting historical narrative by a contemporary figure is the relevant section of Bernardino Corio's history of Milan. Corio had firsthand experience of Galeazzo's court, but his story proves often to be unreliable when compared with other sources.[28] We must find our own way through the court of Milan under Galeazzo Maria Sforza.

Acknowledgments

This study took fifteen years to reach its final form, and dozens of people contributed to it, directly or indirectly. I am grateful to all of them and want here to acknowledge some of their contributions. First, I would like to thank those organizations whose financial support made this study possible, beginning with a Fulbright–Hays scholarship, which facilitated my dissertation research, and an Italian-American Fellowship at the University of California, Berkeley. For postdoctoral support, I am grateful to the Wellesley College Mellon Committee, the American Council of Learned Societies, and, above all, the National Institute of Humanities and Harvard University Center for Italian Renaissance Studies, for a year in scholars' heaven at Villa I Tatti.

I owe to Gene Brucker the opportunity to pursue this project as a seminar project and a dissertation. Thanks are due also to others who taught me much at UC Berkeley: Thomas Barnes, William Bouwsma, Stanley Brandes, Robert Brentano, Natalie Z. Davis, and Randolph Starn. Eugene Irschick shared many insights in postdoctoral discussions. Colleagues and friends in the United States helped me greatly, especially Richard Curtis, Mark Fissel, and Kidder Smith from Berkeley; Frances Gouda, Jonathan Knudsen, and Katherine Park at Wellesley College; and Simon Schama, David Harris Sacks, Elisabeth Swain, and other members of the Cambridge Symposium on Early Modern History. For my work in Milan, thanks go to Giorgio Chittolini, Franca Leverotti, Carlo Paganini, Enrico Gavazzeni, and Grazioso Sironi, as well as my archive companions, Susan Caroselli, Giuliana Fantoni, Fulvia Martinelli, Richard Skinner, and Richard Schofield; and my friends, Luciano and Angela Battistoni, Enzo Pellegrini, and Margherita Uras. Among colleagues encountered while I was at Villa I Tatti, I benefited particularly from the contributions of Paul Barolsky, Bonnie Bennett, Giulia Calvi, Salvatore Camporeale, Bill Connell, Janez Höfler, Bill Kent, Honey Meconi, Diamante Ordine, David Quint, Charles Robertson, Thomas Roche, Patricia Rubin, Janice Shell, and Joanna Woods–Marsden. I am very grateful for the valuable assistance of the staff at Villa I Tatti and the Biblioteca Berenson. My thanks to Craig Hugh Smyth, for inviting me to speak at a 1984 conference there, and to Louis George Clubb, for her directorship while I was a fellow.

For their encouragement of my work as it evolved into a book, I want to thank John Larner, Peter Davis, the late Eric Cochrane, and, above all, my patient editor, Stan Holwitz. Thanks also to all the staff at the University of California Press who contributed their expertise, as well as the first anonymous outside reader of the manuscript, who saw it clearly. Parts of the book have appeared, in substantially different form, in *International History Review, Mitteilungen des Kunsthistorichen Institutes in Florenz,* and *Florence and Milan: Comparisons and Relations,* II (Florence, 1989).

Several people deserve special thanks, beginning with my mentor in Sforza history, Vincent Ilardi, and my colleagues in court studies, Jane Bestor and Evelyn Samuels Welch. Krista Jackson and Ellen Donnelly gave their help and enthusiasm for several years each. Pamela Sichta, Alexa Mason, Fiorella Superbi Gioffredi, and James Lubkin offered vital assistance near the finish line. Gary Bozek read the manuscript and encouraged me to find my own voice. Chögyam Trungpa taught me profoundly about the court's importance. Sabine Eiche deserves extraordinary recognition for her many contributions; my gratitude for her generosity cannot be overstated. Finally, I would like to acknowledge my daughter, Sasha, whose entire life has been shadowed by my work on Milan, and my wife, Kathleen, for her strong support of a project that had me "commuting every day to the fifteenth century."

Author's Notes

Units of Money

Prices and wages in Sforza Milan could be figured in several different monetary units. The two units of account used most commonly during the reign of Galeazzo Maria Sforza were the imperial pound (*libra* or *lira*) and the ducat, which was based on the Venetian unit of the same name and worth roughly the same as the Florentine florin. The pound was divided in the classical Roman manner into 20 *soldi* of 12 *denari* each. The ducat was worth about 80 *soldi*, thus, 4 pounds. A third unit used frequently was the florin of 32 *soldi* (thus, 1.6 pounds or 0.4 ducat). The actual value of coins varied considerably, depending on their metal content and the current ducal monetary policy. Gold was the standard, but it was rarely used in actual transactions; most money was made of silver, and the least valuable coins, of base metal.

While it is difficult to translate the monetary units into modern currency, their relative value can be gauged from some examples. In 1463, one pound's weight of cheese cost 2 or 3 soldi; a pound of wax, 7 soldi; a pound of pork, 1 *soldo,* 6 denari; a pound of veal, 1 soldo, 10 *denari*; a pound of nutmeg or cinnamon, 24 *soldi*; a pound of fine sugar, 15 *soldi*. One *staio* of "good bread" (enough for one person for two weeks) cost 8 *soldi*. In 1476, a good horse could cost 40 ducats. That year, the annual salary of most ducal councillors—who were paid very well—was around 237 ducats. In 1474, a house in Milan fit for such a councillor could cost 1,250 to 1,600 ducats. (For food cost source, see chap. 2; for other figures, see chap. 5.)

A Note on Language

The men and women of the Sforza court spoke and wrote a language considerably different from modern Italian. Even some common names are barely recognizable; "Giovanni" was often spelled "Zohane" or "Zohanne" and could also appear as "Johane," "Johanne," "Zuanne," and so forth. I have modernized the spelling of most names, leaving in quotation marks those for which I found no obvious modern equivalent. Except for a few very well-known names, such as GianGaleazzo Visconti or GianGiacomo Trivulzio, all such double Christian names have been left as two words, as they are in the original documents (e.g., Pietro Francesco Visconti).

Except where noted, I have made all translations from both primary and secondary sources. In this regard, I am grateful for the generous help of many friends and colleagues over the years. All remaining errors are strictly my own. Because of space limitations, I have been unable to include the original text for most passages cited.

Glossary

Cameriere: "Chamberlain" or "valet" are approximate translations, but there is no exact English equivalent.

Cameriere di camera: "Chamberlain of the chamber"; assigned to serve in the duke's bedchamber and to accompany his person.

Cameriere di guardacamera: "Chamberlain of the antechamber/wardroom"; assigned to serve in the chamber adjacent to the duke's bedchamber and to accompany his person.

Cameriere fuori di camera: "Chamberlain outside the chamber"; generally assigned to prestigious household-related work outside the duke's personal presence and innermost chambers.

Sottocameriere: "Underchamberlain"; generally young in age, assigned to tasks involving some intimacy with the duke but not generally as companions.

Collaterale: Comptroller or bookkeeper.

Commissario: Commissar. For a city, the top ducal civil officer, responsible for political matters; often combined with the position of podesta. The ducal administration also included *commissari* who supervised specific activities, such as military administration or construction work.

Galuppo: Mounted servant, with various military and civil functions. A position of low prestige, generally, and not closely linked to the court.

Gentiluomo: Gentleman. The term *gentiluomo* (pl. *gentiluomini*) could be applied generally to anyone who might be considered a "gentleman." It was used often in the Sforza court as a technical term for a specific position within the court: a courtier with a substantial income and high rank, assigned to perform dignified duties in the duke's or duchess's court (and in a few cases, both). The activities of these courtiers varied according to whether they served the duke or the duchess, and some *gentiluomini* had particular responsibilities; for details, see chapter 5. In this study, the more specific usage has been left in the original language, while the more general usage has been translated.

Iconomo: Officer responsible for some local ecclesiastical administration.

Referendario: Supervisor of fiscal activities for local governments.

Referendari-generale had that responsibility for the entire dominion.

Regolatori: Senior fiscal officials.

Archival
Abbreviations

ACM   Archivio Storico Civico, Milan
     BT   Biblioteca Trivulziana

ASMa   Archivio di Stato, Mantua
     AG   Archivio Gonzaga, Corrispondenze Estere, E.XLIX.3
        (b.: *busta* number)

ASMi   Archivio di Stato, Milan
     AS   Archivio (Ducale) Sforzesco (c.: *cartella* number)
     RM   Registri delle Missive

ASMo   Archivio di Stato, Modena
     CDE   Cancelleria Ducale Estense
     DA   Dispacci di Ambasciatori (b.: *busta* number)
     CE   Carteggio Estero (Principi)

ASF   Archivio di Stato, Florence
     MAP   Mediceo avanti il Principato (f.: *filza* number)

SSL   Società Storica Lombarda
     RF   Raccolta Formentini

ASL   *Archivio Storico Lombardo* (periodical)

Secondary sources have been cited in the notes by the author's surname and a short title only. See the bibliography for full publication information on all such works.

Prologue (March 1466)

It is a few days before the Ides of March, in the Year of Our Lord 1466. The winter wind whips through the Gran Croce pass over the Alps. A small band of riders makes its way carefully along the trail, huddling inside their heavy cloaks. One of them feels especially aggrieved by this bitter ride through the mountains. He should be riding in triumph and glory at the head of a great procession, cheered on by admirers and well-wishers. Instead, he travels furtively in a merchant's disguise, with only a few companions. He itches to throw off his drab garments and proclaim himself proudly, but this grim high land is full of bandits and renegades. He fears what will happen if the local people discover that he is Galeazzo Maria Sforza, new duke of Milan.

Twenty-two-year-old Galeazzo was in France with a military expedition when his ducal father Francesco died unexpectedly on March 8. To take his place at the head of the great Sforza dominion, the young heir is hurrying home, without regard for the season, across the Alpine ranges of the duchy of Savoy. Savoy is potentially hostile territory; Galeazzo's mother—Duchess Bianca Maria Visconti—and the Milanese Privy Council have instructed him to take precautions that may safeguard his life and freedom.[1] Thus, the proud young duke hides his identity, traveling in clandestine shame with his handful of followers.

In the event, these precautions are not only humiliating and demoralizing to Galeazzo; they are also inadequate. As the little band of Milanese descends from the pass, it is sighted by a crowd of the local men, who approach the travelers menacingly. Their lords are no friends to Milan or its duke and have little concern for anyone's safety on these mountain roads. The crowd presses

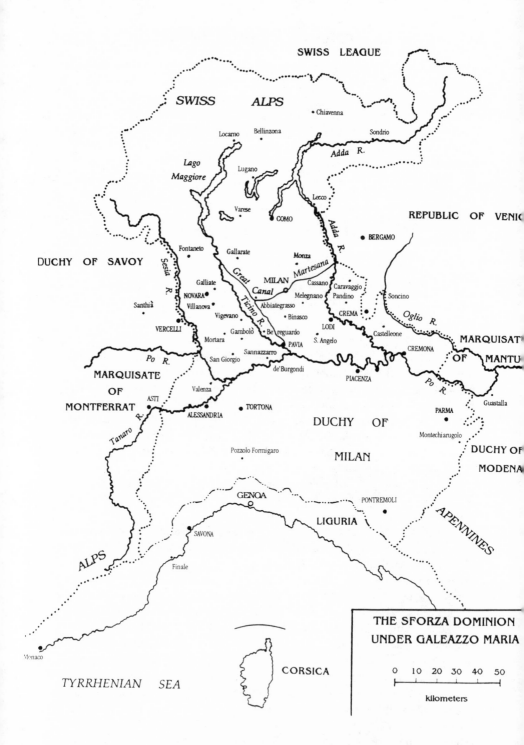

SWISS LEAGUE

SWISS ALPS

- Chiavenna

Locarno   Bellinzona   Sondrio

Lago   *Adda R.*
Maggiore   Lugano

Varese   Lecco

COMO   REPUBLIC OF VENIC

Fontaneto   Gallarate   • BERGAMO

DUCHY OF SAVOY   *Monza*

Galliate   *Great*   MILAN   *Martesana*
NOVARA•   *Canal*   Cassano
Santhià   Melegnano   Caravaggio   • Soncino
Villanova   *Ticino R.*   Abbiategrasso   Pandino
Vigevano   • Binasco   CREMA   *Oglio R.*
VERCELLI   Gambolò   Be' reguardo   LODI   Castelleone
Mortara   PAVIA   S. Angelo   CREMONA   MARQUISAT
Po R.   San Giorgio   Sannazzarro   OF
MARQUISATE   de'Burgondi   PIACENZA   MANTU
OF   *Po   R.*
MONTFERRAT   ASTI   Valenza   Guastalla
Tanaro R.   ALESSANDRIA   • TORTONA   PARMA
                                            DUCHY   OF   Montechiarugolo
                Pozzolo Formigaro   DUCHY OF
                                    MILAN   MODENA
                    GENOA
                                PONTREMOLI
                            LIGURIA   *APENNINES*
ALPS   SAVONA
    Finale

Monaco   THE SFORZA DOMINION
                                            UNDER GALEAZZO MARIA
TYRRHENIAN   SEA   CORSICA
                                    0 10 20 30 40 50

                                            kilometers

in on the travelers, surrounding them and threatening capture. Galeazzo and his companions see a small church nearby, their only hope for refuge. They find sanctuary within, barricade the doors, and wait to be rescued.

For two cold, miserable days, the new ruler of Italy's richest princely state becomes the ignominious prey of a peasant mob. A diplomatic crisis ensues. Count Antonio da Romagnano, a venerable Piedmontese of great learning and considerable influence, intercedes with the ducal government in Turin and the local castellans. Other notables give their support; a Milanese merchant lobbies the Savoyard ducal councillors and lends money to the messengers racing back and forth on this terrible case. Antonio soon secures Galeazzo's release and safe passage, and the duke resumes the road to Milan.

On March 20, 1466, the newly freed prince enters his capital city and is formally enthroned. Antonio da Romagnano is quickly rewarded with an appointment to Milan's Privy Council and an honored place at the Sforza court.[2] Although he is forty years older than Galeazzo, Antonio will outlive his new master. Charming, ambitious, and intelligent, the young duke has every reason to expect a glorious destiny, but a harsher fate awaits him. Galeazzo Maria Sforza will leave his ducal life ten years later in as violent and shadowy a manner as he begins his reign in March 1466. And yet, during his reign, "this duke Galeazzo held the most beautiful court of any prince in Italy."[3]

1

"The Second Prince and Lord in Italy"

The Milanese Dominion and Its Rulers

Galeazzo Maria Sforza entered Milan as its duke on March 20, 1466. When he died, a chronicler from Ferrara remarked, "He was the second prince and lord in Italy." The chronicler went on to explain, "That is, the first was and is the Most Serene Lord King Ferdinand King of Naples, and for the second the . . . duke."[1] At the time, the Milanese dominion held greater wealth and military power than any other princely state in Italy. Yet, accepted practice still ranked the duchy behind the kingdom of Naples—and all other Christian kingdoms—in honor and dignity. The Sforza dukes' feudal overlord, Holy Roman Emperor Frederick III, did not even recognize this young dynasty as the legitimate lords of Milan.

Such tensions between Sforza aspirations and external limitations gave a dynamic twist to the colorful story of this Renaissance court. Conditions internal to the dominion created the foundations for the court's rich and volatile character. Renaissance Milan was a challenging dominion to govern. Not a single one of its nine dukes came to the throne without a struggle and left it peacefully through a natural death. The prosperity and sophistication of the Lombard state made a lavish and populous ducal court possible; political conditions made the creation and maintenance of such a court desirable.

Political Geography of the Dominion

The challenge of maintaining a unified Milanese dominion was rooted in a diversity visible at the most basic geographic level. In 1466, the Sforza dominion included most of western Lombardy, the western half of Emilia, all of

Liguria, and what is now Italian Switzerland. This area was compact, but its topography was varied, with the great Po plain in the center sandwiched between two major mountain ranges. The Alps guarded the north, while the Apennines shielded the Sforza dominion from the south, falling away in Liguria to the coast of the Tyrrhenian Sea. Although the state was relatively secure from those directions, its eastern and western boundaries stretched across the open Po valley, in places bordering the often-hostile states of Venice and Savoy. Milan stood at a crossroads between the Italian peninsula and transalpine Europe, on the main overland routes between Rome or Florence to the south and France or Germany to the north.

The economic character of the duchy reflected this geographic configuration.[2] The ultimate base of the economy was agricultural, farming the rich lands of the great Po plain. Lombardy was essentially self-sufficient in the production of food and most other staples. Some of the Sforza dukes even sought to improve agricultural production and presided over such innovations as the cultivation of rice, which became the most successful cereal crop in the region.[3]

The greatest wealth in this wealthy state, though, derived from the prosperous cities that had long been part of the Lombard landscape. Milan itself was one of the largest cities in Christendom, with thriving industries in armory and cloth manufacture as well as extensive trade. During the later fifteenth century, when the Sforza ruled, manufacture of luxury cloth became the single most important industry for the Milanese economy, with silks, satins, velvets, and brocades being made in considerable quantities.[4] Milan's markets were international; it had few rivals as a center for armor manufacture during the fifteenth century. Genoa, which the Sforza dukes held as a French fief, ranked just behind Venice as an Italian port and center for commerce with the eastern Mediterranean. Other cities of the dominion did not enjoy such size or stature, but they prospered in their own spheres. Alessandria, Como, Cremona, Lodi, Novara, Parma, Pavia, Piacenza, and Tortona were the provincial centers around which the Sforza administration organized its other districts.[5]

These urban centers were linked by relatively efficient and reliable means of transportation and communication. In particular, the many rivers flowing from the Alps and Apennines provided a rapid and economical way to convey both cargo and passengers. Throughout medieval Europe, travel by water was almost always faster and more comfortable than travel by land. The city of Milan proper was serviced by a network of canals, some within the city and others linking the capital to the great rivers Adda and Ticino to the east and west. The Naviglio Grande (Great Canal), which still runs from Milan to Abbiategrasso, provided an easy route by which the dukes could travel to their hunting grounds across the Ticino.

The farms and cities of plain and coast constituted the productive core of the Sforza dominion. The mountains contributed little wealth but formed the backbone of the duchy's defense system. They blocked overland invasion routes and provided a home for the feudal way of life that still dominated much of this area in the later fifteenth century. The traditional political structures of the Sforza dominion reflected their geographic roots. In the Alps to the north and the Apennines to the south, the great feudatories operated often with virtual autonomy. In the lands of the Po plain bordering the territories of Modena and Mantua, other major feudal holdings formed a buffer between princely states. In the central area of the dominion, the villages and farms generally belonged to smaller feudal holdings, while the great cities continued a tradition of urban republicanism with roots dating back beyond the Lombard League. Genoa and Liguria recalled the great commercial empires of the Mediterranean and the closely knit noble clans who had ruled the city and coast for centuries. Every region, city, and feudal holding had its own traditions and interests, and most of them resisted the rule of lords from outside.

Rural Politics and Society

By far the greater part of the duchy of Milan was held in feudal tenure by vassals of the duke. The traditional military aristocracy of the countryside was deeply entrenched in parts of the dominion, especially the Apennines. Such great clans as the Pallavicini and Malaspina could boast lineages of staggering antiquity and proud titles granted by legendary kings or emperors. When Galeazzo threatened to deprive a Pallavicino courtier of his ancestral territory, the noble pleaded that "for about eight hundred years that place of Ravarono has been . . . my family's [de casa mia]."[6]

Only a handful of families could claim continuous possession of major fiefs. Most of the feudatories in Galeazzo's dominion had held their estates for two or three generations at most. In the drive to centralize authority, the great Visconti lords, especially GianGaleazzo, the first duke, had sought to uproot the entrenched feudality and neutralize any threat it might pose to political unification under the prince. However, a constant need for money drove the dukes, both Visconti and Sforza, to refeudalize the duchy, granting out again the land that had been recovered.[7]

The most powerful feudatories in Duke Galeazzo's time were not the most ancient clans. For instance, a veritable "Pallavicino state" had developed in the middle of the century, but after the death of the family head, the estates were divided among his sons and the "state" lost its integrity.[8] Three Pallavicini served on Galeazzo's council of state, and several others acted as military commanders or courtiers.[9] The once-mighty Malaspina had also suffered a diminution of power as a result of divided holdings. The most potent feudal lords under Galeazzo were actually parvenus who had capitalized on refeudalization and the difficulties of transition between the Visconti and Sforza dynasties. The feudatory most capable of exercising true autonomy was Pier Maria Rossi, count of San Secondo. His large and prosperous holdings in the district of Parma also became a virtual "state," its independence facilitated by its distance from Milan.[10] The Rossi were an important family in Parma, but they did not achieve a dominant position until the fifteenth century. Pier Maria held dozens of castles. Twenty-one of them were depicted at his favorite residence, in a Bembo fresco that combines a statement of political domination with a vivid illustration of *amour courtois*. Galeazzo had little effective authority in this region, but Pier Maria caused few problems and even served faithfully on the ducal Privy Council.[11]

Another powerful and independent-minded count, Giovanni Borromeo, held an almost autonomous fief in the Alps around Lago Maggiore. He felt so secure in his holdings that he could risk standing up to a ducal demand and incurring Galeazzo's wrath. Giovanni's social stature can be measured by the marriage connections of his immediate family. His sisters married a Rossi councillor, a Visconti lord, and a Rusca count, and his eleven children married into such distinguished families as Visconti, Medici, Pallavicino, Trivulzio, and Hohenzollern of Brandenburg.[12] Yet, the "Borromeo state" had been in the family's hands only half a century, since Giovanni's father, a wealthy Milanese merchant, had bought the lands and title from Duke Filippo Maria Visconti.[13]

The great feudatories had their own systems of justice, their own rights of appointment to benefices, their own networks of patronage. They employed the same artists as the dukes to decorate residences and illuminate manuscripts; they could even marry into princely families. Although they were not many in number, they played an important role in the duchy, and they could not be ignored. Among other things, these noblemen held strategic geographic positions that no duke could afford to lose, and in the feudal tradition, all of the feudatories could call on local military support to help them hold those positions.

A number of counts palatine bore titles received directly from the emperor. Theoretically, their feudal position bypassed the duke's authority; in practice, most could not survive without the duke's cooperation, and this honor had little meaning. The great majority of the feudatories held their lands and titles from the dukes, under terms colored by the process of refeudalization. Because these vassals lacked continuity of signorial tenure from the preducal era, most also lacked full authority. The dukes insisted that certain legal rights remain in their princely hands, including high (i.e., capital) justice and such revenue sources as the salt *gabelle*. Even Cicco Simonetta, who held the position of first secretary under the early Sforza dukes, was required to pay the *gabelle* on his feudal holdings.[14]

Urban Society

The basic nature of a medieval town was communal and republican, a reaction against feudal hierarchy. Civic office was a crucial part of the commune; even in Renaissance Italy, local councils and offices continued to play important roles, both symbolically and functionally. In the Sforza duchy of Milan, such well-established councils as the Anziani of Parma enjoyed broad latitude to determine the policies of their respective cities. The duke was politically and fiscally represented in the major cities by his *commissario* and *referendario,* respectively.[15]

Although the feeling for self-government, or *libertà,* was strong in the major cities of the Sforza dominion, all of those cities had given way to local and regional lords (*signori*) at some time during the fourteenth and fifteenth centuries. None of the cities had expelled their nobility; consequently, their political systems could be dominated by great families with roots in the country. In some cities, the political factions were identified directly with these feudal patrons.[16] In others, the traditional labels of "Guelf" and "Ghibelline" continued to identify factions centuries after they had lost their original meaning of allegiance to pope and emperor. In 1476, the duke's *commissario* at Cremona prohibited the use of those terms; the fine for each violation was 130 ducats, a sum few men could earn in a year.[17]

Each city had its own particular history, tradition, and value to the state as a whole. Pavia was the second city of the dominion, the traditional rival of nearby Milan and the seat of a large ducal castle. For centuries, Pavia had harbored exiles and rebels from its larger and more powerful neighbor.[18] Under the Sforza, it was the site of the dominion's university, originally founded by the Visconti. The Milanese dukes also kept their large library in Pavia, which they considered their intellectual and cultural capital.[19] Genoa never belonged to the duchy of Milan proper and never accepted the Sforza lordship easily. The memory of independence was always too strong, as was the taste for infighting among the powerful noble *alberghi* of the city. The duke ruled the great port city through a resident vice-governor; it was the only part of his territory in which the threat of military force was usually needed.[20]

Each of the provincial cities had its native aristocracy, and the Sforza court drew heavily from those elites. Some court members belonged to such families as the Beccaria (Pavia), Rusca (Como), and Ponzoni (Cremona), whose ancestors had ruled as *signori* in their home cities. Of course, elites composed a minority of the duke's subjects; the great bulk of the populace consisted of peasants and workers. The city of Milan had a particularly large and active population of artisans, who provided the main support for the short-lived Ambrosian Republic (1447–1450). Under ducal rule, these people exercised little political influence outside their own occupations and neighborhoods.

Neighborhoods constituted an important point of reference in cities of the Sforza dominion. In Milan itself, the six *Porte* (quarters of the city, each named for the major gate in the walls located within its boundaries) provided a vehicle for social identification that was recognized and used by everyone. When the duke married in 1468, he invited the wives of nobles and other prominent citizens to attend the wedding, and the ducal Chancery divided the list of invitees by *Porte*.[21]

Women in Lombard Society

The list of women invited to attend Galeazzo's wedding illustrates the extent to which Lombard society was dominated by men. With the exception of Galeazzo's half-sister Drusiana and "Brigida de Cittadinis, wife of the Church," the two hundred women were listed only as wives (or daughters, daughters-in-law, or fiancées) of the prominent men who provided their political identity: "The wife of Sir Branda Castiglione," "The daughter-in-law of Giovanni Corio," "The wife of the Magnificent lord Pietro Pusterla, and his daughters and daughter-in-law," and so forth. We do not even know from this source who these women were. The social recognition they received derived almost entirely from the men with whom they were most closely linked by blood and by marriage.

Most women in the higher ranks of Lombard society had no choice about their marriage partners; their alliances were a function of political, social, and economic strategies. When Galeazzo was twenty-five years old himself, he arranged the marriage of his sister Elisabetta to his client and *condottiere,* Marquess Guglielmo VIII Paleologo of Montferrat. Following the usual procedure of the time, Galeazzo "had his sister seen [by Guglielmo's representatives], whether she has the physical capacity [*membra et persona*] to be able to bear children."[22] Guglielmo was literally five times her age; Elisabetta said, "I always feared I'd have an old husband, and now I have one." An ambassador who knew the family intimately commented, "I believe her conscience will bother her, seeming that she is going to bed with her father."[23]

A pleasing appearance and a docile disposition were generally considered to be positive attributes for young women from prominent Lombard families. Obesity was not.[24] As such women married, grew older, and bore children, their physical charms became less important than their ability to run a household, rear their children, and contribute in other ways to their husbands' and families' interests. However, women had limited legal rights in Lombard law and custom. Although they could participate in a wide range of activities, they generally needed an adult male to act as their proxies in making contracts and other legal documents. They were also restricted from inheriting property and titles in their own names, although they could transmit property to husbands or children. Widows enjoyed greater freedom of action and, in some cases, could control substantial properties in the names of their minor children.

One widow who appeared occasionally in connection with Galeazzo's court was Maddalena Torelli, *née* del Carretto, daughter of a Ligurian marquess. Her husband, Pietro, had been count of Guastalla, a large and strategically located holding between the states of Milan, Mantua, and Modena. She played an active role as their sons' guardian from Pietro's death in 1460 until her son Guido Galeotto left his minority in 1474. Among other things, sources show her hosting a dinner party for visiting dignitaries, lodging guests for the duke's wedding, and supervising the transfer of Guido's belongings to the court at Pavia in 1474.[25]

The awkward position of a woman, even of Maddalena's status, is evident in a violent dispute that arose between her and Guido before he left her tutelage. The duke himself stepped in to resolve the dispute, designating as mediator the resident Mantuan ambassador, Zaccaria Saggi da Pisa, a longtime member of the Milanese court and a "friend and confidant" of both parties. Guido was demanding control of his share of his father's estate, which Maddalena had handled for fourteen years. Galeazzo gave him "half of all the revenues, of which he can dispose as his things," along with those pieces of his father's furniture that Zaccaria thought Guido needed for his own use. Guido's younger brother, Francesco, had a right to the other half of the estate; the duke decided that, until Francesco attained his majority, his part would remain "in the administration" of Maddalena, as did "the governance of their lands, so long as it . . . will please us."[26]

The duke left Zaccaria to sort out such matters as Maddalena's dowry and arrangements for her four daughters. A dowry was no small thing, especially for a woman of high rank; it was usually all that she possessed in her own name, besides clothes and other personal items. Without a substantial dowry, a young woman from the higher ranks of society could never expect to find a husband of suitable worth. Her parents might even consign her to a convent for life rather than suffer the shame of a dishonorable match.

The Church and Social Control

The institutions of the Roman Catholic Church played a significant role in the Sforza dominion. All of the major cities were episcopal seats, and the archdiocese of Milan had traditionally provided the framework for Lombard unity. One of the Sforza dukes' greatest assets was the authority to grant benefices, uniting secular and ecclesiastical patronage in their princely hands.[27] The mendicant orders were also highly visible; they were more widely respected for their spiritual calling than were the secular clergy or the cloistered houses of monks and nuns, some of which held very substantial properties.

Although heresy had been rife in thirteenth- and fourteenth-century Lombardy, there is little evidence of it by 1466. Control of religious manifestations still formed a crucial part of public order, though, leading to prohibition of debates between Franciscans and Dominicans over the Immaculate Conception of the Blessed Virgin Mary. Displays of open disagreement about religious dogma were potentially subversive, as they could lead to the questioning of authority at all levels.[28] Even public preaching by Franciscans was licensed in some situations only on condition that "they do not concern themselves with matters of state."[29]

The spiritual health of the duke's subjects was an important part of the duke's princely obligation and closely linked to the general health of the body politic. In 1468, the ducal Office of Health investigated an alleged miracle at a village near Milan; the Virgin Mary had supposedly appeared to a farm boy, then left a miraculous fountain behind. Local residents were dunking themselves in the fountain to gain relief from their ailments. The officials' report not only denied the efficacy of the fountain but also condemned the whole idea of "this frivolous and vain religion, . . . this erroneous and false opinion that is against every institute of the church."[30]

Alien elements that did not have a stable role in traditional Christian society were also considered inimical to good order. Duke Galeazzo commanded all gypsies ("cinghali, sive nominati 'de Egypto'") to leave his dominion within three to four days and all Jews to wear a yellow circle on their clothes.[31] The duchy of Milan hosted a Jewish population that was particularly active in commerce and medicine. Although he marked Jews as an alien element in the dominion, Galeazzo employed Jewish physicians for members of his own household and protected their legal interests as he would those of any other ducal servant.[32] His relations with his Jewish subjects were generally cordial, and he carefully maintained their presence in his dominion. During Lent one year, the duke received complaints from Jews in Pavia about a preacher stirring up the populace to run them out of the city. The duke commanded his castellan to stop the preacher, because he would be upset if the Jews were driven out, and "the Jews' residence in the lands of Christians has always been tolerated, especially in those of Holy Church."[33]

The Milanese dominion also attracted a large number of immigrants and transients, in part because of the strategic location of Milan on major trade routes between northern and southern Europe. Immigrants were attracted by the relatively tolerant policies of Milan's rulers, whose state showed both great economic vitality and reasonable political stability. Some of the new arrivals had been specifically invited by the ducal administration, to bring important innovations to Milan. Among them were specialists who helped establish the manufacture of silk cloth, the cultivation and milling of rice, and the remarkable ducal choir.

Milan: The Commune and the Visconti

The combinations of political elements active in the Sforza dominion created a configuration that was difficult to control. The strengths of the urban and feudal sectors gave them resilience and leverage in dealing with their ruler. Although the various cities showed structural similarities, each developed quite distinctly and cherished its own traditions and prerogatives. The sense of local identification (*campanilismo*) was quite strong, and throughout the Visconti-Sforza era, resentments arose against domination by external political forces. During the period of Visconti rule (1277–1447), almost every major provincial city revolted at some point when the central authority was weak and operated independently for a brief period under the leadership of a local nobleman or condottiere.[34]

Even the capital city of the Lombard dominion was uncertain ground for its rulers. The Milanese did not generally identify themselves closely with their masters, especially when those masters were "foreigners" and parvenus, as were the Sforza.[35] For all its size and wealth, though, Milan rarely enjoyed the strong sense of communal identity that characterized many of the great cities of later medieval Europe. The city's symbol was its patron saint, Ambrose, the bishop who had coerced a Roman emperor into acknowledging the supremacy of the church. In his time (the late fourth century A.D.), Milan was the capital of the empire. The legacy of Ambrose shaped Milan's medieval experience, and until the High Middle Ages, the lord of the city was the archbishop. Milan maintained its preeminence as the capital of Lombardy because his ecclesiastical authority extended throughout the region.[36]

The city did have a strong commercial base and a substantial secular nobility (*grandi*). When it received recognition of autonomy from Frederick Barbarossa in 1183, its communal structure was dominated by nobles and great merchants. As in other Italian cities, these elites became embroiled in factional conflict within the walls; in Milan, the factions of the city were never fully reconciled. In the thirteenth century, the struggle manifested between the *grandi* and the common people, led by the merchants. Their respective factions operated two separate governments that warred openly against one another. In the course of these conflicts, strife within the nobility led to the Della Torre family assuming leadership of the popular party. Their rivals for dominance on the Milanese political scene were the Visconti.

The Visconti family name indicates the origins of their political power.

Under the archiepiscopal regime, the archbishop himself was considered the "count" (in Latin, *comes*; in Italian, *conte*). Their lieutenants included a military leader with the title of "viscount" (*vicecomes* or *visconte*). The position became hereditary in a family that then adopted the title as its surname. By the mid-thirteenth century, though, the Visconti had sold back to the commune their last remaining rights from this office. At that time, the family political fortunes were at low ebb.

The Della Torre and their faction enjoyed a brief period of dominance. Then the Visconti triumphed in 1277 under the leadership of Archbishop Ottone Visconti. It was he who effectively established the family's lordship (*signoria*) and the general shape of Milanese political life for centuries to come. Shortly after his entry into the city, Ottone published a list of some two hundred family names, from which would henceforth be chosen the ordinaries of the Metropolitan Church. That list, which included all of the Visconti's noble allies and some of their bourgeois supporters, came to be accepted as the criterion for nobility within the city of Milan. Even in the fifteenth century, the dukes created noble families by adding their names to this list.[37]

Throughout the later thirteenth and fourteenth centuries, the Visconti worked to strengthen their political grip on the city and diocese. New governmental forms were introduced, and new demands were made on subjects, including major financial contributions from the clergy. Matteo Visconti led the secular government as the Captain of the People (*Capitano del Popolo*), and in 1294 he received the imperial vicariate with full sovereign rights over Milan and its territory. Factional strife continued in Milan, mediated unsuccessfully by the emperor, Henry VII, who came to the city for his coronation in 1310. On Henry's death, Matteo was named rector-general by the Milanese general council. The Visconti were careful to operate juridically as magistrates of the commune, even when they had also received a ducal title from the Holy Roman Emperor. That title did not come until 1395; until then, various members of the family ruled—often in tandem—as "lord" (*signore*). In the 1340s, Luchino Visconti disbanded the political parties, outlawed private war, and dismantled the communal army. He and his powerful relatives also initiated a round of palace and castle building. The products of that construction activity dominated the Lombard landscape in the Sforza era and are still visible throughout the former Visconti dominion.[38]

This region flourished in the mid-fourteenth century, and its rulers looked to greater possibilities. From 1353 to 1361, Petrarch resided in Milan and environs, producing not only literary and philological works but also propaganda for the Visconti. He even undertook an embassy to Emperor Charles IV at Prague on their behalf and participated in the marriage of GianGaleazzo Visconti at Paris in 1360. The decade that followed saw many such marriages made by the prolific Visconti brothers Galeazzo II and Bernabò with the noble and royal houses of transalpine Europe. Bernabò made his connections primarily within the Holy Roman Empire, to the Habsburgs, the dukes of Bavaria, and so forth. His co-*signore* Galeazzo preferred to deal with the kingdoms of England and France; besides marrying his heir to Isabelle of Valois, Galeazzo matched his daughter Violante with Edward III's son, Lionel of Clarence.

Between them, Bernabò and Galeazzo ruled a considerable state; however, they divided it scrupulously along territorial lines. Bernabò was lord of Milan and the northern part of the dominion. Galeazzo's capital was Pavia, which had finally been captured in 1359 after a long history of rivalry with its larger neighbor. Galeazzo died in 1378; his son Galeazzo took over his half of the dominion and changed his own name to GianGaleazzo.

GianGaleazzo Visconti was far more ambitious than his predecessors had been, and he was more successful than any other ruler of Milan in asserting his ambitions. He resolved to reunite the dominion under his own rule and to that end, murdered his uncle Bernabò in 1385. GianGaleazzo's sense of guilt about this act contributed materially to the religious life of Milan and its ruling family. Among his acts of contrition the most visible were the founding of the new Duomo in Milan and the Certosa of Pavia, dedicated to Santa Maria delle Grazie (in English generally called the Madonna of Mercy). He instituted a special devotion to this aspect of the Blessed Virgin Mary and vowed that all of his descendants should bear the second name Maria.[39]

GianGaleazzo was the true founder of the duchy of Milan; he received the title of duke from the emperor Wenceslas in 1395. Even before then, however, he had created the basic policies and institutional structures that characterized the duchy throughout its history. He set up the councils of state and other offices of central government and located them in Milan, notwithstanding his personal preference for residence at Pavia. However, Pavia was recognized as the second city of the dominion, seat of the newly established university and of a county assigned to the ducal heir. GianGaleazzo challenged the entrenched feudal interests in the dominion, canceling privileges, limiting the use of armed retainers, and destroying noble castles. He also modified social distinctions within the capital city.

GianGaleazzo's greatest ambitions lay outside the boundaries of his state, in the vast sweep of warfare and diplomacy that almost brought him full control of northern and central Italy before his sudden death from illness in 1402. He was a figure of international stature, continuing his father's tradition of marriage alliances and other social and cultural contacts with the great northern monarchies. When GianGaleazzo died, the duchy of Milan fell on hard times. His sons were minors, incapable of taking command over the far-flung Visconti holdings. Factional conflict reappeared in Milan itself and ultimately led to the assassination of Duke Giovanni Maria in 1412. At that time, the duchy was actually being governed by the condottiere Facino Cane. When GianGaleazzo's young son Filippo Maria entered the city in June of that year, he was duke in name only. He was fortunate to enjoy even that limited recog-

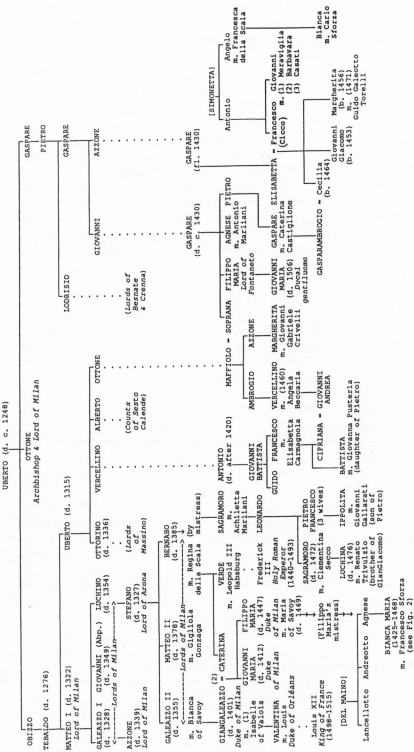

Figure 1. The Visconti lineage (highly simplified)

nition, for the descendants of Bernabò Visconti fought hard to recover the lordship of Milan. Filippo's successful entry owed much to support from certain nobles in military positions, including the Marliani castellan of the Porta Giovia gate in Milan, an Arcelli condottiere from Piacenza, and a Beccaria noble from Pavia. All received fiefs in gratitude.

Filippo had difficulties in many areas, including imperial recognition; not until 1417 did he receive ducal investiture. His reign was filled with unceasing warfare and intrigue, partly as a result of his own contentious and highly suspicious personality. Filippo never recovered all the lands his father had dominated, and in 1427 he lost Bergamo and Brescia to his former military commander, the condottiere Pandolfo Malatesta. This loss formed part of a major defeat suffered against the combined forces of Savoy, Florence, and Venice. As a consequence of the defeat, Filippo agreed to an alliance with Savoy, including a marriage with the count's daughter, Maria. Galeazzo II Visconti had also married a member of the house of Savoy, almost a century earlier.

Filippo's marriage proved to be problematic; he never lived with Maria, and there was some question whether he even consummated their union. The duke did not enjoy the company of women, nor did he like to deal with persons outside a narrow circle of trusted attendants and advisers. As a result, the last Visconti duke spent the latter part of his long reign (1412–1447) almost in seclusion, lurking in the one place he felt safe, Porta Giovia Castle on the edge of Milan.

Because of his constant wars, Filippo followed his father's financial policy, including oppressive taxation and the sale of feudal holdings and privileges that had previously been recovered by the ducal government. The fiefs and immunities did not generally return to the families that had previously held them. Perhaps the most important of these grants went to the Milanese merchant Vitaliano Borromeo, who received land and castles at Angera and Arona on Lago Maggiore, the legendary origins of Visconti greatness.

When Filippo Maria Visconti died in 1447, he left no male heir, only a legitimized daughter of twenty-two years, Bianca Maria. His legacy was as tortuous and problematic as the rest of his life, and no one could claim clear title to the Milanese dominion. Bianca Maria's claim was taken up by her husband, Francesco Sforza, the greatest condottiere of the time. However, many citizens of Milan saw the death of the hated duke as an opportunity to reestablish communal government in the city. A mob tore down Porta Giovia Castle and destroyed the records of the ducal chancery. Freed from the oppressive rule of the lurking prince and the shadow of his fortress refuge, they declared a republic named for the city's patron and symbol, Ambrose.

The Ambrosian Republic was doomed to fail. The city of Milan was not self-sufficient, and other subject cities were unwilling to accept the dominance of the proud Milanese. Elements within the capital lacked political unity and could not avoid a resumption of the loud and bitter conflicts that had characterized the Commune before the Visconti became lords. Lacking adequate food or arms, short of money, and unpracticed at self-government, the citizens were no match for their main opponent, Francesco Sforza. His professional army was the most effective in Italy; with support from Cosimo de' Medici and the Republic of Venice, the veteran general easily starved Milan into submission in March 1450. On his triumphant entry, he was received with honor by leading citizens of the city.

The Sforza Heritage

Milan's new lord in 1450 came from a very different background than did his predecessors. The Visconti had been natives of Lombardy, noble for as long as the concept had had meaning in their city. The Sforza could boast no such pedigree; indeed, their family name was an invention of the fifteenth century. The first to bear it was Giacomo "Muzio" Attendolo, originally a farmer from Cotignola in the Romagna. Muzio left the land and joined a mercenary company. His abilities brought him success in the field, respect from his peers, and rewards from his employers. He became one of the leading *condottieri* of the early Quattrocento.[40]

For Muzio, war was a business and a way of life, one that prospered in the century between the Black Death and the Peace of Lodi. As part of his campaign of self-promotion, Muzio adopted the potent surname Sforza ("Strength" or "Force"). He fought for many of the major and minor states of Italy but became particularly involved in struggles for control of the Neapolitan kingdom, where he received titles and estates.

When Muzio died while on campaign in 1424, his leadership role was assumed by one of his many sons. Muzio had at least fourteen children, nine of them illegitimate. One of the illegitimate sons was Francesco, born in 1401 and reared among the intrigues of southern Italy. He entered the family business early and distinguished himself; by 1440, Francesco outshone every other military leader on the peninsula. The duke of Milan, Filippo Maria Visconti, found Francesco too valuable to lose. In 1441, the duke gave his only child, Bianca Maria, in marriage to Francesco, his commanding general. Filippo Maria did not like the situation, however. He trusted no one, least of all the man clever enough to become his son-in-law. The duke not only refused to attend the wedding, which took place in Bianca Maria's dower city of Cremona, but even disinherited his daughter from the succession. Francesco eventually passed out of Milanese service into the employ of Venice and the Papacy.

Francesco's difficulties mounted with his successes. The very pope who had made him count of the Marches then tried to neutralize his dangerously

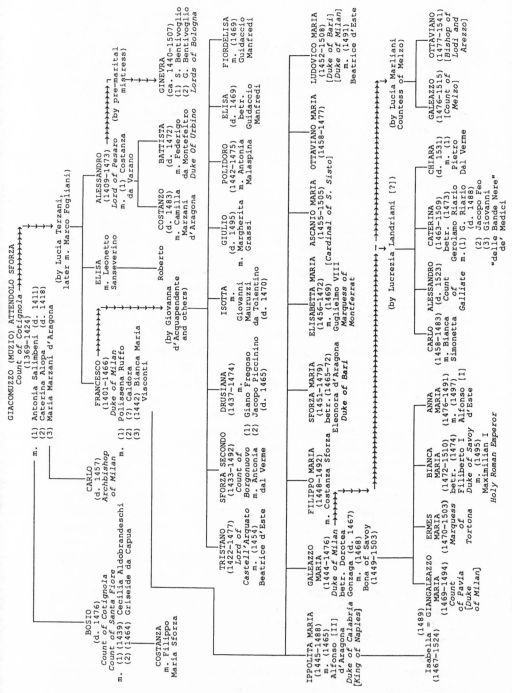

autonomous position within the Papal States. As had often been the case in his life, Francesco was forced to tread a political tightrope to retain the gains he made as a professional soldier. His concerns multiplied with his family. In 1444, his wife bore a son, named Galeazzo Maria at the request of Duke Filippo Maria. The following year, Bianca Maria bore a girl, Ippolita Maria. The two children lived a precarious existence during the years in which their father sought a permanent home somewhere in Italy. A second son, Filippo Maria, was born in 1448, during the campaign to make Milan that home.

Francesco Sforza received formal recognition as duke of Milan from the people of that city on March 22, 1450. At that moment, he became the greatest success story in the history of Renaissance Italy, rising from his illegitimate and obscure origins to authority over the peninsula's wealthiest princely state. The combination of that wealth with Sforza arms and intelligence made the new duke a very formidable player in the ceaseless game of Renaissance warfare and diplomacy. But Francesco's inclinations were not to maintain the conflicts from which he had profited before his accession. Within four years, he had joined forces with Cosimo de' Medici to organize the first great modern peace conference. The establishment of the Universal League at the Peace of Lodi ensured a far greater stability in Italian politics and enabled Francesco himself to concentrate on the difficult task of ruling the duchy of Milan. In addition to the problems previous rulers of Lombardy had faced, Francesco had the burden of unfamiliarity. To help him manage the complex and challenging task of governing Milan, the new duke found loyal and skilled officials both within his existing military administration and among the citizens of his new dominion.

Major Offices of the Sforza Administration

The Sforza administration was divided between civil and military offices, with the Privy Council holding authority over all areas and the Chancery linking them together. The civil administration was divided, in turn, between central and peripheral offices. Each central office bore a specific responsibility: civil justice, finance, public health, and so forth. The chains of command always led back to the Privy Council and the duke himself. The military chains of command leading back to the duke involved primarily the standing army and garrisons. Relatively few condottieri served Milan in peacetime, since the duchy had the most credible standing army in Europe at the time.[41]

Most key decisions about the political direction of the dominion were made in the sphere of the princely court. They were made by the duke himself and by those to whom he delegated authority, the councils and offices of state. These men were termed the *magistrati della corte*; they consisted of the "Privy Council, Council of Justice, Masters of Ordinary and Extraordinary Revenues, and other officers of the court."[42]

The Councils of State and Fiscal Officials   As early as GianGaleazzo Visconti's era, the ducal council of state had been split into two parts. The larger and more important was the Privy Council (*Consiglio Segreto*); the smaller and more restricted was the Council of Justice (*Consiglio di Giustizia*). Both councils had their own chancellors and secretaries, positions that paid well and ranked highly.[43] Some of the wealthiest and most influential subjects of the duke sat on the Privy Council, which exercised sovereign powers subject only to the duke's authority. It dealt with political and diplomatic questions, judicial proceedings of great weight (particularly criminal cases), oversight of state security and finances, public health, and works, even the reception of ambassadors and arrangement of ceremonial procedures for state occasions. The Privy Council served also as the ultimate court of appeal, apart from the duke himself. The Council of Justice had authority only over civil cases. Its members were all distinguished jurists, usually about five in number. Many of them proceeded later in their career to a seat on the Privy Council.

The single largest group of ducal officials in the central administration were those responsible for fiscal matters. Ultimate responsibility for economic policy lay with the duke and Privy Council, but the daily business was overseen by the masters of revenues (*Maestri delle Entrate*). They were divided into two groups, responsible, respectively, for ordinary and extraordinary revenues and commonly referred to as the "Magistrati Ordinari" and "Magistrati Straordinari." The former always preceded the latter on ceremonial occasions; they handled the *gabelles,* customs duties, taxes on horses and woods, and other regular sources of income. The Magistrati Straordinari dealt with feudal revenues, gifts, water use fees, confiscated property, and other irregular incomes.

Other fiscal officials included the *referendario-generale,* who monitored income from the several cities, lawyers and *sindaci fiscali* to protect the duke's legal rights, *collaterali,* responsible for the various fixed military stations, and *vicari generali,* who audited ducal officials when the latter left an office. In all, these men numbered no more than twenty at any given time, plus the treasurer-general and the auditor-general, a legal adviser who helped the duke review and respond to petitions from subjects. Each office also had its own staff, who made calculations, wrote letters, and ran various errands. The higher offices ranked with the highest of all ducal servants.[44]

The Cancelleria Segreta, *or Privy Chancery*   Communication between the various offices of the Sforza court and state, including the ducal office, was the bailiwick of the *Cancelleria Segreta,* the Privy Chancery of the dukes. The Chancery stood at the center of the ducal administration, a vital nexus linking all organs of government. It was one of the most sophisticated and effective bureaucratic institutions in fifteenth-century Europe. Because officials in the Chancery kept the records of acts involving the duke and his agents, their own acts are richly documented.[45]

The Chancery was thoroughly reorganized after Francesco Sforza became duke. Responsibilities were carefully distributed among the persons working in the Chancery: secretaries, chancellors, scribes and coadjutors, ushers, messengers, and other menial servants. Detailed instructions to all of these functionaries were drawn up in 1453–1456 and revised in 1465. The members of the Chancery were to reread these instructions monthly; the regulations covered not only procedures for expediting letters and documents but also the personal behavior of the staff. The instructions even specified the length of time allowed for lunch each day.[46]

Among the persons in the Chancery, secretaries (*segretari*) ranked highest; their work encompassed supervision of all ducal communications, including letters, charters, and proclamations. They ensured that proper forms were followed and procedures executed, including copying all material into the ducal registers. The secretaries' work was not limited to shuffling papers; some bore vital diplomatic responsibilities, maintaining contact between the duke and foreign dignitaries, including envoys resident in Milan. Milanese diplomats resident abroad generally bore the title of secretary in the Chancery. Within the Sforza dominions, secretaries also handled sensitive assignments with political ramifications, such as marriage negotiations initiated by the duke.[47]

Chief among the secretaries were members of the Simonetta family from Calabria. They were led by Angelo, who had served Francesco Sforza before the condottiere became duke. The family had connections to Francesco's first wife, Polissena Ruffo.[48] Angelo's nephews Giovanni and Francesco (Cicco) were brought into the administration, and Cicco became the single most important person in the dominion, after the duke himself. Cicco displayed such political acumen and organizational skills that Duke Francesco named him first secretary immediately on his accession.[49] As first secretary, he functioned in many capacities, from daily logistical arrangements to the most sensitive diplomatic strategies. Angelo remained a secretary until his death in 1472.[50]

Chancellors (*cancellieri*) did most of the actual writing within the Chancery and elsewhere. Writing was not a task that important individuals performed for themselves except in special circumstances. In great families, each adult would have his or her own personal chancellor; the duke's corps of chancellors was the largest in the dominion. The Chancery served also as a humanist training ground, where young men learned to write effectively in neoclassical styles as well as bureaucratic forms.[51]

Within the Chancery, the ushers or doorkeepers (*uschieri*) carried out the logistical functions of ensuring that papers were handled properly, materials were available as needed, and communication within the Chancery was maintained. The chancellors and secretaries generated or received literally millions of pages of material during Galeazzo's brief reign. Outgoing letters had to be copied into one set of registers, formal documents into another, incoming correspondence organized according to place of origin or identity of the sender, and so forth. Files and registers were often needed in other locations, as the ducal court traveled frequently; it was the ushers' responsibility to expedite the transfer. Document searches were occasionally required, with ushers and chancellors poring over registers and files, trying to locate items decades or centuries old.[52]

The ushers were respected members of the Chancery and interacted socially with the chancellors. The messengers did not have the same standing; they have left little trace of their personal affairs. The system of riders carrying messages across the dominion was organized as efficiently as other aspects of this central communications organ. Fresh horses were maintained at vital road junctions, and messengers were required to keep records of the transfer of documents into the hands of others.[53]

Peripheral Administration   The Sforza dominion was governed by a variety of officials in each town or district, as well as from the capital city and the duke's court. Each political entity had its own traditional forms of government, such as town councils and offices to supervise commerce. Most Italian towns and cities also had a podestà, whose function was generally to act as chief magistrate, overseeing the exercise of civil and criminal justice. Such officials were chosen, for a term of one or two years, from men who were not associated with the town and had no vested interests to cloud their even-handed judgment. The right to appoint a podestà belonged typically to whomever exercised the highest jurisdiction over a town, which was usually the duke for the largest towns and his feudal vassals for smaller ones.

The office of podestà was often combined with the political office of *commissario,* a ducal position. Only the major cities had separate *commissari*; smaller towns in areas such as the Gera d'Adda or the Oltrepò shared one for the entire region. The major cities also had separate *referendari,* responsible for the administration of fiscal matters pertaining to the ducal interest, as well as a treasurer who actually handled the money. The constables of the city gates were generally ducal appointees, as were the lieutenants or captains of the dominion's various districts. The men who received appointments to the top positions in the peripheral administration, especially as *commissari* or podestà, were often members of the court.

Allies and Kin

As effective as the Simonetta and other ducal officers were, their very presence caused some persons within the duchy to feel slighted or cheated by the advent of lowborn foreigners. Francesco Sforza was careful to integrate prominent members of the dominion's elites into his government, but without his wife, the duke would probably have been unable to maintain his position. Bianca Maria was not only popular with their subjects but also effective as a diplomat and administrator in her own right. Together, Francesco and Bianca Maria were perhaps the most highly respected couple in fifteenth-century Italy, and they had close personal relations with practically all the dominant figures in Italian statecraft. The success of the Attendoli-Sforza in their military profession also gave them ties of blood or marriage to the lords of Ferrara, Bologna, Urbino, and Pesaro, as well as leading condottieri families such as the Fogliani, Sanseverineschi, and Mauruzzi da Tolentino.

Francesco's tenuous position in Milan was exacerbated by Emperor Frederick III's refusal to recognize him as imperial vicar in Lombardy. The duke did everything he could to reinforce his claim; his Chancery even forged a document of donation from Duke Filippo Maria.[54] Francesco also crafted a careful network of alliances, the most important of which was a close bond with Cosimo de' Medici of Florence. The latter's financial assets saved Francesco time and again from deficits due to massive spending on effective government. Conversely, Milan's strong and well-organized army served as a guarantor of Medici security in their own city.

Francesco also bound himself closely to Italy's only king, Alfonso of Naples, continuing the alliance after 1458 with the new king, Ferdinand (Ferrante). In 1465, the year before his death, the duke saw his eldest daughter, Ippolita, marry Ferrante's son and heir, Alfonso of Calabria. At the same time, Francesco's son, Sforza Maria, was betrothed to Alfonso's sister, Eleonora, and assumed the Neapolitan title "duke of Bari." The third vital element in Francesco's diplomatic network was the greatest of all medieval kingdoms, France. Francesco enjoyed good relations with King Louis XI and strove to bind the two nations closely. Their alliance helped to dispel clouds of fear in Milan about persistent French claims to the duchy.[55] In 1464, Louis granted the former republic of Genoa to Francesco as a fief held from the king, who had himself come into legal possession not long before. As the second-ranking port in Italy, Genoa was a substantial addition to the Sforza dominion.

Francesco also toyed with the idea of a marriage alliance with France; after his death, his heir did in fact marry a relative of Louis XI's. But the early years of the condottiere's reign were too uncertain for him to entertain such ambitions. The first marriage proposals for Galeazzo Maria involved the daughters of Francesco's nearest neighbor and trusted general, Ludovico Gonzaga, marquess of Mantua. A physical deformity in the prospective bride and Francesco's ambition proved obstacles to both the original match and a second betrothal. Despite the ill-will engendered by these slights to their honor, the Gonzaga continued to be close allies and supporters of Milan.[56] Francesco even enlisted their assistance in the education and training of his firstborn, who was sent to escort Pius II on the latter's progress to the

Congress of Mantua in 1459. The Milanese duke also sent his son to Ferrara, where Borso d'Este contributed to the teenage heir's princely training. The Estensi had been the first princely family with whom Francesco had made a marriage connection as duke of Milan. In 1454, his eldest legitimized son, Tristano, had married Beatrice, legitimized daughter of Niccolò III.[57]

Galeazzo's Siblings   The Milanese ducal couple saw their family grow considerably after their accession. Sforza Maria and Ludovico ("il Moro") were born in 1451 and 1452, respectively. Ascanio came along in 1455, Elisabetta in 1456, and Ottaviano in 1458.[58] Ippolita was the only child who married before her father's death. She and Galeazzo were close in age; they were educated together and continued to have a close emotional bond even after she moved to Naples.[59] Filippo, Sforza Maria, and Ludovico were also close in age to one another, and they shared both preceptors and household officers during their parents' lifetime.[60] Francesco Sforza also sired at least seventeen illegitimate children; the most politically significant were Tristano and Sforza Secondo. Galeazzo was the first of Bianca Maria's children, but he was twenty-two years younger than Tristano, the most seasoned soldier and diplomat among their generation of Sforza men.[61]

Educating the Heir to Milan

Two days before Christmas, 1452, Galeazzo Maria Sforza, count of Pavia, wrote his father a letter from Pavia Castle. The eight-year-old heir to the duchy told Duke Francesco that at the latter's urging, he was acquiring "letters and [good] habits, and pursuing true and solid glory, so that I will not degenerate from your glorious and divine virtues, which have allowed you such height of empire [*tanta alteza de imperio*]." The boy reminded his father "not to let me lack horses, dogs, birds, or anything else that would please me."[62]

Galeazzo's interest in things that would please him never changed, but he stopped acquiring good habits even before his father died. It was not for lack of effort on Duke Francesco's part. As Cecilia Ady put it, "He forms . . . a striking example of a child upon whose education every care has been lavished and who nevertheless turns out badly."[63]

"The Manners Which We
Want You to Observe"

In July 1457, the count of Pavia was thirteen years of age, a traditional time for a boy to begin his training for manhood. His father sent him a letter, "considering that now you are of an age to know good and evil." The duke of Milan chose "not to wait any longer to tell you the manners which we want you to observe, so that you may never for any time say you have not had your vices and bad habits admonished and repressed, and that you have never been given the order of life and customs and manners that you have to keep."[64]

Duke Francesco went on to remind his son of the many persons in the ducal household who concerned themselves with his behavior and watched everything he did. "Galeazzo, we have wanted to do the office of the good father and teach you the manners and life that you have to observe. The office of the good son must then be yours, that you put all your thought to knowing these things that we will say to you here below, and with every study and understanding bring them to execution. Doing so, you will be blessed by God and by the most illustrious lady your mother and by us all, and you will keep our love and favor, and by every person you will be commended and praised."

The ten points of "manners" for Galeazzo to observe can be summarized as follows: (1) "to be devoted to God"; (2) to be "reverent and obedient" to his mother, grandmother, tutor, and "every other wise and virtuous person"; (3) "to be reverent and modest" at home or elsewhere and always to honor guests; (4) "to be honest and humane in speaking with everyone, according to their rank, quality and condition"; (5) "not to play with irons, stones or sticks" or to "persevere in anger and hatred"; (6) not to commit "any act of cruelty nor of arrogance" but to use "magnanimity, justice, and clemency"; (7) "not to be hungry for those things that are not worthy or necessary, and not to want all the things that you see and that come into your mind"; (8) neither to lie nor to encourage slanderers, "because the customs of the household which are not laudable bring infamy to the patron"; (9) to be moderate in eating and drinking; and (10) "because you delight in horses and have to use them, see that you never ride a horse with a hard mouth, nor one which has bad feet, or which bucks [levare dritto]."

In later years, Galeazzo would show that he had taken some of these strictures very much to heart but had ignored others completely. His father's instructions did not cover all possible areas of concern, either. The young man probably needed some guidance in the conduct of his sexual relations, but it may have been too late by the time this letter was written. Galeazzo's first illegitimate child was born the following year, when the ducal heir was only fourteen years old. It was the same year his youngest brother was born. By 1465, Galeazzo had fathered four acknowledged illegitimate children.[65]

In general, Francesco's emphasis for his heir's education and training related to the princely role the boy was expected to assume. With his sister Ippolita (later renowned for her literary culture), Galeazzo assiduously studied humanist letters. His education has sometimes been considered a model for a Renaissance prince; at thirteen years old, he read aloud substantial sections from Cicero's De Officiis. At fourteen, he was required to read four hours per day, much of it in Latin.[66]

Letters alone did not suffice to make a prince; Galeazzo also received training in arms and diplomacy. His military training culminated in leadership of the expeditionary force to France; his early diplomatic experience included extended visits to Ferrara, Florence, and Mantua. In these cities, he was feted like a prince; in 1459, the Florentines even arranged a joust in his honor at the feast of San Giorgio. The splendor of Medicean Florence made a great impression on him.[67]

"The Most Beautiful Creature That Was Ever Seen"

Galeazzo himself made a strong impression everywhere he visited. On his visit to Florence, a chronicler there called him "the most beautiful creature that was ever seen in the days of our lives, the cleanest and noblest lord, that well seemed to be the son of the god Mars, newly descended."[68] He was an intelligent and charming youth, capable of speaking well and behaving with princely grace. "The count Galeazzo, when he wishes, has mind and heart enough for every great undertaking."[69]

However, the heir to Milan used his charm to avoid his few responsibilities and indulge his many appetites. In 1459, he gained notoriety for his arrogance, when he refused to dismount while escorting Pope Pius II at the Congress of Mantua.[70] Already in 1457, Duke Francesco was concerned that his son might become spoiled while staying at the court of Ferrara. The duke asked Francesco Pico della Mirandola, who was watching over the young man, to treat Galeazzo "in a domestic manner and familiarly, no longer as a guest." The elder Sforza must have been deeply disappointed by 1460, when he admitted that his son and heir "fears no one and does whatever enters his head."[71]

Political Conditions at Galeazzo's Accession

In general, the duke and duchess of Milan had many reasons to be satisfied with their achievements by 1466. Within the duchy, the structures of the Visconti administration had been adapted and improved by the Simonetta and others to give them arguably the most effective bureaucracy in Italy. Bianca Maria was much loved by her subjects, and Duke Francesco's reign proved to be one of the longest, most peaceful, and most productive periods in the history of the Milanese dominion. With the addition of Genoa, the dominion had expanded to its largest extent in four decades, and Francesco's leadership united it more fully than that of any ruler since GianGaleazzo Visconti.

Francesco and Bianca Maria had also been instrumental in bringing long-lasting peace to the peninsula and in establishing a genuine balance of power between the great powers there. Their alliance with Florence and Naples was in equilibrium with an alliance between the republic of Venice and the Papacy. The latter alliance had been further cemented in 1464 with the election of a Venetian to the Papal See, as Paul II. The dozens of smaller Italian polities had their own relationships with the system of major states. Every ruler had to expend considerable resources on maintaining his position in the complex equilibrium; networks of diplomacy and espionage flourished in the political hothouse atmosphere. Francesco Sforza showed great skill and shrewdness in that area, reinforcing the military skill that had allowed him to create the most effective army in Italy—and to mount the Milanese throne. Francesco's achievement went beyond political and military success; by the end of his reign, he had established himself among the first rank of the Italian aristocracy. His prestigious position was reflected in the marriages his children Tristano and Ippolita had made into the Estensi and Aragonesi as well as the marriages his heir, Galeazzo, had not made into the Gonzaga. Francesco had brought Milan back to a position of prominence beyond the Alps, bringing the duchy directly into the conflicts between France and Burgundy. In 1465, he sent Galeazzo to France for experience with a military expedition supporting Louis XI during the War of the Public Weal. While the young man was there, Francesco died, and his hard-won dominion passed into the hands of his wife and their twenty-two-year-old son. The new ducal team enjoyed a reservoir of respect and goodwill that had been painstakingly accumulated during Francesco's reign. They had reliable allies, a wealthy dominion, an efficient administration, and a period of peace in which to operate. However, they had to reckon with the diverse and contentious nature of their subjects, the substantial debts left by Duke Francesco, and the constantly shifting allegiances that characterized the balance of power. Most difficult of all, they had to deal with Galeazzo's own temperament, which was not well suited to following in his father's footsteps.

2

"To Give Form and Order To Matters of Our Court"

Galeazzo Lays the Groundwork For His Reign (1466–1468)

When Galeazzo Maria Sforza became duke of Milan in March 1466, he was only twenty-two years of age. Because he would not attain his full majority for three years, he had to act under the tutelage of his mother, Bianca Maria Visconti, one of the most highly respected princely figures of her time.[1] For a young man of his pride, ambition, and inexperience, that arrangement was a mixed blessing, and Galeazzo had mixed feelings about it.

The new duke was genuinely concerned about his mother's welfare. A month after his accession, he asked the pope to release Bianca Maria from a meat fast she had vowed following her husband's death. Galeazzo feared her own death would result, and he wanted her to live.[2] However, he bridled at her efforts to guide his development; Galeazzo had great confidence in his own abilities. Within a few weeks of his enthronement, the dowager duchess gave him advice on handling the people of Parma. That city was a perennial trouble spot for the dominion's rulers, home to very powerful and independent-minded feudatories. Nonetheless, the young duke replied tartly, "Let it be known to Your Ladyship that I still know how to lead a goose to drink."[3]

Bianca Maria continued to see Galeazzo with a maternal eye, encouraging his successes as well as trying to educate him. In July 1466, he heard that she was happy because he had dealt skillfully with the citizens of Pavia and because he "always desired to have one of his brothers nearby."[4] In September, she told him he should accept an invitation from the marquess of Montferrat because, "going there, you will be able to see how you like the manners of the marchioness, which will be an example to you of those [manners] of her country, so that when you take a wife from those parts you will know better what to do and how to conduct yourself." The marchioness of Montferrat was

French, and Galeazzo was contemplating marriage to a lady of the French royal house.[5]

Such patronizing suggestions irritated Galeazzo. Formally, he and Bianca Maria shared joint rule over the dominion, but her greater experience, knowledge, and political ability gave her the dominant position. Galeazzo resented being the junior partner. In November 1466, his mother asked him to return to Milan and help expedite certain business. He responded bitterly, "I do not wish to come there to be Your Ladyship's auditor without salary, and now I know to be true that which Your Ladyship has often told me, that I am young and not very wise, because I believed the state to be the common property of Your Ladyship and myself, but now I understand it to be Your Ladyship's alone."[6] Galeazzo's sharp tongue may have been a legacy from his mother, who could speak as pointedly and sarcastically as he.[7] Bianca Maria was a strong-minded woman, and during the first two years of her son's reign, she exercised almost complete authority over matters outside his household.

The Ducal Household

In the sphere where he could make his own decisions, Galeazzo acted quickly. Within three months of his accession, the new duke announced he would "give form and order to matters of our court and to elect and depute a seneschal-general, as is appropriate in courts similar to ours."[8] The nucleus of Galeazzo's court was his household, whose basic responsibility was the well-being of the prince's person. Since the prince's person had the unique value of embodying the whole dominion, his household performed a vital function in keeping that embodiment comfortable, healthy, and content.[9]

Galeazzo Arranges His Household

As the count of Pavia, Galeazzo had had his own household; in 1463, it had included five *gentiluomini,* twelve *camerieri,* four *ragazzi,* a chaplain, a barber, four footmen (*staffieri*), and thirteen others, mainly kitchen staff.[10] *Gentiluomini* were men of good family and reputation whose contribution to the court could include honor, dignity, companionship, and (often) the benefit of experience. First among those serving Galeazzo in his youth was his distant cousin, Ottone Visconti. The *camerieri* constituted the core of the ducal household in many ways, and they performed a variety of crucial functions related to the duke's daily life. They were often, but not always, chosen from persons of high rank, and they might well come from other states.[11] Galeazzo's preaccession *camerieri* were led by another distant Visconti cousin, Vercellino. A few of the footmen were linked to families of some stature, but their role was generally less suitable to persons of rank. Their primary duty was to assist the duke in mounting and dismounting his horses and to accompany him on foot as he rode.[12] The *ragazzi* were "boys," generally of lower rank, who carried out unspecified tasks, probably of a menial nature.[13]

When Galeazzo acceded to the ducal throne in 1466, he inherited responsibility for the entire court, which numbered in the thousands. His household alone grew instantly to several hundred persons, and he inherited the ducal apartments that his father had occupied. They were located in the Palazzo dell'Arengo (generally called the "Corte"), an urban palace near the Duomo, in the very center of Milan.

In June 1466, the new duke began reorganizing the court of Milan from the center of his household outward. The seneschalcy-general stood at the heart of the princely establishment, and the seneschals were the most important of the household officers. Their work at the Sforza court covered every level of activity, from the crudely material to the delicately ceremonial. The seneschals-general bore responsibility for organizing the most visible manifestations of ducal activity. They supervised the preparations for most major undertakings—ducal travels, ceremonial events, visits from foreign dignitaries, and so forth—aided when necessary by the Privy Council and Chancery. Throughout Galeazzo's reign, Giovanni Giapanno and Giovanni da Castelnovate served as seneschals-general; both were also *gentiluomini.*[14]

Galeazzo's reorganization classified *camerieri,* and other members of the court, according to how closely they were stationed to the duke's innermost chambers.[15] Those chambers were the most exclusive space in which Galeazzo operated personally.[16] Galeazzo reassigned "these *camerieri,* old and new, making them into four parts. The first are those who sleep in the Camera del Marmoro and in [the Camera] del Cane." This group, five men in all, were Galeazzo's most intimate attendants. He wanted them to be persons he chose, because they slept in his room, and he would have no privacy from them. "These can come and go to their post except when the Lord discharges them from the chamber."[17]

"Another part is assigned to the Camera della Maestà, and those [*camerieri*] cannot pass further beyond [into the ducal chambers] if they are not asked. . . . Into this same Camera della Maestà, the Lords, ambassadors and these others of the [Privy] Council repair; without leave, they cannot enter [the Camera] del Cane." In that antechamber, the duke created a boundary, protecting his intimate space from unwanted invasions by matters of state and persons outside his innermost circle. He could then choose to invite ambassadors and councillors to speak with him in his chambers. Such conferences were the main reason for sending the *camerieri di camera* out of the innermost chamber. The beds for the *camerieri* were mattresses that were taken up during the day.[18]

"The third squadron cannot pass [beyond] the Camera delle Biscie, and in this [room] stay . . . many others of the old [*camerieri*] of the previous Lord." Thus did Galeazzo establish his independence from his father's looming memory. Creating his own cadre of intimates meant choosing the men who would be close to him and discharging his father's attendants from the household's central space. However, creating his own cadre did not mean that Galeazzo kept the same household officials as before he became duke. Those officials had been his father's choice, not his own; most of them did not stay close to Galeazzo after his accession. "In the Tower Room are the last [*camerieri*], that are almost all of those that were with this Lord before [the accession]. . . . In this room also come all the *gentiluomini*." Thus did Galeazzo draw another boundary. Generally, the *gentiluomini* had neither personal intimacy nor urgent state matters to bring them into the duke's central space.

"It is said, though, that he wants to limit this arrangement of the *gentiluomini* and officials, and give forth a list, so that each one could know there he may go." The new prince intended to systematize conditions of service, payment, and maintenance. He commanded "that all these men find themselves at their places three times each day, that is, in the morning when he rises, at the hour His Excellency dines, and at 19 hours"—roughly 1:00 P.M., counting from sunset. Galeazzo's dinner hour (*hora de disnare*) came early in the day.[19] He planned for his *camerieri* to eat with him sometimes, in groups corresponding to their posts within the household, "so that many times those of the last chamber, the Tower [Room], will be inside [with him], while the others from the other two closer [rooms] will be outside." The handful of persons who shared his bedchamber probably also shared his table every day. The duke also had grand plans for clothing his household officers; he intended "that these *camerieri* of his be dressed two or three times a year from head to toe, and almost all in one livery." He wanted them to be "served like lords."

The Dowager Duchess's Household

Galeazzo's grandiose and detailed vision of his household officers' lives signaled a new approach to the direction of Milan and its court. While he was creating these new policies, his mother maintained much the same household she had had for many years. Bianca Maria's court was smaller than her son's or her late husband's, but it was still substantial, encompassing the households of her eight children and her stepdaughter, Drusiana. In the later years of Duke Francesco's reign, Bianca Maria was personally attended by ten to twenty ladies and damsels, led by Emilia Attendoli and her daughter Antonia. Another two dozen women were charged primarily with the care of various ducal children. Over two hundred men belonged to the duchess's court, from her noble cousins Andreotto and Lancillotto del Maino to dwarfs, porters, and muleteers.[20]

Making Changes

The latter part of the year 1466 was relatively uneventful for the Milanese dominion and its rulers. The Venetian army had made menacing maneuvers after Duke Francesco's death, but no invasion had followed. A political crisis in Florence, in which the Medici might have required Sforza military aid, was resolved without involving Milan. Galeazzo spent much time and attention on hunting, visiting Pavia and the Lomellina district. To the extent that he could, the young duke involved himself also in the business of state.[21] Galeazzo chafed in his limited sphere of action and authority. Spirited and full of restless energy, the young duke often could not contain himself. For most of Christmas week in 1466, he dutifully attended Mass in the mornings and paid his respects to his mother but then gambled with friends the rest of the day, winning and losing as much as 600 ducats per day.

On December 29, Galeazzo was shocked to hear that one of his friends and companions, Donato "del Conte," had fled the dominion. Donato was a member of the Bossi family, ancient Milanese nobles. Because he had received a large income from the duke and had a family in Milan, his departure surprised everyone.[22] The duke's mood turned ugly. He treated Donato as a traitor, confiscating his property and giving his position to a *cameriere* of long standing in the court, Francesco da Varese. Galeazzo held Donato's eight-year-old son as a hostage, and he shamed Donato publicly by having him "painted on cards with a harp in the right hand and a shoe in the left, and attached [them] to the columns of the Duomo and the Broletto." The next day, Donato's image, "painted on a great board in the usual way" (i.e., upside down), was hung over the gate of the Corte Arengo. Galeazzo offered a large reward for his friend's return—dead or alive. The duke blamed his mother for Donato's flight. He took petty revenge on her by, among other things, having his twenty-six horses brought in to gallop noisily around the courtyard of the palace.[23]

"So That When They Want to
Change, They Will Know Where to Go"

Galeazzo turned his bitterness at the close of 1466 into determination at the opening of 1467. He began reordering his world again within a few days of Donato del Conte's flight. "In these days, he has attended to his household arrangements, with which he feels that few have been contented up to now."[24]

However, the new policies were designed less to please courtiers than to protect the finances and security of the ducal establishment.

Galeazzo decided that all of his *camerieri*'s servants must come from his dominion. He wanted a written list of their names, so that the *camerieri* "do not have occasion to change them and take now one of them, now another of them." He put eight more of his father's *camerieri* out of the household and into the armed forces. He also "assigned about 50 other *camerieri* to eat in the household, with one, two, or three servants." Some courtiers were accustomed to having more than three servants eating at ducal expense; they were doubtless displeased at this new policy, as well as another restriction: "These [*camerieri*] are obliged never to leave the Corte without permission" from Galeazzo or a seneschal-general. The duke set the food allowance for "the other *camerieri*, that eat outside the household," at 3 florins per month (per person, including their servants) and cut the salaries of other household officials.

The duke had visions of clarity and order. "He has said he will have made a wardrobe with as many shelves as there are *camerieri*, where their suits, hose, and underskirts [*zupponi*] will be, and written there will be each of their names, so that when they want to change, they will know where to go." Such a system was a logical extension of the decision to put household officers in matching livery. However, Galeazzo was already showing a tendency to change his mind often; no one knew how long the new policies would last.

Galeazzo Moves Out

Galeazzo's changes were unpredictable, and they often proved traumatic to his intimates. "Pietro Pagnani, who up to now has been everything, has fallen far in the last two days. Yesterday he was half desperate." Sometimes the changes shocked persons outside the ducal household. At the end of January 1467, the duke took a bold step, moving out of the Corte Arengo and into Porta Giovia Castle. The idea was received badly by his mother, who reminded him of his father's way of doing things.[25] Older and wiser heads advised against a sudden move to Porta Giovia. Gaspare da Vimercate, a respected friend of Duke Francesco's, recommended that Galeazzo make the move gradually. So, too, did Pietro Pusterla, who had borne the ducal sword at both dukes' accession ceremonies. He advised that such an approach—"little by little to return and reside in that castle"—was the only way to avoid giving offense to the ducal household. He also pointed out the difficulties of proceeding in the face of Bianca Maria's opposition.[26]

Galeazzo's move from the Corte to Porta Giovia carried great symbolic significance. On a personal level, it declared his independence from his parents, both the dead shadow of his father and the living shadow of his mother. They had always ruled their dominion from the Palazzo dell'Arengo, the traditional Milanese residence for most of the Visconti lords. The palace's central location in the capital identified it closely with the people of the city, reflecting the lord's status as a magistrate of the Milanese commune. In contrast, Porta Giovia Castle was "held as a fortress," a forbidding pile of brick at the edge of the city. To have the duke resident in Porta Giovia reminded many people of the dark days when Duke Filippo Maria Visconti lurked there with his schemes and suspicions.

The Castle of Porta Giovia   Now heavily restored, Milan's great castle is known as Castello Sforzesco, commemorating its rebuilding by Duke Francesco and his sons. The name by which it was known in the fifteenth century—"Porta Giovia"—reflected its original function as a fort guarding one of the city gates. By the beginning of that century, it had become the military key to control of the city. In 1412, Filippo Maria Visconti needed the support of the castellan of Porta Giovia to realize his own claim to the ducal succession.[27]

In Galeazzo's time, Porta Giovia Castle faced in toward the city of Milan to the southeast and out toward a large area of undeveloped land to the northwest. The building itself is a huge square structure, two stories high (plus battlements and catwalks) and built of brick, with wide round towers at the corners of the southeast front and square towers at the corners of the northwest wall. The southeast front, facing into the city, is pierced by a large gate in the center; atop it is a tall and elegant clock tower designed for Duke Francesco by the great architect Filarete.

The space inside the castle is divided in half by an internal wall, pierced by two gates. In Galeazzo's era, the half facing toward the city retained a military function, as both parade ground and quarters. It was probably in this section that the less prestigious prisoners were held; the castle always contained a number of them. The half facing away from the city is further divided in half, between the Rocchetta, then housing administrative offices, and the Corte Ducale. Except for the military ceremonies on the feast of San Giorgio, virtually all the activity at Porta Giovia discussed in this book occurred in this rear half. Most of the events involving the court took place in the Corte Ducale area, which now houses the city of Milan's premodern painting and sculpture museum. Many of the support facilities used by the duke and his people were located elsewhere; the enormous ducal stables, for instance, were not attached directly to the castle itself.[28]

In January 1467, when Galeazzo first decided to stay in Porta Giovia, only seven rooms and thirteen beds were available for the court's use. Eight months later, thirteen rooms existed on the same side of the building as the duke's chamber, and the newly constructed ones were being prepared for occupancy.[29] For several years, extensive construction and decoration continued to make the castle comfortable and honorable enough to serve as the ducal residence in the capital. The Corte Ducale was a graceful courtyard built during his reign, around which halls, chambers, and chapels were created for use by the duke, his immediate family, and their personal companions.[30] Notwithstanding all of the money and attention Galeazzo invested in Porta Giovia, it was generally better suited to symbolic and ceremonial affirmations than to making daily life comfortable. Over the period 1468–1476, Galeazzo spent only 18 percent of his nights at Porta Giovia, an average of slightly over two months per year.[31]

Court Logistics

The ducal court of Milan included Porta Giovia Castle, the Corte Arengo, and other buildings throughout the dominion. All of them required furnishing and maintenance, and most were expanded or embellished during Galeazzo's reign. Thousands of human beings and domestic animals played a role in the court. All of them needed to be maintained in a manner suitable to their status and function. The court provided living space and daily necessities for the prince and his extended household. It also held the promise of material advantages for those who participated in its activities. The court was the distribution center for most of the dominion's available wealth and prestige. It was also the dominion's greatest center for economic consumption.

Maintaining the court establishment required an active and efficient logistical organization.[32] Their job was not an easy one. The top officials responsible for logistics fell generally into one of three groups: seneschals (*sescalchi*), who handled lodgings; stewards (*spenditori*), in charge of the kitchen and wardrobe; and masters of stables (*Maestri di Stalla*). Each of them was assisted by subordinates who did most of the physical labor. In addition, the court benefited from the work of cooks, barbers, tailors, and hundreds of other laborers and artisans.

Besides Giovanni Giapanno and Giovanni de Castelnovate, four other seneschals-general were appointed during Galeazzo's reign to handle lodging arrangements.[33] Their work was challenging; they had to find lodgings for several hundred persons when the court traveled outside Milan and Pavia and when distinguished visitors brought their households to the dominion.

The duke and duchess of Milan maintained separate households, eating, and often traveling, apart from one another. Each household had its own set of officials. The table stewards' responsibility was to maintain the pantry (*dispensa*) and ensure that adequate and appropriate food would be available to the principals and their retinues. These stewards were assisted by the *cre-*

denzieri, who looked after the tableware in the *credenza.* At the most menial level, the *apparecchiatori* prepared the dining table for use. At the most exalted level, both duke and duchess had a cupbearer (*coppero*), a carver, and a nobleman "who will bear the platter [*chi porterà el piatello*]."[34]

To provide food for the ducal households, the duke's agents contracted with a victualler who would supply what was needed.[35] The majority of foodstuffs consumed were meats and breads, with some fruits, nuts, and sweets.[36] Evidence from Galeazzo's accounts is sketchy, but Duke Francesco's household table expenses were based on daily consumption of 64 pounds of veal, 8 pounds of lard, 18 pair of assorted poultry and game birds, 5 pounds of sweets, and substantial quantities of bread and wax (for candles, presumably).[37] The court's primary beverage was wine; early in his reign, Galeazzo imported it from the marches of Ancona in lots of 25 or 50 cartloads at a time.[38]

The duke also spent considerable sums on clothing, jewelry, and other items of personal furnishings for the household. The person responsible for those items was the steward in charge of the wardrobe (*guardaroba*); Galeazzo's first wardrobe steward was Ludovico Suardi, an exile from Bergamo.[39] In March 1467, Gottardo Panigarola of Genoa joined the wardrobe as a chancellor; two years later, he succeeded Ludovico as wardrobe steward. Until his own death in 1500, Gottardo remained a pillar of the Sforza administration while also maintaining a prosperous family business in Genoa.[40]

Besides lodging, food, and clothing, persons at court needed horses, the main vehicle for transportation and communication. Both duke and duchess had a master of stables; the importance of this position in Galeazzo's eyes is evident from his choice for his own stables—Count Giovanni Antonio Secco, nicknamed "Borella."[41] The ducal stables handled hundreds of horses, in addition to mules, wagons, and other equipment. The stable staff included wagoners (*carrettoni*), muleteers (*mulateri*), and dozens of stable boys (*ragazzi di stalla*). They lived at the stables, which were generally in a separate building from the residence of the duke and his personal attendants.

Money Troubles

On the same day Bianca Maria expressed her objections to Galeazzo's move from the Corte, the duke received a disturbing letter from a seneschal and a steward. They told him that the household account was running dangerously short of money; if they paid all the previous year's household debts, the current year's allotment would be exhausted by August. They concluded sternly, "How honest and honorable it would be for Your Highness to beg for his livelihood every day, [You] can know [Yourself]."[42] In the orderly Sforza administration, there was an office and a procedure for every type of transaction.[43] Even the duke's household was expected to account strictly for its expenditures. The costs for necessities alone were substantial; Duke Francesco's table expenses, as outlined above, were estimated at more than 2,800 ducats per year. Another 75 *camerieri* and their servants had their expenses paid for eating "in the court," at an estimated annual cost of almost 1,500 ducats. The expenses for 51 dogs and their 31 keepers totaled even more than for the human beings—5,445 ducats per year.[44]

The changes that Galeazzo made to household arrangements at New Year's 1467 reflected concern for the high level of expenses. That problem was never solved during his reign, despite repeated efforts to control costs. In May 1467, the duke commanded that *camerieri* receive money for buying their own meals, rather than being fed at court. It was calculated that such a change could cut food costs in half for some of them.[45] The problem of costs haunted the duchess's court, too; in April 1467, an official had lamented "the intolerable expenses which [Bianca Maria] continually has in the household."[46] To stabilize his household's finances, the duke juggled sources of revenue, seeking to use money more efficiently. In September 1467, he decided to ensure that the household would never be deprived, and he set aside 140,000 ducats of his most reliable annual revenues "for the needs of our chamber [*camera*] and household [*famiglia*], that is, our person and *camerieri, ragazzi, galuppi* [a type of mounted servant], and other servants."[47]

Glory

Financial difficulties notwithstanding, Galeazzo was determined to make his mark. In February 1467, he "decided to make some solemnities and celebrations [on] the day we made the entry into this our duchy." For the occasion, he had the painter Zanetto Bugatti design new coins bearing a likeness of the duke's head. Galeazzo also asked Borso d'Este to lend him an organist.[48] The duke announced a "tournament or battle" to be held at Porta Giovia which would be open to everyone but exiles and rebels. Among those eligible was Donato del Conte, who had returned to Milan and ducal favor.[49] At the same time that Galeazzo was planning to commemorate his accession on March 20, he and his seneschals were preparing for the *annuali* (traditional anniversary observance) of Duke Francesco's death on March 8. These *annuali* would provide an important reminder of the first Sforza duke; every major city in the dominion intended to mark the occasion.[50]

Milanese Exiles and the Venetian Threat

Such public affirmations were satisfying to the proud young duke, but glory could best be won in war. Galeazzo was hungry for glory. He felt he had good reason to consider war as an option; it was, after all, the basis of his family's fortunes. More immediately, the Venetian territories of Bergamo and

Crema lay close to Milan itself. Venice had possessed these districts since the reign of Galeazzo's grandfather, Filippo Maria Visconti. The Serenissima was Milan's main rival for territorial dominance in northern Italy. Although the Venetians had supported Francesco Sforza's conquest of Milan, their consistently aggressive foreign policy caused concern to him and his allies. Galeazzo found the continued Venetian presence in eastern Lombardy an affront to the duchy of Milan and a threat to its security. The "Universal" Italian League created by Francesco Sforza and Cosimo de' Medici had ultimately included all of the peninsula's major powers except Savoy. However, Venice did not participate in negotiations for its renewal; those talks led to a triple alliance between Naples, Florence, and Milan in January 1467.

In the winter and spring of 1466–1467, a number of dissatisfied Milanese subjects fled to Venetian territory. Most of the defectors were young and brash; some belonged to the ducal lineage, including Battista Visconti and Galeazzo's half-brother, Sforza Secondo. When Sforza left in January, the duke confiscated his property.[51] In March, Sforza wrote to Bianca Maria, complaining that Galeazzo had treated him worse than "a rebel or a Turk": "Neither my being a brother to him nor reverence for the happy memory of our father would have defended me from death or perpetual imprisonment." Sforza wrote Galeazzo as well, demanding restitution of his properties and accusing the duke of insensitivity to family obligations.[52]

Not all of the new Milanese exiles were persons whom the duke considered prominent or threatening. One of them was a twelve-year-old boy, Gerolamo Olgiati, son of a ducal official, Giovanni Giacomo (Giacobino) Olgiati. Gerolamo had left Milan under the influence of his teacher, Cola Montano, a minor Bolognese humanist. Cola taught rhetoric in Milan, instructing the sons of Milanese aristocrats in classical language and culture. Unlike most of his colleagues, Cola had an ideological ax to grind, and he promoted republican values very aggressively. Gerolamo and two other students became so inspired that they rode into the Venetian Republic's territory, joining Captain-General Colleoni at his castle of Malpaga. Giacobino had harsh words for Cola Montano. He begged Galeazzo to take a hand in recovering Gerolamo, "suspecting that he is a lamb in the hands of the wolf, and that this most perfidious man will cause him to finish in some disastrous situation [*caso sinistro*]." Furthermore, Giacobino assured his master that "as I recover my son, [Your Lordship] will recover a servant, because my children are raised by me thus, in the devotion and service to Your Excellency, as in the Catholic faith." Gerolamo did return, sent back by Colleoni himself, but Giacobino's words would hold a terrible irony for Galeazzo.[53]

Galeazzo Tries to Be a Warrior

In April 1467, the young duke of Milan considered the threat posed by the Venetian army to be a pressing concern. He wanted to counter a possible invasion with his own show of force, taking thousands of troops on maneuvers near the border. His mother responded scornfully to the plan. She asked if he had received "something new that gives you some suspicion" of Venetian military action, for she knew of none. She went on to rebuke him, because "this display and demonstration seems to us more damaging and dangerous than fruitful in any way." Bianca Maria considered his planned maneuvers a provocative act, and she pointed out that the substantial expense, and inevitable damage to his subjects' property, would outweigh any possible military achievements. Finally, she played on Galeazzo's pride, remarking that observers might think such a show of force "is done out of fear." She advised her son to "think well about this undertaking, and take counsel with those that . . . have more wisdom than you in these matters."[54]

Stung by his mother's belittling words, Galeazzo made a swift return to the capital and prepared for the feast of San Giorgio, the patron saint of Milan's dukes—and of war.[55] Galeazzo made great play of the occasion, having expensive new ducal standards made and bringing "all our servants-at-arms here to accompany our standards." During the following week, he gave gifts of clothing to ducal servants ranging from men-at-arms to councillors of state.[56] Within two weeks, Galeazzo was finally on his way to a real war.[57] Florentine exiles had persuaded Colleoni to invade Florentine territory from the Romagna, and troops of the league responded, facing off against the condottiere's army. The league's overall commander was another leading general of the Renaissance: Federigo da Montefeltro, count of Urbino. Eager to show his mettle on the field of battle, the duke of Milan traveled with his household to the league's headquarters camp near Imola. His pride as a warrior was mixed with irritation at his mother's maternal attitude. Galeazzo had been out of his dominion for barely a week when Bianca Maria sent a messenger to check on him. She even reminded the duke to say his prayers.[58]

Galeazzo remained on campaign for several months. He had not inherited his father's military gifts; although the league's forces defeated Colleoni at the battle of the Riccardina, Galeazzo could take no credit. On the contrary, his presence proved so irritating to the league's commanders that the rulers of Florence extended an invitation to remove him from the battle zone. The invitation led Galeazzo to believe that his presence in Florence was essential for the campaign's success; only later did he realize that he had not contributed at all. At the end of the campaign, though, he had the satisfaction of hearing from Sforza Secondo, who was staying at the ancestral Sforza home in Cotignola. The duke's half-brother declared his intention to "live and die with [Your Lordship], and not depart from your commands."[59]

Soon after his return to Milan in the autumn, Galeazzo departed for a military action on the dominion's western border. His brother-in-law, Filippo of Savoy, had made common cause with Burgundy and threatened invasion from the west. The campaign was brief, and the outcome was favorable. This time, Galeazzo could feel that he had contributed personally. In early November, he held a tournament as a display of arms to impress the dangerous Filippo. After Galeazzo concluded a peace settlement in mid-November, even Bianca Maria told him his reputation would rise.[60]

Family Matters

While Galeazzo was on campaign with the league forces, he continued to receive visits from his mother's messenger.[61] Bianca Maria also wanted him to travel with his brothers, particularly Filippo and Sforza Maria. The latter wrote to Galeazzo in some excitement on May 6, asking the duke to take him along, "my having a strong spirit, intent on the trade [of arms]." Galeazzo agreed to let Sforza Maria and Filippo join him later in May, but Sforza Maria fell ill, and the visit was postponed. In late June, the duke promised that an eager Sforza Maria could visit as soon as he had recovered.[62] Two months later, Bianca Maria wanted again for Filippo and Sforza Maria to join the duke, as he returned to Milan. Sforza Maria fell ill again, but he and Filippo did travel with Galeazzo for about three weeks in late August and early September.[63]

"Not as a Brother But as a Lord"

As duke, Galeazzo was no longer the eldest and most privileged child in his immediate family but rather the head of the ducal lineage. In March 1467, Bianca Maria instructed him on his position as brother, father, and lord to his siblings, emphasizing their need for correction and guidance. When she sent Filippo and Sforza Maria to the duke in August, she insisted that he be stern and fatherly with them.[64] In the ducal lineage, Galeazzo's relationship with his full brothers was the most important after his relationship with his mother. Until the young duke had a legitimate son to succeed him, his brothers were his heirs.[65] They were also among his closest companions, sharing his blood, his values, and his pastimes.

The duke's brothers were a young group, ranging from nine to eighteen years of age in 1467. In November, Galeazzo stated his intentions regarding the households and maintenance allowances of the three teenagers among them: Filippo (18 years old), Sforza Maria (16), and Ludovico (15) were each to receive an annual allowance of 2,000 ducats and a household of at least fifty "notable and virtuous" persons.[66] Two months later, the duke also invested those three brothers with substantial fiefs, which provided further income.[67]

The only ducal brother who was allowed to stay at his own castle consistently during Galeazzo's reign was Filippo, Duke Francesco's second son.

Poor Filippo spent most of the reign at his castles or his house in Milan, struggling to make ends meet. He wanted to live at court but was generally excluded for his unpleasant character.[68] Filippo alienated Galeazzo early in the reign with serious errors of judgment, including direct disobedience to the duke. In March 1468, Galeazzo wrote to Bianca Maria about something Filippo had said to Franchino Caimi's wife, "which seem to me words of an ill nature." A week later, Filippo told his elder brother that "the rage and anger that Your Lordship has demonstrated against me has caused anguish, and gives such anguish to my mind that I don't know what to do."[69] Bianca Maria herself was worried about her second son. When Galeazzo told her Filippo would visit him on campaign, "she became all agitated and upset, and she almost started to weep, and she said that Filippo was already an adult, and he was being spoiled and wasting away in idleness here."[70]

Sforza Maria was formally titled "duke of Bari" during his eldest brother's reign. The title had come with his betrothal to Eleonora d'Aragona of Naples. As a duke, Sforza Maria ranked ahead of everyone in the dominion but his mother and eldest brother. He was a personage of some political significance and Galeazzo's residual heir until 1471. Bianca Maria must have been pleased in June 1468, when Franchino Caimi told her that Sforza Maria was being good and diligent, "and it seems to me he has said good-bye to childish things."[71] However, Sforza Maria displayed the least notable personality of all Galeazzo's full brothers, and his frequent illnesses kept him from playing fully the role of second son.[72]

After Galeazzo, the brother who made the biggest impression on others was Ludovico, not yet referred to as "il Moro." Ludovico spent the first two years of Galeazzo's reign in princely training at their mother's dower city of Cremona. There, he was educated in arms and letters, and he gained experience in entertaining ambassadors, appearing at public functions, and participating in local government.[73] Ludovico was Bianca Maria's favorite; she took a close interest in his welfare and training, clearly anticipating that he would rule someday. Galeazzo believed that she would bequeath Cremona to Ludovico, who the duke reportedly said was "worth more than all the others."[74]

Ludovico showed an interest in all the matters appropriate to his station in life. At one point, he asked for his mother's permission to have his armor sent back to him in Cremona, "to keep it close to me, as is the custom of each good and valorous man of arms."[75] Bianca Maria wanted him to excel at letters as well as arms. In response to her instructions "to attend to making [himself] a *virtuoso,* and to write at least once a week in [his] own hand, in Latin rather than in the vulgar [tongue]," Ludovico promised to do the best he could, "knowing . . . that the *virtuosi* are those that rule and give laws to others."[76] He was inclined to speak in hyperbole and to run afoul of his brother's princely prerogatives. In October 1467, Ludovico tried to intervene in the execution of a man-at-arms. Galeazzo's response was swift and brutal: "We say that you have done ill and most ill to impede this execution. . . . You are a baby; don't put yourself to doing that about which you do not know."[77]

In general, Galeazzo treated his brothers with an uncomfortable combination of vigorous intimacy and callous formality. In the early years of his reign, all of his brothers were eager to join him, wherever he might be. In court or on campaign, the duke was at the center of events, and his brothers wanted to share in the excitement. Filippo, Sforza Maria, and Ludovico had high expectations of their new lord, but they were constantly disappointed by his lack of fraternal warmth. The social distance that the duke maintained was reflected in the formal manner in which he greeted them. Rather than embracing, they merely "touched his hand."[78]

Galeazzo did not trust his brothers fully, either. He was loath to let Sforza Maria and Ludovico enter their own castles. In January 1468, Sforza Maria and Ludovico waited impatiently for Galeazzo to authorize their occupation of newly granted estates; the two brothers had to ask Cicco Simonetta for help in expediting the matter. Later, Ludovico found he needed ducal permission to go hawking at his own estate of Pandino.[79] When Filippo and Sforza Maria visited the duke in March 1468, Sforza Maria remarked sourly that "the acts of kindness he has done us so far have not been very great."[80] Such grumbling from her sons must have torn Bianca Maria between the desire to see her sons get along well and her concern for Galeazzo's princely dignity. When she sent Filippo, Sforza Maria, and Ludovico to stay with Galeazzo in May 1468, she insisted that they treat him "not as a brother but as a lord." She scolded Filippo severely for disobeying the duke.[81]

Ippolita Comes to Visit

In all the world, the person who looked on Galeazzo most fondly was probably his sister Ippolita. Throughout his reign, she served as a valuable informant in Naples. In December 1467, she arrived in his dominion for a visit that would last for many months. Ippolita was a well-educated, well-mannered, well-liked woman. Unlike her elder brother, she was always willing to be guided by her parents. In February 1467, she wrote to her mother from her husband's home at Capua Castle. The dutiful daughter asked "when it seems that I can wear another color than black, because I don't want to change without leave from Your Ladyship." It had been almost a full year that Ippolita had worn mourning for her father.[82] A few months later, she gave birth to Bianca Maria's first legitimate grandchild, a son who would be second in line to the throne of Naples.[83]

A Season of Pleasures   Less than seven months after her son was born, Ippolita arrived by boat in Genoa. On Christmas Day, she was met there by her brother Ludovico and half-brother Sforza Secondo, who escorted her on the four-day trip to meet Galeazzo at Pavia.[84] She came with several Neapolitan noblewomen and was joined in the Sforza dominion by her husband and Federigo da Montefeltro. The men had been with the forces of the league in the Romagna. "Other lords" were also invited, as well as ambassadors from the Italian League powers. On February 4, Pope Paul II imposed a unilateral "Pauline peace" accord, and the League had to formulate a response. Because so many foreign dignitaries were present, "as we desire to show them the greatest honor that will be possible for us, and that our court be honorable," Galeazzo commanded some of his leading feudatories to attend court and "stay here until these festivities [*feste*] are finished." As a matter of honor, the duke paid living expenses for some of the prominent visitors, including Federigo himself.[85]

Galeazzo had ambitious plans; he invited twenty-five prominent military commanders to attend a "beautiful and graceful" joust in January, honoring Alfonso of Calabria and the other visitors.[86] At the end of the Christmas season, Galeazzo had money for living expenses disbursed to sixteen gentlemen of the court, then at Milan. He wanted them to come to Pavia and keep company for an indefinite period with Ippolita and her husband.[87] During the next two months, Galeazzo and his guests were celebrating and conferring almost continuously, moving back and forth between Milan, Pavia, and the Lomellina.

Bianca Maria took little part in the festivities. She did not travel to Pavia at all, and illness largely confined her to the Corte Arengo.[88] Ippolita went to her mother very early in her visit and was received happily. The situation with her brother was more difficult. On more than one occasion during the visit, Ippolita was torn between spending time with him and with her husband. Galeazzo was very possessive of her and not at all gracious when she told him she would travel with Alfonso in early February. Galeazzo tried to make her as jealous as he was; while they were talking, he called their younger sister Elisabetta over, telling her that "if she put on a little flesh, she would be much more beautiful than the lady duchess, her sister." Later in the conversation, he kissed Elisabetta and told her that "even if she wasn't altogether as beautiful as her sister, she had so many more virtues in herself than [Ippolita] had."[89] Ippolita did not change her mind.

The distinguished visitors were entertained with a variety of noble pastimes, especially hunting, dining, sight-seeing, dancing, and costume pageants. Alfonso of Calabria showed a great interest in every aspect of the Milanese court and administration. One day, he went to see "all the offices of the court, down to the wine cellars." Fiscal officials in the Chamber of

Ordinary Incomes were surprised when Alfonso and his companions appeared there. Those officials informed Galeazzo later of the questions the Neapolitans had asked about Milanese revenues and the answers officials had given, skirting some sensitive areas.[90] Six days later, at Pavia Castle, Alfonso toured the great ducal library, then roamed from room to room throughout the castle.[91]

Although Galeazzo was the principal host for this extended visit, others extended their hospitality as well. On January 16, Alfonso of Calabria dined at the Certosa of Pavia with Sforza Maria and Ludovico.[92] Twelve days later, the hostess for supper was Maddalena Torelli, widow (and mother) of the count of Guastalla. On that occasion, the whole company had a good laugh at the expense of Federigo da Montefeltro, generally one of Italy's more dignified princes. He was splattered in the face and chest with savory sauce from a live capon that had been brought to the table, and he had to leave the room and change his clothes.[93] In late February, Galeazzo brought Federigo and the "Conte Camerlengo" (Iñigo d'Avalos, marshal of the kingdom of Naples), along with "a great part of his court," to Mortara, his brother Ludovico's castle in the Lomellina. There, they amused themselves with hunting, eating, and good-humored conversation.[94]

Much of the activity that winter was good-humored and lighthearted. On January 23, after some hawking, Galeazzo and his princely guests went riding in the Giardino behind Porta Giovia Castle. Federigo and Giovanni Francesco Gonzaga rode on individual horses; the rest of the company mounted mules, most of them in tandem. Ippolita rode with one of her mother's court ladies, Margherita Visconti Crivelli, behind her. Ippolita's husband, the duke of Calabria, rode on the same mule as her brother, the duke of Milan. Two Neapolitan counts also participated in the fun; one rode with his wife. The other did not want to take his wife, so she went on foot with her daughter to see the rabbits at a house in the hunting park.[95]

Parties and Pageants   The duke held some grand parties as well. On January 31, "a party was held in the Sala Grande [of the Corte Arengo], where there was a large number of well-dressed gentlewomen." The central figures of Galeazzo's court were present in gorgeous costumes and liveries, and they staged a splendid pageant. First, Sforza Maria and Filippo Sforza entered with their households. Then came a squadron of Galeazzo's young friends and relatives, including his half-brother Polidoro, his longtime friend Guido Antonio Arcimboldi, and the young counts Torelli—"which was a beautiful sight." Finally, Galeazzo himself entered with Bonifacio of Montferrat (son of the marquess), Sforza Secondo, and the duke's close friend, Giovanni Antonio Cotta. They did two dances, then left to change clothes, returning for a light meal. Galeazzo enjoyed himself so much that he decided to hold another party the following week.[96]

In the meantime, the entertainments continued, with more dancing and costuming by the principals. Galeazzo became expansive. He spoke to Bianca Maria about going to Rome and fulfilling a vow, leaving Alfonso of Calabria and Federigo da Montefeltro in charge of "the governance of this state." He told Federigo to send for his wife (Galeazzo's first cousin, Battista Sforza), "because his intention was that [Federigo] should stay here several months."[97] In the midst of all this merrymaking, Galeazzo's close friend, Donato del Conte, fled the court once again. His departure was a surprise once again; in December, he had been one of Galeazzo's closest companions.[98]

On February 7, the duke of Milan held another grand party at the Corte Arengo, with "around 180 ladies" present.[99] Margherita Visconti Crivelli and the wife of Pietro da Gallarate appeared in white damask livery, with their hair and headdresses in Neapolitan style. They were followed by Galeazzo's brothers with twelve companions in green livery, then twelve of Galeazzo's own intimates in a livery based on a portrait of Duke GianGaleazzo Visconti. After that "beautiful sight," a Visconti cousin of Galeazzo's entered with ten companions; they danced a piece, then dramatically removed their long outer garments to reveal dazzling white damask suits, embroidered with pearls. The charming display was observed by several princely figures seated in a viewing stand. Alfonso and Ippolita sat in the place of honor, with Galeazzo, Federigo, and ambassadors from Florence, Ferrara, and Bologna around them. In the lower part of the viewing stand sat several ladies of high rank, including Elisabetta Sforza (dressed in Neapolitan style), Beatrice d'Este Sforza, and the wives of the two visiting Neapolitan counts.

Marriage Proposals   The diplomatic overtones of the splendid gathering on February 7 reflected the importance of such events in the business of Renaissance princes. The season of pleasures in the winter of 1468 had a compelling purpose for Galeazzo; he was making his final selection of a bride. The year 1468 was an appropriate time for the duke to make that choice. His first betrothed, Dorotea Gonzaga, had died in 1467. At that time, the second betrothal his father had made for him, with Bona of Savoy, became more concrete.[100] Several new ideas involving Galeazzo and his siblings came into play. The court of Savoy suggested that Galeazzo and his sister Elisabetta make a double match with Bona and her brother Filippo; Bianca Maria counseled prudence. On January 13, she informed him that messengers had arrived from the duke of Bavaria with another marriage proposal involving Elisabetta.[101] Ludovico and Barbara Gonzaga also continued to pursue a marriage connection with the Sforza, even after Duke Francesco had rejected two of their daughters. The original candidate, Susanna, had developed a physical deformity. Francesco Sforza dissolved the later contract with Dorotea on the pretext of potential physical problems.[102]

In December 1467, the Mantuan ambassador, Marsilio Andreasi, discussed with Galeazzo the marriage prospects of the remaining Gonzaga daughters. The duke was interested in them as much for his brother Ludovico as for himself, but he was especially intrigued by the third daughter, Barbara. Galeazzo wanted Marsilio to ask the Gonzaga about a possible match with her; the envoy did so dutifully, but he added, "I pray God and Our Lady that [Your Ladyship] makes the response that the other marriage arrangement for her has been concluded."[103] Evidently, that arrangement was not made; Barbara was still under consideration by Galeazzo in January 1468, despite her being "of such tender age." The duke's interest in Barbara deepened when a painter, who had been sent to Mantua for the purpose, returned with a portrait of her. The portrait enchanted him; "if he had a spark of love for lady Barbara before, now he has been driven crazy" with love. The painter himself sung the praises of her beauty.[104]

By early February, though, Galeazzo had decided in favor of the match his father had arranged with the king of France. The duke would marry Bona of Savoy, thereby binding Milan more closely to her brother-in-law, King Louis XI. Bona was nineteen years old, born in 1449 to Duke Ludovico of Savoy and Anne of Cyprus. After her sister Carlotta married Louis, Bona and her other sisters spent most of their youth at the court of France.[105] The choice of a bride from the house of Savoy continued a tradition begun by Galeazzo's namesake, Galeazzo II Visconti, and his grandfather, Filippo Maria Visconti. On February 4, Ippolita and Alfonso discussed "this French bride-to-be" with Bianca Maria and Marsilio. Ippolita decided to stay in Milan for her brother's wedding.[106]

The Young Duke Takes Charge

In the winter of 1468, Galeazzo emerged as a decisive and purposeful prince, perhaps in part because of his mother's ill health. In 1467, the duke had corresponded constantly with Bianca Maria about matters of state, even while he was on campaign in the Romagna and Piedmont. However, their relationship continued to be confused and full of conflict. On January 7, 1468, he wrote her, sarcastically acknowledging receipt of "the means and regulations that you will use for the government of our state, all of which I am most certain you will do most wisely, and much better than I would be able to think or recall; and so I sleep a good sleep and rest under the eyes of your Most Illustrious Ladyship." Halfway through the letter, he did an emotional turnabout, lamenting that his mother had written to him "as a stranger, using the *voi*." The duke insisted that if Bianca Maria "considers me her son," she should write him using the *tu* "in the usual way." He ended by declaring she should command him "as your son and servant, as I am and intend to be so long as I live."[107]

Even as Galeazzo was pleading with Bianca Maria to treat him as a mother, he was replacing her as a ruler. By Christmas, he had already decided that "from the New Year forward," all ducal letters would be sent out "solely in our name." He told the Privy Council's secretary to "execute this command secretly."[108] Ousting one's own mother from government was a delicate matter.

Public Audiences

Galeazzo wanted to be a great ruler, dispensing justice, fostering prosperity, and bringing glory. As soon as he had taken over the reins of government, he proclaimed publicly his decision "to give public audience two days each week, that is, Monday and Thursday, to whatever person will want to speak there. . . . And everyone who will have brought a petition or made some other request should return the following Saturday, because a timely response and disposition will be given to all." The duke's stated purpose was to make justice more accessible to his subjects, "to the poor man as to the rich man." If he could not be present personally, his brothers Sforza Maria or Ludovico would stand in for him.

The Ferrarese ambassador observed that this measure was popular with the duke's subjects but less so than a tax reduction would have been.[109] Sforza Maria was unhappy with his own part in the plan. He told Galeazzo he would accept the command "to stay [in Milan] to attend to the audience [that has been] arranged," but he requested passionately that "some times, and most of all on the days when I don't have to attend to the said audience, that I may go for pleasure [i.e., hunting] as far as Desio."[110]

The Ducal Marriage to Bona of Savoy

In early February 1468, Galeazzo showed an intense interest in ruling the Milanese dominion, but his attention soon shifted to his upcoming marriage. For the next six months, he directed much of the dominion's resources to planning, executing, and celebrating his wedding.

The Wedding in France

Lombard marriage customs generally called for two wedding ceremonies, the first at the bride's home and the second in the groom's. Since Bona resided at the French royal court, the duke did not go to the first ceremony in person. A visit to Louis XI's domain could have been physically dangerous, politically disruptive, and personally humiliating to Galeazzo, who would have appeared as inferior in rank to his bride. In his stead, the duke sent his eldest and most distinguished half-brother, Tristano. Tristano was on his way by February 21, having put his personal affairs in order and collected four pieces of velvet as the duke's gifts to the king of France.[111]

At the same time that he was dispatching Tristano to France, the duke began his preparations within the Milanese dominion by planning for the new duchess's household. March was a relatively quiet month, in which the anniversary of Duke Francesco's death was the main public event. Galeazzo chose not to be present personally; instead, he spent three weeks hunting at Vigevano. He wanted Filippo and Sforza Maria to join him there, which disturbed Bianca Maria and the Privy Council; the brothers were expected to participate in the solemn observance. The duke then returned to Milan for the anniversary of his own accession, but he did not celebrate it publicly. In March and April, the league consultations continued, and some of Galeazzo's princely guests, including Ippolita and Federigo, remained in the dominion. Both of them resided mostly in the Corte Arengo, close to Bianca Maria.[112]

At the end of March, Galeazzo received a letter from Tristano, describing Bona of Savoy as she appeared at the French court in Amboise.[113] In April, the marriage activity accelerated, beginning with final negotiations of terms. As Tristano informed his ducal brother, the French custom, "especially [for] the royal blood," required that Galeazzo as groom "should accept the articles [of the marriage agreement] and ratify them before he gets married." The negotiations were painful and embarrassing for Tristano, who had not been prepared for this aspect of his visit to France. "Think, Your Lordship, what my life must be like, that I believed myself to be coming to a wedding and to 'a done deal' [cose f(a)c(t)e]. God grant me the grace to have good patience." He scolded Galeazzo: "My Lord, to me it seems not a great honor to Your Excellency, and a very great disgrace to me, to send me so naked of instructions [nudo de comission]."[114]

Louis XI had particular concerns about guarantees for Bona's dowry, which amounted to 100,000 gold écus, plus her household goods. The agreement accepted by Galeazzo included conditions that he give Bona an honorable and comfortable place to live, let her children succeed to the ducal throne, and ensure that she receive her dowry and an annual income of 15,000 ducats if the duke should die. Galeazzo read the conditions, discussed them with the Privy Council, signed them with his own hand, sealed them, and sent them to Tristano. Then, the wedding could proceed.[115]

The month of April 1468 ended on an auspicious note for the duke of Milan. His marriage agreement settled, he was able to announce that "the Universal Peace of Italy in perpetuity" had been signed five days before. The duke told his mother to have the joyous event proclaimed on May 1 in Milan with fireworks, flourishes of trumpets, and three days of processions.[116] In

May 1468, the court's energies were directed increasingly to the ducal marriage. Galeazzo received letters from Tristano describing the royal court of France, where even dances were arranged in order of rank. The wedding itself occurred on May 10, and Tristano outlined it in detail, including the crown that Bona wore as a member of the royal family.[117] He told Galeazzo also of the symbolic consummation that was performed after the wedding ceremony, in the royal court's presence. Bona and Tristano kissed and climbed into a bed, he on one side and she on the other. There, they "touched one another's bare leg . . . according to the custom."[118]

When Galeazzo received this description, he wrote his mother, calling Bona "my legitimate wife" and stating proudly that the wedding had occurred in the presence of the king and queen "and the other lords and barons of the court, with great festivities [*feste*] and solemnities and ceremonies according to the custom of the royal house [*casa*] of France."[119] Not everyone was happy about his new links to that royal house. Gottardo Panigarola's brother reported from France that "continually in this court it is murmured, especially by the Angevins, that the Most Serene Lord King has broken his neck [*rotto el collo*] in marrying [Bona] to Your Lordship, because she will be badly treated, she will not be able to leave the house, and she will have the worst time that a lady of his family [*casa*] has ever had." Galeazzo was advised to treat his bride well so as to ease the minds of the worried king and queen.[120]

The Wedding in Milan

The year after Galeazzo and Bona were married, the duke drew up a fresco program that showed the central events in their marriage. It outlined

> the first marriage made by the Most Illustrious Lady Duchess, by means of the Magnificent Lord Tristano, in the presence of the King and Queen of France; continuing on the road as she embarks on the sea, disembarks at Genoa, and the Lord [Galeazzo] goes to meet her; the arrival at Milan, the ceremony in front of the Duomo, the presentation of the feudatories, the advent to Pavia, and the change of French clothing to Lombard, with the damsels given by the Most Illustrious Lord, and others of the household, etc.[121]

Within a week after the wedding at Amboise, Bona, Tristano, and their company left for Milan. The hasty departure was suggested by Louis XI, since the wedding had delayed their original schedule. Galeazzo was kept informed of their progress to Aigues Mortes, near Marseilles, where they would board the *Galeaza,* a richly furnished boat, and come to Genoa.[122]

Preparations   In the meantime, Galeazzo threw the dominion into a frenzy of preparations for his bride's arrival. On June 10, he formally announced the upcoming wedding to sixteen of his cities. He told them to hold public celebrations and send ambassadors to the wedding, "since we desire to have all our most faithful citizens and subjects participate in this joy and festivity." The following day, he sent wedding invitations to two hundred feudatories, "desiring to have all our gentlemen, citizens and people [*populi*] participate in this joy and prosperity of ours."[123] A sizable contingent of Milanese nobles would travel to Aigues Mortes and escort her back to the Sforza dominion. Hundreds of persons, led by Ludovico Sforza, were directed to greet her at Genoa. One set of instructions went to fourteen nobles of the dominion, four of their wives, a lady of the court, and the sons of the marquesses of Montferrat and Saluzzo. The instructions came in several phases, culminating in the command to travel to Genoa "in the company of this brother of ours [Ludovico], and honor him and revere him as much as you would our own person." The scope of the preparations is evident from instructions for the 21 persons addressed to bring households totaling 123 horses and 159 persons.[124]

Many more persons were assigned to greet Bona in Milan, and thousands were invited to the wedding itself. The ceremony was originally planned for around June 21 but had to be postponed to the second week of July.[125] Messengers scurried back and forth, carrying commands from the duke to his subjects and appeals or excuses from the subjects to the duke. Pregnancy and childbirth hindered several women from complying with Galeazzo's commands. One of the duke's intimates, Giovanni Giacomo Trivulzio, excused his wife from the trip to Genoa; she had recently given birth to a premature baby, who died and left her suffering with excess milk. The wife of Guido Antonio Arcimboldi was too heavily pregnant to travel, and Guido Antonio himself was away at the baths, healing a foot problem.[126] Lack of money was another obstacle. Sforza Secondo claimed that he could not afford new suits. He requested money or material, "so that I may appear among the others." The fiscal official Fazio Gallerani said that he had no horses and too little money to outfit himself and his wife honorably but that they would prepare as fast and as well as possible.[127] Some of the duke's cities responded similarly. The *commissario* of Lodi told Galeazzo that Lodi had chosen two ambassadors and a gift, "but, truly, this community is very poor."[128]

For some of the duke's subjects, the obstacle to compliance was the confused, or even mutually contradictory, nature of his commands to them. Sforza Secondo's wife had to ask Cicco Simonetta what she was expected to do: "When and how and with how many companions . . . [and whether] I should come to Milan or go to Pavia, or somewhere else." Others were instructed to be in two different places at the same time.[129]

The duke had so much on his mind that he could not keep track of his intentions. Consequently, he established a committee to oversee the wedding arrangements. They were charged with such tasks as finding feathers for the new duchess's feather beds, a master of stables for her household, and a woman of twenty-five to thirty years who was "a good expert [*magistra*]," for doing Bona's hair and headdress.[130] Many of the wedding preparations concerned wardrobe matters, including gifts of cloth for Bona's escorts. Some materials were in short supply and had to be sought as far afield as Florence, Mantua, Ferrara, and Germany.[131] The duke also had Milan's jewelers, goldsmiths, and silversmiths working feverishly to supply the items he intended to give his bride. The list of marriage gifts from him runs to seven closely printed pages.[132] Galeazzo also arranged for participation by more than fifty trumpeters, supplementing his own corps with others from the cities of Milan and Genoa, and the courts of more than a dozen princes and noblemen.[133]

Other resources were poured into Bona's trip from France to Genoa. The *Galeaza* was prepared to lodge over three hundred persons, beyond the sailors, and a ducal official told Galeazzo, "I do not believe it would be possible to find a more worthy boat."[134] However, even the *Galeaza* lacked space for the large company that would be traveling with the new duchess, and additional galleys were required. The boats were all provided with sheets, blankets, and silver plate. The *Galeaza* was outfitted in lavish style; Galeazzo's own silver brocade bed canopy was used to shade the boat's poop deck.[135]

Galeazzo wanted Bona to receive the best possible treatment once she had arrived at Genoa, as well. He instructed the vice-governor there to show her as many "honors and solemnities and demonstrations of joy as are possible," giving her the keys to the city, the ducal fortress, and so forth, "and not otherwise than you would do it for our own person, and much more."[136] The duke also wanted to send two goldsmiths, a glover, a hosier, and a shoemaker to be at her disposal there, "so that the charming lady bride and duchess understands that nothing could be lacking to her."[137]

Six weeks of constant movement by prominent persons, each with his or her own household, caused a logistical nightmare, particularly in Genoa and Milan. In Genoa, horses had to be procured for the party arriving with her by sea from France. They were difficult to find, because the last group of horses lent to visiting dignitaries (Ippolita's company) had been treated badly. At the same time, stable space and straw had to be found for horses arriving from elsewhere in the dominion. Genoa lacked adequate space; some of the gentlefolk coming to greet Bona found that their horses were stabled outside the city entirely.[138]

Housing and household furnishings had to be provided for the entire retinue accompanying the new duchess at every stop on her route from France to the city of Milan.[139] The lodging situation in Milan was difficult because so many persons were coming for the wedding. Summer heat and an outbreak of the plague had driven some residents to their villas in the country. Galeazzo's seneschals-general wrote him worried letters about lodging the princely figures who were expected to attend. For the duke's uncle, Bosio Sforza, "we have provided at [the abbey of] San Simpliciano, with much difficulty." For Corrado Fogliani, half-brother of Francesco Sforza, the persons of the household would be lodged at an abbey, while the horses had to be placed at an inn outside the city gates.[140]

For Bona's own residence, Galeazzo was having Porta Giovia Castle prepared.[141] In the meantime, other dignitaries were reportedly coming from Mantua and Venice and needed accommodations. The son of the marquess of Saluzzo arrived around June 22 and was placed in the best rooms at the Inn of the Well, one of Milan's finest lodgings. The seneschals thought he would be comfortable there, but he was not, so they told the innkeeper "that he should extend to him all the courtesies possible." Still, the visiting prince wanted to move into the marquess of Montferrat's Milan house, to stay with his friend, Bonifacio. They asked the ducal seneschals to provide extra beds for the house, but the seneschals could not help; the plague made it risky to borrow beds from others, and the ducal residences had none to spare.[142]

Borrowing beds, furnishings, and even houses was often necessary in situations of high demand. For the wedding, Milanese residents, including Angelo Simonetta and Maddalena Torelli, were asked to prepare their houses "to lodge as many as possible of those who will come" with the new duchess. The duke's relatives, Giovanni Mauruzzi da Tolentino and Drusiana Sforza, were among those asked to lend tapestries and silver plate for the wedding festivities.[143] Because Galeazzo anticipated a stay of one or two nights at Vigevano Castle, he asked that the "principal and most worthy citizens" of Novara lend up to sixteen "beds, beautiful and well-furnished with beautiful and honorable covers and sheets" for use at that time.[144]

Finally, the duke provided for a system of signals to let him know when Bona had arrived in his dominion. A series of posts would relay the message from Genoa to the duke at Pavia, using columns of smoke (or, at night, fires) and shots from a bombard. The system was not foolproof; smoke and flame from a house on fire caused a false alarm that the duchess was arriving.[145]

The New Duchess Arrives   Bona of Savoy and her French companions stayed at King René of Anjou's estate near Aigues Mortes before they boarded the *Galeaza* around June 23, 1468. For several days, they proceeded in luxury along the Ligurian coast, stopping at the major city of Savona on the way. The voyage had its discomforts; Bona and her ladies were seasick.[146] Nonetheless, on June 28, she landed at Genoa and entered the palace "with great festivity and triumph."[147]

The new duchess did not stay long in Genoa; within a day or two, she was on her way to meet her husband for the first time. The duke would not meet her in Genoa, where his lordship rested on vassalage to her French brother-in-law. Galeazzo had to wait until Bona and her company traveled over the

Ligurian Alps into the duchy of Milan proper. Galeazzo was in a state of high excitement by that time. He led a company that included Federigo da Montefeltro, roaming around the plains between the Po River and the mountains, waiting to encounter Bona. The weather was scorching, and the duke became furious when misleading information about his bride's progress caused him to ride unnecessarily in the heat of the day.[148]

When Bona did finally come into the duchy and his presence, Galeazzo did something very strange: he played a hoax on her. As their respective retinues approached one another in the Alpine foothills, the duke sent a messenger ahead to announce Galeazzo as the duke of Bari, his brother Sforza Maria. Bona believed him and was constrained to treat her husband as her brother-in-law: "She leaned out to him and touched only his hand. Then, immediately, she looked at him, and from the painted likenesses [of him] that she had seen before, and the intimations of the others [escorting her], she recognized him right away. And right away she dismounted from her horse, and the aforesaid Lord did the same, and there with the name of God they embraced and kissed one another quite thoroughly."[149]

It is difficult to understand why the eager bridegroom would play such a game with his bride. Whatever his reasons, the duke soon showed a different sentiment, ordering a commemorative column to be erected on the site of their meeting. Problems arose regarding jurisdiction over "the place where the first congress [*congresso*] occurred, and we were joined together [*se giunsemo insieme*]." Two communes claimed that land, as did Francesco Visconti, distant cousin to the duke. Galeazzo wrote letters demanding that the situation be clarified, and he instructed Francesco, "If the territory be yours, that you yourself have that column made, in memory of that day and act, with the dignity that the matter merits."[150]

After their first meeting, the bridal couple repaired to Vigevano Castle for the real consummation of their match. When Bianca Maria heard that "today they are supposed to sleep together at Vigevano," she asked a physician and two other courtiers to "advise [me of] that which ensues."[151] This consummation was an event of public significance; on July 5, Galeazzo announced in writing to a wide range of government officials that "having done what was required for the regulations of Holy Church, in our castle of Vigevano, we conjoined [*coniunxemo*] with her and consummated the marriage." He went on to declare that the ducal couple would proceed to Milan "to solemnly celebrate our nuptials," and he spoke glowingly of his wife's beauties, good customs, and virtues. Finally, he told those officials to obey the duchess's commands as if they were his own, "wanting, as we do, to honor our said consort, as is our obligation, as much for her virtue as also for reverence of the Majesty of the Most Serene and Christian King of France, her and our brother-in-law, who has sent her home to us most worthily and honorably."[152] Galeazzo's pride and satisfaction at this match glows through every word of his proclamation, and he must have been eager to show off his bride at the wedding ceremony in Milan.

Unfortunately, circumstances did not allow the magnificent display Galeazzo had planned, and the event proved anticlimactic. He himself stated afterward that "we have made small show of these nuptials, on account of the plague." The plague had been troubling Milan all summer, forcing many to retreat to country villas or remain in quarantine. Moreover, the duke had decided—against all advice—to hold the ceremony in the central piazza of the city rather than in the Duomo facing it. Violent storms destroyed many of the temporary structures erected for the occasion, and the damage could not be repaired in time to give the event its full impact.[153]

The Old Duchess Departs   While Galeazzo had prepared frenetically for his bride's arrival, his mother continued to suffer a lingering illness. Bianca Maria maintained an active correspondence with him throughout, but she did not participate in the preparations, except to give some suggestions on the new duchess's household. The dowager duchess lacked both health and wealth at that point. Already in February, she had been reduced to selling her jewels to Galeazzo, who did not offer anything close to their true value. Bianca Maria took him to task for his cheapness, reminding him that "we sell out of extreme need, that we have to satisfy our debts." The ungracious duke accused her of selling the jewels "solely for the purpose of having an excuse, in the arrival of my wife, for not giving her anything of yours."[154] Bianca Maria tried to maintain a cheerful attitude in dealing with her eldest son and his marriage. Sometimes, she showed a flash of the playfulness that characterized her relationship with Galeazzo when things were going well between them. Having heard that he was about to meet his bride for the first time, Bianca Maria asked that "when you have seen her, you will advise us of your opinion about her beauties, with this condition, though—that you not tell us lies."[155]

In mid-May, Bianca Maria went to Cremona for several weeks, accompanied by Ippolita and their respective households. Ippolita asked her brother to allow Giovanni Gabriele Crivelli to come with them, as she wanted his wife, Margherita Visconti, to be part of the company. Ippolita claimed that Margherita would be sad without her husband. The duke had other intentions for Giovanni Gabriele and Margherita, though.[156] Bianca Maria and Ippolita left without them, returning only a few days before the wedding ceremony took place.[157] The dowager duchess was weak from her illness, and she did not relish traveling.[158] There was something pathetic about Bianca Maria's slow and painful progress across the heart of her ancestral homeland. Before the ceremony in Milan, Galeazzo wanted her to make a brief visit to the bridal couple at Abbiategrasso Castle, Bianca Maria's own birthplace. The dowager duchess, last of the Visconti ducal lineage, had to ask her temperamental son "what ladies it seems to you that we should bring with us, and if your brothers and sisters, and your children, should come with us or not." Having received no response, she said the next day that she would bring as few persons as possible, unless she heard otherwise from him.[159]

Bianca Maria had not lost her ability to command, however. The day before arriving in Milan, she gave instructions that her servant Damiano "not enter our wardrobe, nor allow anyone else to enter, but keep the key close to him" and give it to no one. She wanted that "our chambers be well arranged, and do not allow anyone in the world to enter there until we ourselves have entered there." She told the seneschals-general "immediately to put in order [the place] where those in my company, and that of the duchess of Calabria, my daughter, have to dismount. And in this, do not lose time."[160]

Wedding Costs and Gifts   The wedding and its preparations were very costly to the duke, who had already run up substantial debts for the living expenses of visiting dignitaries. By mid-May, the seneschals-general alone owed 12,000 to 14,000 pounds (3,000–3,500 ducats) for the expenses of the Florentine ambassadors to the League talks and of the duke and duchess of Calabria. The masters of revenues refused to supply the seneschals with further credit until the duke stabilized the financial situation.[161] While still supporting those distinguished visitors to the dominion, Galeazzo paid a substantial share of expenses for the persons sent to Genoa for Bona's arrival. Attendance at this event was a duty to the lord, but Galeazzo wanted courtiers and nobles to share his joy. Involving these elites in the proceedings also linked them more closely to the ducal family. Galeazzo counted on the Genoese to pay the costs of outfitting the *Galeaza* and hosting the many visitors to their city, but the local populace would not provide more than 6,000 pounds (1,500 ducats), rather a small sum for the occasion. Galeazzo had to spend 2,500 ducats just for "the expenses of gentlemen going to Marseilles."[162] He called for another 3,000 ducats to pay the expenses of the committee supervising wedding preparations. In his extravagance, Galeazzo also gave cash payments to his trumpeters and large quantities of velvet and other fine stuffs to eighteen *camerieri*. The cloth was to be made into splendid garments, probably for the wedding ceremony.[163]

The wardrobe expenses for the wedding were staggering. Even before May had ended, the duke's treasurer *di camera* said he needed 3,500 ducats for luxury cloth and related items. A month later, he requested 1,000 ducats more for work already done. Galeazzo himself sent two requisition letters to the treasurer-general, demanding 2,354 ducats for a few hundred pearls being sewn into clothes and a headdress for Bona.[164] Two court officers preparing the duchess's household sent more than two dozen letters requesting money for items ranging from bedclothes and tableware to painted decoration on wedding chests. In one case, they requested 50 ducats for her steward "to spend in small matters that would be burdensome to you and to us to make a listing of every little thing."[165] Such expenditures could not be covered by current income. Luxury cloth given to Bona's French escorts was assigned to payment from ducal revenues in 1470–1472—two to four years in the future. Individuals also found themselves going into debt for this occasion. A *cameriere* preparing for Bona's brief stay at Sale pawned 60 ducats worth of personal property to pay for various needs that arose. He asked the duke to pay him at least 30 ducats to help buy back the items before they were lost completely.[166]

In the midst of this lavish spending, Galeazzo exercised some unexpected economies. Although he was paying the expenses of several visiting dignitaries, he did not cover those of some princely wedding guests, including the marquess of Saluzzo's son. The duke planned also to ignore the expenses of his councillors, which brought a respectful rebuke from his seneschals-general. They felt "that it is not an honorable thing" to refuse such generosity to the councillors, who had been "invited to the nuptials on behalf of Your Lordship, because this is the custom in every place, not only for lords but also for every private citizen."[167]

Galeazzo solicited large wedding gifts from the cities of his dominion, leading to the protestations of poverty mentioned above. However, the duke claimed that from the "feudatories and gentlemen" he had invited to the wedding, "we were not expecting any reward from anyone, other than the honoring of the festivity." When Pier Maria Rossi presented him with 100 ducats, Galeazzo said that although "we have not known how to refuse" gifts of "other things which [other guests] have had made . . . neither from you nor others have we wanted to accept money." The duke returned Pier Maria's cash.[168] The gifts that Galeazzo accepted included considerable quantities of worked silver; ducal agents listed them by description and weight. The largest single gift came from the king of France; it totaled 895 "fine" ounces, including a basin bearing the arms of France and Savoy. Federigo da Montefeltro gave items weighing 523 ounces altogether, and the city of Pavia gave items totaling 604 "Ambrosian" ounces. Most of the gifts were under 100 ounces, however; the grand total came to 7,285 ounces.[169]

Pavia Castle

After Galeazzo and Bona were finally wed in Milan, they withdrew to Pavia Castle and passed the rest of July quietly. Near the end of the month, the duke assigned the city of Pavia to his bride, in the expectation that she would bear him a son who would take the title "count of Pavia," traditional for the ducal heirs.[170]

"In the Lombard Style"   It was at Pavia Castle, in July 1468, that Bona made the crucial transition from her French past to her Lombard future. To become fully a part of her new community, Bona had to shed her past, represented literally and symbolically by her French apparel. She had presumably continued to wear these accustomed styles throughout the journey, the wedding, and all the proceedings that introduced her to Galeazzo's domain. When that ceremonial sequence ended, her new Lombard routine began. On July 20, Galeazzo ordered a dozen of the finest veils "in the style which is used presently here in Lombardy" because Bona "from this time forward has to use clothing and headdresses in the Lombard style."[171]

At the same time, the duke gave her companions from France the finest cloth he could find in that time of plague. Some of the recipients refused to accept the gifts, while others sent them back or sold them cheaply. To show Louis XI that he had made worthy offerings to all the visitors, even though some would return to the king empty-handed, Galeazzo wrote to his ambassador in France, enclosing a list of the gifts and recipients.[172]

"We Bear It Special Delight and Love"   Pavia Castle was Galeazzo Maria Sforza's favorite residence. He said that he loved that city more than any other outside Milan, "reputing ourselves to be raised here [in Pavia]. And you can judge and know if we bear it special delight and love, because the greater part of the year we make stable residence [*ferma residentia*] here, with our Most Illustrious Consort and children, and our court."[173] As heir to the duchy of Milan, Galeazzo held the title "count of Pavia" until the birth of his own heir. During the years when he could freely choose his place of residence (1468–1476), the duke spent 35 percent of his nights—over four months per year, on average—in Pavia. He generally went there after the Christmas season and almost always spent much of the late spring and summer there.[174]

Much of the massive brick building survives to suggest how extensive a residence it was. In the mid-fourteenth century, Galeazzo II Visconti had the castle constructed as his signorial seat. Since the city of Milan pertained to his brother Bernabò, Galeazzo Visconti had no access to the family palaces that filled the center of the capital. Pavia Castle was his worthy response. Square in shape and huge in proportions, it now houses a museum, although the north side was destroyed in 1526, and the interiors in general retain little of their original appearance.[175]

The four sides of the castle were equal in size, with rooms on both upper and lower levels and square towers built into the corners. Each side consisted of eleven large vaulted rooms (of which a few were combined to form halls or chapels) and the tower rooms, accessible only through adjoining chambers. Between the circuit of the rooms and the vast central courtyard ran a hall in the form of a portico or loggia, which provided access to the rooms. This portico, divided on each side into sixteen vaults, was roughly two-thirds the width of the rooms themselves. Beyond serving as a passage between rooms, it was a dining venue for the ladies of the court and in summer months, probably housed some of the guards and lesser servants. Although the lower loggia was open, that on the upper floor was largely bricked in to form walls with windows. When the windows were shuttered, the loggia would have been fully functional as an interior space.[176]

Of all the castles in the duchy, only Pavia was equipped to house large numbers of persons from the court, with all the basic facilities needed for daily life. The ground floor housed, among other things, a laundry, a bathhouse, a bakery, and a butchery. The upper floor featured three kitchens, including one each for the households of duke and duchess. Quarters were specifically reserved for the castellan and the *camerieri* in the duke's entourage as well as the logistical and Chancery staff. Persons less central to the court, including visitors, were housed on the ground floor.[177] The stables were connected to the western side of the castle, with an entrance beneath the women's wing. The upper rooms on that side were locked off, to keep the space of the duchess, her household, and her children separate from the areas dominated by men.

Most rooms in the castle were directly accessible from the loggia. The exceptions are particularly notable: the eight tower rooms contained, among other things, the prison, the reliquary and treasury, the library, the Privy Chancery, the count of Pavia's chamber, and the duke's own apartment. The duke's bedchamber could be reached only through an enfilade of three rooms, reflecting the traditional distinctions of proximity to the prince's person. In Pavia Castle, this sequence of rooms was unique; no other suite had more than one room between the entrance from the hall and the most interior space.

Pavia Castle served many purposes beyond its role as the preferred ducal residence. It was a major showpiece, often displayed proudly to honored visitors on tour, even when Galeazzo was elsewhere. Two special features were the library and the reliquary, or treasury. The Visconti-Sforza library was one of the largest in Europe; its greatest prize was a copy of Virgil's *Aeneid* with marginal notes in Petrarch's own hand.[178] The ground-floor room adjacent to the treasury, known as the Chamber of Mirrors (*Camera delli spechi*), was beautifully and uniquely decorated with a mosaic floor and a ceiling covered with stained glass painted with persons, animals, and plants.[179] Pavia Castle was also a major fortress, and its security was extremely important. Duke Francesco had entrusted the castle to Matteo Bolognini, a noble who had helped him conquer the duchy. Francesco even granted Matteo the original ducal surname of Attendoli. In Galeazzo's time, the castellan was Matteo's son, Giovanni Bolognini Attendoli, one of the duke's most highly trusted servants.[180]

Another outstanding feature of Pavia Castle was the Parco or Barco, its hunting park, extending far beyond the city to the north. The justly famous Certosa of Pavia, a Carthusian monastery patronized by the dukes, was founded by GianGaleazzo Visconti within the area of the Parco, on the road from Milan. Galeazzo visited the Certosa rarely, but he spent a great deal of time hunting in the Parco, staying often in a hunting lodge called Mirabello.[181] The duke also experimented there with a version of tent camping, having large pavilions set up for himself and his household. During this experiment, he made use of an interesting device, the portable room: both he and his wife had portable bedchambers of wood, presumably to keep them warm in tents or in the cold drafty stone rooms of their castles in winter.[182]

Galeazzo and Bona Start a New Life

At the end of July 1468, Galeazzo began what amounted to a honeymoon at one of his favorite retreats, Monza Castle. His appearance with a sizable retinue so near Venetian territory caused concern on the other side of the border. The duke wrote to authorities in Bergamo and Crema, assuring them that he had come with Bona "to take some pleasure and recreation, as is our custom to do." He explained that he wanted to "give our exquisite consort some relief from the heat and have her see these delectable and pleasant places."[183]

In the middle of their agreeable sojourn in Monza, the ducal couple spent about a week in Milan to observe "the feast of Our Lady," the birthday of the Blessed Virgin Mary (September 8). Porta Giovia was not yet ready for occupancy by Galeazzo and Bona, so they went to the Corte Arengo. The ducal seneschals planned a festive welcome, and many prominent women of Milan participated. Because no "lady" was then resident in the Corte, Galeazzo's half-sister Isotta was asked to lead and coordinate the women's welcome. About three dozen of them would ride out to greet and escort the new duchess, while another dozen stayed at the Corte with Isotta; "there with festivities and caresses she will receive her honorably." Bona would dismount at the foot of the great stairway and proceed through the halls to her chambers.[184]

The New Duchess's Household

When Bona's French escorts returned home in July, they left her with very few attendants from her childhood home: one elderly woman and two twelve-year-old girls. The elderly woman was probably her nurse [nutrice], who began her life in Milan with a brief but serious illness.[185] Galeazzo's original plans for the new duchess's household were quite specific; the core of her

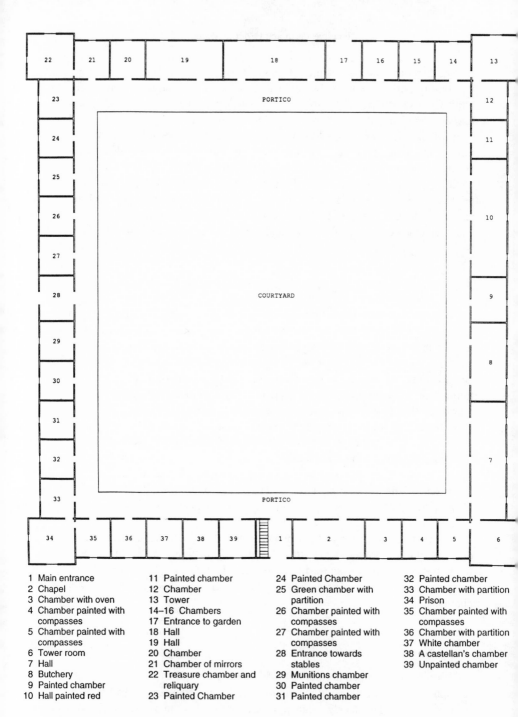

22	21	20	19	18	17	16	15	14	13

PORTICO

23		12
24		11
25		
26		10
27		
28	COURTYARD	9
29		
30		8
31		
32		7
33	PORTICO	

| 34 | 35 | 36 | 37 | 38 | 39 | 1 | 2 | 3 | 4 | 5 | 6 |

1 Main entrance
2 Chapel
3 Chamber with oven
4 Chamber painted with compasses
5 Chamber painted with compasses
6 Tower room
7 Hall
8 Butchery
9 Painted chamber
10 Hall painted red

11 Painted chamber
12 Chamber
13 Tower
14–16 Chambers
17 Entrance to garden
18 Hall
19 Hall
20 Chamber
21 Chamber of mirrors
22 Treasure chamber and reliquary
23 Painted Chamber

24 Painted Chamber
25 Green chamber with partition
26 Chamber painted with compasses
27 Chamber painted with compasses
28 Entrance towards stables
29 Munitions chamber
30 Painted chamber
31 Painted chamber

32 Painted chamber
33 Chamber with partition
34 Prison
35 Chamber painted with compasses
36 Chamber with partition
37 White chamber
38 A castellan's chamber
39 Unpainted chamber

Figure 3. Pavia Castle, approximate ground floor plan

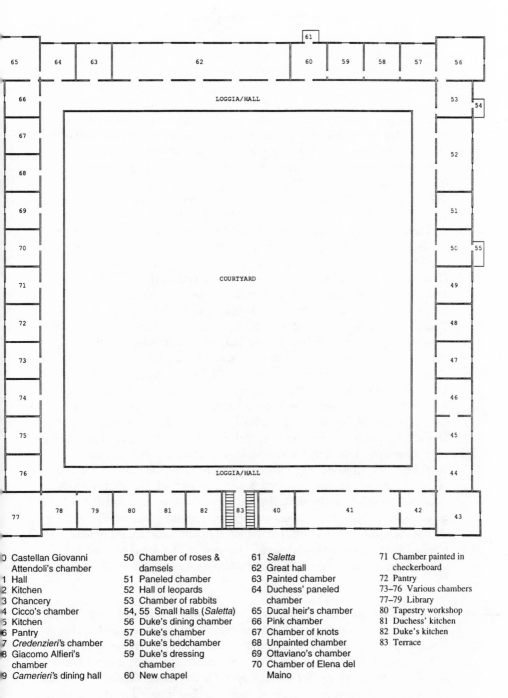

65	64	63	62	60	59	58	57	56

LOGGIA/HALL

61

66		53
67		
68		52
69		51
70	COURTYARD	50	55
71		49
72		48
73		47
74		46
75		45
76		44

54

LOGGIA/HALL

| 77 | 78 | 79 | 80 | 81 | 82 | 83 | 40 | 41 | 42 | 43 |

0 Castellan Giovanni
   Attendoli's chamber
1 Hall
2 Kitchen
3 Chancery
4 Cicco's chamber
5 Kitchen
6 Pantry
7 *Credenzieri*'s chamber
8 Giacomo Alfieri's
   chamber
9 *Camerieri*'s dining hall

50 Chamber of roses &
   damsels
51 Paneled chamber
52 Hall of leopards
53 Chamber of rabbits
54, 55 Small halls (*Saletta*)
56 Duke's dining chamber
57 Duke's chamber
58 Duke's bedchamber
59 Duke's dressing
   chamber
60 New chapel

61 *Saletta*
62 Great hall
63 Painted chamber
64 Duchess' paneled
   chamber
65 Ducal heir's chamber
66 Pink chamber
67 Chamber of knots
68 Unpainted chamber
69 Ottaviano's chamber
70 Chamber of Elena del
   Maino

71 Chamber painted in
   checkerboard
72 Pantry
73–76 Various chambers
77–79 Library
80 Tapestry workshop
81 Duchess' kitchen
82 Duke's kitchen
83 Terrace

Figure 4. Pavia Castle, approximate upper floor plan

company would be four male and four female companions (*compagni* and *compagne*), twelve damsels (*donzele*)—women aged thirty or younger—and ten *gentiluomini*. To serve their needs, she would have several male *camerieri* and female *cameriere*, a seneschal, a chancellor, a treasurer, a cupbearer, a deputy cupbearer, a server, a physician, a carver, and a master of stables, plus five musicians. Galeazzo named them all, except for most of the damsels, and he asked Bianca Maria to choose butlers as she saw fit. The duke wanted his wife's household to include persons who had served his ducal grandfather, Filippo Maria, and grandmother, Agnese del Maino. He did not want to include "any one of those that were active in the Chamber of the lord my father." Bianca Maria, to whom he presented these plans, thought his choices were good ones, but she could not understand his desire to separate Bona's court from Duke Francesco's.[186]

The duty of the four original male companions was "to be with, and honor, [Bona's] person, and act as her company [*compagnia*] with honorable and suitable salary."[187] These four men were chosen from among the most honored courtiers; all were prominent knights and nobles. Among them were Count Antonio Secco, a veteran administrator, and Ottone Visconti, a close companion of Galeazzo's both before and after the accession.[188] By the time Bona actually arrived in Milan, more *compagni*, including Giovanni Gabriele Crivelli, had been added to her company.[189] Among the female companions were Elisabetta Visconti, Cicco Simonetta's wife, and Emilia Attendoli, who had held a similar position in Bianca Maria's court. At the time that Emilia was assigned to Bona's household, her son Giovanni Francesco was Galeazzo's most active *cameriere*. Before Bona's arrival, the duke added more *compagne*, including Giovanni Gabriele Crivelli's wife, Margherita Visconti.[190] Among the damsels, Emilia Attendoli's daughter Antonia took pride of place. She had served in Bianca Maria's household. Galeazzo also chose three other damsels at the same time as the *compagne*, including the wife of his *cameriere*, Giovanni Rusconi da Verona. The duke wanted his mother to choose the rest of the damsels, but she left it to him until the last minute, then relented and made some suggestions.[191] Because of their age, the damsels probably had more in common with Bona than anyone else did in her household.

Paying for the Duchess's Household   Bona's household was funded separately from the duke's; part of each annual budget was set aside as her allotment (*assignatione*). When Galeazzo decided to marry Bona, he was said to be planning a large household of three hundred persons and a generous annual allowance of 25,000 ducats beyond her clothing expenses.[192] When he was drawing up specific plans, though, the duke showed surprising parsimony. He proposed to provide expenses for only one hundred horses, and the allowance of 12,000 ducats that he suggested was so little that his mother thought it would reflect poorly on his honor. The duke wanted limits also on "the expense of the mouths that will eat in the household . . . to avoid the nuisance of so many meals."[193]

When Galeazzo composed actual budgets for his new wife, he found a middle way between those extreme positions. He began her first full year in Milan by allotting over 15,000 ducats to her steward "to spend as much for the living and clothing" expenses of the duchess "and those in her household, as for the pay of *gentiluomini* and other persons assigned to the service of this court, and for expenses of horses, mules and salaries of officials and servants in the stable."[194] The allotment rose to a projected 23,500 ducats for 1473 and 38,810 ducats for 1476.[195] Seven years later, she was receiving ducal support for a household of approximately 170 horses.[196]

The Death of Bianca Maria Visconti

During the period after Bianca Maria's ouster from authority, her many friends throughout Italy felt that Galeazzo was mistreating her. In June 1468, one of them expressed great distress that her unfilial son had driven her from Milan, "that duke being so little loving toward Your Ladyship, as he demonstrates."[197] King Ferrante of Naples told her that he would not send his daughter Eleonora to join her betrothed (Sforza Maria) in Milan. The king explained that his daughter would then be living "in a place where she has to be at [Galeazzo's] discretion, as he would certainly not treat her better than he has Your Highness, but worse."[198]

Galeazzo's treatment of his mother was not the only point of conflict with his parents' allies. The duke's diplomatic agenda put him on a collision course with the king of Naples, in particular. Galeazzo had ambitions to recover Milanese territory lost to Venice forty years earlier. The king supported neither that aspiration nor Galeazzo's efforts to expand Genoa's influence as a mercantile power. Since Naples had been the strongest princely ally of Francesco Sforza and Bianca Maria Visconti, these rifts boded ill for the continuity of Milanese foreign policy.

The Last Pilgrimage

During the summer of 1468, Galeazzo and Bianca Maria maintained an active correspondence, dealing mainly with personal matters pertaining to the ducal family. The duke continued to value intimacy with his mother, even while keeping her at a distance. He was more inclined to exchange pleasantries with her when she was no longer looking over his shoulder. In late May, he sent her a share of his latest hunting bag and asked her to "send in exchange a boatload of fog from the Po, because I hear that Your Ladyship is well supplied with it."[199]

Bianca Maria returned to Milan for her son's wedding in July. At the end of the month, she and Ippolita traveled together to Tortona. There Bianca Maria remained while Filippo escorted his elder sister to Genoa, on her trip home to Naples. He told his mother that Ippolita "left me with many tears (which my nature rarely permits me), that were for the great tenderness and love she showed me."[200] The bridal couple was relaxing in Monza, and Bianca Maria exchanged pleasant letters with her new daughter-in-law. After Filippo returned from Genoa on August 6, Bianca Maria made a brief and leisurely pilgrimage to a shrine in Valenza.[201] Then, she began her slow return to Cremona. The dowager duchess had not shaken the illness that had burdened her all year; perhaps she hoped her visit to the shrine of Saint James might help. If so, she was soon disappointed. At Melegnano, between Pavia and Lodi, Bianca Maria took a turn for the worse.[202]

The Last Illness

August 1468 was a sad and painful time for Bianca Maria Visconti. Her beloved daughter had left, her health was failing, and her son was systematically displacing her. As Galeazzo contemplated bringing his wife to Milan for a short time, he asked if Bona could use the dowager duchess's rooms in the Corte Arengo. Bianca Maria told him to do as he wished and offered sarcastically to move out altogether, so that the new duchess could take her place.[203]

Every exchange between mother and son became another point of contention. Bianca Maria pressed Galeazzo to give 500 ducats to Milan's premier monastery, the abbey of Chiaravalle. The duke agreed but added spitefully, "I have decided at the next [feast of] San Giorgio to go have the display of men-at-arms on the fields of those brothers, and cause them damage totaling more than the 500 ducats." When Bianca Maria wanted a few hunting animals from him, she had to ask repeatedly, through an intermediary.[204]

Yet, even as the young duke was squabbling with his mother, he was asking detailed questions about her health and instructing the ducal physicians to do whatever was needed for her. Over the weeks that followed, all of those physicians congregated in Melegnano, sending back frequent reports to Galeazzo, Bona, and the rest of their households at Monza. After their brief visit to Milan in early September, the duke and his retinue went back to Monza and thence to Abbiategrasso and Novara. For most of that period, Filippo and Ludovico Sforza formed part of the company, while Sforza Maria spent a few weeks in August and September on a goodwill visit to Ferrara.[205]

By mid-October, it was clear that Bianca Maria was dying, and her sons began to gather at her side. Galeazzo did not come until October 20, more than two months after illness had forced her to stop at Melegnano. Three days later, the dowager duchess died. Galeazzo sent over three dozen letters announcing the event to the pope, the Holy Roman Emperor, the king of France, and other princes and nobles in France, Iberia, and Italy.[206] For his mother's funeral, the duke had Bona dressed as Bianca Maria had been for her own mother's and mother-in-law's funerals: "a dress of dark green with two sleeves of black velvet and a veil on the head which covers her to below the eyes, and the usual headdress beneath it."[207] The dowager duchess's exequies "were great and worthy, and she was escorted and mourned by all this land."[208]

The End of an Era

Bianca Maria's passing marked the end of an era in Milanese history; she was the last ruler whose father had been a Visconti. The legacy she left her eldest son was both potent and heavy. Bianca Maria and Francesco Sforza had shown greatness in bringing Milan back to the forefront of Italian, and European, affairs. As duke, Galeazzo benefited from their substantial achievements, but he spent many years trying to emerge from the shadow they cast. He also spent many years paying off the debts his parents—especially Bianca Maria—had accumulated.[209]

While his mother was still battling illness and sorrow at Melegnano, Galeazzo was making a definitive break with his parents' past glories. He instructed his *commissario* of Works that whenever there should be occasion to "have our name painted or sculpted in some place," the form used in his father's time—FRANCISCUS SFORTIA DUX MEDIOLANI QUARTUS— should be replaced by a new one—GALEAZ MARIA DUX MEDIOLANI QUINTUS.[210]

The young duke had come a long way from the inauspicious start of his reign. In a little over two and a half years, he had created a new ducal household, a new ducal seat in the capital, and many new ducal policies. He had also begun a new ducal family. When his mother died, Galeazzo was on the verge of attaining his legal majority, and his newlywed bride was already pregnant with the first child of a new generation.

3

"The Prince Himself Becomes More Eminent"

Galeazzo Establishes His
Princely Presence (1468–1470)

Within a month after his mother's death, Galeazzo instituted an important new policy that reflected his vision of the relationship between the prince and his most distinguished subjects.

> In order that our court be frequented at solemn feasts by distinguished and honorable men, by which it comes about both that the prince himself becomes more eminent and that the noble and excellent men, who are in a state of favor in the prince's eyes, grow in grace and increase in honors; therefore all nobles and barons, feudatories and vassals of our lord who are most dear to our heart, from all of them we have chosen a [certain] number . . . who each year should come to us . . . at the celebrations of the feasts called the Nativity of the Lord, then the Blessed Joseph . . . commemoration of our happy entry into this seat of the duchy, and successively Easter of the Resurrection of Our Lord, which are the greatest solemnities celebrated by us.[1]

Unlike most letters the duke sent to his subjects, this one was composed in Latin, the language of dignity and sacrality. Galeazzo sent it to more than 150 feudal vassals. In extending these compulsory holiday invitations, the duke sought to re-create annually the community of elites that constituted his most important base of support. Their high standing in the dominion merited his recognition, and their presence added luster to his own reputation. Such mutual reinforcement of honor benefited both the prince and his servants.

Sacred Order and "The Greatest Solemnities"

The solemnities of Christmas, Easter, and the feast of San Giuseppe were powerful points of reference in the calendar cycle of the Sforza dominion.

Bringing hundreds of prominent figures together on these occasions could reinforce the idea that the duke stood at the center of the whole dominion. Galeazzo could use these sacred occasions also to remind those present of their relative positions in the order of the world. As the prince, one of his primary functions was to maintain order, not only in the sense of suppressing violence or subversion but also in the sense of keeping his subjects and their possessions in the proper relationships to one another.

Outside the court, the duke could not rely on exercising this authority fully. In 1467, Galeazzo was planning to pass through his cities of Parma, Piacenza, and Lodi for the first time since his accession. The entry into each city would show him the greatest honor possible, including the customary use of a *baldacchino* (canopy) borne by the leading citizens of that city. A baldacchino had profound sacral associations, a potent symbol that blended princely, civic, and divine power. However, the duke instructed his *commissari* in those cities not to use the baldacchino if the leading citizens fell to wrangling over their relative positions in the entries. Galeazzo wanted to avoid "any controversy amongst them over precedence."[2]

In those cities, Galeazzo could not resolve ceremonial disputes without intruding on traditionally recognized local prerogatives. Within the court, though, he was entitled to make such decisions without question. The prince went to some lengths to ensure that those participating in court-related activities knew where they stood. One of the most important means for indicating current status was list making. The lists composed for ceremonial occasions were carefully drawn to reflect precise distinctions of honor and achievement. Even lists composed for mundane daily tasks showed general gradations, particularly in the ranking of offices or functions.[3] In this way, the ducal establishment made clear to all who were watching that the court reflected not only a traditional social and political order but also a higher, sacred order, of which the duke and his servants were the agents.

Easter and the Feast of San Giuseppe

Easter and the feast of San Giuseppe were "the greatest solemnities celebrated" by Galeazzo in the spring during the early years of his reign. Galeazzo came to Milan for observances of San Giuseppe from 1468 to 1470 and for Easter in those years and 1473.[4] Lent and Easter was the time of year at which medieval Christians most fully observed their religious obligations. All good Christians were expected to confess themselves and take Communion at Easter, even if they did not do so the rest of the year. In Galeazzo's Milan, it was not a time for lavish festivities or great displays of ducal power. For the first several years of the reign, Francesco Sforza's death was recalled on its anniversary during the Lenten season. In the city of Milan, that season occurred on different dates than elsewhere, due to the use of the Ambrosian liturgy and calendar.[5]

Although Galeazzo had commanded his feudatories to attend in Milan at Easter, there is no evidence that he actually convoked them for that occasion.[6] He rarely made a public show of this holiest of holidays. One year, the duke withdrew to his chambers for the entire Easter weekend. For half of his reign, he simply celebrated Easter in a modest way wherever he happened to be in the dominion.

During Galeazzo's reign, the feast of San Giuseppe was celebrated more fully at court than was Easter, reflecting the special significance to him of what he termed "our *festa*."[7] The celebration of the lord's accession was a Milanese tradition observed as early as 1289, under Matteo Visconti. Duke Filippo Maria Visconti had also declared his accession day a major holiday.[8] The accession day was unique to each lord—Matteo's was San Vincenzo and Filippo Maria's Santa Giustina—but the practice of commemorating such a day was shared by the whole lineage. Unlike the traditional Christian observance of Easter, San Giuseppe was Galeazzo's addition to the local calendar; it was not even a legal holiday in the city of Milan.[9]

The emphasis of the San Giuseppe observance was dynastic, celebrating the continuity of ducal authority and commemorating the young duke's "enthronement." The climax of the day was a solemn Mass in the Duomo; members of the ducal family and prominent ambassadors headed the list of participants. Galeazzo sometimes allowed feudatories to forgo the journey to Milan, but he always insisted on attendance by councillors, *gentiluomini,* and other members of the court.[10] After 1470, the duke felt that he did not need to attend the annual ceremony. Implicitly, he distinguished between himself as the head of a princely lineage, who was being honored at the occasion, and himself as a living person, who could just as well be elsewhere.[11] When Galeazzo needed surrogates to play his part in the ceremony, he called on the most prestigious members of that lineage; in 1471, he asked his cousin Alessandro Sforza, lord of Pesaro.[12]

That year, Galeazzo was absent from the dominion on March 20. After the observance in Milan, around dinnertime, a man appeared suddenly in the street, shouting, "Long live Saint Ambrose and liberty," and throwing money. Milan's captain of justice had the anonymous agitator arrested and whipped, "which much pleased your [i.e., the duke's] servants, and especially those that were rather ill-treated at the time of liberty [*al tempo de la libertate*]."[13] The connection between Galeazzo's accession day and the loss of Milan's "liberty" was clear to those who resented the duke's dominance in Milan. In turn, those republicans had left scars on the minds and hearts of ducal adherents. Their respective resentments still festered more than twenty years after the "time of liberty" had passed.

Christmas

Christmas was the only major holiday celebrated with great solemnity by all persons in the Sforza dominion. Easter made relatively little impact within the court, and San Giuseppe made relatively little impact outside it. Christmas was long recognized in Milan as the premier holiday of the year, the season of rebirth and renewal. In the capital city's calendar, almost one-fourth of the legal holidays fell within the twelve days of Christmas, five in December and two in January.[14] Moreover, medieval Milan used the style of the Nativity for dating; Christmas Day was officially the first day of the New Year. The ducal Chancery replaced it with January 1 in 1459, but some ducal officials still used the old style as late as 1477.[15]

It was not only the merchants and bureaucrats for whom Christmas marked a pivotal point in the year. The Christmas feast had a long tradition of association with imperial or regal dignities, going back at least as far as the coronation of Charlemagne. Throughout medieval Europe, Christmas marked one of the major milestones in the feudal calendar, a time for paying feudal dues, gathering in feudal courts, and otherwise reaffirming the social bonds that united the rural nobility.[16] Part of Galeazzo's purpose for gathering his feudatories at Christmas in 1468 was to receive their oaths of fealty; representatives of fifty-five families swore their oaths at Porta Giovia on December 26.[17] In later years, the duke also used the occasion of Christmas to enfeoff prominent figures, including his brothers and his cousin, the condottiere Roberto da Sanseverino.[18]

Galeazzo's annual Christmas stay in the capital was the longest period of time he was sure to spend in one predetermined place. That stay never began later than December 23 or ended before January 2. The duke considered attendance at Christmas court a serious responsibility. While feudatories might be excused *en masse* from the solemnities for other holidays, they could not miss Christmas unless they were ill. Every year, the Chancery sent out a letter reminding the feudatories of their obligation to spend Christmas in Milan.[19] The lists of invitees were always carefully updated; each one contained one hundred to two hundred names, many of them collective (e.g., "Cavalchino Guidoboni and brothers)."[20] Galeazzo also invited courtiers, civic notables, foreign dignitaries, and bureaucrats, all the major elites of the dominion.

Christmas has traditionally been a season of generosity. Galeazzo wanted every element of the community over which he ruled to receive a token of his beneficence. Alms were regularly dispensed at this time.[21] Gifts went to members of the ducal household, especially those who facilitated the court's daily activities: trumpeters, castle guards, and doorkeepers. Doorkeepers controlled access to the ducal chambers, and they expected Christmas gratuities; Marsilio Andreasi complained that he would have to give them something, "else they might make me stay outside a few times."[22] Ambassadors themselves, and other persons of high rank, sometimes received gifts from the duke.[23] He also directed his generosity to the lowest elements of the duchy, granting pardons for crimes and releases from imprisonment in his desire to "use our clemency at this celebration of the birth of our Lord." The Christmas spirit extended also to the settlement of disputes.[24]

The Christmas season was devoted to reaffirming the communities of court and state, city and world, microcosm and macrocosm. The customary activities of the week at the Sforza court were demarcated by ceremonies that rarely varied from year to year. The most crucial of these ceremonies took place at Christmas (December 24 and 25) and New Year's (December 31 and January 1). On Christmas and New Year's eves, the immediate ducal family and an intimate group of companions gathered at Porta Giovia for several traditional ceremonies. The most important of these ceremonies was called the "Ciocco"; it was similar to the Yule Log.[25] The days that followed—Christmas and New Year's (the Feast of the Circumcision)—featured Masses. On Christmas Day, the duke heard the traditional three Masses in his chapel, accompanied by his full court.[26] On each holy day of Christmas week, Galeazzo attended mass at an appropriate venue in the capital: December 26 (St. Stephen's) was at Santo Stefano, December 27 (St. John the Evangelist's) at San Giovanni, December 28 (Holy Innocents) at San Francesco, and December 31 (St. Sylvester's) at San Silvestro.[27] The rest of the court was expected to join him or honor each day in some suitable fashion.

Since Christmas week marked the end and beginning of the Milanese calendar year, it was a crucial time for establishing administrative and diplomatic policies. The duke used this time to negotiate contracts with condottieri and rotate appointments within the bureaucracy.[28] Christmas was also a favorite season for marriage negotiations involving the ducal family. In 1467–1468, the duke's own marriage had been under consideration. Later in the reign, his daughter Caterina was pursued by suitors during two consecutive years.[29]

We should not interpret Galeazzo's Christmas court as a throwback to antiquated medieval practice, although the ducal court had a tradition of celebrating this great holiday. In 1466, his first year as duke, he took councillors and courtiers to task for failing to attend him at Christmas.[30] Nevertheless, the policy he instituted in 1468 was new in Milan and unusual in Christendom generally. In the great medieval courts, Christmas was a mobile feast, geographically speaking; Galeazzo's contemporary, Edward IV of England, celebrated Christmas at a different castle every year.[31] By contrast, Galeazzo returned every year to Milan, where his court had a permanent establishment, a physical manifestation of sacred space.[32]

The Princely Court as a Sacred Center

As a center of material life, the court had the glitter of wealth; as a social and political center, it had the lure of power. The most powerful aspect of the court's existence, though, was its role as a symbolic or sacred center.

"As the Saints Do the Divine Majesty"

In December 1468, Giovanni Matteo Bottigella, a courtier from Pavia, found himself too ill to attend the duke's Christmas court in Milan. Bottigella wrote to Galeazzo excusing himself and assuring his princely master that "the greatest pleasure and consolation I could have in this world is when I can see Your presence and contemplate it as the saints do the divine majesty."[33]

This imagery was very powerful in a world still thoroughly Christian. It cast Galeazzo in the flattering role of God himself and his courtiers in the flattering role of the community of saints. The ducal court became an earthly paradise, occupying a special place in the earthly universe. Those who participated in it were presumably blessed with wonders denied to those outside the sacred precincts. According to the logic of the image, the prince's greatness transcended all earthly particularism and united all his subjects and other inferiors on a higher plane, imbued with sacred power. In the later medieval period, secular rulers were absorbing and appropriating the quality of sacrality that had once been a monopoly of the church. The very language of Roman law in the Milanese dominion supported such pretensions, for it spoke of the duke as "the image of the Divine Presence."[34]

Two juridical traditions, current in the later Middle Ages, buttressed princely claims to sacral power. The Judeo-Christian image of the Priest-King (*Rex Sacerdos*) used the figures of David, Melchizedek, and other biblical characters to exemplify direct interaction between God and ruler. It also permitted an identification of the king with Jesus Christ himself, the "mystical body" that incarnated divine power in human form. In this tradition, the king literally embodied his realm, and he interceded with the divine power to ensure the welfare of land and people. This image was particularly useful to the great anointed monarchs, such as the kings of England and France, and lay at the heart of royal healings.[35]

The Roman Empire offered another paradigm, the God-Emperor (*Imperator Deus*). Once deified, the Roman ruler removed himself to a higher plane, and his welfare became a matter of transcendent importance. The stability of the state was no longer merely a human concern, and injury to the prince meant injury to a majesty greater than human—*lèse-majesté*. This tradition was preserved in Roman law and bequeathed to much of Christendom, including Lombardy. Since the duke was recognized by the law within his own dominion as "the image of the Divine Presence," he partook of its sacred majesty.

The Court as Sacred Space

Each of the holidays around which Galeazzo built his annual cycle as prince-in-court marked the "birth" of a "lord"—the birth of Jesus Christ, his rebirth at the Resurrection, and the "birth" of the new duke on his entry into Milan. The identification of Galeazzo with the Son of God was not belabored in ducal communications, but it was embedded in the language of officials, who referred to both Christmas and San Giuseppe as "the feast of Our Lord."[36]

The duke of Milan had considerable resources on which to draw and was thus a person of great power. That power could not be wielded indiscriminately if the welfare of the state—or the prince—were to be maintained. The duke required protection from the dangers and demands of the world at large, and the world required protection from the duke's idiosyncracies. The court functioned as a vessel to contain the precious power of the prince and provide particular points of entry and exit through which that power could be channeled to the rest of the world. Among his other powers, Galeazzo could create and destroy in the social and political spheres. He supervised the creation of structures to define and delimit his court; he also created most of its inhabitants. The words "create" or "make" were used often to denote investiture with a noble title or ducal office.[37] When the duke bestowed such an honor on an individual, he was adding a new person to the social and political world. When that person sprang from relatively obscure origins, as did some of Galeazzo's favorites, their "creation" could alter the nature of ducal society.

Galeazzo and his staff literally put persons at court in their places, positioning them in proper relation to one another. Each occasion had a different list of participants, and a variety of criteria were applied to find their relative ranking. The local order of honorable dignities in Milan, Genoa, and other cities was integrated with hierarchies of office, feudal holdings, marriage connections, and other considerations. The duke could reinforce the traditional orders in any fashion he wished; he could even create a new order. Having invited the most prominent personages in his dominion to court for Christmas in 1468–1469, Galeazzo closed Christmas week in a manner that exemplified the creation and affirmation of social order. For an event at Porta Giovia on New Year's Day, a list was composed, entitled "Order of Those Who Have to Enter into the Saletta of the Castle."[38] From it, one can easily infer some of the main criteria for determining how persons were ranked.

Galeazzo honored first his princely counterparts, then his own family: "All the Lords [*Signori*]," "ambassadors of Lords and Lordships [*Signorie*]," the chancellors of the marquesses of Mantua and Montferrat, and "all the relatives of our Most Illustrious Lord." Princes always ranked ahead of other persons, and ambassadors were generally treated according to the rank of their principals. In a courteous household, guest princes preceded the host family, regardless of their respective dignities.[39]

The persons of princely rank were followed by Milanese ducal officials, specifically the Privy Council, Council of Justice, and masters of revenues (ordinary, then extraordinary). After them came the two chief officers for the capital city, the podestà and the captain of justice. The inclusion of these officers reflects the city's central role in the Sforza dominion, but neither was—or could be—a Milanese citizen. Next to enter the Saletta were men of enormous personal prestige, largely feudatories of the highest rank. They were led by nine powerful Visconti lords, honored probably for their connection to the ducal family. Behind them came the ducal secretary Giovanni Simonetta, then twenty counts, marquesses, and other nobles.

The military servants of the duke were represented at this occasion by the castellan and vice-castellan of Porta Giovia, where the event took place. They are juxtaposed on the list with the agent of the Medici Bank, a person of great importance to the perennially underfunded Sforza. During Duke Francesco's reign, the Medici agent, Pigello Portinari, had held an active and honored place in the Milanese court. After Francesco was succeeded by his son, and Pigello by his brother, the personal relationship gradually evaporated.[40] In the entry on New Year's 1469, Acciarrito Portinari was followed by Bona's secretary and a count from Piacenza. The assemblage was rounded out by a dozen *camerieri*; three of the first four were Visconti, and the other was a Genoese noble from a dogal family. The *camerieri* ranked last because they were attending the event as officers of the ducal household. Household offices were generally not as honorable as offices of state, perhaps because offices of state carried a dignity independent of the duke's person.

"The Heart and Love of Your Subjects and Friends"

January 1469 was a significant watershed for Galeazzo; he attained his twenty-fifth birthday, his legal majority. The duke could proceed from that point with greater confidence, knowing that he had full legal authority within his dominion. His first act on reaching this milestone was to confirm all grants he had made previously.[41] Galeazzo could not claim to be a sovereign prince in the full legal sense; as duke of Milan, he was a feudal vassal of the Holy Roman Emperor, and as lord of Genoa, he was a vassal of the French king. In theory, those overlords could remove him from his offices.[42] Nevertheless, Galeazzo behaved as though he were fully empowered to exercise the ducal office. He sought to be recognized by the emperor, but he did not hesitate to assert his existing authority.

After his twenty-fifth birthday, Galeazzo asked the Council of Justice for legal opinions on whether imperial sanction was truly necessary. The councillors could not agree among themselves on this question.[43] Ducal authority in Milan had two roots. As a vassal of the Holy Roman Emperor, particularly as holder of the ducal title, Galeazzo did need his overlord's acknowledgment. However, the lords of Milan had always based their lordship on recognition by their own subjects. Since the triumph of the Lombard League over Frederick Barbarossa in the twelfth century, the city's political autonomy had been accepted by the emperors. The Visconti lords and dukes exercised their lordship as a magistracy of the commune, and Francesco Sforza took care to gain formal recognition from the citizens of the capital.[44] This local base of support was not affected by the emperor's stance; so long as the duke was accepted by his own subjects, he could claim to be the rightful prince. In the words of a Milanese diplomat, "Your Excellency has an investiture more solid than if it had been written on a table of adamantine, that is, the heart and love of your subjects and friends."[45]

Galeazzo's claim to political legitimacy rested also on his heritage. The Visconti had been accepted as imperial vicars, and their dynasty was unquestionably entitled to continue ruling Milan from one generation to the next. As the eldest son of the only child left by the last Visconti duke, Galeazzo could make a good case for his right to sit on the ducal throne. Although his mother had been explicitly excluded from the succession when she was legitimized, Bianca Maria represented the ancient signorial authority of her family, in the absence of other claimants from the Visconti lineage.

Galeazzo's position was not juridically unassailable, but it was never seriously assailed. Other states treated him as though he were the proper authority, and no power interfered successfully with his rule over the dominion. In 1469, when Emperor Frederick III visited Italy, he avoided Milanese territory, but he did not attempt to remove the duke. Galeazzo told an ambassador he sent to meet the emperor, "Being created and chosen Lord and Duke by all our people of this dominion and also being reputed duke of Milan by His Holiness the Pope and by all the Lords and Lordships of Italy and outside Italy, we will maintain our name, reputation, and dignity."[46]

Later, the duke lost patience with efforts to obtain investiture from his overlord. Galeazzo wrote that since "with the grace of God we find ourselves in peaceful possession of this our dominion and duchy in which our father and lord also stayed for such a long time, we will not work hard anymore about this [quest for imperial investiture]."[47] Nevertheless, Galeazzo continued throughout his reign to seek "our privileges," spurred on by Venetian and Burgundian attempts to obtain title to the duchy.

"For the Good Living and Excellent
Government of the People"

To keep his princely office, Galeazzo had to perform his duties in a manner that respected the concerns of the subjects on whose support he relied. The Sforza library included several books that instructed rulers in how to rule properly, ranging from classical works by Aristotle and Cicero to the High Medieval formulations of Thomas Aquinas, Giles of Rome, and John of Salisbury and early Renaissance writings by such authors as Petrarch. Not only did the library contain multiple copies of Giles's *De Regimine Principum* and John's *Policraticus* but someone in Galeazzo's court was actually reading them in the early years of his reign.[48]

No work of literature or philosophy was produced at Galeazzo's court to articulate his view of the prince's role, but that view was reflected in various words, images, and deeds that emanated from him and his court. He promised equal justice for all and claimed that "from the first day that we succeeded to this Lordship, we have continually put all our study, industry, and intelligence into governing our subjects under the government of justice, . . . the principal thing needed for the good living and excellent government of the people." Accordingly, he told his ducal officers to use diligence in matters related to his revenues, "but under this guise we do not wish that you do any extortion or violence to favor the treasury."[49]

Bernardino Corio, the Milanese historian who had served at Galeazzo's court, later wrote of the fifth duke,

> What was said to him, he listened to attentively. His council was composed of principal men of his domain, and, whatever vices he indulged in, he loved virtuous men beyond measure, and caressed them with gifts; on the other hand, he hated the presumptuous, and the sad, and those of cruel disposition. . . . To his subjects, he willingly gave audiences, and he remunerated his servants.[50]

Galeazzo also encouraged many important innovations in Milanese and Lombard life, including the printing of books, the cultivation of rice and silk, and the collection of detailed records on births and deaths. He ordered dozens, possibly hundreds, of pairs of eyeglasses for members of his court, both myopic and presbyopic. He commanded that every town have a public clock and that dishonest ostlers be prosecuted. He insisted that ducal officials carry out the responsibilities of their office, and he lambasted those who, in his view, had failed to do so.[51]

Winter and Spring (1469)

After his mother died, the temperamental young duke found it difficult to maintain the broad political support his parents had enjoyed. Some prominent members of the court found Galeazzo a less satisfactory master than his father had been, and they left the Sforza service. Among them was the senior ducal physician, Benedetto de' Reguardati of Norcia, a member of the Privy Council and a man of enormous prestige. In January 1469, the physician asked Galeazzo to grant him the favor "of giving me in my departure 2,200 ducats that remain from my pay." Benedetto complained that he had not been paid for many months and had been compelled to borrow at usurious rates.[52]

In general, though, Galeazzo had good reason to be pleased early in 1469. His wife had become pregnant only two or three months after their wedding, and the birth of an heir could be expected within a few months of the duke's attaining his own legal majority. Federigo da Montefeltro returned to Milan to pass another winter; he was still Milan's captain-general, a good friend to the Sforza, and a person of some influence with the duke.[53]

One area in which Galeazzo needed help from his friends in January 1469 was financial. He had overextended the dominion's resources drastically in 1468, and he needed to recover some of the money he had spent. Consequently, he asked all those who had received money from him (including regular income) to give him back half of it. The responses reported by a fiscal official are fascinating. Some loyal courtiers said they would share even their inherited revenues with the duke. Most were happy to comply with the request, but one Milanese nobleman complained that "Your Lordship has given him an income of four and one-half ducats per year and he pays four florins a month [over 21 ducats per year], and he wants to come to Your Lordship to appeal about this undertaking." Another fellow said he was very poor, with four daughters to marry, and would have to sell his belongings to comply with the order. Galeazzo spared no one; the responses came from *staffieri, camerieri, gentiluomini,* physicians, seneschals, bureaucrats, and even his own brothers.[54]

"We Have Reformed and Taken Anew the Courtiers"

Galeazzo continued to reshape the court to his own satisfaction. Just as the duke had reorganized the *camerieri* earlier, so in January 1469, he turned his attention to the *gentiluomini*. On January 17, the duke told the masters of revenues, "We have reformed and taken anew the courtiers that you see noted in the included list." They were all to be paid in the usual manner (nine times per year), "except for those who will conduct themselves at the side of the Lord." The seneschal-general Giovanni Giapanno was given the list of courtiers and their monthly salaries, as well as the task of informing the men. Three days later, he told Galeazzo, "To the greater part of the *gentiluomini* from here [i.e., Milan], which Your Lordship had accepted and reaffirmed in their salary [*provisione*], I have advised them both of their salaries and of the payment schedule [*pagamenti*] and arrangements [*ordeni*] which they have to use. And to all those to whom I have told that up to now, they have accepted and thanked Your Lordship. Tomorrow, I will advise the rest, and so also I have advised those from outside [Milan] by letter."[55]

Later in the year, the duke completed his reorganization by setting a new policy for service by the *gentiluomini*. He instructed the seneschals-general that twelve *gentiluomini* should accompany him at any given time, "including those that are found in that city where it will fall to us to be." Those who were not resident in that city would serve in rotation. The seneschals-general replied that five *gentiluomini* from Milan would be sent immediately to supplement the seven residents at Pavia (where the Duke was then staying), "and these will come for one month, and then they will be changed."[56] Soon afterward, a seneschal noted that certain courtiers from the districts of Pavia and Lodi, located near the capital, "have orders to be found [in Milan] not only at the holidays but every time that the Lord is here."[57]

Jousts and Feasts

The winter and spring passed quickly with the usual seasonal activities, including the anniversary observance of Duke Francesco's death.[58] For the feast of San Giuseppe, the duke excused the councillors from meeting him on his arrival at Milan, saying that he did not consider the occasion to be so important. Nonetheless, preparations were extensive, including an escort of fifty ladies bringing Bona to the Duomo for the ceremonies. For this event, the duke decided also to decorate the chapel of Saint Joseph in the Duomo.[59]

Later in the spring, Galeazzo showed a marked interest in jousting. For the feast of San Giorgio, he staged what proved to be the largest tournament of his reign. The duke invited more than seventy men to take part, including members of his family, client princes, condottieri, captains in the standing army, troops of the *famiglia,* and members of the ducal household. Extensive preparations went into the tournament, and Galeazzo even received reports on practice sessions held during the days before San Giorgio. The duke himself did not joust publicly, but he did so privately in the Giardino with his *cameriere di camera* Giovanni da Verona.[60] Galeazzo considered that tournament an important event; when Guido Rossi asked to be excused because his mother had just died, the duke responded that he shared Guido's sorrow but that the young man should come and participate anyway.[61] Galeazzo must have enjoyed the San Giorgio joust, because he planned another one for May 28 at Abbiategrasso. When he invited Filippo, Sforza Maria, and Ludovico to the tournament, they lamented that they could not get arms for the occasion and asked for their brother's help. Most of the two dozen men who were set to joust that day were members of the duke's household, including Borella and several *camerieri.*[62]

Perpetuating a Dynasty

In 1469, Galeazzo felt he was taking his place fully in the Visconti-Sforza dynasty. He proclaimed the ducal heritage in many forms; his castles were adorned inside and out with the coats of arms and emblems he had inherited. In January 1469, he decided to restore the "walls, towers, and battlements" of his capital city, painting the battlements with "our insignia."[63] He had dozens of emblems from which to choose, commemorating the Lombard, royal French, and imperial heritage of the Sforza dukes. The image most widely associated with the Milanese dukes was the Visconti viper, shown as a large crowned snake, swallowing a "flayed Turk." The ducal coat of arms quartered that frightening image with the imperial eagle.

One of the ducal emblems, a dove bearing a ribbon with the words, "A Bon Droit," had been designed by Petrarch for the marriage of GianGaleazzo Visconti. In July 1469, a courtier noted that the dove emblem was painted incorrectly in Abbiategrasso Castle. To help correct the error, he offered an example of the true emblem from his own home.[64] The same emblem is still visible on the ceiling vaults of the Camera delle Colombine in Porta Giovia Castle; the ceiling vaults of the adjacent Camera dei Ducali bears Galeazzo's coat of arms and initials. The duke would have been pleased to know that his emblems have lasted so long. When he had his coat of arms carved in marble and set over the gate at Soncino Castle, he also had two verses set underneath, with letters of lead "so that they will last forever."[65]

Being remembered in perpetuity was important for spiritual reasons as well as for earthly fame and glory. In a manner typical of late medieval Christianity, the pilgrimage church of Santa Maria del Monte in Varese contained "chapels founded and endowed by the Most Illustrious Visconti Lords, our predecessors," to celebrate the Mass and holy offices. When Galeazzo heard that some of the chaplains were neglecting their duties, he became upset, "as successor to the aforesaid Visconti Lords," and he commanded the archpriest of the church to set them straight.[66]

"You Cannot Have Honor Yourself, That We Do Not Have, Too"

Galeazzo took great pride in his descent from the Visconti. Like his brothers and sisters, the duke used the style "Sfortia-Vicecomes" (Sforza-Visconti) in formal signatures. Members of the Visconti clan held a special position in ducal protocol, as reflected in the New Year's gathering.[67] The duke also acknowledged his Visconti lineage in other ways. When Giovanni Maria Visconti sought the lease on Angera, the Visconti's legendary home, Galeazzo supported that effort, citing his own blood ties (*affinitate*) with the courtier.[68]

The duke identified personally with those who shared the Sforza lineage as well; he saw everything they did as a reflection on himself and his dominion. Galeazzo scolded his uncle, Bosio Sforza, for having a dispute with Tristano, because it had become common knowledge and lowered the family's reputation. The duke told Bosio that such quarreling was improper behavior between uncle and nephew. However, when Tristano staged "some beautiful festivities" to celebrate Carnival, Galeazzo told his half-brother, "You cannot have honor yourself that we do not have, too."[69] The first time Galeazzo left the dominion after he had become sole ruler, he chose a member of the Sforza lineage to serve as temporary governor: his uncle Alessandro, lord of Pesaro. Alessandro headed the second-ranking branch of the Sforza clan and served Galeazzo as a condottiere for a time. He was the only other member of that lineage who ruled a state in his own right.[70]

The Ducal Heir

The most important means of perpetuating a lineage was producing heirs. Bona was due to give birth in May or June 1469, and Galeazzo was keenly aware of the dynastic significance that birth could have. In late May, he asked his castellan in Pavia to undertake research in the ducal library on the names and birthplaces of Galeazzo II Visconti's children by Bianca of Savoy.[71]

Although the castellan found nothing, Galeazzo chose Abbiategrasso Castle as the place for his first child's birth, reportedly because "he likes the comfort of that place very much."[72] The choice had a historic resonance; Abbiategrasso had been a favorite haunt of GianGaleazzo Visconti, whose heir, Giovanni Maria, had been born there. So, too, was Galeazzo's own mother, the daughter of Duke Filippo Maria Visconti.[73]

Galeazzo and Bona took up residence at Abbiategrasso in early May, well before their baby was due. At the end of the month, the duke sent for relics of Saints James, Mary Magdalen, and Bernardino, possibly to aid his wife in childbirth.[74] The birth finally occurred a few weeks later; on June 20, Bona delivered a healthy son. Galeazzo had his first legitimate child—and an heir. After the baby was born, Bona was kept in isolation for "the six days of the birth." At the end of that week, a group of Milanese ladies came to visit her. They were told to leave early and come by boat, on the canal, so that they could stay a few hours and return home by evening.[75]

The birth of the ducal heir was a joyous occasion and prompted the duke to guarantee further the precious things he had given Bona the year before.[76] Public celebrations were held throughout the dominion; in Milan, the Privy Council was involved. Galeazzo sent one of Bona's *camerieri* to France to tell her royal brother-in-law the good news. The duke wanted his messenger "dressed all in the French style" to carry the message.[77] As word of the baby's birth reached Galeazzo's subjects and allies, their congratulations poured in to the duke. He received word of celebrations in such places as Piacenza, Savona, Bologna, and his ancestral home of Cotignola.[78] To ensure that the "gentlemen and citizens" of Milan shared the duke's joy, Galeazzo lifted all the taxes they had paid for quartering soldiers. Henceforth, almost 1,800 troops who had been quartered in the Milanese district would be lodged in three other nearby districts.[79]

The Heir Receives a Name   In the Christian world of Renaissance Europe, a child's baptism held great social and political significance. At that point, the new human being was given a name and welcomed formally into the Christian flock. Galeazzo scheduled the baptism of his son and heir for the feast of Saint James and Saint Christopher, July 25, 1469. It was to be held in the Duomo of Milan, "solemnly and lovingly, as befits such an act." The duke invited a long and distinguished list of guests, including all the feudatories he had invited for Christmas, ambassadors from other states, and two envoys from each of twelve major cities in his dominion.[80]

To serve as godfathers for the baby, the duke invited several persons of high rank, to come in person or by proxy. They included Lorenzo de' Medici, Federigo da Montefeltro, and representatives of the Gonzaga, the Estensi, and the French royal family.[81] Rodolfo Gonzaga, son of Marquis Ludovico, had come to Milan for another purpose, and Galeazzo insisted he stay for the baptism. Rodolfo wrote his mother that "on the one hand, I stayed very readily, to do something that please His Lordship, but on the other hand, I was displeased because I had no clothes into which to change."[82]

At his baptism, the newest member of the Visconti-Sforza lineage received a name that celebrated the founder of the Milanese duchy: Gian-Galeazzo Maria Sforza. Galeazzo Sforza gave his own son and heir the first name that Galeazzo Visconti's son and heir had borne and the second name that all of GianGaleazzo Visconti's descendants bore.[83] As heir to the ducal throne, the infant would hold the title "count of Pavia" and the lands pertaining to it. His mother had received those lands as a marriage portion, in anticipation of this event, and she would now be required to release them to him. In July 1469, she had other concerns, though. Between the time of the birth and the time of the baptism, Bona suffered a bout of tertian fever. Zaccaria Saggi da Pisa reported home to Mantua that her illness "has proceeded from the Lord's lack of restraint, as he is so ardent and enamored of Her Excellency, he could not be held in check."[84]

The Duke's Youngest Siblings

Although Filippo, Sforza Maria, and Ludovico were the most active of Galeazzo's siblings at the ducal court, three others lived in the dominion, as well: Ascanio, Elisabetta, and Ottaviano.

Ascanio was eleven years of age when his brother became duke. He had been destined from the start for a career in the church; his father had sought a cardinal's hat for him but could not persuade Pope Paul II, a Venetian who did not favor Milan. Instead, Duke Francesco procured Ascanio's appointment in 1465 to the abbacy of Chiaravalle, the richest abbey in the dominion.[85] In 1468, Ascanio began to study seriously for a career as a prelate. He moved to the university town of Pavia, where he lived for the rest of Galeazzo's reign. Ascanio spent little time at the ducal court, but he attended regularly at the great occasions, such as Christmas, where the duke gathered the whole family. In 1469, the young cleric had constant problems with servants and other domestic matters as he settled into his life as a student.[86]

Elisabetta was a year younger than Ascanio. Since Ippolita had married and left the dominion before Galeazzo became duke, Elisabetta was his only full sister resident in Milan. She lived in the duchess's household, first her mother's, then (after Bianca Maria's death) her sister-in-law's. The fresco program for Pavia depicted Elisabetta playing ball with her damsels, in a room that also featured the new duchess and some of her household. Because of her youth and gender, Elisabetta was rarely active at court, except during Ippolita's visit in 1468. In August of that year, Elisabetta helped to receive Taddeo Manfredi's proxy, who had come to evaluate her half-sister Elisa for marriage. Bianca Maria would normally have performed that function, but she was then in her final illness at Melegnano.[87]

In June 1469, Elisabetta was suddenly involved in her own marriage. Guglielmo Paleologo, marquess of Montferrat, had lost his first wife, whom Bianca Maria had wanted Galeazzo to use as a model of French manners. The elderly marquess was one of the Sforza's closest neighbors and most reliable condottieri. The duke considered it fitting for Elisabetta to marry Guglielmo, notwithstanding their huge disparity in ages: the groom was five times older than the bride. The marriage agreement was made quickly and the contract ratified without delay. The wedding itself was celebrated within two months, solely at Guglielmo's castle in Montferrat. Sforza Maria led the Milanese delegation that attended it.[88]

Although many of Elisabetta's friends had been concerned about her well-being in such a marriage, it actually proved beneficial to her. Apparently, Guglielmo provided more opportunity for Elisabetta to enjoy herself than Galeazzo had done. Furthermore, her husband had changed her diet. With Galeazzo, "she was ordinarily eating meat four or five times a day, which totally ruined her complexion." In Montferrat, she was "eating more correctly," gaining weight, and generally doing better than ever.[89]

Unlike Ascanio and Elisabetta, Ottaviano never left the Milanese ducal household. Only eight years old at Galeazzo's accession, he spent the early years of his eldest brother's reign living at the ducal residences with the duke's children; Ottaviano was the same age as Galeazzo's eldest natural son,

Carlo. In the latter years of the reign, Ottaviano traveled with the households of the duke and duchess. He was a spirited lad but rarely had an opportunity to participate actively in the court.[90]

Half-Brothers and Half-Sisters

The summer of 1469 was a busy time for the ducal family. Within a week of the ducal heir's birth, Galeazzo's half-sister Elisa died.[91] Her death had important ramifications: she had been promised in marriage to Guidaccio Manfredi, heir to the lordship of Imola. Galeazzo feared that his plans would be ruined; he salvaged them by replacing her with another half-sister, Fiordelisa.[92] The duke's interest in this marriage went beyond diplomatic alliances; he was scheming to take possession of Imola, whose territory included the Sforza's ancestral home at Cotignola.[93]

Around the same time that Elisa died, Galeazzo received a letter from another half-sister, Drusiana, who had just arrived in the Venetian city of Padua. Feeling drastically wronged by the duke, she had fled the duchy after hiding briefly in Milanese convents. Drusiana had had a difficult life altogether; her second husband was Iacopo Piccinino, the condottiere murdered by Ferrante of Naples in 1465.[94]

Drusiana and Sforza Secondo were full siblings, and Galeazzo liked neither of them. Even after Sforza Secondo was reconciled with Galeazzo in 1467, the two half-brothers continued to be in conflict. The duke did not immediately return Sforza Secondo's fief or salary, and Sforza Secondo complained to Bianca Maria, lamenting that "in the other world, the spirit of my father has to be grieving for me."[95] A few months later, Sforza Secondo complained to Galeazzo, "I don't know any Sforzesco who, according to their rank, is in a worse condition than Sforza [i.e., himself]," in regard to holding fiefs. Galeazzo relented and returned Borgonovo to Sforza Secondo by the autumn of 1468.[96] However, Sforza Secondo was in trouble again by March 1469, and he spent some months in the duchy of Modena, pleading for clemency from Galeazzo. By 1472, Sforza Secondo had been rehabilitated and was even named "Captain-General over the Armada and Maritime Army."[97] He did not come to court often during his brother's reign but was regularly called on to join the ducal family for ceremonial purposes.

As Drusiana discovered, being a member of the Sforza lineage did not automatically bring wholehearted support from the duke. Galeazzo's half-brother Giulio sent him several letters requesting support for Giulio's mother. The duke gave short shrift to these pleas, saying caustically that Giulio "makes himself out to be our brother," but that since their father had not provided for him, Galeazzo had no reason to do so. Nonetheless, the duke found Giulio a position with the ducal condottiere and cousin Roberto da Sanseverino.[98] No member of the Sforza lineage was entirely ignored or cut off from

Galeazzo's support. His half-brother Polidoro benefited greatly from Galeazzo's accession; previously, Polidoro had not even been permitted to visit Milan. The new duke granted him a lucrative fief and invited him to all the major *feste* along with Tristano and Sforza Secondo.[99] All three of them served as representatives of the duke in escorting foreign dignitaries.[100]

Members of the ducal family were generally conscious of their special status, and they tended to feel they should be treated accordingly. After the death of her husband, Giovanni Mauruzzi da Tolentino, Galeazzo's half-sister Isotta complained that Giovanni's will had "treated me as though his lady were a private citizen," rather than the duke's sister. When Galeazzo approved the will, Isotta complained of having "lost my husband and my things and also having lost 27 years in which I always served him in his infirmities."[101]

A Fresco Program for Pavia Castle

In the summer of 1469, Galeazzo decided to immortalize his family, his intimates, and his most valued administrators in a fresco program.[102] The scope of the program was vast, covering dozens of halls and chambers on the upper floor of Pavia Castle. Most of those spaces would be painted with figures who actually belonged in them: members of the Chancery in the hall outside the Chancery offices; ducal intimates in Galeazzo's bedchamber; Bona, Elisabetta, and their damsels and entertainers in the hall where the ladies ate, and so forth. Even the infant heir to the duchy was included, receiving caresses from his parents.

The program was quite detailed, with some very specific instructions. In a room to be painted with huntsmen and hounds, the duke wanted to be shown so "that he lightly wounds the stag with the *stambecchina* [a special lance], and there would be those who bear the sword and the cloak, and the footmen."[103] In other rooms, duke and duchess would be shown hunting, eating, and dressing; the more intimate the scene, the more precisely the cast of characters was enumerated. The fresco program was a mirror for the court of Milan. Beyond the scenes of domestic life, it described the Chancery at work, the councillors and ambassadors meeting with Galeazzo, and (in the ducal chapel) the duke's favorite sacred images. The program also had a historical dimension, in the description of Bona's wedding journey to Milan.[104]

Such extensive work was expensive. Bonifacio Bembo of Cremona, one of northern Italy's leading painters in the fifteenth century, made a detailed estimate totaling almost 8,000 ducats, including decorative work on the battlements and some construction. The commission did not consist solely of the new program; Galeazzo wanted existing frescoes from the Visconti era repainted and the Chamber of Mirrors and lower chapel refurbished.[105] If the new images were ever executed, they would have been seen by a very limited audience. The upper floor of Pavia Castle was reserved for the use of the ducal households and Chancery. Only prestigious visitors and persons whose business involved direct contact with Galeazzo might be privileged to enter the halls and chambers for which the program was designed.[106]

A New Decade

Bianca Maria Visconti's death had meant that Galeazzo could consolidate his rule in Milan and impose his princely vision. Outside his dominion, though, the duke could not control events. Throughout Italy, the political landscape began to shift in 1469. Sigismondo Malatesta had died around the same time as Bianca Maria, leaving Rimini subject to a succession struggle. His eldest son, Roberto, had made a prior agreement with Milan and took possession of the city through deception practiced on the pope, his overlord. Paul II was furious and moved against Rimini with his Venetian allies. Roberto relied on the armies of Milan, Florence, and Naples to save him. Galeazzo later argued bitterly that King Ferrante refused to send the troops he had agreed to, although the duke himself was hesitant to become directly involved.[107] It was in the context of this minor crisis that young Lorenzo de' Medici began to participate actively in the world of Italian diplomacy. Near the end of the year, his father, Piero, died, and Lorenzo inherited the reins of leadership in Florence. Thus, the two states that composed the core of the original Italian League had passed into the hands of rulers whose youth and inexperience put them at a substantial disadvantage.[108]

"The Great Love He Has for His Wife . . . Who Has Given Him a Firstborn Son"

As the old decade ended and the new one began, Galeazzo's primary interest lay in the dynastic sphere. He began the 1470s by receiving oaths of fealty to himself and the infant GianGaleazzo as his heir. The city of Milan swore fealty on Christmas Day, 1469, and the other major cities a week later, on New Year's Day.[109] As heir to the duchy, GianGaleazzo had already received the county of Pavia, which had initially been given to his mother. Accordingly, on February 13, 1470, the duke granted her the city and district of Novara. The preamble to the charter spoke of "the great love he has toward his wife . . . who has given him a firstborn son."[110] At the end of the winter in 1470, Galeazzo celebrated the feast of San Giuseppe by receiving all the feudatories of the dominion as they swore fealty to himself and his son.

Milan's leading humanist, Francesco Filelfo, was among the formal witnesses to this major event. At the same time, Bona received oaths of fealty from the city of Novara and the feudatories in its district.[111]

"I Believe That She Will Fill the House for Me"   On May 18, 1470, Galeazzo dictated a will leaving the state to GianGaleazzo, in care of Bona, Ludovico Gonzaga, and Cicco Simonetta. Although the will was composed during a bout of serious illness, it was long and detailed, enumerating bequests to the duke's brothers, *camerieri,* physicians, huntsmen, secretaries, children, seneschals, and other favorites. Despite the tension between Galeazzo and Ferrante of Naples, the duke wanted his son to maintain "good friendship" with the Aragonese king as well as Milan's other traditional allies.[112]

One of the will's provisions regarded the child Bona was carrying at the time. If it proved to be a girl, she would receive a dowry of 100,000 ducats; if it was a boy, he would have an income of 12,000 ducats a year. The duke survived the illness, and within a few days after making the will, he became the father of a second son. At the infant's baptism in June, the new Sforza received the unusual first name Ermes (used by the Visconti) and the ducal family's obligatory second name, Maria.[113] As an aspiring dynast, Galeazzo was very pleased with his wife. Within less than two years of their wedding, Bona had presented her husband with two healthy sons, thus securing the succession and affirming his virility. While she was expecting Ermes, the proud duke had told Zaccaria Saggi da Pisa that "the Duchess is indeed pregnant, and I get great pleasure from it, and I believe that she will fill the house for me [with sons]."[114]

For the most part, Bona played a very conventional role as the duke's wife. In her first few years as duchess, she operated entirely in the duke's shadow, as she became familiar with a new language and a new way of life. She spent most of that time in pregnancy. The duchess was not a domineering character, which doubtless endeared her to Galeazzo. She relied heavily on her nurse, who was said to be the one "that governs and does everything with Her Ladyship."[115] The nurse received her share of ducal favor and was sought by others to procure favor for themselves.[116]

The duchess followed her husband's peripatetic life. The ducal couple generally resided together, and they traveled together more often than not.[117] Bona's court had a much more domestic tone than Galeazzo's. When she received the oath of fealty from a new castellan for Novara, the witnesses included another castellan, her secretary, her nurse, a butler, a doorkeeper, Margherita Visconti Crivelli, and the wife of courtier Battista da Montignana.[118] By contrast, when Galeazzo enfeoffed Lorenzo Terenzi da Pesaro that same year, the witnesses included his brothers Sforza Maria and Ludovico, the ambassadors from Mantua and Montferrat, and three major military leaders.[119]

Security and Uncertainty

In the two years following his marriage, Galeazzo had taken a strong interest in establishing himself as the prince of a major Italian power. Although his efforts to gain imperial investiture had continued to meet resistance, he had enjoyed enough support from subjects and allies to proceed without his overlord's recognition. By the summer of 1470, Galeazzo felt all the more secure because he had two sons who could succeed to the ducal throne and perpetuate the Visconti and Sforza lineages. The eldest had even received an oath of fealty from the entire duchy of Milan. The dominion was peaceful and prosperous, and the court had been reshaped to the duke's taste. Galeazzo had some reason to be pleased; yet, he was beginning to encounter major diplomatic problems, and his position in Italian affairs became uncertain.

4

"He Was . . . Splendid Beyond Measure in His Court"

Galeazzo Asserts His Princely
Style (1470–1472)

> He was most magnificent in furnishings, and in his
> way of life, and splendid beyond measure in his court.
> He presented very rich gifts to his attendants . . . and
> with great salaries he attracted men skilled in which-
> ever science.[1]

Work and Play

In 1470, Galeazzo's world held both promise and menace. His succession seemed secure, but he continued to seek imperial investiture. Within Italy, negotiations continued for the renewal of the Universal League, while a dangerous alliance began to develop between Venice and Naples. The duke was on difficult terms with Louis XI, his most powerful ally. At the same time, the youth of Florence's new rulers and the Venetian sympathies of Pope Paul II made Milan's diplomatic position more tenuous than it had been for years.

In 1470, the Sforza duke was only twenty-six years old, restless and impatient, hungry for glory and pleasure. That May, the Florentine ambassador could still write of Galeazzo in very positive terms, urging Lorenzo de' Medici to remain close to the duke.[2] However, others were less enthusiastic about Galeazzo's character. As early as 1468, Zaccaria Saggi da Pisa had told his Mantuan master that "on account of his dissimulation, [Galeazzo] has very little favor with anyone, and every day it is more widely known." By 1470, the ambassador told the marchioness that "the nature of this Lord worsens 100 percent every day. . . . I understand from some quarters that there is some hope of some improvement, but there is a certainty of worsening, if that is possible."[3] Galeazzo alienated many of the Sforza's friends with his impatience and thoughtlessness; one of them was Federigo da Montefeltro. The duke broke with Federigo in the summer of 1470, reportedly because the count had told Ferrante of Naples not to renew the league with Milan, citing Galeazzo's youth and foolishness.[4] Despite his bad reputation and political isolation, Galeazzo maintained a high level of self-confidence, and the diplomatic picture changed considerably in late summer. The Turkish conquest of Negroponte, a Venetian stronghold in Greece, caused the Italian powers to draw together long enough to renew the league at year's end.

Within the Milanese dominion, the year 1470 was relatively slow for political and diplomatic activity. The only major visit Galeazzo entertained from foreign dignitaries involved French ambassadors. They came in August, when he was reestablishing good relations with his royal brother-in-law. Galeazzo took the opportunity to extend magnificent hospitality, which included a dinner at the Corte Arengo with Bona and "fifty ladies from the most worthy and beautiful damsels of Milan" in attendance.[5] He spent 12,000 ducats to cover his river galley in cloth embroidered with his devices and to dress dozens of *camerieri* in silver brocade. The duke also paid Ludovico Gonzaga 12,000 ducats for a ruby that he wanted to give Louis XI.[6] After all his lavish preparations, the duke was disappointed when the embassy was cut in size from two hundred horses to ninety, and the main emissary, the marshal of France, was too ill to come.[7]

In the meantime, Galeazzo devoted much energy to his new children and other domestic matters. He expanded the size of his household, with both old and new servants: "The Lord was newly restored to their places the greater part of the officials and *camerieri* that belonged to the good memory of his father and has added many *camerieri*. There are more than 70 that he has restored to their places."[8] Throughout the summer and fall, he spent extravagantly on clothing for *camerieri* and others, "and money flowed to make these things, in such a fashion that the artisans all praised the Lord to Heaven."[9]

"He Wanted No One to
Bother Him Until Christmas"

Galeazzo liked to see himself as a major figure on the international stage, and he was often willing to invest much time and money on persons and activities that he considered worthy. However, he did not enjoy ruling the dominion on a day-to-day basis. For that reason, the duke relied heavily on the superb administration maintained by Cicco Simonetta and his colleagues. Galeazzo was always ready to create new institutional structures that delegated responsibility for specific matters to officials of the state or household. The business of state was unrelenting; although Galeazzo had ended his practice of giving regular public audiences shortly after he began it, he could not avoid the ceaseless stream of petitions and questions that flowed to him. The duke conducted most of his princely work in the mornings. Only matters of unusual importance would cause the business day to extend into the afternoon, and it was very rare for matters of state to be raised in the evening. For the court, the day was punctuated by the duke's meals. He rose early, heard his choir sing Mass, then ate breakfast (*colazione*). After the morning's activities, Galeazzo would eat an early dinner (*disnare*), often before midday.[10] The afternoon would end with supper (*cena*), around dusk. When the duke did attend to his work, he would often combine it with travel or recreation, holding audiences and deciding cases while hunting, riding, or watching tennis. When French ambassadors were expected for a working visit one summer, Galeazzo said that he would go hunting with them every day.[11]

When the duke tired of his work, he did not hesitate to put it aside. Occasionally, Galeazzo simply vanished, as Zaccaria found when he sought an audience in August 1470. Galeazzo had gone to Monza "with very few people and in such a way that he did not want his leaving to be known; and he has ordered that no one may go to Monza, because he says he does not want to be bothered for now, but rather to attend to enjoying himself." Two weeks earlier, the duke had threatened to leave for Monza and "made up a list of those who will go there; nor are there on that list any others than those who serve His Lordship and his falconers." Even the duke's brothers were excluded.[12]

Such lists were used also in Milan, to protect the duke from unwanted intrusions. In December 1467, Galeazzo had withdrawn into Porta Giovia Castle "with some of his [companions], saying he wanted to go to Monza, . . . nor did he want that anyone be allowed to enter into the castle except those who are noted on the list for going to Monza, and they are few." The ducal secretary Giovanni Simonetta gained entry, although his name did not appear on the list. The furious duke "gave him such a rebuff that he still stands in fear." The duke also fired the guards who allowed Giovanni to enter and threatened to hang them. Even the Privy Council "was made to wait at the gate for over an hour and a half, although the duke had sent for them."[13] In late October 1470, the duke lost patience totally with his duties. He dismissed all ambassadors and left for Vigevano with his huntsmen, declaring that "he wanted no one to bother him until Christmas."[14]

Hunting

He delighted greatly in hawking, and hunting with dogs, such that one time he spent 16,000 ducats on this for a year. . . . The perches of his hawks, falcons, and other birds of prey were adorned with velvet, embroidered with the ducal arms in gold and fine silver. He had a stable of horses beautiful beyond measure.[15]

It is not surprising that hunting held a prominent place in Galeazzo's personal agenda. The chase played a vital role in the lives of the warrior aristocracy throughout medieval Christendom. Hunting combined practice at arms with a means of obtaining food, and it provided a shared experience with its own conventions, protocol, and techniques. Moreover, hunting was the leading sport available to medieval aristocrats. As a form of recreation, it held enough danger to be stimulating, but it had few of the social, religious, and political complications to be found in tournaments or romantic involvements. In many parts of Christendom, a person's political status could be measured by the extent of his or her hunting privileges.

Galeazzo considered his own hunting prerogatives to be sacrosanct; he established strict regulations, enforced with severe penalties. In doing so, he was following "the arrangements and laudable customs of our ancient predecessors, the Most Illustrious Visconti Lords."[16] When the duke returned from his military campaigns in 1467, he ordered that six districts in the center of the duchy be reserved exclusively for his use. On his return from a visit to Mantua, he temporarily reserved the entire Cremona district for his hunting pleasure.[17] Even his brothers were subject to stringent limitations. When Ascanio requested permission to hunt outside Pavia, the duke granted it solely for Ascanio himself and no one in his household, because Galeazzo wanted "that our hunts be respected."[18] Among the most heinous crimes in Galeazzo's eyes were spoiling hunts and stealing hunting animals; on at least two occasions the theft of hounds sent him into a vindictive rage.[19]

Generally, the duke favored the standard types of hunting—fowl, hares, and deer as prey, hawks and hounds as predators. Sometimes, he would pursue more exotic sport: hunting bears at Varese, boars at Cusago, or wolves at Villanova.[20] He searched frequently for more hunting animals, sending courtiers and huntsmen as far as Scandinavia, Spain, and Britain to find them.[21] Galeazzo demanded gifts of hawks and boars from his own feudatories and officials and sought live deer from feudal lords elsewhere in Italy, to stock his favorite hunting grounds.[22] More than once during his reign, those areas became exhausted of prey. The duke owned an enormous number of hunting animals. He loved his hounds and prized his hawks; the gyrfalcons, most prestigious of hunting hawks, were actually housed much as in Corio's description above. In December 1469, Galeazzo had a room built for them in Porta Giovia Castle, then commanded his wardrobe steward and *commissario* of Works to calculate "how much green velvet it would take to decorate the said gyrfalcons' places, instead of canvas." The velvet was embroidered with ducal emblems before being hung.[23] Corio claims that the duke took one thousand hounds with him to Florence in 1471, and Galeazzo certainly could have brought that many, although evidence shows that Corio exaggerated. The duke traveled with a stable of forty to eighty horses for his own use.[24]

Galeazzo kept a large staff of huntsmen, with some posted to his favorite castles and others deputed to travel with him. They included kennelmen, falconers, and maintenance personnel. Although most of the kennelmen came from within the dominion, some of the duke's favorites were French. Before one visit to France, a Milanese diplomat was instructed to meet with Louis XI's master of hounds and get his help in finding "two good kennelmen who know well how to sound the horn and understand hunting well, that want to come stay with us." Those two huntsmen stayed with Galeazzo until his death.[25] Among the falconers, Greeks formed a large and prominent contingent.[26] Most of these huntsmen were persons of low rank, but their supervisors were men of substance. The captain-general of ducal hunts, Carlo Favagrossa of Cremona, was a ducal *gentiluomo* who had led the hunting staff since Duke Francesco's reign.[27] The head falconer, Pietro Birago, was a Milanese noble and *cameriere di camera* and one of Galeazzo's most intimate companions. His position in Milanese society was sufficiently elevated for Francesco Filelfo, Milan's leading humanist, to give an oration at his wedding.[28]

All of these men and animals were expensive to maintain, as Corio remarked. One of Galeazzo's budgets earmarked 3,000 ducats for the falconers and falcons and 5,000 ducats for the kennelmen and hounds. The duke projected a similar sum of 8,000 ducats total for his stable expenses; to put that figure in perspective, he also earmarked 8,000 ducats each for paying all of his foot soldiers and for a *condotta* to the lord of Forlì.[29]

Despite his fascination with hunting, Galeazzo was not personally a good hawker. On a hunting visit to Mantua, he requested that no one "wiser" than himself accompany him into the field. He insisted that certain men (including the marquess himself) not be present, because it would cause Galeazzo too much shame if his impatience caused him to lose prey that others might take.[30] In his hunting ventures, the duke was often more interested in success than in sport for its own sake. In December 1469, he had huntsmen feed the deer in the Parco at Pavia, to induce them to come closer when Galeazzo came to hunt there. Evidently, this tactic did not work; later that month, he sent orders not to feed the animals, so that they would be hungry and easier to kill.[31]

Other Sports and Games

The duke took an interest in several sports other than hunting. In 1470, he became particularly fond of tennis (*gioco della balla*), played indoors with bats of wood and iron. Galeazzo approached this game as a participant and patron; he employed several professional tennis players. He could also gamble on the outcome of matches; tennis became the premier gambling sport at the Milanese court.[32] The duke built large halls expressly for the purpose in at least three of his favorite castles.[33] In 1471, when planning the construction of such a hall at Porta Giovia, he froze all sales of building stone in Milan, so that he might have enough available for this project.[34]

Another major sport that Galeazzo watched was jousting; he rarely participated. An exception occurred in June 1468, when he held "a beautiful joust, but privately, with no one there other than some *camerieri* and *ragazzi di camera*, and also some of his servants-at-arms, that were eighteen [persons] in total." Galeazzo himself "ran the lance many times, very well."[35] Probably the greatest jousts of his reign were held at the feast of San Giorgio in 1469 and 1471; scores of condottieri, captains, and courtiers participated. Other special occasions marked by jousts included the feast of San Giuseppe in 1467, the Feast of the Assumption in 1471, and Alfonso of Calabria's visit in 1468. In November 1467, a tourney was held as a show of arms to impress Galeazzo's brother-in-law and nemesis, Filippo of Savoy.[36] Several tournaments took place solely as ducal entertainments. For one of them, Galeazzo spent almost 6,000 ducats on the accoutrements of eight *camerieri*.[37]

Some of the games favored at Galeazzo's court were more sedentary, including card games (*triumphi*) played with the tarot deck.[38] Even more than cards, the duke and his court enjoyed playing chess. Some members of the court gained reputations as skilled chess players. Galeazzo placed orders with his wardrobe steward to have chessboards made; when the duke expected them to be used often, he wanted them unpainted, because "the painting goes away too quickly."[39] At the Milanese court, chess was not a genteel pastime. Zaccaria Saggi, himself a chess player, called it "the cursed, bellicose game" and described graphically how much anger and frustration it could engender.[40]

One of the reasons chess was not a genteel pastime was that wagers, sometimes large ones, were often placed on the outcome.[41] Galeazzo and his companions gambled heavily throughout the year, but in particular, gaming and gambling formed a traditional part of the Christmas season.[42] In the first year of his reign, Galeazzo had gambled on both Christmas Eve and Christmas Day. By 1471, his passion was tennis, and he gambled on it throughout the week. On New Year's Eve that year, the duke commanded that everyone present join him in gambling. His interest in these pastimes must have puzzled many persons invited to the Christmas court. Most participants in that New Year's Eve party were unable to ante up the 100-ducat stake Galeazzo required. Even when he offered to give them the money, the majority declined to join him.[43]

"A Beautiful House
for Giving Himself Pleasure"

Galeazzo's passion for sports was reflected in his choice of residences and the features he built into them. The castles of Pavia and Milan were his principal seats, yet only half of his time was spent at one or the other of them during the years he was sole ruler.[44] The duke and his court stayed generally within a relatively small area, a triangle whose longest side measures around

80 kilometers. Seven out of every eight nights (87.5%) were spent at one of the eight ducal residences within this area. The northeastern corner was defined by Monza, the southeastern by Pavia, and the northwestern by Novara. Clustered near Novara, west of the Ticino River, were Vigevano, Villanova, and Galliate. East of the Ticino, about halfway between Vigevano and Milan, lay Abbiategrasso. Galeazzo used these six residences, and others, mainly for hunting trips. The duke spent days or weeks at a time in the Giardino at Milan, living in a hunting lodge called Cassino. He also passed many pleasant days at Mirabello, the hunting lodge in the Parco of Pavia.[45] Galeazzo developed the Giardino and Parco as large hunting preserves for his main residences. The Parco was already well established, and he bought up as much land as he could for the Giardino, expanding it to a considerable size.[46]

Monza, with its famous park, was Galeazzo's favorite escape in the early years of the reign. In all, Galeazzo spent around 4 percent of his nights there during the course of his reign. The only other castle in the eastern part of the dominion which he visited with any regularity was Cassano (1.5%), a fortress on the Adda River, near the border with Venice. In addition, he went occasionally to the Cremona district.

The Lomellina and Western Castles   From the beginning, Galeazzo had spent some time every year in the Lomellina and Novara districts. That part of his dominion lay across the Ticino River, adjacent to Montferrat and Piedmont. As his reign progressed, the duke favored that area more and more, largely abandoning his old haunts at Monza. Three of his favorite residences were located in that area: Vigevano, Villanova, and Galliate. The duke also stayed at several other castles in the vicinity, especially Gambolò and Novara.[47] His fondness for hunting in these districts exhausted the local game; at one point, he ordered feudatories and administrators in the Apennine foothills to send him hares for restocking the area.[48]

Vigevano Castle accounted for some 14 percent of Galeazzo's nights, an average of fifty days per year; it served as the duke's hunting headquarters. He stayed there occasionally during winter but more often in spring and fall, the hunting seasons. Vigevano Castle shared much of the character of Pavia and Milan, although it was smaller. Ludovico il Moro later commissioned extensive and dramatic work on and around it. Because Galeazzo stayed there so often, he arranged to make the castle more convenient for himself and those serving his person; in 1473, for example, he ordered that rooms be prepared for use by his singers whenever he should be in residence there.[49] He also constructed huge facilities to house more horses, hounds, and hawks. The duke found Vigevano a useful base of operations from which to indulge his personal desires and distance himself from burdensome responsibilities. Nevertheless, the amount of time he spent there—almost as much as in Milan itself—meant that he could not always avoid doing princely business while in residence.

Galeazzo passed many additional days and nights in other castles and houses that served him as hunting lodges; chief among them were Galliate (5%), Villanova (2.5%), and Novara (1.5%). Galliate was not a castle held in ducal hands; Galeazzo granted it out—with a comital title attached—to persons with whom he was very close, such as his favorite, Battista da Montignana, and his illegitimate son, Alessandro.[50] Abbiategrasso Castle was used often by Galeazzo as a convenient stop between the Lomellina and Milan. He stayed there for some 6 percent of his nights after 1468 but rarely for more than a few days at a time.

The duke had more ambitious plans for Villanova, a smallish, square, three-story structure that he acquired from its ecclesiastical landlords. In November 1472, he decided to "have built . . . great and beautiful edifices" at Villanova, based on plans drawn up earlier. By March 1474, the castle already contained 69 rooms (probably not counting large halls). Galeazzo had spent more than 3,000 ducats there but still had not obtained possession of the property. In September 1474, a park was being built at Villanova; 4,000 ducats were budgeted for the park in 1476. In December 1474, the duke ordered construction of a *Sala della balla* for tennis. That hall required 4,000 bricks for paving, and he commanded the local inhabitants to make bricks only for that purpose until it was completed—on pain of a 100-ducats fine. In February 1476, Galeazzo's contentious brother-in-law, Filippo of Savoy, congratulated the duke on having made Villanova "a beautiful house for giving himself pleasure."[51]

The logistical impact of the duke's frequent travels was felt not only by the ducal establishment but also by the local inhabitants of districts to which the court moved. These subjects were required to contribute to the provisions and living expenses of the court when it came to the district, an obligation that caused considerable conflict and resentment. Despite such burdens, and the hazards of hosting ducal hunts or other potentially damaging activities, towns with ducal residences generally benefited more than they suffered from the court's presence. Among other things, they enjoyed easier access to ducal largesse, privileges, and exemptions than their counterparts in districts that the court never frequented.[52]

"The Order of the Court"

In the autumn of 1470, Giovanni Simonetta was asked to make a new copy of "the little notebook that I had had made of the order of the court and description of [Your Lordship's] dominion," because it was in tatters. Giovanni sent it to the duke with corrections and additions, reminding Galeazzo that "said little notebook, as [Your Lordship] knows, was not made to keep track in this way of the names of those [persons] of the court . . . but it was done to send to Naples, to His Majesty the King, so that at one time he could see all the order of the court or Your Lordship, and of [Your] relatives."[53]

At the time Galeazzo acceded to the ducal throne, a prince was not yet obliged to maintain a splendid and highly formal court to earn the respect of others. In the early 1460s, Milanese ambassadors had commented on the informality that Louis XI showed in the royal court of France.[54] That informality surprised the Milanese, because the king of France was traditionally Christendom's most prestigious monarch, after the Holy Roman Emperor. During Francesco Sforza's reign in Milan, only the duke of Burgundy's court displayed the lush extravagance of the previous century's great International Gothic court culture.[55]

By the 1470s, interest in court and household was growing rapidly, both within and between individual courts. Several princes commissioned descriptions of their own courts; some, like Ferrante of Naples, also requested or received descriptions of other courts. In 1473, Galeazzo himself received descriptions of Charles the Bold's "very stately and honorable" court of Burgundy.[56] The following year, Olivier de la Marche wrote an extended description of that court, which had been substantially reformed under the *Ordonnances de l'Hôtel* of 1469. De la Marche's work was intended for Edward IV, who commissioned the *Black Book of the Household* in the early 1470s for the court of England. Edward's book gave detailed instructions for the composition and conduct of the royal household, and in 1478, the English king followed his Burgundian cousin by issuing ordinances in that area.[57]

"Court" and "Courtier" in Sforza Milan

In Sforza Milan, the word "court" (*corte*) bore five meanings. Three of the five meanings referred to architectural "courts"; the other two had social or institutional significance. Four of the five meanings, including two of the three architecture-related usages, applied to the princely sphere; they used the duke's person as the central point of reference. One meaning referred to the Palazzo dell'Arengo, and a second to the *Corte Ducale,* the courtyard that Galeazzo had built in Porta Giovia Castle. The third meaning, not a particularly princely one, referred to a type of farm, generally organized around a central courtyard.

The other two meanings of "*corte*" were less well defined. One of them signified the persons traveling or staying with the duke at a given time; alternative translations for this usage would be "retinue" or "entourage." In one instance, Galeazzo traveled from Milan to Pavia with some of his intimates, leaving his wife and "the rest of the court" to follow later.[58] When the duke went on a military campaign in Piedmont, he brought with him "all the court," and he himself referred to "our court" accompanying him. The extent of "the court" in this situation is visible in a letter from two seneschals, who noted that the ducal bodyguard and singers amounted to some three hundred persons between them, and "there would remain . . . Your Excellency, . . . Her Excellency [the Duchess], . . . the councillors, chancellors, and all the rest of the court."[59] Persons accompanying the duke were sometimes termed the *seguito* ("following," "suite"), and those who traveled with him were often said to *seguire la corte* (follow the court).[60]

The fifth meaning of "*corte*" in Galeazzo's era reflected an understanding that the court was an establishment or institution with boundaries that could contain persons and activities. This understanding is reflected in frequent references to "officials of the court" (*officiali dela corte*), "residents in the court" (*residenti nela corte*), "servants of the court" (*servidori dela corte*), events that occurred "in the court" (*nela corte*), and so forth.[61] This dimension of the court was associated particularly with certain locations, such as Porta Giovia Castle, the Corte Arengo, and Pavia Castle. These architectual spaces provided the setting in which most members of the court lived or worked. Wherever the duke might happen to be, part of the court was always operating in those locations. This permanent establishment made the court a constant point of reference, independent of Galeazzo's personal presence.

The distinction between household and bureaucracy was not sharply drawn. The Corte served throughout Galeazzo's reign as a residence for members of the ducal family and for visiting dignitaries. At the same time, it housed vital organs of the central government, including the offices of the seneschals-general and that part of the Privy Council which was based in the capital.[62] In Porta Giovia Castle, a few key officials lived in the wing now called the Rocchetta. The most isolated room of all, in the tower of the ducal wing, was the treasury, where the treasurer-general literally lived with his work; he could not leave the castle without Galeazzo's permission.[63] Some members of the Chancery also stayed there, constantly available for their crucial duties. Even one of the ducal tailors was sometimes required to remain in Porta Giovia and do his work.[64] The huge fortress also housed hundreds of soldiers in its garrison. However, there was little space for the rest of the persons attached to the court; most other ducal servants or officials had to find their own houses in the capital.

The boundaries of the court were not merely physical but social and symbolic as well. The bureaucrats and councillors who constituted the central administration belonged to a court elite that included feudatories, resident courtiers, representatives of provincial elites, and everyone else whom the duke defined as members of his personal space. The court extended beyond the walls of such locations as Porta Giovia or the Corte. Wherever the duke might happen to be, the court was there also. Similarly, the word *cortesano* (modern *cortigiano*)—"courtier"—was applied broadly by the duke himself. He used it for musicians, astrologers, soldiers, and others associated with his personal sphere.[65] In many letters written on behalf of ducal servants, Galeazzo referred to them as "cortesani," even though they might attend in his presence only twice a year.[66] When the duke designated persons as members of the ducal court, they remained members of the court until he removed them. So long as they were considered part of the court, they carried that distinction everywhere they went.

Money and Priorities

As each New Year approached and a new budget was drawn up for the year ahead, Galeazzo was inclined to recall the need for fiscal responsibility. The Sforza finances were always in a perilous state, and the young duke had inherited massive debts from his parents. Perhaps at the prompting of his Medici bankers, Galeazzo instituted several financial and monetary reforms. Among other actions, he revalued Milanese coinage and introduced new types of silver coins.[67]

The fiscal policies of Galeazzo's first few years on the throne failed to cover the costs of the court, and he began the year 1471 with a full-scale effort to rationalize fiscal procedures. As part of that effort, he sent the treasurer-general a list of priorities for disbursing money.[68] By that time, the duke had paid off much of his parents' debt, but he was still behind schedule on compensating the people who served him. His highest priority was to pay all the *salariati*—the salaried officers, including courtiers, singers, and tennis players—what they were owed from the previous year. The second priority was debt service for the duchess's maintenance. Once the treasurer-general had resolved past debts, he could catch up to current obligations: the duke's own income, the marquess of Mantua's pay as ducal condottiere, the merchant provisioners, "and other promises made in the name of the Most Illustrious Lord." Anticipation of debt was also built into the order. The *salariati* outside the household were to be paid their full salaries for 1471 by the end of February 1472; those within the household ranked two steps farther down, along with the rest of the duke's household costs. Before them came money for alms and masses; after them, the money for the duchess's household, the last item on the list.

Money in the Ducal Household

Money disbursed to Galeazzo's household went through the hands of the treasurer *di camera*. However, the more closely to the duke's own person an expenditure was made, the more likely it was to go outside the usual channels. Some very substantial sums were handled by men whose only authority was intimacy with Galeazzo. Without exception, these men served as *camerieri*; in some cases they bore also the title of *maestro di camera,* reflecting their position of financial trust.[69] Giovanni Rusconi da Verona, the *primo cameriere* in 1470–1471, handled much of Galeazzo's financial business. In one transaction, Giovanni spent the staggering sum of 17,000 ducats for Galeazzo, an amount equal to the entire year's budget for the ducal table. In a period of less than two months, Giovanni was consigned 46,000 ducats to spend, mainly during Galeazzo's travels outside the dominion. Giovanni was also involved in paying the military garrison for the Milanese ducal residences; orders flowed from him to the treasurer-general, who disbursed the money to the officer in charge.[70]

Giovanni da Verona was one of Galeazzo's most trusted and honored companions during the first half of his reign. He reached the height of *primo cameriere* (the most highly favored *cameriere di camera*) as early as 1468.[71] His wife was chosen that year as one of Bona's original damsels. On the roller coaster of ducal favor, Giovanni lost his office by February 1470, along with all his gifts from the duke. Within two months, though, Giovanni was restored to his favored place and his role in handling the duke's finances.[72]

The Restless Prince

The young duke of Milan was very restless during the years 1470 to 1472, and he traveled extensively outside the duchy. Galeazzo began 1470 with an ambitious plan to visit Rome with 1,200 persons. That trip never materialized, and later in the year his fancy turned toward France. By January 1471, he was discussing a plan to visit at Lent with as many as 3,600 persons.[73]

A Pilgrimage to Florence

Within a week of considering a trip to France, Galeazzo had changed his mind and began planning a visit to Florence instead. His stated purpose was to make a pilgrimage to the church of Santissima Annunziata, for which his father had had a particular devotion.[74] This plan was also ambitious, projecting a traveling company of over one thousand persons. This time, the duke carried through with it.

Galeazzo's list makers were very busy in the six weeks before his traveling company left. They created four different types of lists, covering the duke's household, the duchess's retinue, and two versions of the company as a whole. The earliest lists show the categories of persons graded according to the relative rank of their offices. The lists begin with the duke himself and fourteen men of the highest rank—three ducal brothers, the marquess of Saluzzo, a bishop, and eight councillors. The rest of the names on the list are grouped under headings in the following order: "Gentlemen" (actually, military leaders), "Physicians and priests," "Seneschals," "Courtiers" (mainly *gentiluomini*), "*Camerieri* and other officials *di camera*," "*Camerieri*" (*fuori di camera*), and "Officials of the household." Clearly separate from the rankings of the ducal party are four ambassadors and the Chancery, which follow the rest of the list. From the Chancery alone, Galeazzo brought 29 named persons, 13 anonymous messengers, and a total of 67 horses. The lists drawn up for the duchess's sizable following show a pattern similar to that of the duke's household. The primary difference is the group of ladies and damsels listed as a group ahead of all male courtiers. Other women from the Sforza lineage also joined Bona's court for this journey.[75]

"With All His Court and Magnificence"   Galeazzo mobilized the entire ducal administration to handle the elaborate logistics for the trek over the Apennines. Among other matters, they attended to details of horses, bridges, food and fodder, wood, lodgings, stables, guards and guides, ferries over the Taro River, and participation in the journey itself.[76] Taking more than one thousand persons on a month-long journey was immensely complex and expensive, especially with the limited technology of transportation available in the Renaissance era. It is remarkable that this visit could be accomplished at all and quite amazing that it was organized on such short notice. The scale of the logistics is evident from instructions given when Galeazzo first conceived the idea. He figured the cost of maintaining the horses at 1 pound each per day, or 30,000 pounds (7,500 ducats) for one thousand horses for a month. He ordered 150 coverings of velvet in the Sforza colors (white and dark red), 45 gold and silver fittings for horses and mules, and new clothes of brocade or velvet for forty *ragazzi* chosen to go along, "all the *sottocamerieri*," and "the *camerieri* who have not had anything from this [last] summer until now." The duke also ordered "beautiful and good horses" for his wife. Moreover, all the persons accompanying him who "do not have [their] expenses [paid] *in casa,* or [a] salary" from the household treasury would have all of their expenses paid while they were "outside of the ducal dominion."[77]

In the meantime, the dominion itself would need a caretaker. Galeazzo deputed his princely cousin, Alessandro Sforza of Pesaro, to serve in that capacity during the duke's absence.[78] Galeazzo and his company left Milan on March 4, 1471, proceeding to the Apennines and crossing the mountains near Parma. After eleven days of travel via Pisa and Lucca, they made a grand entry into Florence on March 15. The splendor of Galeazzo's retinue was staggering.[79] An observer from Siena stated before Galeazzo's arrival that "by everyone, it is attested that it will be, between horses and mules, around the sum of 1,500 or more," plus four hundred persons on foot, "all lords and worthy persons and . . . all in courtly style [*a la cortigiana*], with pomp and without arms." Because of the Lenten season, the Florentines planned no jousts but religious *rappresentazioni* in various churches of the city. The ducal party's lodgings were spread throughout the city, with Galeazzo himself at Lorenzo de' Medici's house and others staying at religious houses or the homes of citizens.[80]

Another Sienese observer, who had seen Galeazzo's grand entry with 1,400 persons into Lucca on March 12, also described the duke's "corte et magnificentia" on entering Florence.

> There was a livery for his greater *camerieri,* all dressed in crimson, and each one well mounted on horseback, with a greyhound on a leash. There were also sixty pages, all dressed in green velvet, on huge coursers, all with fittings of gold and silver, and saddles covered with brocade of various colors and crimson. In similar fashion they led from 65 to 70 mules with coffers and carriages, all with covers of embroidered silk. Of the order and decoration of the Duchess's damsels, and their wagons, I will say nothing; and the same for the great preparations here, which are things almost incomprehensible, and Your Lordships can imagine better than I can describe.[81]

Among other things, this description suggests that Galeazzo's lavish intentions for clothing his household were carried out quite fully. On entering Florence, he went directly to the Annunziata, leading his dazzling retinue through the streets. The following day, March 16, he went to the Palazzo Vecchio "with all his court and magnificence" to address the Florentine *signoria,* who returned the visit at Lorenzo's house the following day. After these formalities had been observed, the rest of the duke's stay was passed without much public activity.[82] On the last evening, a *rappresentazione* was prepared for Galeazzo's entertainment at the church of Santo Spirito. Neither he nor Bona attended, but later that night a fire damaged the church.[83]

The duke and his company returned home by way of Lucca and Genoa, arriving at Pavia exactly one month after they had left. With the exception of unrest in Genoa on the return journey, Galeazzo had been received honorably and graciously everywhere he went. The magnificence of his person and court made a deep impression on the traditionally republican cities of northern Tuscany. Not content with this grand enterprise, in August, Galeazzo conceived of a plan to visit the new pope in Rome; the Venetian Paul II had died and been succeeded by Sixtus IV, a better friend to the duke. Galeazzo had set preparations well in motion before abandoning the idea and sending a delegation with two of his brothers instead.[84]

A Visit to Mantua

In the meantime, the duke spent a month in the summer of 1471 as a guest of the Gonzaga family at the castles of Mantua and (primarily) Gonzaga. Before leaving Milan, Galeazzo had sent them instructions on how to prepare for him, declaring, "I want to live in my own way [*a mio modo*] and as I do every day at home." He was expected to bring over 500 horses with him, including 200 in Bona's household, 100 for his own person, 40 for his brothers, at least 30 for the Chancery, and 60 for his falconers.[85]

The ostensible purpose of the visit was rest and recreation, especially hunting. However, the duke had an ulterior motive for staying at Gonzaga. In the neighboring duchy of Ferrara, Duke Borso d'Este lay close to death, and his succession was in dispute between Niccolò and Ercole d'Este. Galeazzo took a strong interest in the succession. Although he professed to support Niccolò's claim fully, the duke was playing a double, or triple, game. He instructed Donato del Conte to "find out which of sir Niccolò and sir Ercole might have more favor, and might stand more strongly for obtaining that state . . . because it could be that sir Ercole would have more favor . . . and we would not want that, winning, he should remain an enemy to us."[86] Galeazzo remained in Mantuan territory until August 8, ready to swoop like a vulture should Borso's death leave an opening for him. However, Borso did not die until two weeks after Galeazzo had left for Milan.[87]

Looking for Action

After returning to his own dominion, Galeazzo continued to be unusually mobile. In late August, he enjoyed the pleasures of the chase on the eastern borders of his dominion (Romanengo). By September 8, he was planning a trip to the western borders (Novara), asking that paths through the vineyards be cleared for his hunting party. A week after that, he decided to hunt in the southwestern area of the duchy (Alessandria and Tortona). Six days later, he was considering a return to Caravaggio, on the eastern border again.[88]

The duke itched to accomplish something bold and dramatic. In August, he hit upon the idea of challenging the aging Colleoni to a duel.[89] Each leader would have 800 to 1,000 troops, and they would fight—with swords and lances only—in some suitable location chosen in advance. As captain-general of the Venetian army that stood threateningly at the duchy's border, Colleoni was the ideal opponent. Moreover, his reputation for courage and skill gave the challenge a certain dignity and fired the imagination of Italian captains and princes. Many of them offered horses, arms, and even men to one side or the other. Colleoni and Galeazzo both sent out emissaries to buy or borrow such assistance.[90] However, Venice wanted no part of the idea, and the republic refused to permit it while Colleoni was still under contract to them. The contract would not end until early in 1472.

In the meantime, Pope Sixtus IV tried to dissuade the prospective duelists, even threatening them with excommunication. Galeazzo had had second thoughts early on; he realized he could not "do this feat of arms as duke of Milan, but as captain," and he probably feared losing.[91] The duke was not entirely committed to making war at all. On September 20, he told Zaccaria Saggi da Pisa that he had raised his expenditures for condottieri by 50,000 ducats, but he continued, "I am not wise to make such expenditures. What the devil will I do with all these people, that are by contract 50,000 persons and will be 150 squadrons? What the devil will I do with them?" Galeazzo asked Zaccaria if the ambassador thought the duke would ever go to war, particularly against the Venetians. The tactful envoy responded, "Only if they start it," and Galeazzo laughed and said he was probably right.[92] However, neither he nor Colleoni was willing to back down from their duel; their honor was at stake. In October, he met near Vercelli with Duchess-Regent Iolande of Savoy. In December, Giovanni Castiglione, cardinal-bishop of Siena, came to Milan.[93] It was not until February 1472 that Sixtus and King Ferrante succeeded in putting an end to this absurd idea. Galeazzo found little glory in warfare and diplomacy; he turned his attention elsewhere.

Ambition and the Arts

He delighted in painting, in such manner that he once wanted a room painted in one night with most noble figures, and he remunerated well those who served him. He took great pleasure from tennis, gathering those that had experience in this exercise from the farthest parts of Italy, and also had complete rooms made for this purpose, and did the same with musicians.[94]

Galeazzo had lavish tastes, and he enjoyed experiencing skillful masters at work in any field of action. Autumn 1471 marked a turning point in his reign. The visits to Florence and Mantua and the succession of Ercole d'Este in Ferrara made the duke more determined than ever to invest his substantial resources in glory and pleasure. The Medici, Gonzaga, and Estensi were Galeazzo's main rivals as patrons in northern Italy. They posed a challenge to the duke's sense of his own princely dignity. Beginning in September, he initiated several major projects involving patronage of the arts.

"To Adorn Our Chapel with Some
Excellent Musicians and Singers"

The duke enjoyed the art of singing very much, for which reason he had around thirty singers from across the Alps, honorably salaried by him, and among these he had one, Cordier by name, to whom he gave for his salary 100 ducats per month.[95]

Galeazzo's patronage of music was important far beyond the borders of his dominion. He was one of the greatest patrons in all of Renaissance Europe, and his court provided the setting for a major development in the history of vocal polyphony. The duke heard Mass sung every morning, and he took a genuine delight in sacred music. His father had employed very few singers, unlike the monarchs of Naples, France, and the Papacy. As late as March 1471, when Galeazzo traveled to Florence, he was accompanied by only four singers.[96] In September of that year, though, he began to recruit the largest and finest choir in Italy, possibly in all of Europe. The duke's recruitment program was systematic and extensive. It reached directly to the Low Countries, where most great singers were trained, as well as to the choirs of other Italian princes and prelates.

The nucleus of Galeazzo's choir was formed by three singers who had served for many years at the court of Naples; one of them, Alexander Agricola, gained renown as a composer later in the century.[97] Another of them, Raynero, was the agent sent on the first recruitment trip to northern Europe. On a trip to England, he bore a letter to King Edward IV, stating that Galeazzo sought "singers and musicians necessary to us," because he had decided "to adorn our chapel with some excellent musicians and singers."[98] One of the figures brought back to the Milan court by Raynero was Gaspar van Weerbeke, who became vice-choirmaster and later a major composer. In turn, Gaspar was sent to the Low Countries in 1473, with a "shopping list" specifying how many men of each voice Galeazzo desired. In 1474, the ducal choir numbered 40 singers; over the last two years of his reign it stabilized at about 32, still far larger than any of its rivals.[99] Most of Galeazzo's singers were hired from foreign parts, but a few were discovered in the service of local clergy. The brilliant Josquin des Prez sang first with the Duomo's choir, and one "Cardino de Bosco" of Normandy had served the bishop of Como.[100]

Galeazzo's choir was not only very large but very talented as well. Josquin, Gaspar, Agricola, Loyset Compère, and others, revolutionized the writing and performance of the motet, one of the most popular forms of vocal music in the Renaissance. They went so far as to create a new form, virtually unique to the Milanese court, the *motetti missales.* In these Masses, the traditional sung parts (Kyrie Eleison, etc.) were replaced by motets whose subjects were unrelated to their place in the service. These motets were generally set to popular music, a break with the rigid traditions of formal church music. A great innovation of this group of composers was to blend the sacred music in which they were trained with the lively native music of Lombardy.

One of the *motetti missales* cycles from the pen of Compère is called the *Missa Galeazescha*; it was probably written for Galeazzo. Seven of its eight motets celebrate the Blessed Virgin Mary, for whom the fifth duke had a special devotion.[101] She was the subject for many of the *motetti missales,* reflecting the central place she occupied in the Milanese ducal tradition. However, a strong devotion to the Mother of God could not justify replacing the elements of the Mass, long fixed by the church. It was characteristic of Galeazzo to preside over the flowering of a musical form that produced beauty of a high order while subverting religious conventions. The duke had a proactive style as a patron. Although his singers developed the innovative forms that originated at his court, Galeazzo's intimate relationship with them affected what they did. The choir traveled with their master almost everywhere he went, both within the dominion and outside it, even on a military campaign. It was significant that he had rooms at Vigevano Castle maintained for the singers' use; he would generally bring to that castle only persons whom he considered particularly valued or intimate.[102]

The duke was generous to his singers. When Agricola and his companions entered Milanese service in 1469, they were paid 10 ducats per month, more than most courtiers and administrators. That year, Galeazzo twice advanced them three months pay at a time, "so that they may meet their needs."[103] In February 1473, the duke told Zaccaria Saggi da Pisa that he was giving tenors a salary of 12 ducats per month; Galeazzo had also given several singers houses worth 700 to 800 ducats each. In April 1473, the duke was welcoming some of the new singers recruited by Gaspard van Weerbeke. He spent over 1,000 ducats "to buy houses for our singers" and almost 1,100 ducats for "salaries for some singers newly taken," beyond the 4,000 ducats already earmarked for "the expense of the salary for all our said singers for our chapel." Zaccaria told Ludovico Gonzaga, "Certainly, His Excellency has made a very great beginning with these singers, and he spends on them wholesale. He has given one alone that which is worth 400 ducats, in a house, estate, money and clothing . . . and has made him his *cameriere di camera*. [The singer] is a tenor, and very good; and the duke has better."[104]

We know little about the vocal abilities of fifteenth-century singers in general, but one of those recognized by contemporaries as exceptional, Jean Cordier, was hired in 1474 by Galeazzo. The duke reportedly promised a salary of 1,000 ducats per year, but that promise and Corio's claim that the singer was paid 100 ducats per month are characteristic exaggerations. There is no evidence that Cordier received such a sum, which would have been over seven times higher than the highest recorded salary for a ducal singer. The total salary budgeted for the entire choir in 1476, when Cordier was a ducal singer, was 5,000 ducats, roughly the same amount Galeazzo spent in 1473, before Cordier was hired. However, Cordier did receive more than one fief from Galeazzo, which probably brought him a considerable income. The singer was invited to the Christmas court in both 1475 and 1476, on the latter occasion as "Sir Cordier, count and singer."[105]

Instrumental Musicians   Galeazzo's patronage of instrumental music was less extensive. He did maintain a large corps of *trombetti*, or trumpeters. In 1469, the duke ordered that a squadron of them (probably ten in number) accompany him everywhere; the duke employed sixteen to twenty trumpeters at any given time. Pay for these men ranged from 30 ducats per year in 1467 to almost 5½ ducats per month (i.e., 55 ducats per year if they received ten payments) in 1469; they also received an annual gift of hose and a cloak at the feast of San Giorgio.[106]

The trumpeters served Galeazzo in various capacities beyond playing music and providing ceremonial flourishes. Giacomo Sacco of Parma played tennis well enough to take on the duke himself; he and his musical colleague Giuliano da Correggio are both included in one list among the tennis players traveling with the court. Tecla da Firenze helped to recover some of Bianca Maria's belongings after her death, and Luigi da Milano ("Aloisino") served as a messenger to bring the duchy of Bari's revenues back to Milan in 1466. Diego Spagnolo was sent to his native Spain to arrange the release of Milanese courtiers imprisoned there on a horse-buying trip for Galeazzo; six months later, Diego completed their mission.[107]

Galeazzo's fresco programs for his chapels included instrumental musicians, especially trumpeters. Other musicians at his court included nonbrass wind musicians (*pifferi*), guitarists, and lutenists. The wind musicians served on a more regular basis than the others; Galeazzo took six of them to Florence in March 1471. A few months later, he asked Ludovico Gonzaga to lend him some of Mantua's wind musicians, as the duke had thrown all of his own into prison.[108]

The majority of Galeazzo's instrumental musicians came from Germany, but the most renowned musician at the court was Greek: the organist Isacco Argiropulo, son of the great Greek teacher Giovanni and student of the famous organist Antonio Squarcialupi. Isacco came to Milan as a "courtier and harpsichord player" in 1472, after recommendations from Cardinal Francesco Gonzaga and Roberto Sanseverino. Galeazzo prized the musician highly and enlisted his aid in building a fine organ for the chapel in Porta Giovia Castle. In the process, though, Isacco harassed the duke's singers, and the vice-castellan had to keep him under control.[109] Galeazzo had a particular interest in organs; over the course of his reign, he employed or interviewed several organists to build or play instruments for him. In 1476, three organ players were included among the persons traveling with his court.[110] The duke liked to have his favorite musicians of whatever kind with him, wherever he went.

The Visual Arts

When Galeazzo visited Tuscany and Mantua in the spring and summer of 1471, he saw some of the artistic riches in those regions. That experience exercised a strong influence on his activities in the autumn, when he conceived two ambitious projects in the visual arts.

A Mausoleum Plan   At the beginning of November 1471, Galeazzo was very ill, and he feared that death was near. On November 1, he refused to give Zaccaria an audience, because he did not want to be seen with fresh scars from his pox. He even considered canceling the Christmas court that year.[111] On November 3, the duke wrote a will that was far less fanciful than the draft he had dictated eighteen months before. This time, he was serious, and he confined himself to the most vital concerns. Few of the will's basic provisions were altered, but Galeazzo planned for the burials of himself and his wife. He ordered a funerary church made of marble, in the form of a Tuscan baptistery, with a bronze tomb and chapels arranged around it.[112] Such a church would have been audacious and unique, combining elements from the baptisteries of Florence and Pisa (which he mentioned by name) and a project Ludovico Gonzaga was undertaking in the SS. Annunziata of Florence as well as a centrally planned church Leon Battista Alberti was building for the Gonzaga in Mantua. Galeazzo recovered from his illness; the mausoleum was never built.[113]

A Fresco Program for Porta Giovia Castle   When Galeazzo visited Mantua in the summer of 1471, he must have seen Mantegna's frescoes for the Camera degli Sposi, then in progress.[114] He must also have reacted negatively to being outdone by his Mantuan neighbor, who was inferior to him in both rank and wealth. Although the duke had created a grand fresco program for Pavia Castle two years earlier, that program was probably not executed.[115] The Gonzaga could boast the splendid Arthurian cycle by Pisanello as well as the glorious new Mantegna program.[116]

Sometime in 1471, probably late in the year, Galeazzo developed a fresco program for four halls and chambers on the upper floor of Porta Giovia Castle.[117] Two rooms would be painted with decorative motifs. The large hall (Sala Grande) was to feature a hunting scene showing Filippo, Sforza Maria, and Ludovico Sforza joining the duke, fifteen other intimates, and two huntsmen. The small hall (Saletta) adjacent would bear four scenes of Milanese dukes with their wives and inner circles: GianGaleazzo and Filippo Maria Visconti (without a wife), Francesco Sforza, and Galeazzo himself. In that final scene, the fifth duke and his duchess were accompanied by his four secular brothers, Cicco Simonetta, Giacomo Alfieri, six condottieri-princes, and Pietro Pusterla with the ceremonial sword. The two-year-old ducal heir would be shown holding his father's hand, an unusual touch in this gathering of princes.[118]

The commission went through two more versions over the next year or more, each fundamentally similar but with some changes in personnel. Neither of those versions was dated, but a 1472 cost estimate for the job has been associated with the third version. One of the *camerieri di camera* in that version did not come to Milan until November 1472, and another probably did not come into the duke's service until January 1473, so the final program may have originated later than previously thought.[119]

The changes in the programs reflected changes in the population of the court; among the figures in Galeazzo's ducal scene for the final version was his infant daughter Bianca, born in 1472. The programs also reflected changes in the duke's feelings about persons in his world; Sforza Secondo, reconciled and honored in 1472, appeared in that scene. Larger issues were taken into consideration, too, such as rivalries between client princes; the marquess of Montferrat was added for the final version, explicitly placed on an equal footing with his counterpart from Mantua.

Fresco programs such as these provided the duke with further opportunities to create an order based on his own vision. Almost every ducal commission exalted the prince and his family, as they joined the heavenly to the earthly, the past to the future, and the elements of their world to one another. Even Galeazzo's sacred fresco commissions usually included portraits of himself and his immediate family.[120] Secular frescoes also showed the perverse humor in his vision. One of the duke's particular favorites in 1471 was the Albanian Alessio Piccinino, second only to the duke on some lists for the trip to Florence. All three versions of the hunting scene contained instructions "that Alessio be depicted such that a stag has thrown him from his horse, and he is raising his legs to the sky in as attractive a manner as possible."[121]

Other Visual Media   Galeazzo commissioned work in several media besides fresco painting. He planned some monumental sculptures, including the mausoleum and tomb project, a huge bronze equestrian statue of his father, and an altar sculpture for the Duomo. In the event, he had only limited work done, at Porta Giovia Castle, the Duomo of Milan, and the Certosa of Pavia. Much of that work was executed by Milan's leading sculptor, Giovanni Antonio Amedeo.[122] Manuscript illumination was a thriving art in Galeazzo's reign; even some formal documents produced by the ducal Chancery were decorated. The Lombard master Cristoforo de' Predis illustrated magnificent books for Galeazzo himself, including a New Testament, and several other major works were executed for such Milanese noble families as the Borromei and Marliani.[123]

In another genre, Zanetto Bugatti served as the ducal family's favorite portrait painter. In 1468, he did a portrait of Bona for Galeazzo to consider before marrying her. In 1472, Galeazzo commanded him to travel immediately from Milan to Pavia, bringing the equipment needed for "portraying persons from life [*dal naturale*]."[124] Zanetto also designed coins or medals with the duke's likeness. Galeazzo had many such coins and medals made, as well as other portraits and statuettes in silver and gold.[125] In 1471, the duke owed silversmiths over 250 ducats for "the images made in the likeness of the Most Illustrious Lord Count" (the infant GianGaleazzo) and 1,250 ducats for 813 ounces of fine silver worked into statues of seven saints.[126] In March 1472, Galeazzo designated 500 ducats for fifty gold coins or medals with a likeness of his own head. He wanted them to be placed in two small chests on the back of a camel made of gold. The camel would be led by a Moor, also in gold, using a small gold chain. The Moor would bear at his belt the tiny keys used to lock and unlock the small chests. Another 500 ducats were set aside for Moor and camel, which the duke wanted to have done in eleven days.[127]

Patronage of Visual Artists   The visual artists Galeazzo hired did not enjoy the innovative license he extended to composers of vocal music. The duke treated artists as he did other skilled craftsmen, commissioning them in very specific terms to create very specific objects. The commission for the 1469 fresco cycle at Pavia was entitled, "Plan according to which our Most Illustrious Lord wishes that the below-noted places in Pavia Castle be painted and repainted." The detail that makes the programs illuminating of the ducal vision also tied the hands of the artists hired to execute them.

Galeazzo regarded himself as the true creator of both the court sphere and its artistic representations. He hired visual artists to execute what he had envisaged; as a prince, he would not dirty his own hands with the technicalities. Most of the mundane details were handled by Bartolomeo Gadio da Cremona, Galeazzo's *commissario* of Works; sometimes Cicco Simonetta or the secretary Giacomo Alfieri might act for the duke. The commissions were put out to bid, with the lowest bidder generally taking the contract, regardless of relative merit or renown. Gadio had more respect than Galeazzo did for the skill of certain artists, but he would always obey his ducal master's final decisions.[128]

Artists who were eager to curry favor with the duke might offer unusually favorable terms. When Galeazzo wanted some rooms in Porta Giovia Castle painted in 1469, one painter offered to give a 15 percent discount on the job, to forego any advance payment, and to make other variances in standard procedure. Bartolomeo Gadio considered this offer "a very good benefit" to the duke, because other painters would want more money and better terms. However, the other painters bidding on the job countered with a 26 percent discount and won the contract.[129] Final payment for ducal commissions was made on the basis of a valuation by three or four other artists, emphasizing the competitive and commercial nature of the transactions.[130] Differences of opinion could arise and cause ill-will between the artists who had executed a program and those assessing its value.[131]

Galeazzo often employed artists to undertake routine decorative work, sometimes on very short notice. In 1468, a painter was set to work on decorations for the feast of San Giorgio eight days later. Bonifacio Bembo, a major figure in northern Italian art, was hired two years later to "retouch our *Camera dei Conigli* . . . with some millet plants and similar greenery, with some birds, that is, pheasants, partridges, and quail."[132] For Christmas 1469, the duke had painters labor day and night to put decorative patterns and ducal emblems on the halls of Porta Giovia Castle.[133]

The duke did give some support to his artists. When Bembo and another painter were sent to work at Vigevano Castle, Galeazzo told the podestà to have the "community provide them with a house suitable for them and their servants."[134] The duke made the painter Vincenzo Foppa an honorary member of the ducal household (*famigliare*), with the attendant privileges. Galeazzo also recommended Foppa for citizenship in Pavia, noting that the artist had lived there for twelve years.[135]

Bembo was perhaps the most active painter at Galeazzo's court; he also worked on the main chapel at Porta Giovia. He and Foppa participated in painting the huge reliquary at Pavia Castle with what has been called "the last and supreme heraldic and courtly fantasy, truly worthy of the second 'Waning of the Middle Ages' that was the court of Galeazzo Maria Sforza."[136] Their co-worker on this project, Zanetto Bugatti, functioned almost as a "court painter" to the Sforza, although he neither lived nor traveled with the court. Zanetto spent years training under the Flemish master Rogier van der Weyden during Duke Francesco's reign.[137] Presumably, he brought the influence of the Flemish style to his work, but no extant work is definitively attributed to him. As an artist, Zanetto is a shadowy figure, known only from documents.

The greatest Lombard master of visual arts in Galeazzo's time was Foppa, a Brescian who received all of his training in northern Italy. The watershed of his artistic development was a fresco cycle commissioned by the Medici Bank agents, the Portinari, for a chapel in the church of Sant' Eustorgio, Milan. Foppa completed that masterpiece around 1468. He did not work extensively for Galeazzo, nor did he follow the court. Much of his work during Galeazzo's reign bore no connection to the duke whatsoever, and some was not even executed within the dominion.[138] Unlike his father, Galeazzo showed little interest in fostering the work of artists employing neoclassical innovations, although much exciting work was being done in Milan and elsewhere during his time. His taste ran to the gilded and the Gothic.[139] When he commissioned additions or renovations to ducal residences, he was content to replicate the Trecento style of castle building bequeathed by his Visconti predecessors. This choice may have been purposeful, as Galeazzo wanted to recall the Visconti and celebrate their legacy.

A Limited Audience   Galeazzo commissioned many works of visual art, including medals, statuary, and religious frescoes. He used some of the greatest artists of his day, often in trivial ways. The works that could have secured his fame as a patron of art were his three major secular fresco programs: one for Pavia Castle and two for Porta Giovia Castle. However, there is no evidence that the programs were fully executed.[140] All three cycles were intended for spaces close to the center of the court. The Pavia frescoes were designed for the upper floor of the castle, where Galeazzo and Bona had their apartments; the first set of frescoes in Milan would also have occupied walls near the ducal chambers. The third cycle (see chap. 8) was probably meant for a site close to (or overlapping with) that of the earlier program.[141]

Such locations clearly limited the audience. While Galeazzo had coats of arms, ducal emblems, and other attributes of his dignity painted on the public facades of his residences, the more personal images of his major fresco programs were reserved for the select few permitted to enter his personal space. What they would have seen—had the programs been completed—exemplified the Renaissance tendency to blend realism and idealism. The duke's images evoked the daily life of his court and the highest aspirations of his ducal lineage. While the evocations of the lineage would reflect something profound and enduring, though, the depictions of daily life would become obsolete almost immediately. To keep those depictions current, as Giovanni Simonetta had said of listing courtiers, "it would be necessary to redo it every month, as the persons are changed."

Literature and Learning

As duke of Milan, Galeazzo had strong views about the place of music and the visual arts in his princely world. He spent considerable sums on those disciplines, pleasing himself and asserting his vision. He did not have a corresponding interest in the written word. Notwithstanding his own excellent education in Latin letters, Galeazzo showed only minimal concern for the patronage of literature and learning within the court sphere. The Visconti-Sforza library, one of Christendom's best collections, was regarded by the duke as a collection of precious objects more than as a reservoir of knowledge and inspiration. When Alessandro Sforza of Pesaro wanted to borrow "that Virgil annotated by the hand of Petrarch, which is in that library," Galeazzo would not lend it until, "having tasted the sweet wine which you sent me, we have changed our mind."[142]

An inventory from Duke Francesco's reign shows that the ducal library had many books from Petrarch, probably a legacy of the writer's long stay at Pavia Castle during Galeazzo Visconti's time. Another surviving inventory is more interesting, because it lists the books that were "re-placed [*repositi*]" in the library on October 5, 1469, suggesting that they had actually been in recent use (or were new to the library). The list included dozens of books, covering a wide range of subjects. Several treated the principles of government, including Cicero's *De Officiis*, John of Salisbury's *Policraticus*, and

Giles of Rome's *De Regimine Principium.* Others had historical or biographical themes, among them an Italian translation of Livy and both Latin and Italian copies of Lodrisio Crivelli's life of Duke Francesco. A significant number of the volumes dealt with physical health, including two books against poison, one by Benedetto Reguardati, *On Keeping the Person in [Good] Health,* and one "that teaches [how] to gain and lose weight." A few books gave practical advice on other matters, such as agriculture, while several concerned leisure pastimes: books of popular songs, a French book on chess, and John of Salisbury's *De Nugis Curialium* (part of *Policraticus*). Naturally, some of the volumes treated of sacred matters, among them one "on pictures of Heaven" (*De Imaginibus Celi*). The largest single category, though, was composed of orations, verses, and treatises written for members and friends of the ducal family.[143]

Men of Letters   While he continued to support the University of Pavia and its faculty and to ensure that his own children were properly instructed, Galeazzo did little personally to commission literary works or subsidize men of letters.[144] Members of his court did not fill the vacuum in literary patronage; this period produced few written works of note in Milan. Perhaps the most important book in progress at the time was Giovanni Simonetta's biography of Duke Francesco. Giovanni kept its existence secret from his ducal master, as he evidently did not want Galeazzo to have anything to do with it.[145]

The most renowned man of letters associated with Milan in Galeazzo's time was Francesco Filelfo. Although he lived outside the city for most of the reign, Filelfo maintained a residence there, and he was present at the oaths of fealty to Galeazzo and the infant heir.[146] The only written works that Galeazzo requested or received from Filelfo were bits of poetry in honor of such subjects as the ducal mistress or a giant bombard. On receiving the verses for the bombard, Galeazzo promptly lost them, leading him to ask "that you want to have them rewritten *de novo* and sent to us, that is, those same [verses] that were done the other day."[147]

Although Galeazzo did not have a profound appreciation of humanist thought and literature, he did recognize Filelfo as a significant Milanese resource, addressing him on at least one occasion as "poet laureate." The duke responded to Filelfo's various requests and petitions and even paid an allowance to the honored humanist.[148] However, in 1468, that allowance was cut substantially. When Filelfo complained that he had been paid more in the past, Galeazzo replied tartly, "We intend that said allowance begin from the present, and we want to know nothing of the past."[149] Filelfo sought financial support wherever he could find it; even when he was staying in Milan, he did not hesitate to ask the marquess of Mantua for money to help him marry off a daughter.[150] In general, Galeazzo's court did not provide great opportunity for ambitious men with literary skills. An unusual example of advancement through the power of the pen during his reign involves Pietro Andrea Inviciati. He wrote a panegyric to the duke, probably in 1468, and in 1470 received an appointment to the Privy Chancery. The following year, the new chancellor was given permission to attend the university at Pavia, and Galeazzo recommended him to Ascanio Sforza as a servant.[151]

Such modest rewards were all that a literary man could expect at Galeazzo's court. The duke gave great inducements and compensations to his musicians, especially the singers; for whatever reason, he could enjoy and appreciate their work for its own sake as well as for its exaltation of himself. He treated visual artists with less respect and personal interest. Although Galeazzo had grandiose ambitions for the visual arts, he did not appreciate the technical expertise or ingenuity of the artists. His programs were designed to reflect his own vision, not theirs. In the field of letters, Galeazzo took no pleasure. He did not even show an interest in using the medium to affirm or broadcast his own princely image; Giovanni Simonetta may have had good reason to keep his manuscript away from the duke. In the absence of any significant literary patronage by Galeazzo, writers in his era tended to depict him in unflattering colors.

Vices and Virtues

He was avid to amass treasure, for which he deprived many subjects of their money and imposing heavy obligations on them. These things debased his magnificence and excellence.[152]

Such criticisms were among the mildest leveled at the duke by contemporaries. Corio's history dwells with relish on the duke's bizarre atrocities, such as burying a courtier alive, starving a cleric to death, and gazing at corpses. One story, corroborated by Zaccaria Saggi da Pisa, involved the barber Travaglino. Galeazzo had him beaten, apparently for asking to leave the court. The duke then sent for him to say that he would give the barber more of the same if he asked to leave again, "and likewise for [all] those that ask it of me." Galeazzo commanded Travaglino to shave him again a few days later. At the same time, the duke dismissed another barber, recently hired, who had only shaved his master once.[153]

Prone to violent rages, Galeazzo was quick to punish transgressions with great severity. In Corio's words, "In everything, he followed the rigor of justice." When a servant was caught stealing from a courtier, Galeazzo commanded that the criminal's nose and right hand be cut off immediately on arrival at the prison. Later the same day, at the urging of an ambassador, the duke changed the sentence to "twelve blows with a rope."[154] One wonders what would have happened had the first command been executed promptly.

Galeazzo had a habit of cruelty and an inclination toward morbidity. In June 1472, Giovanni da Verona fled the duchy suddenly and mysteriously, forfeiting all of his possessions again. The unexplained flight may have been precipitated by a grotesque act recounted by Corio. He claimed that Galeazzo had "one Giovanni da Verona, his favorite, bound on top of a table" and "had a testicle removed" from him. However, this story is not otherwise confirmed, and Giovanni was back in the duke's service four months later.[155]

Galeazzo's emotional instability affected other aspects of government beyond the administration of justice. Although the duke instituted many procedures to monitor his finances carefully, money and records were handled cavalierly within his most intimate circle. Giovanni da Verona had been entrusted with payment of tens of thousands of ducats for his master in 1470–1471. When he fled in 1472, he left behind a country house near Lodi. The ducal inventory for that house included "a chest with certain books inside . . . where there is written many notations of credits and debits of the Excellency of Our Most Illustrious Lord," "two small sacks with certain instruments and writings inside," as well as a vellum sheet "where there is noted certain clothes of the . . . Lord." Even the fiscal administration was not immune from the duke's whims.[156]

Galeazzo indulged his impulses in all areas. Although the duke observed the Lenten fast with his court, he was not above seeking exemptions for himself, claiming that he was not "in aptitude or disposition" to endure such deprivation.[157] He demanded that his servants and subjects give him gifts, such as horses, hawks, hounds, hunting prey, or even huntsmen.[158] Galeazzo did not share the rugged lack of pretension that contemporaries had admired in his father. He was vain about his own appearance, especially his hands. The duke spent 300 ducats each year on "scented waters and powders" for his own person.[159] He took great care with his hair and beard and employed several barbers. During a 1468 visit to his brother Ludovico at Mortara, Galeazzo talked with a Neapolitan noble about hairstyles. The duke then decided to set a new fashion for his circle, ordering haircuts "alla Catalana" for himself, his brother, a physician, and several *camerieri*.[160] Three years later, he made Bona and some of her companions wear their hair and clothes in a style derived from the portrait of a previous duchess.[161] Galeazzo himself loved to dress in fancy clothes.

The duke cared little about the inconvenience or difficulty he caused others. He could easily call a meeting in Pavia with three councillors and three ambassadors, then cancel it at the last minute, leaving Giovanni Simonetta to handle the situation.[162] Such behavior was sadly characteristic of Galeazzo.

Sexual Joking

Galeazzo's poor judgment was evident also in his humor, which inclined heavily to sexual content. When the duke sent Tristano to marry Bona by proxy, he thanked his half-brother for the latter's restraint with the young bride during the wedding and symbolic consummation. Galeazzo added that he would trust Tristano with anything except Battista da Montignana, "whom I wouldn't trust in your hands for anything" because "I know you wouldn't use [the same] restraint toward him."[163]

Galeazzo joked in the same coarse fashion with every one of the relatives with whom he was on friendly terms. One of them was Pietro Francesco Visconti, a distant cousin who served actively on the Privy Council and in the military. Pietro Francesco's wife had just given birth, and he invited the duke to become godfather to the child. Had it been a boy, it would have received Galeazzo's name; when it proved to be a girl, the duke teased the new father about his inability to father sons. Pietro Francesco replied that to remedy this problem, he had consulted another member of the Visconti lineage, whom he characterized as "an excellent master in such matters."[164]

Galeazzo joked also with his courtiers and nobles. When one courtier requested permission to marry, Galeazzo gave him "license to take a wife, and two, and three, up to a total of ten, without our further permission, but from there on do not take one without our leave."[165] More significant, the duke indulged in sexual joking with his princely neighbors and erstwhile in-laws, Ludovico and Barbara Hohenzollern Gonzaga. He teased them often, usually through the Mantuan ambassador in Milan. His crude jokes involved pretending that Ludovico had many extramarital affairs or that Barbara was pregnant again at age 47—an unlikely event in that era.[166] The marquess and marchioness of Mantua were almost like members of the Sforza family, and Galeazzo treated them at times with the informality appropriate to intimates rather than the formality suitable to fellow princes. Ludovico and Barbara were a dignified and respected couple, though, and the duke's behavior was clearly inappropriate.

The Gonzaga were not the only Italian rulers with whom Galeazzo took such liberties. In April 1468, he received a gift of boars from Borso d'Este, another intimate friend of the Sforza, and replied that Borso could have anything of the duke's, "except two things, that is, our wife and our [favorite horse] Gesualdo, in which we do not want to have company."[167] This joking was not applied indiscriminately; the princely personages involved did have close relationships with Galeazzo and his parents. The quasi-familial bonds between the Sforza and the Gonzaga made the Mantuan ambassadors in Milan, Marsilio Andreasi and Zaccaria Saggi da Pisa, members of the duke's intimate circle. Zaccaria was even received by the duke at times when Galeazzo was dressing, undressing, or simply undressed.[168]

Zaccaria had his own opinions about Galeazzo's outrageous behavior. In 1470, Galeazzo spent a day of Carnival in masquerade, visiting a convent in Pavia. According to Zaccaria, the duke "ended in the ultimate ends of love. . . . By midday he was known to everyone in the manner of Messalina." During Carnival a year later, Galeazzo took Giovanni Bentivoglio and several others, all in masquerade, "and went to give himself pleasure, visiting the convents, greater and lesser, until nightfall."[169] Zaccaria spoke of Galeazzo's behavior as "these subjects worthy of Juvenal and Martial." On another occasion, he observed that Galeazzo's autocratic ways "remind me of the command which Holofernes gave," an unflattering comparison to a biblical tyrant later murdered by a Jewish heroine.[170] Such disapproval brought no retribution from the duke, who may have found it entertaining to tweak the prim ambassador.

Dwarfs and *Buffoni*

Entertainment of all kinds served a critical purpose at court, distracting prince and courtiers from their burdens of responsibility and providing outlets for hostility and anxiety within the enclosed space of the court. Working with this aspect of court life was the particular role of those employed as jesters (*buffoni*) and dwarfs.[171] In the princely courts of Renaissance Italy, professional humorists, grotesques, and scapegoats performed a vital service.

Galeazzo did not rank among Renaissance Italy's most active patrons of dwarfs and *buffoni,* but he did employ a few. He inherited a dwarf named Biagio from his father's court; Biagio probably spent most of this period with the duchess and her children. Later in the reign, Galeazzo numbered one "Sir Gasparo, Spanish Dwarf" among his *camerieri di camera.*[172] The best-documented dwarf of the reign was Giovanni Giustiniani Recanello of Chios. For six months, the duke pressed the vice-governor of Genoa, who had authority over Chios, to get Giovanni to court. When the dwarf finally arrived, he joined Bona's household. Like any other ducal servant, Giovanni used his position to benefit his own family.[173] As of late 1472 or early 1473, Bona probably had a female dwarf in her household as well.[174]

In addition to the dwarfs, Galeazzo kept a resident *buffone,* Giovanni Antonio, often called simply "Signor Buffone." Giovanni Antonio had served previously under Duke Francesco. Like the dwarfs, he probably operated mainly in the duchess's household; in the 1469 fresco program, he and Biagio were included "in the room where the women eat," an appropriate place for humorous entertainers. However, the *buffone* did travel with the duke's court in 1476, and he also acted on his own. In 1471, Giovanni Antonio amazed Ludovico Sforza's party traveling to Venice by arriving there on his own (and without an invitation). Apparently, he was a "clever fool" rather than a genuine simpleton; his correspondence from 1474 reveals both a sizable bank balance and a capable wife.[175]

The Better Side of the Duke

In the eyes of most contemporaries, the fifth duke of Milan had many vices and few virtues. That was not the view of all observers; a Bolognese chronicler recalled Galeazzo in a very positive light.

He governed his people with the greatest justice and clemency, and expanded and beautified the city of Milan, and had constructed many edifices worthy of memory; he was a duke most worthy in many things.[176]

Although it may be an exaggeration to say that Galeazzo acted with clemency, he was quite capable of behaving in an appropriate and princely manner. He could also show glimpses of tenderness, even in the midst of his morbid fascinations. In December 1467, when he was considering candidates for a bride, he talked to the Mantuan ambassador more than once about Dorotea Gonzaga, whose betrothal with him had been broken two years before. She had died that year, and Galeazzo asked if her father and mother had cried at her burial. The duke said that "she was very beautiful, even though she was dead, and that she had not died from anything but anguish and sorrow."[177] One might almost think that he felt a touch of guilt for his part in her suffering.

Although the duke was constantly defying conventional morality, he did not reject it outright, as did his older contemporary, Sigismondo Malatesta. Galeazzo was keenly aware of his religious obligations, and he took care to ensure that they were fulfilled. His traveling household always included at least one chaplain, generally a Franciscan or Dominican friar. Concerned that his chaplains might not be saying Masses daily "at the altars of some of the saints to whom we are devoted," the duke directed his confessor to see that these commitments were respected.[178]

Galeazzo distributed alms regularly, several times each year. On one occasion, he instructed his almoners to redistribute alms intended for "poor and observant convents" bearing the names of twenty-one of his favorite saints, because no such institutions could be found. Galeazzo even made some secret charitable contributions. That he should give alms secretly suggests that he took the act seriously for the salvation of his soul rather than that he merely used it to polish his public image.[179] However, some of his gifts were not anonymous at all; he once had a likeness of himself made in silver—500 ducats worth—and given to Santa Maria delle Grazie in Monza.[180]

Like many Christian princes, Galeazzo had a collection of holy relics, of which he was extremely proud. The duke commissioned a huge display setting to be constructed and painted in the chapel at Pavia Castle for showing off some of his treasures. The relics were used actively to aid in his wife's first childbirth and on other occasions.[181] It is no condemnation of Galeazzo's Christian faith to say that his belief in magical powers extended beyond orthodox doctrine. Almost every Italian prince of his time, including most of the popes, shared a similarly broad view of God's creation. Like his mother, Galeazzo would not travel when the moon was new (in combustione).[182] When a comet appeared in 1472, it caused great concern; on the duke's behalf, Giovanni Simonetta asked two astrologers for opinions on its significance.[183] The duke consulted astrologers regularly. Raffaelle da Vimercate, a Milanese physician, had an active role as astrological consultant to the duke, and one of his relatives was a ducal *credenziere*.[184] Galeazzo also consulted a Dominican friar in Genoa named Giovanni Nanni da Viterbo, one of the most famous astrologers of the period.[185]

Galeazzo understood the impact of comments made publicly about his own health and welfare. Such comments could cause great unrest, and the duke was not inclined to permit them. When a physician from Cremona made an unsolicited public prediction about a ducal illness, the duke threatened to hang him from the walls of the city. The Pavia College of Physicians received a similar threat in response to a public prediction they had issued.[186] The person of the prince was too sacred to expose in that manner.

Family Business

After a season of ambitious projects and near-mortal illness, Galeazzo ended the year 1471 by staging unusually lavish festivities. His brush with death may have brought out some of his more tender feelings. On New Year's Eve, he surprised everyone by allowing his infant sons to stay with him during the evening. This unusual event echoed the duke's fresco program for the Sala Grande, which showed GianGaleazzo holding his hand in the midst of various prominent personages.[187]

In 1472, the duke continued to think often about his family as it continued to expand. His first legitimate daughter, Bianca Maria, was born on April 5. Galeazzo proclaimed three days of continuous festive processions, with "fireworks in the usual places, also having bells rung as on a feast day [*da festa*], as is the custom in similar situations.[188] Her baptism one month later became an occasion for further reinforcing Galeazzo's political base. "[When] the baptism was finished, and the breakfast in the Castle [Porta Giovia] done according to custom, the Lord put himself in the tribunal with the Most Illustrious lady Duchess and the Illustrious GianGaleazzo, his firstborn, where he had brought in the eight Genoese ambassadors, to swear their fealty" to the duke and his heir. The duke also took this opportunity to make his two-year-old son, Ermes, the marquess of Tortona. After *disnare,* Galeazzo brought the Genoese ambassadors to the Corte to watch tennis for three hours. When the game was over, he returned to Porta Giovia and prepared to leave the following morning for Pavia.[189]

Filippo, Ludovico, and Sforza Maria

The grant of Tortona to Ermes was one of several ducal acts in 1471–1472 which reflected the demise of Duke Francesco's agreements with

King Ferrante. As Galeazzo became estranged from the king, he increasingly slighted the brother most closely associated with it. The king had pressured the duke to grant Sforza Maria a substantial appanage, and expectations had centered on Tortona or Cremona.[190] Not only was Sforza Maria deprived of this opportunity but soon afterward his betrothal to Eleonora d'Aragona was also replaced by an arrangement involving Galeazzo's eldest son. The duke had the young count of Pavia betrothed to the child's first cousin, Isabella d'Aragona.[191]

Throughout the years 1470–1472, Sforza Maria and Ludovico continued to travel with Galeazzo most of the time, while Filippo was generally left at his home. When the duke made plans to visit Gonzaga one year, he told Filippo that he was bringing Sforza Maria and Ludovico but that "it seems fitting that one of [the brothers] remain at Milan and stay there in the absence of the others, and we have arranged that that one will be you."[192] In August 1471, poor Filippo was so discouraged that he wanted to take the cloth and become a priest. Galeazzo did not consider it a good idea.[193]

Because Filippo's psychological problems had disqualified him from assuming the responsibilities of a second son, Sforza Maria had taken his place. Notwithstanding the slights Sforza Maria suffered from his eldest brother, he continued to undertake diplomatic responsibilities for Galeazzo. In 1472, Sforza Maria and Ludovico traveled to Montferrat to celebrate the birth of their sister Elisabetta's first child. Elisabetta died while they were *en route,* and they returned immediately.[194] Galeazzo's brothers also participated regularly in the reception and entertainment of visiting dignitaries. According to a protocol drawn up in 1468, the brothers were to greet nonlegatine cardinals and ambassadors of dukes and marquesses; they were also to join the duke in entertaining guests of the highest rank.[195]

Receiving Visitors

In May 1472, Galeazzo entertained two such guests representing two very different types of embassies. One was the great Greek prelate Johannes Bessarion, cardinal of Nicea and papal legate to France. The other was his wife's brother, Filippo of Savoy, accompanied by the powerful Jean de Lescun-Armagnac, count of Comminges and marshal of France. The marshal, who had been expected two years earlier, would finally honor the Sforza dominion with his presence. The two visits were expected to tax the dominion's resources, as the cardinal was coming with 150 horses and the French contingent with 600. The logistics absorbed much of the court's time and energy for several weeks. The welcoming party sent to greet Filippo and the marshal at Vercelli itself amounted to 100 horses, led by Tristano and Polidoro Sforza.[196]

Although Galeazzo's response to both embassies emphasized goodwill and unstinting hospitality, the two visits made an interesting contrast to one another. Cardinal Bessarion had no pressing business to transact with the duke; he was mainly paying a courtesy visit on his way over the Alps to France. In contrast, the French visitors had some serious diplomatic issues to resolve with Galeazzo, and they had come to Milan primarily to treat with him. Moreover, Bessarion's background was profoundly alien to Galeazzo's: the prelate was elderly, Greek, and a man of the cloth genuinely committed to philosophy in every sense. He had no personal or cultural links to Galeazzo and his princely world, while the French noblemen were very much a part of that way of life and even had a family relationship with the duke.

As a consequence, the duke's treatment of the embassies differed radically in form. When Bessarion (called "Niceno" by the Italians) made his entry, Galeazzo sent the Privy Council and other gentlemen ahead, then rode out of Pavia one and a half miles himself, accompanied by his brothers and various attendants. Bessarion, a frail man who died later in 1472, was borne on an enclosed chair between two horses, because it was raining heavily. After the duke met him outside Pavia, they rode back to the city gate, where they were received by clergy with a baldacchino. That canopy covered them on their way to the cathedral. There, the duke accompanied the cardinal to the high altar, where "the usual ceremonies" were conducted. Galeazzo then escorted Bessarion to his lodgings, which were not in the castle.[197] By contrast, at Filippo's entry, Galeazzo mounted up at the last minute to receive him close in to Pavia. On their way into the city, they encountered the duchess Bona, "with a large party of gentlewomen" and the ducal children. The Frenchmen received the keys to the city, then proceeded directly to their lodgings in the castle, "always laughing and joking together" with their host.[198]

The nature of the respective entries clearly reflected the nature of the respective guests. The activities of each visit continued largely in the same vein. After Bona brought some gentlewomen to pay their respects to the cardinal at his lodgings, Bessarion made a return visit to the castle. There, she brought her children to him, and he "made the sign of the cross on their foreheads and kissed them." Galeazzo took personal responsibility for showing the cardinal around Pavia Castle, including the treasury, the relics, and the great ducal library, where they "stayed a good space." When the duke gave Bessarion a gift, it was a book from that library.[199]

Filippo and his companions spent little time in such serious pursuits, although they did have some discussions about their diplomatic business. Even on Corpus Christi day, when Filippo and Galeazzo went to the cathedral "to accompany the Corpus Domini as far as the middle of the Castle," the duke later dressed himself and a dozen intimates "alla francese" to keep his French visitors company.[200] Galeazzo devoted considerable time to tennis during the week, and he kept his guests entertained with traditional noble hospitality, hunting and feasting. After a day in the field, Filippo "confessed that he had never seen in France, Burgundy, or Germany a similar place of such enjoyment, and these servants of his were [ready to be] making this Most Illustrious Lord [a] King in any case." Marsilio Andreasi opined that if the French had stayed in the dominion longer, "being treated as they are, they would make His Excellency [the] Emperor." The Mantuan ambassador, who was hardly unfamiliar with Galeazzo's court, considered it "a wonder the things that they consumed yesterday." For a late afternoon snack, "they had the tables prepared" with meats and confections "not otherwise than at dinner and supper." The Milanese court spicer came in, "saying that here he could not find sugar, and that it was necessary to send immediately to Genoa to have some, so that nothing would be lacking" in the way of pleasures.[201]

High Living

In 1471–1472, Galeazzo indulged himself constantly in fancy costumes, travel, hunting, games, and conspicuous consumption of many kinds. While staying at the Mirabello hunting lodge in June 1471, he decided to "make a good supply of [table] silver beyond that which we have." He wanted expert craftsmen to work the silver for him and have the whole lot done by the feast of the Blessed Virgin's Birthday ("Sancta Maria de Septembre"), when he intended to hold a great joust.[202] On learning that Milanese goldsmiths could not finish it in time, the duke commanded that they all work on this project, to ensure that the work would be completed by Christmas Eve. He exempted only those already doing something else for him. To help speed the process, he resolved to send for masters from Venice, Florence, and other cities. At the beginning of 1472, the project still had not been completed, and Galeazzo sought to have it done by the following Christmas. At that point, Antonio Anguissola told him that there was not enough silver in all of Milan to make the pieces the duke had listed.[203]

During the period of that huge project, Galeazzo also ordered a wide variety of jewelry and clothes. On June 14, silver work that had been done for surcoats was estimated at 1,229.5 ducats. Two weeks later, the duke ordered payment of 6,000 ducats to a jeweler for two large rubies, one set in an eagle brooch and the other in a viper brooch (the symbols of the ducal coat of arms), "to wear on two of our hats."[204] A week after that, as he was commanding all local goldsmiths to work on his silver project, he was ordering payment to a Venetian merchant for a brooch with diamonds and rubies. Two days later, on July 5, Galeazzo promised payment of almost 2,000 ducats to that same merchant for 111 pearls of four carats each, a deal made by Bona's seneschal. On that same day, the duke scheduled payment to another Venetian merchant for other agreements made by her seneschal, totaling 3,000 ducats for a second brooch loaded with diamonds and rubies and 1,000 ducats for two rubies set into two rings.[205] On July 16, Galeazzo ordered payment of another 4,500 ducats to a man who often supplied jewels to the court.[206]

In 1472, Galeazzo's interest in extravagant display extended from jewelry to other aspects of personal adornment, including clothing and scent. He also began hiring new personal servants, including barbers and tennis players.[207] The duke revived his plan to visit Rome but then shelved the idea. However, he did spend the summer at Gonzaga again. In preparation, the duke composed a detailed memorandum demanding certain preparations. They included lodgings for his court and four hundred Milanese soldiers (100 for his bodyguard). He wanted his hosts to ensure an adequate food supply for the people and horses of the Sforza court and to clean the wells to provide "good water." He also told them to clean the ditches "so they do not stink." The duke was evidently still interested in the situation in Ferrara; he also requested a map showing the Mantuan towns bordering on that state.[208]

Confidence

By 1472, Galeazzo had asserted his princely style throughout his dominion and far beyond its borders. While bringing in "men skilled in every science" from many parts of Christendom, he also went out to Florence and Mantua, making an ostentatious show of his "court and magnificence." Although the duke's diplomatic and military undertakings brought him little credit, he continued to have great confidence in his capacity to perpetuate and expand his ducal office. The great wealth of the Milanese dominion, the sophistication of the Sforza administration, and the relative lack of pressure from outside forces combined to reassure him that matters were under control. His subjects and peers may not have agreed, but Galeazzo had seduced his own mind through the lushness of the Milanese court.

5

"He Who Lives at Court Dies in the Poorhouse"

Conditions of Life and Work at Court

In June 1468, when Galeazzo was deep in preparations for his bride's arrival, he received a letter from one of his courtiers, Tommaso Tebaldi da Bologna.

I am a protégé of . . . your grandfather's, and for 33 years, I have been with your family, where by the grace of God—notwithstanding that I am the poorest courtier you have, and that I have nothing from it except the allowance that Your Lordship gives me and just one house so heavily mortgaged that it has almost no value—I am esteemed somewhat, and I have honor that I do not merit, by the grace of Your Excellency. But because, My Most Illustrious Lord . . . I, who have children and great expenses, do not know how to take care of them nor do anything good without the help of Your Excellency, I beg that you might deign to provide me with something stable and permanent where my children may rest . . . when God disposes of me, so that I may flee that proverb . . . the one which says, "He who lives at court dies in the poorhouse [*Chi vive a corte more al spedale*]."[1]

Material security was a source of constant anxiety at the court of Milan, and no one was immune. Tommaso was no marginal character scratching for ducal largesse but an active member of the Privy Council and a major figure in diplomacy and administration.[2] Born around 1415, he had served the rulers of Milan for generations, as secretary and treasurer *di camera* for Filippo Maria Visconti, governor of Piacenza for the Ambrosian Republic, and governor of Como for Francesco Sforza. An able thinker, Tommaso was a noted jurist and humanist, Francesco Filelfo's student, friend, and colleague.[3]

The duke responded to Tommaso's appeal. On New Year's Day 1469,

Galeazzo ceremoniously granted his councillor the "true and honorific" fief of Mandello in the presence of a distinguished group of princes and great nobles.[4] Tommaso later sought support for other family needs as well, such as a benefice that might allow his son to "persevere in studies and make himself a man of merit."[5]

Life at court was fraught with anxiety, even for those with long experience and high office. This anxiety increased during transitional periods, when a new prince was asserting his or her personal style. Those whose livelihood depended on court service trod carefully on the uncertain ground of new standards, tastes, and expectations. Galeazzo exacerbated that uncertainty in May and June 1468, when he was preparing for his bride's arrival. On May 31, Giovanni Gabriele Crivelli was instructed to bring his wife, Margherita, and a modest retinue to Genoa to greet the new duchess. They received those instructions at their villa in Buccinasco, along the Great Canal southwest of Milan. In 1468, the usual discomforts of the capital in summer had been deepened by an outbreak of the plague. The duke's command did not surprise or upset them, although travel was always inconvenient. However, shortly before, Giovanni Gabriele had been directed to execute a ducal embassy that would have taken him somewhere else altogether. The courtier wrote to the duke, concerned that "I do not know how to proceed with what I have to do."

Two days later, Galeazzo clarified the confusion. The couple was definitely to meet the new duchess at Genoa, as Margherita had been named one of Bona's companions. Giovanni Gabriele was preparing to carry out these instructions when he fell ill and wrote to Galeazzo, in some distress, excusing himself from the journey. The duke replied expansively that Margherita should go anyway and that "we have deputed you and your wife to be in the Duchess's company, . . . that is, to hold you as a *gentiluomo* and make you such provision that you will have reason to be happy." Giovanni Gabriele thanked the duke effusively for giving them such honor. "Responding with respect to having set a competent salary, I say that no greater salary nor greater allowance could come to me than to serve Your Lordship." By June 18, the courtier had recovered sufficiently to ride to Genoa after all.[6]

"His Lordship's Courtier"

Many people showed an interest in serving at the Milanese court. One man asked the duke to take him into ducal service in *any* capacity—"either man-at-arms or mounted servant or *cameriere* or *galuppo* or messenger."[7] Giovanni Gabriele Crivelli's relative, Giovanni Antonio ("Brusco") Crivelli, asked Margherita for help in entering court service. He told her, "I do not want to bear arms any longer, but rather, to be His Lordship's courtier."[8] He knew whereof he spoke, for he had served at court under Francesco Sforza before entering the military.[9] Brusco told Margherita he had also written to

Galeazzo directly with his request, and to the duchess Bona. The duke was not the only person in the court who could exercise such patronage; his wife also appointed people on her own initiative. Outside the ducal couple, the most influential individual was Cicco Simonetta, and the first secretary received many appeals for help in finding ducal employment.[10] Brusco's efforts succeeded, one way or another; he became a *cameriere* to Galeazzo.[11]

Rewards and Privileges

Life may have been uncertain for those who lived at court, but it held considerable attractions. In a princely state, service to the princely family offered the greatest potential security, regardless of birth or occupation. Because Galeazzo had full authority in his dominion, he could exempt his servants from any burden and give them substantial rewards and privileges. Members of the court were exempt from all local taxes and tolls, although not from feudal dues. When local authorities forced Leonardo Visconti's family to pay the salt tax and other local charges (*carichi occurrenti*) for personal items, Galeazzo criticized the action as one "which is inappropriate and runs counter to what is customarily done for the others who serve at our court."[12]

The duke and his wife could also manipulate the system of justice, facilitate collection of debts or enforcement of contracts, and investigate crimes against persons in their service.[13] Galeazzo helped his servants in many different ways. A *gentiluomo* escorting the Florentine ambassador came home to find that neighbors had interfered with his mill; Galeazzo ordered the podestà of Milan to undo any damage done.[14] A shoemaker accompanying the duke on campaign feared his creditors would think he had fled to avoid paying debts; Galeazzo ordered that the artisan's reputation and possessions be protected.[15] A soldier serving with the duke asked that his mother be exempted from certain local charges in his hometown, because he was "a poor man" and not home to protect his mother's interests. Galeazzo granted the request.[16]

The duke could also bestow titles, offices, and other honors; grant incomes and estates; guarantee business arrangements; and even use the resources of the church for rewards. Persons employed by Galeazzo received allowances and salaries that could be quite lucrative. Those serving at court might also receive clothing, food, tools of their trade, professional training, and housing at ducal expense. Persons at court were well placed to request and receive fiefs, benefices, gifts, and ducal favor of all kinds. After a condottiere had fled the duchy, leaving behind considerable property, Galeazzo's uncle, Bosio, wrote to request the grant of fief confiscated from the offender. The duke replied regretfully that all the confiscated property had been granted out already—to courtiers who were with his person.[17]

"I Would Not Be Able to Live According to My Rank"   Financial support from the duke spelled survival for some members of the court. Mastino Suardi, one of Bona's *gentiluomini,* belonged to a family of nobles, some of whom had abandoned their native Bergamo when its lordship passed from Milan to Venice. Since he had no ancestral home, Mastino was highly dependent on ducal favor. In 1470, he asked the duke to deliver aid with dowries that Galeazzo had promised for the courtier's four daughters. Later that year, Mastino pleaded with his lord for further financial support, saying that he was pawning his belongings and had no money for "bread nor wine, not wood nor oil nor salt, not straw nor hay." He begged for some kind of gift or income, as a "courtesy," as charity, or even as a loan "to pay back when Your Lordship will have put me in my house at Bergamo"![18]

Ducal support could also help a nobleman maintain his traditional position in society. Giovanni Agostino Isimbardi was a respected member of a noble family in Pavia, a doctor of laws and a man of considerable honor. He served as a ducal *gentiluomo* for many years before suddenly losing favor in 1474. In appealing to the duke for reinstatement, he wrote, "I am a poor gentleman, as Your Excellency can understand, and if it were not for the earnings which I make with my person through the favor of Your Lordship, I would not be able to live according to my rank."[19]

Servants of Stature   Court service was one of the careers appropriate to persons of high social standing and was not limited to those who were natives of the dominion. Galeazzo Marescotti, one of Bologna's leading noble citizens, had fought for Francesco Sforza in his youth. In 1472, he sought a place for his son Ercole at the Milanese court, mobilizing all the assistance he could; Duke Galeazzo received two letters of recommendation from his ambassador in Bologna and one from the Gonzaga cardinal of Mantua. Young Ercole had just left the service of Ercole d'Este, which probably appealed to the Milanese duke's sense of rivalry with his counterpart in Ferrara.[20] When Duke Galeazzo met Ercole Marescotti, he found the Bolognese "an apt and well-mannered youth" and made him a *cameriere di camera.*[21] Ercole was the second Bolognese noble to become a Milanese *cameriere di camera* in less than two years. The first, Enea Malvezzi, had accompanied Giovanni Bentivoglio on a visit to the duchy early in 1471 and had remained in Milan; he, too, had received a recommendation from the cardinal of Mantua.[22]

Galeazzo regarded the office of *cameriere di camera* as one that any young man would be happy to attain. When Francesco Missaglia was ill, the duke told him, "As we have regretted your illness, so have we been pleased to hear that you have improved, and are out of danger; advising you for your consolation that we have chosen you for our *cameriere di camera.* Therefore, attend to making yourself vigorous [*gagliardo*] so that you can come to stay close to us in your office, to serve us with our other *camerieri.*"[23]

While Galeazzo built up his corps of intimates, he was also creating more gentleman courtiers. One of those whom he chose was Tomeino Beccaria, brother of the duke's *cameriere di camera* Gerolamo and son of a courtier who had served Duke Filippo Maria. Galeazzo announced to Tomeino,

> Considering the great faith and devotion of yourself and your family to our state and that of our predecessors, for some demonstration of goodwill toward you, it has occurred to us to choose you among the number of our courtiers, with a salary [*provisione*] of 100 ducats per year. . . . By the tenor of this present letter, we elect you thus from this day forward at our pleasure [*ad nostrum beneplacitum*].[24]

The duke regarded the office of *gentiluomo* as both an honor and a reward. When he bestowed that position on Bernardo Anguissola, a nobleman from Piacenza, Galeazzo told the new courtier,

> From now on may you be in the number of our *gentiluomini,* and so we elect and accept you, seeming to us that your age is better suited to, and sooner calls for, this occupation than that of arms, of which you will not have to take the burden and effort anymore, but attend to enjoying yourself like our other *gentiluomini,* together with whom you will always be well regarded and well treated by us.[25]

Conditions of Life at Court

No one at the court of Milan lived in the luxurious indolence suggested by that letter of appointment. Compared to others, *gentiluomini* were indeed well treated, receiving a substantial income for relatively little—and rather pleasant—work. However, even for persons in that select group, conditions of life at court varied widely. Some of the *gentiluomini* lived in the court on a full-time basis, while most lived in their home districts and served at court only occasionally. Many members of the Milanese court served on a part-time basis or in rotation with others. Only a few key officials were expected to perform their duties continously and remain physically within the boundaries of the court space.

Living Space

Housing was always the most difficult logistical problem at the Milanese court. In Italian Renaissance cities, space was at a premium, and the enclosed space of a court rarely had physical dimensions adequate to contain all the persons recognized as belonging within it. Most members of the court were not fed, housed, or transported by the ducal establishment. They lived in houses they had bought or rented, bought their own food, and provided their own horses.

In particular, members of the court were expected to fend for themselves when they stayed in the capital. Those who did not have houses of their own had to find a place with others, but most persons of any social standing owned or rented housing in Milan. The value of such a house went beyond simply a place to live. At the time of Galeazzo's wedding, the councillor Tommaso Moroni had been in his home city of Rieti, and his house in the capital was being occupied by a visiting prince. The councillor remarked that he would need to recover some of the space his guest had been using, "to have my whole household [*brigata*] and all my horses lodged, because I built my house as it is with the intention of doing myself honor at glorious occasions [*triumphi*] similar to what this one will be."[26]

Galeazzo contributed all or part of the purchase price toward houses for his mistress, some of his singers, his wardrobe steward, and other persons important to him.[27] Giovanni Matteo Bottigella, the noble from Pavia who had likened Galeazzo to "the divine majesty," requested assistance in paying for his new palace. The canny courtier told the duke, "It is fitting that every worthy prince should assist his servants who are constructing a building."[28] The ducal household, including Galeazzo's favorite huntsmen, musicians, and tennis players, used lodgings provided by the duke when they traveled with him outside Milan. These persons were the ones who kept him comfortable; they were, in effect, extensions of his own person. Everyone who traveled in Galeazzo's service received some assistance with housing, including the councillors, *gentiluomini,* and *camerieri fuori di camera.* Few of the ducal castles were equipped to house the entire ducal retinue. When the court traveled, it was necessary to bring along many of the furnishings and borrow others from local inhabitants. In one instance, the duke's agents had to find 160 beds at short notice.[29]

The duchess's court was more compact and self-contained than the duke's, and her courtiers always accompanied her. When Brusco Crivelli wrote to Margherita, the letter was addressed to her "in the court of the duchess at Galliate." Giovanni Gabriele Crivelli had been appointed her *gentiluomo* on June 12, 1468, and by June 21 he was termed "resident in the court" (*residente nella corte*).[30] The phrase was not merely a figure of speech; when Galeazzo wanted a room in Porta Giovia Castle prepared for his physicians' use, he was informed that Giovanni Gabriele and his wife, Margherita, "stay and sleep in that chamber."[31] Some ducal officials were required to sleep at Porta Giovia. Other members of the court were permanently stationed at one residence or another, including caretakers and stable staff.[32] Naturally, castellans and garrisons were bound to their posts as well.

Foreign dignitaries or ambassadors who came to the duke were usually provided housing, according to their rank, in Milan or Pavia but generally had to find their own accommodations if they followed him elsewhere. In Milan, visitors of the highest rank were lodged at Porta Giovia Castle or the Corte Arengo, although some (including the marquess of Montferrat, the count of Urbino, and the Medici) owned their own houses in Milan. For major state occasions in the capital, when dozens or hundreds of feudatories and dignitaries came to the city, the duke commanded that persons with their own houses provide lodging for visitors.[33]

Food, Clothing, and Horses

On August 3, 1470, an anonymous ducal agent drew up a brief estimate of the monthly "expenses for one *cameriere*." The estimate had only three categories of costs: "eating expenses," "expenses for underwear, shirts, and shoes," and "expenses for horses." These items were the basic nonrecoverable costs of maintaining a *cameriere* with one servant. The food expenses (16 pounds) were calculated for two persons; the stable costs (12 pounds), for two horses. In addition to the monthly cost for clothes (6 pounds, 8 *soldi*), a *pro rata* figure of 4 pounds was applied for eight pairs of hose given over a year's time. In all, it was reckoned that a *cameriere* cost 39 pounds, 4 *soldi* (almost 10 ducats) per month to maintain; for fifty *camerieri*, the annual expense was figured at 23,520 pounds, or 5,880 ducats.[34]

Most *camerieri* were among the fortunate members of the court authorized to eat within the household. The 1470 *cameriere* estimate figured 5 florins per person each month for eating costs in the household, but at New Year's 1471, Galeazzo budgeted over twice that amount for the 130 persons eating "in casa."[35] For those dining outside the household, he had allowed a pittance—3 florins per month—in 1467, but the numbers rose. In 1471, the twenty-four *camerieri* posted permanently in Milan were allowed 10 florins per month nine times per year. Another twenty-four who traveled with the duke but "eat out of the household" were to be paid twelve times per year, in amounts varying from 8 to 24 florins each month.[36]

Galeazzo always wanted to minimize court-related expenditures for food. In the same spirit, he limited his expenditures for clothing given to persons at court. Most of the clothing acquired at court did not come from the prince's bounty but was bought from artisans licensed to operate there. One of the *camerieri di camera* bought a new pair of shoes or boots from a court shoemaker every month in 1474. The customers for this shoemaker included not only members of the duke's intimate circle but also a soldier and a member of Bona's kitchen staff.[37] Keeping good records of such accounts was vital, because persons at court bought mainly on credit; cash was always scarce. Risky as such transactions might be, they were vital to the prosperity of many artisans in Milan. In 1472, the *Arti* collectively complained that the duke was spending too little time in the capital, and they were consequently making too little money.[38]

The clothing worn by members of the court provided immediate visual clues as to their position and background. Differences of age, rank, gender, and geographic origin were traditionally reflected in the material and style of their garments. In the fifteenth century, every region of the known world had a particular style of dress. The duchess Bona had been required to change her wardrobe from the French to the Lombard style when she came to reside in Lombardy. Differences also existed among the various regions of Italy as well as between the urban and rural, or highland and lowland, zones within a dominion such as Galeazzo's. At his court, no uniformity of dress was enforced, except among his inner circle and the military. However, certain criteria were broadly observed. Men of greater age and dignity would generally wear longer and darker outer garments.[39] The young duke and his companions sometimes sported colors that were literally dazzling. The young male favorites were the persons most likely to dress provocatively; women at court generally wore clothes that covered everything but their hands, head, and neck. Young men might wear their hair down to their shoulders, but women of rank usually wore their hair up, with a headdress and sometimes a veil.

One article of clothing was politically significant at the Sforza court: wearing hose "alla divisa" (one leg white and the other *morello,* a very dark red) was a sign of personal allegiance to the Sforza. Galeazzo insisted that only persons authorized by him were permitted to wear such hose. He gave them to certain individuals as a sign of favor and to others when they entered his service. In general, hose were probably given more frequently than any other article of clothing. They were less expensive, and needed replacing more often, than the sturdier and finer top clothes.[40]

Although Galeazzo intended from the start to provide clothing for all of his household servants, he thought mainly of those who stayed close to his person. Being out of sight often meant being out of mind. Seven of his Milanese *camerieri* wrote at one point, pleading to be remembered. They pointed out that Galeazzo had "dressed the *camerieri* that find themselves following the person of Your Excellency, the undersigned *camerieri,* most faithful servants of Your Most Illustrious Lordship, assigned to stay in Milan, have thought that they still have not been dressed because they have not been remembered. This being the reason, not having been dressed for not being remembered, by this present letter the undersigned *camerieri* remind and supplicate Your Most Illustrious Lordship to deign to have them dressed, too."[41]

Galeazzo liked to wear rich and beautiful clothes. He dressed often in unusual ways: fanciful finery, masquerade costumes, disguises, and, especially, French clothing. He would also have some of his intimates join in whatever style he was wearing.[42] The magnificent costumes worn on these special occasions were not personal gifts to the *camerieri.* Their clothes pertained to their court offices, and the splendid costumes were lent for each occasion. Cloth for garments made by ducal commission was provided at any given time by a single supplier, with whom Galeazzo would make an exclusive contract. In January 1470, the new supplier was Filippo Pietrasanta and company; they would supply silk, wool, and leather to the court for four years.[43]

After housing, food, and clothing, the greatest necessity of life was transportation, including horses, mules, and wagons. Galeazzo provided or maintained horses at his expense for those who traveled with him and some others. In one unusual show of generosity, the duke gave his seneschal Giuliano da Varese 40 ducats to buy a horse for use in Galeazzo's service. However, the duke was more likely to take horses from his servants than to give them. When the duke held jousts, most of the participants needed to borrow their mounts from others.[44] Some persons who contributed to the court did not ride horses at all, and local artisans and laborers rarely traveled.[45]

The household lists drawn up for logistical purposes usually counted horses, rather than humans. Although the number of horses always bore some correlation to the number of persons, the two totals could differ significantly in any given situation. A list from January 1475 covering table expenses in the ducal household shows 163 boche (human "mouths") in all, while a companion list covering stable expenses totals 90 horses.[46] The discrepancy between these numbers reflects the nature of various household functions. Physicians received substantial salaries and did not travel constantly with the duke, so their eating expenses were not covered. However, the physicians would ride to join the duke if he needed them, so the household treasury did pay for their horses' maintenance. In contrast, the forty men classified under "singers" were all to be fed but were allowed support for only four horses. Their musical function did not require them to travel on horseback, but they did eat in the duke's household every day.[47]

Care of Body and Soul

Medical problems ranked among the greatest preoccupations of persons at court. Illness struck everyone sooner or later and generally lasted weeks or months. Galeazzo lavished medical care on those who were important to him. He often required regular reports on the condition of members of the ducal family or special favorites. In 1467, Battista da Montignana fell gravely ill and remained so for months. At the time, Galeazzo was on campaign in the Romagna; because of a plague scare, Bianca Maria would not allow any physicians to visit the sick. Thus, even though a doctor went every day to the bishop of Parma's house, where Battista stayed, the youth could not be attended. Finally, the physician, Ambrogio Grifi, one of Milan's finest, was permitted to care for Battista. He wrote the duke regularly about the cameriere's condition, and the treasurer di camera also kept the duke informed.[48] When the ducal secretary Giacomo Alfieri fell ill in May 1468, his course of treatment was supervised by the ducal physician Lazzaro Tedaldi, with Galeazzo's authorization.[49]

Although the art of medicine was still based on classical models and closely linked to the practice of astrology, the ducal physicians were generally considered to be excellent healers. When Rinaldo d'Este was stricken by a serious illness while visiting Milan, five physicians attended him, including his own and three provided by the duke. The seneschal Giovanni Giapanno described the situation to Galeazzo, adding that these physicians "would be enough to resuscitate a dead man."[50]

The duke did not usually concern himself with the medical condition of those who were outside his family or inner circle. Other members of the court had to fend for themselves medically, but they did potentially have access to the dominion's best medical resources. Dozens of physicians were available, and their activities are well documented in personal correspondence from court servants of many kinds. Along with problems of money and litigation, medical complaints constituted the topic most frequently mentioned in letters from the Sforza court.

That correspondence was barely anything to say about spiritual matters. Most persons in the Milanese court concerned themselves far more with medical care than with spiritual care. The duke ensured that they could fulfill their religious obligations, though; at Easter each year, Galeazzo brought two to four confessors to the court to "confess courtiers and give them Communion."[51] He also arranged for fish to be provided during Lent, wherever the court happened to be, and he licensed preaching at Easter in ducal castles.[52] Galeazzo himself attended Mass daily, probably accompanied by his favored companions. There is no evidence that other members of the court could, or sought to, attend services so frequently. Few members of the clergy lived and worked at court, and those who did were generally attached to the duke's household as his confessors, chaplains, or singers.

Pay for Service

The central relationship between a prince and his servants was that of service for pay. The thousands of persons participating in the court during Galeazzo's reign exchanged their capacity to serve for his resources of wealth and honor. As Tommaso Tebaldi pointed out, wealth and honor did not necessarily go hand in hand, and payment for court service was promised more often than it was delivered.

Those who held a civil office of any kind (including at court) were termed *salariati,* "the salaried."[53] Members of the court might be paid from nine two twelve times per year in theory, but very few persons in the ducal service received pay for all twelve months of the year. More commonly, payment was made in nine or ten monthly installments. At one point, Galeazzo even thought to pay the *salariati* quarterly; his brothers Sforza Maria and Ludovico were already receiving their maintenance allowances on that basis.[54]

The range of basic pay was broad. A *credenziere* could expect 6 florins per month, probably for ten months, an annual total of 60 florins (24 ducats); one of the most favored ducal kennelmen also received 24 ducats per year. At the other extreme, Giovanni Marliani, the senior court physician in 1470, was assigned 1,000 florins annually (400 ducats).[55] As of 1468, even the masters of revenues made less than half that sum; Melchiorre Marliani's salary was 40 florins (16 ducats) per month (144–160 per year), while Giovanni Andrea Cagnola's pay was 36 florins (14.4 ducats) per month (130–144 per year). At the same time, one of two *referendari-generale,* Fazio Gallerani, received 32 florins monthly. The chancellors of the Privy Chancery received 12 florins per month, twice the *credenzieri*'s salary but only about one-third that of the senior fiscal officials.[56]

Among the duke's servants in arms, ordinary soldiers were paid relatively little; for the ducal garrisons in 1472, the standard wage was only about 5 pounds per month, for ten months (12.5 ducats per year).[57] The senior member of the guard at Pavia Castle in 1472 received 40 ducats annually. Unit commanders fared far better, especially if they also held court offices. Antonio Caracciolo, *cameriere di camera* and co-commander of the ducal bodyguard, enjoyed a salary of 200 ducats in 1473.[58] The councillors of state also occupied the high end of the salary scale. On the most comprehensive list, half of the twenty-six named members of the Privy Council received 86 pounds, 6 *denari* per month for eleven months (almost 237 ducats annually). The ten highest-ranking councillors were listed without pay, because Galeazzo was on an economy drive at the time. Those ten were assigned to remain in Milan; the councillors who were paid would be traveling with the duke or serving in other cities outside the capital.[59] Salaries were always subject to being raised or lowered. The physician Giovanni Matteo da Gradi received 550 florins (220 ducats) per year in 1463–1465, then 600 per year in 1466 and 650 per year in 1467–1469. By 1470, his annual salary was 800 florins. While Bianca Maria was still alive, he also received bonuses of 33 to 50 florins, by her order. In general, physicians were paid more highly, and more consistently, than other ducal servants.[60]

Special Sources of Income   While most *salariati* were paid from the amounts budgeted for the purpose, the more fortunate among them received other forms of income. Some were assigned revenues directly from a particular source, just as Galeazzo had begun by financing his household from the Parco's profits.[61] Some revenues were considered more reliable than others, and thus more desirable. In 1472, the Privy Council insisted on having their salary allotment from "the best revenues that we have, and they do not want to participate at all in the bad [revenues]." Galeazzo did not accommodate their demand.[62]

The duke often supplemented, or even replaced, salaries for ducal servants with fiefs, sinecures, or gifts of money, which they themselves were responsible to manage. The sinecures granted by Galeazzo included the captaincy of the Martesana Canal, which paid 1,000 ducats per year.[63] The duke could also arrange lucrative marriages, grant juicy benefices, or give support to business ventures. He could grant citizenship rights for any of his duchy's cities, thus enabling the recipient to do business on favorable terms in that city.[64] In another vein, Galeazzo gave his choirmaster mining rights to parts of the dominion.[65]

Most persons who were prominent at court received more than one type of income. Giovanni Ghiringhelli, court physician, enjoyed an annual salary of 600 florins (240 ducats) in 1470 and held a lectureship at the University of Pavia. The duke also arranged a marriage for him with a wealthy widow, the stepmother of Porta Giovia's castellan.[66] Physician Giovanni Marliani, whose salary was among the highest of any ducal servant, also held a lectureship at the university. At Christmas 1471, having survived a near-mortal illness, Galeazzo made him a further gift of 100 ducats.[67]

Conditions of Service

Every ducal office had specific duties to perform and conditions under which its officers were expected to operate. The duties for offices of state were usually defined more clearly and explicitly than those for offices of the household, but many persons acted in more than one capacity, and distinctions or classifications were often blurred in practice.

Camerieri and Other Household Servants

In Galeazzo's time, the *camerieri* were divided into three categories: those "of the chamber" (*di camera*), "of the antechamber" (*di guardacamera*), and "outside the chamber" (*fuori di camera*). Their respective roles within the court reflected their degree of proximity to the ducal person. The office of *cameriere di camera* provided the duke formally with his closest companions; they attended on Galeazzo's person, and their station was his bedchamber. The *camerieri di guardacamera* were assigned to the first room outward from the inner sanctum. The *camerieri fuori di camera* performed many mundane logistical functions for the duke. Their primary duties lay in preparing and maintaining residences for the ducal court or visiting dignitaries. They also carried out various types of errands, such as delivering gifts or collecting animals abroad.

Life in the Inner Circle   At least 65 men served Galeazzo as *camerieri di camera* or *di guardacamera* at some time, although 32 of them probably spent a year or less in that capacity. Of the total number, 30 were not natives of the Sforza dominion. Besides a dozen Neapolitans who left soon after being recruited, they included a Bohemian knight, two Spaniards (one a dwarf), and members of several great Italian noble families: the Colonna and Conti (Rome), Caraccioli (Naples), Manfredi (Imola), Malvezzi and Marescotti (Bologna), and Strozzi (Mantuan branch).[68] Of the 35 *camerieri di camera* and *di guardacamera* from within the Sforza dominion, at least 20 came from established families of high rank, including the great marchesal families of Pallavicino (di Scipione), Malaspina (di Fosdenovo), and del Carretto and such prominent Lombard clans as Visconti, Crivelli, Castiglione, Beccaria, Arcelli, and Ponzoni. The *camerieri di camera* were divided between these men of rank—whose office may have been largely honorific—and lesser men recruited for their personal qualities. Several of them, including some of Galeazzo's special favorites, came from families active at the Milanese court.[69]

Some "foreign" *camerieri di camera,* such as Ercole Marescotti, also arrived at the center of Galeazzo's courts through family efforts or connections. Niccolò Petracolli da Cortona came to Milan with his father, a Tuscan condottiere and courtier to Dukes Francesco and Galeazzo.[70] Niccolò himself did not become prominent until Galeazzo's reign; he may have been too young to play a major role under Francesco. As ducal companions, the *camerieri di camera* would generally have been close to Galeazzo in age, but hard evidence is sparse. Pierre d'Olly was twenty-four years of age when he joined the court as a singer in early 1473; he was five years younger than his new master.[71]

For some, the position of *cameriere di camera* or *cameriere di guardacamera* may have been nominal or honorific only, but for many it meant a career of pleasing the prince on a daily basis. Because of its intimate association with the ducal person, the work of *camerieri di camera* and *di guardacamera* was defined by the duke's preferences. These personal attendants were subject to greater fluctuations in favor and disfavor than were other ducal servants.

More than most areas of court life in Milan, the relations between Galeazzo and his *camerieri di camera* are difficult to trace fully through written evidence. Because these men stayed with the duke constantly, little of their interaction appeared in writing. Because their interaction was often of an intimate and personal nature, it was inappropriate or dangerous to record or discuss what had occurred. Some of the *camerieri di camera* and *camerieri di guardacamera* had an intimate relationship with the duke, sharing almost all of his pastimes and escapades. In the 1471–1472 fresco program composed for Porta Giovia, most of Galeazzo's hunting companions were *came-*

rieri di camera, just as they probably were in reality. *Camerieri di camera* also gambled and played games with the duke.[72] They were almost always at his side, and he wanted them to remain there. When Galeazzo granted Carlino Varesino a fief, he made the grant contingent on the courtier's remaining a *cameriere di camera* and not taking up the profession of arms.[73] Soon afterward, when Carlino's sister married Antonietto Arcelli da Piacenza, the groom was required in the marriage contract to travel with the duke at all times.[74]

The leveling quality of companionship provided relief for the duke from his weighty position at the head of the dominion. Nevertheless, Galeazzo did not let his companions forget that he was their master and "father." Many of the duke's closest friends were referred to by nicknames and diminutives that clearly detracted from their dignity; "Carlino" (Carlo) Varesino was one of them. He had little independent standing in the world, but even the noble knight Antonio Arcelli was called Antonietto.[75]

This lack of respect was widely evident in Galeazzo's treatment of his closest companions. During a financial dispute with one of his *camerieri di guardacamera,* Giovanni Antonio da Corbetta (called "Corbettino"), the duke angrily declared, "We resolve not to endure that we be deceived by babies." The "baby" in this case was not too young to be actively collecting offices and money for himself and his brothers as early as 1471.[76] Galeazzo's lack of respect for his *camerieri di camera* was also reflected in his comment to Tristano on Battista da Montignana. When Galeazzo said that he "wouldn't trust [Battista] in your hands for anything," because "I know you wouldn't use [the same] restraint toward him," he implicitly reduced Battista to a casual sex object.[77]

Rewards and Punishments   While *camerieri di camera* routinely endured personal abuse of various kinds from their ducal master, they also received rich rewards from proximity to his princely person. Galeazzo granted them salaries, allowances, fiefs, and other forms of income, arranged marriages for some of them, knighted several, and even became a godfather to the children of a few *camerieri.*[78] He also provided lavish gifts and the use of the finest horses and clothing. Before Christmas 1472, suits were made for twenty-two of these men, in gold brocade for the knights among them and silver brocade for the others. The total cost amounted to almost 4,000 ducats.[79]

Among those housed and fed by the ducal treasury, the *camerieri di camera* always ranked near the top of the lists, generally trailing only the duke's brothers. On average, they were allowed two to four times as many servants at ducal expense as were other members of the household.[80] The pay range for *camerieri di camera* and *camerieri di guardacamera* was also the highest for any household office. It compared favorably to the salary for *gen-*

tiluomini, although the latter did not have the same full-time commitment. Only ducal physicians and members of the Privy Council received consistently higher salaries than the ducal companions. Special favorites such as the *primo cameriere* of the moment probably outpaced even those august gentlemen.[81]

The persons who benefited most from Galeazzo's generosity were generally those who stayed closest to him. In 1469, Pietro Birago, Galeazzo's *cameriere di camera* and head falconer, received revenues totaling 520 pounds per year (130 ducats) from thirteen different sources.[82] On at least three occasions, Antonio Caracciolo, *cameriere di camera* and commander of the guard, received property confiscated from accused criminals.[83] He was also granted two fiefs, one quite prestigious and substantial. However, Antonio also suffered the ill effects of Galeazzo's fickleness. In August 1471, he was dismissed from service and his pay stopped. The dismissal did not last long; within three months, his pay was docked 25 ducats to help Galeazzo buy clothing.[84]

Financially, the most dramatic rise and fall was that of Battista Romari da Montignana. In early 1469, he was granted the county and castle of Galliate, a favored ducal residence with an annual income of 1,000 ducats. Because he could not pay the feudal dues, the grant was revoked, but it was regranted before six months had passed. In August 1470, Battista was stripped of the fief again, then given it back five months later.[85] In 1471, Battista was in such favor that the duke paid to bring his father to Milan, gave the father a position as podestà, and granted Battista an additional 1,000 ducats income from the salt tax for the Novara district. These donations gave the *cameriere* a total income of literally princely proportions.[86] Then, Battista's fortunes took a dip; in December 1471, he was in bad grace, and the duke ordered his patron, the bishop of Parma, not to lend him any money.[87] By October 1472, the feckless count owed Galeazzo 500 pounds, which the duke took directly from the people of Galliate; they, in turn, owed their count 1,700 pounds. Because of this feudal default, Galeazzo not only withdrew Battista's title and incomes but also removed Battista's father from his *podestería* and made him repay the profits from the office. Not long afterward, though, the duke relented and restored the father to his post.[88]

It was not unusual for men to be promoted and demoted between the offices of *cameriere di camera* and *cameriere di guardacamera.* The former were always ranked more highly, and paid more, than the latter. Two lists dating from Christmas 1473–1474 show Battista da Montignana as a *cameriere di guardacamera.* Evidently, he was promoted back to the *camera* again within days and given an annual salary of 300 ducats. In January 1474, Ercole Marescotti was listed as a *cameriere di guardacamera,* with the highest salary in that group (200 ducats).[89] The salaries of *camerieri* were not reliable, because the duke could always change his mind. In March 1474, a document was drawn up showing for the "Transfer and diminution of salaries of the *camerieri* made for Our Most Illustrious Lord." Battista da Montignana's salary had been cut in half, from 300 ducats to 150, and Ercole Marescotti's salary was also reduced to 150 ducats.[90]

Making a career of intimacy with princes was a high-risk gamble. At Galeazzo's court, where the duke was a sporting man, actual gambling was both a required activity and a potential source of further income for ducal companions. In general, one could not expect to win very much when betting against the prince, who held the purse strings. There were exceptions, however; Pietro Birago won 100 ducats in one day from betting on tennis matches.[91]

Other Camerieri   Bernardino Corio stated that Galeazzo had twelve *camerieri* (*fuori di camera*), accompany him at any given time; the duke often organized his courtiers in groups of twelve. One or two at a time were often sent ahead when the court was about to move, so as to organize lodgings in advance. They would also prepare for the coming of foreign princes, ambassadors, and other distinguished visitors.[92] Some tasks required travel abroad for the duke, including trips to buy him horses or hawks. Giacometto del Maino specialized in such travel, going to England at least twice on Galeazzo's behalf.[93] Others bore particular responsibilities within the court; Gaspare Caimi was in charge of the table silver, while Francesco Pagnani was the duke's jewelry expert.[94] Pietro Birago served as both *cameriere di camera* and head falconer for almost the entire reign; Galeazzo's fresco programs featured him in both roles.[95]

The *camerieri di camera* became established as Galeazzo's most intimate officers during the course of his reign. In the first half of the reign, some *camerieri* remaining from Duke Francesco's time still claimed a place in the inner circle. Corio called Vercellino Visconti Galeazzo's "*cameriere* and table companion."[96] Vercellino had been the duke's leading *cameriere* for years before the accession. He accompanied Galeazzo to France in 1465–1466 and was captured with him at Novalesa. In the duke's original household plan, Vercellino was posted among the *camerieri di guardacamera,* close to Galeazzo's person. The *cameriere* bore the duke's ceremonial sword for the magnificent entry into Florence in March 1471. Later, he became less active at court, and in 1475, he was named castellan of Trezzo.[97]

The duke's companions also included some of the most junior members of the court, the *sottocamerieri*. The most favored *sottocameriere* was Battista Cazulo (or Savonaro) da Cremona, called "Nasino." In 1470, Galeazzo paid a gambling debt that Nasino had contracted with another *sottocameriere,* Bernardino da Corte. This colleague appeared often with Nasino; in the hunting scene of the Sala Grande fresco program, they were described together riding with the duke and bearing his horn. In a later fresco program, the two *sottocamerieri* also rode together, Nasino mounted on Galeazzo's favorite horse and carrying some of the duke's ceremonial armor. In Galeazzo's service, Nasino handled such things as his dogs, clothing, and money.[98]

The *sottocamerieri* did not enjoy the honor accorded *camerieri di camera.* They rarely appeared on lists of persons at court, never on salary lists. Judging by a reference in Galeazzo's first will, they may have been below the age of majority.[99] However, *sottocamerieri* performed some very important and delicate functions for the duke which one would hardly expect him to entrust to children. Alessandro da Cotignola (called "Goffino") was sent to Naples to recruit new *camerieri* and was later assigned with another *sottocameriere* to manage the household of the duke's mistress.[100] Goffino himself married during Galeazzo's reign.[101] Another *sottocameriere,* called Morelletto, was the duke's most trusted go-between for casual sexual encounters.[102]

Other Household Officers   Among the other categories of household office, the footmen, *ragazzi,* and *galuppi* totaled 126 persons as of March 1475.[103] Twenty-five to 30 footmen appeared on the court roster at any given time; they received salaries of 32 ducats per year and probably served in rotation.[104] A list of *ragazzi* from Galeazzo's reign shows 21 stationed in Milan, 17 posted to Pavia, and 3 distinguished as "Regazzi di camera," who probably traveled with the duke wherever he went.[105] The *galuppi* were sometimes grouped with court servants, but most of their activities were completely unrelated to the household, such as investigating grain fraud in the area north of Milan. When Galeazzo took on a *galuppo* in 1469, the new servant was furnished with lodgings and "the other necessary things, according to what is provided to our other *galuppi,*" including a cloak *alla divisa* and cloth for a cap.[106]

The duties of most ducal household servants were relatively straightforward; the cooks cooked, the tailors sewed, the huntsmen hunted, and so forth. The men employed as tennis players (*giocatori de balla*) did little besides play tennis, although some servants from other classifications (e.g., trumpeters) played tennis also. Most household servants were paid fairly well; the leading tennis player and barber were both assigned annual salaries of 100 florins (40 ducats).[107] They ran the same risks as their better-paid and more prestigious counterparts; in July 1472, Galeazzo ordered a month's pay withheld from two barbers and three *credenzieri*; the following year, he withheld two months' pay from the cooks and other kitchen staff.[108]

Not all servants held their offices for the full year, which may explain why nine or ten salary payments per year were standard. Many of them probably served in rotation like the *camerieri* and *staffieri,* perhaps all working when the court was at its fullest. Hundreds of the duke's servants never served their lord directly but performed their duties for others in his employ.[109] On some occasions, particular populations within the court suddenly expanded. In 1470, Galeazzo called fifty-four tailors and hosiers to Vigevano from Milan.[110] Most of these men were not attached to the court regularly; only two to four tailors appear at a time on court lists. The most prominent, Emmanuele Lanza, traveled with the duke often, but at times he was confined to Porta Giovia with his work.[111]

Another court tailor, Bassano da Lodi, made a contract with Galeazzo, by which the duke set up an artisan in his own service. The arrangement began with a ducal loan of 100 ducats, enabling Bassano to set up a workshop. The tailor pledged to "do all work that the aforenamed Lord will need and require with all care, speed, and ingenuity," excepting a few categories of product, notably hose and hats. The clothes Bassano produced would be credited against the loan he had received, with accounts being kept by the treasurer *di camera*. The contract included a dire warning that if the tailor violated the contract, "Bassano is content to await that punishment which seems best and pleasing to the aforenamed Most Illustrious Lord."[112]

Gentlemen and *Gentiluomini*

Those who held household offices were greatly affected by the whims of the duke; his personal welfare was the primary focus of their service. Offices of state were generally more clearly defined, and secure, positions. The duke's *gentiluomini*, courtiers *par excellence*, functioned more as officers of state than as personal attendants. Their prestigious backgrounds represented most elites of the dominion, including feudatories, urban merchants and professionals from various cities, and a few longtime civil and military servants of the Sforza.[113] Their presence added luster and gravity to ducal occasions. They greeted Galeazzo on his entry into their city, escorted visiting dignitaries, traveled on diplomatic missions, and attended at great occasions: major holidays, ducal weddings or funerals, ratification ceremonies for treaties, and so forth.

Certain *gentiluomini* had particular responsibilities that they consistently undertook. Carlo Favagrossa da Cremona was captain-general of the ducal hunts.[114] Giuliano da Varese attained both the office of *gentiluomo* and the office of seneschal within eighteen months. As a *gentiluomo,* he succeeded his father, who had died in 1472.[115] Giovanni Giapanno and Giovanni da Castelnovate had long been *gentiluomini* as well as seneschals-general.

The Duchess's Ladies and Gentlemen   The duchess's noble courtiers played a role quite different from the duke's; they actually lived in the castles with her and performed some of the duties that Galeazzo delegated to lesser persons or specialists. Giovanni Gabriele Crivelli himself was used for various errands, including the presentation of petitions to Bona.[116] The duchess's most visible courtiers, the original *compagni* and *compagne,* were quite well compensated for their positions, though. Each was assigned a salary of 50 florins per month (180 ducats per year, at nine payments), more than Galeazzo's own *gentiluomini*—or most of his senior administrators—at the time.[117]

No women served in the duke's household at all, except for his sexual partners. Occasionally, we see a glimpse from the life of a woman at Bona's court. In June 1469, Maria da Gallarate received permission to go to her estate for rest and recreation until her husband (a senior member of the court) returned. Galeazzo assured her that she would be contacted "if you have to come for some need of Our Most Illustrious Consort." A few days later, the duke repeated his generous message and extended it further; he gave Maria permission to go hawking.[118]

Officers of the Ducal Administration

Galeazzo inherited the administrative structure of his dominion, but he treated its officers quite differently than his father had done.

Major Civil Officials   The Privy Council provided stability and continuity of policy for the dominion. As Tommaso Tebaldi's story shows, even some councillors who had served under Filippo Maria Visconti were advisers to the Sforza dukes. Galeazzo and his mother expanded the Privy Council considerably between 1466 and 1469, doubling the membership from Duke Francesco's time.[119] The number of councillors remained steady during Galeazzo's reign, though. Lists of active councillors from both 1469 and 1476 contain twenty-six names.[120] The members had evidently been chosen with an eye to balancing geographic, social, and political interests. Great feudatories, urban aristocrats, high ecclesiastics, professional jurists and scholars, ducal bureaucracy, and the whole geographic sweep of the dominion are represented on both lists.

Precedence on the council carried considerable weight, since its members had been assembled from all of the dominion's men of honor. Pier Maria Rossi's letter of appointment to the council specified that he would be seated "behind Lancillotto del Maino," and the 1469 list of councillors places him in precisely that position. Seven years later, another councillor (Giovanni Borromeo) had risen eighteen places to rank between the two; such mobility was not unusual.[121]

In addition to the active members, the Privy Council included honorary councillors who took no part in substantive proceedings. Among them were foreign dignitaries such as the lord of Imola and the chancellor of Florence. Milanese diplomats sometimes received temporary appointments to enhance their prestige and credibility. Michele Marliani, bishop of Tortona, was named to the council in 1466 only because he was going to Rome; Galeazzo insisted that the nomination was intended "to do him honor, not so that he would take up residence on our council."[122] Of the few ecclesiastics who sat on the Privy Council, most were councillors in name only; these included the duke's brother Ascanio and the archbishop of Milan, a native of Forlì who lived in Rome. Two bishops did participate actively in the council's work: Giacomo della Torre of Parma and Branda Castiglione of Como.[123] The prelates as a group led the order of precedence among council members.

The prestige of the councillors and the gravity of their duties did not mean that they were allowed latitude in directing their affairs. Like other ducal servants, they were expected to be available at all times. In 1470, the duke ordered that he should always have "near us some of those on our Privy Council, as much to honor our person by their presence as to confer with us on the occurrences of our state."[124] Councillors who did not travel with the duke were required to reside in Milan; they convened usually in the Corte Arengo.[125] At one point, Galeazzo instructed six of them, including a bishop and three major feudatories, to "take up residence at your office and not leave without our permission"—quite a demand to make on such prominent personages![126] When Marquess Giovanni Ludovico Pallavicino learned of his appointment to the Privy Council, he and his wife were taking the baths at Acqui. He went to Milan immediately, without returning home to set his affairs in order. He then wrote to the duke with a request to go home, put things straight, and get the money to buy a house in Milan. Determined to please his prince, the noble councillor even offered to go in secret, should Galeazzo think his brief absence would disturb the other councillors too much. Galeazzo was not entirely unreasonable, though. When Giovanni Ludovico fell ill several years later, he received permission to leave the Privy Council and Milan and tend to his health for so long as he needed.[127]

Galeazzo also expanded the numbers of the masters of revenues, doubling them from his father's time to four or five men per group ("ordinary" and "extraordinary").[128] These masters often moved on to higher positions; some later joined the Privy Council, while others became *gentiluomini*.[129] Like the councillors, these officials were usually chosen from high-ranking families of the dominion. They were expected to attend at court occasions, as were all the "magistrati dela corte."

The Treasurer-General   Everything and everyone in the dominion depended on the treasurer-general. From his tower room in Porta Giovia, he received all the monies that came to the central organs of government, kept account of them, and disbursed them according to the duke's instructions. Given the dimensions of the Milanese budget—as much as half a million ducats per year—it is surprising that any individual could stay abreast of the task. The Sforza archives contain literally thousands of orders directed to this official, for he had to authorize every single payment and every occasion on which coins were removed from the treasury. Hundreds of thousands of ducats were literally carried into and out of his rooms; the lists of coins themselves reflect the challenge of the position—pieces ranging from gold ducats to bits of base metal used in daily trade on the streets, including a variety of foreign monies.[130] The treasurer-general was also responsible for drawing up the ducal budget and adhering to it; one can understand why the duke wanted him to stay in the heart of the castle, isolated from all external pressures.

From 1469 to 1473, the treasurer-general was Antonio Anguissola, a noble from Piacenza. He had been a *cameriere* in Galeazzo's household before the duke's accession, and he accompanied the young duke on the traumatic return from France in March 1466.[131] Antonio continued to be intimate with Galeazzo throughout the early years of the reign.[132] The duke required him to remain inside Porta Giovia unless explicitly permitted to leave, but Galeazzo also enjoyed his company and insisted on his attendance at "every feast day," including Sundays. Occasionally, Antonio received permission to take a brief vacation; in 1472, he was granted two days and one night to visit the shrine of Santa Maria delle Grazie in Monza. During that period, he was also allowed to hunt wherever he wished, an unusual privilege that reflected his high standing with the duke.[133] Even before Antonio became treasurer, he had been the only *cameriere* authorized to request money and seek offices for his friends and relatives.[134]

The Privy Chancery   Few members of the court were valued by Galeazzo more highly than Antonio Anguissola; Cicco Simonetta may have been the only one. During Galeazzo's reign, Cicco generally traveled with the duke. When Cicco stayed behind once because of illness, a chancellor wrote that he did not believe it, since he had never before seen the first secretary too ill to work.[135] Cicco presided over the Chancery, worked closely with the Privy Council (of which he was a member), organized Galeazzo's work schedule, and attended personally to many matters that the duke himself neglected. Cicco maintained a diary that survives (in part) for the years 1473–1476 and 1478; its entries indicate the secretary's interests and concerns—official business, some personal matters, descriptions of ceremonial events, and a wide range of miscellaneous information, from "the things that are found excellent in Russia" to a cure for rabies.[136] The diary contains very little secret or scandalous information on the court, but it does illuminate aspects of court activities not visible through other sources.

Cicco's influence with the duke was so great that even councillors of state and Galeazzo's own brothers asked Cicco to intercede with the duke at times. Persons on bad terms with Cicco experienced more than the usual obstacles in dealing with the ducal administration.[137] Cicco profited moderately from his position, acquiring several small to moderate fiefs and controlling patronage adequate to support a large family. Although he had a country seat at Sartirana, his family resided ordinarily in Pavia.[138] Cicco married Elisabetta Visconti, the daughter of a ducal secretary. He had at least nine children, some of them illegitimate. In a social coup of sorts, the first secretary arranged a marriage in 1471 between his daughter Margherita and Guido Galeotto Torelli, the young count of Guastalla; this marriage firmly linked the Simonetta to the great feudal nobility of the duchy.[139]

The Simonetta clan enjoyed an unusual position of stability and dominance in their positions within the Sforza administration. Perhaps more typical was the career of Giacomo Alfieri. Born in L'Aquila, he too had followed Francesco Sforza from the kingdom of Naples to Milan. A chancellor in the early years of Galeazzo's reign, Giacomo joined the duke's inner circle in 1469, becoming chancellor *di camera* and handling outgoing correspondence. Giacomo left the duke's service entirely in April 1474, but by January 1, 1475, he had returned, as secretary to the Privy Council. Like the Simonetta brothers, Giacomo had many personal connections within the Sforza court world. Among other links, he was brother-in-law to both the castellan of Pavia and the treasurer-general.[140]

It may have been Giacomo who wrote to Galeazzo in 1467 about problems of inefficiency and disorder in the Privy Chancery that were so pervasive that the duke was being robbed without knowing it. Moreover, Galeazzo was told, the destruction of the Visconti records in 1447 still hampered Sforza officials twenty years later.[141] This scathing indictment of the Chancery's work marks a notable exception to the usual tone of admiration for its competence, sophistication, and faithful protection of ducal interests.

The number of men working in the Chancery varied during the course of Galeazzo's reign; in 1470, Cicco Simonetta was assisted by two secretaries, thirteen chancellors, three coadjutors, and four doorkeepers. It was expected that one or two chancellors would attend on the duke at all times, even during meals. They were required to travel with him and to be ready for departing at a moment's notice. At least one of the secretaries also traveled with the duke, to expedite his correspondence. In 1472, Galeazzo decided to have two secretaries with him wherever he went; each one was responsible for the correspondence with half of the dominion's districts (plus foreign parts). One of those secretaries was Giacomo Alfieri.[142]

Minor Civil Officials   The civil administration included many offices with more limited duties. The *commissario* of Works (*sopra li lavoreri*) was charged with oversight of all major construction and furnishing projects, including both ducal residences and defensive structures. Bartolomeo Gadio of Cremona, who held that position under Dukes Francesco and Galeazzo, was one of the busiest men in the dominion.[143] His supervisory responsibilities extended to such short-term commissioned workers as fresco painters and other craftsmen, but they mainly involved such long-term ducal servants as engineers, laborers, and suppliers. His most visible subordinates were Danesio Mainerio ("il Danese"), the chief ducal engineer; Benedetto Ferrini da Firenze, an engineer from Florence; and Filippo Corio, head of the Office of Munitions.[144]

The *Judici Stratarum Mediolani* supervised the maintenance of roads and streets. In the capital city itself, Galeazzo wanted the streets paved at the expense of those who owned property along the street frontage.[145] In the countryside, the duke wanted roads maintained so that he, his court, and his ducal messengers could use them as needed. In one case, he complained that the road between Milan and Melegnano was "so damaged that one can ill ride, and our riders [messengers] pass back and forth with danger."[146] Other officials had responsibility for tolls and customs, grain provisioning, waterways, and so forth.

Of all the minor offices, the Office of Health (*Officium Sanitatis*) had the most varied duties. This office may have originated in the Milanese dukes' extreme fear of the plague, but its officials were involved in a variety of interesting projects. Galeazzo wanted to be informed of all births and deaths in the capital and went so far as to forbid baptism or burial to anyone whose birth or death had not been reported. Some reports of deaths showed not only the names, ages, and parishes of the deceased but also the causes of death and even the identity of physicians making diagnoses.[147]

Officials of the Peripheral Administration   Persons who served the duke of Milan rarely remained in the same office or function throughout their tenure. Most were transferred or promoted between various positions in the central administration, the military, the ducal household, and the peripheral administration. Members of the court were sometimes appointed as *commissari,* and many members served as podestà in one town or another. The office of podestà could be lucrative, since it generally collected fees for each case considered and sometimes had a substantial salary attached. For that reason, men actively sought certain appointments and paid the duke for them.[148]

In other cases, such appointments were made as rewards for faithful service. In November 1470, Paolo Castiglione, one of the masters of extraordinary revenues, was granted the *podesterìa* of Alessandria. Paolo told his son Giovanni Francesco, a member of Bona's court, that he did not want that office, and Galeazzo made Paolo podestà of Piacenza instead. Paolo then wrote directly to the duke, thanking him effusively but declining the new honor.

Paolo cited problems with the expenses of moving to a new place, "to have standards made, buy horses, hire servants—and give them clothes, shoes, and salaries—send to furnish the house there, and keep another one furnished here [i.e., Milan], and then hire a judicial vicar, messenger and constable—and keep them paid—when I myself would not be paid." Paolo explained that such expenses would be impossible for him to bear, which was why he had not wanted to go to Alessandria. The administrator continued, "I am a poor gentleman, without a house and without a roof, and almost without any income, and I find myself with many debts and without money . . . and this has happened because I have lived cleanly, and have held honor more dearly than anything else." Paolo ended his letter to Galeazzo by telling the duke that he would be happy to become podestà in Savona or Pontremoli, where the position was well paid. Within a week, the worthy man had received appointment as podestà and *commissario* of Savona.[149]

Regardless of the basis for appointment as podestà or *commissario,* Galeazzo expected those offices to be exercised properly, especially in sensitive areas. In 1469, Stefano da Onate (later a *gentiluomo* to the duchess) became podestà of Soncino, on the border with Venetian territory. The duke gave him strict instructions about doing justice equally for all and maintaining adequate grain supplies as well as keeping the town secure and the territory free of Venetian incursions.[150]

Duty in the peripheral administration could become very burdensome, keeping officials away from home and family for extended periods. In June 1468, Giorgio da Annone, a veteran diplomat and councillor, was serving as *commissario* of Parma. He asked Galeazzo for permission to visit his home in Milan, noting that he had spent fourteen months in France, then two years in Parma, doing ducal business. He wanted to spend some time at home "with regard to my seven small children that are, one could say, without government, their mother being gone and I so far away from them for so long. And furthermore, it has been a good three years since I took another wife, and I have never had time to go and see her."[151]

Military Officials   The ducal authority of the Sforza originated in Duke Francesco's success as a military leader. Armed force guaranteed the security of the Sforza dominion and its leadership, but it rarely needed to be applied, or even threatened, outside the subject state of Genoa.[152] Nonetheless, every city and castle had its garrison, and local residents were taxed to support the soldiers, whether they liked it or not.[153]

The direction of military organization and policy lay with Galeazzo and the Privy Council, but day-to-day supervision of military logistics fell to Orfeo Cenni da Ricavo, Commissioner General for the Armed Forces (*Commissario generale delle gentedarme*). Orfeo was one of the most influential persons in the Sforza court; he traveled with Galeazzo frequently, sat with the Privy Council (to which he was appointed formally in 1474), and participated in the great *feste*. Orfeo was one of the few officials included in both fresco programs composed for Porta Giovia Castle, and he appears often on witness lists for ducal charters. A Florentine native, he came to Cremona, then Milan, during Duke Francesco's reign; his military post was created in 1471, when Galeazzo regularized the entire military structure.[154]

Although Galeazzo ruled in a period of unusual tranquillity, defense was the largest single area of expense in his ducal budgets.[155] Despite a personal lack of military skill, the young duke showed great interest in improving on his father's formidable army. As early as 1469, his officials were looking at ways to reorganize the Milanese armed forces and calculate the costs of maintaining them.[156] Between 1472 and 1474, the ducal administration broke new ground in contemporary practice, drawing up comprehensive mobilization plans for the army in both peace and war.[157] The plans included detailed information on commanders, troop strengths, and chains of command. This precocious example of military planning was characteristic of the Sforza administration's systematic approach to problems. Milan maintained a standing army of several thousand men-at-arms above and beyond the ducal guard, garrisons, and condottieri's contingents. Most of the duke's military commanders were feudatories, an outgrowth of traditional feudal military service. In the later fifteenth century, though, such captains served for pay, what English historians have called "bastard feudalism."[158]

Because Galeazzo's reign was so peaceful, some military commanders found themselves at court more often than in the field. At major *feste* or important consultations, such men as Pietro Francesco Visconti and Giovanni Pallavicino di Scipione could be expected to attend. They commanded units of the standing army, either the *famiglia ducale* or the *lanze spezzate* ("broken lances"), so called because they were hired individually, not in units under a condottiere. The *famiglia ducale* and *lanze spezzate* numbered around 6,000 men under Galeazzo. The *famiglia* formed the core of the duke's standing army but did not function in Galeazzo's reign as a ducal guard. The nucleus of his bodyguard was 100 mounted crossbowmen led by prominent men, including two of his *camerieri*.[159]

The duke also used his brothers and other intimates as military commanders. Each of the brothers (except clerical Ascanio) was responsible for a division of the army in wartime. Some of Galeazzo's favorites, including GianGiacomo Trivulzio and Antonio Caracciolo, served as commanders in the *famiglia,* while remaining close to Galeazzo's person.[160] The duke's old friend, Donato "del Conte" Borri, who had fled the court twice in the early years of the reign, was one of the leading military commanders during the later years. At various times, he led the foot soldiers in the *famiglia* and some of the *lanze spezzate*. He was included in the major fresco programs for Porta Giovia.[161]

Like all Italian rulers of his time, Galeazzo employed the mercenary captains known as condottieri, although few served him actively. The greater part of his army on paper came with condottieri of princely rank: Ludovico Gonzaga of Mantua, Giovanni Bentivoglio of Bologna, Pino Ordelaffi of Forlì, Taddeo Manfredi of Imola, and others. Galeazzo also had professional captains attached more or less permanently to the Sforza service. Many of them had little to do with the court, except at the feast of San Giorgio or other occasions when Galeazzo held jousts.[162]

Continuity and Uncertainty

The Milanese court was characterized by a notable continuity; like Tommaso Tebaldi, most members served from one duke to the next. This continuity resulted in part from inertia; it was always easier to let things continue as they had than to make radical changes. The continuity was also a function of professionalism. Most persons who exercised a ducal office learned to do so carefully and properly. Even the household offices showed a high degree of continuity, especially for those whose place was not strictly contingent on personal intimacy with the duke. The transition from Duke Francesco to his absent son Galeazzo gave an excellent illustration of this process. When Galeazzo reorganized the household three months after his accession, he did not discharge his father's favorite *camerieri* but put them *fuori di camera*. One of the men displaced at this time was Francesco da Varese, who continued to be well paid and highly honored notwithstanding his departure from the charmed circle.[163]

There was also considerable continuity of court service within families. When Giovanni Ludovico Pallavicino became too ill to continue serving on the Privy Council, Galeazzo replaced him with his brother, Pallavicino Pallavicino, so as to keep the honor in their family.[164] Dozens of persons found themselves at court because their parents or guardians had lived or worked there. A typical case was that of Antonio Pallavicino; his father, Federico, marquess of Ravarono, had been a *gentiluomo* as early as 1457. In 1470, Federico responded to a ducal request and sent his son to court as *cameriere*.[165]

"The Lord Giveth, The Lord Taketh
Away, Let the Lord's Name Be Blessed"

Although continuity of service was the norm in the Milanese court, the prince's will was unpredictable. In March 1474, Francesco Pietrasanta was removed from his office as secretary to the Council of Justice. Francesco believed he had offended the duke "with my speech too frank and open," and he wrote a letter to Galeazzo, both appealing for forgiveness and justifying himself. Francesco described his relationship with the duke as follows: "First I was lifted from the crowd (*dal vulgo*), then from the Lords of the Council [of Justice], as Your Sublimity has taken me from that office. I had hoped that my faith and devotion to Your Lordship would be rewarded with ever greater offices; nevertheless, because you may dispose of me as you wish, and I would be rash to try to interpret your wishes, I will say nothing but 'The Lord giveth, the Lord taketh, let the Lord's name be blessed.'"[166]

Francesco was unusual in his outspokenness and his willingness to risk Galeazzo's wrath. The longer one served at court, the more likely one was to experience changes of fortune and position. Men who could endure years in the pressure cooker of ducal office often rose in the ranks; Francesco da Varese was eventually promoted from his longtime post as *cameriere* to the more lucrative and prestigious office of seneschal. Many *camerieri* were promoted to the office of *gentiluomo* as well. A regular ladder of promotion operated in the civil administration. Men who made their career in the law tended to serve on the Council of Justice before being promoted to the Privy Council.[167] Others moved up through the fiscal hierarchy. Melchiorre Marliani had served with the masters of revenues before being promoted to the Privy Council; his brother Antonio then became one of the masters of revenues in his place. When Melchiorre died, Antonio succeeded him on the council.[168]

Naturally, what went up could also go down. Count Ludovico da Barbiano ("de Lugo") was appointed to the Privy Council in May 1467; at that time, he was one of Galeazzo's most trusted advisers. The duke even consulted him about the organization of the household and selection of a seneschal-general. However, a serious scandal in early 1468 caused Ludovico to resign his position after barely a year. He was brought to trial, and although the duke pardoned him in 1468, the trial was not totally annulled until shortly before Ludovico's death in 1471, saving his memory and inheritance.[169]

Demotions occurred regularly, although not often. The *camerieri di camera* who rose to the pinnacle of Galeazzo's passionate favor always fell again afterward, and there was nowhere to go that did not involve a demotion of some kind. Pietro Pagnani, who fell from grace in 1467, continued falling for years; by 1469, he had been stripped of his secretarial post. He held no office from then until 1471, when he was assigned to help Giacomo Alfieri, who had replaced him as secretary. Five months later, a resurgent Pietro was named to the masters of revenues.[170]

While it was often frightening to catch the duke's attention, simple neglect could be equally troubling. In July 1467, a *cameriere* complained to Galeazzo that he had received neither pay nor gifts since the death of Duke Francesco (March 1466), except for 12 ducats at the feast of San Giorgio in 1467. The courtier stressed that he "can't live to honor you without anything" to pay for expenses.[171] In March 1467, Galeazzo's mother had to remind him that one of the courtiers had asked repeatedly to receive velvet for a suit, as Galeazzo had given the other courtiers.[172] The duke needed to be reminded even about his own children's clothing needs; if he was not alerted to such situations, he was unlikely to act on them.[173] Fortunately for those in need, members of the court were not without compassion. In one case, a seneschal asked Galeazzo what to do about a newly hired worker: "This poor little man is almost ill and without hose or clothing. I do not know if Your Excellency wants other provision to be made for him beyond his living allowance [*la provisione de la vita*]."[174]

Leaving the Court

Among the thousands of persons participating in the court over the course of the reign, there were always some coming and others going. In 1467, Giovanni Castiglione asked the duke for permission to leave his office. Giovanni claimed that he was getting too old and could no longer ride well, which prevented him from doing his job properly. Since he worked as a *Judex Stratarum*, responsible for the condition of streets and roads, he had to ride regularly and look at them. Most of all, Giovanni pleaded, he needed to turn his attention to his own business to avoid debtor's prison. His first request brought no response; two months later, he wrote again, describing further his agonies and inadequacies.[175]

Galeazzo sometimes allowed his servants to leave the court, or his service, without objections. One *cameriere* who sought a place in Florence received a letter of recommendation that apparently had no strings attached.[176] However, the duke did not easily allow intimates to leave his side. He was not above the use of subterfuges to keep them close to his person. One of his constant companions was Giovanni Pietro del Bergamino, who experienced the usual ups and downs of intimacy with the duke, gaining and losing revenues, winning and losing money at tennis, hunting, costuming, jousting, and so forth. In 1473, Giovanni Pietro wanted to try his fortune at the court of France. Galeazzo was furious at what he considered an act of desertion. The duke sent his friend a letter about loyalty, dripping with sarcasm. When Giovanni Pietro left anyway, Galeazzo provided a letter of recommendation, but he secretly wrote to Louis XI and the Milanese ambassador in France instructing them to ignore it. The duke hoped to compel his friend's return to Milan, and the plan worked: Giovanni Pietro was back later in 1473, and he spent the rest of the reign as one of the duke's closest companions.[177]

Galeazzo bore great animosity against those who left the duchy without his permission. Like his half-sister Drusiana and the condottiere Giorgio da Galesio, they were generally stripped of all possessions *in absentia*.[178] Those who returned could be rehabilitated, though, as Sforza Secondo and Donato del Conte learned. Only occasionally did the duke himself remove someone "from the number of our courtiers" before that person had left the court or requested leave to do so.[179] Whether one wanted to come, stay, or leave, court membership was always contingent on the duke's pleasure.

"This Condition is Put Forward to Each One That Is Born"

"He who lives at court dies in the poorhouse." If anyone who lived at Galeazzo's court died in the poorhouse, he has not yet come to light. Most members of the court did not "live at court" in a literal sense, although such men as Tommaso Tebaldi or Mastino Suardi, who had left their native cities, lacked local roots outside the court sphere. Most persons associated with Galeazzo's court had a long history in Milan or the other districts of the dominion. In death, these persons generally returned to their families, who faced the same issues of inheritance or succession for them as for anyone.

The imminent death of a relative could also affect the actions of persons at court. In May 1468, Bianca Maria Visconti called for her noble courtier Bonifacio Aliprandi to join her. He asked for a few days grace while he watched over his eighty-three-year-old uncle. Bonifacio's household had all left the city for his summer villa; he was the only one there to help the uncle, who had no teeth and could barely lift his hand from the bed. Because Bonifacio feared that the uncle would die while he was out of the house and that he himself "would have the burden of that on my soul—and also a failure [in the eyes of] the world—I have made the choice to stay and see what end he may make."[180]

Persons at court with few responsibilities and little stature were barely visible in death, as in life. Some persons' deaths had political ramifications or brought changes in the administration of court or state. When Count Ludovico da Barbiano died, it put an end to his disgrace; when Giovanni Francesco Attendoli died, it cut short a promising career. The respected memory of a deceased courtier could translate into continuity of office for members of the family, as when Antonio Marliani succeeded to his brother's seat on the Privy Council. On that occasion, Galeazzo extended his condolences for Melchiorre's death, adding, "But this condition is put forward to each one that is born."[181]

Death in the Ducal Lineage

For those whose offices or personal connections gave them significance in the duke's eyes, the machinery of government became involved in the process of death. As the head of his own lineage, the duke concerned himself particularly with the deaths of persons who belonged by blood or marriage, such as his sister Elisabetta or Giovanni Mauruzzi da Tolentino, his half-sister Isotta's husband.[182] Many persons of both genders were honored by the court at their deaths. All members of the ducal lineage, related "foreign" princes, and persons with positions of trust in the ducal household or major civil offices received funerals if they died in Milan. If they died in another state, their passing was acknowledged with a memorial service.

Of all Galeazzo's relatives who died during his reign, Bianca Maria Visconti was the most important and the most beloved by people of the dominion.[183] The quality of the duke's relationships with members of his family was often reflected in his treatment of their death. The death of his half-sister Elisa was acknowledged and honored with a funeral, then with customary memorial services one week and one month later. The death of half-sister Drusiana was officially ignored, since she died in voluntary exile.[184] Six years after Elisa passed away, her full brother Polidoro died in Milan. Solemnities for him were organized by the ducal seneschals-general, using the same form as had been used for her funeral; then, Polidoro was buried at her side.[185]

In general, funerals and memorial services for members of the ducal lineage were important vehicles for reaffirming social order and the ducal vision. When Alessandro Visconti, a governor of the *lanze spezzate,* died, Galeazzo ordered all of the officers of state "to honor his funeral, as is customary to do for the others of the house of Visconti."[186] The duke took this principle equally seriously for women of the lineage. Luchina Visconti was the daughter of Sagramoro, a major feudatory and Privy Council member who died in 1472. When she passed away in 1476, the duke ordered "all our *magistrati* of the court," except the two councils of state, to "honor her body."[187]

The ducal lineage connection could be honored even when it was quite indirect. Galeazzo considered Andreotto del Maino "our uncle," because Agnese del Maino, Duke Filippo Maria Visconti's mistress, had been Bianca Maria's mother. The death of Andreotto's wife in 1471 was marked with a state funeral.[188] On the Sforza side, Alessandro Sforza of Pesaro was honored at his death in 1473 with a service patterned on the funeral of his mother (Galeazzo's paternal grandmother).[189] A massive service was held for the duke's sister Elisabetta when she died in 1472, even though she had been living with her husband in Montferrat.[190]

Funeral or memorial services were also held for princes who were more distantly related to the Sforza lineage, such as Borso d'Este. To mark the duke of Ferrara's passing, Galeazzo commanded that "all the [secular] clergy, all the religious [houses], and all the friars" of Milan participate, along with all the *magistrati della corte,* as many citizens as possible, Filippo and Sforza Maria Sforza, Polidoro, Tristano and his wife, Beatrice d'Este, "and all the others of our household." Zaccaria Saggi da Pisa, who participated, told his prince that the services were "very solemn and most worthy."[191] Others related to the Visconti and Sforza whom Galeazzo honored with memorial services or funerals included the duchess of Amalfi, the condottiere Giovanni Mauruzzi da Tolentino, and the widow of ducal cousin Luigi da Sanseverino. Corrado Fogliani, a condottiere and half-brother of Duke Francesco, was buried in the Duomo after his 1470 funeral. The duke also ordered "worthy and honorable exequies" for Maria of Savoy, wife of his grandfather, Filippo Maria Visconti, who died in 1469.[192]

Beyond the Ducal Lineage

Galeazzo sent ambassadors to other states for the funerals and memorial services honoring princes past and present. In 1473, he sent two councillors to Savoy for memorial services honoring three members of the Savoyard ducal family. The ambassadors were instructed that they themselves would be "dressed in black," but their servants could dress "in the usual way."[193]

Funerals for ducal officials in Milan were also organized by the seneschals-general. Members of the court posted to Milan, especially the councillors and other *magistrati,* would attend them. This form was observed for officers of both the ducal household and the state administration, such as Raffaelle de' Nigri, of the masters of revenues, who died in 1474, and Domenico Tornielli, "formerly our courtier," who died in 1469. Giovanni Francesco Attendoli's funeral in 1469 occurred after he had already been buried, but it still marked an important recognition by his peers and colleagues.[194]

Although Galeazzo thought it important to recognize the deaths of his loyal servants and princely relatives, he rarely attended such services personally. He did not like to be reminded of death, and he wanted particularly to keep its specter away from festive occasions. At Christmas 1471, several important foreign dignitaries were dressed in brown, a color of mourning; they included the ambassadors from Ferrara and Naples. Galeazzo would not allow anyone to enter Porta Giovia Castle and his presence "if not dressed in colors," which meant that the dignitaries in mourning had to stay away from him or "throw away" their brown clothes.[195] Whatever one's position at court, conditions of life and work always required a keen and constant sensitivity to the prince.

6

"To Gain the Friendship of Many Leading Men"

The Politics of Honor (1472–1474)

By 1472, Galeazzo had become increasingly concerned with gaining the friendship of prominent men. Accordingly, he attempted to treat them with due respect for the nuances of precedence and protocol. In May, when Cardinal Bessarion's visit drew near, the duke convoked the Privy Council to decide key issues of protocol regarding "the receiving and honoring of the Most Reverend Milord of Nicea [Bessarion] in this his entry here."[1]

The central questions involved how far Galeazzo should go to meet the cardinal, "if he should dismount on encountering [Bessarion], [and] if he should send the Privy Council ahead, or rather keep them near His Excellency [the duke]." In the debate, Giacomo della Torre (bishop of Parma), Agostino Rossi (former ambassador to Rome), Tommaso Tebaldi da Bologna, and Cicco argued that Galeazzo should dismount as a sign of special respect. They pointed out that King Alfonso of Naples had done so for the patriarch many years earlier. The opposing argument was made by Tommaso Moroni da Rieti and the Milanese nobleman Pietro Pusterla. They felt that the duke should "save the dignity of the duchy" and remain mounted. Their understanding was that Alfonso had dismounted because "he was a vassal of the church, and he was obliged to dismount." Pietro and Tommaso also said "that they had seen the previous duke of Burgundy [Philip the Good] having come to encounter three cardinals and not having dismounted." Bessarion's status as a legate *a latere,* the highest ranking office in the church below the Papacy itself, influenced the discussion. It was finally decided to follow a suggestion by the bishop of Parma to inform Bessarion in advance that Galeazzo intended to dismount. The councillors were certain that "the Cardinal would not tolerate it, and in this way would be satisfied both the ecclesiastical and ducal dignities." In the event, both the duke and his guest dismounted.[2]

"That No Error of Precedence May Follow"

In October 1472, Galeazzo began to organize a particularly brilliant Christmas court. He asked his client "lords and captains and condottieri" to confer with him, and he invited the hundreds of feudatories, courtiers, and ducal officers who ordinarily shared his Christmas.

The seneschals-general worked to arrange official receptions and holiday lodgings for some of the distinguished Christmas visitors. In early November, Galeazzo decided to accommodate princely visitors in the houses of major feudatories, who were also required to provide household furnishings when possible. The ducal seneschals provided money for food. The lord of Forlì, Pino Ordelaffi, was to be lodged at a house belonging to the heirs of a ducal cousin, one of the Sanseverino family. A more important guest, Giovanni Bentivoglio of Bologna, was placed—with his large retinue of eighty persons—in the house of Count Pietro dal Verme.[3] The Roman condottiere Giovanni Conti was assigned to the house of Lantelmina da Vimercate, widow of the great count Gaspare da Vimercate. She complained of the burden, but Galeazzo shrugged off her objections. He told her, "This should not be a nuisance to you, because he will not make a long stay there, nor will he have to bring many persons, so that they can lodge comfortably enough at your house." The duke urged her to have patience and make the necessary preparations, "because this is a decision that we won't be able to revoke."[4]

In early December, the table steward was seeking information on how much wine, bread, wood, wax, meat, sweets, and so forth, would be needed. He was disbursed the large sum of 1,000 ducats to buy those provisions. Temporary kitchens were erected, with table silver and other furnishings transferred from Pavia Castle. At the same time, the seneschals-general were using a list of guests "that will be seated at table with our Most Illustrious Lord at this blessed feast" to determine how large a table to use and how to arrange the seating. They also concerned themselves with such matters as paying living expenses for the visitors, giving Christmas gifts to resident ambassadors, organizing the entry of the ducal children into Milan, and heating the rooms of Porta Giovia Castle for guests staying there.[5]

Two months earlier, the seneschals-general had been working with the Privy Council and the Chancery to set the lists of invitees in proper order, "that no error of precedence may follow."[6] Giovanni Giapanno advised that they should not "drive themselves mad" trying to deal with the entire list of invitees; accordingly, they dealt only with the list of feudatories. The finished lists were copied and posted in a hall of Porta Giovia, presumably in order that every participant would know his place.

Most decisions on precedence were made by ducal functionaries. Giapanno suggested for this occasion that the bishop of Lodi (Carlo Pallavicino) should precede the Genoese nobleman Prospero Adorno, "for being a bishop, and of good family [*de bona casa*], and for being among the councillors [*sopra li consiglieri*] and in an honorable position [*in loco honorevole*]." Pietro Pusterla was not formally a Privy Councillor during Galeazzo's reign, but he was nonetheless to be ranked highly among the councillors at Christmas 1472. Giovanni Antonio Girardi had used rankings given him by the council's secretary, Vincenzo Amidani. When questions arose over Pusterla's position, Giovanni Antonio returned to Vincenzo "to understand better" what place Pusterla should take. Vincenzo replied that Pusterla was not on his list of council-lors but that "when it befalls that he comes to the council meetings, he goes quite far toward the front." Accordingly, Giovanni Antonio ranked Pusterla fourth.[7]

The one other major problem Giovanni Antonio had encountered with the original list of invitees involved the duke's half-brothers Tristano and Sforza Secondo. Both had been invited to Christmas in 1472, as was usual. In the early years of the Sforza duchy, Sforza Secondo had preceded Tristano, despite the latter's greater age and general reputation, because of a higher-ranking noble title. Then Tristano married a daughter of Niccolò III d'Este and took precedence on the strength of his wife's princely status. During the year 1472, Sforza Secondo was named captain-general of the ducal navy, which, Giovanni Antonio noted, "is indeed a great dignity." It was left to Duke Galeazzo to decide if Sforza should precede again, since the case concerned the princely family. Giovanni Antonio found that everyone else on the original list stood in the proper order, and he sent Cicco Simonetta a revised copy of the list, with the addition of "a few other of the best feudatories who were not written and told they should come."[8]

While the seneschals and Chancery officials attended to precedence among Galeazzo's subjects, the duke asked his ambassador in Rome to check the papal book of ceremonies for information on precedence between the various rulers of Italy. The ambassador wrote back with some surprise that no such written protocol existed at the papal court, where precedence changed according to individual situations.[9] In Milan, a committee of councillors had drawn up a systematic protocol as early as 1468 for the reception and treatment of foreign dignitaries.[10] Early in December 1472, the Privy Council met with the seneschals-general to determine precedence among the princes Galeazzo had invited, especially between the lords of Imola and Forlì. Their decision was guided by the experience of Milanese ambassadors Agostino Rossi at the papal court and Gerardo Colli at the lord of Urbino's funeral.[11]

Such considerations played an important part in relations between princes. At Christmas 1472, the duke wanted to show particular honor to Ludovico Gonzaga of Mantua, his neighbor, ally, and erstwhile father-in-law. However, Guglielmo Paleologo of Montferrat—Galeazzo's neighbor, ally, and (briefly) brother-in-law—insisted on preceding his Mantuan rival. The two marquesses alternated as nominal leader of the Milanese ducal army, and their conflicts over precedence at the ducal court had deep roots. To keep on the best terms with both princes, Galeazzo suggested finally that Guglielmo not come to the Christmas court at all but come instead during the following March at San Giuseppe or Easter.[12] Ludovico Gonzaga did not always triumph in this competition for honor. Soon after honoring him at Christmas 1472, Galeazzo declared the marquess of Montferrat captain-general of the Milanese army, a position senior to that of Ludovico. In a context intended for more permanent use, the 1472 Sala Grande fresco program, the two princes were represented as equals, "in such form and manner that the one does not seem superior to the other."[13]

When the guests had gathered, Galeazzo and his retinue must have presented a dazzling sight. He had taken "all the silver and gold brocade in Milan" to make "suits with wide and open sleeves for all his *camerieri di camera.*" Four of these courtiers received suits of gold brocade, in crimson, "of mid-thigh length, with lining and facing of sable, and beautiful fringe," as well as a gold brocade skirt in sky blue. Seventeen other *camerieri* received similar outfits but in silver brocade. Pietro d'Olly, who was also a singer in the ducal choir, was dressed in dark red velvet with fox lining, in French style. The total cost for these splendid costumes was almost 4,000 ducats.[14]

"Those Who Are on the Vigevano List"

The observance of Christmas proceeded in the usual manner, and the seasonal ceremonies were performed in the presence of the princes and military leaders with whom the duke held his consultations. As part of this particularly grand Christmas season, Galeazzo invested his brothers Filippo, Sforza Maria, and Ludovico with substantial fiefs.[15] On January 3, the conference ended, and the visitors left that day and the following day.[16] On January 7, as soon as the twelve days of Christmas had passed, Galeazzo enclosed himself in Porta Giovia Castle with "few persons, that is, those who are on the Vigevano list." He kept out those, including *gentiluomini* and councillors, who did not belong to his intimate circle. Those persons allowed to enter found that the duke had installed a bell in the tower by the Corte Ducale, and he had the bell rung to call his courtiers to him. Zaccaria Saggi da Pisa told Marsilio Andreasi that Galeazzo's action "reminds me of Holofernes's command" that all should prostrate before a golden statue when certain music was sounded.[17]

The Betrothal of Caterina Sforza

The duke remained at Porta Giovia with his inner circle for five days before riding to Pavia. Less than a week later, he presided over another important ceremony. One of the princely visitors at Christmas 1472 was Count Gerolamo Riario, Pope Sixtus IV's favorite secular nephew. Galeazzo sought to improve his relations with the Papacy after the 1471 election of Sixtus, whose home city of Savona lay in Sforza territory. Among other things, the duke hoped the pope might invest him with Milan if the emperor refused to do so. Galeazzo made Gerolamo a member of the Milanese ducal family in July 1472, allowing the young count to style himself "Visconti." Shortly afterward, in August, Gerolamo was scheduled to visit Milan. In the event, he did not arrive until October, around the time Galeazzo was preparing for Christmas.[18]

Galeazzo and Sixtus had agreed that the young count should marry a member of the Sforza lineage. The duke's initial choice for a suitable bride was the daughter of the late condottiere Corrado Fogliani, Duke Francesco's half-brother. The plan met with bitter opposition from her mother, Gabriella, who was Ludovico Gonzaga's daughter. Gabriella claimed that Gerolamo Riario was not "worthy of such a wife," and her father also discouraged the duke, arguing that the Fogliani dowry was too small and the bride-to-be too young (at eleven years old).[19] Galeazzo was furious when his plans were thwarted. He felt it reflected badly on his honor, and he feared that the papal family would be angry with him. The duke was especially upset, "knowing that . . . King Ferrante has given two of his daughters to two of the pope's nephews." In his rivalry with Ferrante, Galeazzo hated to be outdone. He decided, "so as not to leave the said count [Gerolamo] desperate, and so as not to anger the pope and [Cardinal] San Sisto, and to discharge from our honor" this important commitment, to match Gerolamo with his own eldest natural daughter, Caterina. She was then about ten years old and had been promised some years earlier to a loyal feudatory, Count Amoratto Torelli; Galeazzo's wills had earmarked 10,000 ducats dowry for this match. However, the papal match was far more honorable and politically valuable.[20]

On January 17, 1473, Galeazzo presided over Caterina's betrothal to Gerolamo. The ceremony was small and quiet; it took place in the duke's chambers at Pavia Castle just after Sunday Mass. In attendance were Galeazzo, his cousin Costanzo Sforza of Pesaro, two ducal physicians, and a number of officials, both ducal and papal. Galeazzo promised his new son-in-law the same 10,000 ducats in dowry previously earmarked for Caterina—"to be paid at whatever time he should be of age to consummate the marriage." Within three days, Gerolamo gave his betrothed a substantial collection of velvets, diamonds, rubies, emeralds, and other jewelry, including thousands of pearls. On January 20, the pope's nephew mounted up and left for Rome.[21]

Galeazzo was satisfied with the Riario match for Caterina, but he was mightily displeased with the Fogliani and Gonzaga. He told Ludovico Gonzaga that the marquess would have to take responsibility for the marriage of Gabriella Fogliani's daughter. The duke also began a vindictive legal proceeding against Gabriella and her lover, whom Galeazzo imprisoned for "sleeping with her" and for taking money and table silver from the Fogliani estate.[22]

A Wedding at Court

Galeazzo was capricious and fickle in his interests, frequently restless and easily bored. At the end of January, he declared grandiose intentions to promote music throughout Italy and to collect the peninsula's greatest choir. On February 10, Zaccaria Saggi da Pisa noted that the duke "lives gaily and attends to nothing other than . . . giving himself pleasure and good times by all means and forms for which he has an appetite." Less than a week later, the ambassador wrote that Galeazzo was "in despair, impatient with pleasure and good times, and he says that [the despair] flourishes in him all the more because he does not see that anything can be born in Italy which would give rise to something new."[23]

On February 26, the duke, "disguised in French clothing, together with his friends and *camerieri di camera,* mounted his horse secretly and went to Milan."[24] When he arrived in the capital, he "went to dismount at the Inn of the Well, pretending to be an ambassador of the king of France that had just arrived here. Then he went about the city with three companions, without anyone knowing who he was." The following day he went out once more, but on foot. On his return, he said that if he ever went out in disguise again, he would do so on horseback, "so as not to wear himself out so much."[25]

On the same day, Galeazzo gave orders that a double wedding and a "ladies' party be held in the castle" of Porta Giovia two days later. Cicco Simonetta described the wedding in his diary.

> His Excellency the Lord having decided that Carlino Varesino and Messer Antonietto da Piacenza should take wives, that is, the said Carlino a daughter of Messer Giacomo da Cusano and the said Antonietto a sister of Carlino, today after dinner he had the said brides come here into Porta Giovia Castle, where an infinite number of the city's ladies also attended, as well as many other courtiers and gentlemen. The courtyard next to the Sala Verde was honorably prepared for this solemn festivity with dances and music, etc., in this fashion: about 23 hours, His Excellency the Lord and his Lady had the said brides go into the hall above the Sala Verde, and in the presence of Messer Santo, the Sienese ambassador, who sat on the left hand, on the equal level with the Lord and the most exquisite Lady, who was on the right side, and also the councillors, the said youths were married solemnly, with a ring, etc. His Excellency the Lord held both brides' hands and Messer Agostino Rossi said the words.[26]

This occasion was far grander than the previous month's betrothal of Caterina, although the principals in the wedding were of less exalted rank. The grooms were Galeazzo's *camerieri di camera* Antonietto Arcelli and

Carlino Varesino. Antonietto came from a noble family in Piacenza that had seen better times. Carlino's background can be traced back no farther than one generation: his father and uncle both served in the Sforza administration.[27] Antonietto married Carlino's sister Elisabetta, and Carlino married Maddalena Cusani, daughter of the prominent councillor and jurist Giacomo Cusani. Their lineage boasted both great antiquity and civic distinctions. They also exemplified the professional urban aristocracy. Three of Giacomo's sons followed his footsteps into the law, while one became a physician and another a notary. The head of the family in each generation earned a respected place in the ducal service; Giacomo's father had served as physician to Duke Filippo Maria.[28] In contrast, Carlino appeared to be a parvenu and adventurer of the worst sort. He had been invested with feudal estates barely two years before his wedding and had no hereditary patrimony at all. Carlino's only claim to prominence was his favor with the duke, and his position could not be guaranteed from one day to the next. Giacomo Cusani must have had grave doubts about Carlino's ability to support Maddalena properly.[29]

Galeazzo orchestrated every step of the marriage process. He determined the dowry arrangements and contributed to them himself, thus binding the family relationship of the participants to the relationship between prince and subjects. In making the double match, Galeazzo united his inner circle with the bureaucracy and civic elite of Milan. He also bound members of this intimate circle more closely to one another and to himself. Antonietto was required by the marriage contract to travel with the duke and keep his wife at court (or at least in a commensurate style of life).[30]

Beyond acting as father to both the brides and bridegrooms, the duke also presided over the ceremony himself, with his wife but, apparently, without clergy. The only other active participant mentioned by name was Agostino Rossi, a noble jurist esteemed Milan's best orator. The "words" he spoke were heard by representatives of most elites in the dominion, and the presence of the Sienese ambassador transformed the wedding into an international event. The event also had a light and festive side; Galeazzo staged music and dancing. Seldom did large numbers of women appear in the duke's court, and it was particularly rare to see the ladies and their presumed frivolity juxtaposed with the gravity of the councils of state. Here, though, all were united within the duke's sphere: the wedding was held in the hall closest to the duke's own apartments in Porta Giovia. Galeazzo was lending his *camerieri* considerable honor with this grand occasion.

The Avenues of Honor

In the Renaissance world of political action, honor was the primary currency. The various forms and degrees of honor available in the Sforza dominion reflected that state's heterogeneity. There were powerful mercantile elites, urban professionals, an influential and highly varied feudal nobility, and officeholders in city, state, and church. Each city or district had its own criteria for determining who mattered in the local universe; only at court were these particularist interests consistently integrated. The representation of traditional orders at court was a major concern; precedence and protocol carried great weight, and determining the relative standings of these different elites formed a critical part of the court's function. The order visible in the court went beyond the recapitulation of traditional points of view. A new synthesis was created which sought to balance the legitimate interests of the duchy's elites against the proper functioning of daily life for all and to reinforce the duke's own position as guarantor of his subjects' welfare.

From a certain perspective, few of the duke's subjects were politically significant; the rest lacked adequate honor. Nonetheless, the mass of subjects were not simply forgotten or exploited. Many of Galeazzo's court servants were persons of low birth; for them, the court offered a wonderful opportunity for social mobility and access to favor for self and family. Battista da Cremona, who served as governor to the duke's illegitimate sons Carlo and Alessandro, was "a poor youth burdened with father, mother, brothers, and sisters to marry."[31] His progress in the ducal service came largely as a result of his own merit. Although it is not clear how he arrived at court, he did understand how to take advantage of his good fortune. When Battista made requests for additional income from the duke, Alessandro Sforza supported his appeals.[32]

"There Is Always Less
Suspicion of a Gentleman's Integrity"

In the duchy of Milan, no single social group or community enjoyed a monopoly of honor. Aristocracies of birth held leading positions in both urban and rural society but showed great diversity among themselves. In the rural reaches of the dominion, the traditional orders of medieval society prevailed as they had for centuries. Ludovico della Rocca, "one of the principal gentlemen of Corsica . . . had to marry one of his daughters to a villein [*villano*], which caused him great shame and trouble."[33] Among other problems, he could no longer find good husbands for his other daughters. The duke heard of the problem from the commander of the ducal garrison at Milan, in which Ludovico had just begun to serve. The commander requested a leave of three months for the Corsican to go home and set matters straight, because Ludovico was "noble and useful." The obverse of honor was shame; to cheapen one's nobility by tainting it with villein blood undermined one's honor and interfered with the proper order of life.

The distinction between a person who was noble (*nobile* or *gentile*) and one who was not (*popolare*) could hold great significance, even in a major commercial city. Nobles as a group simply possessed greater honor than non-nobles. For a difficult legal case in Genoa, the duke told his vice-governor to ensure that "those whom the parties shall choose be of noble house, and gentlemen, because there is always less suspicion of a gentleman's [*gentiluomo*] integrity than of a commoner's [*popolare*]."[34] One did not need to bear a feudal title to claim nobility; the tradition of noble families in Lombard cities never ended. Conversely, some fiefs such as Battista da Montignana's Galliate, were "nobile"; others, such as Tommaso Tebaldi's Mandello, were not.[35] In the city of Milan, dozens of families were recognized as noble. Most of them probably had ancient feudal roots, but their noble status in the capital came from inclusion on Archbishop Ottone Visconti's *Matricula Nobilium* of 1277.[36] Because of this list, nobility in the city of Milan was clearly demarcated in theory; those on the list were nobles, and those not on the list were not, regardless of their wealth or political influence.

Persons who were not considered *nobili* were *popolari*. In the latter stages of the Ambrosian Republic, the *popolari* had become impatient with the nobles who had initiated the republic, and a government largely composed of guildsmen had tried to resist Francesco Sforza.[37] The city of Milan did not have a strong tradition of communal identity, which worked to the disadvantage of the *popolari*. The guilds and other institutions that dominated life in many cities were generally overshadowed in Milan by the nobility and the *signori*. Nonetheless, *popolari* could be every bit as wealthy, even politically influential, as nobles. In many situations, no difference was visible between the lives of nobles and of commoners with similar economic resources. In general, wealthy families built grand palaces and lived splendidly.[38] In general, wealthy Milanese were capitalists, noble or not, investing their family wealth in business ventures. During Galeazzo's lifetime, the growth area for investment was the burgeoning luxury cloth industry.[39]

Citizenship and the Professions

Great wealth was the key that opened most doors in a Renaissance city, but political standing and many economic opportunities rested on citizenship. It was difficult to obtain citizenship where one was not a native, and Galeazzo often granted citizenship in a specific city to one of his servants.[40] Even he could not exercise this authority in an unrestrained manner, though, for cities were very jealous of their prerogatives.

An important route to greater honor in cities was office-holding, a hallowed tradition in the Italian civic world. In each city, offices were renewed frequently, and election to office served often as an index of a citizen's respect in the community. Major cities had a strong sense of autonomy, and when communes such as Parma or Genoa sent delegations to treat with the duke or Privy Council, those delegations were treated as embassies from another government.[41] Citizens in the dominion's cities could also gain great honor from membership in one of the professions. Jurists and physicians ranked most highly, with notaries somewhat below them. The colleges of "doctors" (in law or medicine) figured among the most influential bodies in any city, particularly in the university town of Pavia. They were considered true "experts" and flourished in a society plagued by illness and litigation. Most members of these professions were *popolari*, but some of the jurists, and even the occasional physician, came from noble families.[42]

City and Country

The prominent citizens of Milan and most Lombard cities did not live in isolation from the surrounding rural environment. Most noble families held feudal tenures, some quite extensive; the Beccaria family, which dominated politics in Pavia during the fourteenth and fifteenth centuries, was heavily endowed with fiefs to the south and west of their city.[43] Most urban aristocrats wielded more authority in their rural holdings than in the city. It is not surprising that ambitious men such as Vitaliano Borromeo and GianGiacomo Trivulzio sought to transcend the confines of urban politics and establish themselves as rural lords.[44]

The overlap of rural and urban aristocracies in the duchy of Milan operated in both directions. Feudal nobles had a substantial stake in the political systems of certain cities. Urban electoral politics in Parma were dominated by four great landed families: the Pallavicini, Rossi, Sanvitali, and Correggeschi. Not only were the city's four parties (*squadre*) named after their feudal patrons but the city council and other offices were divided to ensure that each of the parties would be equally represented.[45] In Piacenza, a similar domination was exercised by a few local families whose influence carried through from the High Middle Ages to the sixteenth century.[46]

Honor in the Church

Another avenue of honor available to noble and *popolare* alike was the church. Bishops figured among the most influential policymakers in Galeazzo's court, and the duke's personal confessors were always bishops or abbots.[47] Most prelates in the dominion were men who began with social and political advantages, such as Branda Castiglione, bishop of Como and son of a Milanese count. Most secular benefices were in the hands of the local nobility, especially the duke himself. Appointment to the secular clergy was usually the result of political favor. Because the duke of Milan was authorized to provide to benefices within his dominion, he could use church offices as he used those of the civil administration, to reward adherents and solidify his political authority.[48]

Galeazzo could also use his secular authority to support the church's interests on occasion. In 1471, he heard that "our gentlemen and courtiers of the

Porte [in Milan] throw themselves very tepidly" into the "acts and solemnities" of public religious ceremonies such as Corpus Christi. In particular, the duke was concerned that they failed to "pay out promptly and with good spirit and without letting anything lack from what is needed for their portion and jurisdiction, in making processions [*triumphi*] and offering [*oblatione*] continuously." Galeazzo listed two dozen courtiers and other worthies in each of two *Porte,* who were to be prodded for contributions to the upcoming Corpus Christi celebrations.[49] Since the secular arm exercised such a powerful influence over the ecclesiastical establishment, the duke rarely encountered opposition from independent-minded clerics. One exception occurred in 1469, when Galeazzo was enraged to learn that confessors were absolving his toll collectors for embezzling the customs duties. He asked the dominion's bishops to stop that practice, threatening to make up any lost revenues from the benefices of those responsible for the affected areas.[50]

Giovanni Arcimboldi Gets a Red Hat   An illustration of links between secular politics, ecclesiastical honors, and personal favor in the court is the career of the Arcimboldi brothers, Giovanni and Guido Antonio. Their father was a count and Privy Councillor under Duke Francesco. Both sons were courtiers who turned late in life to careers in the church. Giovanni trained as a jurist and studied under Filelfo, among others. When his wife died, Giovanni became an apostolic protonotary and, in 1467, bishop of Novara. As such, he was a valuable diplomatic agent for Galeazzo, who named him to the Privy Council that year.[51]

In May 1473, Giovanni and the archbishop of Milan were elevated to the cardinalate by Sixtus IV as part of the *rapprochement* with Galeazzo. The duke made great play of the honor, which he felt reflected well on him personally. The archbishop was resident in Rome, but Giovanni was very much part of the Milanese court, and Galeazzo saw the new cardinal as an extension of ducal authority and splendor. The duke even sent Carlino Varesino to talk to Giovanni about the new servants the cardinal would hire. Giovanni responded by sending Galeazzo a list of persons being considered for those positions.[52] Initially, the duke wanted the ceremony for Giovanni's elevation to be held at Pavia, where Galeazzo was staying. He commanded that "all those on our council together with all our *gentiluomini* and courtiers that have a salary from us" come to celebrate and accompany the new cardinal and his prince. The duke also gathered all the dominion's bishops together. He requested that the senior bishop (in length of tenure), Giacomo della Torre, sing an Ambrosian Mass for the occasion. When asked, though, Giacomo said he "could not sing either an Ambrosian or Roman Mass, any more than fly," without danger to his life, because of a problem with catarrh that had kept him from singing Mass for fourteen years![53]

Galeazzo was determined that the elevation ceremony be a major social and political event, and it took place in the Duomo of Milan on May 28. The duke could not be present "because of certain important matters"; the councils of state represented the princely authority.[54] Giovanni was escorted from his house to the council chambers by some colleagues from the two councils as well as other courtiers and *magistrati*. At the chambers, the rest of the councillors joined them, and the whole group proceeded to the Duomo next door. The cardinal-elect walked between the next two highest-ranking councillors, the bishops of Parma and Como. Inside the cathedral, Giovanni was seated in the tribunal's seat of honor (generally the place of the duke or his featured guest), accompanied by the councils of state. The two senior bishops again had the most honorable places beside him, along with Tristano Sforza, who often represented the duke's person on ceremonial occasions.

This ceremony was not held solely for the benefit of the ducal family and administration. Seated below the principals were not only courtiers and bureaucrats but also civic worthies—"doctors and merchants." The elevation of a cardinal representing the dominion was an event for all to celebrate. It could benefit everyone to have a Milanese voice heard in the papal Curia, even if Giovanni himself was not Milanese but a native of Parma and his family owed their prominence largely to Duke Francesco's favor. The central part of the ceremony commenced with a Mass sung by the Duomo's archpriest; the archbishop himself remained in Rome. The Mass was followed by a reading of the papal briefs to Galeazzo, Giovanni, and Giacomo della Torre, who was charged with performing the actual "ceremonies which were contained in the instructions sent from Rome." Giovanni put the new cardinal's hat on his back and knelt before Giacomo while "all the words" were said. Then the hat was placed on his head and a choir sang the "Te Deum." After the whole event was completed, the new cardinal "was accompanied solemnly to his house, with trumpeters and pipers, etc."

Cardinal Riario's Visit   In September 1473, only a few months after Giovanni Arcimboldi received his red hat, Galeazzo hosted another cardinal, Pietro Riario. He was Gerolamo's brother and Sixtus IV's favorite ecclesiastical nephew. His Milanese visit complemented Gerolamo's stay earlier in the year and completed some of the unfinished business in the developing Milanese-papal alliance. As a cardinal, Pietro Riario was a prince of the church, and as the pope's nephew, he belonged to one of Italy's ruling dynasties. Galeazzo received him and his retinue of over 220 persons accordingly. The solemn entry of a prince was an occasion of great pomp and magnificence, designed to display the Milanese court and state at their best as well as to provide a fitting reception for the distinguished guests.[55] Characteristically, Galeazzo wanted the arrangements to be perfect without his personal involvement. On September 9, he replied to questions from his steward as to whether "those in the cardinal's party who will eat at court should be served by their own servants or by others. We marvel that you should bother us with such things, which you—who are in charge of this matter—must understand better than we. You will do what you think best, and do not bother us with such trifles."[56]

For Pietro's entry, Galeazzo sent his brother Ludovico, the counts Torelli, and many other gentlemen to greet the approaching cardinal several miles from Milan. The duke then sent the new cardinal Arcimboldi and the Privy Council to meet Pietro a short distance from the capital. Galeazzo himself, accompanied by the Neapolitan ambassador (Antonio Cicinello), "his *magistrati,* courtiers, and *gentiluomini,* who were a great number," met Pietro two miles outside the city. When they made contact, the duke honored his guest by dismounting, and the two principals embraced. Cicinello followed suit. When the whole party remounted to enter the city together, the duke and the ambassador rode in the first rank, while the two cardinals rode together behind them. Pietro rode on the right, the most honorable position. When they entered the city gate, the princely party was accompanied by a solemn procession with a baldacchino, emphasizing the sacral quality of the occasion. They dismounted at the Duomo, "according to the custom of cardinals," then proceeded without the baldacchino to Porta Giovia. Galeazzo accompanied Pietro to the foot of the stairs in the ducal wing, then sent his guest up to his lodgings escorted only by his own traveling company.[57]

Unlike Cardinal Bessarion's visit to Milan in 1472, Pietro's stay was not merely a courtesy visit.[58] The pope's nephew had many important matters to discuss with Galeazzo, and they wasted little time, meeting the next morning after Pietro had taken a walk in the Giardino. In the afternoon, they conferred with Ambassador Cicinello. During the following two days, Pietro met intensively with the duke, Cicinello, and the Privy Council. The cardinal's chambers became the primary venue for diplomatic formalities during this visit. Galeazzo and his guest dined there one evening, joined by two of Pietro's companions, Ludovico Sforza, and a ducal *cameriere di camera.* On another occasion, the duchess made an appearance, respectfully kissing the cardinal's hand. On their last day in Milan (September 16), the two principals dined at midday with Count Giovanni Borromeo.

On September 17, Galeazzo, Pietro, and several courtiers took a boat down the canals from the Giardino in Milan to Pavia Castle, where they stayed for the next three days. On September 18, the duke and cardinal conferred, completing their substantive consultations. On Sunday, September 19, they went in the morning to the cathedral, then to see the galleons at the Arsenal. That afternoon, the visit climaxed with a collective Confirmation ceremony for Galeazzo's legitimate children as well as his illegitimate sons Carlo and Alessandro. Cardinal Riario stood as *compare* for all of them while a bishop performed the ceremony. Early the next morning, Pietro embarked on a boat for Mantua, on his way to Venice and Rome. He "left here well content and satisfied" with the agreements he and the duke had made. Galeazzo gave Pietro personal gifts worth 6,000 ducats, took on the expenses of supporting two condottieri previously paid by the pope, and sold the city and county (*contado*) of Imola to Riario's brother.[59] Many years later, Galeazzo's daughter Caterina earned historical notoriety at the city she received from him at this time.[60]

The Sad Case of Taddeo Manfredi

Galeazzo did not possess the city and county of Imola when his reign began. It was held as a papal fief by the Manfredi family of Faenza, who took over Imola from the Alidosi earlier in the fifteenth century. Members of the Manfredi clan squabbled bitterly over control of Imola, and ultimately they turned to the duke of Milan to settle the dispute. Galeazzo had a personal interest in Imola, because its territories included the Sforza's ancestral home of Cotignola.[61] In general, the Manfredi family had had a friendly and productive relationship with the Sforza. Taddeo attended Galeazzo's Christmas court in 1468, not long before his son Guidaccio married Fiordelisa Sforza. Guidaccio came to live with her in 1469, and in the same period, Taddeo's son Galeazzo Manfredi had become a *cameriere* to the duke. By 1471, the elder Manfredi was receiving a substantial stipend from Milan for himself and Guidaccio. Taddeo was even granted honorary membership on the Privy Council.[62] These honors did nothing to clarify the situation in Imola, but in 1471 the duke was casting covetous eyes on the city for himself. It might be a useful outpost in the Romagna, or even a valuable bargaining chip.

Galeazzo invited the embattled Taddeo to Milan, and the Romagnol lord arrived in January 1472, just after the Christmas season. He brought a company of twenty-five that included his son Galeazzo. As a signorial household, the Manfredi party was received with great honor, and its expenses were fully paid by the ducal treasury.[63] Expense payments were halted in February, but Taddeo continued to receive honorable treatment throughout the year. In April, he joined the duke in receiving Savoyard ambassadors for the feast of San Giorgio; in December, he was numbered among the *signori* who would attend at Christmas. By September, the Manfredi household included two ducal *gentiluomini* assigned to "keep company" with them and maintain liaison with Galeazzo. In November, Taddeo's wife and sisters joined him in Milan.[64]

Honored or not, Taddeo was unhappy as early as February 1472 with Galeazzo's arrangements for his household and with ducal commands to consign Imola to Galeazzo's ambassador in Bologna. The duke chose a Pallavicino noble as the Milanese governor for the city and its *contado*. A year later, that governor was replaced by Taddeo's first *gentiluomo* companion, the only Milanese noble he knew well.[65] In December, Taddeo claimed to be so poor that he had nothing left to sell but two suits, "which I keep back so that I can come be with you [at Christmas]." By 1473, Taddeo had entered a sad limbo. The second *gentiluomo* assigned to his household, Gabriele Stampa, was instructed in March 1473 to "keep His Lordship [of Imola] and his people well disposed." Poor Taddeo was consumed throughout his life with the ambition to control his native city. He longed to escape from the velvet cage of Milan, but the duke's agents remained vigilant. Gabriele was told to keep the closest possible watch on their "guest," not to leave Taddeo alone for long periods, and to check every evening whether Taddeo was preparing to depart from Milan. A ducal secretary monitored Taddeo's mail. Four ducal *camerieri* were assigned to serve him and to take turns sleeping in his house. The duke's fears were well-founded; in early February, Galeazzo Manfredi had fled the duchy with the help of a priest from Faenza.[66]

In May 1473, Taddeo agreed to the formal transfer of Imola to Galeazzo, receiving in exchange the fief of Castelnuovo Terdonese.[67] The transfer did not resolve his awkward position in Milan or lessen his desire to escape. In September, Galeazzo was so anxious Taddeo might flee that he had guards from the Porta Giovia garrison supplement the *camerieri* in Taddeo's household.[68] As a gentleman, Taddeo still had some latitude of action, though. In April 1474, he was permitted to spend Easter at his feudal estate, then to visit his sister in Genoa. Of course, Gabriele Stampa accompanied him.[69]

For the rest of Galeazzo's reign, Taddeo depended on financial support from the duke of Milan, and his situation continued to worsen. By 1474, Taddeo had been deprived of Castelnuovo, and the lesser estates replacing it were endangered by unpaid debts in Imola and Bologna. In 1475, he had to remind the duke to pay his allowance and incomes from feudal possessions. The supplicant pointed out that he needed the money to maintain himself and his children in honorable style.[70] For a few years after 1472, the Manfredi in Milan enjoyed little honor from their ducal hosts. Taddeo and his family became permanent fixtures on the margins of court life. Until 1476, they were not invited to ducal residences for major occasions or daily activities. Taddeo and his wife, Marsobilia, lived in Milan, although in October 1474, he was considering a move to their estate at Cusago. Marsobilia died in 1476, on which occasion Galeazzo sent condolences but offered no memorial.[71]

Guidaccio Manfredi and Fiordelisa Sforza depended wholly on ducal generosity. In 1474, Guidaccio announced to Galeazzo the birth of a ducal niece. Guidaccio lamented that poverty kept him from being able to support the baby and pleaded for help from the duke. The young couple lived a shadowy existence in Milan and outlying towns, never quite a part of the court and always displaced from houses when others needed them. They were housed in Porta Giovia Castle for that birth, and Fiordelisa was permitted a visit by her mother-in-law and the latter's three damsels. In 1475, when Fiordelisa was pregnant again, they were living on Taddeo's estate at Cusago and would have been evicted had not the leaseholders kindly allowed her to stay until she had recovered from childbirth.[72]

"Keeping Company"
with Foreign Dignitaries

When Gabriele Stampa was assigned to serve in Taddeo Manfredi's household, it became his full-time occupation. Gabriele was required to execute commissions for the duke that related to Imola, such as obtaining restitution of money owed to a Milanese man-at-arms by a Jew of Imola. Gabriele's responsibility extended even to resolving domestic disputes in the Manfredi household, such as an argument between Taddeo's seneschal and brother-in-law.[73]

Like his father and brothers, Gabriele was a loyal feudatory and a reliable agent for the Sforza dukes. He served Galeazzo as a customs official, a *commissario,* and above all as a *gentiluomo* in the court. Gabriele specialized in "keeping company" with foreign dignitaries; he was used particularly for Venetian envoys.[74] *Gentiluomini* and *camerieri* who worked as companions performed a variety of functions, especially meeting foreign dignitaries when they arrived, escorting them on tours of Milan or Pavia, and providing liaison with Milanese institutions and resources. These courtiers usually did their work in groups of two to four, but as many as eight *gentiluomini* might be assigned to form the honorable escort for a visitor of high rank. This aspect of court service was vital to creating and maintaining Milan's reputation as a great state and court. This escort duty was a skilled occupation, and few members of the court were considered qualified for it. When Gabriele Stampa was unable to accompany the Venetian ambassador to Vigevano for a meeting with Galeazzo, Giovanni Giapanno chose not to replace him. The seneschal-general sent the envoy with just one other courtier, because "here there is no other person that satisfies me."[75]

Diplomats at the Sforza Court

Since diplomacy was a major component of princely business, diplomatic activity at court never ceased. Galeazzo received new embassies at a rate of at least one per week during the latter years of the reign.[76] The visits of these foreigners followed certain patterns common to diplomatic practice throughout late medieval and Renaissance Europe. The Sforza understood well the importance of diplomacy: Milan was the first state to send a resident ambassador north of the Alps, to France. The Sforza dukes maintained one of the most extensive networks of resident envoys in Italy. Galeazzo kept such ambassadors for all or part of his reign in Rome, Naples, Savoy, Florence, Bologna, France, and Burgundy.[77]

During Galeazzo's reign, several states kept resident ambassadors in Milan. The duke felt mightily offended if states to which he had dispatched envoys did not follow suit. The corps of residents in Milan was led by his main allies, Florence and Naples (replaced in 1475 by Venice). Mantua, Milan's most trusted client state, was represented continuously; the lords of Urbino, Modena/Ferrara, and Montferrat also sent envoys to Milan for varying periods during the reign.[78] These men were based in the capital, where they maintained regular lodgings. Although the ambassadors generally resided in these houses, they were often "on the road," since the duke spent most of his time outside Milan and would summon them for audiences and consultations.[79]

The ambassadors from allied states held a special place in the Milanese court and administration. Because of their friendly status, they were regarded as more than just agents of foreign powers. These envoys consulted regularly with Galeazzo and even met with the Privy Council at times.[80] Their importance went beyond the political realm, into the social; the ambassadors participated in various court activities, depending on their personal qualities and the state they represented. Antonio Cicinello, the Neapolitan ambassador during the later years of the reign, was one of the most visible diplomatic agents in Milan. He appeared at major state occasions, even in a fresco commission for Porta Giovia Castle. Cincinello carried on a very active correspondence with the duke when the two were not meeting in person. Their contact sometimes held great urgency, despite—or because of—the tensions that developed between their states. Cincinello had succeeded his uncle as ambassador to Milan; in turn, he brought his own nephew to meet the duke and spend time at the Sforza court.[81] The Neapolitan was not the only foreign envoy to introduce the next generation of his family into Galeazzo's world; Angelo della Stufa of Florence brought his son Sigismondo there and even told the duke that the young man "would have it most highly dear" to "have from Your Excellency a letter of *familiarità*."[82]

Antonio's intimacy with Galeazzo and his regular inclusion in major public events may have been related to his continuous presence at court. Like most of the princes represented at the court of Milan, the king of Naples kept his envoys there for several years at a time. As a noble from a princely state, Antonio probably shared many of the Milanese court's values. Della Stufa was unusual among the envoys from Florence in his relationship with the duke and court; Galeazzo even knighted him in 1470. Generally, the Florentine representatives were active in their business dealings with the duke but not socially prominent at court. They were not nobles, and their civic ideology discouraged emulation of the extravagant behavior appropriate to the second estate. Moreover, Florence rotated her ambassadors frequently. Most of them served more than one stint in Milan, which was Florence's closest ally following the Peace of Lodi.[83]

One of the functions of resident ambassadors was to evaluate the Milanese court and administration. The most sensitive material was usually presented to their principals personally, when the diplomats returned to their native states, or passed along orally through messengers and special envoys. Nevertheless, the ambassadors' letters to their princes often contained surprisingly frank observations and appraisals. The outspokenness of these letters is particularly striking given that Milanese agents could intercept the correspondence. One of the most scathing indictments of Galeazzo's policy that survives from his time is a copy the Privy Chancery made of a letter apparently written by a Neapolitan diplomat to Urbino's ambassador.[84]

Modern studies of diplomacy in this period have emphasized the emergence of resident ambassadors, but only a few states actually maintained them. Galeazzo transacted most of his diplomatic business with special ambassadors who were sent for limited visits with specific agendas. Cicco Simonetta's diary records embassies from more than forty different princes, republics, and major figures during the years 1473 to 1476, ranging from the queen of Cyprus to the city of Parma, from the Swiss League to the "Great Sultan" of Egypt and Syria.[85]

Protocol and Language

Galeazzo had a keen sense of social distinctions. Being correct in his formal behavior was a matter of some importance, especially insofar as it reinforced his princely dignity. The duke always used the imperial plural in his own communications, except when addressing persons of superior rank. He employed the forms of address appropriate to his correspondents: for lesser or younger persons, the familiar *tu*; for prestigious persons, the neutral *voi*; and for parents, popes, and kings, the respectful *lei*.[86]

The Privy Chancery maintained a scrupulously correct titulary, carefully weighing terms of respect and intimacy.[87] Members of the ducal lineage— even a nun—were termed "affine" (*affinis*). Other major correspondents were addressed by honorific words ranging from "like a father" (*tanquam pater*) for kings and Ludovico Gonzaga to "friend" (*amicus*) for certain Italian nobles and the archbishop of Canterbury. The duke of Burgundy was addressed as "blood kin" or "brother" (*consanguineus*), the lord of Albania as "despot" (*despotus*). Some persons were "lord" or "lady" (*dominus, domina*), others merely "magnificent" (*magnificus*) or "admirable" (*spectabile*). The criteria for differentiation could be subtle; Lorenzo de' Medici was addressed as "magnificus," his brother Giuliano as "spectabile." The Malaspina marquesses of Verrucola and Fosdenovo were honored with "magnificus"; the Malaspina marquesses of Villafranca and Mulazzo received the less prestigious "spectabile." These careful distinctions were structured into Milanese diplomatic practice. A councillor sent to greet the emperor in 1468 carried with him an all-purpose introduction kit, including three letters identical in content but differing in forms of address: one each for superiors, peers, and inferiors.[88]

It was crucially important that each person receive the honor he or she was due, and forms of address were important within the court. Correspondence always reflected the relative standings of the persons involved. The duke himself was addressed by his servants as "Most Illustrious and Excellent Lord," or some variation on it. In closing, they would "humbly recommend" themselves to him and sign themselves, "Most Faithful Servant Of Your Most Excellent and Illustrious Lordship." Only a few writers went to the lengths of calling themselves a "true and sincere servant and slave of Your Excellency," or, at the most extreme, "your dog and slave."[89] When referred to in the third person, Galeazzo was normally termed "Our Most Illustrious Lord."[90] Cicco Simonetta was usually addressed as "Magnificent Lord" or "Magnificent Knight," with a flattering "most honored" or "most respected" prefixed. His subordinates and other lesser officers might call him "father" and "benefactor" as well. Other councillors could term him "like a brother." His actual brother Giovanni addressed him as "Magnificent knight, most honored brother." The treasurer-general was addressed as "Admirable and most honored, like an older brother" by lesser ducal officers.[91]

For personal meetings between persons of rank and dignity, gracious words were *de rigueur,* and appropriate gestures also contributed to affirming relationships. "Touching the hand" (*toccare la mano*) was the standard greeting between persons who were not intimate, conveying respect and acceptance. Embraces or kisses were reserved for persons with a more intimate relationship—or for those with whom one wished to visibly establish a closer bond. When Bona was fooled into greeting Galeazzo as if he were Sforza Maria, she simply touched his hand until she realized he was actually her husband.[92]

"He Created 100 Courtiers"
(Christmas 1473)

In the court of Milan, the year 1473 featured several festive occasions with political overtones, and Galeazzo ended it with a Christmas celebration that was even larger than the previous one. The foreign dignitaries invited this time included the noble condottieri Giovanni Battista Anguillara, Roberto da Sanseverino, Niccolò Mauruzzi da Tolentino, and Giovanni Conti. Conti, who had also attended in 1472, was lodged (by ducal command) at the house of Count Pietro dal Verme. The year before, Pietro had hosted Giovanni

Bentivoglio with a household of 70 to 80 persons. This time, Galeazzo reassured him, he would be inconvenienced less; Conti's party numbered only 20 to 25. The guests were asked to arrive six days before Christmas "with not too many horses."[93] That limitation was well considered. On another occasion, the seneschals had reminded Galeazzo "that in this city, when it is at the best it can be, there are not [many] lodgings capable of holding 30 or 40 horses."[94]

The ceremonial observances in 1473 were unusually open to large groups of the duke's elite subjects. The Ciocco on Christmas Eve was celebrated in the large Sala Verde of Porta Giovia Castle, attended by Galeazzo, his wife, all his children and brothers, an unspecified number of feudatories, and "many noble ladies of this city." On Christmas Day, the duke heard the usual Masses in his chapel with his brothers, councillors, feudatories, and *gentiluomini*. Among the usual consultations, negotiations, and administrative actions of the Christmas season, Galeazzo spent part of Christmas Eve closeted with councillors and the ambassador from Naples. On the day after Christmas, he received an envoy from the condottiere Antonello Ordelaffi. On December 27, Galeazzo created a committee of eight distinguished men to investigate problems in Genoa. On December 30, he received envoys with the payment from Rome for the city of Imola. The envoys also gave the duke gifts of birds, fruit, and jewels.[95]

All of these activities were fairly typical of the Christmas observances at Galeazzo's court, but he invited more people to join him at Christmas in 1473 than in any other year. In addition to hosting princes, condottieri, and the usual crowd of ducal dependents, he considerably expanded the court itself.

> At Christmas of the year 1474 [O.S.], he created 100 courtiers with an allowance of 100 ducats per year, and among them was my father. Forty of these he gave to the duchess; they were dressed in dark red velvet, and his own in crimson.[96]

Corio saw this event from the inside, as his father, Marco, was promoted from the post of *cameriere* to the more honorable and lucrative office of *gentiluomo*. The "courtiers" Corio describes were, in fact, all *gentiluomini*. In October, the duke had ordered a committee from the Privy Council to find "in our dominion 100 gentlemen apt for the court." The five councillors making the selections all had extensive experience with the Sforza court, including Tommaso Tebaldi, Pietro Pusterla, and ducal cousins Lancillotto del Maino and Pietro Francesco Visconti.[97] Until this time, the ducal *gentiluomini* had numbered around thirty-three during Galeazzo's reign, as they apparently had in his father's time. That number was quite substantial, but tripling it gave the duke of Milan an enormous reservoir of honorable men from which he could ornament his court. The forty-one *gentiluomini* assigned to his wife constituted a remarkably large and distinguished group; they included ten courtiers who had previously been (and continued to be) among Galeazzo's *gentiluomini*. These courtiers were an expensive investment, as Corio indicates. The duke did indeed allot each of these *gentiluomini* a salary of 100 ducats, resulting in a total annual outlay of 10,000 ducats—three times the previous level.[98]

This addition to the active courtiers paralleled Galeazzo's expansion of other ducal offices, such as the councils of state, masters of revenues, kennelmen, and musicians. In this case, the duke had an important political purpose.

> Because of the death of the aforementioned Cardinal [Riario], Galeazzo Sforza felt strong unhappiness, seeing all his plans cut in half and knowing that, because of his greatness of spirit, not only were some Italian rulers angrily against him but Charles, duke of Burgundy, also threatened him. Because of this, he sought as much as was possible to gain the friendship of many leading men of his cities.[99]

In reality, the situation was not quite as Corio painted it here; Cardinal Riario did not die until January 5, 1474, months after the duke had decided to create new courtiers. Nonetheless, Galeazzo was clearly looking for support through representation from the leading lineages of his dominion. He also instructed the committee of councillors not to choose too many men from "any single family" (*una medesima casa*). Only two surnames appear more than three times, with the largest contingent being from the Visconti: six, half of them new creations. The Crivelli were the only other family honored with three new nominations; they had previously boasted one member among the *gentiluomini*.

The councillors choosing these courtiers were probably encouraged to balance the geographic distribution as well. One list explicitly classifies the one hundred *gentiluomini* by city of origin.[100] The majority of them were residents of Milan itself; among the thirty-two "old" courtiers, only ten came from districts outside the capital: Lodi (2), Novara (1), Pavia (5), and Parma (2). Of the sixty-eight new creations, thirty originated from places other than Milan.[101] At this time, the duke honored all of the major districts in his dominion, with at least three courtiers selected from each of the areas not previously tapped: Alessandria, Como, Cremona, and Genoa. Pavia contributed six of the new *gentiluomini,* making a total of eleven from the duchy's second city.

On the whole, these courtiers were quite a distinguished lot. The lists of *gentiluomini* from this time indicate twenty-two knights and four counts among the one hundred men. Very few of the *gentiluomini* could be considered the heads of their respective lineages, though. Most were chosen from among the brothers and sons of "leading men of his cities." Some, such as Marco Corio and Giorgio Marliani, were ducal servants who had demonstrated their competence to the duke as well as their honorable ancestry.

Others, such as Giovanni Andrea Lampugnani and Gerolamo Olgiati—long since returned from his adventure with Colleoni—were brothers and sons of respected ducal servants.[102]

Alessandro Castiglione, selected as a new *gentiluomo* for Bona at this time, was an ideal nominee, a solidly respectable Milanese noble. He and his brothers had participated in the Ambrosian Republic, then the Sforza administration. Alessandro served under both Duke Francesco and Duke Galeazzo as a fiscal official and podestà in several ducal cities.[103] The story of his early years as a courtier illustrates the disparate—and sometimes conflicting—interests of the ducal court, civil administration, local citizens, and family. In December 1473, Alessandro was completing a two-year term as podestà and *commissario* of Pontremoli. Tax farming was a thriving business in the dominion, and the office of *podestà* was one of the most widely farmed. In some cities, such as Pontremoli, that office was combined with the ducal office of *commissario*. The more vital ducal offices, such as those of *commissario* or *referendario* in a major city, were carefully distributed to competent and reliable administrators. On December 12, 1474, the duke commanded Alessandro "to come to Milan this next Christmas, since we have made you our courtier," but insisted that the new courtier stay in Pontremoli until his office had been properly audited. That auditing procedure was followed for all ducal officials leaving an office that bore financial responsibilities; it ensured that their books balanced and that they had not looted the public treasury. Galeazzo would not waive the audit even for a noble whom he had just created a courtier.

In the meantime, Alessandro was chosen for a two-year term as podestà of Novara. Because his audit dragged on longer than expected, he could not take up the new post immediately. Instead, he sent his son Giovanni Antonio to exercise the new office while the audit was completed on the old one.[104] The audit was resolved without further complications, but Alessandro still found himself with two new positions, as the duchess's *gentiluomo* and podestà of Novara. Bona's *gentiluomini* were generally resident at court, and the duke himself may have encouraged Alessandro to stay near his person. Whatever the reason, over the next eight months, Alessandro lived mainly at court, while his son served in Novara for him.

This irregular situation could not continue; the duke had Cicco call Alessandro in to correct it. The new courtier protested that he had ducal permission for this arrangement but agreed to reside in Novara, going to Milan only "at Christmas and those times that the courtiers are obligated" to do so.[105] The good people of Novara liked his son's work, though, and Alessandro never did take up his office of podestà. In December 1475, Galeazzo commended Giovanni Antonio's achievements and awarded him the standard of the city as well as other marks of recognition. Five days before Christmas that year, the duke gave Giovanni Antonio—"podestà of that city of ours,

Novara"—permission to come to Milan and convalesce from an unspecified physical ailment. With some irony, Galeazzo commanded that Alessandro take his son's place in Novara until the latter's final audit was completed. Shortly afterward, in an unusual move, the duke removed Alessandro from Bona's court and made him a ducal *cameriere di camera*.[106]

Alessandro was not the only courtier who also held an office in the peripheral administration. Francesco Birago, also a *gentiluomo* created at Christmas 1473, later found that he needed additional income. He asked Galeazzo's brother Ludovico to make him captain of Domodossola, over which Ludovico had jurisdiction. Once granted that post, Francesco asked Galeazzo if he should take up residence there, promising, "I will always find myself at Milan at the feast of [Your Lordship]"—San Giuseppe—"and at the Birth of Our Lord"—Christmas—"and so many times as would be necessary."[107]

"We Will . . . Give Them All Good Treatment According to Their Rank"

He also chose 100 *camerieri,* which were also dressed by the magnanimous duke, with a salary of 100 florins per year. Twenty of these he kept close to him, so that they would follow him wherever he went, and to them he provided 80 ducats per year, beyond 25 ducats which he gave them for a horse. Among their number was myself, Bernardino Corio, the present author, at the age of fourteen years.[108]

On December 9, 1473, Galeazzo sent a letter to the ducal governor of every major district in the dominion, announcing that "if in that our city there be some youths, sons of gentlemen," who "might wish to come stay with us . . . they should come to us at this next Christmas feast."[109] He had in mind to create new *camerieri* along with the new *gentiluomini.* When Corio's father became a *gentiluomo,* the historian-to-be became a *cameriere,* although only fourteen years of age. Galeazzo also sent a *sottocameriere* to Naples to recruit a dozen *camerieri* there. By early 1474, Galeazzo had boosted the number of *camerieri* from 53 to 126, a massive increase.[110]

Galeazzo deliberately ornamented his court with young men of noble family. His reputation as a great prince benefited from their presence in his household. In addition to the Bolognese Marescotti and Malvezzi, he had among his *camerieri* a Caracciolo from Naples and one of the Strozzi from that family's Mantuan branch. Among the new selections at Christmas 1473 was Marcello Colonna, from the great Roman family. However, the duke's primary focus was on the "leading men of his cities," and these domestic elites provided most of his *camerieri.* Galeazzo drew from the Pallavicini, Rossi, Malaspina, Visconti, Castiglione, Rusca, Beccaria, Anguissola, and other dominant noble families.

Inducements were needed to bring "sons of gentlemen" to the court and keep them there. In his announcement of December 9, Galeazzo promised that "if they should please and satisfy us, we will . . . give them all good treatment according to their rank and condition."[111] Like the *gentiluomini,* these *camerieri* constituted a substantial investment. Corio's figures are at least partially confirmed by a document from spring 1474 which shows one man receiving "80 ducats a year as have the new *camerieri* who follow the court."[112]

A list drawn up in January 1474 shows thirty-four *camerieri fuori di camera* deputed to accompany the duke (plus another thirty-four *camerieri di camera* and *di guardacamera*). Among the *camerieri fuori di camera,* all but four men were marked 60 (ducats, presumably); two others were marked 70 and 80, respectively. The grand total for the thirty-four men in this one category was exactly 2,000 ducats. A separate list shows how much the *camerieri di camera* and *di guardacamera* would be paid; the respective totals were 2,900 and 1,910 ducats. Thus, in all, these sixty-eight *camerieri* traveling with the duke would cost 6,810 ducats annually in salary alone, plus maintenance expenses.[113] In addition, dozens of *camerieri fuori di camera* were paid to stay in Milan. The scope of the duke's creation of new courtiers at this Christmas is reflected in the financial figures. Altogether, the 168 *gentiluomini* and *camerieri* whose salaries are specified would cost the ducal treasury 16,810 ducats per year, fully 5 percent of budgeted expenditures for the entire dominion in 1473. The expense was worthwhile to Galeazzo if he could gain the friendship of his leading subjects and the respect of his peers.

The Infant Bianca is Betrothed

Because Galeazzo needed friends to help stabilize his political and diplomatic situation, he filled the court that Christmas with hundreds of new faces from within and outside his dominion. In mid-December, Iolande, duchess of Savoy and regent for her eight-year-old son, sent two ambassadors to Milan. On December 17, they arrived at Vigevano to see Galeazzo "and hear the order and form which will be used around the act of marriage [*parentado*] that will be done at Milan during the Christmas season, between the daughter of the Lord and the duke Filiberto, duke of Savoy."[114]

Galeazzo invited almost 150 members of the court of Savoy to help him finish the Christmas season on this positive note. A year earlier, he had betrothed his eldest illegitimate daughter to the pope's nephew. Now he was publicly committing his eldest legitimate daughter to a far more important match. Little Bianca was still an infant—under two years old—at this time, but she already bore a great diplomatic value to her ambitious father. The Visconti-Sforza tradition of marrying into the house of Savoy had a sound practical basis, given Savoy's strategic position between Milan and France. Galeazzo had wed Filiberto's aunt, and the duke's grandfather and great-

great-grandfather had also married Savoyards. Relations between Savoy and Milan had often been thorny, but the close dynastic link between Savoy and France led Galeazzo to improve relations with his western neighbor. The need to do so seemed particularly acute as Charles the Bold cast covetous eyes across the Alps, trying to create a kingdom for himself. One of Charles's hopes was to persuade Emperor Frederick III to grant him the ancient Carolingian crown of Italy, a title traditionally bestowed in Milan itself.

About 150 members of the Savoyard court and nobility arrived on New Year's Eve to join in the last week of Christmas festivities, culminating in the betrothal.[115] They were led by the bishops of Turin and Vercelli, the marshal of Savoy, the governor of Nice, and the president of Turin. Galeazzo met them outside the city gates, "accompanied honorably by all the council, courtiers, and gentlemen, and by the illustrious brothers of our most illustrious Lord." The Milanese contingent escorted their guests to their lodgings at the Corte Arengo. Later, the ambassadors joined Galeazzo and his court at Porta Giovia Castle to celebrate the Ciocco, then returned to the Corte. The New Year began in 1474 with the ambassadors from Savoy joining the duke at Porta Giovia. They were accompanied by the councillors and other gentlemen. Galeazzo went to the entrance of the Sala Verde to greet them, then the whole group mounted up and rode to the Duomo to hear Mass "with all the feudatories, *gentiluomini,* courtiers, and *camerieri.*" Afterward, the envoys returned to Porta Giovia and dined formally with the duke. That evening, Cicco Simonetta went quietly to the Corte to arrange the form of the marriage contract with the Savoyards. He went back two days later to complete those arrangements.

The betrothal ceremony took place at dusk on Epiphany (January 6). For the Milanese, the persons in attendance included the duke, duchess, and ducal children, Galeazzo's full brothers and three half-brothers, the Neapolitan ambassador, "all" the feudatories, councillors and magistrates, *gentiluomini, camerieri,* and "an infinite number of ladies." The bishop of Turin gave an oration in Latin "by which he demonstrated with what sincerity and affection" Iolande of Savoy agreed to this marriage alliance. Galeazzo responded in Italian, and the solemnities were appropriately balanced with banquets and entertainments.[116] As the ceremony began in the Sala Verde of the castle, the iron "key" of the ceiling vault fell. The crowd emptied out into the courtyard and completed the ceremony in the cold of the winter evening. It must have seemed a grim omen.[117]

Making Knights   The last part of the betrothal solemnities extended the political significance of the occasion even further: "After the above-mentioned contract was made and celebrated, the Lord made knights." Such ceremonial knightings by the duke were not common in the Sforza period;

they occurred generally at events of paramount significance, such as Duke Francesco's accession in 1450.[118] In the late Middle Ages, knighthood was one of the most important marks of social distinction, and knighting was one of the most solemn of all ceremonies. Galeazzo's court was not a chivalric paradise; nonetheless, in Sforza Milan, knighthood was one of the few marks of distinction always recognized in formal proceedings and usually on administrative lists (denoted by the prefix "d." for "dominus"). Even when the duke's intimates were called by diminutives, their knightly status was acknowledged.[119] When the duke outfitted his intimates before Christmas 1472, he distinguished the knights among them by dressing them in gold brocade, and the others in silver.[120] Knights were referred to as "gilded" because of the golden spurs traditionally given with the honor.

By the fifteenth century, only sovereign monarchs—kings, emperors, and popes—were juridically entitled to "make" or "create" knights, although originally any knight could do so.[121] Galeazzo created knights without any apparent qualms, or explicit objections from others, about his apparent lack of credentials. He held himself to be a sovereign prince and behaved as such; in doing so, he was following the lead of his father, who had knighted a group of prominent Milanese nobles when entering the ducal office.[122]

Knighting was a special sign of ducal favor, a reward rarely granted, and all the more precious for that. Bianca's betrothal was the only occasion on which Galeazzo made knights *en masse*. His penchant for numbering by dozens led him to choose twelve men for this special honor.[123] The list of recipients reflected his effort to gain support from various elites. The first on the list was his own natural son Alessandro, the second Giuliano Anguillara, son of a leading Roman condottiere in Milanese service. Half of the recipients were members of the ducal household: four *camerieri di camera,* one *cameriere di guardacamera,* and a seneschal. All but one belonged to very distinguished Italian noble families, including the Bevilacqua, Caraccioli, Colonna, Del Carretto, Malaspina, and Pallavicini. The exception was Galeazzo's *cameriere di camera* Carlino Varesino. The last three men on the list were scions of the dominion's nobility, among them Giberto Borromeo, whom Galeazzo would try to bring into his household the following year.[124] By Galeazzo's own admission, Marcello Colonna was knighted in order to draw stronger support from his branch of the Colonna clan.[125] The duke probably had similar motives for honoring the sons of Giovanni Battista Anguillara, Giovanni Borromeo, Manfredo Landi, and Pietro Pusterla.[126]

Galeazzo also knighted other individuals during the course of his reign. In 1470, the honor was extended to the ambassador from Florence, Angelo della Stufa. That envoy was very unwilling to receive a knighthood, although it is not clear whether his hesitancy sprang from diplomatic considerations or the effects on his standing in Florence.[127]

Altogether, Bianca Sforza's betrothal must have struck participants and observers as an event of great importance to duke and duchy. For the girl herself, the event was not so important; she continued to live as one of the Sforza children, traveling with her brothers from castle to castle, looked after by a governor and a wet nurse.[128]

Marriage as Ducal Policy

Marriage played a vital role in social relations within the Milanese court. Even outside the circles of his family and intimate companions, Galeazzo considered the marriages and betrothals of his servants and subjects to be worthy of his attention and participation. In the ten years of his reign, he arranged, approved, or intervened in hundreds of them.

Marriages in the Ducal Family

Because Galeazzo did not want his close male relatives to pose a threat to the unity of his dominion, he allowed none of them to marry and create a cadet branch during his reign. However, female members of the family were exploited for their political value as marriage partners to princes. In a period of five years, the duke arranged marriages for two sisters into the ruling families of Montferrat and Imola and betrothals of two daughters into the ruling families of Rome and Savoy.

Marriage Strategies and Princely Authority

Marriage played an important role in family strategies for all members of the Sforza court.[129] Unlike conditions in Renaissance republics, it was not sufficient for a prominent family to ally itself with peers and counterparts. In a princely state, the greatest political and economic clout rested in the hands of the prince. Thus, the criteria for advancement often depended on an authority that most families could not influence. The duke became a player in the marriage negotiations of any individual or family whom he deemed sufficiently important or interesting.

In most cases, Galeazzo's hand fell lightly on prospective marriages, merely approving arrangements already made by the parties involved. He did not approve all of them, though; courtiers and nobles learned to ask permission before planning a wedding. The duke sometimes stepped in entirely on his own initiative to discourage or facilitate certain matches. Often, he intervened at the request of one of the parties. In roughly one-third of the cases, the duke himself was largely responsible for making the arrangement.

Galeazzo's first matchmaking venture dates from 1467, before he himself was married. He complained, "I do not understand these matters of marriages [*parentadi*]," and the effort failed.[130] By the last years of his reign, Galeazzo had become practiced and confident. Every social group was subject to his attentions, from his own sisters to his wife's stablehands, from local merchants to ducal pages.

Most of Galeazzo's attention went to nobles and ducal servants. Assistance with marriages was one of the duke's most effective vehicles for rewarding and supporting persons he considered loyal, useful, or deserving. In September 1474, he stepped in on behalf of his auditor-general and councillor, Lorenzo Terenzi da Pesaro. Lorenzo was having difficulties with the Milanese nobleman who was about to become his new son-in-law. The nobleman had failed to "adorn and clothe said bride-to-be, as is the custom of Milan," once the full dowry had been paid by the bride's father. Galeazzo commanded that the groom-to-be pay without argument or penny-pinching "as is done . . . between persons of similar quality and rank."[131]

"A Fine Dowry and a Beautiful Damsel"   One revealing case of ducal matchmaking involved Luigi Castiglione, whose distant cousin Baldassare later wrote the definitive book on the gentleman courtier. Luigi had been a ducal *gentiluomo* for barely two months when he concluded a marriage agreement in February 1474. His prospective mother-in-law was Countess Orsina Sanvitale, widow of a major feudatory from Parma. Luigi dutifully went to the Lomellina, seeking approval from the duke, and he received it on February 19. However, even as the courtier was returning to Milan, Galeazzo changed his mind. He wrote to Giovanni Simonetta in the capital, notifying Luigi that approval had been withdrawn.[132]

The duke did more than simply cancel Luigi's plan; Galeazzo proposed a match with one Elisabetta Malletta. The duke deputed Giovanni Simonetta to see the match through; after some initial hesitation from Luigi, agreement was reached. On February 23, Giovanni drew up a marriage contract with a dowry of 4,500 florins, plus 1,000 florins for clothing and shoes. When the contract was completed, the secretary reported Luigi's pleasure at acquiring "a fine dowry and a beautiful damsel." On February 26, Luigi himself wrote to Galeazzo with a notable display of obsequious gratitude.[133]

The Castiglione family claimed a prominent position among the Milanese nobility. Luigi's father, Guarnerio, had been an imperial Count Palatine, a member of the Privy Council, and a military captain of distinction. Guarnerio himself had married the daughter of the great condottiere Carmagnola, and the marriages of his children show a clear pattern of links with leading feudal and military families.[134] Luigi's proposed Sanvitale match fit well with this pattern, but his marriage to Elisabetta did not maintain the tradition. The Malletta family originated in Montferrat; they had neither a long history as landed nobility in the duchy of Milan nor a strong military heritage.

Galeazzo was not unwilling to join the Castiglione and Sanvitale families in marriage. A month after Luigi had first approached him, the duke had Giovanni Simonetta persuade Luigi's brother to complete the match Luigi was forced to relinquish.[135] Galeazzo had canceled Luigi's match as a favor to Giovanni Pallavicino di Scipione, who was a councillor, major feudatory, military commander, and vice-governor of Genoa. The reasons he wanted Luigi's marriage quashed are obscure, although one of Giovanni's own daughters married a Sanvitale in 1475. In February 1474, the duke proposed another marriage between the Pallavicini and a major feudal family. He asked Maddalena Torelli to marry her second daughter to Giovanni Manfredo Pallavicino because he was "from a good family, had much property, is virtuous, thoroughly noble and good [tutto gentile e da bene], and pleasing to us."[136]

The Pallavicini di Scipione were also connected to the Malletta through one of Giovanni's daughters. She married Elisabetta's brother Pietro Maria, a ducal gentiluomo. The Malletta marriages of this generation owed much to ducal patronage; sister Antonia also married a ducal gentiluomo. In all probability, Galeazzo played such a dominant role because the family lacked a traditional base in the duchy. Their father was a count from Astì who settled in the western part of the Sforza dominion.[137]

The duke's intervention in Luigi Castiglione's match was peremptory and autocratic, but he displayed some respect for his courtier. The use of the ducal secretary Giovanni Simonetta as go-between shows that the matter was considered a function of statecraft, not merely a domestic affair. It also shows that Galeazzo did not intend to dirty his own hands with the details. He remained on a hunting trip while the matter was resolved.

"He Does Not Have Enough Property to Merit the Girl"   Not all ducal matchmaking efforts involved important personages. Giuliano da Robiano, Pa sottocameriere, was the nephew of a cameriere di camera. Although he was reared around the court, his family had little social standing and left few family records.[138] Nevertheless, Galeazzo favored the youth and tried several times to create a marriage for him. The first effort involved an affluent Milanese citizen with a nubile daughter; he rejected the match. A year later, Galeazzo tried again, this time suggesting a girl whose father had recently died. The effort failed, primarily because the girl was only six years old. The enraged duke prohibited her from ever marrying, although he later relented.[139] Galeazzo then tried a different match, to no better end. The prospective bride's mother and grandfather protested that the girl was only four years old, that she was too closely related to Giuliano, and that in any case the young man "does not have enough property to merit the girl" and wanted her solely for her money.[140]

They were absolutely right. At least two of the heiresses Galeazzo tried to procure for Giuliano stood far above the youth in rank and far below him in age. Unlike Luigi Castiglione, the principals in these cases were not addressed as persons of substance, nor were they contacted through a figure like Giovanni Simonetta. In all three cases, the duke's efforts failed to bring about the desired matches, and he did not use heavy coercion to enforce them. Neither Giuliano nor his prospective brides swung great political weight, and the *sottocameriere* was not one of the duke's particular favorites. The greater Galeazzo's emotional and political investment, the more pressure he applied.

A Visit from the King of Denmark

After the Savoyards left Milan, it was not long before Galeazzo had another opportunity to welcome an important personage and display his own magnificence. In mid-February 1474, Galeazzo received a message from King Christian I of Denmark. The king, who was brother-in-law to the marchioness of Mantua (Barbara Hohenzollern of Brandenburg), was making a trip to Mantua and Rome and wanted to stop for a visit in Milan. It was not the first message Galeazzo had ever received from Christian; in 1469, the king had requested a suit of armor for his own person. The duke had ordered one from Milan's best armorer, Antonio Missaglia, and had paid for it.[141]

Galeazzo received few guests whose personal dignity was superior to his own, and Christian was the first reigning sovereign to visit during his reign. The duke leaped immediately into action, mobilizing "all the newly made *gentiluomini, camerieri,* and most honorable feudatories to honor His Majesty." He also volunteered his brothers and half-brothers Ascanio, Filippo, Polidoro, and Tristano, who could be sent wherever the seneschals thought they were needed.[142] When Galeazzo received Christian, he staged a splendid entry that honored both the visiting monarch and native elites. During the course of the royal visit, Galeazzo gave more, displayed more, and did more honor to Christian than to any other person who visited during his reign.[143] Four councillors, ten *gentiluomini,* and two ducal brothers escorted Christian on his progress from the Venetian border to a town near Milan. Galeazzo arrived nearby, accompanied by "the most worthy of his feudatories" and his *camerieri di camera.* The duke dismounted and embraced the king, then spoke to him in "beautiful words" (through an interpreter).

After this generous greeting, the two rulers rode to Milan, "accompanied by all the court in the grandest order, that was a stupendous thing to see." The two courts proceeded in the following order: servants of *gentiluomini, camerieri, gentiluomini* (with trumpeters alongside the horses), the Privy Council, ducal brothers, king and duke, king's retinue, and Galeazzo's one hundred mounted crossbowmen. On their way to the city gate, they passed the ducal falconers with falcons in hand and a panther with its ducal keeper. The road was lined with onlookers; councillors, *gentiluomini*, feudatories, and other courtiers were stationed all along the route. Outside the gate, Ascanio and Sforza Maria were posted with a crowd of gentlemen and *camerieri*. They presented Christian with the keys to the city, offering him "their persons, the state, and all rights" in addition. This act of courtesy made their home symbolically his home and recognized the king's superiority.

The next stage of the entry added a sacral element to this princely hospitality. Only the innermost circles of the princely households—Christian's retinue and twelve to sixteen ducal *camerieri di camera*—actually accompanied their principals into the city. At the gate, these special few were greeted with a baldacchino; before stepping under it, Galeazzo and Christian genuflected and kissed the Cross. The solemn procession that followed featured regular clergy with "all the relics that they have," while groups of prestigious Milanese laymen bore the great canopy in relays. At the Duomo, the company left the baldacchino.[144] Galeazzo and Christian entered the cathedral, repeating their genuflection at the high altar. The archpriest and ordinary of the Duomo then said "the necessary solemnity and oration," and a "Te Deum" was sung, enlisting divine sanction for the king's visit.

After the benediction, Galeazzo escorted Christian across the piazza to the Corte Arengo. Having introduced the king to the politically and spiritually active segments of his community, the duke now brought Christian into an elaborated version of his domestic sphere. Bona greeted the king inside the palace, accompanied by her three children and 150 ladies from court and city. The two retinues then accompanied the king to his chambers, in which Duke Francesco had resided. The chambers were "prepared and put in order not otherwise than if the Pope or the Emperor were coming there" and as richly furnished for the occasion "as is done at the feast of Christmas." Galeazzo even had an altar installed for Christian's use; it was decorated as lavishly as the duke's own.[145] Having done everything possible to honor this solemn occasion, Galeazzo left his guest and returned to Porta Giovia Castle.

Because King Christian's visit was primarily social, affairs of state occupied little of the time the two princes spent together.[146] The morning after the king's arrival, Galeazzo went to his lodgings and brought him back to Porta Giovia, where they dined and exchanged gifts. The duke's contributions included two mules and a sapphire worth more than 1,200 ducats. Galeazzo also showed off his chapel and choir at Mass; the chapel was "prepared worthily and furnished with many good singers in perfection that was a thing most worthy of any great lord and king." The following day (March 16), Galeazzo gave his guest an exhibition of hunting with hounds, falcons, and a female panther. The king greatly enjoyed this morning of noble recreation. In the afternoon, the duke offered Christian a riding tour around the city, which he displayed proudly, crowning the itinerary with a stop at Antonio

Missaglia's shop.[147] On the morning of March 17, the king went to Porta Giovia, accompanied by Galeazzo's brothers and other courtiers. The duke used this occasion to show off the Giardino, his prime hunting venue. Later that day, the princes and their retinues (including the duke's brothers) traveled by boat to Pavia, where Galeazzo staged a display of tennis. According to Corio, the duke showed his guest the ducal treasury, library, and reliquary.

A guest's departure, while by no means as important as his arrival, was always acknowledged ceremoniously, with an emphasis on the duke's lavish generosity. Christian and his company of 141 persons took their leave on March 18. The duke escorted the king from Pavia Castle to the embarkation point for Mantua, which Christian would reach on the Milanese ducal river galley (*bucintoro*). Galeazzo gave everyone in the royal party gifts of gold brocade and velvet, graduated according to the rank of the recipients. The two princes parted on extremely cordial terms, and Galeazzo sent the king on his way, accompanied by several major Milanese feudatories.

Striving for Greatness

The visit from Christian of Denmark left Galeazzo feeling confident and expansive. Christmas 1472 had marked a watershed in the duke's reign, when he began a full-scale effort to establish himself as a great prince. Galeazzo extended his hospitality to the utmost for the "distinguished and honorable men" who attended court at that time and a year later, when he created so many new courtiers. He hoped that those courtiers would help to reinforce his support from his subjects. Similarly, he hoped to gain support through entertaining the pope's nephews and the Savoyard court and through betrothing his daughters to Gerolamo Riario and Duke Filiberto. In an age when honor was the currency of aristocracy, the duke sought to gain and hold as much honor as possible. By any measure, ruling Milan was an expensive business.

7

"With the Greatest Pleasure and Contentment of the Heart"

Love and Hate at the Court
of Milan (1474–1475)

After King Christian of Denmark left Pavia for Mantua in March 1474, Galeazzo and the Milanese court resumed their usual activities. The next day, the duke took his retinue to hunt in the Lomellina for almost two weeks, staying at Vigevano and Villanova. The court then spent about the same length of time in Abbiategrasso, where Galeazzo celebrated Easter on April 11. That Easter was shared with very few companions; he sent his brothers and all the *gentiluomini* back to Milan, keeping only about ten *camerieri* with him.[1]

By April 15, the duke was back with the court in Milan. He had stayed away long enough to allow the Council of 900 to meet in the capital. The council was a relic of the city's communal traditions, and all major Milanese families were represented on it. Galeazzo had them convoked at this time to approve his comprehensive new monetary policy, revaluing coins then in circulation and creating some new types of coins. The duke proclaimed the new system in June. Among the coins introduced was the *testone,* a silver coin worth a pound, so called because it bore a likeness of the duke's head (*testa*).[2] The council was also asked to repeal the hated *inquinto* tax, an extra fifth levied on top of regular imposts. The repeal was an act well received by all, but the duke did not actually stop levying the tax. Galeazzo was personally represented at the council by Tristano Sforza; his half-brother Polidoro also attended, as a Milanese noble. Galeazzo gave permission for his sons Carlo and Alessandro to take part as well, "not as someone sent by us but as brothers and sons."[3]

"Principally for his Regal Dignity"

Over the weeks that followed the duke's return to Milan in April, he received a variety of foreign dignitaries, among them a Venetian ambassador traveling to Burgundy. Another papal nephew, Antonio Fuppo, came through en route to Bologna, and Gerolamo Riario's brother-in-law visited on his way to serve as *commissario* for Imola. For three days, beginning on April 18, another relative by marriage of Ludovico Gonzaga passed through Milan: Eberhard, count of Württemberg, was returning to Germany. When the count entered Milan, Galeazzo had him "accompanied honorably" by ducal brothers "and other courtiers." As a guest of princely rank, Eberhard was lodged in the Corte Arengo, using the rooms of the late duchess, Bianca Maria. The duke visited him there the day after his arrival. When the count left, Galeazzo ordered all his expenses paid throughout the dominion.[4]

Galeazzo was very touchy about his princely dignity, despite—or because of—his lack of formal recognition. He sent surrogates to greet Eberhard, instead of going personally, and only later asked the Privy Council if he should have met the count himself. They pointed out that the duke had greeted lesser lords in the past and should have honored this one accordingly. Galeazzo responded that "these ultramontane [lords] are arrogant and they do not respect anyone but themselves." He may have been offended because Eberhard's first request to visit Milan had not specified an audience with the duke. Galeazzo reinforced his contention that the Germans were arrogant by referring to a letter from the Hohenzollern margrave of Brandenburg, a close relative of the marchioness of Mantua. The duke felt that the margrave had insulted him by calling him "dearest friend."[5]

On April 24, 1474, the court participated in the annual observance of the feast of San Giorgio. Two days later, Galeazzo convoked an important meeting of both councils of state to discuss obtaining the "privilege of the Duchy, etc., and on the erection of the Duchy into a Kingdom, etc." Eight councillors were deputed to write the documents of feudal investiture, and so forth, to be sent with Milanese ambassadors to the emperor. The duke continued to receive envoys from other states, including Savoy and Aragon. On May 1, he celebrated May Day in the Parco at Pavia with his brothers and *camerieri*. It was customary to celebrate May Day at the court; the previous year, in the Giardino at Milan, the duke had been joined by "all the councillors and *gentiluomini*, and a great number of ladies."[6]

On May 21, King Christian arrived at Pavia on his return trip to Germany. Galeazzo sent feudatories to escort him from Cremona, and the duke himself came out a short distance from the city to meet Christian. Visits made on a return journey never occasioned the spectacular entries and receptions of the outbound journeys. The king's return was further obscured by an accident of timing, for he was expected at the same time as a major French embassy. Galeazzo deputed the Privy Council to bring Christian into Pavia with baldacchino and procession; the king had entered Lodi and Cremona in similar fashion. Galeazzo himself received the French ambassadors; despite Christian's own high rank, the king of France (even when represented by a proxy) was more important to the duke.[7]

On this second entry to Pavia, Christian received the keys to the city and castle. He stayed in the same rooms he had previously occupied in the castle, but his retinue was lodged in hostelries. After two days, the king wished to leave so that he could attend the Imperial Diet in Germany. Galeazzo insisted that he stay, arguing that heavy rains made travel difficult, but Christian departed on May 23. The king had previously requested a loan of 4,000 ducats to pay for his travel expenses over the Alps. At Christian's departure, the duke presented him publicly with a gift of 4,000 gold *testoni* in a large basin. Galeazzo escorted his guest to the foot of the stairs in Pavia Castle; Christian left in a carriage, "because of the great rain." The duke commanded that all costs be paid for the king's travel through the dominion, as had been done for the Danish court's previous passage. No expense was spared to "make some demonstration of the love that His Lordship holds" for His Majesty of Denmark.

Galeazzo was well pleased with himself. He thought that he had found an appreciative ally of high rank and considerable influence with the Holy Roman Emperor. The duke showed every possible honor to King Christian, in his own words, "principally for his regal dignity."[8] It was characteristic of Galeazzo to emphasize rank and dignity, but more was at stake here. The duke hoped that Christian would help him attain a regal dignity of his own. Galeazzo's most fundamental political problem was the continued refusal of Emperor Frederick III ro recognize a Sforza as the legitimate ruler of Milan. Galeazzo sought at the very least to obtain that recognition ("the privilege of the duchy"), but he wanted more. He asked the king to intercede with Frederick to have the duchy of Milan raised to a kingdom and the county of Pavia raised to a duchy. The duke was willing to pay as much as 200,000 ducats for the regal title.[9] In 1474, Galeazzo was especially anxious to move on the matter because Charles the Bold of Burgundy had been seeking the emperor's investiture for Milan, in exchange for returning imperial territories to Frederick. In late 1473, Venice had also offered 200,000 ducats for that investiture, although the duke was assured that Frederick "would sooner have invested the Turk" with Milan. Galeazzo had prepared an embassy to accompany Christian back to the Imperial Diet. It was headed by the dominion's leading orator, Agostino Rossi.[10]

Galeazzo cherished great ambitions for his dynasty and its political destiny. At the end of February 1474, he had organized a large and elaborate ceremony in Pavia for the translation of GianGaleazzo Visconti's body from a church in Pavia to the magnificent Certosa. The latter religious house had been founded by GianGaleazzo himself, and it became the prize jewel of Milanese ducal patronage in sacred architecture.[11] Galeazzo was determined to go beyond GianGaleazzo Visconti's achievement and gain a royal title. It was rumored that he had made a secret agreement with Pietro Riario to obtain a royal investiture if Riario ever became pope. Before the Sforza duke enlisted Christian's help with the imperial investiture in 1474, he had tried to gain the crown of Cyprus, through a claim in his wife's right.[12]

Galeazzo's pursuit of regal dignities cannot be ascribed solely to megalomania. Milan had a royal tradition dating back to the Lombards, and medieval kings of Italy (a title borne by Holy Roman Emperors) were crowned in Milan. The wealth and military strength of Galeazzo's dominion put it well beyond the level of other Italian princely states such as Mantua and Ferrara. In all of Europe, the only princely rulers who could draw on greater resources were a few kings and the duke of Burgundy. Even most sovereign monarchs—including the kings of Naples and Denmark—were less affluent than the dukes of Milan. Francesco Sforza had reinforced the idea that the Milanese ducal office was a great dignity when he replaced the original Gonzaga marriage plan for his heir with a link to the royal house of France. The young Sforza heir also heard from those around him that he was fit, or even destined, for a royal title. A book-length horoscope composed for him in 1461 includes a dedicatory poem linking him with regality. The beautiful frontispiece shows him being crowned by the hands of God reaching down from Heaven.[13]

Galeazzo resented the inferiority of his princely dignity to the dignities of royal personages. The duke wanted particularly to match the status of King Ferrante of Naples, the only secular Italian prince who outranked him. Galeazzo had grown bitter about his relationship with the king. Ambassador Antonio Cicinello claimed that Galeazzo had called Ferrante "a bastard and a traitor."[14] Within a year after the match between Sforza Maria and Eleonora d'Aragona had been dissolved in 1472, Ferrante had staged a marriage between Eleonora and Ercole d'Este, always a rival to Galeazzo. When the angry duke of Milan sent an embassy to the wedding festivities at Ferrara, he insisted that his envoys were there "to honor the [Ferrarese] groom and not the [Neapolitan] bride."[15]

Musical Politics

Galeazzo's relations with King Ferrante had not been good in 1473 and early 1474. Indeed, in May 1474, the duke had imprisoned two ex-Neapolitan singers in his choir, because he learned that they had received a "lettera de familiarità" from the king. At the same time, Galeazzo hired one of the best singers of the time, Jean Cordier, away from Ferrante.[16] Throughout 1473, the duke had been pirating singers from the royal choir, all the while claiming to have no part in their move to Milan. In March 1474, Galeazzo sent his singer Giovanni Martini secretly to lure a singer away from the king's ally,

Ercole d'Este of Ferrara.[17] This piracy was a two-way street, and Galeazzo guarded his own investment jealously. In 1474, he suspected some singers of trying to flee the dominion, and he instructed thirty-one bridge- and gatekeepers on the borders not to let any singers pass without ducal authorization.[18]

Galeazzo, Ferrante, and Ercole all spent lavishly on their choirs, but the duke of Milan invested more in vocal music than any other Italian prince of his time.[19] In the period 1473–1474, Galeazzo's choir was at its zenith in terms of size and quality, including five men who later figured among the most prominent composers in Renaissance Europe: Josquin, Compère, Agricola, van Weerbeke, and Martini. It was probably in this period that most of the *motetti missales* were written.[20] The magnificence of the ducal choir did not come about by accident. In January 1473, Galeazzo had noted that "having for some time before now taken greater delight in music and in singing than in any other pleasure, we have put effort into having singers to make a Chapel, and up to now we have brought a good number of Singers, from beyond the Alps and from various countries, and have begun a distinguished [*celebre*] and worthy chapel."[21] The duke's ambitions for patronage of vocal music transcended his own court. He wanted to "promote [*suscitare*] music in Italy," and he sought papal authorization to create choirs in the dominion's cathedrals, which would then supply their best talents to him. "And then when there would come to him the desire to hear a great noise he would send for all of them and have them cry out at one stroke [*cridare ad una tratta*] in such a manner that their voices would go up to the Heavens."[22]

Suspicion and Intimacy

The summer of 1474 was a relatively uneventful time at the Milanese court, a time of waiting. Galeazzo was waiting for his royal ambitions to bear fruit, waiting for word from Germany, waiting to be acknowledged as one of Christendom's great princes. In the meantime, the activities of the court reflected the season's hottest diplomatic issue, Sixtus IV's effort to reduce Città di Castello. Armies were mobilized in various states, and diplomats were dispatched throughout the peninsula. The issue had many ramifications for the alignment of the Italian powers; since Florence opposed the papal campaign, the recent *rapprochement* between Florence, Milan, and Rome was threatened.[23]

Intrigue lurked everywhere. One day in July, the ducal secretary Francesco Pietrasanta was escorting Giovanni Palomaro, a special ambassador from Naples, to the house of Antonio Cicinello, Naples' resident envoy.

We were barely outside the entrance to the monastery when someone came up very suddenly, touched the said Palomaro's hand, and greeted him on behalf of

Antonio d'Orli, governor of Nice. The said Palomaro made a sign to him, and he shut up, then Palomaro quickly took leave of me and went to talk to Messer Antonio [Cicinello] for a good while. Later, he told me he would leave Milan tomorrow, although he originally said he would stay six to eight days longer. I knew that he had just been waiting here for a reply or messenger from Madama [the duchess of Savoy], through the said Antonio d'Orli.[24]

Later that day, the ducal secretary had a long discussion with Cicinello and the Florentine resident ambassador, Tommaso Soderini. Francesco noted that Soderini expressed suspicions of Sir Antonio's "cunning."

In the summer of 1474, efforts were afoot to reconcile Galeazzo and Ferrante. The duke was anxious to break the alliance between Venice and Naples, and he initially tried to return to previous configurations of the Italian League, or some anti-Venetian alliance with Naples.[25] While Giovanni Palomaro was visiting Milan on his return from Burgundy, the Sforza capital was also hosting special envoys from France, Florence, Venice, and Genoa. The resident diplomats from Mantua, Florence, and Naples met with Galeazzo regularly, and he consulted the Privy Council often.

The court was constantly on the move during that summer. From July 4 to September 22, Galeazzo and his retinue spent only seventeen days at Milan and none at Pavia. They went east for most of July, to Cassano and Monza. While they were based there, some members of the court, including several singers, a *cameriere di camera,* and Tommaso Soderini, visited Trezzo Castle, on the border of Venetian territory. Soderini came to see Galeazzo at Cassano and confer over the situation at Città di Castello. Because the ambassador was not physically able to ride at the time, the duke provided a boat to bring him from Milan, complete with dinner and whatever else Soderini might need for the trip. That month, the sexagenarian marquess of Montferrat was getting married again, his Sforza wife having died almost two years earlier. His new bride was related to Filippo of Savoy, one of Galeazzo's worst enemies. Nevertheless, the duke lent the marquess tapestries and table silver for the wedding. Galeazzo spent the feast of the Assumption (August 15) in Milan, hearing Mass at Santa Maria della Scala. He left the next day for another hunting trip in the Lomellina, where he continued to receive ambassadors.

The Duke's Companions

Among his attendants and companions, he was witty, unpretentious, and familiar.[26]

One of the most important contributions that the court made to the duke's well-being was to provide him with companionship in his daily life. Whatever Galeazzo did, he surrounded himself with men who would share his pleasures and pastimes. Ambassadors from princely states such as France, Naples, or Mantua were usually welcome to join him. The ambassadors' standing sometimes gave them influence with the duke that others did not enjoy. On several occasions, the intercession of resident ambassadors saved criminals from vicious punishments that Galeazzo had ordered in a fit of rage.[27]

Occasionally, the duke could enjoy himself in the company of his peers, as when Giovanni Bentivoglio came to Milan for Carnival.[28] The duke's partners and opponents in games included not only men employed for the purpose (his professional tennis players) but also trumpeters and *sottocamerieri*, even Borella, the master of stables.[29] Wherever Galeazzo went, he brought along a coterie of companions. Some of them held offices that formally constituted them as his inner circle, while others were simply with him because he wanted them there.

Carlino Varesino Takes a Holiday   On June 22, 1474, the duke sent a letter of passage and safe conduct to "Spectabilis eques D. Carlinus Varesinus, camerarius n[oste]r primus de camera," entitling the young man to take a company of four on a pilgrimage to Santa Maria di Loreto.[30] Ducal companions rarely took trips away from Galeazzo, but making a pilgrimage was a favorite purpose for such trips. The duke himself had claimed that his extraordinary 1471 journey to Florence fulfilled a pilgrimage vow. Throughout medieval Christendom, pilgrimages provided the best rationale for leisure travel.

The June 22 letter of passage for Carlino was the second one the duke sent him for the trip to Loreto. Galeazzo had heard that Carlino "was leading more persons in your company than we have ordered" and had sent the more restrictive letter. He also sent a letter to a ducal official who was to see that no persons or towns along the route gave Carlino "any honor, nor even spoke with him, but let him go on his way like an unknown person." The duke claimed that such treatment was what Carlino himself had requested, to travel "with more contrition to his devotion." In fact, it was probably Galeazzo himself who felt Carlino required more contrition.[31] Over the next few days, the duke sent a series of personal letters to Carlino, who was making his way through Emilia. Galeazzo wanted the courtier back home, claiming that Carlino's leg "is not yet in such condition that you can comfortably follow this road." Sometimes, the duke told him, "it is better to follow the opinion of others than to persevere in one's own."[32] Galeazzo's next letter had a stinging tone that the duke often adopted when his intimates upset him. He even recalled to Carlino that "our reminders to you are commands." But he sent an attendant to the *cameriere* with money needed for the trip, "even though it would be better for you that you were without it." Then, two days later, "for certain good reasons," the duke ordered Carlino to return home immediately.[33]

The Rise and Fall of a Primo Cameriere   Serving as a ducal companion was a risky business, and individuals did not last long in the position of highest favor. Whether due to Galeazzo's emotional instability or their own arrogant reactions to success, their careers followed similar meteoric courses. Carlino himself became a *cameriere di camera* as early as 1471 and the duke's favorite sometime in 1473. He was the courtier responsible for buying "scented waters and powders" for the duke's person.[34] The gala double wedding shared with Antonietto Arcelli reflected an unusual degree of ducal favor. Carlino's knighting at Bianca Sforza's betrothal showed clearly that the young man had arrived at the highest level of preference, given that he lacked the social and political standing of his eleven fellows in the ceremony.

By the end of 1474, Carlino's fall from grace was equally obvious. Galeazzo declared his intention to deprive his *cameriere* of the fief of Ronchetto, granted in 1471. The duke reminded his companion that the original grant had been made for "faithful service" and continuous attendance on the ducal person. Because Carlino needed money to "be able to live more honorably," the young man had thought to take up a military career. Galeazzo had not wanted him to leave the court, and "so that in your life you not have a legitimate reason to absent yourself," the duke had given Carlino "a fitting state and income to be able to live honorably without having to seek other circumstances of employment."[35] Although Galeazzo did not make good on a threat to give Ronchetto to the Opera del Duomo of Milan at the end of 1474, a beleaguered Carlino needed to sell the estate and stabilize his finances. Throughout 1475, he tried to arrange the sale, which was complicated because his wife Maddalena's dowry was secured by Ronchetto. Carlino wanted to transfer that security to his other property at Frascarolo, but Maddalena's father, the councillor Giacomo Cusani, had to consent to the sale. Giacomo became alarmed about her financial position and his own reputation, insisting that Maddalena's interests should be protected and that he himself should not suffer "shame or injury" on this account.[36]

The status of a courtier's estates was one measure of ducal favor; the number of persons he could maintain at ducal expense was another. In January 1474, Carlino had been one of three *camerieri di camera* entitled to maintain a household of five persons, the highest number permitted to any of these twenty-two ducal companions. In January 1475, he was only allowed a household of three, half as many as the duke's new favorite.[37] The new *primo cameriere di camera* in 1475 was Francesco Pietrasanta, not to be confused with the secretary of the same name. He was a young man reared at court; his mother had been a damsel to Bianca Maria Visconti. Francesco occupied the modest office of footman as late as 1472, when he was promoted to *cameriere di camera*. The promotion came in time for him to be included among the *camerieri di camera* in the 1472 fresco commission and the lavish outfitting for Christmas that year.[38]

Francesco benefited from the duke's extravagant generosity throughout 1475. He received many gifts from Galeazzo, including the honor of a knighting on May 21. The duke enfeoffed him three times in the spring and summer; Francesco received Cantù only two days after it was vacated by the death of Polidoro Sforza. In August, Galeazzo added Gambolò, one of his favorite hunting lodges in the Lomellina, which had belonged to the powerful Beccaria family.[39] In October 1475, Francesco received permission to take a pilgrimage to Florence and Santa Maria di Oliveto, with a company five times as large as Carlino had been allowed in June 1474. Even at the start of 1476, Francesco maintained his position of favor. The ducal treasury was supporting a household of twelve for him, twice as many as most of his colleagues and two more than the duke's next rising favorite. Fortunate Francesco also enjoyed a lucrative marriage; he and two brothers wed three sisters and co-heiresses.[40]

"Those Four Gentlemen Who Would Go with Him Continually"   The formal structure of court society—rank, office, family, and so forth—did not fill all of life. Some of the most intimate and emotionally powerful relationships within the court were informal, linking men and women in ways that had more to do with basic human desires than calculated social or political strategies. Princely prerogative included the power to choose one's own companions regardless of their formal position, and Galeazzo believed strongly in his prerogative.

Among the officers of the court, the *camerieri di camera* were formally constituted as the closest ducal companions. However, the four courtiers most consistently intimate with Galeazzo were not part of this group. The Mantuan ambassador called them "those four gentlemen who would go with him continually, . . . His Excellency being accustomed to joke and enjoy himself quite a bit with them."[41] These four men—GianGiacomo Trivulzio, Guido Antonio Arcimboldi, Giovanni Pietro del Bergamino, and Giovanni Antonio Cotta—were usually grouped together in court documents. All four appeared often as witnesses to ducal charters, reflecting their frequent proximity to the duke's person.[42] Fresco programs, household lists, and even a ducal budget placed them generally in a category of their own, after the ducal brothers and before the *camerieri di camera*.[43] All four men were very active at games, especially tennis; two were also invited to jousts.[44] In effect, these four were collectively Galeazzo's "best friends."

Their official duties varied widely. Giovanni Antonio Cotta's career was the least notable of the four. A Milanese aristocrat and minor feudatory, he served Dukes Francesco and Galeazzo on diplomatic missions but probably acted as a *cameriere* during the early years of the latter's reign. In the 1470s, he bore military responsibilities, including a captaincy in Ludovico Sforza's squadron.[45]

Giovanni Pietro del Bergamino also served Galeazzo in a military capacity. As early as 1468, he was a squad leader in the ducal guard (*famiglia*), a position he held still (or again) in 1475. Giovanni Pietro sprang from an old Bergamasque noble family, the Carminati di Brembilla; his surname "del Bergamino" derived from a nickname given his father, who had served the Sforza dukes as a military captain. Giovanni Pietro himself was a page at Duke Francesco's court by 1450, when he was approximately twelve years old; the courtier was about six years older than Galeazzo.[46]

Guido Antonio Arcimboldi had been a favorite of Galeazzo's from youth. He was the eldest son of a councillor from Parma who owed his high position to Duke Francesco; the Arcimboldi were not ancient nobility.[47] Unlike Giovanni Antonio and Giovanni Pietro, Guido Antonio never had a military career but maintained a close personal relationship with the duke. On some occasions when Guido Antonio was away from court, Galeazzo called him back just to enjoy his company.[48] Guido Antonio's brother Giovanni was the bishop of Novara who became a cardinal in 1473. The brothers had close relations with one another; Guido Antonio relayed messages between Giovanni and the duke and accompanied Giovanni to his new diocese. In turn, Giovanni often interceded with the duke when Guido Antonio had angered Galeazzo.[49]

The last of Galeazzo's four special companions was ultimately the most renowned—ironically, for his service against Sforza Milan. GianGiacomo Trivulzio, who served as a military captain under Galeazzo, later became the grand marshal of France. He led the army that conquered Milan, and Galeazzo's brother Ludovico, in 1499. GianGiacomo's family were Milanese nobility of some antiquity, with major feudal holdings. These holdings were further expanded in 1473, when GianGiacomo received fiefs that the duke had confiscated from a fugitive condottiere. Like other ducal companions, GianGiacomo received his share of rewards and punishments, including a brief dismissal from ducal service. Like most of the others, he also had relatives in Galeazzo's employ; his uncle Pietro was an important figure in the ducal administration.[50]

GianGiacomo, Giovanni Antonio, Giovanni Pietro, and Guido Antonio performed rather ordinary functions and sprang from rather ordinary backgrounds. They were rewarded by rather ordinary means: grants of money, fiefs, and other property, time with the duke, and perhaps some special privileges and activities. However, they stood out among Galeazzo's companions for the constancy of their close relationship to his person. Most noticeably, the duke himself grouped them together into a special category of their own, transcending their formal positions. Evidence of personal companionship is rare in official documents, especially between individuals where the duke was not involved; one interesting example features GianGiacomo and Guido Antonio. In 1476, they departed for a pilgrimage to the Holy Land, accompanied by another courtier, the squad leader Galeotto da Barbiano, count of Belgioioso. Galeotto, over thirty years the duke's elder, was recalled to Milan by Galeazzo, who wanted his company.[51]

"The Two Most Dismal Men in the World"

Galeazzo was in Galliate on August 19, 1474, when his ambassadors to the Imperial Diet returned and reported to him. As no further word arrived from the emperor within a few weeks of their return, the duke realized that his hopes for recognition would again be disappointed. He became very bitter about his erstwhile royal ally Christian as well as the obdurate Frederick. On learning that those two worthies had been depicted in Mantegna's fresco for the Camera degli Sposi in Mantua, Galeazzo called them "the two most dismal men in the world." The duke was monstrously offended that they were included while he, the Gonzaga's neighbor and patron, was not.[52]

With the failure of his efforts to gain imperial or papal investiture, Galeazzo's attitude began to change. He never ceased trying to achieve full political legitimacy—in 1475, he was willing to offer 300,000 ducats for the erection of the duchy into a kingdom—but his patience wore thin. The duke's frustration and discouragement affected his judgment, which had never been very good. His extravagances and austerities became more extreme, his foreign policy shifted radically, and his actions became more outrageously unconventional than ever.

Galeazzo stayed at Pavia from late September to late October, when he went to Milan for one night. "He was very sober this time, and quieter than usual, and in the evening he stayed in his chamber with few people, nor did he call me otherwise, as he usually does. Then he, and those he had called in, came out and said that, at Venice," a league had been concluded with Florence and Venice. In making this alliance, Galeazzo broke a long tradition of enmity with the Serenissima and friendship with Naples. The duke blamed his change of policy on King Ferrante.[53] The following morning, he left the capital early and spent six days traveling with his companions and his wife before reaching Varese. There, the ducal couple fulfilled a pilgrimage vow at Santa Maria del Monte, the premier pilgrimage shrine within the dominion. They stayed there for three days, and Galeazzo did some bear hunting before making a fast return to Milan. The whole trip lasted nine days.[54]

The duke stayed only five days in Milan, then went to Bereguardo until the beginning of December. While he was away, the "solemnity of the publication of this league" with Venice and Florence was celebrated in the capital. The procession staged on November 20 included councillors, fiscal officials, other ducal officers, attorneys, physicians, merchants, courtiers, gentlemen, and many Franciscan friars. Galeazzo requested and received a detailed description of the event from his seneschals-general, but he did not stir from his country retreat.[55] When he did come back to Milan in early December, the quality of court life changed near the center, and an important new character was added to the *dramatis personae*.

The Duke Falls in Love

"This Most Illustrious Lord was counseled by his physicians that His Excellency should do everything to live cheerfully and with goodwill. At his present age, he is leaving old age and going into decrepitude, and for the time that remains to him to live, he should seek to spend it with the greatest pleasure and contentment of the heart that is possible for him, by this means taking the place of worries and continual thoughts of wars and great things." Thus, following the advice of "his most discreet physicians," Galeazzo had "newly fallen in love with a most beautiful woman, citizen and noblewoman of this city, married though, to a descendant of the illustrious house of Gonzaga," a reputed natural son of the condottiere Carlo Gonzaga. "The lady is nineteen years of age and she is . . . esteemed in truth the most beautiful woman in Milan."[56]

Two days after Christmas 1474, Zaccaria Saggi da Pisa wrote to the marchioness of Mantua with this interesting news. She may have been surprised to learn that Galeazzo was passing from old age to decrepitude; she was probably not surprised that he had taken a married lover. The letter, however, was not Zaccaria's idea but another example of the duke's sexual joking with Barbara and her Gonzaga husband: "This Most Illustrious Lord has made me promise to write about this matter to Your Highness. . . . It will be necessary for you to make me some response, so that I may show it to His Excellency." The references to Galeazzo's old age probably reflected a period of depression he was suffering as well as his perverse sense of humor. The notion that his affair was a medical necessity was typical of that humor. The affair was no fantasy, though. "His Most Illustrious Lordship has so far spent wholesale to have her, and in a short time. First, he bought [*compra*] her from her husband for 4,000 ducats of goodwill money, then he immediately married off two of her sisters, to whom he gave 2,000 ducats each for dowry." This was an expensive undertaking, and a profitable one for the young lady's husband. The arrangement was his idea: "This did not happen by her consent, but she was sold by her husband and mother-in-law." Nonetheless, the new ducal mistress was "most obedient to this Lord, and His Lordship is not ungrateful toward her."[57]

In fact, Galeazzo spent wholesale once he had her as well. "He has dressed her with many clothes of gold brocade in damasks, crimsons . . . and other cloths of silk in various colors in such manner that she is dressed like a queen." The duke bought new jewelry for her, with a value of 16,000 ducats or more; three-fourths of that value was accounted for by one brooch. For another 4,000 ducats, Galeazzo purchased the former Milanese residence of the late count Pietro Torelli, his widow, Maddalena, and their children. The duke gave the house to his new mistress, and, in three days, he had it furnished entirely anew with a "most beautiful credenza of table silver," tapestries, and bed coverings of silk, velvet, and brocade. The cost of the furnishings exceeded 1,000 ducats. To maintain this lavish way of life, Galeazzo gave the young lady a monthly allowance of 200 ducats as well as a yearly income of 1,000 ducats from the Martesana Canal. Her husband received the title that went with that income (Captain of the Martesana) and further income from the same source. He was also named podestà of Como, an honorable and lucrative office, without the usual payment.[58]

The duke's new female companion was not merely dressed as a queen and given a princely income; Galeazzo also assigned two *gentiluomini* to accompany her wherever she went. Altogether, he wanted her to maintain a household of thirty persons. For 3,000 ducats, he bought her a country estate located about half a mile from the Giardino, where he could visit her easily whenever he wished. In fact, "His Highness has gone to see her every evening since he fell in love, and lives with as much joy as one could say is possible. He has put her in the [Torelli] house newly bought for her, in which he can go to her very comfortably by day or by night, as he wishes, pretending to go to the stable and see his horses. And so today [December 27], His Lordship went to her after dinner." The whole affair was conducted as secretly as possible at first: "Up to now the Most Illustrious Milady Duchess has had some suspicions, and thrown out a few words about it. But His Excellency has given her to understand that it is not true, and that this lady is the beloved of the Most Illustrious Lord Ludovico, his brother." The sly duke pointed out signs of lovesickness in Ludovico, and he terrified the duchess's retinue so much that they dared not reveal anything to her about the matter. In the meantime, Galeazzo "persevered in giving exquisite Milady all the good treatment that he has done up to now, and in such manner that I believe truly that she has gained rather than lost from this."[59]

Galeazzo Creates a Princess

Galeazzo created a princess of his new paramour. She was not altogether a Cinderella, though. Her name was Lucia Marliani, and her paternal family had a distinguished history among the Milanese nobility. As castellan of Porta Giovia Castle in 1412, Vincenzo Marliani had enabled Duke Filippo Maria Visconti to take his ducal seat in the face of rival claimants.[60] At the time Galeazzo's relationship with Lucia began, he had just visited her uncle, Giovanni Antonio, the archpriest at Santa Maria del Monte. Giovanni Antonio's brother was Michele Marliani, a bishop and nominal member of the Privy Council. Lucia also had relatives within the court; her uncle Giorgio was a *cameriere* until Christmas 1473, when he was promoted to *gentiluomo*.

Lucia herself came from a family of women. Her father, a wealthy merchant, had died when she was young, leaving her mother with six daughters to rear, one of them born after he died.[61] Since women were not legally empowered to make their own contracts, Lucia's mother needed the help of male procurators to maintain herself and her children. Lucia was the third to be betrothed and the second to be married; her husband was Ambrogio Raverti, a Milanese merchant in his early twenties. He became procurator for the family even before he and Lucia were wed. They were still in their second year of marriage when she caught the duke's eye and left her conjugal household.[62]

Galeazzo did not take his new relationship lightly. Five days before Zaccaria wrote to Mantua, describing the situation, the duke began creating a series of formal documents codifying his grants to Lucia. The first one gave her the income from the Martesana, and the second gave her the right to keep whatever he granted her, for herself and her children by him. Both contained a clause to the effect that Lucia "not intermingle herself with her husband in a carnal bond [*carnalem copulam*] without our special permission in writing, nor to have it with any other man except our person, whenever it should chance that we wish to have coitus with her [*cum ea coire*]." The donations would be voided by any failure to comply with these extraordinary provisions.[63]

Galeazzo did not stop there. After the Christmas season, he abandoned efforts to keep the relationship secret. On 8 January 1475, he formally granted his mistress the former Torelli house, subject to the same conditions. The same day, she received something far more precious and unusual: "From our plenitude of power, we make and create that Lucia, and children to be born from her and us, Visconti and of the Most Illustrious family of Visconti. From this day forward, let Lucia and [those] children . . . be so in perpetuity, and let them be known and named and called Visconti and of the Visconti family, and may they be able and obliged to bear the sign of the Viper, which is proper and peculiar to the Visconti."[64] This act was a stunning departure from Renaissance conventions. It is particularly remarkable in light of the tremendous value Galeazzo placed on his Visconti lineage. The duke went even further, though. The next day, he gathered an extraordinary group at Lucia "Visconti"'s new residence. Eighteen of the most honorable and influential men in Milanese court circles were assembled there: Filippo, Sforza Maria, and Ludovico Sforza; the ambassadors from Mantua and Montferrat; eight privy councillors; Galeazzo's four closest companions; and Francesco Pietrasanta, *primo cameriere di camera*. They were convoked to witness a donation to Lucia. In their presence, and thus with their formal approval, the duke created his mistress a noblewoman. He gave her a newly minted title— "countess of Melzo"—and coat of arms, quartering the Visconti viper with a dove. He made the grant heritable by any children she might bear him.[65]

The duke must have made this grant in the knowledge that Filippo Maria had rewarded Vincenzo Marliani's support with the fief of Melzo.[66] This elevation of Lucia into the ranks of the comital nobility flouted many conventions of Lombard law and princely behavior. Women were not legally permitted to bear such titles in their own right, and only the "prefatus Princeps, cum suae potestatis plenitudine" could have put himself above the law to create such a situation. Moreover, the donation bore the same conditions regarding sexual intercourse that were included in his earlier grants. By compelling the eighteen notables to witness this charter, he made them legitimize an illegitimate act. The councillors, ambassadors, and ducal brothers must have found their position extremely embarrassing.

Twelve days later, Galeazzo ended his first round of grants to Countess Lucia with a "Declaration and Mandate of the Most Illustrious Lord Duke that the Lady Duchess, her Illustrious Firstborn and other successors may not disturb the aforesaid Lady Lucia, Countess, in the things granted." The document was literally a curse on those who would interfere with any of Galeazzo's donations to Lucia, even his own firstborn and heir: "We curse him and we call on omnipotent God so that in vengeance for us, if he acts against this as described above, He may curse him by the curse with which Dathan was cursed, and Abyron, whom the earth would not bear, but swallowed alive; and so Judas Iscariot, betrayer of our Redeemer." The duke went on to state that his heir GianGaleazzo would be disinherited if he should try to revoke his father's donations, and the ducal title would pass to the second-born son, Ermes. If Ermes should also contravene his father's wishes, he, too, would be cursed and disinherited, and Ludovico Sforza, Galeazzo's brother, would assume the ducal mantle.[67] There could be no more convincing illustration of Galeazzo's devotion to his new love and his general loss of political judgment. Galeazzo made every effort to formalize his relationship with Lucia, but there was no proper procedure for installing a mistress in the Italian Renaissance court. Lucia was treated with a wary respect by the ducal officials; once she had received her title as countess of Melzo, they always referred to her as "La Contessa."[68]

"Lust . . . in Full Perfection"

This Galeazzo was much subject to Venus, and to filthy lust, in such manner that his subjects were greatly disturbed by this.[69]

Even after "buying" Lucia from her husband, Galeazzo indulged often in anonymous casual liaisons, only a few of which have come to light. His household accounts refer occasionally to money or wardrobe items disbursed "per certi nostri secreti," most of which were sexual contacts. He promised financial support to some prospective bedmates; one widow petitioned after his death with a circumstantial tale of her daughter's seduction and impregnation. Surprisingly, Galeazzo was not without concern for his anonymous bastards. In one case, he wrote officials at Cassano concerning "a girl which is said to be our daughter," commanding them to provide for her and thanking a local cleric for baptizing her.[70]

Galeazzo's sexual inclinations led him to seduce women from all social backgrounds, and his casual treatment of "respectable" ladies proved particularly disturbing to some of his subjects. The duke's taste for attractive ladies even caused husbands and fathers to offer their wives and daughters in hopes of gaining favor. In one of the milder instances, Galeazzo later wrote the husband a letter commenting on the husband's pleasure

> that we kissed your wife when we were at Galiavola. In one action we came to satisfy two people, that is, your father-in-law, who insisted that we should kiss her, and you, that show yourself to be similarly quite happy with it. . . . But to speak quite freely with you, by this action we do not want to be the cause for interruption of your custom, that is, of allowing your women to be kissed, . . . that certainly seems to us a not-unbecoming custom, and one that pleases us.[71]

The duke himself was conscious that his sexual behavior passed all bounds. At Easter one year, he gave a mock confession to Zaccaria Saggi da Pisa, saying that his only true sin was "lust—and that one I have in full perfection, for I have employed it in all the fashions and forms that one can do."[72]

Sexual Violence and Group Sex

> And worse, when he had satisfied his dishonest desire, he had [the women] raped by a great number of his [companions].[73]

There is little evidence to corroborate Corio's charge that the duke shared his conquests with his companions. However, in testimony dating from 1477, one man retroactively accused Galeazzo of "leading his daughters to the brothel."[74] Evidence is also lacking about sexual violence on the part of the duke and his companions within the court, but a case from Cremona illustrates the attitudes of Galeazzo and his men. The case involved one of the *camerieri di camera,* Cosme Ponzoni. Cosme belonged to a powerful family that had briefly held the lordship of Cremona. He joined the court sometime before 1471 and was a *cameriere* by March of that year. Less than a year later, he and five other men were accused of committing a violent rape in a

Cremona hostelry. The others included at least two nobles and at least one other ducal officer, a squad leader in the duke's personal guard.[75]

Galeazzo responded to news of the crime by ordering the podestà of Cremona to proceed against the accused. At the same time, he sent a ducal official on a special investigation into the case. The duke had no particular illusions about Cosme's innocence, but he did not banish the *cameriere* from court. On March 4, 1472, he ordered the podestà to allow Cosme to defend himself through a procurator, rather than appearing personally, "staying as he is here at our service." The official's investigation was slow in developing, but the podestà proceeded apace. By late April, the trial had already begun, and Galeazzo encouraged the podestà to be "ministering justice in this case notwithstanding anything to the contrary."[76]

Late in May, the case was decided. The podestà found Cosme guilty but felt that "the matter cannot be punished except with a *pena arbitraria,*" which only the duke could impose. Galeazzo fined his *cameriere di camera* the astronomical sum of 10,000 ducats, to be paid into the ducal treasury. Moreover, "we do not want him to stay nor live in the Cremona district," unless Cosme paid another 10,000 ducats. The other men involved were sentenced to "confiscation of all their property" and banishment from Cremona, their home district.[77] The severity of this penalty reflected the duke's genuine interest that justice be done within his dominion. It also reflected Renaissance ideas about criminal penalties, which served to fill the government's coffers, redistribute the property of malefactors, and deprive the latter of their home base. In July 1472, Galeazzo gave a member of the ducal guard the property of one nobleman convicted of the rape.[78]

However, Cosme Ponzoni himself was less harshly treated. While the initial investigation was still under way, he received a license to transport grain from his home district "for his use and that of others in our court." Even in August 1472, after sentencing, the duke helped the convicted rapist pursue a debtor, as Cosme was occupied "in the care of our person." In November, the *cameriere* was included among his colleagues in the preparations for Christmas. It does appear that Cosme was held briefly in his brother's custody before January 1473, when the duke ordered his release. On April 29, 1473, though, exactly one year after his sentencing, Cosme was awarded a ducal pardon for his crime. The only condition was that he could not return to Cremona without Galeazzo's written permission. The following day, the duke gave Cosme that permission in order for the *cameriere* to obtain some money there.[79]

Homosexual Interests

When Galeazzo said that he had practiced lust in every possible form, he was almost certainly including homosexuality. Although no explicit descriptions of homosexual activities at his court have come to light, implicit references are numerous. The duke's coarse joke to Tristano about Battista da Montignana reflected more about his own practices than his half-brother's. A strong sexual undertone pervades Galeazzo's relations with his intimates, especially the *camerieri di camera,* who slept in his room.

When the duke recruited new *camerieri* from Naples in 1473, one of his motives may have been sexual; he asked for youths of "noble and beautiful appearance." One such youth, Bernardino da Sorrento, came to the attention of Milan's ambassador to Naples after Goffino had already left. The ambassador told Galeazzo about Bernardino, insisting that "he could not be more to [Your Lordship's] purpose and appetite": the youth was twenty-two years old, "as big as Carlino [Varesino], and Carlino knows him well from when he was at Naples." The envoy's confidence was justified; Galeazzo responded that Bernardino should be sent immediately.[80]

Male homosexual encounters were not rare among the Renaissance nobility; the classical tradition gave them an ideological rationale, and medieval traditions made them seem less dangerous to many than sexual acts with women. After telling Galeazzo about Bernardino da Sorrento, the ambassador to Naples also mentioned the duke of Calabria's inability—in the grip of an illness—to "restrain himself from coitus, as much with women as with men."[81]

Other Sexual Liaisons at Court

Few illicit sexual liaisons are visible from written records. We know of Gabriella Sforza-Fogliani's affair with Gerolamo Corti only because the vengeful duke exposed it. Galeazzo's own wife had an affair with a *cameriere* from Ferrara, Antonio Tassino. Their relationship became so scandalous after the duke's death that Tassino was forced to leave the court.[82] Pier Maria Rossi had one of the most romantic affairs of the fifteenth century with Bianca Pellegrino, the wife of a Milanese aristocrat; their love was immortalized by the Bembo frescoes in Rossi's home castle of Torrechiara.[83] Sforza Secondo conducted an affair for years with a married woman who lived with him as his "concubina" until Galeazzo made him send her back to her husband; previously, the duke had colluded in the arrangement.[84] No doubt other such affairs took place among the court's many members, but there was no web of sexual intrigue, merely individual relationships undertaken for personal reasons.

"The Most Deadly Enemies That I Have"

The emotional intensity of love affairs had its counterpart in the enmity between some members of the court. Traditional rivalries and feuds were brought to court, and new ones arose there. The duke's enemies did not appear at court often, if at all; Galeazzo preferred that they stay away. The Correggeschi, major feudatories in the Parma district, were almost all on bad terms with him, and only one member of the family ever came to Milan during his reign.[85] The duke's antipathy toward them was so great that he would not allow Tristano Sforza's wife, Beatrice d'Este, to visit her son by her first marriage to Niccolò da Correggio.[86]

Among members of the court, some feuds were brought from home. In June 1468, Boschino d'Angheria complained to the duke of a plot against him by Giorgio Marliani (Lucia's uncle) and two of his Marliani cousins. The issue escalated, and two months later Boschino had Melchiorre Marliani's factor seized by Milan's captain of justice. Boschino told the duke that Melchiorre had convoked the Privy Council over the matter and that he himself feared what the council might do. After all, Boschino explained, Melchiorre had been treated very well by Galeazzo; as a result, the councillor "lives in such arrogance that he appears to be another Cosimo de' Medici in Florence."[87]

Traditional enmities also surfaced when members of the court lost favor suddenly. Giovanni Agostino Isimbardi blamed a persistent enemy in the court for his fall from grace in 1474.[88] The *gentiluomo* Francesco Salvatico declared that his own troubles were caused by "my adversaries, these Lampugnani." He claimed they were trying to influence the duke "with their insinuations and insolences."[89] The *cameriere* Filippo degli Oddi, imprisoned by ducal order, insisted that his unjust punishment resulted from a rival's slander. As a nobleman (from Perugia), he claimed the right to test the truth of the accusation through trial by combat, should his accuser be capable of bearing arms.[90] Physical violence did not flare up often at Galeazzo's court. In a rare case soon after his accession, his first master of stables was murdered by three *galuppi,* who then fled to Colleoni at Malpaga.[91]

Other conflicts within the court were less momentous. The veteran *cameriere* Francesco da Varese exchanged harsh words with Fioramonte Graziani da Cotignola, a ducal *gentiluomo,* and another veteran from Duke Francesco's time. The *cameriere*'s son had appeared unexpectedly at Fioramonte's house and demanded lodgings, which the *gentiluomo* did not want to provide.[92] Even the duke's most reliable servants could find themselves in conflict. Ambrosino da Longhignana, vice-castellan in Milan, bore great ill-will toward Bartolomeo Gadio, calling him "a poltroon" and "a big shit [*merdazo*]," among other things. Bartolomeo told Galeazzo, "I would write [the name of] that Ambrosino in the book of the most deadly enemies that I have."[93] Disagreements also arose between the women at court. Bianca Maria Visconti received a vitriolic letter from her servant called "La Comatre," complaining that the "cursed witch" who ran the duchess's household had taken her room away from her.[94]

Despite the duke's volatile nature, his court was generally well behaved, and disputes were usually addressed quickly. The duke himself sometimes settled differences between persons of high rank; in 1474, he ordered the feuding Balbiani brothers, counts of Chiavenna, to bring their dispute to his court for resolution at Christmas.[95] Such disagreements between family members were all too frequent. Similarly, disputes over such matters as property boundaries and water rights often disrupted relations between neighbors.[96]

Ancient Nobility versus Recent Arrivals

Most disputes within Galeazzo's court were personal in nature, and overt political conflict occurred rarely. Although the factional networks of Guelfs and Ghibellines were ubiquitous in the cities of the dominion, they carried little ideological force and did not produce strong competing blocs at the ducal court. However, the court was pervaded by an underlying tension between the ancient nobility of Milan and the new arrivals brought to prominence by the Sforza—including Galeazzo himself. In particular, Cicco Simonetta was hated by many of the capital's traditional leaders, such as Gaspare da Vimercate and Pietro Pusterla.[97]

Galeazzo's relationship with Pietro Pusterla, and the Milanese nobility in general, was fraught with mutual suspicion and resentment. Galeazzo relied heavily on the Simonetta family and other "new men," such as Orfeo Cenni da Ricavo and Giacomo Alfieri; some resentment was bound to arise among those who felt displaced. The duke needed his subjects' support to maintain his position, especially in the face of opposition from his feudal overlord. Yet, the traditional leaders of Milanese society were not inclined to give that support blindly. In turn, the duke had his own cause for resentment. His tense relationship with his mother may have exacerbated the conflict with Milanese nobles, to whom she was the last ruler of "their own." When Galeazzo decided to move to Porta Giovia Castle, Pietro and Gaspare da Vimercate reminded him of opposition from the ducal household in general and Bianca Maria in particular.[98] Nine months later, the duke complained to his mother about a letter she had written.

> I am disturbed again that it appears Your Ladyship believes so easily . . . whoever says something bad about me. . . . As for having noted the many speeches of our malcontent subjects, I say that I do not know those who would be malcontent with good reason. . . . It could be that they are those to whom some inconvenience has been done with reason and justice, and perhaps others also [make complaints, being] not very happy . . . because they do not have everything that they would like, and in these could be Pietro Pusterla, because he is insatiable by nature.[99]

The Pusterla were an ancient Milanese noble family, and Pietro had been important at court as early as Filippo Maria Visconti's time. His position in Milanese society is reflected in the marriages of his children to great noble families of Milan: Visconti, Bossi, Castiglione, Crivelli, Stampa, and the counts Rusca of Como.[100] At the accessions of both Dukes Francesco and Galeazzo, Pietro presented the ceremonial sword, and he continued to enjoy great prestige throughout their reigns. He was active in diplomacy and actions of the Privy Council; although he did not receive a formal appointment to the council while Galeazzo was alive, he ranked highly among the members when he sat with them.[101] From Pietro's perspective as a longtime member of Milan's ruling elite, it is easy to understand why the reckless, irreverent, foreign-born duke gave grounds for complaint. From Galeazzo's perspective as an inexperienced ruler in a world of entrenched interests, it is easy to understand why such complaints seemed unreasonable.

Galeazzo did not like Pietro's disapproving attitude, but he showed respect for Pietro's influence, intelligence, and integrity. Notwithstanding his own suspicions, the duke trusted the nobleman to help choose new *gentiluomini* in 1473 and to negotiate Ludovico Gonzaga's *condotta* in 1470. Galeazzo honored Pietro often, including him in appropriate positions of precedence at such great occasions as the Christmas court and the trip to Florence. The duke even knighted the nobleman's son at Bianca Sforza's betrothal.[102] Galeazzo did not appoint Pietro or Gaspare to the Privy Council, but in that omission he did no less than his father had done. Duke Francesco never named them to the council, even though he had had them bear the sword and scepter at his enthronement procession and had counted them among his closest friends and advisers. When Galeazzo composed the fresco program for the Sala Grande of Porta Giovia Castle, he placed Pietro and Gaspare in the lineage cycle scene with Duke Francesco, Bianca Maria, her uncle Andreotto del Maino, Antonia Attendoli, and Cicco Simonetta. Viewed against the political and genealogical background, that combination of persons seems very judiciously balanced.[103]

It has been argued, especially by the historian Riccardo Fubini, that Pietro Pusterla and the Ghibelline nobles of Milan were victimized by Galeazzo and tacitly supported acts against the duke. There is no question that such prominent nobles as Giovanni Borromeo and Donato "del Conte" Borri were illtreated by the duke at times, but so were others; Galeazzo gave almost everyone a reason to be dissatisfied with him.[104] Some pieces of evidence cited to illustrate Pietro's alienation from the duke illustrate also the complexity of the situation in Galeazzo's reign, which did not reflect a simple division of allegiances along obvious lines of lineage or faction. Fubini has noted that Pietro's daughter Giovanna married Battista Visconti, who fought with Colleoni against Galeazzo, and Evelyn Samuels Welch has remarked that Galeazzo replaced Pietro as sword bearer for the trip to Florence.[105] The duke chose instead Vercellino Visconti, his own longtime *cameriere*. Not only was Vercellino himself a distant cousin of Battista Visconti's but Vercellino's son later married Battista's sister. Vercellino's favor with Galeazzo exemplifies the unreliability of all such generalizations about the duke's preferences, for the *cameriere* was a protégé of Duchess Bianca Maria, for whom Galeazzo had such ambivalent feelings. Vercellino's first cousin Margherita kept company with her (and later Bona), and his own marriage had been arranged by Bianca Maria.[106]

Brothers and Sisters at Court

When persons at the Milanese court needed allies, they turned most often to members of their family. Having a strong family, and good relations within it, was virtually a necessity for survival in Renaissance Milan. Close relatives relied on one another for support of various kinds, and those persons who succeeded at court typically used their positions to benefit their kin. Members of one's immediate family were often business partners and companions. At a court whose population came from many different backgrounds, it was helpful to return to the shared values and experiences that generally came with a shared lineage.

The Duke's Brothers

The most visible family at Galeazzo's court was his own; in particular, the duke's brothers continued throughout the reign to have an important place near his person. Ludovico and Sforza Maria, or Ottaviano, led lists of persons traveling with the ducal household.[107]

As the ducal brothers grew toward adulthood, the main activity that brought them together was sport, especially hunting. This passion for the chase was part of an aristocratic ethos that all of them shared. Their correspondence is filled with references to hunting; when Sforza Maria was bedridden with an illness, he and Galeazzo conducted a lively epistolary debate over the relative merits of hares and deer as prey. Galeazzo teased Sforza Maria coarsely, advising his brother to be "fleeing from sexual intercourse, so as not to debilitate the stomach any more than it already is."[108] Sforza Maria also participated in another of Galeazzo's favorite pastimes, tennis; in January 1472, the duke won 30 ducats from his brother betting on the game.[109] Ottaviano was not yet able to join Galeazzo as a companion and was still treated as a child. Galeazzo did not share hunting animals with him but in 1475 made him a gift of a tame lion.[110]

Outside recreational contexts, Galeazzo preferred that his brothers act in a ceremonial capacity. They appeared prominently at great occasions, and all but Ascanio, the cleric, held honorary positions as commanders in the ducal army.[111] Some of the brothers represented the duke as special emissaries to other states.[112] When Ludovico was sent to Venice in 1471, he was instructed to tell the Serenissima that "as my brother and lord, when he was a minor, used to make similar trips, and also we his brothers, so now he intends that his sons, when they are of suitable age, do likewise."[113] Sforza Maria's trip to Venice in 1474–75 was planned on a grand scale. He was assigned fifty horses in his personal retinue, and thirteen councillors and gentlemen accompanied him.[114] These diplomatic ventures had little substance, though; Ludovico's instructions for the trip to Venice specified that he would make no concrete replies to serious policy questions. The brothers were even deprived of substantive contact with foreign ambassadors in Milan; a Ferrarese envoy was warned not to see Filippo or Sforza Maria except in Galeazzo's presence and then only if it were "a light visit."[115] Systematic exclusion from political activity must have been particularly galling to Ludovico, who had been trained by his mother for princely life.[116]

Because Ascanio spent Galeazzo's reign training for a career in the church, he spent most of this period living and studying in Pavia but joined his brothers at most solemn occasions. The duke even insisted that Ascanio attend the feast of San Giorgio, the warrior saint, prompting Ascanio's governor to complain that Galeazzo was interrupting his brother's studies.[117] In January 1475, Ascanio himself was named to the Privy Council and "constituted the head of the council, so that he precedes all."[118] The honor was as nominal as others that Galeazzo bestowed on his brothers, but it was fitting for a ducal brother destined to be a cardinal. The duke made active efforts to secure Ascanio's elevation to the cardinalate, but during his reign, Ascanio had to be content with the abbacy of Chiaravalle, whose lucrative income he shared with the monks who lived there.[119]

Other Families At Court

The most influential "court family" in Milan was the Simonetta, whose domination of the Chancery might have created a dynasty. The secretaries and brothers Cicco and Giovanni were indispensable to the early Sforza. Giovanni served as secretary to the Privy Council, liaison between Galeazzo and visiting dignitaries, conduit for news from abroad, and the duke's agent for many delicate matters within the court. Privately, he wrote the most comprehensive contemporary biography of Francesco Sforza, a major achievement in humanist historiography.[120] The next generation of Simonetta were also involved in the Chancery; Cicco's son Giovanni Giacomo joined as a chancellor at age seventeen, in 1470, and quickly became an active and valued part of the family and the Sforza government.[121]

The working relationship between the Simonetta brothers was excellent, but their intimate contact was relatively limited. When Cicco's daughter was married in October 1475, Giovanni was not listed among the dinner guests, who included Giovanni Bolognini Attendoli, Cicco's son-in-law, Guido Galeotto Torelli, several Visconti lords related to him by marriage, and the son of Count Pietro dal Verme.[122] That same month, though, Giovanni and his wife each made a separate visit to Cicco's wife, who was confined by illness to their home in Pavia.[123] Both Giovanni and Cicco married the daughters of major feudatories. Cicco wed Elisabetta Visconti, and he maintained a close relationship with some of his Visconti in-laws. Giovanni's second wife, Caterina, was a daughter of Count Marcellino Barbavara; one of her sisters married the ducal cousin and military commander Pietro Francesco Visconti. Giovanni's relationship with his Visconti in-laws was a useful vehicle for gathering news; family networks were among the best sources of information in an age of slow and difficult communications. When Colleoni's Venetian army threatened the Sforza dominion in 1467, one of the men in his household was the son of a damsel of Pietro Francesco Visconti's wife. The son passed news of the Venetians through his mother to Pietro Francesco, who in turn sent it to Giovanni Simonetta, his brother-in-law. Giovanni then conveyed the information to Galeazzo.[124]

Giovanni Simonetta was also linked by marriage to the brothers Pietro and Francesco Birago. Francesco, captain of Domodossola and new *gentiluomo* at Christmas 1473, had wed another daughter of Marcellino Barbavara. In May 1475, Francesco was having trouble with Pietro, who claimed full title to the fief they shared. Giovanni wrote his own brother, Cicco, on Francesco's behalf, asking for help in the matter.[125] Pietro and Francesco Birago were not always in conflict with one another. When Francesco sought to become podestà of Valenza, Pietro interceded with the duke for him. They also cooperated to help a third brother, Daniele, seek preferment in the church. Daniele was an apostolic protonotary, resident in Rome, but he aspired higher. A cleric about to resign a benefice wanted to name Daniele as his successor, and support was needed in persuading the general of the order to accept him. Francesco wrote to Pietro, seeking letters of support for Daniele from the duke and the general's brother, also a Milanese courtier. The duke obligingly wrote and nineteen months later was writing again on Daniele's behalf, this time for the abbacy of a monastery near Parma. In the meantime, Daniele gave something substantial to Pietro and Francesco, which caused Galeazzo to write with warm approval that Daniele was a "good and loving brother."[126]

Pietro Birago was involved not only in his own network of brothers but also in a family syndicate led by the young *gentiluomo* Giovanni Andrea Lampugnani. Pietro belonged to the family because he had married a niece of Giovanni Andrea's. The syndicate held a lease on property belonging to the abbacy of Morimondo, a lucrative monastery on the Ticino near Abbiategrasso. Although Galeazzo had initially prohibited Pietro from participating in the lease, he relented in November 1473, when Giovanni Andrea wanted Pietro to share in the syndicate's losses. Such syndicates were commonly used as a vehicle for making shared investments, especially among family members.[127]

Brothers and Sisters   Persons close to the duke and duchess routinely used their positions to benefit their own families. Elisabetta da Palenzona of Tortona was appointed damsel to Duchess Bona in late 1468, after an uncle in ducal service told Galeazzo that she had been a "most faithful servant" to Bianca Maria. In early 1470, Elisabetta herself requested an administrative office in Tortona for her brother, which the duke granted. A few years later, a second brother joined the court as a *cameriere*.[128]

Most family networks crossed court boundaries. The countess Lucia's Marliani uncles included Giorgio, a courtier in Milan; Michele, a bishop in Rome: Giovanni Antonio, an archpriest in Varese; and feudatories living on the family estate.[129] Because their occupations kept them apart, the brothers were rarely in close contact; Michele's deathbed was probably the first place they had been reunited in years. Lucia's immediate family consisted entirely of women. When she took up residence in Milan during her first pregnancy, she often enjoyed the company of close relatives, especially sisters who had married into the court under Galeazzo's aegis.[130]

In some families, several members participated extensively in the court; the Camposilvio offer an outstanding example. Tommaso da Camposilvio (called "Angelo del Conte") had been a companion and courtier to Duke Francesco. He died before Galeazzo acceded, leaving a widow and four children active in the court.[131] The widow, Elisabetta, was one of Bona's four original *compagne,* while two of her daughters figured among the new duchess's original damsels. At least one of those daughters, Daria, remained in that office throughout the reign, and she married at court in 1470.[132] Both sons, Carlino and Giovanni Antonio, served Galeazzo as *camerieri.* The latter was among the young duke's favorites in the early years, but he died in 1469. Carlino, an excellent jouster, had risen to *cameriere di guardacamera* by 1474, but he left the following year to seek a position in Florence.[133]

New Partners

For capable young men to change employers was no rarity in Renaissance Italy. Professional mobility occurred easily on the peninsula, where many autonomous states shared a similar sophisticated culture. That shared culture made possible the political balance of power that was such a remarkable and precocious feature of this period. Alliances, too, could be changed easily. However, underlying conditions made certain combinations awkward and unlikely. The states centered on Milan and Venice were natural rivals in northern Italy, where each could gain territory and influence only at the expense of the other. It was a surprise to many when Galeazzo proclaimed his new alliance with Venice in 1474. About ten days after Galeazzo made Lucia a member of his ducal family, he celebrated the first exchange of resident ambassadors with his new ally. He had already sent Sforza Maria to Venice with a large retinue in November, and his brother was there when the Milanese envoys arrived. On their departure from the dominion, those envoys were cheered on by a crowd of ducal subjects, as bells rang and bombards boomed "not otherwise than if the doge of Venice were making an entry." The incoming Venetian ambassadors were greeted with equal or greater fanfare. The duke even instructed his officials to make roads for them through the snow.[134]

Naples, Burgundy, and France

By 1475, Galeazzo had become excruciatingly impatient with his political status. The duke was still eager to receive the full recognition he felt he deserved, and he was willing to spend extravagantly to obtain it. In July 1475, he offered the Holy Roman Emperor as much as 200,000 ducats for ducal investiture—and 300,000 for a royal title.[135]

"The House of Visconti Is Not Inferior in the Least to That of Aragon"
Relations with Naples continued to worsen. When the duke broke their alliance in the autumn of 1474, he blamed the king's bad faith. In May 1475, the duke forbade Sforza Maria from using the style "d'Aragona," granted with the ducal title of Bari in 1465. Galeazzo declared in a proud fury that "the house of Visconti is not inferior in the least to that of Aragon."[136] Conflict between those two Italian powers gave the French an excellent opening on the peninsula, especially when the Neapolitans could incite rebellion in Genoa. Galeazzo's main concern with his northern neighbors was their respective interests in Italy itself; Charles of Burgundy had already shown himself to be greedy for Milan, and Louis XI had dynastic claims to both Milan and Naples.

Although pride and anger distorted Galeazzo's policymaking, splendor and hospitality continued to be his stock in trade. Even while he dismantled the Neapolitan alliance, he entertained the king's son, Federico, in style and comfort, housing the royal guest in the Corte Arengo because Porta Giovia could not accommodate the traveling party.[137] Federico was first expected in November 1474, but his progress was postponed until after Christmas. When he came in mid-January 1475, he was ironically present for the exchange of ambassadors between Milan and Venice.

During the period when Galeazzo was breaking with Naples, relations worsened also with Milan's other royal ally, France. Any movement toward

Venice brought Galeazzo closer to Burgundy, the Serenissima's longtime ally. Moreover, the duke was concerned about Louis XI's overtures in late 1474 to Ferrante and an alliance with the Swiss that brought French interests to the very borders of the duchy. That alliance resulted from menacing incursions into Switzerland by Louis's archrival, Charles the Bold of Burgundy. Galeazzo was well informed about Burgundy from the reports of a resident Milanese ambassador, Giovanni Pietro Panigarola (Gottardo's brother).[138] Since the duke of Milan had learned in 1473 that Charles was seeking the Milanese investiture from Frederick III, news from Burgundy had become more important than ever.[139] By Christmas 1474, though, Galeazzo feared Burgundy far less than France. Moreover, the duke of Milan was intent on defying traditional patterns. Tired of being a junior partner to his royal brother-in-law and concerned about Louis's intentions in Italy, the duke looked instead to Charles of Burgundy as an ally. On January 30, 1475, at Moncalieri in the duchy of Savoy, Milan made its first and only alliance with Burgundy. The duchess Iolande mediated the agreement, which was a bold stroke of diplomacy. In some ways, Moncalieri stands as a high-water mark in the history of Milan, when the Sforza state was recognized as an independent power capable of making such treaties without reference to any feudal overlords.[140]

The Bastard of Burgundy Pays a Visit   Galeazzo's greatest show of hospitality in 1475 celebrated this new alliance, hosting a Lenten visit by Antoine, Bastard of Burgundy. "Monsignore lo Bastardo" was the honored but illegitimate half-brother of Charles the Bold, the most brilliant prince of the time. The Bastard was traveling to Milan and Naples to gain support for his brother's plan to seize the title of Holy Roman Emperor and use its prestige and resources against Louis XI. Galeazzo first learned on February 26 of the Bastard's impending arrival, and he sent a barrage of logistical questions to his agents in Savoy, though which the visitor was coming. The duke also ordered the Bastard's closest counterpart, Tristano, and a half-dozen *gentiluomini* to meet the visitor at Vercelli, on Savoy's side of the border. They would escort him throughout his stay in the Sforza dominion. Because it was Lent, Galeazzo wanted to entertain his princely guest with dinners of large fish and commanded that such fish be sought throughout the Lake District, especially Lago Maggiore.[141]

The Bastard of Burgundy arrived in the dominion on March 9, 1475, with his son and a company of 115 horses. They came first to Mortara, then proceeded the next evening to Vigevano. Galeazzo rode out to greet them but did not dismount when they met. The Bastard and his retinue stayed with Galeazzo over the weekend; on Monday, March 13, the visitor went to Milan, embarking at Abbiategrasso on a boat ornamented with the ducal arms. The

Privy Council came to meet him on another boat, accompanied by the duke's sons, GianGaleazzo and Ermes, and an enormous crowd of courtiers.[142] In Milan, the Bastard was to be lodged in the Porta Giovia chambers where the marquess of Montferrat usually stayed. Problems arose with that arrangement, because Galeazzo was having a secret stairway built into the wall of the castle, and the seneschals could not get access to prepare for the guest's coming. Instead, the Bastard used the rooms that Cardinal Riario had occupied in 1473. In March 1475, those rooms were being used by the duke's sons, who were moved to Bona's section of Porta Giovia for the duration of the Burgundian's stay.[143]

Being moved from their rooms was not the only way in which Gian-Galeazzo and Ermes were affected by the Burgundian's visit. For the first time, the young boys (almost six and five years old, respectively) were called on to participate in the entertainment of a distinguished foreign guest. On the boat where they met the Bastard, the little count of Pavia "received him graciously, and with such lordly and measured manner and sweet words, asking him about his well-being and that of the Lord Duke of Burgundy, as though he were 25 years of age." When the boat arrived at the Porta Giovia Castle gate, the precocious ducal heir and his brother mounted on horseback with their guest and escorted him as far as the entrance to his rooms. There they dismounted, and the little count "on his own initiative took the Lord Bastard by the hand and accompanied him into the room . . . and stayed there a little. The Illustrious Count said with a gracious manner to the Lord Bastard. 'Your Lordship must be tired. You should rest.'" GianGaleazzo took his leave from a princely guest who was very impressed with the child's courtesy.[144]

The two boys went every day to entertain the Bastard in his chambers. On his first full day in Milan, little Ermes danced the moresca with a dwarf; their guest was amused and admiring. Later that day, Tristano took the Bastard to Antonio Missaglia's and other armorer's shops. The Burgundian ordered armor for himself, his son, and others.[145] On the morning of March 16, the boys went with the Privy Council to escort the Bastard from his chambers. As they had done when they brought him into Porta Giovia Castle a few days before, the ducal sons rode on either side of their guest on the way to the city gate. "There, he embraced and kissed both of them cordially and tenderly" before departing southward. Although Galeazzo had remained in Vigevano, the Burgundian had been worthily entertained and honored in Milan by the ducal lineage, the Privy Council, and the bulk of the Milanese court.[146]

New Affirmations

Galeazzo had made many changes in a year's time. The new friendships with Venice and Burgundy marked a radical departure from the foreign policy of his father's time. The duke was turning his world upside down, and nowhere was the upheaval more visible and shocking than in the creation of Lucia Marliani as countess and Visconti princess. After his efforts the previous year to gain support from prominent figures within and outside the dominion, Galeazzo now gave them every reason to recoil from him. His emotional equilibrium, never strong, had been profoundly shaken by Christian's failure to help with the emperor. Galeazzo felt that the old ways had failed him; it was time to affirm in new ways the strength and independence of his dominion.

· GALEAZ · MARIA · DVX · QVINTVS ·

Incipit opusculū super declaratione arboris consanguitatis et affinitatis cō questis tractatibz oīus impedimentoz matrimonioz ꝙuestioibz seruēbus ꝑea mā matrimonij ꝓpositi per clarissimū .ff. dꝛ. datorem. d. Jeronimū a sagariam papiēsē lectū legēre i sclia studio papiēsi ordinariā iuris canoici ꝺ anno dnī 1464 ad laude dei ac illustrissimi principis et excelentissimi Galeaz marie sforcie viceꝯꝰitis ducis 4ti papie igloriecᷓ coīts Januē ac cremone dni que altitudo ꝑseruare dignet.

Dū sī ꝑ oīus certo tꝑis spado mẽmisso a lectura ordinaria vacare cōtingeret nollem ur per ipm ocius viribz ingenij i met theulis in bealiores fierent et per neglām que oīus calamitarū et vicioz aliue est et mater i nutrita i laborib ꝑsuata ꝯꝑerter sed per omnjū ꝯeticentj suscipere incrementur

ur lege legans f. ꝗ ornaricibz .ff. tele. nꝰ requisitus ut ipmis aqnā pluribus auditoribz oignis scolastieis scire et irel ligere plura cupiēnbus iur̄ philosofij ꝯes homines naturá scire ārstoerat et scar eth rem per cūm cognoscere ut arbore cōsanguinitatis et affinitatis legere et declare vellem et eius lectura operā nauur ut ꝙ multis icognitum, est et obscuriū ꝑ inspeorem oeculoz planis et cognituz relinquat' altine cōsiderant ꝙ et sī in hee eis more gerere pulcrum et lauoabile esset, pulcrius tú ee matias oīus impedimentoz matrimonij ipi acere et sb quadam ꝓpedto ipsius arboris declationi amectere, cū multis ꝙoibz iacēobz et eigenntbz ao ipam inuz ao laudem dei oiporenci et priapis gloriosissimi stimaú sforcie ducis 4di 2c papie anglieꝗ coīts cremone ac Janue dni per morte superueciete ipsius pncipis distulli nunitiue mors acerba coegit et tituli ipi operis corde socido mẽte deuota erala cū .iio ipsius operis titulus ad magnalis

Galleazzo Maria Sforza. Portrait by Antonio and/or Piero Pollaiolo. *Galleria degli Uffizi, Florence. By permission of Alinari.*

Above: Galeazzo Maria Sforza. Portrait attributed to Zanetto Bugatti. *Foto Saporetti, Milan. Below*: Bona of Savoy kneeling beside female saint. Detail of painting attributed to Bernardo Zenale. *Foto Saporetti, Milan.*

Above: Francesco Sforza. Portrait attributed to Bonifacio Bembo. *Below*:
Bianca Maria Visconti. Portrait attributed to Bonifacio Bembo. *Photos courtesy
of Pinacoteca di Brera, Milan.*

Aerial view of Castello Sforzesco (former Porta Giovia), Milan. *Foto Saporetti, Milan.*

Above: Corte Ducale of Castello Sforzesco, Milan, surrounded by ducal wing.
Below: ducal chapel of Castello Sforzesco, Milan. *Foto Saporetti, Milan.*

Left: rear facade of Castello Sforzesco, Milan, ducal wing. *Foto Saporetti, Milan. Right*: Ludovico "il Moro" Sforza. Detail from Pala Sforzesca. *Pinacoteca di Brera, Milan.*

Above: *Camera dei ducali* of Castello Sforzesco, Milan. Ceiling vaults with Galeazzo's arms and initials, overpainted with Ludovico il Moro's. *Foto Saporetti, Milan. Below*: Ludovico III Gonzaga, marquess of Mantua, with his wife, Barbara Hohenzollern of Brandenburg, and some children and court servants. Ludovico is speaking with Marsilio Andreasi, sometime envoy to Milan. *Fresco by Andrea Mantegna in Camera degli Sposi of Castello di San Giorgio, Mantua. By permission of Alinari.*

Above: Vigevano Castle. *Below*: Vigevano Castle, showing passageway built by Galeazzo. *Photos courtesy of Comune di Vigevano.*

Facade of Pavia Castle. *Photo by Sabine Eiche.*

Above: courtyard of Pavia Castle. *Below*: upper loggia or hall of Pavia Castle. *Photos by Sabine Eiche.*

Above: Villanova Castle courtyard. *Below*: Villanova Castle courtyard. *Photos by Sabine Eiche.*

Above: Villanova Castle exterior. *Below*: Galliate Castle. *Photos by Sabine Eiche.*

Galeazzo Maria Sforza being crowned by God while receiving book of his horoscope from author Raffaelle da Vimercate. *Archivio Storico Civico, Milan, Biblioteca Trivulziana, cod. 1329, fo. 2.*

Opening page of charter to Lucia Marliani, with Galeazzo's arms at the top. The arms he granted her appear in the first letter of the text. *Archivio Storico Civico, Milan, Biblioteca Trivulziana, cod. 1333, fo. 1.*

L'AMENTO DEL DVCA

GALEAZO MARIA, DVCA
DI MILANO.

Quando fu morto nella Chiefa di Santo Stefano
da Giouan'Andrea da Lampognano,

Title page of printed "Lamento del duca Galeazzo Maria Sforza." *Archivio Storico Civico, Milan, Biblioteca Trivulziana.*

8

"To the Praise and Glory of . . . All the Triumphant Celestial Court"

Splendor, Intimacy, and Death (1475–1476)

In 1475, Easter fell on March 26, ten days after the Bastard of Burgundy's departure. Galeazzo, who stayed in Vigevano for the entire month, withdrew from public view. "His Highness has been in seclusion all this Holy Week and had not allowed anyone to talk to him or see him, except for a *cameriere* who dresses him and two *sottocamerieri* and a *ragazzo* who attend his chamber; and he has commanded that no person dare come to disturb him or speak to him until the three days of Easter have passed."[1] As soon as Easter had ended, the duke emerged to order preparations for one of the most lavish displays of ducal splendor in Sforza history. The occasion was an annual ducal holiday, the feast of San Giorgio. In 1475, that feast had a special significance, for Galeazzo made the public proclamation of his alliance with the duke of Burgundy. The new alliance was dedicated "to the praise and glory of omnipotent God and the most glorious Virgin Mary, and of the most blessed Saint Ambrose and the glorious knight Saint George, and of all the triumphant celestial court."[2]

The Feast of San Giorgio

"The glorious knight Saint George" was patron saint to the dukes of Milan, an appropriate figure for the warrior Sforza dynasty.[3] Except for Genoa, none of the dominion's major cities had a special veneration for this saint. Galeazzo's observances of this feast emphasized his authority over the whole dominion, transcending local interests. The martial nature of Saint George's image also reinforced the martial nature of Milanese ducal authority; it was the army that had brought the Sforza to the throne and ensured that they remained there. Galeazzo made the regular observance of San Giorgio a high priority. As early as 1467, he insisted on returning to Milan "to be able to provide in time for the matters of San Giorgio."[4] It was the only occasion outside the Christmas season that he always spent in the capital once he had taken his ducal seat. The date of this observance—April 24— was unique to Milan, where the feast was celebrated according to the Ambrosian calendar. Elsewhere in Christendom, the feast of Saint George was celebrated on April 23.

Galeazzo's observance of San Giorgio remained essentially the same throughout his reign, although it varied in scale from year to year. San Giorgio was an occasion for great pride, when military emblems symbolizing ducal power were sanctified by the church with the participation of court, household, administration, and princely clients. The duke rode with an honorable following in procession from Porta Giovia Castle to the Duomo, where leading prelates of the duchy blessed the ducal military standards. On his return to Porta Giovia, the duke held a military parade and inspection, the most elaborate annual display of military strength. For San Giorgio 1475, Galeazzo pulled out all the stops. He planned for over 4,000 soldiers to participate in the display, among them the *galuppi,* ducal mounted guard, household troops, ducal brothers' squadrons, and other elements of the standing army as well as a division from condottiere Giovanni Conti. The logistics were overwhelming. All of the troops had to be housed; those living within fourteen miles of the capital—as far away as Abbiategrasso—stayed at their homes, while the rest were billeted within twelve miles of the city. Every household in the Milanese district was either used or taxed for that billeting, except those of monasteries and gentlemen.[5]

On March 30, Galeazzo ordered the wardrobe steward, Gottardo Panigarola, to provide new liveries for 33 singers, 30 footmen, 61 *galuppi,* 35 pages, 26 kennelmen, and the 100 mounted crossbowmen of the ducal guard. "To the footmen (*stapheri*) you will make for each one a *zuparello* of green velvet, or sky blue, but all of the same color. For use over that you will make them a cloak in the Sforza colors [*a la divisa*] with the viper [Visconti emblem]."[6] Each group was to have its own uniform dress, with a distinctive color and emblem. Gottardo Panigarola had also to provide new cloaks "*ala divisa Sforzescha*" (white and dark red) and new breastplates for 1,205 menat-arms. Their 750 pages were furnished with matching clothes and a pennant on a lance. The 87 squad leaders received cloaks of velvet; the others, cloaks of ordinary wool cloth. The squad leaders in each of the six divisions bore a different emblem; for the *lanze spezzate,* for instance, it was the *semprevive,* a plant that Galeazzo used often as an emblem.[7] The duke also made sure that his own family, including the countess Lucia, sported splendid new clothes for San Giorgio in 1475. Little GianGaleazzo and Ermes received armor and long *zupponi,* covered by sky blue cloaks embroidered with the same emblems their father wore over his armor. Lucia was clothed in a dazzling creation of gold brocade in white.[8] Even one of the physicians received a scarlet cloak and crimson velvet robe for the occasion.[9]

Galeazzo invited several foreign dignitaries to attend the observance of San Giorgio in 1475, including envoys from Savoy, Venice, and Ferrara and the marquess of Mantua in person. Ambassadors were lodged at ducal expense in Milan's finest inns; the marquess was housed in Porta Giovia Castle. Galeazzo spent much of April 22 and 23 in his chambers consulting with the emissaries, after hearing Mass. The Savoyards discussed "the threats which the king of France made against them," among other things. Ludovico Gonzaga had nothing substantive to discuss with Galeazzo, and they just went hunting in the Giardino later.[10]

On the day of San Giorgio, April 24, Galeazzo "went to the Duomo, armed with all arms, and had the standards blessed according to custom, then the solemn Mass was sung. And with His Excellency were to be found the illustrious lord Marquess of Mantua, the Governor of Nice and Balochino, ambassadors from Savoy, [the ambassador] of the duke of Ferrara and Clemente, secretary of the Signorìa of Venice."[11] The following day, after Mass, Galeazzo and Ludovico Gonzaga went out to the Giardino, where all the troops were arrayed by squadron. The duke made a detailed review of them, one by one, even the pages and foot soldiers, "and he wanted all the squad leaders and men-at-arms to put on their helmets and bear their lances, to see how apt they were in their trade." Galeazzo spent two hours with his soldiers before sending them out of the Giardino "all in step together, which was a beautiful sight. The standards were borne back into the Castle with the sounds of horns, pipes, drums, and guns, so that all the air resounded." The duchess watched the whole parade from a window on the upper floor of Porta Giovia.[12] After reviewing the troops, Galeazzo and the marquess reentered the castle; each went to his own chambers to dine, the duke downstairs and his guest above. Early the next morning, the two princes took a boat to Pavia, where they stopped off for a bit of deer hunting at Mirabello before proceeding to Pavia Castle. Bona came to Pavia in a separate boat, later. The countess Lucia had made the trip to Pavia the evening before.[13]

A Fresco Program for San Giorgio

In 1474, Galeazzo had also staged a lavish display for San Giorgio and commanded that all *camerieri* and other courtiers come to Milan for it. The total cost for wardrobe work alone was estimated at 11,000 ducats.[14] That year, the duke drew up a detailed fresco program depicting the San Giorgio observance at its most splendid. The program was intended for the Sala della Balla of Porta Giovia, although it was probably not executed.[15]

The program consists of four parts, each one probably intended for a different wall. The first scene presents the festal procession issuing from Porta Giovia. Galeazzo and his footmen are at the gate, preceded by his *camerieri,* among them Guido Antonio Arcimboldi, bearing the ceremonial golden sword and talking with Carlino Varesino. The two *sottocamerieri* Nasino and Bernardino da Corte ride ahead of them, bearing princely regalia. Nine other *camerieri di camera* ride near them, including Francesco Pietrasanta, Pietro Birago, and Cosme Ponzoni, the pardoned rapist. Ahead of them ride a "company of *camerieri,*" dressed lavishly and approaching the Duomo, "to accompany his Excellency and the standards." The scene includes unarmed courtiers moving "toward the Duomo like people that go to see the celebration and accompany the Lord." Following the duke come persons of princely rank, led by the Neapolitan ambassador, the marquesses of Mantua and Montferrat, and six condottieri. The Sforza family are represented by seven of the duke's brothers and half-brothers who led military squadrons; behind them ride the four governors of the *lanze spezzate.* Their names are to be painted in gold "and similarly the names of the best horses they have." The military leaders are followed by the administrative and ecclesiastical contingent, primarily the two cardinal-bishops, the Privy Council, and the Chancery. Interspersed throughout the scene are trumpeters and common soldiers.

The second scene of the fresco program features all the armed men gathered at the Corte, where Galeazzo is shown with his following, surrounded by foot soldiers and musicians. The principals move from that palace to the adjacent cathedral, where the chaplain is saying Mass at the altar of Saint George and the cardinal-archbishop of Milan blesses the standards. The choral responses to his benediction are provided by the duke's own choir. The ceremony finished, the third section of the fresco program illustrates the return to Porta Giovia Castle. The fourth part describes the armed men in full parade at the castle, viewed by the unarmed observers and depicted in great detail.

Other San Giorgio Observances

Galeazzo rarely celebrated the feast of San Giorgio quite so lavishly as in this fresco program, or in the observance of 1475, but he never skimped on the occasion. In 1467, he was already prepared to spend 1,300 ducats on five hundred pennants to be carried by the household troops and "the *camerieri* who bear arms."[16] In 1469 and 1471, he used the occasion to hold tournaments.[17] In 1472, all the feudatories who were usually expected in Milan at San Giuseppe were told to attend at San Giorgio instead, and ambassadors from Savoy and Genoa were present for the display. Troops who had come to accompany the ducal standards caused damage in the Milanese district.[18] The next year, Galeazzo sought to prevent similar damage; he commanded that the troops not arrive in the district so early, "because we would not want them to spend so many days on the backs of poor men." He gave the *galuppi* double pay and soldiers from the *famiglia* (*famigli d'arme*) triple pay for the occasion. The pay was not high for these men—4 pounds (1 ducat) per month was the basic rate—but it added up quickly when given to 466 soldiers.[19] Three years later, in 1476, the celebration was modest, including only the men-at-arms of the ducal guard and the troops already stationed in the district.[20]

The Ambrosian Tradition

The city and people of Milan and its district were not particularly moved by the feast of San Giorgio. This ducal saint was not their saint, and the ducal celebration was not their celebration. They bore the cost of bringing hundreds or thousands of soldiers to their homes, where those soldiers caused damage and inconvenience. The great activities of the day occurred in places where ordinary citizens could not go, including the cold, forbidding Porta Giovia Castle, which those citizens had attacked in 1447. The occasion reminded them of their subjection to a dynasty that was no longer even native to their city.

Milan had its own traditions, its own great patron saint. The civic and liturgical identity of the Sforza capital was dominated by the figure of Saint Ambrose. Milan had its own unique form of the Mass, its own form of chant, it own ritual calendar. Because of Ambrose, the great ducal celebrations of San Giorgio and San Giuseppe fell on dates observed nowhere else in Christendom. Because of Ambrose, Mass was not celebrated on Fridays during Lent, and Carnival was observed on different dates than elsewhere.[21] Because of Ambrose, the citizens of Milan could feel that they had a special distinction. The saint was also the symbol of Milanese *libertà*. His name graced the short-lived republic that preceded the Sforza dominion. When the city was briefly the Roman imperial capital, Bishop Ambrose was more powerful than the emperor himself. It was in Milan that Christianity became the official religion of Rome. After the fall of the Lombard kings, Ambrose's episcopal successors resumed that tradition of authority. It was the diocesan authority of Milan that gave that city its dominance over Lombardy in the Middle Ages, and it was the archbishops who controlled Milan itself. They were the "counts" to whom the Visconti were "vice-counts." Ultimately, it was an archbishop who established the Visconti family as Milan's lords and who created the list of those families whose noble status would henceforth be recognized.[22]

Although Galeazzo Maria Sforza did not control the archiepiscopal office in Milan, he used the Ambrosian political heritage to reinforce his own image. Like his predecessors, the fifth duke placed the image of Milan's patron saint on coins minted during his reign. However, Galeazzo was not content with the traditional iconography of the church father in a pastoral posture; he had Ambrose depicted on horseback, striking down heretics.[23] This militant mounted Ambrose was no longer merely a historical bishop; the duke's imagery recalled papal, imperial, and chivalric pretensions. The identification of Ambrose with the Sforza dominion reaffirmed the latter's legitimacy. Galeazzo felt the Ambrosian Mass was the proper observance for certain occasions with major political ramifications. The annual masses commemorating Duke Francesco's death were held according to the Ambrosian Rite.[24] When Giovanni Arcimboldi was elevated to the cardinalate in 1473, the bishop of Parma was asked to sing an Ambrosian Mass as part of the celebration.[25] The saint's feast (December 6) was a high point of the ritual year in Milan, and "servants of the court" resident there were presented with gifts, according to traditional practice.[26]

Saint Ambrose was a beloved figure only within the Milanese district; elsewhere in the dominion, he was a symbol of oppression by the capital city. One reason for Francesco Sforza's success in conquering Milan was that other parts of the duchy had rejected the Ambrosian Republic and its particularist interests. A prince from outside Milan might have more regard for the dominion as a whole than the citizens of Milan had shown. Personally, Galeazzo had little attachment to the capital's patron saint. The duke rarely spent the feast of Sant 'Ambrogio in Milan, and his traveling court made little show of the occasion. His daily Mass was celebrated according to the Roman, or Gregorian, Rite, and his testament specifically requested that Gregorian Masses be celebrated for the sake of his soul.[27]

The Bastard Returns

Galeazzo spent much of May and June 1475 in consultation with ambassadors from various powers, including his own Genoese subjects. He also set preparations in motion for a second visit by Antoine, Bastard of Burgundy, on his return trip from Naples.[28] The Bastard reached the Sforza dominion on the first day of July. The following day, he arrived at Milan and was greeted by the usual crowd of courtiers, councillors, and other ducal officers as well as Tristano Sforza. The honored guest was lodged at the Inn of the Well and kept company throughout his week's stay by eight of the duke's most honorable *gentiluomini,* including Gabriele Stampa. The seneschals presented him with "a most worthy gift of edible things," including large quantities of bread and wine, 3 wheels of aged cheese (weighing 26–30 pounds each), over 500 fowl of six different types, 120 pounds of candles, and sweets such as marzipan (18 pounds), fruits, nuts, and 6 loaves of fine sugar. For a dessert wine, he received 24 flasks of Malvasia.[29]

Although ready to extend his generosity to the Bastard, Galeazzo himself remained at Pavia and refused to see his guest at all during the week; the duke felt insulted. Charles the Bold had directed his half-brother to execute a special embassy to Galeazzo, pursuant to the new alliance between the two states. The duke of Milan felt this arrangement dishonored him, since the Bastard had originally been authorized as an envoy to another state. Even worse, that state was hated Naples. Consequently, Galeazzo resolved to wait until Charles the Bold could send "an honorable embassy," to which Galeazzo intended to reply by sending his own brother, Ludovico.[30] The Bastard was upset by Galeazzo's refusal to see him, suspecting that the duke was entertaining French ambassadors instead. Antoine went about his business for the week, while Galeazzo kept secretly informed about purchases of armor and other items by his guest. The Bastard's departure was honored with an escort of courtiers, councillors, and other ducal officers. He rode with Branda Castiglione, bishop of Como and Privy Councillor, "because up to our adolescence, we were acquainted with one another together in Brabant." The Bastard discussed the awkward situation with his childhood friend, explaining his own position and asking about Galeazzo's. "And," as bishop Branda related to his ducal master, "he said many other stinging words to me about this."[31] Even Galeazzo's generous hospitality could not assuage his guest's wounded princely pride.

Extravagance

The lavish gift of edibles to the Bastard of Burgundy reflects the sensual extravagance that characterized the last two years of Galeazzo's reign. The court's use of luxury items increased even beyond its previous high level, and the duke kept Gottardo Panigarola, the wardrobe steward, constantly busy. Gottardo had to make the arrangements to manufacture or purchase whatever Galeazzo demanded, then deliver it within the brief period the impatient prince was willing to wait. These demands ranged from paper on which Josquin des Prez would write music to chessboards and included collars for dogs, covers for mules, and huge quantities of cloth and jewelry.[32]

Demands came to the wardrobe almost every day for cloth or finished clothing to give members of the ducal family, courtiers, administrators, visiting dignitaries, Galeazzo's mistresses, and anyone else to whom the duke felt generous. A random sample of wardrobe orders from 1475 shows him outfitting the head of his choir for Christmas, giving a gold brocade garment to his ambassador in Venice, and having clothes of silver brocade and other expensive stuffs made for two new *camerieri*. Galeazzo's letters to his household treasurer show him spending almost 113 ducats on live pheasants to stock his hunting grounds and almost 350 ducats on construction at the house he gave Countess Lucia.[33] As a result of such payments and the grandiose plans for

San Giorgio 1475, the 1476 budget shows 53,000 ducats owed to Gottardo "for expenditures made in the year 1475," not including the brocades mentioned above. Those items and others given in the Christmas season were not to be paid for until 1477. The 1476 budget also bears debts of 46,380 ducats for jewels. Altogether, these figures dwarf the 38,810 ducats that the 1476 budget set aside for maintaining the duchess's household all year, or the 60,338 ducats earmarked for the salaries of all Galeazzo's officials.[34]

"For Her Incredible Love Toward Us"

Galeazzo's fondness for the Countess Lucia did not wane during 1475–1476, and he continued to shower her with the best of everything. In May 1475, he requested from Lorenzo de'Medici a huge and famous ruby the latter possessed. In September 1475, Milan's leading humanist, Francesco Filelfo, wrote the duke praising Lucia "with prudence and elegance."[35] The young lady also received property from another source in October, when her uncle Michele, bishop of Piacenza, died. Because of "the love that we bear" her and her family, Galeazzo sent a ducal servant to visit Michele in the latter's final illness. He also commanded the *commissario* of Piacenza to visit the ailing ecclesiastic. After Michele's death around two weeks later, the bishop's brother Giovanni Antonio asked Galeazzo to ensure that the Marliani were not deprived of their inheritance. In response, Galeazzo told the *commissario* to make inventories of the late bishop's property and allow Michele's brothers and servants to bring his personal property home to Milan. Lucia inherited all of it.[36]

In December, the countess received 4,000 ducats from the ducal treasury, and on the last day of the year, Galeazzo gave her property in Vigevano that had previously belonged to the former *primo cameriere,* Carlino Varesino. In the charter, the duke declared his desire to "acknowledge the Magnificent Lady Lucia Visconti, Countess of Melzo, for her incredible love toward us" and many other appealing qualities. On June 13, 1476, he made another major grant to her: a feudal investiture adding Desio and Marliano (her family's town of origin) to her comital lands. The grant was not merely nominal; when Galeazzo told the masters of revenues that she had received Desio, he also informed them that she possessed the right to choose the town's podestà.[37]

In addition, Galeazzo brought Countess Lucia with him as he traveled about the duchy, arranging side trips for her to nearby places of interest. While the court was at Cassano in August 1475, Lucia visited Trezzo; from Galliate three months later, she went to Novara. Earlier in the year, with the court in the Gera d'Adda district, she had visited the *commissario* and two courtiers with estates in the area.[38]

Austerities

Throughout his reign, Galeazzo steered an erratic fiscal course between extravagance and austerity. In 1471, even as he had been collecting Italy's largest choir and taking his retinue of 1,400 persons to Florence, he had sought petty economies in his own and his wife's households.[39] The duke's efforts to systematize the institutions of court and state were motivated in part by a preoccupation with the budget. He wanted to increase revenues and limit what he considered unnecessary spending, while spending liberally when the spirit took him. At the end of 1475, he was particularly concerned about the fiscal health of his dominion. On December 19, he arrived in Milan, after which he "attended solely to curbing costs, deciding he wants to restore the excess expenditures made this year."[40]

"In this beginning of the year [1476], the Lord has ordered that some of his councillors be distributed as *commissari* of the cities and towns of his dominion." Among these men were courtiers and administrators newly named to the Privy Council, such as Antonio Secco, one of Bona's four original *gentiluomini*.[41] Sending councillors to serve as *commissari* was an act of economy; in those offices, they would save Galeazzo the salary of an additional administrator. He also chose a group of ten councillors to remain at work in Milan "without any pay at all." He planned to curb payments to all of the civil administration. "To the Magnificent Messer Cicco, he has said that [Cicco] should bring with him only six chancellors, and that two others would remain at Milan with his brother Giovanni Simonetta, and that all the rest would be discharged." Those discharges probably did not occur.

The seriousness of Galeazzo's intentions at this time was reflected in his intention to suspend the pay of his four closest companions (Trivulzio, Cotta, del Bergamino, Arcimboldi) and leave them "in Milan at home." For the *camerieri* "to whom His Lordship has given their own [property] and granted them a fief or other income, he has taken away their pay entirely, wanting them to serve him at their own expense. [He is] not giving them any other expenses except for eating [*la boccha*], and that because, since they are obliged to stay near His Lordship continually, it is necessary that they eat in court according to custom." Galeazzo's plans for other *camerieri* included limits on their pay and expense allowances, "and there will be few who remain, because he shows that he wants to discharge many and limit himself to keeping only those that are necessary to him for service of his person." The implication that the duke surrounded himself with crowds of unneeded attendants reflects the princely magnificence that Galeazzo generally sought to project. That tendency to self-aggrandizement always had its counterpart in Galeazzo's desire to control and systematize his sphere. "It has not been yet made public who [of the *camerieri*] would be discharged and who would remain. He had said that, when His Lordship leaves [Milan], after the [Christmas] holidays are over, he will leave the rota signed by his own hand, by which it will be known what everyone will have to do." The duke began discharging footmen and claimed he "did not want to keep more than twelve *ragazzi* in the household."[42]

The duke's intention to cut costs extended to almost every area of his court. All the *gentiluomini,* for both himself and the duchess, were deprived of their pay "for a year at least," and salaries were suspended for a year to all other "officiali de la corte" and administrators outside the Privy Council. At the same time, he planned to collect more taxes, cut the pay of major condottieri, and generally impose an austerity so strict that it would bring his budget back into balance. The written budget for 1476 shows a positive balance of 100,000 ducats, but it may have overestimated income and underestimated expenses.[43] Whatever the case, most of the planned austerities were probably not put into effect.

"Our Friendship and Compaternity"

One area in which Galeazzo did not intend to impose austerities was where his heart beat most strongly. The countess Lucia began the year 1476 in the second trimester of pregnancy. On April 16, Galeazzo wrote her to say, "We are pleased that you have arrived [in Milan] safe, sound, and joyful, and we encourage you to remain so, with a happy mind." He himself left Vigevano for Milan on the following day, three hours after she had borne him a son. That son is referred to in the grant of Desio and Marliano as "the magnificent Galeazzo Sforza Maria Visconti." The new estate, with its ancestral connection to Lucia herself, was probably a reward for producing this male child.[44]

On May 5, 1476, Galeazzo ordered Ambrogio Raverti to visit him in Pavia, where a ducal chancellor was waiting to "tell you some things on our behalf." Those "things" probably related to the son whom Ambrogio's wife had just borne and the duke was about to baptize as his own.[45] For the baptism of his natural son, Galeazzo, the duke needed to establish a new network of ritual kinship among men suitable as *compari* for an illegitimate cadet. The one formal social relationship that was undertaken purely as a matter of personal choice was *comparaggio,* or ritual co-parenthood. Parents (generally, fathers) chose *compari* (literally, co-fathers) for the baptism of each child.[46] The construction of networks of interest through the medium of baptism was a vital process in traditional Catholic society.[47] *Comparaggio* created fictive kin of theoretically equal standing. It expanded or reinforced an individual's network in ways that could be politically or professionally useful as well as personally pleasant. Because the choice of *compari* could be different for each child, a parent could create variations on this basic theme, acknowledging new friendships, reaffirming old ones, and generally re-creating networks with greater flexibility than ties of marriage or blood could afford. It was not necessary for a *compare* to appear in person at the baptism; just as Galeazzo became a husband by proxy, many individuals became *compari* by proxy.

Galeazzo invited the same group of very honorable men to participate, personally or by proxy, in the baptisms of his first three legitimate children: Lorenzo de' Medici, Federigo da Montefeltro, Giovanni Bentivoglio, Cicco Simonetta, Giovanni Bolognini Attendoli (castellan of Pavia), and the powerful French cardinal Rohan. Another member of the group, Angelo Simonetta, died a month before Bianca Sforza's baptism in 1472. For that occasion, the duke also invited two prominent members of the Visconti clan to participate. The rest of the group represented all the primary supporters of Galeazzo's position: his princely peers, client princes, civil and military administrations, the Medici of Florence, and the kingdom of France. Naturally, these prominent personages did not always appear themselves; even for the baptism of the duke's heir, Cardinal Rohan sent an abbot as proxy.[48]

The choice of *compari* for Lucia's son was a delicate one. The duke could not invite the figures who stood as *compari* to his legitimate children, yet he sought persons of similar dignity who maintained good relations with him. His three choices were Roberto da Sanseverino, Giovanni Arcimboldi, and Giovanni Conti.[49] Roberto was Galeazzo's first cousin; his mother had been Duke Francesco's sister. In 1476, he also held the second-largest contract with Milan for military services. As a former courtier, Arcimboldi had close personal relations to the duke, and as a cardinal, he held an influential position. Conti, a noble Roman condottiere, was already linked to Galeazzo's household through his own son, Giovanni Battista, a ducal *cameriere*. Galeazzo scheduled the baptism for Sunday, May 19, 1476, and suggested that Giovanni Battista act as proxy for his father.[50]

On those occasions when Galeazzo's *compari* invited him to return the favor, he sent his own proxies. At least three times, the duke had his ambassador in Bologna stand in at the baptism of Giovanni Bentivoglio's children. The same ambassador also acted for his master in the baptism of Roberto da Sanseverino's son.[51] Although baptism was the most usual occasion for which *compari* were invited, it was not the only one. When Cardinal Riario visited Milan in 1473 as part of the papal-Milanese *rapprochement,* he stood as *compare* at the confirmation (*cresmò*) of the duke's three legitimate children and two illegitimate boys.[52] This event occurred in the same year that Gerolamo Riario was betrothed to Galeazzo's daughter Caterina and further reinforced the network of interest between Sixtus IV and the duke.

"For the Goodwill You Bore Your *Compare*"

In general, *comparaggio* was not so important a vehicle for bonding at the princely level. Princely networks formed and dissolved much more rapidly than those of their subjects, and the spirit of collegiality and benefaction that characterized *comparaggio* was part of the expectations of princely office.[53] Galeazzo condescended to join in *comparaggio* with certain courtiers and favored subjects. When Carlino Varesino's wife gave birth to a son, Galeazzo told Giovanni Simonetta that "we have heard that Maddalena, wife of Messer Carlino Varesino, our *cameriere,* has had a son, which is very pleasing to us. . . . We have constituted you our procurator to make *compatricio* in our name with Sir Carlino and Maddalena . . . for the son." After the baptism, Giovanni informed the duke that the baby had been given the name Galeazzo. Later that month, Giovanni served as the duke's proxy for the baptism of Pietro Birago's daughter; Galeazzo helped choose her name.[54]

The usefulness of *comparaggio* for establishing a network in the Milanese court is apparent from its widespread application. Cicco Simonetta had the most extensive network of *compari* at court; he was much more accessible than the duke himself. Because Cicco could facilitate any procedure in the ducal administration, a relationship of compaternity with him was widely sought. Among those who addressed him as "compare" were the archbishop of Milan, Tristano Sforza, Pigello Portinari, Federigo da Montefeltro, various condottieri, and members of the Sforza administration.[55] Cicco benefited from these connections, too, as he could gain compliance and cooperation more readily from persons who had such a personal link with him.

Appeals for assistance on the basis of *comparaggio* occurred regularly within the court. In 1469, Cicco had received one from the duke's *referendario-generale,* Fazio Gallerani. Addressing Cicco as "compare," Fazio explained that Ottaviano Porro, "your godson and son of the late Bartolomeo Porro, your *compare* and mine," had begun holding a minor office in the ducal administration, but the formal letters of appointment had yet to be completed. He asked Cicco to have the letters expedited "as much for the goodwill you bore your *compare* as for [Ottaviano] being godson to you, and also because he is my nephew."[56] It is worth noting the distinction between Cicco's relationships with the son (his *figliozo,* or godson) and the father (his *compare*). Although one relationship could hardly exist without the other, each was seen in a different light; a *compare* was a person of equal dignity, while a godson held a junior position.

Cicco was not the only desirable *compare* at Galeazzo's court. Within the Chancery, the secretaries, chancellors, and ushers were linked to one another several times over in this way. When Giovanni Pietro Pagano had his son and daughter baptized, he invited ten colleagues from the Chancery to join him as *compari.*[57] *Comparaggio* could thus reinforce the collegiality of a group whose internal relations must have been fairly close already. *Compare* relationships could also transcend professional or social groupings, as in the cases of Michele Bonicci (ducal chancellor) with Lazzaro Tedaldi (ducal physician), Giovanni Rusca (count from Como) with Fabrizio Marliani (bishop of Tortona and Galeazzo's confessor), Angelo Simonetta with Domenico del

Ponte (physician from Lodi) and the Flemish vice-choirmaster Gaspar van Weerbeke with Pietro da Carcano, Milanese doctor of canon law.[58]

"[My wife] has newly had a girl which I want to have baptized next Sunday. Because I believe that Your Magnificence will not be able to be here, I want to draw up a proxy for Your Magnificence, in the name of whomever you would like. He has to come and participate for Your Magnificence at the baptism of that girl for reaffirming our friendship and compaternity. I offer and recommend myself to Your Magnificence." Thus wrote Count Giovanni Borromeo to the ducal secretary, Giacomo Alfieri, already his *compare* for a previous daughter. The respectful tone of the letter does not reflect the two men's respective backgrounds. Alfieri, a native of the kingdom of Naples, was in no way the count's social equal, let alone his superior.[59]

Comparaggio was not an exclusively male institution, and women could also call on compaternal relations for favors. Calling herself his "commater," Anna Scaccabarozzi Fossati, widow of a ducal seneschal, asked Galeazzo for help on behalf of a brother-in-law who was in trouble. She appealed to "the singular favor which I consider myself to have with Your Excellence through the medium [*per el mezo*] of our compaternity."[60] The following year, when the duke was trying to arrange a marriage for her, he wrote, "*Comare,* we have continually desired your welfare and honor, for the love that we bore toward the good memory of the late Francesco, your husband and our *compare,* and also that we bear toward you."[61]

The Ducal Household in 1476

The love Galeazzo bore for Lucia Marliani Visconti became increasingly visible in 1476. However, when Lucia traveled with the court, she was not accompanying Galeazzo in lieu of his wife. "This morning, the Lord and Milady Duchess embarked on a boat and came to Binasco by the canal, and tonight they stayed here." On January 3, 1476, Galeazzo and Bona started the annual travel cycle together. The relationship between the ducal couple is oddly difficult to assess, and the voluminous records from the Sforza archives include no direct communications between Galeazzo and Bona. The duke was a remarkably fickle man, and he had many brief obsessions and preoccupations during his reign. However, he did not lose interest quickly in his wife. As late as the summer of 1473, the duke had a private passage built between his chamber and Bona's in Porta Giovia Castle. Galeazzo specifically instructed the *commissario* of Works that he did not want to be seen going to his wife.[62] In September of that year, he had referred to his wife as "young and beautiful," commenting (in a characteristic letter to his ambassador in Rome) that "considering that we too are young, and that we are adequate to

satisfy her very well, we do not care about her going where she pleases"—
such as "convents of the religious."[63]

A Strange Ménage

Lucia was not the only woman who bore Galeazzo a child in 1476. On
July 19, the duchess Bona gave birth at Pavia to a daughter, later named
Anna. Bona herself sent the letters notifying ambassadors that her daughter
had been born. Galeazzo took little interest in his new daughter's baptism
and early care.[64] The ducal family's domestic situation was altogether unconventional during much of the year. While Galeazzo had handled the baptism
of another man's wife in April, his own daughter's nurse was being chosen
in July by his own wife's favorite, Antonio Tassino.[65] The court must have
seemed a strange ménage to observers when the duke traveled with both his
mistress and his wife, who brought along her lover as well.[66]

Notwithstanding the intimacy that the duke and duchess shared with others, they continued to travel together often. After wintering at Pavia, they
both proceeded to Vigevano, where Bona remained while Galeazzo went to
Milan for San Giorgio and Lucia's childbirth. The ducal couple reunited in
May at Pavia, where they stayed through the summer. Within two months
after Bona gave birth to Anna, she and Galeazzo went to Galliate for an extended stay in the Lomellina. She may have remained there while the duke
made a brief trip to Varese for bear hunting. In mid-November, they left
Galliate, traveling together until their return to Milan for Christmas.[67]

The Duchess and the Countess   Bona began to assert herself more in
1476, probably with Tassino's support and encouragement. She laid claim to
more of the ducal resources, as when she ordered a seneschal to assign half of
the stable facilities at Galliate Castle to her own court. On another occasion,
she ordered that the duke's seneschals not be allowed in her bedchambers
without her special permission, even if she was not present.[68] Bona became
more active also in other areas of court life, arranging marriages, assist-
ing courtiers, and giving clothes and other gifts. She even exerted pressure on
important ducal officers, such as the treasurer-general and the constable of
Milan's Porta Tosa gate.[69]

For her part, the countess Lucia spent several months at her house in
Milan after giving birth in April. Her household staff had been chosen by the
duke, and two of his *sottocamerieri* kept him informed of her activities. On
August 25, they told him that she had been in the house all day, "quite cheerful," dancing with her young companions. Her uncle Giovanni Antonio, archpriest of Santa Maria del Monte, also visited during the day, and her brother-

in-law Alessandro da Rho dined with her. The following day, two daughters of Pietro Pusterla paid Lucia a visit. They all danced together, and the visitors "stayed to dinner with her, constantly joking." Later in the afternoon, she wanted to go out and asked Giovanni da Castelnovate to send around "her *gentiluomini* which Your Excellency previously ordered should keep her company." Evidently, she had not made this request before, for two of them had long since been appointed seneschals and become unavailable for this duty. Of the other two, one was absent from Milan and the other ill in bed. The seneschal-general had to substitute four other *gentiluomini* on the spot.[70]

Within her own sphere, Lucia did not hesitate to assert herself. In December 1475, she had interceded with Galeazzo to pardon a young *cameriere* who had been banished by him. In April 1476, she took advantage of her favored position to seek help for a convent in which one of her sisters lived.[71] When her son had a mild illness at the age of eight months, she was not shy about telling the attending physician her ideas for curing the infant.[72]

Children at Court

The Sforza court was not a nursery, and few children outside the ducal family were reared at court. The ducal residences were not designed to house whole families, and even the duke and duchess rarely kept their young children with them. As vital as children were to the perpetuation of lineage, they were not socially integrated until they had reached sufficient age to be married (if girls) or trained as warriors and courtiers (if boys). At twelve or thirteen years, young men and women could become a contributing part of the court establishment. Younger children generally lived at family homes elsewhere.

The Ducal Children   The duke's own children did have their place at court, but it was not generally with their parents. The children lived under the care of governors and wet nurses in one or another of the main ducal residences: the castles of Pavia, Milan, Abbiategrasso, and Vigevano and the hunting lodge called Cassino.[73] Galeazzo took an active interest in his children's upbringing, especially the boys'. He involved himself personally with issues of wet nursing, such as having a wet nurse replaced when her own child proved to be mute; it was feared that her milk might render the duke's son mute, too. Galeazzo also approved the weaning of the ducal heir at the age of three years.[74] The duke showed concern for his children's health. He commanded in one case that the children not play near moats or other water hazards and in another that they not travel in rainy weather. Bona was also concerned about her children's welfare; when she feared that her firstborn was ill, several physicians and courtiers worked to set matters right.[75]

Responsibility for the ducal children was shared between Galeazzo and Bona, and the legitimate children were maintained as part of her household. Despite this arrangement and the assertions of modern historians, the duchess did not reside with her children, except when the whole family stayed at Pavia.[76] On one occasion, she made a visit to them at Abbiategrasso which could not have lasted more than a few hours, for she was with Galeazzo in the morning at Gambolò and rejoined him in the evening at Villanova.[77] The legitimate children did not spend much time with their parents during Galeazzo's reign; only at the Christmas season was the family consistently united.[78]

Each child had a governor or governess, all of whom tried to advance their own interests. Pietrina Aliprandi was governess to Ermes in 1476, when she sought the privilege of appointing Bosco's podestà. She reminded the duke that she had four daughters of her own, for whom she had to provide dowries. Caterina Corti, Bona's midwife in 1472, held the lucrative office that set grain prices for the city of Milan. By 1476, she was Bona's *comare* (co-mother) for GianGaleazzo, which meant that she slept with the boy every night. When she was away from the court and unavailable, Bianca Sforza's wet nurse substituted for her in GianGaleazzo's bed.[79] Carlo and Alessandro shared a governor, Battista da Cremona, who was young and socially inconsequential. In contrast, Margherita Toscani, governess of their sister Caterina, was a lady of rank who had spent many years at court under Bianca Maria Visconti.[80]

Significant differences in the treatment of the various children reflected the importance of legitimacy and gender. The legitimate children were generally preferred over their half-siblings; in the Sala Grande fresco program, for instance, only the legitimate children were included. However, illegitimacy was not a major obstacle within the Sforza family; both of Galeazzo's own parents had been of illegitimate birth.

Legitimate or illegitimate, the boys received more attention than the girls. Galeazzo's natural sons, Carlo and Alessandro, were the eldest of his children, reaching their teens during the latter years of the reign. The duke began to include them in the ceremonial life of the court during the 1470s, and he enfeoffed them both. Carlo was temperamental and disrespectful, even to his father, who disposed of responsibility for him by marrying twelve-year-old Carlo to a daughter of Angelo Simonetta.[81] Galeazzo left Carlo in the care of his in-laws; despite their advocacy, Carlo did not receive much from his father for a few years. The will that Galeazzo dictated just after Carlo's marriage in 1470 left the boy nothing but "the wife given him presently." By 1476, though, Carlo had returned to favor and received the title of count.[82]

The more highly favored Alessandro had been granted the county of Galliate even before he was knighted in 1474.[83] Accordingly, he ranked ahead of Carlo in ceremonial precedence, and he participated in diplomatic receptions. Like his father, Alessandro had a keen enjoyment of good living; in 1476, he requested money from Galeazzo for the purpose of gambling.[84]

Galeazzo took a hand in his sons' education. In 1473–1474, he turned attention to Carlo's lessons, which were conducted in part by a disciple of Filelfo's. When the duke heard that Carlo had been "very obstinate toward your master in all things," he commanded that the boy be obedient and attend to learning, or else "we will give you such punishment that you will be left very unhappy."[85] Galeazzo's other sons had somewhat less distinguished preceptors. As of 1473, Alessandro was studying with Lorenzo Ferrari of Cremona. From March 1476 or earlier, Mattia da Trevio was teaching the ducal heir, GianGaleazzo, who began reading at this time. That November, when Mattia returned from an illness, Galeazzo set a limit of one hour per day, and one-half hour per sitting, on his son's reading time. The duke himself had been forced to read as much as four hours per day.[86]

While the duke's legitimate children were in residence with their governors and governesses, they often received visitors, including foreign dignitaries of princely rank. It was not uncommon for persons associated with the court to pay their respects to the young ones, especially the ducal heir. The children's stay at Cassino in November 1473 prompted many social calls of this kind; the callers included their half-brother Carlo and (separately) his betrothed, a number of *gentiluomini* (and at least one *gentiluomo*'s wife), a councillor, a physician, and resident ambassadors from Mantua and Naples.[87] In 1475, a painter received permission to visit GianGaleazzo to execute a portrait.[88]

Taking Care of Children   Parental responsibility had a powerful influence on the actions of persons at court. It was probably an appeal from "Piccetto" (Giacomo del Piccio), one of Galeazzo's seneschals-general, that resulted in a benefice being granted to the preceptor of that courtier's children.[89] Tommaso Tebaldi's appeal for a fief was motivated by a desire to provide his children with financial security. Many appeals to Galeazzo, such as Pietrina Aliprandi's, were made in the name of the children who needed dowries, clothing, education, medical attention, or other kinds of care.

The need to care for children could also affect ducal servants' ability to perform tasks for Galeazzo. When the duke went on campaign in 1467, he told both Antonio Guidoboni and Antonio's son to accompany him. Antonio pleaded that one of them be allowed to remain home to run their household because "I have so much—and such a—family, and for the most part women and little ones."[90] The plea did not reflect a lack of confidence in the women's capacity to manage the household but rather a recognition of the legal impediments to their doing so fully.

"Those . . . to Whom
One Has to Give Lodgings"

In 1476, a ducal official drew up a "List of those assigned to ride with the court of our Most Illustrious Prince and Most Excellent Lord, to whom one has to give lodgings."[91] The fifty-three categories total well over one thousand horses, plus dozens of pages, kitchen and pantry servants, barbers, kennelmen, foot soldiers, and others who did not have horses to be counted. Unlike the lists for the journey to Florence in 1471, this one does not include ambassadors, *gentiluomini,* or military captains; court members in those categories were not routinely provided lodgings as part of the ducal household.

At the head of the list, following the duke himself, are his brothers Ludovico and Sforza Maria, then two councillors and Galeazzo's four favorite companions. Between them, these eight men were entitled to lodgings for 112 horses (and their corresponding humans). The end of the list shows 170 horses for the duchess's court, among them 14 for Galeazzo's brother Ottaviano. Bona's household was always itemized separately, and this list gives only a total number, "including carts, wagons, and every other thing." It is substantially smaller than her retinue for the Florence trip, which had included over 300 horses. Apart from the addition of Bona's household at the end, the list is organized in order of rank and function. The first section following the councillors and ducal brothers contains four clerics (confessors and chaplains), three physicians, the court spicer, and four seneschals. As might be expected, the next categories are those closest to the duke's person: 23 *camerieri di camera,* 18 *camerieri di guardacamera,* and 12 *sottocamerieri.*[92] They are followed by the Privy Chancery, led by Cicco Simonetta and his son Giovanni Giacomo, then singers, organists, the master of perfumes, a clockmaker, tennis players, barbers, tailors, the kitchen, pantry, and stable staff, huntsmen, and "Signore Buffone." The list is rounded out by footmen, mounted crossbowmen of the ducal guard, foot soldiers, porters, and a few miscellaneous figures.

Finding suitable lodgings for so many persons, and their horses, must have posed a daunting challenge to the seneschals. When the duke went on campaign late in 1476, a concerned seneschal noted that the ducal bodyguard and singers amounted to some three hundred between them, and "there would remain . . . Your Excellency, . . . Her Excellency [the duchess], . . . the councillors, chancellors, and all the rest of the court."[93] Very few castles anywhere had the capacity to house so many people without considerable strain.

In all these lodging plans, the countess Lucia was never included, and no provisions were made explicitly for her. In that sense, she was never a part of

Galeazzo's household at all; the logistics of her own travel were arranged separately. At times, Lucia traveled entirely independently of the duke and his household. A week after traveling with Galeazzo and Bona in the Lomellina, she made a devotional visit to Santa Maria delle Grazie in Monza, staying at the castle there. Several days later, she was back in Milan, dining at the house of her brother-in-law, Alessandro da Rho, a ducal official. By Galeazzo's command, he had married Lucia's youngest sister.[94]

"The Exequies Were So Worthy . . . And There Was Not the Least Little Scandal"

On March 17, 1476, a solemn event in Milan brought together persons from many backgrounds, to an extent even Galeazzo had not anticipated. The occasion was the funeral of Bosio Sforza, half-brother of Duke Francesco and Galeazzo's uncle. Born in 1411, Bosio was a legitimate son of Muzio Sforza. He inherited the Romagnol county of Cotignola and gained more estates by marrying well. Through his first wife, Bosio acquired the substantial properties and title of the count of Santa Fiore, in Tuscany. In 1464, long after his first wife's death, he married Griseide da Capua, daughter of the Neapolitan duke of Atri. Some of her male relatives came to Galeazzo's court; one brother served briefly as a *cameriere di camera.* Bosio himself served the duke mainly as a military captain and feudatory in the Parma district, where he held two fiefs. Bosio resided in Milan part of each year, but he did not attend at his nephew's court much outside the great *feste.*[95]

Bosio's death did not come as a surprise. Before it occurred, Galeazzo had instructed that Bosio be honored with a state funeral, then buried in the Duomo. The duke had also written in advance to Griseide, promising her help with collecting debts, and so forth. When Bosio died, in Parma, Galeazzo sent the widow his condolences and told the *commissario* to send the remains to Milan.[96] On March 15, 1476, the duke gave the seneschals-general their orders for Bosio's funeral. Like Alessandro, his half-brother, Bosio would be associated in death with Duke Francesco's mother, Lucia Terzani da Marsciano, and his exequies would be performed as hers had been. Ironically, Bosio was not her son, since he was legitimate, but Galeazzo thought to do him the greatest possible honor by this association with the mother of the first Sforza duke. Indeed, Galeazzo wanted Bosio to be buried in the Duomo "next to this Madonna Lucia, removing the others that are in that place." The duke ordered Gottardo Panigarola to provide silver brocade to cover the casket and crimson cloth to cover the tomb at the funeral. He wanted all four of his sons to attend, dressed entirely in *morello,* the dark red ducal color.[97]

As usual, the duke himself did not attend the funeral; he remained at Vigevano, receiving descriptions afterward from the seneschals and Ermes's governor.[98] What made this event remarkable was that so many individuals and groups wanted to take part in the occasion; the old count was a much-loved man. The seneschals themselves were unusually proud of the occasion: "The exequies were so worthy and with such a multitude of gentlemen and other persons of every manner, as much to accompany the casket as to watch its progress [concorso] as no others have been, from the death of the late Most Illustrious Madonna your mother until now. And [these exequies were conducted] with such order that there was not the least little scandal."

The event fell into five sections, beginning with the gathering of the principals. At around 18 to 19 hours (12:00–1:00 P.M.), the councillors and many courtiers, who had gathered at the Corte Arengo, mounted on horseback and rode to Porta Giovia Castle with Tristano Sforza and Zaccaria Saggi da Pisa. They all returned to the Corte to sit with the body in a place specified by the duke. The order in which "the relatives" (li parenti) sat shows a careful balance of politics, protocol, and kinship. The Privy Council set the order, as they usually did when the precedence of princes was involved. The ducal heir, GianGaleazzo, came first, with the ambassador from Ferrara at his side; behind them was Ermes with Zaccaria. Behind them, in turn, came Tristano with Galeazzo's son Alessandro, then Carlo Sforza with Guidaccio Manfredi, followed by Lancillotto del Maino, Francesco Visconti, Andreotto del Maino, "and then, hand in hand, all the other relatives according to their rank." The ambassador from Ferrara preceded the Mantuan ambassador because the Este duke outranked the Gonzaga marquess. Guidaccio Manfredi was presumably included because his wife, Fiordelisa, was a Sforza relative of Bosio's. His place in the order was at the end of the princely figures, just ahead of three Milanese noblemen related to the ducal lineage through the late duchess's Visconti and del Maino heritage. Bosio had not been related by blood to any of them.

The bereaved "relatives" were men only. Although several of the mourners were related to Bosio through female lines, no women participated in the public exequies. In contrast, a great many men who were not part of the family joined in the funeral procession, the third section of the program. The procession wound around streets of central Milan, starting from the Corte and ending at the Duomo. It was led by "all the clergy," holding forty crosses and candles. Following them walked "all the servants [servitori] of the court," then about twenty household servants (famegli) of the deceased. They were all dressed in brown, a color of mourning.

After Bosio's household came "all the camerieri of Your Excellency who are found in this town, who are a good crowd," the gentleman courtiers (gentiluomini aulici) of duke and duchess, then "all the . . . mourners hand in hand, accompanied by two [members] of the Privy Council as long as they lasted, and then successively by two of the other magistrati." Leading the mourners was GianGaleazzo, escorted by the bishop of Cremona and Taddeo

Manfredi, as the highest ranking councillors. The ambassador from Ferrara went next, escorted by Galeazzo's onetime rescuer, Antonio da Romagnano, and Pietro Pusterla. Behind these most honorable figures came the city's participants: the jurists and physicians, "who were a great number," the merchants, and "the neighbors from the parishes, . . . a great multitude."

At the Duomo, all were seated in order again. A large group of clergy entered behind them, followed by the casket preceded by a hundred poor men "with black hoods and a torch in hand for each," walking two by two, and followed by a hundred more. The casket was deposited in the choir area of the cathedral, then a friar preached the sermon, which lauded Bosio "and the whole house of Sforza [tutta la casa Sforzescha]." Afterward, the duke's sons were escorted back to the castle. During the whole series of ceremonies, a group of "ladies who came to honor the said exequies" stayed in a hall upstairs in the Corte Arengo. There was "a very great quantity of them," with the relatives arranged in order. Tristano's wife, Beatrice, ranked first, then Galeazzo's half-sisters, Isotta and Fiordelisa. The rest were linked by blood or marriage to either the Sforza or the Visconti, led by Bianca Simonetta, wife of Galeazzo's son Carlo, and her mother, Francesca della Scala. Others named in the description were the daughters of Lancillotto del Maino and wives of Pietro da Gallarate, Pietro Francesco Visconti, and the late Gaspare da Vimercate.

What impressed the seneschals-general about this day was that so many people participated who were not mandated by command or custom. Men came from Parma to honor their fellow citizen, and they were very pleased at the great show Galeazzo had made "of the love that he bore for said Lord Bosio." In the evening, the body was brought out of the city for burial. So many of the Milanese turned out to pay their respects and so many clergy accompanied the body that "it was no less beautiful a spectacle in its own way than was today's funeral." The seneschals-general were amazed that people acted with "such love and eagerness" that there was no need to give commands: everyone was ready to do what was needed.

Threats and Fears

Galeazzo did not feel as well loved as his uncle Bosio. As the reigning prince, he perceived threats on all sides, and he feared for the safety of his person and his dominion. His three most powerful fears were specters that troubled many rulers: assassination, plague, and foreign domination.

Sedition and Assassination

By the last years of his reign, Galeazzo had offended virtually everyone with whom he had dealings. He had lost the personal charm that had prompted Benedetto Dei to liken him to "the son of the god Mars, newly descended" in 1459.[99] Rather, the duke had shown himself to be harsh, peremptory, and defiant of social conventions. He behaved abusively toward those within his power and reacted with extreme emotions to situations that hardly merited them. When Galeazzo lost a favorite dog "which he would keep in his chamber," he had it publicly proclaimed that anyone who stole a dog—from himself or any other person—would suffer the confiscation of all their property. Informers would receive 5 ducats for their help.[100] When a dog sent him by Edward IV of England died, Galeazzo sent a *cameriere* back to Edward for a replacement, saying, "It seems that Fortune permits that to the person who allows himself the most pleasure comes the greatest perturbation."[101]

Galeazzo had many reasons to be perturbed. He had developed many political rivals and even more personal enemies. It is not surprising that he thought his life and government were threatened by sedition and assassination plots. Such fears were not unreasonable for any prince, whose lives were often at risk, and the lords of Milan had a long history of rivalry, treachery, and violent death. Emotionally unstable though he was, Galeazzo never sank to the level of unrelieved paranoia that afflicted his grandfather, Duke Filippo Maria. Still, Galeazzo feared what might happen if his control over his world broke down. The duke's precautions against assassination included the crowd of personal attendants who accompanied him almost constantly. He maintained a personal guard of 100 mounted crossbowmen who traveled with him, 50 at a time, except when he was in disguise or at play. He also installed 100 extra guards at the castles in both Pavia and Milan and brought 100 guards from Milan when he visited the castle of Cassano in 1470. To protect himself from poisoning, Galeazzo ordered that wells "for the use of our mouth" at sixteen castles where he sometimes stayed (including all of his favorites) be locked when he was in residence.[102] In October 1469, two books "against poison" were replaced in his library, having apparently been used recently.[103]

The duke's awareness of security issues extended beyond his own borders. In September 1476, he spoke to the Ferrarese ambassador, whose prince (Ercole d'Este) had just quashed an attempted coup by his half-brother Niccolò. Galeazzo expressed surprise that Ercole would go about accompanied only by two footmen, as if he were "one of the least gentlemen." The Milanese duke said that he himself took special care "around the guard of his person" because he wanted "*Miserere mei Deus* to be sung at another's house, but not at his house." After that allusion to the two princes' shared musical interests, Galeazzo went on to remind Ercole "that, even though he has nothing to fear from his brothers or others . . . he nonetheless always brings with him a guard for his person of 50 footmen and 50 mounted crossbowmen." Galeazzo urged his Este cousin to maintain better security. Having seen what had happened to Ercole, he wanted to add 100 men-at-arms to his own guard.[104] Galeazzo's concern was not merely rhetorical. On September

7, he commanded that all the *famigli d'arme* in his ducal guard escort him while he hunted deer at Galliate. They were to bring their horses, body armor, and boots and ride with "their sword at their side."[105]

Galeazzo's security concerns were not limited to armed attacks; he also entertained suspicions of subversion. At one point, his vice-castellan in Milan investigated guests at a supper whose conversation had touched on sensitive state matters. The host was a prominent noble, Francesco Castiglione, and the guests included Filippo Pietrasanta, Gaspare Trivulzio, and other men of repute. The witnesses insisted that nothing was said against the duke, although the host had suggested that the Simonetta owed their prominent position at the Sforza court to the alliance between Milan and Naples. The supper had occurred before Galeazzo broke with Ferrante.[106]

Plague

What Galeazzo feared most was the plague, and that fear was shared by all of his contemporaries. The lords of Milan had traditionally taken strict and thorough precautions to protect themselves and their subjects.[107] Galeazzo imposed the usual quarantine (literally, a forty-day isolation period) on places and people suspected of exposure and refused entrance to the duchy to all persons arriving from known plague spots. This exclusion even applied to persons the duke would normally have seen with pleasure, such as musicians and high-ranking ambassadors.[108] The primary responsibility of the ducal Office of Health was to combat the plague, and their careful recording of deaths was evidently related to that effort. In 1468, the Privy Council recommended against permitting public preaching in Milan for Lent until no cases of plague had occurred in the capital for twelve days. The same year, Bianca Maria alerted the Office of Health that a possible case had occurred in Melegnano, and she asked them to investigate.[109] That year was a difficult one for the plague in Milan; an outbreak in the capital ruined the ducal wedding ceremony in July. Weeks before the wedding, Galeazzo had begun a concerted campaign against the deadly disease, constituting several noblemen as "deputati supra facto pestis." He also instructed the Office of Health to bring into the campaign court physicians and the gentlemen in charge of Milan's *Porte*.[110]

The duke took the threat of plague very personally. In 1472, when he was hunting at Bereguardo during an outbreak in the Oltrepò, he ordered that no person should "presume nor dare to come there while we will be staying there"—on pain of death—"except those from the area whom you know have not been frequenting a suspect place [*loco suspecto*]." Others were not allowed within four miles of the castle.[111] In 1475, the duke further tightened his stringent precautions against the plague. His concern arose in anticipation of pilgrims making their way to Rome for the jubilee. He appointed Andreotto del Maino, Melchiorre Marliani, and two other trusted ducal officers to deal with "the jubilee and the plague in the ducal dominion." They were instructed to meet at least twice a week and plan how to keep the dominion free from contagion.[112] In 1476, the duke's plague fears worsened with outbreaks in Rome, Venice, and other major cities. He became especially concerned when the disease appeared in Pavia.[113]

The Sultan's Ambassador   Galeazzo's personal precautions regarding the plague almost caused him to miss a most unusual embassy from the sultan of Egypt and Syria.[114] When the ambassador reached Milan on October 7, the duke was hunting bears in Varese, and he instructed the Privy Council to receive the envoy on his behalf. In the meantime, Galeazzo received word that the visitor had complained of being "badly lodged and honored." The duke thought the complaint might have been triggered by a visit he received at Varese from a Venetian ambassador; the Venetians and Turks were not on good terms. To smooth the troubled waters, Galeazzo directed Cicco to treat the sultan's envoy well.[115]

The following day (October 14) the council convened with suitable magnificence in the Corte Arengo. They lined the walls of the upstairs *Saletta* with tapestries and set up a tribunal under a canopy of gold brocade. The ambassador was honored with the center seat in the tribunal; six councillors and Zaccaria da Pisa sat on his right side, and seven other councillors sat on his left. Across the room were the Council of Justice, *magistrati, gentiluomini,* and other courtiers. The ambassador presented his mission, which involved Venetian and Genoese merchants who had allegedly harmed some of the sultan's subjects. The sultan, in turn, was detaining Genoese and Venetian merchants with their goods. The ambassador had already visited Venice to make this problem known and seek a resolution. Now he had come to Milan to see the prince who ruled the Genoese.[116]

In the meantime, Galeazzo himself returned to Galliate, where he remained. He had the Privy Council convene in the Corte again on October 19, and announce that the ambassador "should not make the effort of going to Galliate to see His Lordship." The reason given was "suspicion of the plague," since the ambassador had been in plague-troubled Venice. To make up for this lack of hospitality, Galeazzo allowed the ambassador and his retinue to tour Porta Giovia. Several days later, on October 22, the duke relented and invited the ambassador to see him at Novara. Although Galeazzo told the envoy to bring along the gifts the sultan had sent, he did not accept them for fear of contagion. Nonetheless, the ambassador remained in Novara until November 8, when he went back to Genoa with a letter from the duke.[117]

On Campaign in Piedmont

The years 1475–1476 were characterized by an extraordinary degree of complexity in the relations between the powers of Europe. Alignments, real and potential, shifted rapidly, and their scope began to expand beyond the traditional areas of interest and concern. Ferrante of Naples married his daughter Beatrice to King Matthias Corvinus of Hungary, bringing that eastern European monarch more closely into Italian affairs. Charles the Bold and others (including Galeazzo himself) sought agreements with the pope which might bring them the title of emperor from the defunct Eastern Roman Empire. For some months, the Italian powers collectively feared a possible alliance between France, Burgundy, and the emperor, directed against the pope and the Italians generally.[118]

By the autumn of 1476, Galeazzo's diplomatic situation had become a serious problem. His Burgundian alliance had been shaky from the start. In 1475, Louis XI of France had scored several diplomatic successes, chief among them the Treaty of Picquigny with England. In January 1476, Galeazzo sent a distinguished embassy to Burgundy, led by four councillors: Branda Castiglione, bishop of Como (and childhood friend of the Valois dukes), ducal cousin Pietro Francesco Visconti, Giovanni Pallavicino di Scipione (briefly vice-governor of Genoa), and Luca Grimaldi, a Genoese jurist.[119] On hearing of this projected embassy, the young *gentiluomo* Gerolamo Olgiati asked the duke to let him join the company, "desiring always to learn and see more things." Gerolamo assured Galeazzo that he had discussed this idea with his father, Giacobino. The duke replied, "We commend your proposals, seeming to us that they arise in good part," and he granted permission for his courtier to go.[120] The ambassadors stayed with Charles the Bold's court for months but accomplished little, besides watching Burgundian fortunes decline.[121] Charles of Burgundy was losing prestige rapidly, and two defeats by the Swiss in 1476 made him an even less attractive ally.

Early in 1476, the Milanese duke had reopened relations with France, hoping to establish a new understanding and balance the fading alliance with Burgundy. By August, Galeazzo had cast his lot definitively with his brother-in-law. Charles the Bold sent troops over the Alps into the duchy of Savoy, and Galeazzo could not allow hostile armies to run loose so near his own borders. Worse yet, the Burgundians had captured Iolande of Savoy and her ducal children, one of whom was betrothed to Galeazzo's daughter. By early October, Iolande had escaped from Charles and taken refuge with her brother, Louis XI, at Tours. Louis thus had effective control of her son, Duke Filiberto, and the direction of Savoy. Throughout much of the year, Galeazzo faced the possibility that the French might take over this neighboring state.

To counter both the French and Burgundian menaces, Galeazzo began sending his own troops to his western borders, then finally into Piedmont. He was particularly concerned about the areas that owed allegiance to Filippo of Savoy. On November 15, Galeazzo himself crossed the Sesia River into the duchy of Savoy, "with his guard only." After making the crossing, he called for his household squadron and "all the court." It was this situation that led a harried seneschal to bemoan the lack of lodgings in this unfamiliar territory for the hundreds of persons traveling with the court, including the duchess, councillors, chancellors, and even the ducal choir. The court remained in Piedmont, mainly at the towns of Santhià and Moncravello, until December 8, when the duke returned to his own lands.[122] Wherever the court went, it remained at the center of the duke's sphere, even on campaign; men-at-arms stayed "in the surrounding places."[123]

"I Am Dead" (Christmas 1476)

Galeazzo stayed in the Lomellina for about a week in December 1476. He went on to Cusago for a few days, probably for more hunting, before arriving at Milan to honor Christmas. That Christmas was not destined to be the usual festive occasion, though. The fear and suspicion that shadowed the autumn of 1476 extended to the end of the year. Many of the distinguished persons who normally spent Christmas with the duke were absent that year, by his own command. On November 30, he had sent his brothers Ludovico and Sforza Maria to France. Galeazzo claimed that they were eager to make the trip, but he did not honor them with a substantial retinue or a ceremonial departure. It has been argued that he suspected them of designs against his life.[124] The duke also barred Ascanio from attending at Christmas because the plague had recently been detected in Pavia, where Ascanio was studying at the university. Galeazzo "excused" all gentlemen and feudatories resident in Pavia from attending that Christmas.[125]

Corio and others describe many ominous portents that occurred on or after December 20, 1476, when Galeazzo returned to Milan. On Christmas Eve, Galeazzo celebrated the Ciocco in the customary way with his wife, his sons, his brothers Filippo and Ottaviano, and his councillors. Filippo and Ottaviano placed the great log in the fireplace personally.[126] On Christmas Day, the duke attended the customary three Masses in Porta Giovia Castle. Then he retired to the *Camera delle Colombine*—painted with the Petrarchan emblem, "A Bon Droit"—and talked of the Sforza lineage and how long it should last, with so many young and vital members. He spent most of the day hunting with falcons. On the morning of December 26, Galeazzo was anxious, cold, and disturbed; even the duchess had had nightmares. He chose not to wear his usual breastplate beneath his splendid clothes and put on a rich suit of crimson and the Sforza colors, dark red and white. At the last minute, he considered hearing Mass in Porta Giovia Castle, instead of going to Santo Stefano, but his chaplain and singers had already gone to the church. Galeazzo had his sons GianGaleazzo and Ermes brought to him, and he kissed them affectionately.

The day was cold, and the assembled councillors, ambassadors, and feudatories did not look forward to the walk across Milan to the church of Santo Stefano. Galeazzo decided to go on horseback, and he rode among the throng of honorable men to the church. He entered Santo Stefano with a small retinue—two ambassadors, Orfeo da Ricavo, twelve *camerieri,* and several other attendants. When he reached the middle of the church, his *gentiluomo* Giovanni Andrea Lampugnani approached him, as if to seek an audience. Galeazzo waved him off, saying it was not a suitable time. Suddenly, the young nobleman pulled out a knife and stabbed the duke. Two other conspirators— *gentiluomo* Gerolamo Olgiati and ducal chancellor Carlo Visconti—joined in the deed, along with some of their servants. The duke was stabbed fourteen times. He cried, "I am dead," and expired almost instantly.[127]

"Death is Bitter, but Fame is Eternal"

As soon as Galeazzo was attacked, his companions and guards reacted. The head of his personal guard was wounded trying to defend the duke, and a footman was killed. The church was thrown into a panic, with horrified worshipers fleeing for their lives. All of the conspirators escaped except Giovanni Andrea Lampugnani himself. He was killed while trying to hide among the women in the congregation.[128] Galeazzo's corpse was left where it had fallen while everyone fled the church. The councillors headed for the castle to establish order. The conspirators sought to save themselves, as did frightened courtiers and citizens, who feared a political cataclysm. The ducal authorities moved quickly to ensure that no uprisings would ensue, warning all Milanese soldiers to be ready for action. Ludovico Gonzaga was asked to Milan as a friendly prince and wartime head of the Milanese army. Prominent citizens, including Count Giovanni Borromeo, appeared before crowds in Milan to reassure them and encourage their support for the authorities.

Giovanni Andrea Lampugnani's corpse was dragged through the city by a group of youths, while others hit and stabbed it; the remains were fed to pigs. A mob sacked his house as well as the houses of his brother and nephew. A Lampugnani servant who participated in the murder took sanctuary in another church but was arrested anyway. Brought to Porta Giovia Castle, he was tortured until he revealed the names of the other conspirators. Carlo Visconti hid for a few days before, exhausted and confused, he sought his relative Pietro Francesco Visconti, the ducal councillor. The elder Visconti turned him in to the ducal authorities, who took his confession and condemned him to death.

Gerolamo Olgiati hid for several days in the houses of his family, the parish priest, and other unsuspecting neighbors. His father, torn between paternal feelings and loyalty to the duke, probably told the authorities where to find the young assassin. Gerolamo was taken to Porta Giovia Castle and tortured to a confession; he was then condemned to death. With Carlo Visconti and one of their servants, Gerolamo was quartered alive at the castle before dawn on January 2, 1477. Just prior to dying, Gerolamo declared proudly, "Mors acerba, fama perpetua"—Death is bitter, but fame is eternal. He had already presented his inquisitor, ducal chancellor Marco Trotti, with Latin epigrams attacking the duke and exalting Giovanni Andrea Lampugnani. The remains of the executed assassins were displayed from the city gates, and their decapitated heads were placed on the campanile of the Broletto in the center of Milan.[129]

Gerolamo's confession tells the story of the conspiracy, starting with his inspiration by Cola Montano to free Milan from the tyrant.[130] Carlo Visconti was avenging his sister's seduction by the duke. He himself had been a chancellor to the Council of Justice since 1474.[131] Giovanni Andrea Lampugnani assassinated his prince because of an investment gone sour. His syndicate leasing property from Morimondo Abbey had been dispossessed when Branda Castiglione, bishop of Como, took over patronage of the abbey. The bishop had removed the previous abbot for his "evil life" and canceled the leases. The syndicate applied to the duke for support, but Branda was a senior councillor, a highly respected and valued ducal servant. Galeazzo declined to intervene, telling Giovanni Andrea to deal with the bishop himself. Branda would not consider an accommodation, nor would Galeazzo hear further pleas from his young *gentiluomo*. An embittered Giovanni Andrea had begun plotting the duke's death earlier in 1476.[132]

A Tragic End

The dramatic manner in which Galeazzo died was almost an inevitable consequence of his provocative and insensitive behavior. The fifth duke had alienated many of his subjects and peers; it is no surprise that some were outraged or disgruntled enough to commit violence against his person. In his last two years, the moods of the restless prince swung between extremes more than ever, and the solid foundations of his princely world seemed increasingly shaky. His finances were eroding, his family's cohesion was crumbling, his political situation was awkward, and his circle of intimates was undermined by his own instability. A pall of uneasiness hung over the court of Milan by the latter part of 1476, and the duke's assassination was a fitting, if tragic, end to his life and reign.

9

"His Court Was One
of the Most Brilliant
in the Whole World"

Galeazzo's Court in Historical Perspective

While the young assassins of Duke Galeazzo Maria Sforza were being hunted and punished, Duchess Bona took charge of the government, as her late husband had specified in his will.[1] She acted as regent for her seven-year-old son, GianGaleazzo, assisted by Cicco Simonetta, who had many years of experience guiding the Sforza dominion. The councillors and leading citizens of Milan agreed on a package of popular measures to reassure and distract the public. The measures included restoration of salt taxes taken in advance by the ducal tax collectors, liberation of all persons imprisoned for debts or unpaid fines, the sale and transportation of food without customs payments, and even the final abolition of the hated *inquinto*.

The conspirators in the assassination had counted on some great upwelling of popular revulsion following years of Galeazzo's oppressive and extravagant rule. Unfortunately for them, the Milanese were not interested in overthrowing the Sforza regime; in the capital, the duke's death was followed by nothing worse than a heightened level of fear and suspicion. Among the other subjects of the duchy, little turmoil occurred, beyond some unrest in Parma; that city had never fully accepted the Sforza dukes. Only in Genoa did serious threats arise against the ducal regime; a revolt after Galeazzo's assassination was suppressed by force of arms.

The new rulers proclaimed additional popular measures in the early days of their regime, while the various elements of the city, the ducal administration, and the dominion in general took oaths of fealty to them. The duchess's position was not easily secured, though. Galeazzo's brothers, especially Sforza Maria and Ludovico, felt that they should rule the dominion. In the spring of 1477, the brothers attempted a coup, which failed. Ludovico and

Sforza Maria went into exile at Perugia. Filippo, who retired once again to his castle, and Ascanio, who went to Rome, were not considered responsible parties in the revolt. Ottaviano, his young heart full of courage and his young mind full of heroic thoughts, refused to surrender. With ducal troops in hot pursuit, he drowned in the River Adda while trying to cross the border.

GianGaleazzo Sforza was formally enthroned as duke of Milan at the ducal feast of San Giorgio in 1478. His mother did not play the role of regent for long. The following year, Ludovico and Sforza Maria Sforza returned again and successfully ousted the duchess. Soon thereafter, Sforza Maria died suddenly of an illness, and Ludovico "il Moro" directed the fortunes of the dominion for the next twenty years. One of his first acts was to behead Cicco Simonetta and replace him with Bartolomeo Calco, who had been Bona's secretary. In 1480, Ludovico forced Lucia Marliani to resign her title and estates in favor of her son, Galeazzo Visconti, who participated without fanfare in the court of Milan when he reached an age to do so. His younger brother, Ottaviano, born to Lucia after Duke Galeazzo's death, was also recognized as the son of a prince. He made a career in the church, ultimately becoming the bishop of Lodi and then Arezzo. Lucia returned to her husband and bore him at least four children. She continued to maintain and defend the privileges Galeazzo had granted her.[2]

A magnificent prince like his eldest brother, Ludovico was more politic to others and less haunted by spectacular vices. He presided over the Golden Age of Milan in the 1480s and 1490s, hiring such artistic geniuses as Leonardo da Vinci and Donato Bramante, expanding the institutions of court and state further, and plunging into diplomacy with great energy and some ability. The high points of Ludovico's stewardship were weddings staged between 1489 and 1495 for young Duke GianGaleazzo (with Isabella d'Aragona of Naples), himself (with Beatrice d'Este of Ferrara), and his nieces, Anna and Bianca Sforza (with Alfonso d'Este and Emperor Maximilian I, respectively).[3]

Shortly after GianGaleazzo attained his legal majority in 1494, the feckless young man died. His uncle Ludovico has long been suspected of involvement in that death, but there is no solid evidence against him. Ludovico succeeded to the ducal office, ruling in his own right until 1500. In connection with the marriage of Bianca to Maximilian, Ludovico even.obtained imperial investiture as rightful duke of Milan. The ill-starred Sforza dynasty did not enjoy that recognition for long. Although a better diplomat than Galeazzo had been, Ludovico overestimated his own ability to manipulate events, especially when they involved the great monarchs of Europe. In 1500, Ludovico Sforza was permanently dispossessed of Milan by the army of France. Ironically, that army was led by Grand Marshal GianGiacomo Trivulzio, once an intimate companion of Duke Galeazzo's. Ludovico was taken to France as a prisoner of Louis XII; he died there in 1508. Milan never again enjoyed true political autonomy; although two Sforza dukes reigned between 1500 and 1535, they did so under shadow of domination by France, Spain, and the Swiss. Italy had become the battleground and prize for powers across the Alps.

Few of Galeazzo's immediate family lived to see the end of their dynasty's rule. His sister Ippolita died in 1488, just before her daughter Isabella married GianGaleazzo. Galeazzo's brother Filippo died quietly in 1492. Ascanio lived until 1505 as a leading member of the Papal Curia, a cardinal and patron of art and music. His best composer was Josquin des Prez, once a singer in his eldest brother's choir. Galeazzo's second son, Ermes, died in 1503 as a nobleman of little moment. Galeazzo's daughter Bianca died in 1510, in a far higher station. Her betrothal to Filiberto I of Savoy had been dissolved on the death of the little Savoyard duke in 1482; thirteen years later, she became an empress. Her younger sister, Anna, was betrothed to Alfonso d'Este of Ferrara in 1477, married him in 1490, and died in 1497. Their mother, the former duchess, Bona, spent her later years in quiet obscurity. She received a pension from the king of France to live modestly in a Savoyard castle until her death in 1503. Of Galeazzo's illegitimate children, Carlo died in 1483, Alessandro in 1523, and Chiara in 1531. Chiara's first husband had been count Pietro dal Verme. Caterina, who married Gerolamo Riario—and two other husbands after him—died in 1509. She became the most famous of Galeazzo's children through her bold actions as lady of Imola, in defense against Cesare Borgia. The lord of Imola whom she and Gerolamo had replaced, Taddeo Manfredi, left Milan during GianGaleazzo's reign. He went on to serve both Florence and Venice, but he never regained his native city.[4]

"He Was . . . Desirous of Glory and of Being Feared"

When Galeazzo died, his world feared what would follow. On hearing the news, Pope Sixtus IV said, "Today the peace of Italy has died."[5] As little as the duke of Milan was loved, his death shook the peninsula's balance of power and put a chill in the hearts of his fellow princes.

Almost every urban chronicler from northern and central Italy had something to say about the disturbing event and its causes. Most of them blamed the victim, seeing Galeazzo's assassination as a natural conclusion to his life of extravagance, cruelty, and lust. Benedetto Dei, once so thoroughly charmed by Galeazzo as a youth, said that the duke's death was due to his "having become libidinous and lustful beyond measure, putting aside all ducal dignity." Benedetto, whose sources in Milan were better than those of most foreign writers, said, "Galeazzo Maria was doing things to be assassinated every day by his own [courtiers]."[6] Another Florentine chronicler agreed that the murder was a "worthy, manly, and laudable undertaking."[7] Machiavelli later followed their lead, seeing the assassination as a caution to tyrannical princes. He described the event and its background in vivid detail.[8]

Some commentators held the opposing view. One contemporary characterized Lampugnani as an "assassin and traitor, moved by a diabolical spirit and by the rage and poison of a mortal hatred."[9] A chronicler from Ferrara called the murder "this unheard-of excess" and a "most abominable act."[10] Not all observers had a personal opinion. A chronicler from Forlì took pains to describe the assassins' raging passions without adding his own.[11] Few contemporaries had a neutral opinion about the duke, though. As a Bolognese chronicler wrote, "He was the most feared lord to be found in Italy at that time."[12] It would have pleased Galeazzo to read those words, for, in Corio's courtier's-eye view,

> He was exceedingly generous, desirous of glory and being feared. He held it dear that one could say with truth that his court was one of the most brilliant in the whole world.[13]

Galeazzo Maria Sforza was very much a man—and a prince—of the Renaissance era. The duke shared Petrarch's lust for glory, Machiavelli's respect for those who inspire fear, and Castiglione's appreciation of a brilliant princely court. Machiavelli and Castiglione were not yet born when Galeazzo acceded to the throne in March 1466. They wrote about his world; he did not imitate theirs. The duke was also a proud and demanding ruler, by his own admission. As he told one young man who had displeased him, "Lords want to be obeyed in everything . . . and this you should remember in every place where you may find yourself."[14]

"Youth"

Galeazzo's character was not simple and straightforward. He had a brilliant capacity for innovation and a strong inclination to maintain tradition. He tried unceasingly to rationalize his responsibilities, creating systems to manage court and state efficiently, yet he often acted on impulse and broke his own rules. He initiated admirable monetary and fiscal policies while overspending dramatically on the most frivolous and luxurious items. His taste for cruelty and outrageous sexual behavior was matched by his fear of God and respect for religion and the occult arts. His desire to be heard, seen, and acknowledged was contradicted by a taste for secrecy and disguise.

The youth and audacity of great figures in his ducal choir, with their innovative musical forms and bright polyphony, made a good match for the prince who was their patron. There is little doubt that these innovations took place under Galeazzo's watchful eye. Given his active interference in all areas of life and his daily attendance at Mass where these pieces were sung, it is inconceivable that he did not approve them, at the very least. In many ways Galeazzo's behavior fit closely the Renaissance idea of *giovinezza,* "youth." Youth was a dangerous time, especially in men, whose aggression and sexuality were expected to disrupt the social fabric if they were not somehow harnessed or neutralized. For this reason, the great republics of Renaissance Italy would not permit such youths to participate fully in the political process. Matters of policy needed cool heads, which youths could not be expected to possess. Philippe de Commynes remarked disapprovingly of Lorenzo de' Medici that the latter was "a young man ruled by young men."[15] The same could have been said of Lorenzo's friend Galeazzo. Indeed, of all the major rulers in Europe during Galeazzo's reign, only Lorenzo was younger than he, and Lorenzo was not even a true prince.

The qualities of prudence and cool wisdom that contemporaries admired so much in Francesco Sforza and Bianca Maria Visconti were conspicuously absent in their eldest son. His entire reign can be understood in many respects as a reaction against the burden of living up to the image—and the expectations—of his parents. Galeazzo could not possibly have surpassed his father on the field of battle or in the diplomatic arena. He could never have attracted greater love and respect from the people of the dominion than his mother had enjoyed. The areas in which he asserted himself most effectively were those in which he could outshine them both. His princely court was a powerful vehicle to greatness.

The Court

Renaissance scholars have long written of Galeazzo's era as that of a "new generation of princes."[16] Among these "princes" were Charles the Bold of Burgundy (1467–1477), Lorenzo de' Medici in Florence (1469–1492), Ercole d'Este of Ferrara (1471–1503), even Edward IV of England (1461–1483). Ludovico il Moro, Galeazzo's younger brother, belonged to the same generation. All of them had a lively appreciation for the value of *magnificentia*—great displays of splendor—in maintaining their political grip and extending their influence.[17] Galeazzo had a keen interest in what his peers were doing throughout Italy, as well as in France, Burgundy, and the other princely states of Christendom. Their generation saw the birth of Machiavelli, for whom Galeazzo Maria Sforza was the very model of an extravagant tyrant, and Castiglione, for whom the court of Milan was a crucial training ground.

These princes did not constitute the first generation to self-consciously cultivate an international network of courts; such networks had previously developed in the twelfth and fourteenth centuries. In Galeazzo's time, though, the network of princely courts endured and evolved into the great court culture of early modern Europe. The period of Galeazzo's reign was unusually peaceful; between 1467 and 1478, no major warfare broke out in Italy. The duke was not challenged by a crisis of survival, nor was he required to make the financial sacrifices of wartime. He wanted to extend the revival of Milan's greatness that his father had initiated, especially to recover what Venice had taken away four decades before.

Galeazzo could draw on the considerable resources of the duchy of Milan without either the financial drain or opportunities for glory that war represented. This combination of circumstances influenced profoundly his choices for investment of personal energy and money. The Milanese duke preferred situations he could manage and predict, particularly without deep involvement in them. He wanted to indulge his own interests while delegating the dreary routine business of state and household to others. Because the ducal court provided an ideal setting in which to embody the Milanese dominion with the full panoply of *magnificentia,* it was an obvious choice for the investment of Galeazzo's resources. His investment in the court formed part of his search for a competitive edge in the princely world of the later fifteenth century. He sought to match such luminaries as the king of France and the duke of Burgundy and to outdo everyone else. In particular, he wanted to best the prince he had come to hate above all others, Ferrante of Naples. He did not create the court of Milan, in which thousands of men and women had served during his youth. In a state so wealthy and important as the Sforza dominion, even such a relatively austere ruler as Duke Francesco maintained a large establishment. Galeazzo did not indicate where he found the models for all the forms and practices he used, but he did keep a close eye on what was done in the other courts of Christendom. There was nothing austere about Galeazzo, and he added considerably to the court in every way but moral stature.

Contained Space

The ducal court of Milan changed constantly—through deliberate policy, accidental events, the comings and goings of individuals, and many other factors. On Christmas Day, there may have been two thousand persons in attendance; when the duke was hunting at Monza, there may have been twenty. These visible variations were significant indicators of the prince's activities and policies, but they do not tell us much about the court except that it could contain variations. If the space in the court was more filled, it looked more full, but that did not mean the court had fundamentally changed. A strong framework of special ceremonies, routine tasks, and regular procedures ensured that these variations could be tolerated, or even applied deliberately.

The highly visible changes in the Milanese court under Galeazzo Maria Sforza can distract observers from recognizing the remarkable continuity in the underlying structure of the court. The princely court of Milan contained the duke's space. The duke himself stood at the center of the center. As the prince was central to the state, so the court was central to the dominion, operating at many levels to integrate and articulate the society and economy of Milan and its territories. The court was the space in which the interests of the prince's person converged with the interests of others from within his state and beyond. All of these individuals and communities had a variety of choices as to the investment of their money, time, energy, and prestige. Because the competition was fierce, they needed to make their investments efficient. The court had the virtue of being enclosed and defined, thus more manageable and predictable than the world at large. Moreover, the court provided all the elements that converged there with access to resources and exchanges that might not otherwise have been available to them.

It is difficult to discuss the nature of space in clear, precise language. In the case of a princely court, it is important that empty space not be overlooked. Had Galeazzo's court been absolutely full of servants, courtiers, art objects, musical instruments, horses, account books, and other items, it could not have functioned. The virtue of the court in this regard was that the duke and his agents could determine where the boundaries of that space should be, how to partition it internally, how to distribute people and things within those compartments, and so on. Within this space, people, objects, and ideas that would not ordinarily have encountered one another were brought together in systematic and purposeful ways.

The princely court was characterized by extraordinary flexibility contained within a well-defined formal framework. That combination facilitated essential aspects of material sustenance, political direction, social integration, and symbolic representation. The court could be altered or adjusted more easily than most institutions, because it was relatively well defined, self-contained, and subject to the immediate authority of one person and his agents. As the duke wished to change degrees of access to his person, patterns of residence, daily timetables, artistic styles, or anything else, he could do so with some ease. This observation applies particularly to the fifteenth century, before a canon of courtly practice had been established.

An Expensive Investment

The ducal court was an important vehicle for Galeazzo's aspirations. In his time, it was distinguished by a lavishness rare even in wealthy Milan, embellished with paintings, tapestries, fine clothes, jewels, and other gorgeous accoutrements. This wealth and splendor was widely known outside the dominion; even Zaccaria Saggi da Pisa, who spent many years as the Mantuan ambassador in Milan, was moved to write, "It is truly a worthy court to see."[18] Without cultural sophistication and wealth, a brilliant court would not have emerged in Milan. Without internal heterogeneity and external pressure, the investment in a court might not have seemed worthwhile. That investment was very substantial; in the ducal budget for 1476, almost 200,000 ducats are devoted to household cost, wardrobe debts, salaries, building projects, musical patronage, family allowances, and other items that could be considered aspects of "the court."[19]

Galeazzo's emphasis on the court was not an arbitrary exercise of frivolity or escapism; it developed in response to compelling interests. The values and imperatives of the duke's subjects varied widely one from another, and competition was intense, even within the dominion. The duke was expected to provide order and security, which enabled families and communities to pursue their own particular interests and ensure their own survival. In some cases, it was insufficient to maintain existing conditions; misfortune or ambition might lead them to seek advancement. Survival and advancement went beyond material sustenance, important though that surely was. For the elites of the duchy, honor also carried great weight, for it offered a means by which they could maintain their social identity. Different elites identified themselves according to such different criteria as title, civic office, and antiquity of lineage. Even citizenship was an important privilege that distinguished those who mattered in a given city.

Within a limited budget, the prince sought to maintain his position and enlist the support of subjects and peers in his efforts to impose a princely sense of order. He was responsible for the presentation and promotion of his state outside its borders, in both peace and war. Within the borders, he wanted to integrate the elements of his dominion as fully as possible, reinforce his own image as a legitimate and effective ruler, and bring his people prosperity. Like any other head of a family, he was obliged also to maintain the interests of his own lineage.

Those who served Galeazzo well were rewarded commensurately, as Bernardino Corio emphasized: "He loved virtuous men beyond measure and caressed them with gifts." "He presented very rich gifts to his attendants . . . and he remunerated his servants."[20] The wealth available through ducal patronage was enormous; not only did Milan boast considerable secular resources but the duke also had an unusual degree of control over appointments to ecclesiastical benefices. Because the court was the space around his person, it naturally attracted many who sought to gain from his bounty. Conversely, the promise of abundance could be used by the duke as lure to draw persons of honor from within and without the duchy closer to him and more fully under his control. The benefits of ducal service were attractive to many, although the burdens proved too much for some. Galeazzo demanded a great deal from his servants, leaving little time for family or personal business. He was generous enough, however, to mitigate some of these disadvantages; for most families in the dominion (and some outside), the advantages of placing

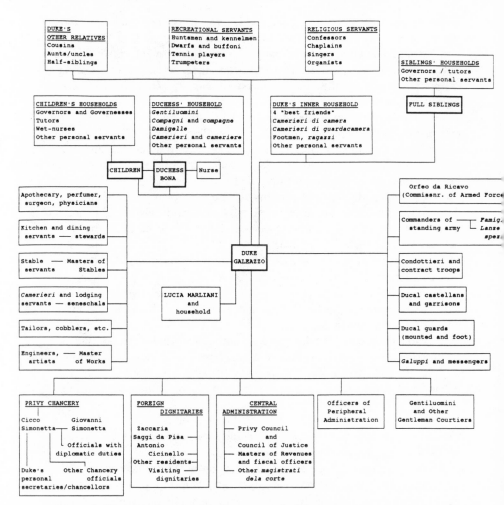

Figure 5. Diagram of court-related persons and offices

at least one relative in his service were worth the risks. Few members of the court found life safe or easy, though; the level of anxiety was always fairly high.

Literally thousands of men and women were entitled to consider themselves members of this court, and their numbers had broad social and economic impact. The ducal court was unquestionably the greatest center of consumption in the dominion. Although it may have produced little, it served a vital function as market for both staples and luxury goods. The duke spent huge sums on food, drink, jewelry, and clothes—as much as half the income of Italy's wealthiest princely state. To his outlay were added all the expenditures of court members who lived outside the walls and spent their own money on sustenance and display. Every commercial provider in the dominion (especially in Milan and Pavia) was affected directly or indirectly. The two best hostelries in the capital housed a continuous stream of foreign dignitaries coming to treat with the duke. Even the great Milanese industries of armory and luxury cloth benefited from the presence of the court, which had a voracious appetite for their wares.

In the long run, the most outstanding characteristic of court service at Milan was the underlying stability of its structures, regardless of princely whims or political circumstances. With all the continuity of office and opportunity in the Milanese court, though, the security that Tommaso Tebaldi da Bologna had sought was elusive. He died in February 1475, and after Galeazzo's death, the regent Bona granted Tommaso's fief of Mandello to Galeazzo's natural daughter, Chiara, and her husband.[21]

Honor and Order

The creation and maintenance of political and social order was central to the responsibilities of princely office. The overall political direction of the Sforza dominion lay in the center, at the court. The process of making and executing policy at the highest levels constituted an important part of the court's purpose and shaped much of its structure. Conversely, what occurred in the court affected the making of policy. Because the court was central to the state, it was important that social order be clearly established there, for the benefit of the dominion as a whole.

The integrating function of the court stands out as one of its most notable characteristics. The court furnished a context for bringing together disparate political, social, and professional elements in the prince's presence. What made this integration possible was the framework of court structures. That framework was composed of ranked lists, official positions, cycles of ritual observance, special festivities, and other clearly defined points of reference. These points of reference furnished social reinforcement of various kinds. Those who already held positions of honor in their home environment might be recognized in a much wider sphere through their appearance at court events. Those who did not enjoy such recognition on the basis of family status or civic office might find new avenues for gaining honor within the court itself or through the duke's favor.

Support from honored and influential personages, whether subjects or peers, was a vital part of the Sforza duke's survival as a prince. Galeazzo had to strike a balance between his princely desire to "befriend the leading men" and his personal prerogatives and preferences. The integration of diverse ranking systems called for a set of ducal priorities that honored every dignity appropriately with respect to its traditional pretensions—and to the prince's vision. The Christmas disinvitation to Guglielmo of Montferrat and the exaltation of Carlino Varesino at Bianca Sforza's betrothal offer clear examples of the duke's liberty to choose his own priorities in his own court.

Order based on rank gave the court a predictable shape and framework that were invaluable for social and political orientation. Put more simply, the court provided various means by which participants could know where they stood. Rank is an essentially linear concept; each rank follows that which precedes it and precedes that which follows it. Rank is not reciprocal or symmetrical; one end of the scale is defined as superior to the other. The independent dignities attached to offices of state, feudal titles, ecclesiastical benefices, and so forth, brought a greater degree of honor than offices in the household or ambiguous intimacy with the prince. But honor and order were not everything. As Tommaso Tebaldi da Bologna reminded the duke, one could not eat honor, and relations between members of the court were far more varied and complex than a simple chain of command.

Circles and Networks

The thousands of men and women at the court had families, friends, lovers, and business associates both within and beyond the court's boundaries. They traveled, changed offices, lost favor, married, died, and generally behaved as human beings in a community. What gave their life at court its texture and richness were circles of intimacy and networks of interest. The immediate personal relationships of court members created the circles of intimacy; shared aspirations, business ventures, geographic background, or political imperatives could create networks of interest.

The flexibility of intimacy and shared interests worked in both formal and informal ways to counter the linear, rigid order of ranked relations. These circular and reciprocal bonds added dimensions to that order; intimacy and interest could extend the range of behaviors appropriate between persons of unequal social or political standing. Even the duke had intimates of lower rank who could behave—at appropriate moments—as though they were his equals. The interactions between these individuals are among the most difficult items to find in documents, but they are also among the most important. Circles of intimacy and networks of interest defined the social topography of life for those participating in the court.

Family relationships created natural alliances and provided points of departure from which individuals could operate in the court world. Bonds of marriage and *comparaggio* strengthened existing associations and created new networks. They formalized friendships and furnished channels to sources of social and political influence which aided in the ceaseless effort to maintain and improve the well-being of individuals and their families. Within the duke's Privy Chancery, for instance, chancellors, secretaries, and support staff bound themselves to one another time and again through marriage and *comparaggio,* reinforcing their professional association with personal bonds. The duke himself encouraged connections between persons of diverse backgrounds at court. Such bonds reinforced his own position at the head of a unified dominion.

The development of a bureaucratic elite was a key element of Milan's Renaissance court, as exemplified most fully by the Privy Chancery. The shared professional experience of its members gave them a sense of mutual solidarity, but they were not isolated from other elements of court and state. Officers of the Chancery were linked by blood, marriage, friendship, and professional service to the full range of society in the Sforza dominion.[22]

No one at court remained an outside observer; everyone who entered within the boundaries became a participant, if only temporarily. The presence of foreign dignitaries in the Milanese court expanded the duke's world in two directions. Bringing them under his aegis added to the honor and universality of his dominion and extended the duke's authority to the world at large. In the other direction, all those who came into Galeazzo's sphere carried away with them gifts, impressions, and a taste of the Sforza style. The higher the dignity of the visitors, the more they added, the more they were honored, and the more they took away with them.

Sacred Space

Galeazzo Maria Sforza had been trained well in the symbolic aspect of princely rule. He understood how to employ rituals and ceremonies in affirming traditional values and extending those values in new directions. In particular, Galeazzo realized that explicit presentations of the imagery of princely power and courtly splendor constituted one of his most effective tools for proclaiming the universal nature of his authority.

The nature of a prince's authority has been considered by some scholars to underlie any study of a princely court. Elias used the categories of Max Weber in formulating his "court-aristocratic figuration." According to this formulation, a court could only arise under a ruler whose authority is predominantly institutional, rather than "charismatic." In this theory, the ruler's charisma has been transformed into a matter of routine. Elias saw the court as part of a stabilizing process and the director of that process as a prince whose function was to maintain the status quo rather that to cause radical change.[23]

Elias's view arose from the study of a court society that was declining from its era of dynamic usefulness (eighteenth-century France). The perspective changes when looking from the other end, at a court still taking shape. For a prince such as Galeazzo, the space of the court could be open and creative, permitting him to make radical changes if he chose to do so. He and his agents were creating some of the institutions of the court. Those institutions were not fashioned purely from the duke's imagination, however; he used existing forms and reshaped them.

Because Duke Galeazzo needed the acceptance of his subjects and the respect of his peers, he sought to give them a stake in supporting him. As Giovanni Matteo Bottigella realized, the court had a quality of transcendence and could be viewed as the saints gathered around the divine presence. It was not merely a place for the most important people to gather, or the most important decisions to be made. From a certain perspective, the court was a sacred space and as such, an exemplary microcosm of ideal society.[24] This conception of the court as microcosm is evident in the duke's letter to his feudatories requiring their presence at court for "the greatest solemnities observed by us." The profound importance of the command is reflected in the use of Latin, the language of ritual, rarely used in correspondence between prince and subjects. In the letter, Galeazzo spoke not only of honor but also of a more elevated and precious gift he could bestow—grace: "So that . . . the noble and excellent men who are in a state of grace and favor in the prince's eyes grow in grace and increase in honors."[25]

Using the existing framework of ritual observances, Galeazzo created a new cycle of major holidays. This ducal calendar revolved around his princely interests, both co-opting and transcending particularist local traditions. It is clear from his actions that the duke sought to use holidays as vehicles to symbolically affirm his role as sovereign prince at the head of an integrated dominion based upon, but not subject to, the city of Milan. The emphasis on lineage at the feast of San Giuseppe, and on military force at the feast of San Giorgio, furnished powerful reinforcement for Galeazzo's princely office. He made Christmas the year's most important point of reference for the dominion as a whole, instituting a regular pattern of observances that blended the sacred and secular. Ironically, the very regularity of this pattern made it possible for the duke's assassins to plan their murder well in advance; as members of the court, they knew that Galeazzo would attend Mass at Santo Stefano with few personal attendants and guards near him.

The duke thought also to cast the images so vital to his own vision in less ephemeral forms of visual art. Such imagery carried vivid and immediate messages that Galeazzo could personally enjoy and that others could see and absorb. The prince's vision of order as it would have appeared in these works could inform viewers how they should see the world. Galeazzo's vision was not consistently fixed; he exercised the same arbitrary discretionary powers here as in setting boundaries for the court. That which pleased him was included; that which displeased him was not. Most of the visual art Galeazzo planned and commissioned does not survive, was never completed, or was never begun. The great works that would have reflected his glory and vision never came to fruition. Galeazzo would undoubtedly be much better remembered had he succeeded in fixing symbolic images in the lasting and grandiose forms he saw so clearly in his own mind.

Failure and Success

Galeazzo used his court as a space for bringing together all the most important elements of his universe. He sought to join Heaven and Earth, to link past with future, and bind together everything within his dominion under his own authority. He tried to enlist the adherence of subjects, peers, and even superiors in support of this proud vision. Galeazzo's death on the feast of Saint Stephen is heavy with ironic significance. His presence in the church, surrounded by the galaxy of Milanese elites, was a manifestation of his desire to bring all together around him. It also reflected an understanding of the role ritual and ceremony could play in binding himself to his dominion and the elements of the dominion to one another. For his assassins to rend the fabric of his princely world at that point in space and time reflected their own appreciation for the power of the occasion.

The assassins' action also illuminates the flaws and distortions in Galeazzo's personality. His youth and audacity did not accord well with his desire to establish the court as a symbolic center. His resentment and defiance against his parents—and their success—caused him to abandon much of what his people admired and respected about the ducal regime. Obsessed with a lust for greatness and an urge to be free of conventional restrictions, the fifth duke of Milan gave too little weight to the traditional values and aspirations of his people. Their collective vision was superseded by the vision he imposed, one they did not perceive as wholesome, even-handed, or sympathetic. Instead of uniting the Sforza dominion under his leadership, Galeazzo's own actions crystallized the opposition against that leadership.

Consistency and clarity of purpose are fundamental attributes of an individual or institution to which one can look for guidance about proper behavior and manifestations of shared values. Unfortunately, Galeazzo Maria Sforza lacked these qualities. To the three young noblemen who murdered him, the prince who should have been their benefactor and protector had become a threat to themselves, their families, and the people of Milan. On a day celebrating martyrdom, the fifth duke was sacrificed for the welfare of those people. The Christmas season was an ideal time for such a sacrifice to be made. It marked the traditional beginning of the New Year for the Milanese, when rebirth and renewal arose from the darkest time of the year.

Many of Galeazzo's policies and preferences perished with him, and the great ambitions he cherished were destroyed from within the court in which he nurtured them. Yet the ducal court continued to flourish after he was gone, even though his successor was too young to direct it personally. The contained space of the court became a central point of reference for the increasingly complex and sophisticated world of Renaissance Milan. The guiding hand of Galeazzo's brother Ludovico brought Milan to its brief but memorable Golden Age, manifesting most brilliantly in the court Galeazzo had fostered. Looking back on his own youth there, Baldassare Castiglione could later write of "the Castle of Milan, once the vessel for the flower of the world's men."[26]

Epilogue (December 1476)

It is two days after Christmas in the Year of Our Lord 1476. The season is icy cold, and the city of Milan is dark and troubled. Normally, Duke Galeazzo would attend Mass the next morning at the church of San Francesco. The Mass would commemorate the feast of the Holy Innocents, children slaughtered by a brutal and frightened king. But tonight Galeazzo lies lifeless in the sacristy of Santo Stefano, wearing a new suit of gold brocade that he had especially requested for use after death. His wife has sent 300 ducats' worth of rings and other jewelry from Porta Giovia Castle to complete his deathly splendor.

That much grace the murdered duke is granted, but no more. It is about halfway through the night now, when all good folk are abed, and only the city guard keeps watch. A few ducal servants converge on Santo Stefano for a sad grisly errand. They collect the duke's corpse and carry it the short distance to the Duomo, huge and ominous at this unnatural hour. Their torches flicker feebly in the cavernous emptiness. Unceremoniously, the servants place their dead master's corpse in the casket of his father, Duke Francesco. They leave father and son to rot together in the cold, grand stone of Milan's great cathedral.

Galeazzo Maria Sforza never receives a funeral or any memorial service. He has no tomb of his own, no great mausoleum of marble and bronze, not even a modest stone bearing his name. Only a few persons know where he is buried, "so that in aftertimes, one could not show it, saying, 'Here is placed the duke Galeazzo, who was killed.'" For the sake of public order, about which Galeazzo cared so much, he is quickly abandoned to his soul's journey, with nary a public Mass to help it along. Because of fear, the fifth duke of Milan, who set such store by ceremonial splendor, ends his reign in the same muffled, clandestine manner in which he began it.[1]

Appendix 1
Itinerary of
Duke Galeazzo Maria Sforza,
1468–1476 (per night)

WINTER

(Christmas Week 12/25–1/1; Epiphany 1/6)

1467–68
Milan 12/25–31
Pavia 1/1–25 ....
Milan 1/28–2/12
Abbiate 2/13
Vigevano 2/14–21
Mortara 2/22
Vigevano 2/23–3/15
Milan 3/16–19

1468–69
Milan 12/25–31
Vigevano 1/1–2/28
Mortara 3/1
Villanova 3/2–16
Abbiate 3/17 ....
Milan 3/19

1469–70
Milan 12/25–1/2
Pavia 1/3–11
Mortara 1/12
Robbio 1/13
Bulgaro 1/14–17
Vigevano 1/18–28
Pavia 1/24–3/8 ....
Vigevano 3/10–11 ....
Novara 3/13 ....
Galliate 3/15
Abbiate 3/16–18
Milan 3/19

1470–71
Milan 12/25–1/7
Monza 1/8–31
Milan 2/1–7 ....
Vigevano 2/10–15 ....
Pavia 2/17–26 ....
Milan 2/28–3/3
Pavia 3/4
Piacenza 3/5
Borgo S. Donnino 3/6–7
Belleto 3/8
Pontremoli 3/9–10

1471–72
Milan 12/25–1/5 ....
Vigevano 1/7–29 ....
Pavia 1/31–2/24
Vigevano 2/25–3/19

(1471)
Lucca 3/11
Pietrasanta 3/12–14
Florence 3/15–19

1472–73
Milan 12/25–1/11
Pavia 1/12–2/23
Milan 2/24–3/1
Vigevano 3/2–19

1473–74
Milan 12/25–1/6 ....
Pavia 1/8–2/15
Bereguardo 2/16
Mortara 2/17–18
Villanova 2/19–20
Vigevano 2/21–28
Galliate 3/1–2
Fontaneto 3/3–10
Galliate 3/11
Abbiate 3/12
Milan 3/13–16
Pavia 3/17–19

1474–75
Milan 12/25–2/7
Abbiate 2/8–9
Pavia 2/10–24
Vigevano 2/25–3/19

1475–76
Milan 12/25–1/2
Binasco 1/3–4
Pavia 1/5–3/6
Vigevano 3/7–19

SPRING

(San Giuseppe 3/20; San Giorgio 4/24)

(Easter 4/17) 1468	4/2 1469	4/22 1470	4/14 1471	3/29 1472	4/18 1473	4/10 1474	3/26 1475	4/14) 1476
Milan 3/20–23	Milan 3/20–4/13	Milan 3/20–25	Florence 3/20–23...	Vigevano 3/20–22...	Abbiate 3/20–21	Bereguardo 3/20	Vigevano 3/20–4/4	Vigevano 3/20–23
Abbiate 3/24...	Abbiate 4/14–21	Abbiate 3/26–29...	Pietrasanta 3/25	Milan 3/25–5/5	Villanova 3/22	Vigevano 3/21–30	Villanova 4/5–12	Abbiate 3/24...
Milan 3/29–30	Milan 4/22–5/2	Novara 3/31–4/4...	Carrara 3/26–27	Pavia 5/6–6/26	Novara 3/23–31	Villanova 3/31–4/2	Abbiate 4/13–19	Vigevano 3/25–4/17
Abbiate 4/1–9	Abbiate 5/3–6/26	Fontaneto 4/6–15...	La Spezia 3/28		Abbiate 4/1–9	Abbiate 4/3–12...	Milan 4/20–26	Milan 4/18–29...
Milan 4/10–19...		Pavia 4/17...	Genoa 3/29–4/1...		Milan 4/10–5/7	Milan 4/15–30	Pavia 4/27–6/26	Pavia 5/1–6/26
Abbiate 4/21–23		Milan 4/19–30	Novi Ligure 4/3		Pavia 5/8–28...	Pavia 5/1–6/26		
Milan 4/24–26		Pavia 5/1–6/26	Pavia 4/4...		Bereguardo 6/1–22			
Abbiate 4/27–5/4			Vigevano 4/6–19...		Milan 6/23–6/26			
Milan 5/5–12			Abbiate 4/22					
Abbiate 5/13–16			Milan 4/23–30					
Milan 5/17–18			Pavia 5/1–6/26					
Pavia 5/19–6/26								

SUMMER

1468	1469	1470	1471	1472	1473	1474	1475	1476
Tortona 6/27	Abbiate 6/27–7/20	Pavia 6/27–7/28	Pavia 6/27–7/15	Pavia 6/27–30	Milan 6/27–7/5	Pavia 6/27–7/3	Pavia 6/27–8/9	Pavia 6/27–
Alessandria 6/28–29	Milan 7/21–25	Abbiate 7/29–30 . . .	on Po River 7/16	Belgioioso 7/1–4 . . .	Bruzzano 7/6	S. Angelo 7/4–5	S. Angelo 8/10	8/31 . . .
Pozzolo Formigaro 7/26–8/16 . . .	Monza 7/26–8/16 . . .	Milan 8/1–2	Guastalla 7/17	Bereguardo 7/6–15	Monza 7/7–14	Lodi 7/6	Lodi 8/11	Galliate 9/10–15 . . .
6/30 . . .	Milan 8/18–19	Monza 8/3–8	Borgoforte 7/18	Pavia 7/16	Milan 7/15	Cassano 7/7–24	Pandino 8/12	
Vigevano 7/2–4	Vigevano 8/20–23	Milan 8/9–16	Mantua 7/19–20	on Po River 7/17–19	Pavia 7/16–8/23	Monza 7/25–27	Cassano 8/13–26 . . .	
Abbiate 7/5 . . .	Pavia 8/24–9/15	Monza 8/17–25	Gonzaga 7/21–8/7	Gonzaga 7/20–8/8	Gropello 8/24–30	Milan 7/28–8/14	Galliate 8/30–9/3	
Milan 7/8–10		Cassano 8/26–9/9	Guastalla 8/8–11	on Po River 8/9–17	Gambolò 8/31 . . .	Turbigo 8/15	Villanova 9/4–12 . . .	
Pavia 7/11–8/4		Lodi 9/10 . . .	Cremona 8/12–24	Pavia 8/18–9/15	Vigevano 9/2–3	Galliate 8/16–30	S. Giorgio 9/14–15	
S. Angelo 8/5		Parma 9/15	Castelleone 8/25–9/5		Galliate 9/4–10	Villanova 8/31–9/2		
Monza 8/6–9/4 . . .			Pavia 9/6–10		Milan 9/11–15	Galliate 9/3		
Milan 9/6–8			Gropello 9/11–12			Gambolò 9/4–9		
Monza 9/9–14 . . .			Garlasco 9/13			S. Giorgio 9/10		
				------------			------------	
				(1471)			(1474)	
				Gambolò 9/14			Mede 9/11	
				Vigevano 9/15			Sannazzaro de' Burgondi 9/12–15	

AUTUMN

1468	*1469*	*1470*	*1471*	*1472*	*1473*	*1474*	*1475*	*1476*
Abbiate	Pavia	Parma	Vigevano	Bereguardo	Milan	Pavia	Sannazzaro	...
9/17–29	9/16–10/20	9/16–21	9/16–17	9/16	9/16	9/16–10/26	de'Burgondi	Gambolò
Novara	Milan	Cremona	Galliate	Abbiate	Pavia	Milan	9/16–19	9/28–30
9/30–	10/21–31	9/22–25	9/18–30	9/17–19	9/17–10/30	10/27	Gropello	Villanova
10/17...	Lainate	Pizzighetone	Novara	Novara	Gambolò	Castano	9/20–21	10/1
Melegnano	11/1	9/26–29	10/1	9/20–26	10/31–11/1	10/28	S. Giorgio	Galliate
10/20–23	Castiglione	Pavia	Sannazzaro	Galliate	Vigevano	Lonate Pozzolo	9/22–23	10/2
Milan	11/2	9/30–10/21	Sesia	9/27–10/6...	11/2–12/17	10/29	Sannazzaro	Gallarate
10/24–11/26	Varese	Vigevano	10/2	Milan	Abbiate	Gallarate	de' Burgondi	10/3
Abbiate	11/3	10/22–25	near	10/8–12...	12/18–24	10/30	9/24	Varese
11/27...	"Guani"	Galliate	Vercelli	Monza		Fagnano	Lomello	10/4–11
Milan	11/4	10/26–27	10/3–5...	10/14–18...		10/31	9/25	Varese
12/1–14...	Vigevano	Novara	Milan	Pavia		Castiglione	Sannazzaro	10/12
Vigevano	11/5	10/28	10/7–21	10/20–29		Olona	de' Burgondi	Galliate
12/19–21...	Galliate	Vigevano	Monza	Gropello		11/1	9/26...	10/13–
	11/6–27	10/29–12/2	10/22–24	10/30		Varese	Villanova	11/11...
	Vigevano	Pavia	Milan	Ottobiano		11/2–4	10/1–10	Novara
	11/28–	12/3–16	10/25–11/7	10/31		Gallarate	Varese	11/13
	12/19	Milan	Vigevano	Cozzo		11/5	10/11–24...	Sannazzaro
	Milan	12/17–24	11/8–12/24	11/1–4	------	Milan	Luino	Sesia
	12/20–24			Robbio	(1472)	11/6–10	10/26–29	11/14
				11/5–7	Fontaneto	Villanova	Varese	Greggio
				Galliate	11/20–24	11/11–12/1	10/30–31...	11/15
				11/8–19	Vigerano	Vigevano	Galliate	Santhià
					11/25–27...			
					Milan			
					12/1–16...			

AUTUMN (continued)

1472	1473	1474	1475	1476	
Fontaneto 11/20–24	Milan	12/2	11/2–12/6	11/16–20	
Galliate 11/25–27 ...		Abbiate 12/3	Villanova 12/7	near S. Germano 11/21–25	
Vigevano 12/1–16 ...		Milan 12/4–24	Gambolò 12/8–12 ...	Santhià 11/26	
Milan 12/22–24			Abbiate 12/14	Moncravello 11/27–12/3	
			Cusago 12/15–18	Santhià 12/4–7	
			Milan 12/19–24	Sannazzaro Sesia 12/8	
				Novara 12/9–14	(1476)
					Villanova 12/15
					Abbiate 12/16
					Cusago 12/17–20 ...
					Milan 12/22–25

Notes:

1. "..." indicates unknown locations for date(s) here.

2. The starting dates for winter (12/25) and spring (3/20) reflect important landmarks in the annual calendar. The starting dates for summer (6/27) and autumn (9/16) have been chosen for convenience.

3. The name of Abbiategrasso has been abbreviated to "Abbiate," the form used during Galeazzo's reign.

Appendix 2
Persons to be Lodged When Traveling with the Milanese Ducal Court, 1476

("1476. Lista de li deputati acavalcar[e] dreto ala corte del n[ost]ro Ill[ustrissi]mo Principe et Ex[cellentiss]imo Sig[no]re ali quali se ha adare alogiament[i]," ASM, AS, c. 932)

	ca.li			
El u.ro Ill.mo P. et Ex.mo Sig.re		d. Karlino v.exino	vj
Lo Ill.mo Duca de Barro	xxxij	d. Antonieto da piesentia	iiij
Lo Ill.mo Sig.re Ludovico	xxxij	d. Hyeronimo de Becharia	iiij
d. Petro da Gallara	x		
d. Orpheo	x		
d. Jo. iacobo treultio	vij		
d. Guido antonio arcimboldo	vij		
d. Jo antonio cotta	vij		
Jo. petro del B. gamino	vij		

(*fo. 1r*)
ca. li

(*col. 2*)

d. Petro de birago	vj
d. Baptista e }	vj
Andrea sclaffenato }	
d. Baptista de p.ma	x
Francisco de strozi	viij
Nicolo de cortona	vj
B. tolomeo de locarne	iiij
Jo. petro crivello	viij
Alesandro de castiglione	viij
Covelle de s.cto severino	v
Jo. Bapt. a del conte	viij
Castellino Vesconte	v
Berlingere caldoro	vj
Alesio de durazio	ij
d. Gasparo nano spagnolo	iiij
d. Alfonso spagnolo	iiij
Gasparro Vesconte	iiij

El Rmo. Mon.re de Piacenza — x
d. lo Abbate de Sa.cto Sevino — iiij
d. lo Abbate de Quartaziola
Fra Francisco

Mro. Giohan.e M.liano — iij
Mro. Lazaro — iij
el conte Galeoto bivilaq.a — vj

Mro. Ambrosio de binasco — iij
El Spiciaro
Juliano de V.exe — vj
Cosma de Briosco — iiij
Piseto — iiij

camereri de camera
d. Francisco de petras.cta — xij
d. Antonio carazo — x
d. Georgio del careto — vj

Camereri de guardacamera
d. Jo. francisco pallavicino — iiij
petro de oly — iiij
Marchino de Abia — vj
Johanne de V.ona — iiij

Roberto Vesconte	iiij	Cavalarij	x
El Bruscho	iiij		
Nicolo Maleta	ij	*Uschieri dela canz.a*	
Jo. luchino crivello	ij	Ruspino	j
Jacobino del castelatio	ij	Francino	j
Aluysino de cornegliano	ij		
Francisco de olza	ij		*(col. 2)*
Jacobino de caponago	ij	d. Fabricio	vij
Baldesare choyro	ij	d. Gabriello pagliaro	vij
Brecella	ij	Cavalarij de s.s.to	x
El Fazardo	ij	d. Jacobo Alfero	vj
B. nardino del misalia	ij	Jo. de novate	iiij
		B.nardino de Treultio	
	(fo. 1v)	S. Gasparo Ghilimberto, scriptore	

Sotocamereri		*Cantatori*		
Fidelle		d. lo Abbe	e }	iiij
Goffino		d. Bovis	}	
Nasino		d. Cordiere	e }	vij
Hyeronimo da Sena		d. Rollando	}	
Baptistino B.bavara		Brant	e }	iiij
Zentille		d. Gulielmo	}	
Morelleto		d. henricho	e }	iiij
Danielle de palu		elloy	}	
euxebio da Lode		Gaspare	e }	iiij
Francisco de cotignola		daniello	}	
Alesandro da cremona		Avignono	e }	ij
Faxano		Guinet	}	
		Ruglerio	e }	iiij
Uschieri ducali		Cornellio	}	
Franc.o Choyro		Peroto	e }	iiij
Ciorino		Perotino	}	
		Pruglij	e }	ij
La ducale canzeleria		Ottinet	}	
El Mag.co d. Cicho	xij	Jannes	e }	iiij
d. Jo. iacobo, suo figliolo	iiij	Gillet	}	
Marcho Troto	iiij	d. Antonio	eL }	ij
Alesandro coletta	iiij	p.pos. de Scta. tegia	}	
Filipo feruffino	iiij	Cardin	e }	iiij
Francisco Rizio	ij	Aluyseto	}	
Tomasio de hexio e }	iiij	Michel de Torsa e	}	ij
Nicolo toschano }		Juschin	}	
d. Antiquario	ij			
Francisco da Tolentino	j		*(fo. 2r)*	
Jo. petro comino	ij	Anto. ponzo	}	ij
Jo. petro de caxale,		d. Raynere	}	
offi.ale deli cavalarij		Jannes	}	ij

Marcho   }
Jannes Franau   }   iiij
Jannes B.bero   }

Sonatori da orghani
Fra Matheo Garza
Jo. andrea da cerusa
Georgio da Viana
El Mag.ro di P.fumi   ij
Mag.ro Zanino darrelori
Mag.ro Franc.o bombardero
Malpaga stambechinero   j
Boniforte stambechinero   j

Giochatori da balla
Corazina
El Maystreto   ij
Nicollo
El Bresano
Rizo
chito grande
El Florenzoto
Juliano Trombeta   j
Sacho Trombeta   j
Gulielmo

Barberi
Mag.ro Bono
Mag.ro Donato

(*col. 2*)
Travaglino
Tomasio piacentino
B.bero Mato

Credenzeri
Anto. de Vicomercato
El Cavalere
Ambrosio

Soto crede.zeri
Matheo
Roffino
Jacometo
Ambroseto

Spenditori e dispensatori
d. Aluyse de petras.cta   ij
Matheo del Castelatio
B.tolomeo
Jo. Anto. de Castello S. Zohane
Andrea bosso
Ardizone

Sertori
Cazardo Mag.ro
Antoniolo
El calzante
Paulino calzolaro
Sig.re Buffone

Ap.egiatori de salla
Furiano, mag.ro de salla   ij
Xp.oforo
Apolinario
petro

Soto ap.egiatori
Georgino
Marchiano

Fornari
                                  (*fo.2v*)
Georgio
Jo. antonio

Bechari
Tomasio
Andriolo fasolo

Canevari
d. nico
petro

Polarolli
Bapt.a
Moreto

Cochi
Nicolo da meda
Mag.ro Gulielmo
Mag.ro Thomaso
Mag.ro petro

Mag.ro Hyeronimo
Mag.ro B.tho

Soto cochi
Bonadies
Guido
Bono

Scotini
Romagnollo
Scarpagiodi
Guerino
Gulielmo

Stalla Ducale
P. la p.sona del n.ro Ill.mo
  p. et Ex.mo Sig.re   L
el conte Borella   vj
Spagnollo   ij
Jo. Anto. B.baresco spenditore
Nicollino soto spenditore
Mag.ro Rollando marescalcho
Mag.ro Gotardo sellaro
Matheo dala mandolla
Mag.ro maffeo b.bero

(col. 2)
Victore dispe.sere cibario
Jo. Maria dispe.sere del feno
  e de biada
Mag.ro Johanne cocho
Martino ap.egiatore
Jacobo da cremona cavalcatore
Thenchone cavalcatore
Mulateri da stalla   X
Mulateri da cam.a   iiij
cavagli de fatione   Lxxx
el vesconte sopra li infr.i

Ducali regazi
Reversino de fontanella
Karlo da seregnio
Clemente de pavia
v. Nocente de mantoa
Tadeo da Pisa
Jo. antonio da m.lo
Petro zohane de cayro

Jo. matheo da lode
v. ludovico de p.ma
Scarioto
Sasseto
Evangelista
Jacobo da corte
Jacobo da monza
Ludovicho del guasco
Batayno
Francisco de Birago
B.nardino de piacentia
Jo. antonio de vigieveno
B. tolomeo todeschino

Galupi di quali sono et.
alcuni Usellatori
Jo. antonio uselatore
Venturino
Bataglino   (fo. 3r)
Bbeta. usellat.
Diana usellat.
Biancho uselat.
Tachino uselat.
Roberto uselat.
Turcheto usellat.
Antonio de valentino
pixanello
Bichino
Xp.oforo da m.lo sopra li infr.i

Caretoni et Mulateri		j
Cecharello mulatero	m.	ij
Augustino	m.	ij
Xp.oforo mezatesta	m.	j
Aluysio Mulatero	m.	ij
Furgusino	m.	ij
Antonio del conte	m.	ij
Girardo	m.	ij
Jeronimo	m.	ij
Steffano da mlo.	m.	ij
Johanne de Romane.go	m.	ij
Lenzo	m.	ij
Bagio	calo.	j.
Petro dela bella	m.	

Caretoni
Francesco	cali.	iiij

Adam	iiij		Barbiglio	j
Vicentio	iiij		Jacobo d'Abia	j
Johanne todescho	iiij			
Malvaia	iiij		(*fo. 3v*)	
Morello	iiij		Xpoforo.de vigieveno	j
Borino	iiij		Antonio da Mlo.	j
Bossino	iiij		Gulielmo	j
Fontana	iiij		Laure.tio da rognano	j
Joh.e Mato	iiij		Antonio de mixinti	j
Leonardo	iiij		Joh.e antonio da m.lo	j
petro todescho	iiij		Bapt.a	j
zentilhomo	iiij		B.tolomeo	j

(*col. 2*)

canat. a pede

Johe. petro cocho — j

Corero

Pizino sopra le legne — j

Capelleto de casora

Mag.ro Francisco mares }
Calcho }
Bozera } v
Beltramino }
Gienoveze }
Cornezano }

Comello da ligurno

canateri da sausi

Stanghelino
El priore
Mazaloste

d. Karlo de cremona — xij
[com]put. *carete due p.*
portare pane e cani

El prioreto
Magro. Stanghero
Simone todescho
Lazarino

*Canateri da brachi
del n.ro Ill.mo Sig.re*

Barone
Martelino

Xpoforo. de bolla — j
Lansalloto de Bolla — j

Chitolla
Granzino de cusago
Johanne da pioltino

Canateri da cam.a

Antonio de Buste — j
Gulielmoto — ij
B.trame de ligurno — j
Morello da rognano — j
Gulielmino

*cazadori p. provedere
ale caze*

Mazono de cusago
Ambroseto de moreto
Andriolo da corsicho
Sancto da moreto
Xp.oforo da corsicho
Simone da corsicho
Antonio de bexana

Canateri da livreri a cavallo

Antonio de belolo — j
B.nardo da Mlo. — j
Righino — j
Donato da moreto — j
Francisco da sexto — j
Nicolino — j
Ambrosio d'Abia — j
Nicolla — j

Uselatori ducali

Jacobo de mag.ro Niccolo greco — ij
Jacomello — ij
Hestor — ij
Lezaro — ij

(col. 2)

Bochazino	ij
fioravante	ij
pillato	ij
Beltrame capello	j

Uselatori ch[e] vene dreto
ala Invernata

Rizo	ij
Donato	ij
Tadeo	ij
Johanne greco	ij
Mag.ro Leone	ij
Georgio greco	ij
Georgio delarte	ij
Georgio albanese	ij
Carleto	ij
Zane	ij
Augustino	j

Uselatori de la Illma. madona
duchessa

Guido	e	}	iij
Andoardo		}	

Uselatori de [blank]

perino	e	}	iij
Francisco de Nicolo de Rizo		}	

Stafferi ducali

Johane grande	
xp.oforo de buste	ij
San xp.oforo	
Sforza de castellione	
Jacobino crivello	
Giemigniano de pontremolo	
Stefano da cremona	
Gallo boza	
B.tola lita	
Ambrosio porro	
D.m.co de Castiono	
Antonio de Carlione	

(fo. 4r)

Baptistino de Gavi
Cexaro de traieta
Joh.e. antonio porro

Donato basso
Gigante de ferara
B.tolomeo pegoraro
Johe. de Riva
B.nardino dela tarcheta
Francisco de Rippa
Andrea dalza
Pedroleone
Todeschino
B.nardino de V.exe
Gaspero de romane.go

Rosso capitane dela	ij
guardia	

It. provisionati a pede

Balestrieri a cavallo

Gasp.eto	e	}	xxvij
Silvestro		}	
Conte			xxvij
Greagheto		}	xxvij
Simone		}	
Covelle		}	xxvij
Parmesano		}	

(col. 2)

d. Jo. Angello de florentia	viiij
d. Jo. Bapt.a da cotignola iij	
xp.oforo da Bolla	v

Lista della Ill.ma et ex.ma madona		
duchessa [com]put. cavalli xiiijo. del		
Ill.o Sig.re Ottaviano et		
[com]put. carete mulli et ogni altra		
cosa /	e in s.a	cLxx

Lista computatis om.ib.s extracto		
fora perino, franc.o, et		
El Biancho, uselatore		
	e in s.a	xxxx

Fachini	viij

Appendix 3
Princes and Feudatories Invited
to Milan for Christmas, 1472

[Codex in ASM, AS, c. 1483–feste, giuochi, spettacoli.]

[doc. #158]

Infr[ascript]i s[u]nt principes & d[omi]ni & proceres & Barones ac Feudatarij
& Nobilis venturi M[edio]l[anu]m ad celebrandum proximu[m] festum natale
d[omi]nicum apud Ill[ustrissimu]m principem & Ex[cellentissimu]m
d[omi]n[u]m n[ost]r[u]m d[omi]n[u]m ducem Mediolani.

Ill. d.n.s Marchio Mantue
Ill. d. Marchio Montisferrati
M.cus d. Pinus de Ordelaphis Forlivij
&c.
M.cus d. Robertus de S.ctoseverino
M.cus d. Johannes de Bentivolijs
M.cus Johannes Comes
Ill. d.n.s Filippus maria sfortia
Vicecomes
Ill. d.n.s Sfortia maria sfortia Vicecomes
dux Barri
Ill. d.n.s Lodovicus maria sfortia
Vicecomes comes Mortarij
Ill. & R.dus d.n.s Ascanius maria
Vicecomes
Ill. d.n.s Ottavianus maria Vicecomes
M.cus d.n.s Bosius Sfortia de Attendolis
M.cus d.n.s Sfortia secundus comes
Burginovi
M.cus d.n.s Tristanus Sfortia
M.cus d.n.s Polidorus Sfortia
d. Petrus maria de Rubeis
co. Petrus de Verme
d. Lancilotus de Mayno
d. Andreotus de Mayno
co. Johannes &   }fr.es de Bonromeis
co. Vitalianus   }

d. Thomas de Reate
d. Sagramorus & } fr.es Vicecomites
Petrus franciscus
d. Johannes lodovicus & } fr.es Marchiones Palavicini
d. Palavicinus   }
d. Prosper Adurnus
d. Petrus de Pusterla
d. Thomas de Bononia
d. Laurentius de Pisauro
d. Gerardus de Collis
d. Johannes filippus de Trechate
d. Antonius de Romagnano
d. Petrus de Trivultio & Nepotes
d. Franciscus Vicecomes
d. Johannes jacobus Ritius sive
d.n.s Johannes stefanus eius filius
d. Petrus de Galerate
d. Cichus Symonetta
d. Jo. Petrus & Nepotes Vicecomites
                    [doc. #159)
co. Manfredo de Lando
co. Marsilius & fr.es de Torellis
co. Guido galeotus & } fr.es de Torellis
co. Franciscus maria }
R.dus d.n.s Karolus Marchio
Palavicinus Ep.us Lauden.

Johannes franciscus Marchio
Palavicinus
Johannes manfredus Marchio
Palavicinus
co. Ugo de S. ctoseverino
co. Petrus Rusca
co. Johannes Rusca
d. Johannes aloysius & Frater Vicecomites
Lucas Crottus
d. Augustinus de Becharia
d. Johannes matheus Bottigella
d. Johannes Stampa
co. Otto de Mandello
co. Ugolotus Crivellus
co. Johannes bartholomeus Crivellus
d. hieronymus &   } fr. es de Maletis
d. Petrus maria   }
d. Johannes antonius & fr.es. de Cottis
Gasparinus Vicecomes
d. Albertus Vicecomes
Jo. Maria Vicecomes
co. Galeotus de Bivilaquis
d. Baptistinus de Campofregosio
co. Hieronymus de Becharia
d. Manfredinus & } fr.es de Becharia
Raynaldus   }
Baldesar de B. zijs
Donatus de Burris de Mediolano
Georginus de Galesio
d. Franciscus de Valperga
Johannes georgius & } fr.es. de
Lampugnano
Franciscus   }
d. Antonius & fr.es de Lonate
d. B.nardus de Lonate
Jacobus de Eustachio

[doc. #160]

d. Conradus de la Porta
Ritius de Cortona
d. Johannes augustinus Isimbardus
Floramons de Gratianis de Cottignola
d. Petrus de Birago
co. Franciscus de Castiliono de
Venegono

Christoforus de Casate
Alpinolus de Casate
d. Alexander Vicecomes & Nepotes
d. Franciscus &   } de Castiliono quon.
d. Guarnerij
Fratres   }
Nobiles de Besutio
d. Johannes aloysius & } fr.es de Bossis
Johannes Franciscus }
co. Bartholomeus Scotus
co. Albertus Scotus de Casalegio
co. Jacobus Scotus
Hector de Rubeis de Placentia
Daniel Radinus dictus Todiscus
co. Johannes de Balbiano
co. Gabriel de Balbiano
co. Angelus & Frater dela Pergula
d. Antonius Guascus
d. Martinus de Nibia
Carolus Cacharanus
Nobilis de Valperga
d. Franischus Vicecomes de Azareto
Bonifacius &   } fr.es ceterisque
Marchiones Vartij
Nicolosius   }
d. Zanardus de Torniellis
d. Matheus &   } de Anfossio
Fratres   }
d. Johan[n]es & } de Putheo
Fratres   }
d. Daniel de Rubeis
d. Gabriel Vicecomes
Johannes Spinula quon. Cacianimici

(doc. #161)

Amphitrio de Girasio
Johannes Malvicinus
Daniel & Con[ ]vites de Scarampis
Cavalchinus & } de Guidobonis
Fratres   }
d. Lazarus &   } fr.es de Spinulis de
Cassino
Johannes   }
Heredes quon. d. Petrini & Sanguinoli
dela Somalia

Antonius &   } fr.es de Belcredo
Stefanus   }
Heredes quon. d. Thomasij & Johan.is
  cacini de Cacijs
Johannes nicolaus de Nicellis
Conradinus & } de Georgijs
Fratres   }
Comites Mede
Rafael Zacharia &
Ruffeninus de Curte
Georgius &   } quon. Zonfrini de
            Merliano
Fratres   }
Petrus paulus &   } Fratres de Lanello
Tartalia   }

Johannes franciscus Stangha
Nobiles de Sissa
Baldesar &   } de Trottis
Fratres   }
Nobiles de Busseto de Bagnaria
Magister Gabriel Pavarus
Heredes quon. d. Antonij & Gabrij de
  Malvicinis
Galeaz de Gromello
Nobiles de Gambarane
Nobiles Sparovarie
Nobiles Cond.ni Rochete Tanagri
Nicolaus de Arena
Petrus antonius & } de Villa
Nepos   }

Appendix 4
Persons in Ducal Party
for 1471 Visit to Florence

From codex captioned on outside cover, "1471. Le Liste dela andata delo Illmo. Sigre. duca Galeaz duca de mlo. a Fiorenza & certe altre liste" (ASM, AS, 898). A handful of additional copies are scattered throughout the *Sforzesco* series. The codex contains 15 separate lists for the Florence journey, each falling into one of four types. The most common type, dated 21 January 1471, lists Galeazzo first, his favorite Alessio Piccinino Albanese second, then the ducal brothers and other notables, court officers, and the traveling household. Some examples of this type bear headings for each category of persons listed. Another type, dated 14 February 1471, lists only the household, with Alessio ranking below his position in the earlier list. A third type (undated) shows Bona's full retinue, divided under various category headings and into the groups (*squadre*) in which her court traveled. The fourth type of list, also undated (but probably composed close to the March 4 date of departure) bears no such headings but includes elements from the other three types. This Appendix includes the first list in the codex, probably the first draft composed when the duke conceived of the trip, with examples of the second and third types.

I [fos. 2r–v]

Modoetie, xxj Januari 1471

	ca.		ca.
El nro. Illmo. S.	80	d. Alberto vesconte	6
Alexio Picinino dala stafa	3	d. Colla gayetano	6
Lo Illmo. S. Filippo	20	d. Jo. jac. trivulci	5
Lo Illmo. S. duca de barri	20	Orpheo	6
Lo Illmo. S. ludovico	20		
Monre. de Novara	14	Mro. Jo. da marliano }	
d. Thomaso dariete	12	Mro. Jo. ghiringhello }	10
petro da pusterla	12		
d. Thomaso da bologna	10	(*fo. 2r*)	
d. Petro da trivulci	8	El Spiciaro	1
d. Alexo. spinola	8	Confessore et duy capellani	7
Nicodemo	8		
d. Hyeronimo maleta	6	d. Jo. petro vesconte	6
Petro de Galarate	8	d. Jo. aluise vesconte	5
		d. Alex. vesconte	5
d. palavicino palavicino	6	d. Manfr.ino da Becaria	4
Jo. franc.o palavesino	6	d. Petro maria maleta	4

	ca.		*ca.*
Johanne da Castilion.	4	B.nardino de eugobio	2
d. Jo. Aug.o Isimbardo	4	Clemente da Concorezo	2
Marchese de varese	4	Johanne da castelonoate, Jo.	
	ca.li 314	chiapano co. 1a camara et	
		p. apte ad s.[ire]	20
(col. 2)		Conte Galeoto	5
Rizo da Cortona	4	Pizeto	4
Petro da birago	4		
Carlo de Cremona	4		
Donato da Milano	5	Li credenzeri et sotocreden.	6
d. Hyeronimo de beccaria	4	Cochi et scoti	7
Petro franc.o Vesconte	8	Martino sop.cogo	
Johanne de V.ona	3	Bono [et] Donato barberi	4
Nicolo da cortona	3	Manuelo [et] Bassano Sertori	4
B.tolomeo da locarno	2	Guiniforte [et] Malpaga	2
Antonio carazolo	3	stambechineri	
d. Guido ant.o	4	El Cavalero, Xp.oforo,	
Carlino Varesino	2	apolinario	3
Antonieto da Piasenza	2	Gasparro da p.ma	3
Gasparre Cayme	2	Johane [et] Nicolo	2
Bapt.a de Mon.re	2	Bassano spendit. }	
Francisco da Varese	3	Ceresa }	
Jo. luchino crivello	2	Andrea dispensat. }	5
Yasone marescotto	2	B.t.o [con]script. }	
Gosme Ponzono	2	Jo. da lorilozie }	
Zorzo dal Carreto	3	Coracina }	
Xp.oforo Ussero	2		
Sotocamareri vj	6	Cantori iv	6
Jo. petro del B.gamino	4	Piferi vj	8
d. Vercelino	4	Tro.beti xx	30
d. Baptistino da campofregoso	5	Xpo. da milano [et] mulat.	100
Antonio palavicino	2	canateri	10
Damiano da Barci	2	Falconeri	25
Francesco pagnano	2		ca.li 234
Aluise da maregnano	2		
Jacomino dal castellazo	2		
Branda da castiglione	2	d. Cicho [con] la cancellaria	50
Manfredo da Campofregoso	2	La. Franc.o da casa [con] cavall.	14
Corbetino	2	La Ill.ma Madon.a [con] le done	
Nicolo maleta	2	sarano in soa compagnia	300
El Bressano	2	Fioramo.te [et] la mogliere	8
	ca.li 97	M.co d. la Turcho	12
(fo. 2v)		d. Francesco dini	12
Aluise zorzo	2	d. Xp.of. rangone	10
Jo. bassano	2	Zacaria da pisa	8
El Piasentino de Johanne Jac.o	2	Martino da nibia	8
		Gabriel Pagliaro	2

II [fos. 9r–v] "Lista de landata da
fiorenza facta et ordinata a di 14 de
februario de lanno 1471"

	ca.	bo.
Il n.ro Ill.mo S.re cum	45	45
cavalli [et] ragazi		
della stalla sua		
Sotocamareri	6	6
Pompeo et coracina	2	2
Xp.oforo Speciaro	1	1
Bono barbero	2	2
Manuello [et] bassano S.tori	4	4
El Ceresa cum la dispensa	4	4
Antonio crendenzero [cum]	6	7
la credenza		
Il cavalero de salla }		
Xp.oforo et }	3	6
Apolinaro [et] Fachini }		
M.ro Jacomo cogo [cum]	6	6
la cusina		
Borella [et] Spagnolo cum		
li off.li dalla stalla	39	22
M.ro Zohanne da rolorio	1	1
Alessio da durazo	3	3
M.ro Zohanne da Marliano }		
M.ro Zohanne Ghiringhello } medici		
M.ro Lazaro }	10	10
Il Conte Galeoto sescalco [et]		
Martino sop. cogo	7	7
Piceto sescalco	4	4
d. Jeronimo da Becharia	4	4
Petro pagnano	6	6
d. Zorzo dal caretto	3	3
Baptista da mons.re	4	4
Antonieto da piasenza	2	2
Carlino Varesino	2	2

(col. 2)

	ca.	bo.
Zohanne da V.ona	3	3
B.tho. da locarno	3	3
Carlino de angello	3	3
Nicolo da crotona	3	3
Gusme ponzono	3	3
Aluysino da cornagliano	2	2
Jason Malscotto	2	2

	ca.	bo.
Jo. luchino crivello	2	2
Corbetino	2	2
Branda da castigliono	2	2
Jacomino dal castelazo	2	2
B.nardino da Ugobio	2	2
Nicolo malleta	2	2
Gabriel pagliaro	3	3
Zoh.e fran.co bosso	2	2
Enea malvezo	3	3
Xp.oforo da lode uschiero	2	2
Malpaga [et] Boniforte	2	2
Do.ico da bregno et el } canepari		
[com]pagno }	2	2
Zorzo da Ello et al } fornari		
[com]pagno }	2	2
d. Zohanne artono	2	2
Franzoseto canatero	1	1
Zannetto calzante	1	1

Staferi

Johanne grande	1
Xp.oforo da busti	1
Sancto Xpo.f.o	1
Stefano da Cremona	1
Jacomino crivello	1
Fenochio	1

(*fo. 9v*)

Baptistino da gavio	1
Sforza da casteliono	1
Zimignano	1
Gallo	1
Fran.co da P.tasancta	1

Fachini

Il Bizaro	1
Manno de lacomayore	1
Cavigia da bregno	1
Michele da bregno	1
Rosseto da bregno	1
Marzo da bregno	1

Famigli da stalla

Guielmo da bregno	1
Scaramuza de Milano	1

	ca.	bo.
Petro rosso		1
Fran.co de calavria		1
Martino todescho		1
do.ico da Meglio		1
Julliano da moza		1
Laurenzo da Allexan.		1
Baldasar dal Monte de brianza		1
Berlenda da bregno		1
Petro picardo		1
Thadeo da bregno		1
Petro da soncino		1
Andrea da villa		1
Galupo novarese		1
Antonio da B.gamo		1
Xp.oforo da Montaldo		1
Paulo todesco		1
Jacomo todesco		1
Rolando da Casate		1
Jacomo da bregno		1

(col. 2)

	ca.	bo.
Antonio da Cantu		1
Petro Sgiava		1
Zuliano da Abbia		1
Otto todesco		1
Peruchino		1
Jacomo da Gra		1
Boscheto de domodossella		1
Jacomo da meriguano		1
Cemerino da Milano carratono		
per la carreta		
dalla busula	4	2

| Johanne petro panigarola | 4 | 4 |

III [fos. 16r–17r]
"Inf.s.ti sonno quili che Anno andare a fiorentia in anze de la n.ra Ill.ma madona in d.cta cavalchata p. la prima squadra"

(fo. 16r)

	bo.	ca.
Primo d. Joh.ne maria Vesconte		
[com] la muiere	x	x
Fioramonte da codignola		
[com] la muiere	viij	viij

	bo.	ca.
d. B.nardo la lona		
con la muiere	viij	viij
d. Joh.ne antonio meza barba		
[con] la muiere	viij	viij
d. Hotto Vesconte	iiij	iiij
d. Antonio secho	iiij	iiij
d. Mastino suardo	iiij	iiij
d. Antonio porro	iiij	iiij
d. Jacobo becheto	iiij	iiij
Steffeno stampa	iiij	iiij
Aluysio da dugni.o	iiij	iiij
Joh.ne da galara	iiij	iiij
Venturino rabia	iiij	iiij
Boldrino crivello	ij	ij
M. Alberto capelano	ij	ij
M. Matregni.o sertore	iij	iij
Albertino guardaroba	ij	ij
Mulateri	muli	xL

"Inf.s.ti sommo quili che anno andare in anze de la n.ra Ill.ma p. la seconda squadra in d.cta cavalchada"

(fo. 16v)

	bo.	ca.
P.o La magnifica d.	xv	xv
biatriza sforza		
d. Antonia da peroza	iij	ij
d. Isabeta dangelo [et]	iij	ij
daria sua fiola		
Hellena deL maigno	j	j
Madalena nana	j	j
Joh.ne gabrielo crivello	iiij	iiij
Domenicho mentono	iij	iij
V.gilio crivello	iij	iij
Joh.ne zorzo del maigno	iij	iij
Domenicho cristiano	j	j
Donado uschiero	j	j
Brunelo uschiero	j	j
Jacobo montena	j	j
Joh.ne da lecho	j	j
Biaxe nano	j	j
Joh.ne de m.gliano	j	j
Pagij vj	vj	vj
Lorenzino	ij	ij

	bo.	ca.
Felixe di mag.ri	j	j
Andrea cremoneze	j	j
Antonio galuppo	j	j
M. donado barbere	j	j
El fameglio de d. antonia da p.oza	j	j
M. Antonio s.cogo	j	j
Joh.ne muto scotto	j	j
Beltramino fiolo de zuchino	j	j
Gabrielo dal torgio	ij	ij
Danielo da grupelo	j	j
M. Somelino selaro	j	j
Famiglij de stala	viij	ij
Mulateri	muli	xv

"Inf.s.ti sonno quili che anno andare con la n.ra Ill.ma Madona in la t.za squadra"

	bo.	ca.
P.o La n.ra Illma. Madona	j	iiij
Fiordeliza sforza	j	i
d. Francischa da castigliono	ij	j
Nutrice	ij	j
Violante	j	j
Malgarita di crivelli	ij	j
Madalena da V.ona	j	j
Izabeta da tertona	j	j
Caravaze iiij	iiij	0
Don zuliano capelano	ij	ij
M.ro Ambrozio griffo	iiij	iiij
Pedro da landriano	iiij	iiij
Joh.ne fran.cho da castiglio	iij	iiij
Hector de d. antonelo	iij	iiij
Coralo	ij	ij
Zacharino	ij	ij
Pagij iiij	iiij	iiij
Francescho credenzere	ij	ij
Martino soto credenzere	j	j
Donado da varexio	j	j

	bo.	ca.
B.tolameo crede.zere de le done	j	j
Antonio barbante	j	j
Joh.ne m.cho rolando	j	j
Angelo dal barra	j	j
Batista da comischio	j	j
Agustino guardaroba	j	j
Domenicho fachino	j	j

(col. 2)

Xpo.foro da galara	j }	
Raignaldo staffero	j }	ij
Donado pestono	j }	
Scalabrino staffero	j }	
Aluyxio resta spe.ditor	j	j
Rafaelo despe.sadore	j	j
Zorzo parixe soto despe.sadore	j	j
Martino sarnaro	j	j
Joh.ne da varexio	j	j
M.ro Xp.oforo spiziaro	j	j
Agustino da pavia	j	j
M. S.melino cogo	j	j
M. Beltramo cogo	j	j
Guidino scoto	j	j
Scotino scotto	j	j

(fo. 17r)

Scotini ij	ij	ij
Fachini iiij	iiij	0
Zuchino M.ro da stala	ij	ij
Mafiero rognia	j	j
M.ro Staffeno meneschalcho	ij	ij
Famiglij da stala	xvj	iiij
Mulateri	muli	xv

Notes

Preface

1. Baldassare Castiglione, *Il Libro del Cortegiano,* introd. by A. Quondam (Milan, 1981):15.

2. The literature on Louis XIV and his court is very substantial. Ragnhild Hatton provides a useful starting point; see *Louis XIV and His World* (London and New York, 1972), and chap. 11 in A. G. Dickens, ed., *The Courts of Europe* (New York, 1984; first published London, 1977).

3. Castiglione, 16.

4. Walter Map, *De Nugis Curialium,* ed. by M. R. James, revis. by C. N. L. Brooke and R. A. B. Mynors (Oxford, 1983): 2–4. The translation is my own, using James's Latin text, his original translation (1914), and a translation by Frederick Tupper (1923). As Trevor Dean has observed, the courts of Renaissance Italy were quite similar to those described by Map, whose work may not have been known to Renaissance Italy, and his fellow Briton, John of Salisbury, whose work certainly was known. See "Notes on the Ferrarese court in the later Middle Ages," *Renaissance Studies* III, no. 4 (1989): 358; comment on Map and Salisbury drawn from preface by Benjamin Kohl and James Day in their translation of Giovanni Conversini da Ravenna, *Two Court Treatises* (Munich, 1987): 7. In fact, John's *De Nugis Curialium* was part of Galeazzo Maria Sforza's library and was read; see Giuseppe Mazzatinti, "Inventario dei codici della biblioteca visconteo-sforzesco, redatto da Ser Facino da Fabriano nel 1459 e 1469," *Giornale Storico della Letterature Italiana* I (1883): 58.

5. Giovanni Papagno, "Corti e cortigiani," in Adriano Prosperi, *La Corte e "Il Cortegiano"* II: *Un Modello Europeo* (Rome, 1979): 197.

6. A. T. Carter, *A History of the English Courts,* 6th ed. (London, 1935): 14–15.

7. George Burton Adams, *Court and Council in Anglo-Norman England* (London, 1965): 9 and 6, respectively.

279

8. Giovanni Simonetta to Galeazzo Maria Sforza, 5 Nov. 1470, Milan (Archivio di Stato-Milan, Archivio Sforzesco, cartella 896).

9. Lauro Martines, *Power and Imagination* (New York, 1979): 221.

10. Quoted in Sergio Bertelli et al., *Italian Renaissance Courts,* trans. M. Fitton and G. Culverwell (London, 1986): 8.

11. Norbert Elias, *The Court Society,* trans. Edmund Jephcott (New York, 1984): 40; originally published as *Die Höfische Gesellschaft* (Neuwied, 1969).

12. Emmanuel Leroy Ladurie, ["Les Cabales de la Cour de France sous Louis XIV, d'après les *Memoires* de Saint-Simon"], in *Annuaire de la Collège de France* (1976): 634. For a general sense of the progression from medieval to modern courts, see the collection of essays in Dickens, *The Courts of Europe.*

13. Elias, *Court Society,* 2.

14. Martines, *Power and Imagination,* 229.

15. Bertelli, *Italian Renaissance Courts,* 8–9.

16. Ibid., 17–20.

17. The Centro Studi "Europa delle corti" has published several books, mainly *atti* of conferences on early modern Italian courts. For a good summary of the publications through 1982, see John Larner's review article, "Europe of the Courts," *Journal of Modern History* 55 (1983): 669–672.

18. J. A. Burrow, "Introduction," in V. J. Scattergood and J. W. Sherborne, *English Court Culture in the Later Middle Ages* (London, 1983): ix. Burrow saw the court's fluidity as conceptually problematic; six years later, Dean showed greater comfort with such flexibility ("Notes on the Ferrarese court," 358).

19. *Oxford English Dictionary* III (Oxford, 1989): 1057; *Grande Dizionario della Lingua Italiana* III (Turin, 1964): 854–856; C. T. Lewis and C. Short, *A Latin Dictionary* (Oxford, 1975): 205–206, 501.

20. In October 1987, I had an opportunity to speak at a conference on these two duchies; for the proceedings, see Centre Européen d'Études Bourguignonnes, *Milan et les États bourguignons: Deux ensembles princiers entre Moyen Age et Renaissance,* no. 28 (Brussels, 1988). Werner Parravicini spoke on the Burgundian court; his work is illuminating and precise. The most useful major studies in English on Burgundy are biographies of the Valois dukes by Richard Vaughan. Chapter 5 of *Charles the Bold* (London, 1973) has a particularly good treatment of the court. The classic presentation of this court is Otto Cartellieri, *The Court of Burgundy* (New York, 1929).

21. No other work served as a model for this one, but Gervase Mathew's *Court of Richard II* (London, 1968) inspired consideration of a single court in many dimensions. Peter Lewis, *Later Medieval France* (London, 1968), also gives unusually acute and attentive consideration to the court's role. Bernard Guillemain, *La cour pontificale d'Avignon* (Paris, 1966), is an ambitious study exploring household administration and broad demographic issues.

22. Jakob Burckhardt, *Civilization of the Renaissance in Italy* I (New York, 1958): 42.

23. For Ludovico's court, the dominant work is still Francesco Malaguzzi Valeri, *La Corte di Lodovico il Moro,* 4 vols. (Milan, 1913–1917), although it is factually suspect and has been superseded in many areas. Several conferences relating to Ludovico's court took place in Milan in the early 1980s, in particular, *Milano dell'età di*

Ludovico il Moro, with proceedings published by Archivio Storico Civico & Biblioteca Trivulziana (Milan, 1983).

24. Cecilia Ady, *A History of Milan under the Sforza* (London, 1907). For some works of the recent authors, see Bibliography.

25. Fondazione Treccani degli Alfieri, *Storia di Milano,* 17 vols. (Milan, 1953–1962). Santoro's *oeuvre* is huge, and Chittolini has also been prolific; the Bibliography lists only works contributing directly to this study. Chittolini has also participated in various publications of the Centro Studi "Europa delle corti." The *Archivio Storico Lombardo (ASL)* contains a wealth of articles on Milanese and Lombard history, with many printed documents.

26. The most useful *fonti* in the Archivio di Stato, Milan, have been the *Registri delle Missive* and *Archivio Ducale Sforzesco.* The Sforzesco series is subdivided into the *Potenze sovrane, Potenze estere, Carteggio interno,* and *Trattati ed atti* series, but all are numbered continuously, and the specific categories are not needed to identify the *cartella* in question. The *Potenze sovrane* contains letters and documents from members of the ducal family; the *Potenze estere* from locations outside the dominion; and *Trattati ed atti,* unbound documents, such as treaties and investitures. The *Carteggio interno* contains letters and documents from within the dominion, classified by city or district, with the file for Milan itself serving as a catch-all for items from various sources, including draft letters from the duke and duchess. I have used material also from the *Registri Ducali, Famiglie, Feudi Camerali, Araldica (Parte antica)* and *Autografi* series, as well as the *Archivio Notarile, Archivio Crivelli,* and Giovanni Sitoni di Scozia's work in the *Acquisto Riva Finolo* and *Theatrum Genealogicum.*

27. In the Archivio Civico, Milan, I consulted material from the Biblioteca Trivulziana. I have also used manuscripts from the Biblioteca Ambrosiana and Società Storica Lombarda library.

28. Bernardino Corio, *Storia di Milano* (Milan, 1503); the edition cited in the present study is in 2 volumes, edited by A. M. Guerra (Turin, 1978). For Corio himself, see *Dizionario Biografico degli Italiani (DBI),* XXIX: 75–78.

Prologue

1. As one of the councillors wrote to the duchess, "It seems to me . . . the return of Count Galeazzo manifests itself to be very dangerous, because of which . . . he should not come [back] in the same manner in which he passed through to France . . . but that His Lordship should return in the guise of a pilgrim with companions [and] . . . the best horses and most alert soldiers that he has always following about half-mile or mile or two or three [behind], so that the one group can see the other, until he has passed through the mountains and be in some secure place" (Giacomo Stanga to Bianca Maria Visconti, 8 Mar. 1466, Milan; ASMi, AS, c. 878). In "Galeazzo Maria Sforza, prigione nella Novalesa," Magistretti collected many sources to determine who was responsible for what occurred, but he reached no definitive conclusion.

2. Antonio was appointed on April 2, 1466 (Santoro, *Uffici,* 8).

3. Caleffini, *Diario,* fo. 87. I owe the reference to Jane Bestor, who discovered it while researching her study, "Kinship and Marriage in an Italian Ruling House: The

Este of Ferrara in the Reign of Ercole I (1471–1535)" (Ph.D. dissertation, University of Chicago, 1992).

1: "The Second Prince and Lord in Italy"

1. Caleffini, *Diario,* fo. 87. The duke of Ferrara was considered the third-ranking prince. I owe the reference to Jane Bestor (see Prologue, n. 3).

2. For general introductions, see Barbieri, *Economia e politica nel ducato di Milano*; Treccani, *Storia di Milano,* Vol. VIII, Pt. III.

3. Motta, "Coltura del riso," 395; Galeazzo to Gabriele Paleari, 9 Dec. 1473, Vigevano (ASMi, AS, c. 915) (first rice mill, with experts from Genoa). The Milanese were viewed as pioneers; see Zaccaria Saggi da Pisa to Ludovico II Gonzaga, marquess of Mantua, 7 Mar. 1474 (ASMa, AG, b. 1624); and Niccolò Roberti to Ercole d'Este, 29 Sep. 1475, Milan (ASMo, CDE, DA, Milano, b. 1).

4. For movement of capital into the luxury cloth industry (and away from the struggling wool business), see Mainoni, "L'attività mercantile," 577.

5. For administrative organization, see Santoro, *Uffici,* xv and xxiv.

6. Federico Pallavicino to Galeazzo, 24 Dec. 1470, Milan (ASMi, AS, c. 897).

7. For a full discussion, see Chittolini, "Infeudazioni e politica feudale"; see also his essay, "Entrate e alienazioni di entrate."

8. See Chittolini, "Particolarismo signorile e feudale in Emilia."

9. Santoro, *Uffici,* 8, 9, and 13 (council appointments); Simonetta, *Diari,* 104–107 (courtiers); Litta, d. 77, t. xvii.

10. Chittolini, "Particolarismo signorile e feudale in Emilia," *passim.*

11. Woods-Marsden, "Pictorial Legitimation of Territorial Gains." Pier Maria revolted later; see Bueno de Mesquita, "Ludovico Sforza and His Vassals."

12. Calvi, *Famiglie Notabili Milanesi,* II, Borromeo, t. 6; *DBI,* XIX: 53–55.

13. Cognasso, *Visconti,* 500.

14. For Cicco's *gabelle,* see document headed "1473, Le rason[e] del sale ch[e] paga le terre feudale de d[omi]no Cicho ogni anno" (ASMi, AS, c. 1602).

15. Santoro, *Uffici,* xvi, xxx–xxxiii.

16. See chap. 5.

17. Galeazzo to *commissario* of Cremona, Aug. 1476 (ASMi, RM, no. 123, fo. 322r).

18. Cognasso, *Visconti,* 123.

19. Pellerin, *Bibliothèque*; Cognasso, *Visconti,* 358.

20. See, e.g., Santoro, *Sforza,* 81–82, 139–140.

21. List headed "Mulieres invitate pro diebus VI et VII Julij" (printed in Beltrami, *Dame milanesi,* 13–21).

22. Z. Saggi to Barbara Hohenzollern Gonzaga, 12 June 1469, Abbiategrasso (ASMa, AG, b. 1623). The match was made after the Gonzaga had refused to marry one of their young daughters to Guglielmo.

23. Z. Saggi to Barbara H. Gonzaga, 13 June 1469, Abbiategrasso, and 18 Aug. 1469, Milan (ASMa, AG, X.3, b. 1623). Elisabetta was 13 years old when she married, and her husband about 65; see chap. 3.

24. For some positive attributes, see Z. Saggi to Barbara H. Gonzaga, 22 Dec.

1474, Milan (ASMa, AG, b. 1624). For obesity, see Marsilio Andreasi to Barbara H. Gonzaga, 9 Jan. 1468, Milan (ASMa, AG, b. 1623). In 1469, the Sforza library included a book on how to gain and lose weight ("che insigna ingrassare et smagrare"); see Mazzatinti, "Inventario," 59.

25. For dinner and lodgings, see chap. 2. On Guido's belongings, see Giovanni Niccolò Bergonzi to Galeazzo, 25 Feb. 1474, Pavia (ASMi, AS, c. 855). See also Litta, d. 103, t. ix.

26. Simonetta, *Diari,* 109.

27. See Prosdocimi, "Conferimento dei benefici" and "Stato sforzesco"; and Ansani, "Politica ecclesiastica" and "Provista dei benefici." For the Milanese church in general, see Enrico Cattaneo in Treccani, *Storia di Milano,* IX: 509–706.

28. Galeazzo to Privy Council, 2 Apr. 1475 (ASMi, RM, no. 120, fo. 141r).

29. Galeazzo to vicar of Episcopal Curia, *commissario,* and *referendario* of Novara, 29 May 1474 (ASMi, RM, no. 115, fo. 338v).

30. "Servitori Dep[uta]ti Off[ici]o Sanitatis" to Galeazzo, 8 June 1468, Milan (ASMi, AS, c. 884). Galeazzo also sent his castellan at Pavia to investigate stories of miracles wrought by the recently discovered body of a saint (Galeazzo to castellan, 24 Feb. 1469; ASMi, RM, no. 90, fo. 41v).

31. For gypsies, see Galeazzo to *commissari,* 4 June 1476 (ASMi, Rm, no. 123, fos. 217r–v). For Jews, see proclamation of 30 Aug. 1473, Milan [draft] (ASMi, AS, c. 914). Dukes of Milan were unusual in exempting some Jews from wearing special marks; even Galeazzo's order was not enforced strictly (see Simonsohn, *Jews in Milan,* I: xxi. His introduction is the best survey of Jews in the duchy. The multivolume history is a collection of documents; for Galeazzo's reign, see I: 413–677.

32. Galeazzo to castellan of Pavia, 27 Mar. 1469 (ASMi, RM, no. 90, fo. 80r); summarized by Simonsohn on p. 473.

33. Galeazzo to Magistro Jacobo Ebreo de Cremona and Galeazzo to podestà of Cremona, 23 Oct. 1471 (ASMi, RM, no. 99, fo. 141v). The Jewish physician was asked to cure a son of a Christian ducal physician. In December 1471, the duke had Maestro Jacobo return to heal a condottiere (ASMi, RM, no. 103, fo. 85r; and no. 106, fo. 88v). (Simonsohn missed the first summons; he summarizes the second and third letters on 570 and 578, respectively. See 556–557, for formal appointment of Jacobo as a ducal physician, 23 Aug. 1471.)

34. Many local histories discuss the Milanese dominion from their particular viewpoint. Treccani, *Storia di Milano,* VI and VII; Cognasso, *Visconti*; and Santoro, *Sforza,* treat the issue from the central authority's perspective.

35. See chap. 6.

36. Susan Caroselli has argued that Milanese aristocrats were actively hostile to their dukes; see *Casa Marliani,* chap. 1. The discussion of the Visconti period that follows here derives mainly from Cognasso, *Visconti,* and Treccani, *Storia di Milano,* VI.

37. See chap. 7.

38. Caroselli, *Casa Marliani,* chap. 1.

39. Cognasso, *Visconti,* 358.

40. The discussion on the Sforza that follows is based mainly on Santoro, *Sforza,* and F. Catalano in Treccani, *Storia di Milano,* VII.

41. For the civil administration's hierarchy and military offices, see Santoro, *Uffici,* xv–xvi, and her contribution (Pt. III, Chap. IV) in Treccani, *Storia di Milano,*

VII. For an assessment of the Sforza army, see Mallett, *Mercenaries and Their Masters*, chap. 5.

42. "Filza de tuti li magistrati dela corte . . . ," 13 Sep. 1479 (ASMi, AS, c. 1607).

43. Santoro, *Uffici*, xix–xxii (Privy Council); xxii–xxiii (Council of Justice), 12 and 40 (Cusani); Treccani, *Storia di Milano*, VII, 521–524.

44. Santoro, *Uffici*, xxvii–xxix.

45. Documentation internal to the Chancery appears throughout the *Sforzesco* series; c. 1606 and 1607 hold particular concentrations of such material.

46. *Codex Ducalis Cancerelliae Mediolani 1476* (MS in Biblioteca Ambrosiana); ACM, BT, cod. 1325, fos. 86r–101r, including updates from Galeazzo's reign.

47. Secretaries abroad included Gerardo Cerruti in Bologna (Santoro, *Uffici*, 50; Cerioni, *Diplomazia Sforzesca*, I: 165) and Sagramoro Menclozi [Sagramori] da Rimini (Santoro, *Uffici*, 49; Cerioni, *Diplomazia Sforzesca*, I: 220–221). For a mission within the duchy involving the secretary Francesco Pietrasanta, see letters in ASMi, RM, no. 107, fos. 304r–305r (14 Oct. 1471). Francesco also went on embassies abroad and was posted to France by 1476 (Cerioni, *Diplomazia Sforzesca*, I: 209).

48. Litta, d. 3.

49. Santoro, *Uffici*, 8 and 49. Cicco Simonetta's *Diari* is Vol. I of the *Acta Italica* series and was also published serially in *ASL*. The original forms ASMi, RM, nos. 111A (1473–1474) and 111B (1475–1478).

50. Santoro, *Uffici*, 4.

51. For chancellors' orders, see ACM, BT, cod. 1325, fos. 89r–91r. Ianziti emphasizes this aspect of the Chancery. In 1474, Galeazzo gave a new *cameriere* permission to enter the Privy Council's chancery and learn to write like coadjutors, as the youth wanted "to learn something" (Galeazzo to [unknown], 19 Mar. 1474, Pavia [copy], ASMi, AS, c. 922).

52. For ushers' functions, see ACM, BT, cod. 1325, fos. 91r–93v; ASMi, AS, c. 1606; for searches, see, e.g., Galeazzo to Giovanni Simonetta, 10 Mar. 1469 (ASMi, Rm, no. 89, fo. 192r).

53. For riders' orders, see ACM, BT, cod. 1325, fos. 93v–94v.

54. F. Cusin wrote extensively on Francesco's relations with the emperor; see Bibliography. For forgery, see Giampietrino, "Pretesa donazione," and Motta, "Ancora sulla pretesa donazione." The Chancery also forged alterations to the Papal document that allowed the dukes of Milan to fill benefices (see Ansani, "Provista dei benefici").

55. The claim derived from a marriage between GianGaleazzo Visconti's daughter Valentina and the duke of Orléans. GianGaleazzo's first wife also belonged to the French royal family.

56. See Beltrami, "L'Annullamento del contratto."

57. Tristano, a distinguished knight, was born in 1422, legitimized in 1448, and died in 1477 (Litta, d. 1, t. 2).

58. All of Duke Francesco's legitimate children bore the second name Maria, a tradition established by GianGaleazzo Visconti. The name is rarely used in historical accounts except for Sforza Maria, to avoid confusion with other members of the family who bore the given name Sforza.

59. For their shared education, see Cesari, "Orazione inedita di Ippolita Sforza." For Ippolita in general, see ASMi, AS, c. 1479-Ippolita.

60. For a lively example of their shared education, see Valagussa, "Ceremoniarum quae celebrantur in Natalitiis." In 1463, they still shared their household officers with their three younger siblings (SSL, RF, cod. 5, fo. 180r; Valagussa received a salary of 20 florins per month, second highest of all their household officers). As late as 1467, Sforza Maria and Filippo still shared a chaplain, master of stables, etc. (Sforza Maria to Bianca Maria, 18 Aug. 1467, Lodi; ASMi, AS, c. 1481-Sforza Maria).

61. Sforza Secondo was born in 1433, legitimized in 1448, and died in 1492. He was called "Secondo" because he was the second of Francesco's illegimate sons to be named Sforza. He married into a great feudal family, the Dal Verme counts of Bobbio (Santoro, *Sforza,* 104–105).

62. Galeazzo to Francesco Sforza, 24 Dec. 1452, Pavia (ASMi, AS, c. 1461).

63. Ady, *Milan under the Sforza,* 94; her chapter on Galeazzo is not bad. The only full-length biography of Galeazzo is a romanticized work by Cesare Violini. Santoro, *Sforza,* Chaps. XIV–XXI, are useful, although sometimes inaccurate. For discussions of politics during Galeazzo's reign, see Pontieri, *Età dell'equilibrio*; Pillinini, *Sistema degli stati italiani*; and Riccardo Fubini's contributions to Lorenzo de' Medici, *Lettere.* For a political narrative from the Milanese perspective, see Franco Catalano in Treccani, *Storia di Milano,* VII: 227–309; Vols. VII, VIII, and IX of the series include relevant sections on art, warfare, and music, respectively.

64. Full text in Orano, *"Suggerimenti di buon vivere,"* 15–20.

65. Carlo was born in 1458, Alessandro around 1460–1462, Caterina in 1463, and Chiara around 1464–1465.

66. Niccolò "de Carinus" to Duke Francesco, 16(?) Aug. 1457, "Oscellate" (ASMi, AS, c. 1461) (Cicero); Lancillotto del Maino to Francesco Sforza, 18, 19, 22 Sep. 1458, Pavia (ASMi, AS, c. 1461) (4-hour sessions); Cappelli, "Guiniforte Barzizza"; Cesari, "Orazione di Ippolita Sforza," 50–64; Jahn, *Bianca Maria,* 236–237.

67. Hatfield, "Descriptions of the Medici Palace," and correspondence of April and May 1459 in ASMi, AS, c. 1461. For the joust plan, see Count Giovanni Balbiani to Duke Francesco, 5 Apr.; Galeazzo himself described his entry into Florence (letter to Duke Francesco, 17 Apr.).

68. Benedetto Dei, *Cronica,* 67 (fo. 22v).

69. Cristoforo da Soncino to Duke Francesco, 7 Aug. 1457, "ex terra Porti" (ASMi, AS, c. 1461).

70. Vincenzo Scalone to L. Gonzaga, 1 May 1459, Milan (ASMa, AG, b. 1620).

71. Cited in Ady, *Milan under the Sforza,* 95, from Cappelli, "Guiniforte Barzizza." Bianca Maria and Francesco were both disappointed with their eldest son; see Terni de Gregorij, *Bianca Maria.* For 1457 comment, see Francesco Sforza to Galeazzo, 7 Aug. [no location] (ASMi, AS, c. 1461).

2: "To Give Form and Order to Matters of Our Court"

1. Initial oaths of fealty were sworn to Bianca Maria alone; e.g., oath from vassals in Piacenza district, 11 June 1466, Milan [draft] (ASMi, AS, c. 878).

2. Galeazzo to Agostino Rossi, 19 Apr. 1466, Milan (ASMi, AS, c. 1459).

3. Galeazzo to Bianca Maria, 8 Apr. 1466, Milan (ASMi, AS, c. 1461).

4. Ambrogio Cavalero to Galeazzo, 9 July 1466, Milan (ASMi, AS, c. 878).

5. Bianca Maria to Galeazzo, 10 Sep. 1466, Milan (ASMi, AS, c. 878), and

18 Sep., Milan [draft] (ASMi, AS, c. 1459). The marchioness at that time was Marie, daughter of Count Gaston of Foix (Cappelli, *Cronologia,* 308).

6. Galeazzo to Bianca Maria, 5 Nov. 1466, Vigevano (ASMi, AS, c. 878).

7. See, e.g., Bianca Maria to Galeazzo, 10 June 1468, Cremona, and 21 Aug. 1468, Melegnano (ASMi, AS, c. 1460).

8. Galeazzo to Count Ludovico "da Lugo" [Barbiano], 25 May 1466 (ASMi, RM, no. 72, fo. 165r).

9. The terms used most often for the household were *caxa* (modern *casa*) and *familia* (modern *famiglia*). *Caxa*—literally, house—was the term applied to the household as a place in which things occurred, such as courtiers eating "in casa" (e.g., in "Assignatione del piatello ducale 1471 facta die p[rim]o Januarij," ASMi, AS, c. 1603). *Caxa* was also used to mean "family" or "lineage" (e.g., in Galeazzo to vice-governor of Genoa, Oct. 1475, ASMi, RM, no. 124, fo. 10v; Galeazzo to Giovanni Giapanno, 21 Oct. 1473, Milan [draft], ASMi, AS, c. 914). *Familia* was the term applied to a collection of persons who had "familiarity" (*familiarità*) with the prince, generally in a capacity of service (e.g., in Galeazzo to *Regolatori* and masters of revenues, 7 Sep. 1467, from camp near Casalino [Novarese], ASMi, AS, c. 1483-*spese*-"famiglia tratamento"). For another Sforza court, see Eiche, "'Famiglia' of the Sforza court at Pesaro." A *famiglio* was a servant, rather than a family member or relative (*parente*). *Famigli d'arme* were literally "servants of arms." The core of the Milanese standing army was called the *famiglia*. A prince might make an artist or musician his "familiar" (*famigliare*) to show his favor (see chaps. 4 and 7). A relationship linking one person to another through blood or marriage was called *parentado* (see, e.g., Privy Council to Galeazzo, 12 Feb. 1471, Milan, ASMi, AS, c. 898; and Galeazzo to Battista Visconti, 27 Apr. 1474, Milan [draft], ASMi, AS, c. 923).

10. SSL, RF, cod. 5, fos. 178v–179r.

11. In Galeazzo's preaccession household, Borso Scrovegni (Padua), Galeotto Bevilacqua (Verona), and Ludovico Suardi (Bergamo). Galeotto's and Ludovico's families had moved to Milan.

12. See, e.g., Galeazzo to Antonio Anguissola, 3 July 1470, Pavia (ASMi, AS, c. 894). The term *staffiere* (generally spelled "stafero" or "staphero" in Sforza documents) derives from *staffa* (stirrup).

13. Lower rank is reflected in the anonymity of *ragazzi* listed for Galeazzo's preaccession household and the use of first names only for some listed elsewhere as "Ducali Regazi" (Appendix 2) or "Ragazi" (Porro, "Lettere," 1878, 657, and 1879, 257). Exceptions included d. Sillano de' Nigri and Francesco Birago.

14. Simonetta, *Diari,* 105.

15. For the description that follows, see Marsilio Andreasi to Barbara Hohenzollern Gonzaga, 27 June 1466, Milan (ASMa, AG, b. 1623).

16. The treasury and the duchess's chambers were protected more carefully than the duke's chamber. See Elias, *The Court Society,* Chap. III, and Girouard, *Life in the English Country House,* on the organization of space.

17. A fresco program for Pavia Castle depicted Galeazzo dressing in the company of "all the *camerieri di camera*" and a few other intimates (see discussion in Welch, "Galeazzo and the Castello di Pavia," 363–364).

18. See, e.g., Gallassio Gallassi to Galeazzo, 16 Jan. 1474, Milan (printed in

Welch, "Galeazzo and the Castello di Pavia," 365; and Beltrami, *Castello* [1894]: 330–331).

19. M. Andreasi to Barbara H. Gonzaga, 27 June 1466. This system did not last long, but Galeazzo always expected his servants to be at their posts on time. For pay docked from footmen who failed to do so, see Galeazzo to A. Anguissola, 3 July 1470, Pavia (ASMi, AS, c. 894); 17 Oct. 1471, Cassino (two letters in ASMi, AS, c. 901); 6 June 1472, Pavia [draft], and 14 July 1472, Bereguardo (both ASMi, AS, c. 905).

20. For Bianca Maria's court at its most extensive, see SSL, RF, cod. 5, fos. 178r–184v. For a more limited group, including Ippolita and Drusiana, see undated list in ASMi, AS, c. 1460 (filed under the year 1468).

21. For this period, see ASMi, AS, c. 878, and ASMi, RM, no. 72, *passim.*

22. M. Andreasi to Barbara H. Gonzaga, 25, 28, and 29 Dec. 1467 [O.S.], Milan (ASMa, AG, b. 1623).

23. M. Andreasi to Barbara H. Gonzaga, 30 and 31 Dec. 1467 [O.S.], Milan (ASMa, AG, b. 1623).

24. For the description that follows, see M. Andreasi to Barbara H. Gonzaga, 4 Jan. 1467, Milan (ASMa, AG, b. 1623).

25. Bianca Maria to Galeazzo, 30 Jan. 1467, Milan (ASMi, AS, c. 1459). For Pietro, see M. Andreasi to Barbara H. Gonzaga, 4 Jan. 1467.

26. Gaspare da Vimercate to Galeazzo and Pietro Pusterla to Galeazzo, both 1 Feb. 1467, Milan (ASMi, AS, c. 879). Galeazzo's brother, Filippo Maria Sforza, had to move out when Galeazzo decided to move in.

27. For Filippo Maria Visconti, see Cognasso, *Visconti,* 393. The best secondary source on Porta Giovia Castle is still Beltrami's *Castello* [1894]; he directed its nineteenth-century reconstruction. See Welch, "Frescoes for Castello," for revisions to his plans of Porta Giovia's ducal wing.

28. See, e.g., Zaccaria Saggi da Pisa to Barbara H. Gonzaga, 21 Dec. 1474, Milan (ASMa, AG, b. 1624).

29. G. Giapanno to Galeazzo, 31 Jan. 1467, Milan (ASMi, AS, c. 879); Giovanni da Castelnovate and G. Giapanno to Galeazzo, 8 Sep. 1467, Milan (ASMi, AS, c. 881).

30. See Beltrami, *Castello* (1894), Pt. I, chaps. 8 and 9; and Welch, "Process of Sforza Patronage." The ongoing construction is reflected in Galeazzo's correspondence with Bartolomeo Gadio da Cremona, ducal *commissario* of Works; see especially ASMi, Autografi, c. 88.

31. See Appendix 1.

32. The most thorough discussion of logistics from an Italian Renaissance court is *Ordini et offitij alla corte . . . d'Urbino,* ed. G. Ermini. The author had experience of courts across Italy, including Duke Filippo Maria Visconti's. For a summary of offices he outlines and those of the Sforza court at Pesaro, see Eiche, "'Famiglia' of the Court at Pesaro," 79–87. Dr. Eiche kindly pointed me to two other studies of princely households: Blackley and Hermansen, eds., *Household Book of Queen Isabella*; and Parsons, *Court and Household of Eleanor of Castile.*

33. Antonio Meraviglia and Francesco da Varese were named seneschals-general in 1474, Giuliano da Varese and Cosmino da Briosco in 1475 (Santoro, *Uffici,* 112).

All but Francesco became *gentiluomini* in 1473; he remained a *cameriere*. Galeazzo's other seneschals included Count Galeotto Bevilacqua and Giacomo del Piccio ("Pizeto") (see Appendix 2).

34. For appointments of Galeazzo's stewards, see Santoro, *Uffici,* 114. See Porro, "Preventivo," 130, and "Lettere" (1879): 261, for examples of their activity. See below for the initial composition of Bona's household.

35. The most comprehensive source for provisioning of the Sforza court comes from Duke Francesco's reign; SSL, RF, cod. 5, is an eighteenth-century copy of "Entrata e spese camerali del 1463." It is a general account of expense and salary rates for all persons and offices associated with ducal service. The transcription seems reliable, which is not true of a partial printed version (Formentini, *Rendiconto del ducato*).

36. SSL, RF, cod. 5, fo. 141r, shows "old price" for foodstuffs from provisioner Antonio Cancellieri in 1459 and "new price" from provisioner Gabriele Mondinari in 1460. Fo. 141v shows prices (in two unlabeled columns, possibly "old" and "new") of wax, spices, and sweets from ducal spicer Antonio da Perugia. Among prices charged to Duke Francesco, a pound's weight of cheese cost 2 or 3 soldi; of wax, 7 soldi; of pork, 1 *soldo,* 6 *denari*; of veal, 1 soldo, 10 *denari*; of nutmeg or cinnamon, 24 *soldi*; of fine sugar, 15 *soldi*. One *staio* of "good bread" (enough for one person for two weeks) cost 8 *soldi*; and a pair of peacocks, 16 *soldi*.

37. SSL, RF, cod. 5, fo. 142r.

38. ASMi, RM, no. 75, fos. 170r (25 cartloads) and 182r (50 cartloads).

39. Santoro, *Uffici,* 114; for his activities, see ASMi, RM, no. 89, *passim.* He died in 1469. His father was one of Bona's original *compagni* (see below).

40. For chancellorship, see L. Suardi to Galeazzo, 28 Mar. 1467, Milan (ASMi, AS, c. 879); for stewardship, see Galeazzo to Filippo Morosini, 4 Apr. 1469; and to *Regolatori* and masters of revenues (ASMi, RM, no. 89, fos. 226r and 227v). For dual career, see Gino Barbieri, "Gottardo Panigarola mercante e spenditore sforzesco."

41. For Borella as master of stables, see, e.g., Porro, "Lettere" (1878): 260; for background, see Santoro, *Uffici,* 23. His nickname was the name of his county in Calabria; he also received a fief from Galeazzo. Borella's father, Antonio, served the Sforza in various capacities and became part of Duchess Bona's court. Borella's sister Lantelmina was prominent early in Galeazzo's reign; her husband, Count Gaspare da Vimercate, died in 1467. Borella's father-in-law was Franchino Caimi, a courtier in Bianca Maria's household (Sitoni di Scozia, *Theatrum Genealogicum,* 403). Under Galeazzo, Borella served also as co-commander of the ducal bodyguard (Porro, "Lettere" [1878]: 258–259) and went abroad often (see, e.g., ASMi, RM, no. 74, fo. 96v; ASMi, RM, no. 84, fo. 150r; Galeazzo to A. Anguissola, 23 June 1472 and 26 Aug. 1472, Pavia, ASMi, AS, c. 905 and 906, respectively).

42. G. da Castelnovate and Luigi Pietrasanta to Galeazzo, 30 Jan. 1467, Milan (ASMi, AS, c. 879).

43. Santoro describes the fiscal mechanisms in *Uffici,* xv and xxv–xxix.

44. SSL, RF, cod. 5, fo. 142v for dogs, fos. 146r–v for *camerieri,* and intervening pages for other persons and animals. For January 1475, costs of maintaining 163 persons and 90 horses in Galeazzo's traveling household amounted to 892 florins (almost 357 ducats) (Porro, "Lettere" [1879]: 261–264).

45. Pietro Pagnani to Galeazzo, 21 May 1467, Milan (ASMi, AS, c. 880). The cal-

culation was made in 1470, when it was decided to give expense money, not meals *in casa,* to twelve *camerieri* posted to Milan (Luigi Pietrasanta to Galeazzo, 30 Apr. 1470, Milan, ASMi, AS, c. 893). In September 1469, seven ate *in casa* (Giov. Francesco Attendoli to Ercole del Maino, 21 Sep. 1469, Pavia, ASMi, AS, c. 1478-Giov. Francesco Attendoli). The phrases "eat in the court" (*mangiare in corte*), "eat in the household" (*mangiare in casa*), and "have their expenses [paid] in the court" (*havere le spese in corte*) were interchangeable.

46. Gaspare Ambrogio Barzizza to Galeazzo, 9 Apr. 1467, Milan (ASMi, AS, c. 879).

47. Galeazzo to *regolatori* and masters of revenues, 7 Sep. 1467, from camp near Casalino [Novarese] (ASMi, AS, c. 1483-spese-"famiglia tratamento").

48. For coins, see G. Giapanno to Galeazzo, 4 Mar. 1467 (ASMi, AS, c. 879). For organist, see Galeazzo to Borso d'Este, 14 Feb. (ASMo, CDE, CE, Principi-Milano, b. 1). Galeazzo also gathered some of his soldiers for the event; see Domenico Guiscardi to Galeazzo, 21 Feb., Milan (ASMi, AS, c. 879).

49. Galeazzo to *commissari* of all major cities, 11 Feb. 1467 (ASMi, RM, no. 74, fos. 136v–137v).

50. See instructions to cities, 16 Feb. 1467 (ASMi, RM, no. 80, fos. 13r–16v); and G. Giapanno to Galeazzo, 26 Feb. and 4 Mar. (ASMi, AS, c. 879).

51. Galeazzo's full brother Sforza Maria was invested with Sforza Secondo's fief of Borgonovo; see investiture document, dated 25 Jan. 1467, Milan (ASMi, AS, c. 1481-Sforza Maria).

52. Letters to Galeazzo and Bianca Maria, both dated 22 Mar. 1467, Orzinuovi (ASMi, AS, c. 1480-Sforza Secondo). Sforza Secondo himself had betrayed his father at one point.

53. Giacobino Olgiati to Galeazzo, 5 May 1467, Milan (ASMi, AS, c. 880; partially printed in Belotti, *Gerolamo Olgiati,* 39–40). See Belotti, Chap. III, for more; also Calvi, *Famiglie Notabili,* v. 3, Olgiati, t. 2; and Santoro, *Uffici,* 97.

54. Bianca Maria to Galeazzo, 20 Apr. 1467, Milan (ASMi, AS, c. 1459).

55. Galeazzo to Bianca Maria, 20 Apr. 1467, Piacenza (ASMi, AS, c. 879); Galeazzo to Bianca Maria, 21 Apr., Lodi (ASMi, AS, c. 1461). He had been planning the ceremony since at least February 18 (L. Suardi to Galeazzo, 18 Feb., Milan, ASMi, AS, c. 879).

56. Galeazzo to officials in nine districts, 2 Apr. 1467 (ASMi, RM, no. 80, fo. 42v). For more on men-at-arms, see Domenico Guiscardi to Galeazzo, 15 Apr., Milan (ASMi, AS, c. 879). For standards, see Marchino d'Abbiate to Galeazzo, 6 and 15 Apr., Milan (ASMi, AS, c. 879). They were apparently painted by Costantino da Vaprio; see letters of 16 Apr. (ASMi, RM, no. 80, fos. 56r–v). For gifts, see Galeazzo to A. Anguissola, 30 Apr., Lodi (ASMi, AS, c. 879).

57. See ASMi, AS, c. 880, for many letters from the first week of May 1467, related to intensive preparations for the trip. Galeazzo had been planning it since at least March 31 (ASMi, RM, no. 80, fos. 199r–v).

58. Bianca Maria to Galeazzo, 21 May 1467, Milan (ASMi, AS, c. 1459). For more correspondence related to this campaign, see ASMi, AS, c. 167.

59. Sforza Secondo to Galeazzo, 12 Sep. 1467, Cotignola (ASMi, AS, c. 1480).

60. Galeazzo to Bianca Maria, 3 Nov. 1467, Agamo (ASMi, AS, c. 882); Bianca Maria to Galeazzo, 15 Nov., Milan (ASMi, AS, c. 1459). Filippo, son of the late Duke

Ludovico and brother of Amedeo IX, was a violent man who attacked persons in his own family and court. His alliance with Burgundy was revenge for two years of imprisonment at the hands of Louis XI. Filippo "Senza Terra" became count of Bressa and survived to be duke of Savoy (as Filippo II) in 1496–1497 (Argegni, ed., *Condottieri, Capitani, e Tribuni*, III: 186–187).

61. See, e.g., Bianca Maria to Galeazzo, 11 July 1467, Milan [draft] (ASMi, AS, c. 1459); Galeazzo to Bianca Maria, 9 July, Villa S. Prospero (ASMi, AS, c. 1481-Sforza Maria).

62. Sforza Maria to Galeazzo, 7 May 1467 "in feza"; Galeazzo to Sforza Maria, 22 June, camp on banks of Senio (ASMi, AS, c. 1481-Sforza Maria); Cicco to Bianca Maria, 16 June, near Faenza; Bianca Maria to Galeazzo, 21 and 26 May, Milan (both ASMi, AS, c. 1459). On Sforza Maria's illness, see also Benedetto Reguardati to Galeazzo, 18 May, Milan (ASMi, AS, c. 880). Galeazzo received many letters on his brothers' health, e.g., Ambrogio Grifi to Galeazzo, 27 May, 9 June, 22 June, 10 and 14 July, Milan (ASMi, AS, c. 1461).

63. Bianca Maria to Galeazzo, 17 and 18 Aug. 1467, Milan (both ASMi, AS, c. 1459); Filippo and Sforza Maria to Bianca Maria, 19 and 21 Aug., Piacenza (and nearby camp); 25 Aug., Valeggio; 28 Aug., Oleggio; 29 and 31 Aug., Casarino; Filippo to Bianca Maria, 2 Sep., Abbiate; Franchino Caimi to Bianca Maria, 26 Aug., Valeggio (all ASMi, AS, c. 1477-Filippo); Galeazzo to Bianca Maria, 4 July, Villa S. Prospero [draft]; Franchino Caimi to Bianca Maria, 16 and 25 Sep., Casalino (all ASMi, AS, c. 1461).

64. Bianca Maria to Galeazzo, 11 Mar. and 17 Aug. 1467, Milan (ASMi, AS, c. 1459).

65. See Dina, "Ludovico il Moro," 763, and Fubini, "Crisi del ducato," 73, n. 47, for Ludovico as Galeazzo's heir, replacing Sforza Maria in 1471.

66. Franchino Caimi to Bianca Maria, 16 Nov. 1467, Vigevano (ASMi, AS, c. 1461; cited in Dina, "Ludovico il Moro," 756). By 1469, allowances had been doubled (Galeazzo to A. Anguissola, 9 Feb. 1469, ASMi, RM, no. 89, fo. 115v), but in March 1472, Galeazzo had "all 2,000" ducats of Filippo's allowance withheld (Galeazzo to A. Anguissola, 12 Mar. 1472, Vigevano, ASMi, AS, c. 904). A budget estimate for 1473 set aside 8,000 ducats for "the Most Illustrious brothers," possibly 2,000 ducats each for Filippo, Sforza Maria, Ludovico, and Ottaviano (ASMi, AS, c. 1483-*bilanci*-Galeazzo [#195]). The 1476 budget reserved a total of 10,525 ducats in allowances for Sforza Maria, Ludovico, and Ottaviano (Porro, "Preventivo," 132).

67. Sforza Maria received the county of Valenza [Po], which had been held by the late Gaspare da Vimercate (Sforza Maria to Bianca Maria, 13 Jan. 1468, Pavia, ASMi, AS, c. 1481-Sforza Maria; see also ASMi, RM, no. 81, fo. 61r). He had previously been invested briefly with Borgonovo, forfeited by Sforza Secondo (see above). Ludovico received Mortara (Sforza Maria and Ludovico to Bianca Maria, 16 Jan. 1468, Pavia, ASMi, AS, c. 1481-Sforza Maria; see also ASMi, RM, no. 58r). Filippo became count of Corsica, a title he gave up in 1472 (see renunciation, dated 1 Jan. 1472, Milan, ASMi, AS, c. 1539).

68. For Filippo's pleas and requests to be at court and receive money for living expenses, see ASMi, AS, c. 1477-Filippo Maria, *passim.*

69. See Galeazzo to Bianca Maria, 5 Mar. 1468, Vigevano (ASMi, AS, c. 883);

and Filippo to Galeazzo, 12 Mar., Milan (ASMi, AS, c. 1477-Filippo). For another example of Filippo's poor behavior, see Filippo to Galeazzo, 18 Sep. 1470, Melegnano (ASMi, AS, c. 896). Filippo was something of a simpleton; his nickname was "Testa Mata," Foolish Head (Jahn, *Bianca Maria*, 295).

70. Giovanni Simonetta to Galeazzo, 30 Oct. 1467, Milan (ASMi, AS, c. 1460).

71. Franchino Caimi to Bianca Maria, 19 June 1468, Pavia (ASMi, AS, c. 846); for Sforza Maria as duke of Bari, see Ferorelli, "Ducato di Bari."

72. For Sforza Maria's correspondence, see ASMi, AS, c. 1981-Sforza Maria.

73. See Dina, "Ludovico il Moro," 750–753, for his upbringing. ASMi, AS, c. 1468 and 1469, contain Ludovico's own detailed accounts of his activities. See also Fubini, "Crisi del ducato," 73, n. 47.

74. M. Andreasi to Barbara H. Gonzaga, 7 Dec. 1467, Milan (ASMa, AG, b. 1623).

75. Ludovico Sforza to Bianca Maria, 28 Aug. 1467, Cremona (ASMi, AS, c. 1468).

76. Ludovico Sforza to Bianca Maria, 11 Sep. 1467, Cremona (ASMi, AS, c. 1468).

77. Galeazzo to Ludovico Sforza, 16 Oct. 1467, in camp near Caresana Vercellina [copy]; Ludovico to Bianca Maria, Cremona, 23 Oct. (year lacking but must be 1467, although filed under 1466) (both in ASMi, AS, c. 1468).

78. Sforza Maria to Bianca Maria, 7 Mar. 1468, Vigevano (ASMi, AS, c. 1481-Sforza Maria); Ludovico to Bianca Maria, 7 Mar., Vigevano (ASMi, AS, c. 1468).

79. For complaints about the delay in occupation of estates, see Sforza Maria (and Ludovico) to Bianca Maria, 13, 16, 18, and 20 Jan. 1468, Pavia (ASMi, AS, c. 1481-Sforza Maria). Sforza Maria was excited when Galeazzo allowed him to enter Valenza in May 1468 (Sforza Maria to Bianca Maria, 23 May, Pavia, ASMi, AS, c. 1481-Sforza Maria). Ludovico received permission to hunt at Pandino but was recalled three days later (Galeazzo to Ludovico, 25 and 28 July 1473, Pavia, ASMi, AS, c. 914). He paid 8,300 ducats for Pandino in 1469 (Galeazzo to A. Anguissola, 13 Dec. 1469, Vigevano, ASMi, AS, c. 891). The three eldest brothers also received houses in Milan (Sforza Maria to Bianca Maria Visconti, 19 June 1468, Pavia; ASMi, AS, c. 1481-Sforza Maria).

80. For the brothers' desire to be with Galeazzo, see Sforza Maria to Galeazzo, 7 May 1467, "in feza" (ASMi, AS, c. 1481-Sforza Maria); and Ludovico to Bianca Maria, 10 Aug. 1468, Monza (ASMi, AS, c. 1468). For the brothers' disappointment, see Sforza Maria to Bianca Maria, 7 Mar. 1468, Vigevano (ASMi, AS, c. 1481-Sforza Maria).

81. Bianca Maria to Galeazzo, 16 May 1468, Milan (ASMi, AS, c. 884).

82. Ippolita to Bianca Maria, 12 Feb. 1467, Capua (ASM, AS, c. 1479-Ippolita).

83. Ippolita to Bianca Maria, 1 June 1467, Capua (ASM, AS, c. 1479-Ippolita).

84. Galeazzo to Agostino Rossi, 24 Dec. 1467, Milan (ASMi, AS, c. 1479-Ippolita); Sagramoro Visconti, 26 Dec., Genoa (ASMi, AS, c. 1468); Ludovico to Bianca Maria, 24 Dec., Busalla; 27 Dec., Borgo dei Fornari; 28 Dec., Serravalle; and 29 Dec., Sale (all ASMi, AS, c. 1468). Two weeks before Ippolita landed, Galeazzo told Bonifacio of Montferrat to join Ludovico in meeting her (Galeazzo to Bonifacio, 9 Dec.; ASMi, RM, no. 74, fo. 173v). The duke began preparing for her arrival at

Pavia a week before she reached Genoa (Galeazzo to castellan of Pavia, 17 Dec., ASMi, RM, no. 79, fo. 251r).

85. Galeazzo to Pietro dal Verme, 11 Dec. 1467, Milan [draft] ASMi, AS, c. 882. For expenses, see Galeazzo to masters of revenues, G. da Castelnovate and G. Giapanno, 24 Dec. (ASMi, RM, no. 79, fo. 263v). See also Galeazzo to podestà and castellan of Abbiate, 14 Feb. (ASMi, RM, no. 81, fo. 117r); League envoys would stay there.

86. Galeazzo to 25 captains, 17 Dec. 1467 (ASMi, RM, no. 79, fo. 254r).

87. Galeazzo to G. Giapanno, 7 Jan. 1468 (ASMi, RM, no. 81, fos. 5r–v).

88. Bianca Maria to Galeazzo, 6, 8, 13, and 17 Jan. 1468 (ASM, AS, c. 1460).

89. Bianca Maria told Galeazzo of Ippolita's feelings (6 Jan. 1468, Milan, ASMi, AS, c. 1460). For Galeazzo's bad grace, see M. Andreasi to Barbara H. Gonzaga, 6 Feb. (ASMa, AG, b. 1623).

90. M. Andreasi to Barbara H. Gonzaga, 9 Jan. 1468, Milan (ASMa, AG, b. 1623); Giovanni Botta and Lancillotto [da Figino, probably; surname ripped off] to Galeazzo, 9 Jan., Milan (ASMi, AS, c. 883). The sensitive areas included the Chamber of Extraordinary Revenues, in particular. When asked if the annual ordinary income of the dominion totaled as much as 200,000 ducats, the officials said it did not.

91. Sforza Maria and Ludovico Sforza to Bianca Maria, 15 Jan. 1468, Pavia (ASMi, AS, c. 883). For more on visitors (including "all these magnificent ambassadors" of the League), see Pietro Landriani to Bianca Maria, 15, 19, 22, and 14 Jan., Pavia (ASMi, AS, c. 846).

92. For Certosa dinner, see Sforza Maria and Ludovico Sforza to Bianca Maria, 16 Jan. 1468, Pavia (ASMi, AS, c. 1481-Sforza Maria).

93. M. Andreasi to Barbara H. Gonzaga, 29 Jan. 1468, Milan, ASMa, AG, b. 1623). Maddalena's original plan to give a supper (cena) for Alfonso was thwarted, and Galeazzo arranged another one (Galeazzo to Maddalena, 18 Jan. 1468, Pavia, ASMi, RM, no. 81, fo. 36r).

94. Ludovico Sforza to Bianca Maria Visconti, 23 Feb. 1468, Mortara (two letters, ASMi, AS, c. 1468). Galeazzo changed his mind several times about dining and lodging arrangements, turning an honor into an inconvenience.

95. M. Andreasi to Barbara H. Gonzaga, 23 Jan. 1468, Pavia (ASMa, AG, b. 1623).

96. M. Andreasi to Barbara H. Gonzaga, 1 Feb. 1468, Milan (ASMa, AG, b. 1623).

97. M. Andreasi to Barbara H. Gonzaga, 8 Feb. 1468, Milan (ASMa, AG, b. 1623); see also his letter of 5 Dec. 1467, Milan, for early plans.

98. See various letters from Feb. 1468 in ASMi, AS, c. 883. For closeness to Galeazzo, see M. Andreasi to L. Gonzaga, 4 Dec. 1467 (ASMa, AG, b. 1623). Donato returned to Milan in October (Galeazzo to Bianca Maria; and to masters of extraordinary revenues, 15 Oct. 1468, ASMi, RM, no. 82, fo. 108v).

99. M. Andreasi to Barbara H. Gonzaga, 8 Feb. 1468, Milan (ASMa, AG, b. 1623).

100. For some documents related to this marriage, see Magenta, Castello di Pavia, II: 255–282. They include negotiations in 1465 (255–258) and preliminary agreements made in 1467 (261–263).

101. Bianca Maria to Galeazzo, 11 July 1467, Milan (ASMi, AS, c. 1459), and 13 Jan. 1468, Milan (ASMi, AS, c. 1460).

102. Beltrami, "L'Annullamento del matrimonio."

103. M. Andreasi to Barbara H. Gonzaga, 7 Dec. 1467, Milan (ASMa, AG, b. 1623).

104. M. Andreasi to Barbara H. Gonzaga, 23 Jan. 1468, Milan (ASMa, AG, b. 1623). See also his letter of 4 Feb.

105. See *DBI*, XI: 428–430; Arici, *Bona di Savoia.*

106. M. Andreasi to Barbara H. Gonzaga, 4 Feb. 1468, Milan (ASMa, AG, b. 1623). For prior matches with Savoy, see chap. 1.

107. Galeazzo to Bianca Maria, 7 Jan. 1468 (ASMi, AS, c. 1461).

108. Galeazzo to Vincenzo Amidani, 19 Jan. 1468 (ASMi, RM, no. 81, fo. 51v). This command did not apply to letters regarding Genoa; Bianca Maria was still involved there, because Galeazzo had not yet been invested by Louis XI (see, e.g., G. Simonetta to Galeazzo, 9 Oct. 1467, Milan, ASMi, AS, c. 882).

109. For announcement, see Morbio, *Codice Visconteo-Sforzesco,* 390–391, or ASMi, RM, no. 81, fo. 81r (copy on fo. 93r). For ambassador's comment, see Ugolotto Facino to Borso d'Este, 29 Jan. 1468, Milan (ASMo, DA, Milano, b. 1).

110. Sforza Maria to Galeazzo, 15 Feb., Milan (ASMi, AS, c. 1481-Sforza Maria).

111. Galeazzo to L. Suardi, 14 and 18 Feb. 1468 (ASMi, RM, no. 81, fos. 118r and 128r); Tristano Sforza to Galeazzo, 15 and 19 Feb., Milan (ASMi, AS, c. 1481-Tristano). The use of a proxy was customary; when Ercole d'Este married Eleonora d'Aragona, Sigismondo d'Este went to Naples as proxy for the wedding (Francesco Malletta to Galeazzo, 17 Apr. 1473, Naples, ASM, AS, c. 224).

112. See *regolatori* and masters of revenues to Galeazzo, 19 Feb. 1468, Milan (ASMi, AS, c. 883), and Bianca Maria to Galeazzo, 6 Mar. (ASMi, AS, c. 1460). For Federigo in Milan, see his letters to Cicco and to Galeazzo, 1 Apr., Milan (both in ASMi, AS, c. 883), and a letter from Pietro dal Verme to Federigo, 1 May, Milan (ASMi, AS, c. 884). For Federigo's residence, see G. da Castelnovate to Galeazzo, 14 May, Milan (ASMi, AS, c. 884).

113. Tristano Sforza to Galeazzo, 23 Mar. 1468, Amboise (ASMi, AS, c. 534; printed in Magenta, *Castello di Pavia,* II: 273).

114. Tristano to Galeazzo, 2 Apr. 1468, Tours (ASMi, AS, c. 534).

115. Galeazzo to Tristano, 23 Apr. 1468, Abbiate (ASMi, AS, c. 1463; see also full dowry contract in ASMi, AS, c. 1463, and letter printed in Magenta, *Castello di Pavia,* II: 280–282).

116. Galeazzo to Bianca Maria, 30 Apr. 1468, Abbiate (two letters in ASMi, AS, c. 883); proclamation, 1 May, Abbiate (ASMi, AS, c. 884). The treaty was universal only in name, actually affirming the alliances between Milan, Naples, and Florence (pro-France), on the one hand, and Venice and Savoy (pro-Burgundy), on the other. The pope sided with Venice.

117. See Tristano to Galeazzo, 8, 10, 12, 14, and 21 May 1468, Amboise (all in ASMi, AS, c. 534; 10 and 21 May letters printed in Cantù, "Nozze di Bona Sforza," 179–182). When Tristano went to Naples for Ercole d'Este's wedding in 1473, he recalled his reception by Louis XI in 1468 (Tristano to Galeazzo, 14 and 17 May 1473, Naples, ASMi, AS, c. 224).

118. Description repeated in Galeazzo to Tristano, 21 May 1468 [copy] (ASMi, AS, c. 1461; printed in Cantù, "Nozze di Bona Sforza," 183–184).

119. Galeazzo to Bianca Maria, 21 May 1468 (ASMi, AS, c. 1461).

120. Giovanni Pietro Panigarola to Galeazzo, 20 June 1468, Lagny Castle (ASMi, AS, c. 534).

121. De 'Rosmini, *Istoria di Milano,* IV: 148.

122. For departure from Amboise, see Galeazzo to Bianca Maria, 26 May 1468 (ASMi, AS, c. 1461). For information on the trip through France, see letters from Tristano to Galeazzo, and G. P. Panigarola to Galeazzo, in ASMi, AS, c. 534; and from Galeazzo to Bianca Maria, in ASMi, AS, c. 1461.

123. ASMi, RM, no. 83, fos. 259v–260r and 260v, respectively.

124. ASMi, RM, no. 83, fos. 259r (10 June 1468) and 273r (15 June), respectively. For instructions to gentlemen, see Galeazzo to *referendario-generale* [Fazio Gallerani]; and to Francesco Castiglione, both 3 June 1468 (ASMi, RM, no. 83, fos. 198r and 198v, respectively). Ludovico worried that his household was too scanty for the occasion (Ludovico Sforza to Bianca Maria, 15 June, Pavia, ASMi, AS, c. 1468; also 10 June, Pavia, ASMi, AS, c. 1468, and her reply, 11 June, Cremona, ASMi, AS, c. 1469).

125. Galeazzo invited 206 prominent Milanese women for July 6 and 7 (Beltrami, *Dame Milanesi,* 13–21). See also Filippi, *Matrimonio di Galeazzo.*

126. Giovanni Arcimboldi to Galeazzo, 28 May 1468; and Giovanni Giacomo Trivulzio to Galeazzo, 5 June, both Milan (ASMi, AS, c. 884). See also Niccolò da Tolentino to Cicco, 31 May 1468, Bereguardo (ASMi, AS, c. 846).

127. Sforza Secondo to Galeazzo and Sforza Secondo to Cicco, both 29 May 1468, Borgonovo (ASMi, AS, c. 1480); and Fazio Gallerani to Galeazzo, 4 June, Milan (ASMi, AS, c. 884).

128. Francesco Malletta to Galeazzo, 11 June 1468, Lodi (ASMi, AS, c. 1463). See also Pietro Pasino to Galeazzo, 13 June, Tortona (ASMi, AS, c. 1463).

129. Antonia dal Verme Sforza to Cicco, 15 June 1468, Borgonovo (ASMi, AS, c. 1473-Antonia). See also Beatrice d'Este Sforza to Galeazzo, 3 June, Portigo (ASMi, AS, c. 1475-Beatrice); Marsilio Torelli to Galeazzo, 17 June, Milan; and Tommaso Moroni da Rieti to Galeazzo, 18 June, Rieti (ASMi, AS, c. 1463).

130. Galeazzo to Bianca Maria, 25 May 1468 (hairdresser); Deputati sopra apparati delle nozze to Galeazzo, 15 June (master of stables); and Deputati to Bianca Maria, 3 and 8 June (feathers) (all Milan, ASMi, AS, c. 1463).

131. See, e.g., Bartolomeo da Cemo to Galeazzo, 31 May and 5 July 1468; L. Suardi to Galeazzo, 16 June; and Filippo Morosini to Galeazzo, 18 July (all Milan, ASMi, AS, c. 1463).

132. Santoro, "Codice," 281–287; guarantees on 270–273, with the promise of 25,000 ducats annual income after Galeazzo's death. Original documents (22–26 July 1468, Pavia) are in ASMi, AS, c. 1463; copies in ASMI, Registri Ducali, no. 24. For jewelry work, see Francesco Pagnani to Galeazzo, 13 and 15 June 1468, Milan; and Cristoforo Pagnani and Pietro Landriani to Galeazzo, 31 May (3 letters), 1 June (3 letters), and 9 June, Milan (all ASMi, AS, c. 1463); and F. Pagnani to Galeazzo, 7 June, Milan (ASMi, AS, c. 884).

133. See Claudio Sartori in Treccani, *Storia di Milano,* IX: 791–794.

134. L. Beccaria to Galeazzo, 29 and 30 May 1468, Genoa (ASMi, AS, c. 1463).

135. S. Visconti to Galeazzo, 1 and 7 June 1468, Genoa (ASMi, AS, c. 1463).

136. Galeazzo to Sagramoro Visconti, 1 June 1468 (ASMi, RM, no. 83, fo. 181r).

137. Franchino Caimi to Bianca Maria, 19 June 1468, Pavia (ASMi, AS, c. 846); and Gallassio Gallassi to Galeazzo, 2 June, Milan (ASMi, AS, c. 884).

138. Galeazzo to Giannono Corio, 4 June 1468 (ASMi, RM, no. 83, fo. 210r); and Sagramoro Visconti to Galeazzo, 7 June, Genoa (ASMi, AS, c. 1463).

139. See, e.g., Giovanni (Malvicini?) da Fontana, Teodorino Besozzi, and Damiano Barzi to Galeazzo, 12 June 1468, Sale (ASMi, AS, c. 846).

140. G. da Castelnovate and G. Giapanno to Galeazzo, 21 June 1468, Milan (ASMi, AS, c. 1463).

141. B. Gadio to Galeazzo, 20 and 31 May 1468, Milan (ASMi, Autografi, c. 88).

142. G. da Castelnovate and G. Giapanno to Galeazzo, 21 and 23 June 1468; and G. Simonetta to Galeazzo, 21 and 22 June (all Milan, ASMi, AS, c. 1463). See also ASMi, RM, no. 83, fos. 349v–350r.

143. Galeazzo to sons and heir of the late Giovanni Pietro Castiglione; to Drusiana Sforza; to Giovanni Mauruzzi da Tolentino; and to Tommaso Grassi; Galeazzo to Angelo Simonetta; to Marcellino Barbavara; and to Maddalena Torelli; all 16 June 1468 (ASMi, RM, no. 83, fo. 280v). Maddalena sought to excuse herself because of plague in her household (Maddalena to Galeazzo, 17 June 1458, Settimo, ASMi, AS, c. 1463).

144. Galeazzo to *referendario* of Novara, 11 June 1468 (ASMi, RM, no. 83, fo. 246r). For preparations at Vigevano Castle, see Ettore Rossi da Piacenza and Giovanni Pietro Caccia to Galeazzo, 1 July, Vigevano (ASMi, AS, c. 846).

145. Galeazzo to Pietro dal Verme, 22 June 1468 (ASMi, Rm, no. 83, fo. 327v) (instructions); and G. (Malvicini?) da Fontana, Teodorino Besozzi, and Damiano Barzi to Galeazzo, 24 June 1468, Sale (ASMi, AS, c. 846).

146. See letters from various persons to Galeazzo, 24 to 28 June 1468, from San Remo, Savona, and Genoa (ASMi, AS, c. 1463).

147. A Meraviglia and L. Beccaria to Galeazzo, 28 June 1468, Genoa (ASMi, AS, c. 1463).

148. Galeazzo to Tristano, 30 June 1468, Novi (ASMi, AS, c. 1463); mentioned also in Alessandro Colletta da Cremona to Cicco, 30 June, Pozzolo [Formigaro] (ASMi, AS, c. 1463).

149. Alessandro Colletta da Cremona to Cicco, 30 June 1468, Pozzolo [Formigaro] (ASMi, AS, c. 1463).

150. Galeazzo to Francesco Visconti of Assaretto, 9 July 1468 (ASMi, RM, no. 74, fo. 191v). The duke also commanded the podestà of Alessandria to erect the column (11 July 1468; ASMi, RM, no. 84, fo. 1 tris). The use of sexually suggestive terms was typical of Galeazzo's sense of humor (see chap. 3).

151. Bianca Maria to Guido Parati, Franchino Caimi, and Filippo "de Barbis," 2 July 1468, Lodi [draft] (ASMi, AS, c. 1460).

152. Galeazzo to both councils, the podestà and captain of justice of Milan, *regolatori* and masters of revenues, *vicari generali, referendari,* and *collaterali* of the City of Milan, 5 July 1468, Abbiategrasso [draft] (ASMi, AS, c. 885).

153. Galeazzo to Roberto Sanseverino, 10 July 1468 (ASMi, RM, no. 84, fo. 3 bis) (plague); G. da Castelnovate and G. Giapanno to Galeazzo, 1 July 1468, Milan (ASMi, AS, c. 1463) (storms).

154. Galeazzo to Bianca Maria, 22 Feb. 1468, Vigevano; and Bianca Maria to Galeazzo, 27 Feb., Milan (ASMi, AS, c. 1483-argenterie, gioie, etc.-Galeazzo).

155. Bianca Maria to Galeazzo, 30 June 1468, Lodi (ASMi, AS, c. 1460). See also

Galeazzo to Bianca Maria, 6 Mar., Vigevano (cited in Malaguzzi Valeri, *Pittori*), about a portrait of Bona he commissioned from Zanetto Bugatti.

156. Ippolita to Galeazzo, 16 May 1468, Milan (ASMi, AS, c. 1479-Ippolita). For more on Giovanni Gabriele and Margherita, see below and chap. 4.

157. See letters from Galeazzo to Bianca Maria, 21 May to 27 June 1468, Pavia (ASMi, AS, c. 1461); and from Bianca Maria to Galeazzo, 19 May to 17 June, Cremona, and 24 June to 3 July, Lodi (ASMi, AS, c. 1460).

158. Bianca Maria to Galeazzo, 17 June 1468, Cremona (ASMi, AS, c. 1460).

159. Bianca Maria to Galeazzo, 3 July 1468, Lodi, and 4 July, Milan (ASMi, AS, c. 1460).

160. Bianca Maria to Giovanni da Gallarate; and to G. da Castelnovate and G. Giapanno, both 3 July 1468, Lodi [draft] (ASMi, AS, c. 1460).

161. G. da Castelnovate to Galeazzo, 14 May 1468, Milan (ASMi, AS, c. 884).

162. L. Beccaria To Galeazzo, 30 May 1468, Genoa (ASMi, AS, c. 1463) (expenses in Genoa); Galeazzo to A. Anguissola, 31 May, Pavia (ASMi, AS, c. 1463) (expenses for France).

163. Galeazzo to A. Anguissola, 27 June 1468, Tortona (ASMi, AS, c. 1463) (committee); Galeazzo to regolatori and masters of revenues, 1 and 9 June (ASMi, RM, no. 83, fos. 182r and 232r) (trumpeters); Galeazzo to L. Suardi, 20 June (ASMi, RM, no. 83, fo 306v) (*camerieri*).

164. B. da Cemo to Galeazzo, 31 May and 2 July 1468, Milan; Galeazzo to A. Anguissola, 10 and 15 June, Pavia (ASMi, AS, c. 1463).

165. Cristoforo Pagnani and Pietro Landriani to A. Anguissola, 31 May (3 letters) and 1, 9 (3 letters), 14, 15, 17 (2 letters), 18, 20 (3 letters), 22, 27 (3 letters), 28 (2 letters), and 30 June, Palazzo Arengo, Milan (all ASMi, AS, c. 1463). The painting work, by Costantino da Vaprio, is in the 15 June letter; the steward's petty cash in 14 June.

166. L. Suardi to Galeazzo, 16 June 1468, Milan (ASMi, AS, c. 1463); and Teodorino Besozzi to Galeazzo, 20 June, Sale (ASMi, AS, c. 846).

167. G. da Castelnovate and G. Giapanno to Galeazzo, 23 June 1468, Milan (ASMi, AS, c. 1463).

168. Galeazzo to Pier Maria Rossi, 8 July 1468 (ASMi, RM, no. 84, fo. 7r). For acceptance of 500 ducats from a city, see Galeazzo to city and men of Novara, 15 Aug. (ASMi, RM, no. 84, 175r).

169. Codex headed "Infrascripti sonno li argenti donati a la Exa. del Sigre. nro., e consignati . . . [torn] Gasparo Cayme" [no date] (ASMi, AS, c. 1483-inventari-Galeazzo). (Note on back of codex shows gifts were for wedding.)

170. Charter dated 26 July 1468, Pavia (ASMi, AS, c. 1463, in codex with wedding gift list; printed in Santoro, "Codice," 270–272).

171. Galeazzo to Nicodemo Tranchedini, 20 July (ASM, RM, no. 84, fo. 55r).

172. Galeazzo to G. P. Panigarola, 21 July 1468 (ASMi, RM, no. 84, fo. 64v–65r); and list (fos. 68r–69v, and copy in ASMi, AS, c. 1484-drapperie).

173. Galeazzo to "Deputati Officii Provisionum" of Pavia, 20 Jan. 1474 (ASMi, RM, no. 116, fos. 176r–v).

174. See Appendix 1.

175. The best discussion of Pavia Castle in English is in Welch, "Galeazzo and the

Castello di Pavia." Appendixes 1 and 2 describe the ground floor's "stantie del castello de Pavia" (ASMi, Autografi, 229) and the upper floor's "lochi del castelo de Pavia da depingere" (ASMi, Autografi, c. 96). For the castle's history, see Magenta, *Castello di Pavia*; with the "stantie" document on II: 330–332. ASMi, Autografi, c. 226, contains documents on Pavia Castle.

176. In Porta Giovia Castle, Galeazzo called an open loggia adjacent to the ducal apartments the *sala aperta* (open hall); each loggia space in Pavia Castle was also termed "sala."

177. See, e.g., a 1468 letter from Galeazzo to castellan of Pavia (ASMi, Autografi, c. 226; printed in Welch, "Galeazzo and Castello di Pavia," 366).

178. See Pellerin, *Bibliothèque des Visconti et des Sforza.*

179. See Welch, "Galeazzo and the Castello di Pavia," 359.

180. For the Bolognini Attendoli's honorary status, see Santoro, *Uffici,* 612 and 31, n. 7. Galeazzo also invited Giovanni to be a godfather for the duke's first legitimate daughter (ASMi, RM, no. 103, fo. 343r).

181. Bertelli, *Italian Renaissance Courts,* 8, reproduces a nineteenth-century map showing Mirabello in the center of the Parco.

182. Galeazzo to B. Gadio, 16 Aug. (Sep.?) 1472 (ASMi, RM, no. 105, fo. 219r); and B. Gadio to Galeazzo, 27 Nov. 1468, Milan (ASMi, Autografi, c. 88). Such a chamber is now displayed at the Palazzo Ducale of Urbino.

183. Galeazzo to "d. Rectorib[us] Pergami"; and to captain and podestà of Crema, 9 Aug. 1468 (ASMi, RM, no. 84, fo. 149v).

184. G. da Castelnovate to Galeazzo, 4 Sep. 1468, Milan (ASMi, AS, c. 885). See the list of women, identified by husbands' (or fathers') names; Isotta Sforza is shown as Giovanni da Tolentino's wife ([undated], ASMi, AS, c. 1463).

185. Galeazzo to Bianca Maria, 8 June 1468, Pavia (ASMi, AS, c. 1461); and Giovanni Marliani to Galeazzo, 22 Aug., Pavia (ASMi, AS, c. 1463) (illness).

186. Galeazzo to Bianca Maria, 16 Feb. 1468, Pavia (ASMi, AS, c. 1461); Bianca Maria to Galeazzo, 18 Feb., Milan (ASMi, AS, c. 1460); and Galeazzo to Bianca Maria, 20 Feb. (ASMi, RM, no. 81, fo. 133v–134r).

187. Galeazzo to Antonio Secco; to Antonio Porro; to Mastino Suardi; and to Ottone Visconti, 18 Feb. 1468, Vigevano (ASM, *Sforzesco,* 883).

188. Antonio Secco, Borella's father, was a *commissario* when he was appointed *compagno.* Later, Galeazzo named him to Privy Council (Santoro, *Uffici,* 13, 407, 554). For Ottone's position, see SSL, RF, cod. 5, fo. 178v (1463); and M. Andreasi to Barbara H. Gonzaga, 4 Dec. 1467 (ASMa, AG, b. 1623).

189. See chap. 4.

190. For original appointments, see Galeazzo to Bianca Maria, 20 Feb. (ASMi, RM, no. 81, fos. 133v). For Emilia in Bianca Maria's household, see, e.g., undated list in ASMi, AS, c. 1460 (filed under 1468). Emilia and Giovanni Francesco both died in 1469 (see ASMi, RM, no. 89, fos. 135v–136r, for her, and chap. 5, for him); for his activities, see ASM, RM, no. 89, *passim.*

191. Galeazzo to Bianca Maria, 26 and 28 May and 8 June 1468, Pavia (ASMi, AS, c. 1461).

192. Z. Saggi to L. Gonzaga, 4 Feb. 1468, Milan (ASMa, AG, b. 1623).

193. Galeazzo to Bianca Maria, 20 Feb. (ASMi, RM, no. 81, fo. 134r). In 1470, Galeazzo sought to pare down the duchess's household and reduce expenses further; see "Lista de bocche cassate de la casa de la Ill[ustrissi]ma duchessa" (ASMi, AS, c. 1602).

194. Galeazzo to *regolatori* and masters of revenues, 7 Jan. 1469, Vigevano [draft] (ASMi, AS, c. 1463).

195. See 1473 budget in ASMi, AS, c. 1483-bilanci-Galeazzo (#195). For 1476, see Porro, "Preventivo," 132. Instructions of 1476 to her household treasurer put the actual allotment at 107, 420 pounds (27,810 ducats), including payment to courtiers (Bona to G. da Gallarate, 17 Mar., Vigevano, ASMi, AS, c. 929). From 1471–1472, her *gentiluomini* were paid directly by the treasurer-general (Galeazzo to A. Anguissola, 7 Jan. 1471, Milan; and 1 June 1472, Pavia; ASMi, AS, c. 892 and 905, respectively).

196. See Appendix 2.

197. [Unknown] to Bianca Maria Visconti, 7 June 1468, Naples (ASMi, AS, c. 1460). The writer noted the hostility between Galeazzo and Ferrante. He may have been Sforza envoy Antonio da Trezzo, whose similar letter is cited in Jahn, *Bianca Maria,* 284–285, and Terni de Gregorij, *Bianca Maria Visconti,* 195.

198. Quoted in Ferorelli, "Ducato di Bari," 428.

199. Galeazzo to Bianca Maria Visconti, 23(?) May 1468, Pavia (ASMi, AS, c. 884); her pleasant reply is dated 23 May, Cremona (ASMi, AS, c. 1460).

200. Filippo to Bianca Maria, 4 Aug. 1468, Cornigliano; see also Filippo to Galeazzo, 28 July and 6 Aug., Tortona; and Filippo to Bianca Maria, 1 Aug., Busalla, and 2 Aug., Cornigliano (ASMi, AS, c. 1477).

201. Bona to Bianca Maria, 9 Aug. 1468, Monza; and Bianca Maria to Bona, 1 Aug. [draft] (ASMi, AS, c. 1463). For itinerary, see ASMi, AS, c. 1460.

202. For letters reflecting her illness, see ASMi, AS, c. 1460.

203. Galeazzo to Bianca Maria, 20 Aug. 1468, Monza; and Bianca Maria to Galeazzo, 21 Aug., Melegnano (ASMi, AS, c. 1460).

204. Galeazzo to Bianca Maria, 20 Aug. 1468, Monza (ASMi, AS, c. 1460). For requests, see Bonifacio Aliprandi to Bianca Maria, 12 and 20 Aug. 1468, Monza (ASMi, AS, c. 1460), and 28 Aug. 1468, Monza (ASMi, AS, c. 1477-Filippo).

205. Ambrogio Grifi to Bianca Maria, 14 Aug. 1468, Monza (ASMi, AS, c. 1460). For many letters on her illness from August to October 1468, see ASMi, AS, c. 1460 and 885. For Galeazzo's activities in that period, see also ASMi, AS, c. 1461 and ASMi, RM, no. 84. For Filippo and Ludovico, see ASMi, AS, c. 1477-Filippo and 1468, respectively. Sforza Maria described his visit to Ferrara in vivid letters (see ASMi, AS, c. 1481-Sforza Maria). He found the Este court poorer than Milan's (e.g., Sforza Maria to Bianca Maria, 8 Sep., Belfiore).

206. For announcements, see ASMi, RM, no. 82, fos. 121r–122(a)v.

207. Galeazzo to G. Giapanno, 22 Oct. 1468 (ASMi, RM, no. 82, fo. 114r).

208. Z. Saggi to Barbara H. Gonzaga, 27 Oct. 1468, Milan (ASMa, AG, b. 1623). Bianca Maria made hundreds of bequests to religious and charitable institutions (see documents in ASMi, AS, c. 1460).

209. ASMi, AS, c. 1460, has lists of creditors and debts; see also Caffi, "Creditori." Galeazzo was still paying her debts in 1475 (ASMi, AS, c. 1460).

210. Galeazzo to B. Gadio, 27(?) Aug. 1468 (ASMi, RM, no. 84, fo. 243v).

3: "The Prince Himself Becomes More Eminent"

1. 23 Nov. 1468 (ASMi, RM, no. 82, fo. 219v). Marsiglio Andreasi wrote that Galeazzo had told "all of his feudatories and gentlemen that he wants that they should appear in an orderly fashion [*in ordine*] to honor His Excellency at three *feste* each year, that is, at Christmas, at Easter, and at San Giuseppe, at the 20th of March, when the Lord entered" (24 Nov. 1468, Milan [postscript]; ASMa, AG, b. 1623).

2. Galeazzo to *commissari* of Parma, Piacenza and Lodi, 31 Mar. 1467 (ASMi, RM, no. 75, fo. 199v).

3. Such lists had been composed in Filippo Maria Visconti's time (Decembrio, *Vita Philippi Mariae,* 281). For examples from elsewhere, see Eiche, "'Famiglia' of the Court at Pesaro" (also for Urbino and Ferrara), and Polichetti, *Palazzo di Federigo da Montefeltro,* 374–380.

4. See Appendix 1.

5. The Ambrosian liturgy affected the anniversary of Francesco's death when the anniversary fell on a Friday; it did not permit Masses on Fridays during Lent. On memorial services, see Giovanni Giapanno to Galeazzo, 26 Feb. 1467, Milan (ASMi, AS, c. 879); masters of revenues and *regolatori* to Galeazzo, 19 Feb. 1468, Milan (ASMi, AS, c. 883); and Giovanni Simonetta to Galeazzo, 7 Mar. 1471, Milan (ASMi, AS, c. 898).

6. The duke considered an Easter court in 1471 (Baldassare Barzi to Galeazzo, 8 Apr. 1471, Milan; ASMi, AS, c. 899) but also considered going hunting (Zaccaria Saggi da Pisa to Ludovico Gonzaga, 6 Apr. 1471, Milan; ASMa, AG, b. 1624). He spent that Easter at Vigevano (see Appendix 1).

7. See, e.g., reference in ASMi, RM, no. 89, fo. 196r.

8. Cognasso, *Visconti,* 83 (Matteo); Jahn, *Bianca Maria,* 10 (Filippo Maria).

9. Morbio, *Codice Visconteo-Sforzesco,* 383–384.

10. See below for 1469. For other years, see G. da Castelnovate to Galeazzo, 18 Mar. 1470, Milan (ASMi, AS, c. 892); G. da Castelnovate and G. Giapanno to Galeazzo, 17 Mar. 1472, Milan (ASMi, AS, c. 904); G. da Castelnovate to Galeazzo, 20 and 21 Mar. 1473, Milan (ASMi, AS, c. 913); ACM, BT, c. 1325, fos. 119r–122r (1476 invitees) and Giovanni Agostino Olgiati to Cicco Simonetta, 20 Mar. 1476, Milan (ASMi, AS, c. 1462). In 1472, feudatories were to attend at San Giorgio instead, and Galeazzo decided not to invite the Venetian ambassadors (Galeazzo to various officials, 20 Feb., 18 and 20[?] Mar. 1472, ASMi, RM, no. 106, fos. 61v, 150v, and 157r–158r; and G. da Castelnovate and G. Giapanno to Galeazzo, 17 Mar., ASMi, AS, c. 904).

11. See Appendix 1 for Galeazzo's various locations at San Giuseppe.

12. Alessandro Sforza da Pesaro and Privy Council to Galeazzo, 21 Mar. 1471, Milan (ASMi, AS, c. 898). In 1475, Galeazzo commanded Tristano Sforza "to represent our person . . . [in] the usual manner" (ASMi, RM, no. 120, fos. 113r–v). In 1476, Galeazzo's heir may have represented his father (Galeazzo to G. A. Olgiati, 18 Mar., ASMi, RM, no. 125, fo. 9r).

13. Giovanni Marco Toscani to Galeazzo, 20 Mar. 1471, Milan; see also Alessandro and Privy Council to Galeazzo, 21 Mar. (ASMi, AS, c. 898).

14. The Christmas holidays only composed one-fifth of the total number of holidays in the calendar. See Lubkin, "Christmas at the Court of Milan," for a fuller discussion of Galeazzo's Christmas court.

15. Cappelli, *Cronologia*, 13. Santoro asserts that the use of January 1 (the style of the Circumcision) was "rarer" in Sforza documents (*Uffici*, xvi). For the Old Style still in use, see Princivalle Lampugnani to Bona, 31 Dec. 1477 [i.e., 1476], La Spezia (ASMi, AS, c. 1462; printed in Belotti, *Gerolamo Olgiati*, 191–192). Mantua still used the Old Style in this era.

16. Simonetta, *Diari*, 110, records a feudal contract in which payments were due on two successive Christmases and the Easter between them.

17. See Calvi, "Castello Porta Giovia," 241–242.

18. Galeazzo to masters of revenues and Antonio Anguissola, 27 Dec. 1472 (ASMi, RM, no. 110bis, fos. 147v–148r) (brothers); Galeazzo to Sagramoro Sagramori, 14 May 1474, Pavia (ASMi, AS, c. 1476-Chiara Sforza) (Roberto).

19. For letters, see ASMi, RM, nos. 112, fo. 302v (1473); 118, fo. 319r (1474); and 127, fo. 68r (1476). See also ACM, BT, cod. 1325, fos. 122v (1474), 125r (1475), and 127r (1476). Some major feudatories were specifically told they need not attend at Christmas (ASMi, RM, no. 89, fos. 46v–47r).

20. See Appendix 3 for the list from 1472; for originals, see ASMi, RM, no. 82, fos. 219v–222v (1468); no. 89, fos. 47r–49r (1469); no. 112, ff. 302r–303r and 332v–334r (reordered) (1473); and no. 118, fos. 319v–321v; ASMi, AS, c. 1483-feste-Galeazzo (1472 and 1475). See also ACM, BT, cod. 1325, fos. 122v–124v (1474) and 117v–118v (probably 1476).

21. "Li dinari dati la vigilia de la Festa de Natale a frati et monache amore dei," 24 Dec. 1470, Milan (ASMi, AS, c. 897). A special grant for a Cremona convent was added in July 1469 to alms regularly given at Christmas (Galeazzo to Giovanni Francesco Attendoli, 3 July 1469, ASMi, RM, no. 86).

22. Marsilio Andreasi to Barbara Hohenzollern Gonzaga, 31 Dec. 1467 [O.S.], Milan (ASMa, AG, b. 1623).

23. Galeazzo to Giovanni da Castelnovate and G. Giapanno, 14 Dec. 1472 (ASMi, RM, no. 110bis, fo. 127v) (Este ambassador), and Galeazzo to masters of revenues and A. Anguissola, 27 Dec. 1472 (ASMi, RM, no. 110bis, fos. 147v–148r) (fiefs to brothers).

24. ASMi, RM, no. 110bis, fos. 144r–v (3 pardons dated 25 or 26 Dec. 1472); Galeazzo to Gabriele Balbiani; and to Giovanni Balbiani, 16 Nov. 1473 (ASMi, RM, no. 112, fo. 337v) (dispute resolution).

25. The fifteenth-century sources spell the name "zocho"; the modern Italian (i.e., Tuscan) word is *Ceppo* (F. Weiser, *Handbook of Christian Customs*, 97). Giorgio Valagussa, preceptor to Galeazzo's brothers, wrote a humanist dialogue giving a fascinating analysis of elements in the Sforza's Christmas rituals (*De originis ceremoniarum in Natalitiis*). Santoro, *Sforza*, 168–169, describes the Ciocco as a ducal custom, dating from the Visconti period. For contemporary descriptions, see M. Andreasi to L. Gonzaga, 24 Dec. 1472, Milan (ASMa, AG, b. 1623; Simonetta, *Diari*, 150) (1474); Corio (1978), II: 1399 (1476); and Bartolomeo Gadio da Cremona to Giacomo Alfieri, 15 Dec. 1471, Milan; ASMi, Autografi, c. 88. For the Yule Log, see Weiser, *Handbook*, 97–98, and Frazer, *Golden Bough*, X, 247ff.

26. Simonetta, *Diari*, 65 (1473), 150 (1474); Corio (1978): 1399 (1476). The three masses were traditional—and unique—to the liturgical celebration of Christmas (Weiser, *Handbook*, 69–70).

27. M. Andreasi to B. H. Gonzaga, 28, 29, and 31 Dec. 1467 [O.S.], Milan

(ASMa, AG, b. 1623); M. Andreasi to L. Gonzaga, 31 Dec. 1472 [O.S.], Milan (ASMa, AG, b. 1624).

28. See, e.g., Simonetta, *Diari,* 66 and 188.

29. The daughter was Caterina. Galeazzo's eldest legitimate daughter was betrothed at Epiphany 1474; see chap. 6 for both. For negotiations in general, see, e.g., Simonetta, *Diari,* 3, 65–74, 151, and 188. For 1467–1468, see chap. 2.

30. M. Andreasi to Barbara H. Gonzaga, 25 Dec. 1467 [O.S.], Milan (ASMa, AG, b. 1623).

31. Edward hosted as many as 2,000 people at Christmas court (Dawson, *Christmas,* 89).

32. In 1471, when Galeazzo was ill, he prepared to celebrate the Ciocco at Pavia, rather than Milan (Galeazzo to B. Gadio, 30 Nov. and 2 Dec., ASMi, RM, no. 99, fos. 170v and 172v).

33. Giovanni Matteo Bottigella to Galeazzo, 7 Dec. 1468, Pavia (ASM, AS, c. 846).

34. Massetto, "Le fonti del diritto."

35. For the fullest discussion of this tradition, see Kantorowicz, *King's Two Bodies,* and "Mysteries of State."

36. For application of this phrase to San Giuseppe, see Giovanni Agostino Olgiati to Galeazzo, 20 Mar. 1476, Milan (ASMi, AS, c. 1462).

37. For dictionary definitions of "create" or "creare," see *Oxford English Dictionary,* III (Oxford, 1989): 1134, meanings 1 and 3; and *Grande Dizionario della Lingua Italiana,* III (Turin, 1964): 936–937, meanings 10, 11, and 14. For its use by Galeazzo, see letter to Giovanni Leonardo Vismara, 25 Dec. 1470 (ASMi, RM, no. 100, fo. 12v).

38. "Ordine de quilli che hanno a intrare in salleta in castello," 1 Jan. 1469 (ASMi, AS, c. 887); on the reverse: "Household Arrangements (*Ordini de casa*) of the Most Illustrious Lord."

39. The policy of treating ambassadors according to their principals' rank is reflected in the 1468 protocol (Maspes, "Prammatica," 148–150). All lists drawn up for ceremonial occasions at the Sforza court placed "lords" (*signori*) and their representatives first.

40. Acciarrito Portinari did not appear at court in the 1470s. For the Portinari as bank agents, see De Roover, *Medici Bank.*

41. For announcement that Galeazzo was no longer "in tempo di minore etate de anni xxv," see Galeazzo to both councils of state, 24 Jan. 1469 (ASMi, RM, no. 89, fos. 71v–72; see also fos. 86r–87r); and Cicco Simonetta to "Magnifici Domini" [Privy Council], 18 Jan., Vigevano [draft] (ASMi, AS, c. 887).

42. Santoro, *Sforza,* chaps. 3 and 23; and F. Catalano, in Treccani, *Storia di Milano,* VII: 258, discuss the issue. See also the works of F. Cusin.

43. G. Simonetta to Galeazzo, 26 Jan. 1469, Milan (ASMi, AS, c. 887).

44. See Cognasso, *Visconti,* 506; and Santoro, *Sforza,* chap 3.

45. Carlo Visconti to Galeazzo, 9 Nov. 1473, Trier (ASMi, AS, c. 572); printed (#18) in Paganini, "Documentazione fra Milano e l'impero," 36.

46. Instructions to Tommaso Moroni da Rieti, 4 Jan. 1469, Milan (ASMi, AS, c. 66); cited in Treccani, *Storia di Milano,* VII: 258.

47. Galeazzo to cardinal of Siena, 12 Oct. 71, Gropello (ASMi, AS, c. 572), printed in Paganini, "Documentazione fra Milano e l'Impero," 37.

48. See Mazzatinti, "Inventario," 55–59.
49. Galeazzo to [unknown], 26 Mar. 1472 [no loc.; draft] (ASMi, AS, c. 904).
50. Corio (1978), II: 1409.
51. For printing, see Biscaro, "Panfilo Castaldi," and Treccani, *Storia di Milano,* VII, Pt. IX. Galeazzo supported the new art actively (see also ASMi, RM, no. 106, fos. 105v and 156v). For baptisms and burials, see chap. 5. For public clocks, see Galeazzo to podestà of Villanterio, 10 May 1476 (ASMi, RM, no. 123, fo. 178r); and to *commissario* of Lodi, 8 Aug. 1476 (ASMi, RM, no. 125, no. 291r). The Lodi clock was made by Galeazzo's personal clock maker, a German who traveled with the duke (see, e.g., B. Gadio to Galeazzo, 27 Nov. 1468, ASMi, Autografi, c. 88; and Appendix 2). For eyeglasses, see Ilardi, "Eyeglasses," 348–350; also "Occhiali alla corte," 16–20, and "Doni di occhiali," 54–55. For ostlers, see ASMi, RM, no. 123, fo. 139v. For criticism of officials, see Galeazzo to Nicodemo Tranchedini da Pontremoli, 24 Jan. 1476 (ASMi, RM, no. 123, fo. 56r); and to Dombello Riccardi, 30 Sep. 1468 (ASMi, RM no. 80, fo. 168r).
52. Benedetto Reguardati to Galeazzo, 10 Jan. 1469 (ASMi, AS, c. 887); Galeazzo paid 200 ducats soon after (ASMi, RM, no. 89, fo. 140v). Benedetto must have been assigned a very high salary; for his activities, see letters to Galeazzo, 26 Feb. 1467, Milan (ASMi, AS, c. 879), and 18 May, Milan (ASMi, AS, c. 880). He had sought to leave for Florence in February 1468, but Bianca Maria had blocked his departure (Bianca Maria to Galeazzo; and Bianca Maria to Cicco, both 15 Feb. 1468, Milan, ASMi, AS, c. 883).
53. For his house and expenses, see Galeazzo to G. Giapanno, 24 Jan. 1469 (ASMi, RM, no. 89, fo. 69r); G. Giapanno to Galeazzo, 25 Jan., Milan (ASMi, AS, c. 887); G. da Castelnovate to Galeazzo, 20 Mar. (ASMi, AS c.888). See ASMi, AS, c. 89, fo. 39v, for use of his influence.
54. Giovanni Botta to Galeazzo, 17 and 28 Jan. and 22 Feb. 1469, Milan (ASMi, AS, c. 887).
55. Galeazzo to masters of revenues; and to G. Giapanno, 17 Jan. 1469 (ASMi, RM, no. 89, fos. 49v, and 50v–51r); G. Giapanno to Galeazzo, 20 Jan., Milan (ASMi, AS, c. 887). The money would come from grain tolls.
56. Galeazzo to G. da Castelnovate and G. Giapanno, 25 Aug. 1469 (ASMi, RM, no. 88, fo. 200v); G. da Castelnovate and G. Giapanno to Galeazzo, 27 Aug., Milan (ASMi, AS, c. 889).
57. G. Giapanno to Galeazzo, 10 Dec. 1469, Milan (ASMi, AS, c. 891).
58. G. da Castelnovate and G. Giapanno to Galeazzo, 7 Mar. 1469, Milan (ASMi, AS, c. 888).
59. Galeazzo to G. da Castelnovate and G. Giapanno, 13 Mar. 1469 (ASMi, RM, no. 89, fo. 200r) (councillors); G. da Castelnovate to Galeazzo, 12 Mar. (ASMi, AS, c. 888) (ladies); G. da Castelnovate and G. Giapanno to Galeazzo, 3 Mar., Milan, and Galeazzo to A. Anguissola, 10 Mar., Villanova (ASMi, AS, c. 888) (decoration).
60. Lists of jousters and horses in ASMi, RM, no. 89, fo. 215r, and ASMi, AS, c. 1483-giostre (#222 and 224); G. F. Attendoli to Galeazzo, 20 Apr. 1469, Milan (ASMi, AS, c. 888) (practice); Baldassare Arrivabene to Barbara H. Gonzaga, 26 Apr., Milan (ASMa, AG, b. 1623) (Galeazzo); Z. Saggi to Galeazzo, 15 Apr. 1469; and G. da Castelnovate to Galeazzo, 21 Apr. (both Milan, ASMi, AS, c. 888).

61. Galeazzo to Guido Rossi, 6 Apr. 1469 (ASMi, RM, no. 90, fo. 85r).

62. Filippo, Sforza Maria, and Ludovico to Galeazzo, 5 May 1469 (ASMi, AS, c. 888); "Giostratori che hanno ad giostrare zobia p[ro]x[imo] in Abia (ASMi, AS, c. 891).

63. Galeazzo to Franceschino da Castel San Pietro, G. Giapanno, B. da Cremona, and Bartolo da Novate, 8 Jan. 1469 (ASMi, RM, no. 89, fo. 12v).

64. Antonio Porro to Galeazzo, 31 July 1469, Milan (ASMi, AS, c. 889). Galeazzo noticed also the state of ducal emblems painted on Milan's civic palace (B. Gadio to Galeazzo, 12 June 1469, Milan; ASMi, AS, c. 889). For descriptions of emblems, see Santoro, *Sforza,* 403–404; and Beltrami, *Castello* [1894], 712–725.

65. Galeazzo to B. Gadio, 20 and 24(?) Aug. 1474 (ASMi, RM, no. 118, fos. 128r and 134v).

66. Galeazzo to archpriest of Sta. Maria del Monte, 10 July 1476 (ASMi, RM, no. 125, fo. 234r).

67. For signatures, see Sforza files in ASMi, Autografi. For precedence, see also "Invitati per i gravi . . . [of Francesco Sforza]" (undated, ASMi, AS, c. 1458, filed under year 1466).

68. Galeazzo to *regolatori* and masters of revenues, 24 Apr. 1467 (ASMi, RM, no. 80, fo. 51r). Evidently, Giovanni Maria succeeded; see Galeazzo to *regolatori* and masters of revenues, 4 July 1467 (ASMi, RM, no. 79, fo. 52r).

69. Galeazzo to Bosio, 3 Nov. 1470 (ASMi, RM, no. 97, fo. 84v); and to Tristano, 28 Feb. 1474 (ASMi, RM, no. 115, fo. 144r).

70. For documents relating to Alessandro's governorship, see ASMi, AS, c. 898 and 1473-Alessandro. For the Sforza of Pesaro generally, see Santoro, *Sforza,* Chap. XLIX, and the works of Sabine Eiche. Alessandro served against Galeazzo in 1467 but was reconciled to him in 1470. Alessandro died in 1473.

71. Giovanni Attendoli to Galeazzo, 25 May 1469, Pavia (ASMi, AS, c. 847).

72. Z. Saggi to Barbara H. Gonzaga, 26 May 1469, Milan (ASMa, AG, b. 1623).

73. For Bianca Maria and her father, see Bueno de Mesquita, *Giangaleazzo Visconti,* 177. For Giovanni Maria, see Cognasso, *Visconti,* 358. Galeazzo II Visconti had given the castle to his new wife, Bianca of Savoy; their son GianGaleazzo gave it in turn to his bride (Bignami, *Castelli Lombardi,* 30).

74. Galeazzo to G. Attendoli, 28 May and 1 June 1469 (ASMi, RM, no. 90, fos. 154r and 165r; both printed in Caffi, "Castello di Pavia," 558). The eyeglasses had been an object of devotion for his grandfather, Duke Filippo Maria (Ilardi, "Doni di occhiali alla corte sforzesca," 55).

75. Galeazzo to G. Giapanno, 20 June 1469 (ASMi, RM, no. 88, fo. 26r).

76. See Santoro, "Codice," 273–274.

77. ASMi, RM, no. 88, fos. 25r and 26r (celebrations); fo. 27r (messenger).

78. See letters dated 21 to 30 June 1469 in ASMi, AS, c. 1464.

79. ASMi, RM, no. 88, fos. 88v–89r. The announcement was to be made on the day of the child's baptism. See ASMi, RM, no. 89, fos. 167v–168r, for Galeazzo's recognition that this tax weighed on the Milanese.

80. For invitations, see Galeazzo to Bosio Sforza, 3 July 1469, Abbiate [draft] (ASMi, AS, c. 889); ASMi, RM, no. 88, fos. 112r–113r. A few feudatories were added to the list used for Christmas 1468. ASMi, AS, c. 1464, contains letters from

Princivalle Lampugnani (12 July 1469) and Francesco Malletta (20 July) announcing the ambassadors elected in Piacenza and Lodi, respectively. For payment of baptism expenses, see Galeazzo to A. Anguissola, 15 July, Abbiate (ASMi, AS, c. 889).

81. For precedence among the *compari,* see Galeazzo to G. da Castelnovate, 19 July 1469 (ASMi, RM, no. 88, fo. 111v). Galeazzo's *compari* were largely the same for all his children's baptisms; see M. Andreasi to L. Gonzaga, 2 and 5 May 1472, Milan (ASMa, AG, b. 1624). In 1469, Rinaldo d'Este came as proxy for Duke Borso; see letters in ASMi, AS, c. 889, including Galeazzo to A. Anguissola, 21 July 1469, Abbiate; and Cicco to Galeazzo, 30 July, Milan. See also ASMi, RM, no. 88, fos. 125v–126r, 155r and 156r.

82. Rodolfo Gonzaga to Barbara H. Gonzaga, 23 July 1469, Milan (ASMa, AG, b. 1623). For more on Rodolfo's visit, see Galeazzo to A. Anguissola, 12 July, Abbiategrasso (ASMi, AS, c. 889); and Z. Saggi to Barbara H. Gonzaga, 24 and 26 July, Milan (ASMa, AG, b. 1623).

83. GianGaleazzo Visconti's name at baptism had been simply Galeazzo; see chap. 1.

84. Z. Saggi to Barbara H. Gonzaga, 10 July 1469, Milan (ASMa, AG, b. 1623).

85. Pellegrini, "Ascanio Maria Sforza," 223–225.

86. For Christmas, see above; see also chap. 8, for the feast of San Giorgio. For domestic problems, see letters in ASMi, AS, c. 1465.

87. For proxy's visit, see Bianca Maria to Galeazzo, 19(?) August 1468, Melegnano (ASMi, AS, c. 1460); for Bona's household, see below (fresco program).

88. For Elisabetta's reaction, see chap. 1. See ASMi, AS, c. 1476-Elisabetta Maria, for marriage contract and related documents. For wedding, see Sforza Maria to Galeazzo, 21 Aug. 1469, Casale [Monferrato] (ASMi, AS, c. 1481-Sforza Maria). See also Motta, "Elisabetta Sforza" and "Ancora di Elisabetta Sforza."

89. Z. Saggi to Barbara H. Gonzaga, 8 Oct. 1469, Milan (ASMa, AG, b. 1623).

90. For earlier years and lively character, see letters in ASMi, AS, c. 1479-Ottaviano Maria. For travel with the duke and duchess, see Appendix 2 and Porro, "Lettere" (1878): 261.

91. On Elisa's death, see chap. 5. For the marriage plan, see Galeazzo to Bianca Maria Visconti, 9 Sep. 1468, Milan (ASMi, AS, c. 885); more generally, see ASMi, AS, c. 1476-Elisa (sister of Galeazzo). Motta recognized her existence in "Elisabetta Sforza" and "Ancora di Elisabetta Sforza." She should not be confused with Duke Francesco's sister (and Galeazzo's aunt) Elisa, countess of Biandrate, mother of Roberto da Sanseverino (see, e.g., 1473 draft budget, ASMi, AS, c. 1483-bilancie).

92. Fiordelisa may have replaced Elisa in the plan months before Elisa's death; in March 1469, someone was sent by the lord of Imola to see "Madonna Fiordelisa, betrothed of the Magnificent Guidaccio" (G. Simonetta to Galeazzo, 9 Mar. 1469, Milan, ASMi, AS, c. 1476-Drusiana; see also Galeazzo to G. Simonetta, 6 Mar., ASMi, RM, no. 89, fo. 180r). Elisa had been examined and approved by a Manfredi emissary in August 1468 (Bianca Maria to Galeazzo, 19[?] August 1468, Melegnano, ASMi, AS, c. 1460).

93. Alessandro Visconti suggested that Taddeo Manfredi be offered money and a chance to regain his own ancestral home, Faenza (letter to Galeazzo, 2 June 1469, Pavia, ASMi, AS, c. 847).

94. Drusiana's personal property was sent to Sforza Secondo, who had to pay for

it (Galeazzo to *referendario* of Novara, 11 Mar. 1469, ASMi, RM, no. 89, fo. 190v). She stayed in exile until her death in 1474, still seeking return of her property (letters in ASMi, AS, c. 1476-Drusiana). See Galeazzo to Sforza Secondo, 12 and 15 June 1474 (ASMi, RM, no. 119, fos. 45r and 50r) for reaction to her death. In 1463, Drusiana's household had been supported by her father (SSL, RF, cod. 5, fo. 180v). See also Santoro, *Sforza,* 103–104.

95. Sforza Secondo to Bianca Maria, 9 Oct. 1467, "Monte Inagro" Vercellese; for Galeazzo's intentions, see "Memoriale de le cose rascionate che el Signore N[ost]ro vole fare ad Sforza Secundo" (ASMi, AS, c. 1480).

96. Sforza Secondo to Galeazzo, no date or location [but before late April 1468]; for return to Borgonovo, see Sforza Secondo to Galeazzo, 30 Nov. 1468, Borgonovo (both in ASMi, AS, c. 1480).

97. For March and April 1469, see Sforza Secondo's letters to Galeazzo from S. Ilario; for his return, see letter of 1 Oct., Borgonovo (all in ASMi, AS, c. 1480). For his appointment, see Mattia da Trevio to Galeazzo, 7 Feb. 1472, Borgonovo (ASMi, AS, c. 1480).

98. Galeazzo to Roberto da Sanseverino, 25 Feb. 1474 (ASMi, RM, no. 117, fo. 69v); Giulio's letters are in ASMi, AS, c. 1478-Giulio. Despite his poor relations with Galeazzo, Giulio was included in the duchess's household for the 1471 journey to Florence (see Appendix 4).

99. Polidoro was born in 1442 (probably), legitimized in 1448, and died in 1475; see Giulini, "Polidoro Sforza" (p. 258 for separation from court). A good marriage was arranged for him with a Malaspina. If it is true that Polidoro was exiled from court because Bianca Maria disliked his mother, his recall by Galeazzo may have been a piece of deliberate mischief. Polidoro joined in the festivities of winter 1468 (M. Andreasi to Barbara H. Gonzaga, 1 Feb. 1468, Milan; ASMa, AG, b. 1623). For enfeoffment with Cantù, see "Quaternum novarum provisionum . . . ," fo. 8v (ASMi, AS, c. 885). For participation in San Giorgio jousts, see letters to Galeazzo, 19 Apr. 1469 and 10 Apr. 1471, Milan (ASMi, AS, c. 1479-Polidoro).

100. See, e.g., letters of instruction to him regarding Giovanni Bentivoglio (9 Jan. 1471; ASMi, RM, no. 97, fo. 168v) and Gerolamo Riario (19 Nov. 1472; ASMi, RM, no. 110bis, fo. 28v).

101. Isotta Sforza da Tolentino to Galeazzo, 27 Mar. 1470, Milan (ASMi, AS, c. 894); 29 Mar. 1470, Milan (ASMi, AS, c. 1479-Isotta). Isotta received an allowance of 400 ducats for 1473, but Galeazzo stopped paying her after that year (see 1473 budget [#195] in ASMi, AS, c. 1483-bilanci, and her undated petition to duchess Bona in ASMi, AS, c. 1479-Isotta). Isotta never shrank from making complaints or appeals; see ASMi, AS, c. 1479-Isotta, *passim.*

102. On this program, see Welch, "Galeazzo and the Castello di Pavia." The date is deduced from the presence of both the "Count of Pavia" (GianGaleazzo) and Elisabetta Sforza in the program.

103. Welch, "Galeazzo and the Castello di Pavia," 373. She has printed the entire program and has shown on a plan where each painting would go. De'Rosmini also printed the program in *Istoria di Milano,* IV: 147–149. The original is in ASMi, Autografi, 96.

104. See chap. 2.

105. See chap. 2; and Welch, "Galeazzo and the Castello di Pavia," 366.

106. Welch, "Galeazzo and the Castello di Pavia," 373–374; De'Rosmini, *Istoria di Milano,* IV: 149–150.

107. "Copia unius partis lrarum. d. Jo. Bapte. ad Camillum," (no date; ASMi, AS, c. 890). The letter, copied by the Sforza Chancery, was probably from Giovanni Battista Coppola of Naples to Camillo Barzi, Urbino's ambassador. For a modern view of the crisis, see Lorenzo de' Medici, *Lettere,* I: 541–546.

108. See Lorenzo de' Medici, *Lettere,* I: 44–47, 546.

109. ASMi, RM, no. 91, fos. 116–120r; and ASMi, AS, c. 1535. On January 21, Galeazzo announced the succession arrangement to sixteen rulers and certain cities of his dominion (ASMi, RM, no. 91, fos. 120r–122v). Genoa was added in 1472 (M. Andreasi to L. Gonzaga, 5 May 1472, Milan; ASMa, AG, b. 1624).

110. See Santoro, "Codice," 274.

111. ASMi, AS, c. 1536 and 1537, consist entirely of the feudatories' oaths (Novara in c. 153; printed in Santoro, "Codice," 275–278); for preparations, see ASMi, RM, no. 91, fos. 167r and 172v (Novara), and 174r–175r.

112. 18 May 1470, "in camera cubicularum," Pavia (ASMi, AS, c. 1461).

113. See letter of congratulations from the government of Florence, 7 June 1470 (ASMi, AS, c. 1476-Ermes Maria). For Visconti use of name, see grant of lease to Giovanni Maria Visconti, 24 Jan. 1469, Vigevano (ASMi, AS, c. 887).

114. Z. Saggi to Barbara H. Gonzaga, 29 Nov. 1469, Milan (ASMa, AG, b. 1623).

115. Z. Saggi to Barbara H. Gonzaga, 3 Aug. 1469, Monza (ASMa, AG, b. 1623); he continued that "she says it isn't true." His letter of 6 Jan. 1469 (also b. 1623) remarks on Bona's silence and lack of assertiveness.

116. Favors granted to the nurse included gifts of property (letter-patent, 4 Jan. 1472, Vigevano, ASMi, AS, c. 903) and a house (given before 19 Mar. 1472; ASMi, RM, no. 104, fo. 83r). For a favor sought from her, see "Zuanno de Chinno" to Simona, 26 July 1476, Milan (CI 931).

117. For their travel around the duchy together, see, e.g., Simonetta, *Diari,* 14, 27, 39, 42, 47, 188, 197, 211; and M. Andreasi to Barbara H. Gonzaga, 26 Apr. 1475, Milan (ASMa, AG, b. 1625).

118. Santoro, "Codice," 280.

119. See charter investing Lorenzo with Bellano et al., 23 May 1472, Pavia (ASMi, AS, c. 1539).

4: "He Was . . . Splendid Beyond Measure in His Court"

1. Corio (1978), II: 1409.

2. Angelo della Stufa to Lorenzo de' Medici, 30 May 1470, Milan (ASF, MAP, f. XLVIII, #1).

3. Zaccaria Saggi da Pisa to Ludovico Gonzaga, 12 Nov. 1468, Milan; and to Barbara Hohenzollern Gonzaga, 24 Jan. 1470, Vigevano (ASMa, AG, b. 1623). See also Lorenzo de'Medici, *Lettere,* II: 528–529, for a French ambassador's negative view as of April 1470.

4. Cristoforo Rangoni to Borso d'Este, 3 Aug. 1470, Milan (ASMo, CDE, DA, Milano, b. 1).

5. Galeazzo to Giovanni de Castelnovate, 7 Aug. 1470 (ASMi, RM, no. 95, fo. 165v); see also G. da Castelnovate and Giovanni Giapanno to Galeazzo, 6 Aug.,

Milan (ASMi, AS, c. 894), and Galeazzo to castellans of Pavia, 15 Aug. (ASMi, RM, no. 95, fo. 170r).

6. Galeazzo initially paid only 10,000 ducats, and Ludovico Gonzaga had to ask for the balance; see Z. Saggi to L. Gonzaga, 3 and 11 Aug. 1470, Milan (ASMa, AG, b. 1623); Galeazzo to L. Gonzaga, 11 Aug., Milan [draft]; L. Gonzaga to Galeazzo, 13 Aug., Borgoforte; and receipt ("Confessio") by Zaccaria for the additional 2,000 ducats (17 Aug., Milan) (ASMi, AS, c. 1483-argenteria, gioie, porcellane, abiti-Galeazzo).

7. Z. Saggi to L. Gonzaga, 7 Aug. 1470, Milan (ASMa, AG, b. 1623).

8. Z. Saggi to L. Gonzaga, 3 Aug. 1470, Milan (ASMa, AG, b. 1623).

9. Z. Saggi to L. Gonzaga, 25 Oct. 1470, Milan (ASMa, AG, b. 1623).

10. For *disnare* being served in the morning, see Z. Saggi to L. Gonzaga, 7 Aug., Milan (ASMa, AG, b. 1623). Galeazzo sent a daily memo to his seneschals-general around dinnertime; see G. da Castelnovate and G. Giapanno to Galeazzo, 13(?) July 1476, Milan (ASMi, AS, c. 1462).

11. Simonetta, *Diari,* 118 (hunting); Galeazzo to Giovanni Simonetta, 8 July 1474 (ASMi, RM, no. 118, 49v) (French ambassadors); "Brevissima extracto [*sic*] de la cavalcata de XXIII de Julio 1476," and similar working notes dated 29 July and 1 Aug. 1476 (ASMi, AS, c. 931); also C. Rangoni to Borso d'Este, 15 July 1470, Pavia (ASMo, CDE, DA, Milano, B.1) (riding); Alessandro da Foligno to Galeazzo, 10 July 1475, Milan (ASMi, AS, c. 927) (tennis).

12. Z. Saggi to L. Gonzaga, 18 and 3 Aug. 1470, Milan (ASMa, AG, b. 1623).

13. M. Andreasi to L. Gonzaga, 4 Dec. 1467, Milan (ASMa, AG, b. 1623). Giovanni did gain entry the next day (M. Andreasi to L. Gonzaga, 5 Dec).

14. C. Rangoni to Borso d'Este, 26 Oct. 1470, Milan (ASMo, CDE, DA, Milano, b. 1); also Z. Saggi to L. Gonzaga, 17 Oct. 1470, Pavia (ASMa, AG, b. 1623).

15. Corio (1978), II: 1408–1409.

16. Galeazzo to C. Favagrossa da Cremona, 18 Oct. 1470, Pavia (ASMi, AS, c. 896), with many instructions. For GianGaleazzo Visconti's hunts, see Bueno de Mesquita, *GianGaleazzo Visconti.* Malaguzzi Valeri, *Corte di Lodovico il Moro,* I, is full of half-digested information on the Sforza hunts. For representative documents related to the hunts, see ASMi, AS, c. 1483-*cacce.*

17. He later limited the reserved area; see Galeazzo to *commissario* of Cremona, 27 July and 1 Sep. 1471; and to podestà and men of Castelleone, 20 Aug. 1471 (ASMi, RM, no. 101, fos. 157v, 257v, and 212v). Districts reserved in 1467 were Milan, Pavia, Lodi, Lomellina, Novara, and Oltrepò (Galeazzo to C. Favagrossa de Cremona, 27 June 1467, camp near Faenza, ASMi, AS, c. 880).

18. Galeazzo to Ascanio, 5 July 1472, Mirabello (ASMi, AS, c. 905).

19. See, e.g., Galeazzo to podestà of Mortara, 10 Nov. 1469 (ASMi, RM, no. 91, fo. 15v); to *commissario* of Cremona, 27 July 1471 (ASMi, RM, no. 101, fo. 157v); to vice-governor of Genoa, Apr. 1472 (ASMi, RM, no. 106, fos. 213r–v); letter of command from Galeazzo, 23 Sep. 1472 (ASMi, RM, no. 109, fo. 98r); copy of proclamation, 20 Apr. 1476 (ASMi, RM, no. 125, fo. 56r).

20. *Diari,* 146 and 211 (Varese); 65 and 188 (Cusago); and 155 (Villanova).

21. For expeditions abroad, see, e.g., Galeazzo to Ludovico Suardi, 14 July 1468 (ASMi, RM, no. 84, fo. VIIIr) (Norway); Galeazzo to A. Anguissola, 18 Dec. 1470, Milan (ASMi, AS, c. 897) (England); Ghinzoni, "Rettifiche," (Scandinavia); Gale-

azzo to Gabriele Paleari, 1 Sep. 1473, Gambolò (ASMi, AS, c. 914) (Corsica); Gottardo Panigarola to Galeazzo, 14 Oct. 1473, Milan (ASMi, AS, c. 914) (Spain). For horse buying in Sicily, see Galeazzo to G. Paleari; Galeazzo to Gallassio Gallassi [draft]; and Galeazzo to Antonello da Castelleone [draft] (4 Sep. 1473, Galliate; ASMi, AS, c. 914).

22. For examples, see Galeazzo to *commissario* of Lodi; to Pallavicino Pallavicini; to marquess of Soragna; and to Scaramuccetto, 3 Dec. 1470 (ASMi, RM, no. 95, fo. 249r) (hawks); to three podestàs; to five captains of military districts; to *commissario* of Val de Taro; to seven feudal families in Apennines; and to vice-governor of Genoa, 13 Dec. 1470 (ASMi, RM, no. 97, 137r–138r) (boars). For deer request, see draft letters to lord of Piombino; to Braccio (Montone?) da Perugia; to Orsini count of Pitigliano; to Counts Farnese; and to count of Santa Fiore [Bosio], 16 Feb. 1474 (ASMi, AS, c. 922).

23. Galeazzo to Gottardo Panigarola, 2 Dec. 1469 (ASMi, RM, no. 87, fo. 90r). The duke also considered covering three other rooms in Porta Giovia with velvet, including the ceilings (G. Giapanno to Galeazzo, 27 Jan. 1469, Milan; ASMi, AS, c. 887).

24. Corio (1978), II: 1381 (hounds); Appendix 4, Porro, "Lettere" (1878): 263 (horses), and undated list for Mantua trip in ASMi, AS, c. 395. Some of the horses were probably used by his household.

25. Galeazzo to Cristoforo da Bollate, 19 Apr. 1471 (ASMi, RM, no. 98, fo. 289r). For French kennelmen ("Guglielmoto Franzoso" and "Guglielmino Franzoso"), see Appendix 2 and Porro, "Lettere" (1878): 259. Gugliemotto appeared in the fresco commission for Porta Giovia's Sala Grande (see below).

26. See, e.g., Appendix 2.

27. For two lists of kennelmen, see Appendix 2, which includes falconers also. For Carlo's hunting position, see undated document in ASMi, AS, c. 908, which confirms him as captain-general of hunts, as he had been under Duke Francesco. He is listed with huntsmen in Appendix 2. For post as *gentiluomo,* see Galeazzo to G. Giapanno, 17 Jan. 1469 (ASMi, RM, no. 89, fo. 51r); also ASMi, RM, no. 81, fos. 5r–v, for Carlo as one of the courtiers escorting Ippolita Sforza and her husband.

28. For hunting position, see, e.g., document granting water rights, 26 July 1468, Pavia (signed by "Paulus" and "Francischinus"; ASMi, AS, c. 885). He was included in the 1469 fresco commission with falconers and hawks, the 1472 commission in the hunting scene, and the 1474 commission with *camerieri di camera.* The wedding occurred in 1458; the oration was published in 1492 (*DBI,* X 609).

29. Porro, "Preventivo," 132–133. In a 1473 budget, both falconers and kennelment were allotted 3,000 ducats, plus 720 ducats for the kennel at Pavia (ASMi, AS, c. 1483-*bilanci*-Galeazzo [#195]).

30. Z. Saggi to L. Gonzaga, 30 June 1471, Pavia (ASMa, AG, b. 1624).

31. Galeazzo to C. Favagrossa da Cremona, 14 Dec. 1469 (ASMi, RM, no. 87 fo. 102r); and 30(?) Dec. (ASMi, RM, no. 92, fo. 81r).

32. ASMi, AS, c. 1483-*giuoco della palla*. See also "Lista delli denari del zocho della balla che sonno stati vincti & persi prout infra," 13 Oct. 1471, showing wagers won and lost on various matches, with the players named. The verso shows wagers for a game called *sbarraglino.* For May 1472, see letters from M. Andreasi to L. Gonzaga (ASMa, AG, b. 1624).

33. Motta, "Giuoco della palla." For castles, see Bartolomeo Gadio da Cremona to

Galeazzo, 7 Dec. 1470, Milan (ASMi, AS, c. 897) (Cassino); Galeazzo to castellan of Abbiategrasso, 19 Dec. 1474 (ASMi, RM, no. 118, fo. 352v) (Villanova); B. Gadio to Galeazzo, Feb. 1474, Milan (several letters) (ASMi, Autografi, c. 88) (Porta Giovia).

34. Filippo Corio to Galeazzo, 8 Aug. 1471, Milan (ASMi, AS, c. 1483-giuoco della palla). For measurements of the planned hall, see Giacomo Oliari to Galeazzo, 27 July 1471, Milan (ASMi, AS, c. 1483-giuoco della palla); the total cost was estimated at 7,000 pounds or more.

35. Sforza Maria to Bianca Maria, 13 June 1468, Pavia (ASMi, AS, c. 846). See also chap. 3, for private jousting in 1469.

36. ASMi, RM, no. 79, fo. 254r (17 Dec. 1467; Alfonso's visit); no. 98, fo. 300r (Assumption); Galeazzo to Bianca Maria Visconti, 3 Nov. 1467, Milan (ASMi, AS, c. 882) (Filippo). For San Giorgio, see chap. 8. See also much additional material in ASMi, AS, c. 1483-giostre-Galeazzo.

37. See expense list "Sopra lassignatione de Filippo de Petrasancta" (#153, n.d., ASMi, AS, c. 1483-spese-Ludovico [sic]); the joust date of 1 Aug. 1473 is clarified in Galeazzo to Marchino d'Abbiate; to GianGiacomo Trivulzio and Giovanni Pietro "del Bergamino" (both 28 July 1473); and to Antonio Missaglia, 29 July (all ASMi, RM, no. 110, fo. 147v).

38. See, e.g., Pavia fresco program, with Elisabetta and damsels playing cards and other games (Welch, "Galeazzo and the Castello di Pavia," 373). When the young Galeazzo was in Ferrara, he had played cards and tennis with Francesco Pico della Mirandola when it rained (see, e.g., Galeazzo to Duke Francesco, 2 Aug. 1457, Belriguardo, ASMi, AS, c. 1461).

39. For Galeotto, see Motta, "GianGiacomo Trivulzio in Terra Santa," 870–871 (same document also in Morbio, Codice Visconteo-Sforzesco, 467). For chessboard, see Porro, "Lettere" (1879): 256.

40. Z. Saggi to L. Gonzaga, 11 Mar. 1473, Milan (ASMa, AG, b. 1624).

41. See, e.g., citation for Galeotto da Barbiano in n. 39.

42. Medieval English kings considered confining the use of cards and dice to the twelve days of Christmas (Dawson Christmas, 86 and 91).

43. M. Andreasi to Barbara H. Gonzaga, 31 Dec. 1472 [O.S.], Milan (ASMa, AG, b. 1624). For 1466, see chap. 2. Duke Francesco had disapproved of gambling on tennis using credit (letter to Galeazzo, 7 Aug. 1457 [no loc.], ASMi, AS, c. 1461).

44. See Appendix 1 for Galeazzo's location on 97% of the nights during these nine years. The chart was drawn up from evidence in Simonetta, Diari, and the locations given in charters and correspondence from the Registri delle Missive, Registri ducali, and various series of the Archivio Sforzesco.

45. Cassino and Mirabello have not been distinguished from Milan and Pavia, respectively, in Appendix 1.

46. See chap. 2. For efforts to buy all Giardino lands still out of ducal ownership, see ASMi, RM, no. 109, fo. 79v (Galeazzo to masters of extraordinary revenues and Michele Bonino; and to masters of revenues and Giovanni Botta, both 19 Aug. 1472). For leasing and stocking Giardino lands, see ASMi, RM, no. 95, fos. 213r and 219v (Galeazzo to masters of ordinary revenues, 26 Oct. 1470; and to Luigi da Parma, 3 Nov. 1470). For earlier history, see Beltrami, Castello (1894): 199–214 and 687–690.

47. In the Lomellina, Galeazzo also stayed at San Giorgio, Candia, Mede, Lomello, Garlasco, Gropello, and Sannazzaro de' Burgondi (see Appendix 1).

48. Galeazzo to eleven noble addressees, including Pallavicini, Rossi, Scotti, and Borromeo, 12 Nov. 1476 (ASMi, RM, no. 127, fo. 36r).

49. On Vigevano Castle generally, see Schofield, "Ludovico il Moro and Vigevano." For singers' rooms, see G. Paleari to Galeazzo, 26 Nov. 1473, Milan (ASMi, AS, c. 915); 100 ducats were earmarked for the purpose.

50. ASMi, *Feudi Camerali,* 260; Galeazzo to *referendario* of Novara, Galeazzo to people of Galliate, both 19 July 1469 (ASMi, RM, no. 86, fo. 114r); to *referendario* of Novara, to people of Galliate, both 2 Aug. 1470 (ASMi, RM, no. 95, fo. 158r); and to *referendario* of Novara, 6 Jan. 1471 (ASMi, RM, no. 99, fos. 2v–3r). Galeazzo to *iconomo* of Pavia, 19 May 1473 (ASMi, RM, no. 114, fo. 92r), refers to Alessandro as count of Galliate.

51. Galeazzo to B. Gadio, 3 Nov. 1472 (ASMi, RM, no. 105, fo. 248r); B. Gadio to Galeazzo, 23 and 31 Mar. 1474, Milan (ASMi, AS, c. 922); Galeazzo to Gerardo Cerruti, Sagramoro da Rimini, and abbot of San Bartolomeo of Novara, 23 Mar. 1474, Vigevano [draft] (ASMi, AS, c. 922); Galeazzo to Sforza Maria, Sep. 1474 (ASMi, RM, no. 119, fo. 164r); Galeazzo to castellan of Abbiategrasso (ASMi, RM, no. 118, fo. 352v); Z. Saggi to L. Gonzaga, 28 Feb. 1476, Milan (ASMa, AG, b. 1625); and Porro, "Preventivo," 134. See also Galeazzo to Sagramoro Sagramori da Rimini [in Rome], 26 Feb. 1474 (ASMi, RM, no. 117, fo. 70v); and Galeazzo to captain of Lomellina, 15 Dec. 1476 (no. 124, fo. 88v) for other works at Villanova. Galeazzo's death cut short his plans; the castle is now a *casa agricola.*

52. For local residents who refused to pay their share of expenses, see Galeazzo to Privy Council, 22 Mar. 1474 (ASMi, RM, no. 115, fo. 186v); for local authorities slow to gather provisions, see Galeazzo to podestà and *referendario* of Novara, 31 Mar. 1474 (ASMi, RM, no. 115, fo. 228r). Fodder was also important; see letters from Galeazzo to authorities in Abbiate and Novara (ASMi, RM, no. 125, fos. 9r and 319r, respectively). For interaction between dukes and Vigevano's populace, see Fossati, "Le relazioni fra una 'terra' e i suoi signori." For more on Vigevano in the ducal era, see Chittolini, *Metamorfosi di un borgo.*

53. G. Simonetta to Galeazzo, 5 Nov. 1470, Milan (ASMi, AS, c. 896). On the court of Naples, see Ryder, *Kingdom of Naples.*

54. Cited in Lewis, *Later Medieval France,* 121. Louis XI was widely known for his informality, but see chap. 2 for Tristano Sforza's reports from France on the elaborate festivities for the duke's proxy marriage.

55. For a brief introduction to the International Gothic court culture, see Mathew, *Court of Richard II,* chap. 1.

56. G. Simonetta to Galeazzo, 24 Oct. 1473, Milan (ASMi, AS, c. 914); and Simonetta, *Diari,* 58–60 (23 Oct. 1473). In 1469, Galeazzo had told Rodolfo Gonzaga that the latter's father was doing him no good by sending him to the court of Burgundy, where the young man would "never learn anything that will give me a good reputation here" (Rodolfo Gonzaga to Galeazzo, 23 July 1469, Milan, ASMa, AG, b. 1623). When Galeazzo sent Giovanni Pietro Panigarola as ambassador to Charles the Bold, he did not ask specifically for reports on court activities (Instructions, 2 Feb. [1475], Milan, ASMi, AS, c. 516; printed in Sestan, *Carteggio Diplomatico,* I: 399–402).

57. De la Marche, *La maison du duc Charles le Hardy.* Werner Parravicini has studied the Ordonnances.

58. Cicco Simonetta, *Diari,* 12.

59. Giuliano da Varese and Cosmino da Briosco to Galeazzo, 28 Aug. 1476, Palestro (ASMi, AS, c. 856).

60. See, e.g., Simonetta, *Diari,* 12 and 220; and Galeazzo to Giuliano da Varese, 13 Nov. 1476 (ASMi, RM, no. 126, fo. 41r). "Compagnia" and "brigata" were terms used often for persons accompanying a dignitary; both can be translated as "company."

61. G. da Castelnovate, G. Giapanno, and G. Simonetta to Galeazzo, 17 Mar. 1476, Milan (ASMi, AS, c. 1475-Bosio Sforza). When Giovanni Battista Conti became a ducal *cameriere,* Galeazzo wrote that he "had newly come to make his residence in our court [*fare residentia in la corte n(ost)ra*]" (letter to A. Anguissola, 3 Apr. 1475, Abbiate, ASMi, AS, c. 913). Santoro, "Codice di Bona," 270, and *Uffici,* 113 and 177, show the Latinate term *aulico* for "courtier." It derives from the classical *aula,* used for "court" in Latin documents from Galeazzo's Chancery (e.g., ASMi, RM, no. 82, fo. 219r).

62. Santoro (*Uffici,* xxi) and others have claimed that the Privy Council sat at Porta Giovia in this period, but see chap. 5.

63. Galeazzo to A. Anguissola, 2 Jan. 1469, Abbiategrasso (ASMi, AS, c. 887); and 12 June, Abbiategrasso (ASMi, AS, c. 889).

64. When Gabriele Paleari became a personal secretary to the duke, he began lodging in Porta Giovia (ASMi, RM, no. 110bis, fo. 107r). For tailor, see Galeazzo to Filippo Eustachi, 19 Nov. 1472 (ASMi, RM, 110bis, fo. 29v); and to Ambrosino da Longhignana, 6 and 7 Sep. 1473, Pavia (ASMi, AS, c. 914).

65. Alessandro Castiglione was expected to serve as podestà of Novara and come to Milan "at Christmas and those times that courtiers are obliged to do so" (Declaration of 30 Aug. 1474, Galliate, ASMi, AS, c. 925).

66. E.g., Galeazzo to A. Anguissola, 13 Oct. 1472, Monza (ASMi, AS, c. 908) (Isacco Argiropulo, organist); Galeazzo to *referendario* of Pavia [undated draft] (ASMi, AS, c. 854) (Giovanni Artono, astrologer/philosopher); ASMi, RM, no. 106. fo. 126r (Egidio ["Riccio"] Petracolli da Cortona, "our courtier and soldier"); and ASMi, RM, no. 117, fo. 92r (Fioramonte Graziani da Cotignola, "our *cameriere* and courtier").

67. See Cipolla, *Moneta a Milano*; Leverotti, "Scritture finanziarie"; and Chittolini, *Entrate e alienazioni di entrate.* The policy changes began in 1466 and continued through most of Galeazzo's reign.

68. "Ordini dati p[er] Il n[ost]ro Ill[ustrissi]mo S[igno]re dati ad Antonio Anguissola g[e]n[er]ale thesaurere in qual modo se debia governar[e] circa li pagam[en]ti se havi vano ad far[e] ne lanno p[rese]nte m cccclxxj" (ASMi, AS, c. 1603).

69. For a *maestro di camera* (Niccolò Petracolli da Cortona) handling 3,387 ducats for the traveling household's expenses, see Galeazzo to A. Anguissola, 29 Apr. 1473 (ASMi, AS, c. 913). See also Porro, "Lettere" (1878): 120.

70. "Dinari spexi della assignatione del n[ost]ro Ill[ustrissi]mo S[igno]re del anno presente 1471 pagati alli infr[ascript]i de ordinatione de soa Ill[ustrissi]ma. S[igno]ria," 1 Apr. 1471, redone 26 Sep. 1471 (ASMi, AS, c. 1483-*spese*-Galeazzo); Galeazzo to A. Anguissola, 6 Jan. 1471, Milan (ASMi, AS, c. 898), and letters from Aug. to Oct. 1471 (Galeazzo to A. Anguissola, ASMi, AS, c. 901).

71. Galeazzo to Ludovico Suardi, 20 June 1468 (ASMi, RM, no. 83, fo. 306v).

72. Galeazzo to Bianca Maria, 20 Feb. 1468 (ASMi, RM, no. 81, fo. 134r) (wife); Galeazzo to Giovanni Rusconi da Verona, 26 Jan. 1470; and to podestà of Vigevano, 28 Jan. and 27 Apr. 1470 (ASMi, RM, no. 95, fos. 15r, 17v, 66r).

73. For Rome trip, see "Lista del andar[e] ad Roma . . . ," 14 Feb. 1470 (ASMi, AS, c. 1603); for French visit, see letters of 10 Jan. 1471, ASMi, RM, nos. 97, fos. 169v–170r, and ASMi, RM, no. 98, fo. 55r; also Z. Saggi to L. Gonzaga, 6 Oct. 1470, Pavia, and 5 Dec. 1470, Milan (ASMa, AG, b. 1623). The reference to 3,600 persons is in "Thomas" ["da Hexio"?] to Gerardo Cerruti, 14 Jan. 1471, Milan (ASMi, AS, c. 898).

74. See Eiche and Lubkin, "Mausoleum Plan of Galeazzo," n. 9.

75. Codex of "Le liste de landata del Sig[no]re Duca de M[i]l[an]o a Fiorenza con altre liste aligate," 4 Mar. 1471 (ASMi, AS, c. 898). See Appendix 4.

76. See letters in ASMi, RM, nos. 97 and 98; and ASMi, AS, c. 898.

77. Codex of "Le liste de landata . . . a Fiorenza," fo. 4r.

78. For Alessandro's governorship, see ASMi, AS, c. 898 and 1473-Alessandro.

79. Machiavelli's famous condemnation of the duke's corrupting influence (*Florentine Histories,* 307) was a retrospective view; the writer was only two years old in 1471. Corio's exaggerated description of the ducal entry ([1978], II: 1379–1383) was equally remote; he was only eleven years old then and not yet part of the court. Better testimony comes from the *ricordi* of the Rinuccini family in Florence and letters to the government of Siena from two neutral observers (Paoli, *Venuta di Galeazzo in Firenze*).

80. Paoli, *Venuta di Galeazzo in Firenze,* 29–32 (Lorenzo Antonio Venturini to priors of Siena, 10 and 11 Mar. 1470 [1471], Florence). Baldino Dominici sent a list of the retinues to Siena with a letter of March 8 from Lucca (19–24).

81. Paoli, *Venuta di Galeazzo in Firenze,* 33–35, 37–38 (B. Dominici to priors of Siena, 13 Mar. 1470 [1471], Lucca and 16 Mar., Florence).

82. Paoli, *Venuta di Galeazzo in Firenze,* 39 (B. Dominici to priors of Siena, 16 Mar. 1470 [1471], Florence).

83. Rinuccini, CXV–CXVI. He did not editorialize.

84. For Rome preparations, see letters of 19 Aug. 1471 (ASMi, RM, no. 101, fos. 222v–223r); and G. Giapanno and G. da Castelnovate to Galeazzo, 2 Aug., Milan (misfiled in ASMi, AS, c. 925). See also letters to Galeazzo from ten councillors, courtiers, and ducal relatives, all 20 Aug., Milan (ASMi, AS, c. 901). The crotchety bishop of Parma, Giacomo della Torre, agreed to go, "notwithstanding that the sea is very bad for me, because I cannot urinate there." For delegation Galeazzo sent later, see letter to councillors, courtiers, and bishops, 26 Aug. (ASMi, RM, no. 100, fos. 302r–v).

85. Z. Saggi to L. Gonzaga, 14 May and 30 June [cited] 1471, Milan (ASMa, AG, b. 1624); see also letter of 27 Feb., Milan, and M. Andreasi to L. Gonzaga, 5 Mar., Milan (ASMa, AG, b. 1624). An undated list shows 494 horses in the company, including 40 for Galeazzo personally and 150 for Bona. Galeazzo began discussing such a visit in 1470 (Z. Saggi to L. Gonzaga, 31 July, Milan, ASMa, AG, b. 1623).

86. "Instruction sep[ar]ata: donato de Mediolano," 22 June 1471, Pavia (ASMi, AS, c. 395); the "public instructions," supporting Niccolò, had been shown to the marquess of Mantua. See also various correspondence and documents in ASMi, AS, c. 395, including plans to grab land from the Este territory (documents 78–81).

87. For itinerary, see Appendix 1. For Borso's death, see chap. 5.

88. For hunting near the Venetian border, see Galeazzo to podestà and men of Romanengo, 16 Aug. 1471 (ASMi, RM, no. 101, fo. 206r); see also below. For the western plans, see Galeazzo to Filippo Maria Visconti, 8 Sep.; and Galeazzo to captain of the Alessandria and Tortona district, 15 Sep. (ASMi, RM, no. 101, fos. 267v and 278r, respectively). For the Caravaggio idea, see Galeazzo to Antonio Secco, 21 Sep. (ASMi, RM, no. 102, fo. 39v).

89. See Fumi, "Sfida del duca Galeazzo Maria," which documents this situation fully and discusses Galeazzo's espionage against Colleoni.

90. In November, Galeazzo demanded horses from his subjects for this purpose (ASMi, RM, no. 103, fos. 29r–v).

91. Galeazzo to Colleoni, 4 Sep. 1471, Castelleone (printed in Fumi, "Sfida del duca Galeazzo Maria," 372).

92. Z. Saggi to L. Gonzaga, 21 Sep. 1471, Novara (ASMa, AG, b. 1624).

93. See ASMi, RM, no. 102, fos. 79v–80r and 83v (duchess); and fos. 222v and 254r–v (cardinal).

94. Corio (1978), II: 1409.

95. Corio (1978), II: 1398.

96. See Guglielmo Barblan in Treccani, *Storia di Milano,* IX: 820. For the Florence trip, see Appendix 4.

97. Agricola and his two companions came to Milan in 1469; see Galeazzo to A. Anguissola, 13 May, Abbiategrasso (ASMi, AS, c. 888); and 5 Sep., Pavia (ASMi, AS, c. 890). For their background in the Neapolitan court, see Barblan in Treccani, *Storia di Milano,* IX: 820; Atlas, *Music at the Court of Naples,* chap. 5, and "Antonius Cicinellus S.R.M.," 30 May 1474, a Milanese copy of a letter from the Neapolitan ambassador to his king (ASMi, AS, c. 923).

98. Quoted in Treccani, *Storia di Milano,* IX: 820, and Motta, "Musici," 301.

99. Simonetta, *Diari,* 128–129, divides the 40-man choir into "chapel" and "chamber" choirs. Other lists date from March 1475 (33 singers) and December 1475 (26 singers). They are printed in "Musici," 322–324, and Treccani, *Storia di Milano,* IX: 830 and 836. Appendix 2 here is the latest list in date (1476) and has not been published before (32 singers).

100. For Cardino, see Galeazzo to vicar of the court of the archbishop of Milan, 24 Aug. 1472, Pavia [draft]; and bishop of Como to Galeazzo, 23 Aug., Milan (ASMi, AS, c. 906). The bishop, Branda Castiglione, spent much of his youth in Brabant and probably had contact there with musical centers. Motta, "Musici," tried to identify all musicians at the Sforza court; many facts have come to light since he wrote. For Josquin, see, e.g., Lowinsky and Blackburn, eds., *Josquin des Prez.*

101. See Ward, *"Motetti Missales"*; *New Grove Dictionary of Music,* XVII; and Noblitt, "Ambrosian Mottetti Missales."

102. For campaign to Savoy, see Giuliano da Varese and Cosmino Brioschi to Galeazzo, 28 Aug. 1476, Palestro (ASMi, AS, c. 856); for Vigevano, see above.

103. Galeazzo to A. Anguissola, 13 May 1469, Abbiategrasso (ASMi, AS, c. 888); and 5 Sep. 1469, Pavia (ASMi, AS, c. 890).

104. Z. Saggi to L. Gonzaga, 5 Feb. 1473, Milan (ASMa, AG, b. 1624); Galeazzo to A. Anguissola, 29 Apr. 1473, Abbiategrasso (ASMi, AS, c. 913).

105. For hiring and promise, see letter headed "Antonius Cicinellus S.R.M.," 30 May 1474 [copy] (ASMi, AS, c. 923). For Christmas, see ACM, BT, cod. 1325,

fos. 126v (1475) and 118v (1476). For 1476 budget, see Porro, "Preventivo," 133. For other details, see Barblan in Treccani, *Storia di Milano,* IX: 845.

106. See Barblan in Treccani, *Storia di Milano,* 787–795; Galeazzo to G. da Castelnovate and G. Giapanno, 25 Aug. 1469 (ASMi, RM, no. 88, fo. 200v); and Motta, "Musici," 38–39. A 1468 list not printed elsewhere shows 20 ducal trumpeters (ASMi, RM, no. 83, fo. 232r). The same number went to Florence with Galeazzo in 1471 (see Appendix 4). These numbers had not changed much from the time of Duke Francesco, who had 18 trumpeters in 1463.

107. For persons mentioned, see Appendix 2 (court list); "Lista delli dinari . . ." (8 Oct. 1471) in ASMi, AS, c. 1483-*giuoco della palla* (Sacco); Galeazzo to Antonio Anguissola, 18 Jan. 1469, Vigevano (ASMi, AS, c. 1460) (Tecla); Bianca Maria to Galeazzo, 18 Sep. 1466, Milan (ASMi, AS, c. 1459) (Aloisino); Galeazzo to Alberto Litta, Milanese merchant, 3 Apr. 1473 (ASMi, RM, no. 113, fo. 99v); and Gottardo Panigarola to Galeazzo, 14 Oct. 1473, Milan (ASMi, AS, c. 914) (Diego).

108. For musicians in chapel frescoes, see, e.g., "1472. Spese facte per M. Zanete et compagni . . ." (ASMi, Autografi, 96) (Vigevano). Musicians depicted in the Castello chapel's vault are still visible (as restored) today. For instrumental musicians in general, see Motta, "Musici," 43ff. (request to Mantua on p. 47); and Barblan in Treccani, *Storia di Milano,* IX: 797–806.

109. Motta, "Musici," 297–299; and "Giovanni e Isacco Argiropulo"; Barblan in Treccani, *Storia di Milano,* IX: 809–811; and Galeazzo to Ambrosino da Longhignana, 22 July 1473, Pavia (ASMi, AS, c. 914). Soon after being taken on, Isacco received 100 ducats from the treasurer-general as an advance on his salary (Galeazzo to A. Anguissola, 13 Oct. 1472, Monza (ASMi, AS, c. 908). Pietro Riario requested a performance by Isacco when visiting Milan (Galeazzo to Isacco, 21 July 1473, Pavia, ASMi, AS, c. 914).

110. For organists traveling with the court, see Appendix 2. See also Barblan in *Storia di Milano,* IX: 811–814; Porro, "Lettere" (1879): 252 (ducal organist building or repairing organs); Galeazzo to podestà of Vigevano, 22 Nov. 1474 (ASMi, RM, no. 119, fo. 269v) (two organists from Genoa); to podestà of Pavia, 28 Jan. 1476 (ASMi, RM, no. 123, fo. 58v) (Spanish organist "in our service"); and to Cristoforo Pradella, 17 Mar. 1476 (ASMi, RM, no. 123, fo. 116v) (organist invited to Pavia by bishop).

111. Z. Saggi to L. Gonzaga, 7 Nov. 1471, Milan (ASMa, AG, b. 1624); Galeazzo to Privy Council, 19 Nov. (ASMi, RM, no. 102, fo. 186v).

112. Will dated 3 Nov. 1471, Milan (ASMi, Archivio Notarile, f. 1480); prior draft dated 18 May 1470, Pavia (ASMi, AS, c. 1461).

113. For more detail, see Eiche and Lubkin, "Mausoleum Plan of Galeazzo." He did consider founding chapels in the Duomo dedicated to seven saints (see letters from Nov. 1471 in ASMi, AS, c. 902). To reassure officials in volatile areas about his health, Galeazzo wrote on November 4 to the vice-governor of Genoa (ASMi, RM, no. 102, fo. 146r) and the *commissari* of Parma, Lodi, and Cremona (ASMi, RM, no. 103, fo. 4r). He assured them he was "without any danger."

114. Galeazzo knew of the fresco as early as 1470, when he received a description from two councillors negotiating Ludovico Gonzaga's *condotta* with Milan (Tommaso Tebaldi da Bologna and Pietro Pusterla to Galeazzo, 10 Apr. 1470, Mantua, ASMi, AS, c. 395; published, with commentary, in Tissoni Benvenuti, "Un nuovo documento").

115. See chap. 3.

116. See Woods-Marsden, *Pisanello's Frescoes.*

117. For a full discussion of this program, see Welch, "Frescoes for Castello." The document is dated only "1471," but she assumes it was composed after the trip to Mantua. The inclusion of "Guglielmotto" suggests it was done no earlier than summer; he probably did not arrive from France until then (see above). It is also unlikely that Galeazzo had developed the program, or meant to execute it, as of mid-August. He gave Bonifacio Bembo, who had worked on frescoes for Pavia Castle, permission to visit his native Cremona, because the duke intended to have no more painting done at the time, at Pavia or elsewhere (Galeazzo to Bonifacio, 10 Aug., ASMi, RM, no. 100, fo. 258v).

118. Program printed in Welch, "Frescoes for Castello," 181–182 (original in ASMi, Autografi, 96).

119. Programs and estimate printed in Welch, "Frescoes for Castello," 182–184 (originals in ASMi, Autografi, 96). Her dating of the undated versions is based in part on information from my dissertation and personal communications. Further information has come to my attention since then, including the arrival of Ercole Marescotti in November 1472 (see chap. 5) and Pierre d'Olly in early 1473 (see above).

120. See, e.g., commissions for chapels in Vigevano, "1472. Spese facte per M. Zanete et compagni . . . ," (ASMi, *Autografi,* 96); Caravaggio (B. Gadio to Galeazzo, 28 Jan. 1474, Milan; ASMi, Autografi, 88). Those without the family (e.g., ceiling of Porta Giovia Castle's ducal chapel) showed the Holy Trinity surrounded by singers and musicians bearing banners with a red cross, signifying the Christian kingdom and the city of Milan.

121. Welch, "Frescoes for Castello," 181–183.

122. Spencer, "Il cavallo di bronzo per Francesco Sforza" (statue); Schofield, Shell, and Sironi, *Giovanni Antoni Amedeo* (altar).

123. For a facsimile of the New Testament, see *Il codice varia 124 della Biblioteca Reale di Torino, miniato da Cristoforo de' Predis* (Turin, 1987). Another book he did for Galeazzo is in the Wallace Collection. A book on consanguinity written for Galeazzo opens with a miniature of his court (Paris, Bibliothèque Nationale, MS Lat. 4586, fo. 1).

124. Galeazzo to "Mag[ist]ro Zanetto pittore in M[i]l[an]o," 15 Aug. 1472 (ASMi, RM, no. 110, fo. 28r); a similar letter went to Bonifacio (Bembo) da Cremona (see fo. 29r).

125. For Galeazzo's coinage generally, see *Corpus Nummorum Italicarum,* V: 162 ff. For Zanetto, see chap. 2.

126. "1471. Lista de uno debito da pagarsi ad M[agistr]o Maffeo et ad altri per imagine fatte de argent[o] et altre cose" (ASMi, Autografi, 96). See also Galeazzo to A. Anguissola, 31 Dec. 1472 (ASMi, AS, c. 909), for two more portraits in silver of GianGaleazzo.

127. Galeazzo to Antonio Anguissola, 17 Mar. 1472, Vigevano; also Antonio to Galeazzo, 17 Mar., Milan, and 18 Mar. note of estimate for starting camel (ASMi, AS, c. 1483-argenteria, gioie, porcellane-Galeazzo).

128. See Welch, "Process of Sforza Patronage," 371–375. For Gadio's relations with artists from Cremona, see Wittgens, in *Storia di Milano,* VII: 807.

129. See Welch, "Process of Sforza Patronage," 375–378. For quotation, see

B. Gadio to Galeazzo, 22 June 1469, Milan (printed in De'Rosmini, *Istoria di Milano,* IV: 145–146). See chap. 3 for estimate on 1469 Pavia fresco; Beltrami and Welch also print a 1472 estimate for a program in Porta Giovia.

130. See, e.g., B. Gadio to Galeazzo, 17 July 1473, Milan (ASMi, AS, c. 914).

131. See, e.g., B. Gadio to Galeazzo, 30 Apr. 1470, Milan (ASMi, AS, c. 893), for a program in Porta Giovia.

132. Galeazzo to "Mag[ist]ro Bonifacio" [Bembo] (ASMi, RM, nos. 95, fo. 12bis); and letters from Galeazzo, 16 Apr. 1468 (ASMi, RM, no. 80, fos. 56r–v) (Costantino [da Vaprio?] for San Giorgio). Work for San Giorgio was supervised by Roberto da Sanseverino. For more on the Bembo family, see Malaguzzi Valeri, *Pittori Lombardi,* Chap. III; Pirovano, 50–52; Samek-Ludovici. Chap. V.

133. Galeazzo to B. Gadio (ASMi, RM, no. 91, fo. 68v). See Welch, "Secular Fresco Painting," Chap. VIII, on artists at Galeazzo's court.

134. Galeazzo to podestà of Vigevano, 27 Aug. 1472 (ASM, RM, no. 110, fo. 39r).

135. B. Gadio to Galeazzo, 20 Mar. 1473, Milan (ASMi, Autografi, c. 88).

136. Wittgens, in Treccani, *Storia di Milano,* VII: 781. See original letters from B. Gadio in ASMi, Autografi, c. 88 and c. 96; and others printed in Caffi, "Castello di Pavia," 554–556.

137. Wittgens, in Treccani, *Storia di Milano,* VII: 786, 811; see also Malaguzzi Valeri, *Pittori,* Chap. V.

138. Besides Welch, see Wittgens in Treccani, *Storia di Milano,* VII: 759, 761; and *Vincenzo Foppa.*

139. See Wittgens, in Treccani, *Storia di Milano,* VII: 781; and Welch, "Process of Sforza Patronage," 381–384.

140. For fullest discussion of the secular frescoes and their contexts, see Welch, "Frescoes for Porta Giovia," and "Galeazzo and the Castello di Pavia."

141. See Welch, "Frescoes for Porta Giovia."

142. Galeazzo to castellan of Pavia, 14 Feb. 1471 (ASMi, RM, no. 97, fo. 237v); and to Alessandro, 14 Feb. (ASMi, RM, no. 98, fo. 164r[bis]). Duke Francesco and his castellan had been concerned also about borrowed books that were not returned (Mazzatinti, "Inventario," 34).

143. See Mazzatinti, "Inventario," 54 (Petrarch, 1459), and 56–59 (1469).

144. For university faculty, as projected for 1475, see ASMi, RM, no. 118, fos. 179v–280v. For the ducal children's education, see chap. 8. Galeazzo did declare that a Greek scholar, Andronico da Constantinopoli, was coming to Milan "to our service," sending his Greek and Latin books ahead (Galeazzo to *commissario* of Cremona, 21 Mar. 1475, ASMi, RM, no. 121, fo. 56r).

145. See Ianziti, *Politics and Propaganda.*

146. He also left his wife and children in Milan; see Robin, *Filelfo in Milan,* 142–143. For oaths of fealty, see above.

147. Galeazzo to Filelfo, 4 Feb. 1472 (ASMi, RM, no. 104, fo. 33r) (bombard); 18 Feb. 1472 (ASMi, RM, no. 106, fo. 58r) (lost verses); 2 and 17 Sep. 1475 (ASMi, RM, no. 122, fos. 103v and 122r) (mistress).

148. Galeazzo to Filelfo, "poet laureate," 2 Mar. 1472 (ASMi, RM, no. 106, fo. 96v) (debt relief); 14 Sep. 1468 (ASMi, RM, no. 80, fo. 80r) (allowance); May 1475 (ASMi, RM, no. 120, fos. 192v and 209v) (complaints about neighbors).

149. Galeazzo to Filelfo, 24 Aug. 1468 (ASMi, RM, no. 84, fo. 233v). See also Robin, *Filelfo,* 138.

150. Filelfo to L. Gonzaga, 27 July 1476, Milan (ASMa, AG, b. 1625).

151. The panegyric is filed with papers from 1468 (ASMi, AS, c. 1461). For Chancery appointment, see Galeazzo to masters of revenues and Antonio Anguissola, 20 Jan. 1470 (ASMi, RM, no. 91, fo. 160r). For recommendation, see Galeazzo to Ascanio, 20 Nov. 1471 (ASMi, RM, no. 103, fo. 40v).

152. Corio (1978), II: 1408.

153. Corio (1978), II: 1408; and Zaccaria to [unknown], 3 Feb. 1470, Pavia, ASMa, AG, b. 1623).

154. Galeazzo to masters of extraordinary revenues, 25 June 1472, and to officials of Lodi, 13 Oct. 1472 (ASMi, RM, no. 105, fos. 13v and 289v) (flight and return); reference to letters sent Giovanni, 20 Oct. 1472 (ASMi, RM, no. 110, fo. 95r), and Corio (1978) II: 1408. The *sottocameriere* Eusebio suffered an "accidente . . . de uno testiculo chella" in 1474 and required serious medical attention (ASMi, RM, no. 118, fo. 138r). Giovanni left again in 1474 and was recommended to the marquess of Montferrat (ASMi, RM, no. 117, fo. 246v), but he had returned by 25 May 1475 (ASMi, RM, no. 120, fo. 263v).

155. Galeazzo to vice-podestà and *commissario* of Pavia, 10 Oct. 1469 (two letters) (ASMi, RM, no. 87, fo. 53r–v); Corio (1978), II:1408.

156. "Descriptio bona mobilia Johannis de Verona olim duc[a]lis camerarij in loco de Cernignano dep[ut]atus Laude," 22 June 1472 (ASMi, AS, c. 1602).

157. Galeazzo received an exemption in 1467 and requested another in 1468, with four companions (Galeazzo to Lorenzo da Pesaro [in Rome], 21 Feb. 1468, ASMi, RM, no. 81, fo. 139v).

158. E.g., Galeazzo to Ludovico Beccaria, 30 Aug. 1472 (ASMi, RM, no. 107, fo. 222r) (hawk); Lancillotto and Andreotto del Maino and Tommaso Tebaldi da Bologna to Galeazzo, 23 Sep. 1471, Milan (ASMi, AS, c. 901); Galeazzo to Lancillotto, Andreotto, and Tommaso, 25 Sep. (ASMi, RM, nos. 103, fo. 60r) (horses); Galeazzo to Giovanni Borromeo, Nov. 1472 (ASMi, RM, no. 110bis, fo. 57r) (hounds), and 4 Nov. 1473 (ASMi, RM, no. 112, fo. 319r) (huntsman).

159. Porro, "Preventivo," 133; and Galeazzo to A. Anguissola, 11 July 1472, Bereguardo (ASMi, AS, c. 905). See also Galeazzo to "Pelegro Salvago," 21 Feb. 1472 (ASMi, RM, no. 106, fo. 63v).

160. Ludovico Sforza to Bianca Maria, 23 Feb. 1468, Mortara, and 23 Feb., Vigevano (ASMi, AS, c. cart. 1468).

161. Z. Saggi to L. Gonzaga, 25 June 1471, Milan (ASMa, AG, b. 1624).

162. Galeazzo to Niccolò Roberti (Este ambassador) and G. Simonetta (two letters), 1 Aug. 1475 (ASMi, RM, no. 122, fos. 32r–v).

163. Galeazzo to Tristano Sforza, 21 May 1468, Pavia (ASMi, AS, c. 1461).

164. Galeazzo to Pietro Francesco Visconti, 7 July 1472 (ASMi, RM, no. 105, fo. 48r); Pietro Francesco Visconti to Galeazzo, 6 July 1472, Milan (ASMi, AS, c. 905). The Visconti "master" consulted by Pietro Francesco was Duke Filippo Maria's half-brother.

165. Galeazzo to Gaspare Gavirana da Parma, *cameriere,* 21 Mar. 1476 (ASMi, RM, no. 123, fo. 123r); within a few weeks, Gaspare received more serious permission to marry an heiress from Parma (ASMi, RM, no. 123, fo. 141v).

166. E.g., Z. Saggi to L. Gonzaga, 8 Mar. 1470, Milan (ASMa, AG, b. 1623), and 15 Apr. 1473, Milan (ASMa, AG, b. 1624); to Barbara H. Gonzaga, 31 Oct. and 29 Nov. 1469, Milan (ASMa, AG, b. 1623). For jokes on the Gonzaga that were slightly less sexual, see letters to Ludovico of 31 July and 3 Aug. 1470, Milan (ASMa, AG, b. 1623). For Barbara, see *DBI,* VI: 41–42.

167. Galeazzo to Borso d'Este, 14 Apr. 1468 (ASMi, RM, no. 83, fo. 44v).

168. E.g., Z. Saggi to L. Gonzaga, 25 Jan. and 15 June 1471, Milan (ASMa, AG, b. 1624).

169. Z. Saggi to [unknown], 3 Feb. 1470, Pavia (ASMa, AG, b. 1623); and to L. Gonzaga, 2 Feb. 1471, Milan (ASMa, AG, b. 1624). In June 1471, Galeazzo commanded that three lax convents in Pavia be walled to keep them living "religiously" and chastely (ASMi, RM, no. 101, fo. 80r).

170. Z. Saggi to [unknown], 3 Feb. 1470, Pavia (ASMa, AG, b. 1623) ("Juvenal"), and to L. Gonzaga, 7 Jan. 1973, Milan (ASMa, AG, b. 1624).

171. For Renaissance *buffoni* and dwarfs in general, see Luzio and Renier, "Buffoni, nani, e schiavi," and Swain, *Fools and Folly.* During Galeazzo's reign, these figures flourished most under Este patronage at Ferrara; see references in letters from Sforza Maria to Galeazzo, 23 Aug. 1468, Medellana, and 8 Sep. 1468, Belfiore (ASMi, AS, c. 1481).

172. For Biagio, see Motta, "Musici," 280 (1451 mention), and De'Rosmini, *Istoria di Milano,* IV: 149 (fresco).

173. Guido Visconti to Galeazzo, 6 and 12 Jan. 1474, Genoa (ASMi, AS, c. 1484-buffoni e nani); ASMi, RM, nos. 115, fo. 57r and 118, fos. 35v, 83v–84r (letters of Jan. and July 1474 to Genoa and Chios); Francesco Giustiniano Recanello to Giovanni, 3 Feb. and 18 Apr. 1476, Chios (family). See also Bona to Gaspare Ambrogio Barzizza, 27 June 1476, Pavia (ASMi, AS, c. 1484-buffoni e nani), in which she orders silver fittings for his cloak.

174. "La nanneta" is mentioned in the final fresco program for the Sala Grande in Porta Giovia (Welch, "Frescoes for the Porta Giovia," 184).

175. For Giovanni Antonio under Duke Francesco, see "Quaterno . . ." of Antonio Anguissola (1460–1466), fo. 3v (ASMi, AS, c. 1483-*spese*-Francesco). On Venetian odyssey, see Antonio Meraviglia to Galeazzo, 17 Jan. 1471, and Ludovico Sforza to Galeazzo, 22 Jan., Venice (ASMi, AS, c. 1469); Giovanni Antonio returned home with Ludovico's entourage. For the distinction between a clever fool and a simpleton, see Swain, *Fools and Folly,* 54–55. Correspondence from 1474 related to "Signor Buffone" includes ASMi, RM, no. 115, fos. 148r, 231v, 232bis; and Marchese Bigli to Galeazzo, 1, 6, and 24 Mar. 1474, Milan (ASMi, AS, c. 922).

176. *Corpus Chronicorum Bononiensum,* 444–445.

177. M. Andreasi to Barbara H. Gonzaga, 7 Dec. 1467, Milan (ASMa, AG, b. 1623).

178. Galeazzo to Paolo [di San Genesio], bishop of Eneapolis, 4 Apr. 1472, Milan (ASMi, AS, c. 904).

179. Galeazzo to Giovanni Arnulfo [Vismara] and Boldrino [Crivelli], 31 Dec. 1469 (ASMi, RM, no. 87, fo. 111v). See also Morbio, *Codice Visconteo-Sforzesco,* 455–456, for 500 ducats to be given "observant friars and nuns" at May Day 1475. The 1476 budget reserved 4,000 ducats for alms and masses (Porro, "Preventivo," 133). For alms given secretly, see Galeazzo to A. Anguissola, 27 Apr. 1470, Milan (ASMi, AS, c. 894).

180. Galeazzo to A. Anguissola, 26 July 1473, Monza (ASMi, AS, c. 914).

181. Wittgens in Treccani, *Storia di Milano,* VII: 781 (display). For use of relics, see chap. 3; and Galeazzo to castellan of Pavia (ASMi, RM, no. 99, fo. 14r) (Mary Magdalen and Bernardino).

182. See, e.g., Galeazzo to G. da Castelnovate, 17 July 1469 (ASMi, RM, no. 86, fo. 113r); and Galeazzo to Privy Council, 20 Nov. 1475 (ASMi, RM, no. 122, fo. 189bis). For Bianca Maria, see, e.g., letters to Galeazzo, 17 June 1468, Cremona, and 3 July 1468, Lodi (ASMi, AS, c. 1460).

183. G. Simonetta to Galeazzo, 21 Feb. 1472, Milan (ASMi, AS, c. 903).

184. Raffaelle da Vimercate to Galeazzo, 10 Nov. 1474 and 2 Sep. 1475, Milan (ASMi, AS, c. 925 and 927, respectively); Galeazzo to Raffaelle, 26 Sep. 1475 (ASMi, RM, no. 122, fo. 133r); Galeazzo to G. Simonetta, 4 Nov. 1475 (ASMi, RM, no. 122, fo. 161v); and G. Simonetta to Galeazzo, 21 Feb. 1472, Milan (ASMi, AS, c. 903).

185. Galeazzo to Giovanni da Viterbo, 25 Nov. 1476 (ASMi, RM, no. 126, fo. 48v); Galeazzo to vice-governor of Genoa, 4 Nov. 1475 (ASMi, RM, no. 122, fo. 180v); Thorndike, *A History of Magic,* IV: 263ff. and 439. For the latter years of Galeazzo's reign, complete *giudizi* survive from various astrologers, plus briefer predictions about more specific matters (ASMi, AS, c. 1569).

186. Both on same draft page, dated 7 Aug. 1468, Monza; ASMi, AS, c. 885.

187. M. Andreasi to Barbara H. Gonzaga, 31 Dec. 1472 [O.S.], Milan (ASMa, AG, b. 1624).

188. Letters to various cities of dominion, 5 Apr. 1472 (ASMi, RM, no. 106, fos. 186v–87r). The celebrations were not to begin until April 7, as April 6 was the day on which the duke of Savoy's funeral would be held.

189. M. Andreasi to L. Gonzaga, 5 May 1472, Milan (ASMa, AG, b. 1624). Later in the year, he gave his wife a higher standing in the dominion by publicly reaffirming that her commands were of equal authority to his own. (Galeazzo to a long list of officials, feudatories, and ducal relatives, 22 Nov. 1472, ASMi, RM, no. 110bis; fos. 36v–39r.)

190. Ferorelli, "Ducato di Bari," 428–429; Fubini, "Crisi del ducato," 59; and Lorenzo de' Medici, *Lettere,* I: 342.

191. Galeazzo announced this betrothal in letters (Italian or Latin) to the princes of Montferrat, Savoy, and France (and his own envoys there), plus Giovanni Arcimboldi, Cardinal Bessarion, the vice-governor of Genoa, and the Privy Council. Milanese envoys expedited other letters to Ferrara, Bologna, Forlì, Pesaro, and the Swiss League (see notes and draft letters, 23 July 1472, Gonzaga, ASMi, AS, c. 1464).

192. Galeazzo to Filippo, 5 July 1472, Mirabello [Pavia] (ASMi, AS, c. 905).

193. Galezzo to Filippo, 22 Aug. 1471 (ASMi, RM, no. 100, fo. 282v).

194. Galeazzo to Sforza Maria and Ludovico, 2 Sep. 1472 (ASMi, RM, no. 107, fo. 231r).

195. Maspes, "Prammatica pel ricevimento degli ambasciatori," 148.

196. See, e.g., ASMi, RM, no. 103, fos. 368r–374r; no. 106, fos. 268r–269r, 296r (numbers), 305v–306r, and 339r; and no. 107, fos. 7v–8r, 12r, 16v, 20r, and 53r. For welcome at Vercelli, see M. Andreasi to L. Gonzaga, 24 May 1472, Pavia (ASMa, AG, b. 1624).

197. M. Andreasi to L. Gonzaga, 19 May 1472, Pavia (ASMa, AG, b. 1624).

Marsilio noted "that it was not believed by anyone" that Galeazzo would escort Bessarion to his lodgings; the duke rarely did so for any visitor.

198. M. Andreasi to L. Gonzaga, 24 May 1472, Pavia (ASMa, AG, b. 1624).

199. M. Andreasi to L. Gonzaga, 21 May 1472, Pavia (ASMa, AG, b. 1624); for the book, see ASMi, RM, no. 107, fo. 45v.

200. M. Andreasi to L. Gonzaga, 28 and 29 May 1472, Pavia (ASMa, AG, b. 1624); see list of those dressed "alla francexa" 28 May 1472 [no location] (ASMi, AS, c. 1483-feste, giuochi, spettacoli); and Galeazzo to Gallassio de Gallassi, 26 and 28 May 1472, Pavia [drafts] (ASMi, AS, c. 904).

201. M. Andreasi to L. Gonzaga, 29 and 31 May 1472, Pavia (ASMa, AG, b. 1624).

202. Galeazzo to A. Anguissola, 20 June 1471, Mirabello [Pavia] [draft] (ASMi, AS, c. 1483-gioie, abiti, etc.-Galeazzo).

203. Galeazzo to A. Anguissola, 24 June and 3(?) July 1471, Mirabello [Pavia] [draft]; 3 Jan. 1472, Abbiategrasso; and A. Anguissola to Galeazzo, 4 Jan. 1472, Milan (ASMi, AS, c. 1483-gioie, abiti, etc.-Galeazzo).

204. Gottardo Panigarola to Galeazzo, 14 June 1471, Milan; Galeazzo to Antonio Anguissola, 27 June, Mirabello [Pavia] (ASMi, AS, c. 1483-gioie, abiti, etc.-Galeazzo).

205. Galeazzo to A. Anguissola, 3(?) and 5 July 1471, Mirabello [Pavia] [drafts] and duchy dated 5 July, Mirabello [Pavia] (ASMi, AS, c. 1483-gioie, abiti, etc.-Galeazzo).

206. Galeazzo to A. Anguissola, 16 July 1471, on boat between Pavia and Torricella (ASMi, AS, c. 1483-gioie, abiti, etc.-Galeazzo). Galeazzo encountered many problems with the jeweler, Lorenzo da [Borgo] Val di Taro; see Galeazzo to "Johan. Boco nec non Anto. Anguissole," 30 Oct. 1470, Vigevano; Francesco Pagnano to Galeazzo, 10 Aug. 1471, Pavia (ASMi, AS, c. 1483-gioie, abiti, etc.-Galeazzo); and Galeazzo to F. Pagnano, 9 Aug. (ASMi, RM, no. 101, fo. 197).

207. For clothing, see above (May 1472) and ASMi, AS, c. 905, passim. For scent, see above. For new barber, see Galeazzo to Luigi Pietrasanta, 28 Mar. 1472, Milan [draft] (ASMi, AS, c. 904); the barber, Travaglino, was to receive 10 florins per month 10 times per year (40 ducats total). For tennis players, see Galeazzo to A. Anguissola, 1 Sep. Pavia, and 23 Sep., Novara; and to masters of revenues and A. Anguissola, 23 Oct., Milan (ASMi, AS, c. 908).

208. "Memoria ad Marsilio de quello ha ad scrivere. . . ," [undated] (ASMi, AS, c. 905). The document has a note stating it was given to Francesco da Varese on June 9, presumably to pass on to the Mantuan ambassador. Marsilio Andreasi was resident ambassador in Milan that year; Zaccaria Saggi da Pisa had been there when Galeazzo planned his 1471 trip.

5: "He Who Lives at Court Dies in the Poorhouse"

1. Tommaso Tebaldi to Galeazzo, 17 June 1468, Milan (ASMi, AS, c. 884).

2. Santoro, Uffici, 8; for Privy Council attendance in 1473–1474, see Cicco Simonetta, Diari. Tommaso was active as councillor and diplomat in 1467–1468 (ASMi, AS, c. 1460, passim). He had been at the Sforza court since 1432 (Ilardi, Dispatches, I: xlv).

3. Tommaso was one of the councillors choosing *gentiluomini* for the duke in 1473 (Galeazzo to Giovanni Giapanno, 21 Oct. 1473 [draft]; ASMi, AS, c. 914). He traveled with Ascanio to Savoy in January 1474 (ASMi, RM, no. 115, fos. 67r and 74r). His wife attended the wedding in Milan and greeted Bona in the Sep. 1468 entry (Beltrami, *Dame Milanesi*, 17; and undated list in ASMi, AS, c. 1463). Tommaso was invited to the Christmas court each year.

4. Charter dated January 1, 1469, in ASMi, Notarile, fo. 1580; see also Santoro, *Uffici*, 267, n. 1.

5. Tommaso da Bologna to Galeazzo, 25 Oct. 1470, Milan (ASMi, AS, c. 896).

6. Galeazzo to Giovanni Gabriele Crivelli, 10 June 1468 (ASMi, RM, no. 83, fo. 234v); G. G. Crivelli to Galeazzo, 12 June, Buccinasco (ASMi, AS, c. 1463). See also G. G. Crivelli to Galeazzo and to Cicco, both 31 May, Buccinasco (ASMi, AS, c. 886); Galeazzo to G. G. Crivelli, 2 June (ASMi, RM, no. 83, fo. 190v); and G. G. Crivelli to Cicco, 18 June, Buccinasco (ASMi, AS, c. 1463).

7. Galeazzo Pagnani to Duke Galeazzo, 25 Jan. 1468, Milan (ASMi, AS, c. 883). Pagnani had been a *cameriere* in June 1466 (see ASMi, RM, no. 72, fo. 189v).

8. Brusco Crivelli to Margherita Visconti Crivelli, 22 Oct. 1476 [no loc.] (ASMi, AS, c. 932). Brusco's identity is clarified in the witness list of a *procura* for "Hector de Faffis" and wife, 18 Mar. 1470 (ASMi, AS, c. 1535).

9. For Brusco as *cameriere* in 1463, see SSL, RF, cod. 5, fo. 146r. He became a *famiglio d'arme* in July 1471 (ASMi, RM, no. 100, fo. 237r).

10. For an example of Bona's patronage, see letters to Elena Lampugnani Visconti, 10 and 21 Aug. 1476, Pavia [drafts] (ASMi, AS, c. 929 and 931, respectively). For some appeals to Cicco, see chap. 7.

11. See Appendix 2 (1476).

12. Galeazzo to podestà of Castelnuovo Terdonese, 29 Mar. 1474 (ASMi, RM, no. 116, fo. 268r). In 1475, Galeazzo told the podestà of Vigevano that a ducal kennelman was "exempt like his other peers" from paying local charges (ASMi, RM, no. 121, fo. 158v [178v]).

13. For example, G. G. Crivelli received aid from the duke and duchess with several debts and contracts (see ASMi, RM, no. 97, fo. 132r; Bona to all *podestà*, captains, etc., 21 July 1473, Pavia, ASMi, AS, c. 914; and to captain of justice of Milan, 12 June 1476, Pavia, ASMi, AS, c. 931) and with prosecution of a man who stole from him (Bona [?] to captain of Binasco, 13 Sep. 1476, Galliate, ASMi, AS, c. 929).

14. Galeazzo to podestà of Milan, 28 Feb. 1467, Pavia [dr.] (ASM, AS, c. 879).

15. Galeazzo to Bianca Maria, 6 May 1467, Lodi (ASMi, AS, c. 879). Courtiers were not to avoid paying their debts "sotto favore de essere cortesano"; in August 1475, all Milanese merchants owed money by courtiers were invited to bring their accounts for settlement at the Christmas court (Galeazzo to "Abbatibus Mercatorum Mli.," ASMi, RM, no. 122, fo. 69r).

16. Galeazzo to Bianca Maria, 13 July 1467, in camp "contra Mordanum" (ASMi, AS, c. 881).

17. Galeazzo to Bosio, 4 Oct. 1473 (ASMi, RM, no. 116, fo. 26v); Cicco Simonetta recorded the confiscations and new grants on October 1 (*Diari*, 55).

18. Mastino Suardi to Galeazzo, 27 Aug. and 4 Sep. 1470, Milan (ASMi, AS, c. 894 and 896, respectively) (dowries), and 9 Dec. 1470, Milan (ASMi, AS, c. 897) (plea). Even the Suardi still in Bergamo were strong supporters of Milan (see ASMi, RM, no. 100, fos. 271v and 329v).

19. Giovanni Agostino Isimbardi to Galeazzo, 17 Feb. 1474 (ASMi, AS, c. 922). He was a *gentiluomo* in 1469 (ASMi, RM, no. 89, fo. 51r). See also Calvi, *Famiglie Notabili,* I, Isimbardi, t. 1.

20. See letters from Galeazzo in November 1472 on ASMi, RM, no. 111, fos. 89r (to Gerardo Cerruti), 100r (to Galeazzo Marescotti), and 100v (to Cardinal Gonzaga). Ercole appeared on lists of *camerieri* beginning in that month.

21. Galeazzo Marescotti had at least ten children (Litta, d. 67). Within six months of Ercole's arrival, Duke Galeazzo recommended his brother Agamemnone to be podestà of Perugia (ASMi, RM, no. 111, fo. 213v).

22. For Enea's arrival, see *Corpus Chronicorum Bononiensum,* 426. He also appeared in the 1471–1472 fresco commissions.

23. Galeazzo to Francesco Missaglia, 17 Nov. 1469 (ASMi, RM, no. 91, fo. 23r).

24. Galeazzo to Tomeino Beccaria, 12 Jan. 1474, Pavia [draft] (ASMi, AS, c. 922). For family, see ASMi, Acquisto Riva Finolo, no. 4, fasc. 10, and below.

25. Galeazzo to Bernardo Anguissola, 9 June 1469 (ASM, RM, no. 90, fo. 179r).

26. Tommaso Moroni da Rieti to Galeazzo, 18 June 1468, Rieti (ASMi, AS, c. 1463).

27. For singers, see chap. 4; for mistress, see De'Rosmini, *Istoria di Milano,* IV: 111–113. For steward (Gottardo Panigarola), see Galeazzo to A. Anguissola, 13 July 1472, Bereguardo (ASMi, AS, c. 905). See also Antonio Bracelli to Galeazzo, 10 Sep. 1474, Milan (ASMi, AS, c. 925), for help previously promised with buying a house; he had found two houses, one at 5,000 pounds, the other at 1,600 ducats. Gottardo's house cost only 150 ducats.

28. Giovanni Matteo Bottigella to Galeazzo Maria Sforza, 21 Apr. 1970, Pavia (ASMi, AS, c. 914).

29. Galeazzo to castellan of Monza, 22 Aug. 1475 (ASMi, RM, no. 122, fo. 77r); for other examples, see ASMi, RM, no. 95, fo. 175r (Cassano, 1470); ASMi, RM, no. 115, fo. 128r (Villanova, 1474); ASM, RM, no. 102, fo. 21r (Galliate, 1471); ASMi, RM, no. 110bis, fo. 125v (Abbiategrasso, 1472); and (ASMi, RM, no. 110, fo. 89v) (Monza, 1472). Beds were usually consigned to *cameriere* organizing lodgings. Vigevano had an official "sopra li alogiamenti de la n[ost]ra corte," with an annual salary of 30 florins (Galeazzo to podestà of Vigevano, 22 June 1476; ASMi, RM, no. 123, fo. 256r).

30. Santoro, "Codice di Bona," 274.

31. Beltrami, *Castello* (1894): 247. G. G. Crivelli, his wife, and a niece were among those with highest priority "when one cannot house everyone together" (see undated document, probably from Bianca Maria's household, headed "Quando non se po allogiare tutti insieme . . . ," ASMi, AS, c. 1602).

32. See chap. 2.

33. On lodging arrangements for envoys to Milan, see Lubkin, "Strategic Hospitality," 176, 179, and 180. See also chaps. 2, 6, and 7.

34. Document headed "Mcccclxx die iij aug[ust]i. Ordine de la spex[a] p[er] uno camarero" (ASMi, AS, c. 894).

35. "Assignatione del piatello ducale 1471 facta die p[rim]o Januarij" (ASMi, AS, c. 1603). The same rate applied in November 1471 ("1471. Lista de le spexe facte p[er] Aluysio da petrasancta in lo mese de novembr[e] ale boche infrascr[ipt]e . . . ," ASMi, AS, c. 1603).

36. Almost all those on both lists were *camerieri fuori di camera* (lists from 2 Jan.

1471, and duplicate from 31 Dec. 1471 [O.S.], beginning "D. Antonio Compadre hon[oran]do" and "D[omi]ne Antonio compater honora[n]de," respectively [ASMi, AS, c. 1603]).

37. See lists of debts owed Matrignano Brasca by court figures, including *camerieri di camera* Antonietto Arcelli da Piacenza (1474–1475) and Giorgio del Carretto (1474) (ASMi, AS, c. 1602). See also list of Giovanni Simonetta's clothing debts in ASMi, AS, c. 1604.

38. M. Andreasi to L. Gonzaga, 12 Apr. 1472, Milan (ASMa, AG, b. 1624).

39. E.g., Privy Council to Galeazzo, 28 Nov. 1475, Milan (ASMi, AS, c. 928). For the role of clothing in later medieval French court life, see Piponnier, *Costume et vie sociale.*

40. See chaps. 2 (winter 1468), 4 (summer 1472), and 6 (winter 1473).

41. See contract in ASMi, AS, c. 892; Filippo's predecessor, Cristoforo Barberini, went out of business. See also contract between Barberini and Galeazzo, 29 Sep. 1468, Abbiate [with draft] (ASMi, AS, c. 1484-*drapperie*).

42. Hose *alla divisa* was rarely granted (5 Jan. 1475; ASMi, RM, nos. 120, fo. 1v); for restrictive proclamations, see ASMi, RM, no. 88, fo. 141v (1469); and no. 118, fo. 282v (1474).

43. Undated petition signed by Antonio Meraviglia et al. (ASMi, AS, c. 1484-*camerieri, ecc.-s.d*). It originated before Christmas 1473, when two signatories were promoted to the office of *gentiluomo.*

44. See, e.g., a list of jousters and horses in ASMi, AS, c. 1483-*giostre*-Galeazzo (#226). For Giuliano, see Galeazzo to *collaterali generali*, 17 June 1476 (ASMi, RM, no. 125, fo. 171v).

45. Gallassio Gallassi to Galeazzo, 2 June 1468, Milan (ASMi, AS, c. 884).

46. Porro, "Letter" (1879): 261–264 (originals in ACM, BT, cod. 1384).

47. Several physicians also held lectureships at Pavia University; in 1463, they were Giovanni Marliani, Benedetto Reguardati, Guido Parati, Giovanni Ghiringhelli, and Giovanni Matteo da Gradi (SSL, RF, cod. 5, fos. 109r–111r).

48. Ambrogio Grifi to Galeazzo, 21 May 1467, Milan (ASMi, AS, c. 880), 27 May and 9 June 1467 (ASMi, AS, c. 1461); Ludovico Suardi to Galeazzo, 8 June 1467, Milan [postscript] (ASMi, AS, c. 880); for a later illness, see Giacomo della Torre, bishop of Parma, to Galeazzo, 3 Nov. 1475, Milan (ASMi, AS, c. 928).

49. See account of expenses for this cure, in ASMi, AS, c. 1620.

50. The physicians were Giovanni Marliani, Guido Parati, and Cristoforo da Soncino (G. Giapanno to Galeazzo, 2 Aug. 1469, Milan, ASMi, AS, c. 880).

51. Galeazzo to prior of San Marco fuori le mura of Milan, 18 Mar. 1475 (ASMi, RM, no. 120, fo. 117r); see also Galeazzo to "D. Guardiano St. Angeli Ord. Minor. Mli.," 31 Mar. 1474 (ASMi, RM, no. 115, fo. 211r); and Galeazzo to Antonio de Alasia, vicar of the Episcopal Court of Novara, 19 Mar. 1476 (ASMi, RM, no. 125, fo. 10v).

52. For Lenten fish, see Galeazzo to podestà of Trecate, 23 Feb. 1475 (ASMi, RM, no. 120, fo. 76r); and Bona to constable of Porta Tosa, 12 Mar. 1476, Pavia (ASMi, AS, c. 929). For a February 1, 1472, contract between ducal seneschals and two named suppliers, see ASMi, AS, c. 903. For preaching licenses, see Galeazzo to Privy Council, 13 Feb. 1474 (ASMi, RM, no. 115, fo. 117v), and to castellan of Galliate (ASMi, RM, no. 115, fo. 122r).

53. Their salaries were usually called *provisioni*; the *provisionati*, however, were

poorly paid members of the military garrisons. In general, payment was made differently to the civil and military administrations; for those holding offices in both spheres (including most commanders of the standing army), the civil office took precedence.

54. In March 1474, Galeazzo ordered his new treasurer-general to pay all *salariati* three times per year, except ambassadors outside Milan and lecturers at Pavia University (letter to Antonio Landriani, 19 Mar. 1474, Pavia, ASMi, AS, c. 922). When Galeazzo made Tomeino Beccaria a *gentiluomo,* he said Tomeino would be paid quarterly (12 Jan. 1474, Pavia [draft], ASMi, AS, c. 922). For his brothers, see Galeazzo to Gabriele Paleari, 27 Aug. 1473, Milan (ASMi, AS, c. 914); they had complained that their allowances were not being paid quarterly, as was intended (Galeazzo to A. Anguissola, 20 Aug. 1473, Milan, ASMi, AS, c. 914). In 1473, Galeazzo decided to pay household expenses bimonthly (Galeazzo to A. Anguissola, 18 Feb. 1473, ASMi, AS, c. 911).

55. Galeazzo to masters of revenues and A. Anguissola, 9 Feb. 1470 (ASMi, RM, no. 91, fo. 189r) (G. Marliani); and Galeazzo to Luigi da Pietrasanta, 28 Mar. 1472, Milan (ASMi, AS, c. 904) (a *credenziere*). For kennelman Guglielmotto "Franzoso," see entry in 1473 draft budget (28 Nov. 1472; ASMi, AS, c. 909).

56. "Quaternus novarum provisionum . . ." showing pay for various officials as of 1466–1468 (ASMi, AS, c. 885). For chancellor's pay, see Galeazzo to masters of revenues and A. Anguissola, 20 Jan. 1470 (ASMi, RM, no. 91, fo. 160r).

57. See detailed (but partial) pay list for the Pavia Castle garrison headed "1472. Infrascritti sonno li p[ro]visionati ch[e] se ritrovano nel Castello de pavia . . ." (ASMi, Autografi, 229); and a full list of "provisonati Balestrerei et schioppiteri ducali" assigned to Porta Giovia and Corte Arengo as of February 25, 1469 (ASMi, AS, c. 1602). By 1476, the pay of 1,251 infantry and 200 gunners at Porta Giovia had risen to 2 ducats each; their 74 *capi* received 3 ducats (gunners) or 4 ducats (infantry) each (Galeazzo to Alessandro da Foligno, 19 Oct. 1476, ASMi, RM, no. 124, fo. 72v).

58. See n. 57 and Galeazzo to A. Anguissola, 3 Mar. 1473, Vigevano (ASMi, AS, c. 913).

59. "Reverendi & Mag[nifi]ci d[omi]ni de ducale Consilio Secreto pro anno 1476" (ASMi, AS, c. 929). For explanation of which councillors were paid, see Zaccaria Saggi da Pisa to Ludovico Gonzaga, 22 Dec. 1475, Milan (ASMa, AG, b. 1625). Compare to a 1463 list of 13 councillors, most paid at 60 florins (24 ducats) per month (SSL, Raccolta Formentini, cod. 5, fo. 97r). In 1469, five councillors were not paid salaries for that office, "because [each] has his separate salary," which would be supplemented for expenses (Galeazzo to *regolatori* and masters of revenues, 8 Feb., ASMi, RM, no. 89, fo. 114v).

60. "Ratio d. Mri. Johanne mathey de Gradi" [no date] (ASMi, AS, c. 887); Galeazzo to masters of revenues and A. Anguissola, 9 Feb. 1470 (ASMi, RM, no. 91, fo. 189r).

61. Galeazzo's favorite source for such revenues was the Val di Lugano; see, e.g., Galeazzo to A. Anguissola, 15 and 25 Feb. 1469, Vigevano (ASMi, AS, c. 887); and to masters of ordinary revenues and A. Anguissola, 31 May 1470, Pavia [draft] (ASMi, AS, c. 893).

62. Galeazzo to A. Anguissola, 16 Mar. 1472, Milan (ASMi, AS, c. 904).

63. Santoro, *Uffici,* 205; De'Rosmini, *Istoria di Milano,* IV: 108–110. For fiefs' replacing salaries, see, e.g., unheaded list; on reverse: "1474. Liste facte delanno 1474 ma renovate vz. de camerieri" (ASM, AS, c. 925).

64. Ducal registers are full of such grants; see, e.g., ASMi, *Registri Ducali*, nos. 174–177, *passim*, or Santoro, *Registri delle lettere ducali*, 168.

65. 10 Jan. 1476 (ASMi, RM, no. 122, fo. 264r).

66. Galeazzo to masters of revenues and A. Anguissola, 9 Feb. 1470 (ASMi, RM, no. 91, fo. 189r) (salary), and Galeazzo to Caterina, widow of Antonio Eustachi (?), 3 Apr. 1470 (ASMi, RM, no. 92, fo. 190v) (bride search); see also Galeazzo to castellan of Porta Giovia Castle (Filippo Eustachi), 9 May 1470, Pavia [draft] (ASMI, AS, c. 893). When Giovanni went with Sforza Maria on a trip to Venice, he had to find a substitute for his university lectures (Galeazzo to G. Ghiringhelli, 6 Jan. 1471, ASMi, RM, no. 97, fo. 63r).

67. SSL, cod. 5, fo. 110v (lectureship); and Galeazzo to masters of revenues and A. Anguissola, 5 Jan. 1473 (ASMi, RM, no. 109, fo. 123r) (gift).

68. See Appendix 2; Simonetta, *Diari,* 104–105; Galeazzo to G. Giapanno, 29 Sep. 1472 (ASMi, RM, no. 105, fo. 262) (Sigismondo da Bohemia); Galeazzo to G. Giapanno, 9 Feb. 1470 (ASMi, RM, no. 91, fo. 187r) (Galeazzo Manfredi).

69. For Francesco Pietrasanta (*primo cameriere* in 1475), see chap. 7. Gerolamo Beccaria (*primo cameriere* in 1470) was the son of a ducal *cameriere* (Sitoni di Scozia, ASMi, *Acquisto Riva Finolo,* 4, fo. 10r; and Galeazzo to A. Anguissola, 14 Nov. 1470, Vigevano, ASMi, Sforzesco, 896). For Giovanni Francesco Attendoli, see chap. 2. Pietro Birago's uncle Andrea was principal *cameriere* to Filippo Maria Visconti (see charter of investiture, 2 Dec. 1471, Vigevano, ASMi, Notarile, f. 1580).

70. For early references, see Galeazzo to L. Suardi, 20 June 1468 (ASMi, RM, no. 83, fo. 306r) (Galeazzo's wedding), and letters dated 28 June 1468 (ASMi, RM, no. 83, fos. 349r–v) (investiture with fiefs of Ludovico da Barbiano). Niccolò's father, Egidio, left the duchy in 1473, and Niccolò received his fief (investiture, 9 Apr., Abbiategrasso, ASMi, AS, c. 1540). Father and son were included in the first two versions of the Sala Grande fresco program.

71. Z. Saggi to L. Gonzaga, 5 Feb. 1473, Milan (ASMa, AG, b. 1624).

72. See chap. 4.

73. See draft of feudal investiture for Ronchetto, 20 Dec. 1474 ("1 januari 1475" lined out), ASMi, AS, c. 925. The presence of *camerieri di camera* near the ducal person is evident in lists of witnesses from documents.

74. "1474. Pacta et conventione facte inter d. Antonietum et d. Karlinum Varesinum," ASMi, Famiglie, 195 (Varesini). Illnesses were excused.

75. Antonietto's surname was rarely used in ducal lists, although acknowledgment of his knightly title was used often. An equivalent translation to this combination ("d. Antonietto") might be "Sir Little Anthony"; see, e.g., Appendix 2; lists in ASMi, AS, c. 925; and Cicco Simonetta, *Diari,* 106. For surname, see ASMi, RM, no. 110, fos. 22r and 32v.

76. Galeazzo to masters of ordinary revenues, 22 June 1472 (ASMi, RM, no. 109, fo. 61v) ("baby"); see related letters on fos. 60r, 64r, and 127r. For Giov. Antonio's seeking money, see, e.g., his letter to Galeazzo, 11 June 1472, Milan (ASMi, AS, c. 905). The *cameriere* was married by 1476, when his wife received ducal assistance in collecting a debt (Galeazzo to captain of Lomellina; 4 July 1476, ASMi, RM, no. 123, fo. 270v).

77. Galeazzo to Tristano Sforza, 21 May 1468, Milan [copy] (ASMi, AS, c. 1461).

78. E.g., Galeazzo to G. Simonetta, 3 May 1475 (2 letters) (ASMi, RM, no. 120, fo. 201r); and G. Simonetta to Galeazzo, 18 May, Milan (ASMi, AS, c. 926).

79. "Lista de li ducali camereri de camera quali vole lo n[ost]ro Ill[ustrissi]mo

Sig[no]re siano vestiti prout infra," 9 Nov. 1472, Galliate; Gottardo Panigarola to Galeazzo, 18 Nov. 1472, Milan; Galeazzo to A. Anguissola, 14 and 23 Nov., Milan (all ASMi, AS, c. 909). Galeazzo used all the gold and silver brocade in Milan for this purpose (Z. Saggi to L. Gonzaga, 16 Nov. 1472, Milan, ASMa, AG, b. 1624).

80. See Appendix 2 and household list in Porro, "Lettere" (1879): 261–264.

81. For the salaries and household numbers of *camerieri di camera* and *di guarda-camera* as of January 1474, see unheaded list (composed before 6 Jan.), labeled on the reverse: "1474. Liste facte delanno 1474 ma renovate vz. de camereri" (ASMi, AS, c. 925). Some received no salaries, because they had income from estates granted by Galeazzo.

82. Galeazzo to *regolatori* and masters of revenues, 28 Jan. 1469 (ASMi, RM, no. 89, fo. 81r).

83. Galeazzo to A. Anguissola, 5 Mar. 1469 (ASMi, RM, no. 86, fo. 41v); to Pietro Pasino, podestà of Cremona, 10 Sep. 1469 and 25 Nov. 1469 (ASMi, RM, no. 87, fos. 25r and 85r); and to Guglielmo "Guazardo," 4 Mar. 1473 (ASMi, RM, no. 110, fo. 146r; also ASMi, RM, no. 109, fos. 130v and 135r). Antonio represented one of Naples' greatest families; his branch were the Caraccioli Pisquizio, counts of Nicastro (Galvani, *Galleria Araldica,* "Caraccioli").

84. For revenues and fiefs, see Galeazzo to A. Anguissola, 3 Mar. 1473, Vigevano; ASMi, AS, c. 913; to masters of ordinary revenues, 26 Mar. 1470 (ASMi, RM, no. 95, fo. 52r); and to Gabriele Paleari, 28 Nov. 1473, Vigevano (ASMi, AS, c. 915); investiture dated 3 Sep. 1473, Vigevano (ASMi, AS, c. 1540); and *cameriere* lists in ASMi, AS, c. 922. For dismissal and pay docking, see Galeazzo to Domenico Guiscardo, 31 Aug. 1471 (ASMi, RM, no. 99, fo. 120r), and to A. Anguissola, 20 Nov. 1471, Vigevano (ASMi, AS, c. 902).

85. ASMi, *Feudi Camerali,* 260 (first grant); Galeazzo to *referendario* of Novara, and to people of Galliate, 19 July 1469 (ASMi, RM, no. 86, fo. 114r (first confiscation and restoration); Galeazzo to *referendario* of Novara and to people of Galliate, 2 Aug. 1470 (ASMi, RM, no. 95, fo. 158r) (second confiscation); Galeazzo to *referendario* of Novara, 6 Jan. 1471 (ASMi, RM, no. 99, fos. 2v–3r) (second restoration).

86. Galeazzo to A. Anguissola and masters of ordinary revenues, 21 Apr. 1471, Abbiategrasso (ASMi, AS, c. 899) (tax). A list dated 25 Apr. 1471 shows Battista with annual incomes of 1,000 ducats from salt tax in Galliate, 610 ducats from Galliate, and 130 ducats from tax on horses (ASMi, AS, c. 1603). For his father at court, see Galeazzo to Giovanni Antonio Romari da Montignana, 1 June 1471, Pavia [draft] (ASMi, AS, c. 900) (travel expenses); and Galeazzo to *commissario* of Alessandria and Tortona, 27 Aug. 1471 (ASMi, RM, no. 101, fo. 243r) (*podesterìa*).

87. Galeazzo to Giacomo della Torre, bishop of Parma, 17 Dec. 1471 (ASMi, RM, no. 102, fo. 271r).

88. Galeazzo to masters of revenues and A. Anguissola, 28 Sep. 1472 (ASMi, RM, no. 109, fo. 98v) (nonpayment); to masters of ordinary revenues and A. Anguissola, 3 Jan. 1473 (ASMi, RM, no. 109, fo. 122v) (cancellation of repayment); and to podestà, *commissario,* and men of Galliate, 6(?) Oct. 1472 (ASMi, RM, no. 110, fo. 85r) (money owed by town); Giacomo della Torre to Galeazzo, 17 Nov. 1472, Milan (ASMi, AS, c. 909).

89. "Translatione et diminutione de salarij facti . . . de li camereri" [undated but after 23 Mar. 1474] (ASMi, AS, c. 922). Compare with lists in Appendix 2 and Simonetta, *Diari,* 106.

90. "Translatione et diminutione . . ." (ASMi, AS, c. 922).

91. "Dinari exbursati di quali resto haverne li buletini" [undated] (ASMi, AS, c. 1604).

92. Corio, *Storia di Milano*, II: 1400. The *gentiluomini* serving at court also numbered twelve, except at special occasions; see below. For examples of *camerieri* sent-ahead to prepare lodgings, see ASMi, RM, no. 72, fos. 172v, 174r, 196v–197r, 281r, 354r, and 371r; and no. 75, fo. 199r.

93. Galeazzo to Acciarrito Portinari, 29 Sep. 1475 (ASMi, RM, no. 122, fo. 135v), and 2 Nov. 1476 (ASMi, RM, no. 124, fo. 82r) (Giacometto); Ghinzoni, "Rettifiche alla storia di Bernardino Corio," 60 (Bernardino del Missaglia to Denmark); Galeazzo to A. Anguissola, 4 Feb. 1470 (ASMi, RM, no. 91, fo. 177v) (gift delivery).

94. On Gaspare Caimi and the table silver, see, e.g., Galeazzo to A. Anguissola, 16 Feb. 1469 (ASMi, RM, no. 86, fo. 29r); and Galeazzo to Gaspare Caimi, 4 Nov. 1472 (ASMi, RM, no. 110, fo. 108r). For Francesco Pagnani and jewelry, see ASMi, AS, c. 1483-argenterie, gioie, etc.-Galeazzo, *passim*.

95. In a grant of water rights dated July 26, 1468, Pietro is called "camerarius et superior aucupator" (Pavia; ASMi, AS, c. 885); he appears on every list of *camerieri di camera* through the reign and was involved with hawking at least as late as October 1475 (Porro, "Lettere" [1879]: 254).

96. Corio (1978), II: 1373. Vercellino was a first cousin of Margherita Visconti Crivelli (Litta, d. 12, t. XIV).

97. Gottardo Panigarola to Galeazzo, 18 Feb. 1471, Milan (ASMi, AS, c. 898), and Corio (1978), II: 1380 (Florence trip); M. Andreasi to Barbara Hohenzollern Gonzaga, 27 June 1466 (ASMa, AG, b. 1624) (household office); Galeazzo to Marchetto Marliani, temporary custodian of Trezzo Castle, 15 Jan. 1475 (ASMi, RM, no. 120, f. 13v) (castellany). See also Litta, d. 12 (Visconti), t. 4.

98. "Lista de li denari a dare via Johane da Verona . . ." (undated, but internal evidence suggests 1470; ASMi, AS, c. 1483-spese-Ludovico [*sic*]) (gambling debt); Beltrami, *Castello* (1894): 280 and 366 (fresco commissions); Galeazzo to Carlo Favagrossa da Cremona, 19 Jan. 1470 (ASMi, RM, no. 95, fo. 9v) (dogs); Galeazzo to masters of ordinary revenues, 24 Oct. 1473, Pavia (ASMi, AS, c. 914) (expenditures).

99. See Galeazzo's will, 18 May 1470, Pavia [draft] (ASMi, AS, c. 1461). For lists, see Appendixes 2 and 5.

100. For Goffino's return from Naples, see *Diari,* 61. The 1476 reports on the mistress are in letters from Alessandro da Cotignola and/or Daniele da Palude to Galeazzo, 25 Aug. (ASMi, AS, c. 1462), 26 Aug. and 16 Oct. (ASMi, AS, c. 931), and 21 Nov. (ASMi, AS, c. 932), all from Milan.

101. Galeazzo to Ambrosino da Longhignana, 18 Aug. 1473, Pavia (ASMi, AS, c. 914). With Galeazzo's help, Goffino's sister married a physician from Pizzighettone, who was then named the town's official physician, with a ducal salary (ASMi, RM, no. 103, fos. 183r and 356v).

102. E.g., list headed "1471" in ASMi, AS, c. 1603; some payments to "certi nostri secreti" may have been to spies (e.g., "al Fra di Pisa"), not lovers.

103. Porro, "Lettere" (1879): 256–257.

104. For numbers, see, e.g., Porro, "Lettere" (1879): 256–257 (30 *staffieri*) and Appendix 2 (26). For pay, see Galeazzo to Antonio Anguissola, 3 July 1470, Pavia (ASMi, AS, c. 894), showing a new *staffiere* receiving 8 florins per month 10 times per year, "as for our other *staffieri*." For withholding of pay, see that letter and others

to Antonio, dated 17 Oct. 1471. Cassino (two letters in ASMi, AS, c. 901); 6 June 1472, Pavia [draft], and 14 July 1472, Bereguardo (ASMi, AS, c. 905).

105. ASMi, AS, c. 1604. "El Sig[no]re Buffone" is listed with *ragazzi* there, as he was in 1463 (SSL, RF, cod. 5, fo. 144v). "Signore Buffone" turns up also with stable staff awaiting payment for 1476: "Lista de li Officiali e Famigli de la duchale stalla quali restano h[ave]re da Joh[an]e Antonio da S[an]c[t]o Angello p[er] resto de la provisone loro delan[n]o 1476" (ASMi, AS, c. 1604).

106. For new *galuppo,* see Galeazzo to Dombello Riccardi and to Giovanni Francesco Attendoli, 17 May 1469 (ASMi, RM, no. 89, fo. 310v). The *galuppi* were included with the court for 1475 San Giorgio preparations (Porro, "Lettere" [1879]: 255–256) and were mentioned in Galeazzo's first will (18 May 1470, Pavia, ASMi, AS, c. 1461). For activities, see, e.g., Galeazzo to Dombello Riccardi or his lieutenant Gerolamo, 7 Jan. 1468, Milan [draft]; Dombello to Galeazzo, 6 June 1468, Galbiate (ASMi, AS, c. 886-ducato).

107. Galeazzo to Luigi Pietrasanta, 28 Mar. 1472, Milan (ASMi, AS, c. 904).

108. Galeazzo to L. Pietrasanta, 25 July 1472, Gonzaga (ASMi, AS, c. 905), and to A. Anguissola, 18 Mar. 1473, Milan (ASMi, AS, c. 913).

109. Servants working for members of the court are reflected in traveling lists such as Appendix 2; they generally account for the extra numbers of "mouths" or "horses" beyond the persons of the named figures.

110. Galeazzo to Gottardo Panigarola, 30 Jan. 1470 (ASMi, RM, no. 91, fo. 177v).

111. For Emmanuele's travels with the household, see Appendixes 2 and 5. For his confinements to Porta Giovia, see Galeazzo to Filippo Eustachi, castellan of Porta Giovia, 19 Nov. 1472 (ASMi, RM, 110bis, fo. 29v), and Galeazzo to Ambrosino da Longhignana, 6 and 7 Sep. 1473, Pavia (ASMi, AS, c. 914).

112. "Pacti et conventioni fra el n[ost]ro Ill[ustrissi]mo S[igno]re et Bassano da Lode, ducale sarto," 24 Aug. 1470, Monza (ASMi, AS, c. 894).

113. For the *gentiluomini* as of January 1, 1469, see ASMi, RM, no. 89, fos. 50v–51r.

114. For Carlo as *gentiluomo,* see, e.g., Galeazzo to G. Giapanno, 7 Jan. 1468 (ASMi, RM, no. 81, fo. 5v); and 17 Jan. 1469 (ASMi, RM, no. 89, fo. 51r). He has held the hunting office under Duke Francesco (Santoro, *Uffici,* 183).

115. Giuliano's father, Marchese da Varese, called himself a "marchese senza marchesato" (letter to Galeazzo, 16 Jan. 1469, Milan; ASMi, AS, c. 887). Giuliano was marquess of Clivio (Santoro, *Uffici,* 112). When the marchese died, Giuliano asked Galeazzo's help in keeping executors from plundering the estate (Galeazzo to Privy Council, 12 Feb. 1472; ASMi, RM, no. 106, fo. 39r). Giuliano began his career as a military captain, and he continued to serve as such even after becoming a courtier (Marchese da Varese to Galeazzo, 1 May 1467, Milan, ASMi, AS, c. 880; "Giostratori che giostrarano el di de Sancto Zorzo" [1469], ASMi, RM, no. 89, fo. 215r–v; Porro, "Lettere" [1878]: 266).

116. Giovanni Gabriele presented a petition (*supplicatione*) from Stefanina da Corte to Bona; a decision was rendered February 8, 1474, at Pavia (ASMi, AS, c. 922).

117. Galeazzo to Bianca Maria, 20 Feb. 1468 (ASMi, RM, no. 81, fo. 133v). The *compagni* were termed Bona's "gentiluomini" in 1474 lists (e.g., Simonetta, *Diari,* 103).

118. Galeazzo to Maria da Gallarate, 16 and 21(?) June 1469 (ASMi, RM, no. 88, fos. 15r and 28v).

119. Santoro, *Uffici,* xx, cites two sources for Francesco's era, showing the Privy Council with 12 and 15 members, respectively.

120. Galeazzo to *regolatori* and masters of revenues, 31 Jan. 1469 (ASMi, RM, no. 89, fo. 91r), and document headed "Reverendi & Mag[nifi]ci d[omi]ni de ducale consilio Secreto pro anno 1476 alio non aparente" (ASMi, AS, c. 929).

121. Galeazzo to Vincenzo Amidani (secretary of Privy Council), 18 Jan. 1469 (ASMi, RM, no. 89, fo. 53r), and lists in preceding note.

122. Galeazzo to Cicco, 16 Sep. 1466, Candia (Lomellina) (ASMi, AS, c. 878). Michele's formal appointment is dated 25 Aug. 1466, three weeks before the duke actually gave his approval (Santoro, *Uffici,* 9). For Taddeo Manfredi and Bartolomeo Scala, see Santoro, *Uffici,* 11.

123. The archbishop of Milan was Stefano Nardini; he served the Sforza as a diplomatic agent (Santoro, *Uffici,* 7; Cerioni, *Diplomazia Sforzesca,* I: 197).

124. Galeazzo to Cicco, 22 Feb. 1470 (ASMi, RM, no. 92, fo. 150v).

125. The Privy Council changed its Milan venue on occasion; in June 1475, they asked to use a chamber in the Corte Arengo where Bianca Maria had slept. They were denied the use of that chamber but permitted the use of another one in the Corte (ASMi, RM, no. 122, fo. 14r). See also a change of rooms in August 1473 (Galeazzo to Bartolomeo Gadio da Cremona, 5 Aug.; ASMi, RM, no. 112, fo. 88v). See also Filippo Corio to Galeazzo, 25 Sep., Milan (ASMi, AS, c. 914), for renovations of the Corte for the Privy Council. For records of some Privy Council meetings from April to June 1474, see ASMi, AS, c. 926. Simonetta, *Diari,* records 19 Privy Council meetings from 1473 to 1476.

126. Galeazzo to Branda Castiglione, to Giovanni Pallavicino, to Antonio da Correggio, to Pier Maria Rossi, to Antonio da Romagnano, and to Gerolamo Spinola, 1 Aug. 1474 (ASMi, RM, no. 118, fo. 100v).

127. Giovanni Ludovico Pallavicino to Galeazzo, 12 and 31 July 1468, Milan (ASMi, AS, c. 885); and Galeazzo to Giovanni Ludovico, 21 Mar. 1474 (ASMi, RM, no. 115, fo. 182v).

128. Santoro, *Uffici,* xxv-xxvii.

129. E.g., Santoro, *Uffici,* 13, 65, 75, 76 (Antonio Marliani); and Cicco Simonetta, *Diari,* 105 (Franceschino da Castel San Pietro, a *gentiluomo* in 1473).

130. For the treasurer-general's duties, see Santoro, *Uffici,* xxvii-xxviii. Lists of coins brought to him in 1471 and 1473 appear in ASMi, AS, c. 1603.

131. Antonio served from 1469 until his death in 1473. See Santoro, *Uffici,* 109 (appointment); Corio (1978), II: 1374 (French expedition); Galeazzo to Gallassio d'Abbiate, 23 Aug. 1473 (ASMi, RM, no. 112, fo. 150r) (death). He was succeeded by Antonio Landriani (see Calvi, *Famiglie Notabili,* III, Landriani, t. 3; Santoro, *Uffici,* 16, 17, 26, 99. For Landriani's appointment, see Galeazzo to Antonio, 19 Mar. 1474, Pavia (ASMi, AS, c. 922).

132. Antonio appeared in the ducal bedchamber scene of the 1469 fresco program (De'Rosmini, *Istoria di Milano,* IV: 148) and among the *camerieri di camera* in Galeazzo's first will (18 May 1470, Pavia [draft], ASMi, AS, c. 1461).

133. Galeazzo to A. Anguissola, 12 June 1469, Abbiategrasso (ASMi, AS, c. 889) (holiday order); 1 Jan. 1469, Abbiategrasso (ASMi, AS, c. 887) (confinement); and 15 Mar. 1472, Vigevano (ASMi, AS, c. 904) (vacation).

134. Galeazzo to *regolatori* and masters of revenues, 14 Aug. 1468 (ASMi, RM, no. 84, fo. 172v).

135. Giacomo Malumbra to Cicco, 13 Sep. 1475, Milan (ASMi, AS, c. 927). For other instances of Cicco's separation from Galeazzo, see ASMi, AS, c. 923 (Aug. 1474) and 925 (Oct.–Nov. 1474).

136. Simonetta, *Diari,* 111 and 175–176, respectively.

137. For councillor applying through Cicco, see Tommaso Tebaldi da Bologna to Cicco, 12 Feb. 1474, Milan (ASMi, AS, c. 922); for ducal brother, see Filippo Sforza to Cicco, 15 Aug. 1471, Vimodrone (ASMi, AS, c. 902). For a feudatory who suffered Cicco's enmity, see Giovanni Borromeo's entry in *DBI,* XIX: 53–55.

138. Santoro, *Uffici,* 363 and 374, note (fiefs). For Cicco's family affairs, see ASMi, AS, c. 1083, devoted wholly to his papers; also letters from Giovanni Antonio Girardi da Pavia (a chancellor) to Cicco dating from 1472 (ASMi, AS, c. 905 and 906) and 1475 (ASMi, AS, c. 927).

139. See marriage contract, 20 Apr. 1471, Milan (ASMi, AS, c. 1538); Zaccaria Saggi and Orfeo da Ricavo were among the witnesses. See also Litta, d. 3, t. 1.

140. Santoro, *Uffici,* 31 and 54; ASMi, RM, no. 86, 50v (chancellor *de camera*); Galeazzo to *regolatori* and masters of revenues, 5 Jan. 1469 (ASMi, RM, no. 89, fo. 34r) (replacing Pietro Pagnani); Welch, "Galeazzo and Castello di Pavia," 373 (fresco program); Galeazzo to masters of revenues, to A. Anguissola, and to *vicarius provisionum Mediolani,* 1 Dec. 1472 (ASMi, RM, no. 110bis, fos. 77v–78r; also printed in Porro, "Lettere" [1878]: 116) (dividing correspondence duties); document giving leave from service, 26 Apr. 1474 (ASMi, AS, c. 923).

141. "Aquilanus" to Galeazzo, 8 Nov. 1467, Milan (ASMi, AS, c. 882).

142. Santoro, *Uffici,* xxiv. This division of responsibility is still visible in the way certain records are organized in the ducal archives.

143. Evidence of Bartolomeo's work appears throughout the Sforza archives; ASMi, Autografi, c. 96, is devoted to him. For secondary references, see especially Beltrami, *Castello* (1894), and Welch, "Sforza Patronage."

144. For work on Castello, see Beltrami, *Castello.* Danesio was a ducal engineer as early as 1467 (Santoro, *Uffici,* 125). Filippo held his position from at least 1461 (Santoro, *Uffici,* 119 and 121). Benedetto served the Sforza from 1453 (Beltrami, *Castello* [1894]: 194).

145. Initial paving order (dated 4 Sep. 1470) in Santoro, *Registri delle lettere ducali,* 133; original in ASMi, Registri ducali, no. 3, fos. 215r–217v. Galeazzo appointed a committee (*Deputati super solandis stratis Mediolani*) to oversee paving; see, e.g., ASMi, RM, no. 125, fo. 21v.

146. Galeazzo to *Judici stratarum,* 21 Mar. 1475 (ASMi, RM, no. 120, fo. 125r). Other ducal officials also monitored road conditions for the duke; see, e.g., G. da Castelnovate to Galeazzo, 17 Oct. 1469 (ASMi, AS, c. 890).

147. E.g., "Hector de Marchesis" to Galeazzo, 4 Dec. 1468, Milan (ASMi, AS, c. 886). For more letters from him reporting births and deaths, see ASMi, AS, c. 886, 914, 926, and 927. For commands, see Galeazzo to vicar of archbishop of Milan, 4 Apr. 1472 (ASMi, RM, no. 106, fo. 184r), and to Privy Council, 20 Oct. 1472 (ASMi, RM, no. 105, fo. 312r).

148. Uguzzone Besazia, a noble from Cremona appointed as Bona's *gentiluomo* in 1473 (Simonetta, *Diari,* 103) became temporary *commissario* of Pizzighettone in July

1474 (see letters from Galeazzo in ASMi, RM, no. 119, fos. 88r–v) and still held that office in April 1475 (Galeazzo to Uguzzone, 18 Apr., ASMi, RM, no. 121, fo. 89r). For podestà payments, see, e.g., list (headed "1474") of podestà for 1474–1475, with payments owed for each position (ASMi, AS, c. 922). Alessandro Castiglione (see above) owed 15 ducats for his new post at Novara.

149. Paolo Castiglione to Galeazzo, 10 and 18 Nov. 1470, Milan (ASMi, AS, c. 896). In July 1473, Giovanni Francesco persuaded the duke to grant Paolo (then at Savona) Cremonese citizenship (draft document dated 26 July 1473, Pavia, ASMi, AS, c. 914).

150. The full instructions were to (1) do justice equally for all; (2) be good to friends of the Sforza state, and "guard yourself from . . . partisans of St. Mark" (i.e., Venice); (3) not open gates at night, except for important state matters; (4) take care of grain supplies, and keep in touch with officials locally and in Milan; (5) keep an eye on Venetian activities; (6) keep walls of forts strong; (7) not let any Venetian soldiers spend any nights on Milanese soil; (8) not let any Milanese soldiers get out of hand, and punish them if they do (Galeazzo to Stefano da Onate, 5 Jan. 1469; ASMi, RM, no. 89, fos. 33r–v). For appointment as podestà, see Santoro, *Uffici,* 425; for appointment as *gentiluomo,* see Simonetta, *Diari,* 103.

151. Giorgio da Annone to Galeazzo, 13 June 1468, Parma (ASMi, AS, c. 1463). Giorgio had served Filippo Maria Visconti and Francesco Sforza as a diplomat; appointment to the Privy Council and the Parma post came in 1466. When the Parma position expired in 1468, he became *commissario* of Alessandria and Tortona. He died in July 1472 (Santoro, *Uffici,* 8, 457, and 527).

152. See Santoro, *Sforza,* 138–139; and F. Catalano in Treccani, *Storia di Milano,* VII: 284–285. The Genoese did not even want Galeazzo to stay in the Castelletto (Genoa's fortress) when he was returning from Florence (Galeazzo to vice-governor, 26 Mar. 1471, Carrara, ASMi, RM, no. 98, fo. 252v).

153. Documents on the billeting of troops appear throughout the *Sforzesco* series, especially in *cartelle* 1601–1604. As a special concession in honor of his heir's birth, Galeazzo relieved the Milanese of their obligation to support troops (see chap. 3).

154. Santoro, *Uffici,* 12; Cerioni, *Diplomazia Sforzesca,* I: 165; Welch, "Frescoes for Castello," 183; Beltrami, *Castello* (1894): 368. A 1476 list of councillors ranked Orfeo ninth of 26 ("Reverendi et mag[nifi]ci domini . . ."; ASMi, AS, c. 929); he appears also among the traveling household (Appendix 2 and Visconti, "Ordine dell' esercito sforzesco," 466). For his frequent appearance on witness lists, see ASMi, AS, c. 1535–1542, *passim,* and De'Rosmini, *Istoria di Milano,* IV: 121 and 133.

155. See, e.g., Porro, "Preventivo," 131–132; see also Leverotti, *Crisi finanziaria,* 129, for summaries of other budgets from Galeazzo's reign.

156. See ASMi, AS, c. 1603, for lists of captains and squadrons from 1469 and others dating as early as 1467.

157. See Visconti, "Ordine dell'esercito," and *Storia di Milano,* VIII.

158. For general practices, see Dean, *Land and Power.*

159. Treccani, *Storia di Milano,* VIII; Mallett, *Mercenaries and Their Masters,* 119; Porro, "Lettere" (1878): 267 (*lanze spezzate* commanders).

160. For squad leaders (*capi de squadra*) of the bodyguard and *famiglia* in 1475, see Porro, "Lettere" (1878): 258–259 and 265–266, respectively.

161. See previous two notes; also Welch, "Frescoes for Castello," 181–184; and

Beltrami, *Castello* (1894): 367–370 (fresco programs); Argegni, *Condottieri, capitani e tribuni,* I: 102–103; Calvi, *Famiglie Notabili,* vol. 3, Borri, t. IV. Donato was also a feudatory and a relative of Galeazzo through his del Maino mother.

162. See lists in Visconti, "Ordine dell' esercito," 453–455. The Sforza archives contain extensive lists of ducal condottieri, especially in ASMi, AS, c. 1601–1604. For jousts, see chap. 4.

163. On changes, see chap. 2. Francesco appears near the head of *camerieri* lists throughout Galeazzo's reign.

164. Galeazzo to Giovanni [Ludovico] Pallavicino, 28 Dec. 1475 (ASMi, RM, no. 123). For brother's appointment, see Santoro, *Uffici,* 13, and Cicco Simonetta, *Diari,* 188.

165. Federico Pallavicino to Galeazzo, 29 May 1470, Milan (ASMi, AS, c. 893).

166. Francesco Pietrasanta to Galeazzo, 23 Mar. 1474, Milan (ASMi, AS, c. 922). For the original appointment, see Santoro, *Uffici,* 45; for first removal, see Galeazzo to Council of Justice, 21 Mar. 1474 (ASMi, RM, no. 115, fo. 182r), and to Francesco, 26 Mar. (ASMi, RM, no. 115, fo. 199r). He had become a secretary in 1471 (masters of extraordinary revenues to Galeazzo, 23 Dec. 1471, Milan; ASMi, AS, c. 902). Francesco was reinstated, then removed again when he refused a mission to Corsica, claiming he feared pirates. The duke forgave him, because he was a useful diplomatic agent (ASMi, RM, no. 120, fos. 79r, 80 r–v, 81v, 90v, 91r–v, and 192r; and Francesco to Galeazzo, 25 and 27 Feb. 1475, Milan, ASMi, AS, c. 926). He had been removed from the council post to go on missions abroad; for some of those missions, see Galeazzo to masters of revenues, 7 July 1472 (ASMi, RM, nos. 105, fos. 49r–v); five letters dated 14 Oct. 1472 (ASMi, RM, no. 107, fos. 304r–305r); and Cerioni, *Diplomazia Sforzesca,* I: 209. He became ambassador to France in 1476.

167. Santoro, *Uffici,* 10, 13, 65, and 76; A. Marliani to Galeazzo, 24 Oct. 1475, Milan (ASMi, AS, c. 927). After Antonio was promoted, Fazio Gallerani asked to replace him among the masters of revenues (Fazio to Galeazzo, 18 Dec. 1475, Milan, ASMi, AS, c. 928).

168. Santoro, *Uffici,* xxii, and numerous examples.

169. Calvi, *Famiglie Notabili,* I, Barbiano and Belgioioso, t. II; Santoro, *Uffici,* 9; letter from Galeazzo about renunciation, 21 Nov. 1468 (ASMi, RM, no. 82, fo. 213r).

170. For Pietro's fall in January 1467, see chap. 2. In 1475, he still owed money for cloth consigned to his tailor in 1467 (list dated 1475 of debts owed Gottardo da Seregno, "mercante de drapi de seta," ASMi, AS, c. 926).

171. Papi de Burgo to Galeazzo, 9 July 1467, Milan (ASMi, AS, c. 881).

172. The courtier was Princivalle Lampugnani (G. Giapanno to Galeazzo, 4 Mar. 1467, Milan, ASMi, AS, c. 879).

173. E.g., G. da Castelnovate and L. Suardi to Galeazzo, 28 Feb. 1467, Milan (ASMi, AS, c. 879) (Carlo). The same letter requests that newly hired Gottardo Panigarola be dressed ("vestirli") from the duke's wardrobe. In 1470, Panigarola reminded Galeazzo to provide for Caterina Sforza (see response in ASMi, RM, no. 98, fo. 13v). The same year, her governor, Guido Visconti, made two similar reminders (letter to Galeazzo, 6 Sep. 1470, Milan, ASMi, AS, c. 896; response to second reminder in ASMi, RM, no. 98, fo. 13v).

174. G. da Castelnovate to Galeazzo, 13 Sep. 1467, Milan (ASMi, AS, c. 881).

175. G. Castiglione to Galeazzo, 22 Oct. and 22 Dec. 1467, Milan (ASMi, AS, c. 882).

176. Carlino da Camposilvio (Galeazzo to Filippo Sagramori da Rimini, 1 Oct. 1475; ASMi, RM, no. 124, 4v).

177. See ASMi, RM, no. 91, fo. 172v; Galeazzo to A. Anguissola, 6 Jan. 1471, Cassino (ASMi, AS, c. 898), and 17 Jan. 1472, Vigevano (ASMi, AS, c. 903) (rewards and punishments). For Giovanni Pietro's general background and career, see chap. 7. Giovanni Pietro left for France in early 1473; he may have been upset because he was forced to return money to the ducal treasury (see Galeazzo to A. Anguissola, 6 Apr. 1473, Villanova; ASMi, AS, c. 913). Galeazzo was upset himself over a minor accident he had just suffered; he sent Giovanni Pietro a sarcastic letter suggesting the courtier wait to depart until he knew whether the duke would survive (Galeazzo to "Illustri Regio armorum capitaneo Johanni Petro Bergamino tanquam fratri n[ost]ro carissimo," 13 Mar. 1473, ASMi, RM, no. 113, fo. 6v; see also Z. Saggi to L. Gonzaga, 15 Mar., Milan, ASMa, AG, b. 1624). For Duke Francesco's practice of writing recommendations coded to be ignored, see Ilardi, "Crosses and Carets."

178. See Simonetta, *Diari*, 11, for Giorgio; and ASMi, AS, c. 1476-Drusiana (*passim*) for Drusiana, whose estate had already been stripped.

179. Galeazzo to A. Anguissola, 13 Jan. 1472, Vigevano, and 13 Sep. 1472, Pavia (ASMi, AS, c. 903 and 908, respectively).

180. Bonifacio Aliprandi to Bianca Maria, 28 May 1468, Milan (ASMi, AS, c. 884).

181. ASMi, RM, no. 124, fo. 13r (two letters and one document, all dated 21 Oct. 1475).

182. See chap. 2.

183. See chap. 3.

184. See chap. 3.

185. Galeazzo to G. Giapanno, 5 Mar. 1475 (ASMi, Rm, no. 120, fo. 91v); G. Giapanno to Galeazzo, 6, 7 (two letters), 8, 10, and 12 Mar., Milan (ASMi, AS, c. 926); Porro, "Lettere" (1878): 127.

186. Galeazzo to G. da Castelnovate and G. Giapanno, 31 Oct. 1476 (ASMi, RM, no. 126, fo. 16v).

187. Galeazzo to G. da Castelnovate and G. Giapanno, 8 June 1476 (ASMi, RM, no. 125, fo. 156v); for her given name, see Litta, d. 4 (Trivulzio).

188. Galeazzo to Privy Council, to Andreotto del Maino, and to G. da Castelnovate, 29 May 1471 (ASMi, RM, no. 100, fos. 62r–v).

189. Galeazzo to Privy Council, 7 Apr. 1473 (ASMi, RM, no. 113, fo. 118r).

190. Galeazzo to A. Anguissola, 4 Sep. 1472, Pavia (ASMi, AS, c. 908); and expense list dated 9 Sep., Milan (ASMi, AS, c. 906).

191. The ambassador from Montferrat was not invited to take part (Z. Saggi to L. Gonzaga, 27 Aug. 1471, Milan; ASMa, AG, b. 1624). See also Galeazzo to Privy Council and to G. Giapanno, 23 Aug. (ASMi, RM, no. 100, fo. 289r); Galeazzo to A. Anguissola 23 Aug., Cremona [draft]; G. Giapanno to Galeazzo, 27 and 28 Aug., Milan (ASMi, AS, c. 901). Afterward, Tristano and Beatrice d'Este Sforza thanked Galeazzo for honoring her half-brother (27 Aug., Milan, ASMi, AS, c. 901).

192. For duchess, see Galeazzo to A. Anguissola, 13 Mar. 1469; and G. da Castelnovate and G. Giapanno to Galeazzo, 16 Mar. (both Milan, ASMi, AS, c. 888). For Mauruzzi, see G. da Castelnovate and G. Giapanno to Galeazzo, 18 Mar. 1470, Milan (ASMi, AS, c. 894). For Sanseverino widow, see ASMi, RM, no. 89, fo. 201v; and G. da Castelnovate and G. Giapanno to Galeazzo, 16 Mar. 1469, Milan (ASMi,

AS, c. 888). For Fogliani, see G. Simonetta to Galeazzo, 20 and 22 Sep. 1470, Milan; Tristano Sforza to Galeazzo, 23 Sep., Milan (all ASMi, AS, c. 896). For Maria, see ASMi, RM, no. 91, fo. 107r.

193. Galeazzo to Branda Castiglione and Alessandro Visconti, 24 and 25 Mar. 1473 (ASMi, RM, no. 113, fos. 51r and 55r).

194. Galeazzo to Privy Council, 23 Aug. 1474 (ASMi, RM, no. 118, fo. 132v) (Raffaelle); Galeazzo to Privy Council, 24 Aug. 1469 (ASMi, RM, no. 88, fo. 200v) (Domenico); G. Simonetta to Galeazzo, 28 Nov. 1469, ASMi, AS, c. 890 (Giov. Francesco).

195. M. Andreasi to L. Gonzaga, 26 and 31 Dec. 1472 [O.S.] (ASMa, AG, b. 1624). They may have been mourning Borso d'Este, who had died four months before. For brown clothing as mourning attire, see also Privy Council to Galeazzo, 28 Nov. 1475, Milan (ASMi, AS, c. 928).

6: "To Gain the Friendship of Many Leading Men"

1. Marsilio Andreasi to Ludovico Gonzaga, 18 May 1472, Milan (ASMa, AG, b. 1624).

2. M. Andreasi to L. Gonzaga, 18 and 19 May 1472, Milan (ASMa, AG, b. 1624).

3. Giovanni da Castelnovate and Giovanni Giapanno to Galeazzo, 11 Dec. 1472, Milan (ASMi, AS, c. 909); Baleazzo to G. Giapanno, 3 Nov. (ASMi, RM, no. 105, fo. 349r) (Ordelaffi); Galeazzo to Pietro dal Verme, 4 Nov. (ASMi, RM, no. 107, fos. 338v–339r). See also Zaccaria Saggi da Pisa to Ludovico Gonzaga, 12, 15, 18, 19, and 27 Nov. 1472, Milan (ASMa, AG, b. 1624).

4. Galeazzo to Lantelmina da Vimercate, 3 and 10 Nov. 1472 (ASMi, RM, no. 105, fos. 349r and 363r—passage cited). Lantelmina objected because she had already committed herself to house Francesco Gonzaga (Z. Saggi to L. Gonzaga, 12 Nov. 1472, ASMa, AG, b. 1624).

5. G. da Castelnovate and G. Giapanno to Galeazzo, 7 Dec. 1472; Galeazzo to Antonio Anguissola, 24 Dec. 1472 (both Milan, ASMi, AS, c. 909); Galeazzo to G. da Castelnovate and/or G. Giapanno, 9, 12, 13, and 14 Dec. (ASMi, RM, no. 110bis, fos. 107r–v, 117r, 122r, 123v, 127v, and 130r).

6. Giovanni Antonio Girardi to Cicco, 29 Oct. 1472, Milan (ASMi, AS, c. 908), and 6 Nov. 1472, Milan (ASMi, AS, c. 909).

7. G. A. Girardi to Cicco, 6 Nov. 1472, Milan (ASMi, AS, c. 909).

8. See Appendix 3, the Christmas invitation list for 1472.

9. Giovanni Arcimboldi and Giovanni Andrea Cagnola to Galeazzo, 14 Dec. 1472, Rome (copied in Biblioteca Ambrosiana, *Codex Ducalis Cancelleriae Mediolani 1476*, fo. 68v).

10. Maspes, "Prammatica," 148–150.

11. Privy Council to Galeazzo, 2 Dec. 1472, Milan (ASMi, AS, c. 909). See also Galeazzo to Giovanni Simonetta and to Privy Council, 1 Dec. 1472 (ASMi, RM, no. 110bis, fo. 77r). Galeazzo told them to meet with the seneschals-general and determine precedence among Ludovico Gonzaga, Pino Ordelaffi of Forlì, Taddeo Manfredi of Imola, Giovanni Bentivoglio of Bologna, Roberto da Sanseverino, and Giovanni Conti.

12. Z. Saggi to L. Gonzaga, 23 Oct. 1472, Pavia, and 2 and 4 Dec. 1472, Milan

(ASMa, AG, b. 1624); in a letter to Galeazzo, 2 Dec. 1472, Milan (ASMi, AS, c. 909), the envoy argued Ludovico's case.

13. See Welch, "Frescoes for Porta Giovia," 178–179. She notes that Guglielmo was added to the final version of the program, in part because he was Galeazzo's brother-in-law, but his wife, Elisabetta Sforza, had died by the time that version was written (see chap. 4). Both Ludovico and Guglielmo were named as executors for Galeazzo's will, along with Federigo da Montefeltro, Roberto da Sanseverino, Cicco Simonetta, and Bona (ASMi, Archivio Notarile, filza 1580; summarized in Giulini, *Memorie spettanti,* VI: 593–596).

14. Z. Saggi to L. Gonzaga, 16 Nov. 1472, Milan (ASMa, AG, b. 1624); "Lista de li ducali camereri de camera . . . ," 9 Nov., Galliate; and Galeazzo to A. Anguissola, 14, 17, and 23 Nov., Milan (ASMi, AS, c. 909).

15. Filippo became count of Bassignana, Sforza Maria received Sezzadio, and Ludovico was granted the lordships of Domodossola and Corte di Mortarella (Galeazzo to masters of ordinary and extraordinary revenues and A. Anguissola, 27 Dec. 1472; ASMi, RM, no. 110bis, fo. 148r).

16. For the chronology, see Simonetta, *Diari,* 3.

17. Z. Saggi to L. Gonzaga and to Marsilio Andreasi, 7 Jan. 1473, Milan (ASMa, AG, b. 1624). The biblical reference is apocryphal.

18. For ducal letters regarding Gerolamo's visit, see ASMi, RM, no. 107, fos. 158v–159v, 179v, 310v, 337v, 339v, and 353.

19. L. Gonzaga to Cicco, 6 Jan. 1473, Pavia (ASMi, AS, c. 396); Galeazzo to L. Gonzaga, 18 Jan., Pavia [draft] (ASMi, AS, c. 396); and Z. Saggi to L. Gonzaga, 18 Jan., Milan (ASMa, AG, b. 1624). Galeazzo may have planned the Fogliani-Riario match as early as February 1472 (Marsilio Andreasi to L. Gonzaga, ASMa, AG, b. 1624).

20. Galeazzo to L. Gonzaga, 18 Jan. 1473, Pavia [draft] (ASMi, AS, c. 396); see draft will of 18 May 1470, Pavia (ASMi, AS, c. 1471), and final will of 3 Nov. 1471, Pavia (ASMi, Archivio Notarile, f. 1580; summarized in Giulini, *Memorie spettanti,* VI: 593–596). In 1471–1472, the lord of Camerino's heir came to Milan at Christmas, seeking a match with Caterina (ASMi, RM, no. 102, fos. 320v and 373v).

21. *Diari,* 4–5; see also Ghinzoni, "Usi e costume principeschi," and ASMi, AS, c. 1476-Caterina, for lists of marriage gifts from Gerolamo.

22. See testimony from Gerolamo and Matteo da Candia, the main witness against him, 15 and 19 May 1473 (ASMi, AS, c. 1478-Gabriella Sforza/Fogliani).

23. Z. Saggi to L. Gonzaga, 5, 10, and 16 Feb. 1473, Pavia (ASMa, AG, b. 1624). For music, see also chap. 7.

24. Simonetta, *Diari,* 11.

25. Z. Saggi to L. Gonzaga, 26 Feb. 1473, Milan (ASMa, AG, b. 1624).

26. Simonetta, *Diari,* 12–13.

27. For the Arcelli as feudatories, see their oath of fealty, 20 Mar. 1470 (ASMi, AS, c. 1537). Earlier in the century, an Arcelli had declared himself *signore* of Piacenza (Cognasso, *Visconti,* 402). For Carlino's father, see Santoro, *Uffici,* 224, 295, 506; for his father's death, see Bianca Maria to Galeazzo, 31 May 1466, Milan (ASMi, AS, c. 878). The uncle's later success owed something to Carlino's influence; see, e.g., Galeazzo to Giovanni Botta or A. Anguissola, 24 July 1472 (ASMi, RM, no. 110, fo. 7r).

28. For the Cusani, see Calvi, *Famiglie Notabili,* III.

29. For first investiture, see draft document headed "20 dicembre 1474" ("1 januari 1475" lined out) (ASMi, AS, c. 925).

30. "1474. Pacta et conventione facte inter d. Antonietum et d. Karlinum Varesinum" (ASMi, Famiglie, 195-Varesini). Galeazzo gave jewels to the brides; see "Infrascripte sono le zoye consignate al nro. Illmo. Sigre. per mi, Franco. Pagnano, per la dona de Carlino Varexo., die xxvi Februarij 1473, et de d. Antonieto, ducali camareri" (ASMi, AS, c. 1483-spese-Galeazzo).

31. Battista da Cremona to Galeazzo, 28 July 1474, Pavia (ASMi, AS, c. 855). Battista began serving as governor to Galeazzo's son Carlo and supervised both sons briefly, then was assigned to Alessandro alone (Alessandro and Carlo Sforza to Galeazzo, 28 Aug. 1469, Milan, ASMi, AS, c. 889; Andreotto del Maino to Galeazzo, 9 May 1470, Milan, ASMi, AS, c. 893; Galeazzo to Battista da Cremona, "filiorum Ill[ustrissi]mi principis custodi," 26 May 1470, ASMi, RM, no. 95, fo. 88v).

32. Alessandro Sforza to Galeazzo, 15 Mar. 1476, Milan (ASMi, AS, c. 929).

33. Alessandro da Foligno to Galeazzo, 16 Mar. 1473, Milan; ASMi, AS, c. 913. The Della Rocca ruled Corsica for parts of the thirteenth to fifteenth centuries (see Cappelli, *Cronologia,* 323–324).

34. Galeazzo to vice-governor of Genoa, Oct. 1475 (ASMi, RM, no. 124, fo. 10v).

35. The distinction is clear in the original grants: "feudi recti honorifici nobilis & gentilis" (Battista) versus "veri et honorifici" (Tommaso) (grant of Galliate made May 12, 1469, Abbiate; grant of Mandello made January 1, 1469, Milan; both in ASMi, Archivio Notarile, f. 1580).

36. The original list is printed in Crivelli Visconti, *Nobiltà Lombarda,* 7–9, with a different version on 10–11.

37. Cognasso, *Visconti,* 506.

38. The Palazzo Borromeo, destroyed in World War II, was a splendid example. For a good introduction to the subject, see Caroselli, *Casa Marliani.*

39. Mainoni, "L'attività mercantile e la casate milanesi," 577.

40. Santoro printed many examples in *Registri delle Lettere Ducali.*

41. For the red-carpet treatment accorded one Genoese embassy, see Lubkin, "Strategic Hospitality," 181–182.

42. Simonetta, *Diari,* 119–122 and 184–185, lists the "doctors" in Milan and Pavia as of June 11, 1474, and November 18, 1475 (Milan only), respectively.

43. Cognasso, *Visconti,* 31; ASMi, Famiglie, 15; ASMi, Acquisto Riva Finolo, 4, fasc. 10.

44. On the Borromei, see *DBI,* XIX: 53–55, and Cognasso, *Visconti,* 500. On Trivulzio, see De'Rosmini, *GianJacopo Trivulzio.*

45. See Santoro, *Sforza,* 183–184, for the factions' troublesome activity after Galeazzo's death.

46. Bueno de Mesquita, "Ludovico Sforza and His Vassals," 186.

47. Galeazzo's confessors included Paolo di San Genesio, bishop of Eneapolis and suffragan of Milan (Eubel, *Hierarchia Catholica,* II: 180), and Fabrizio Marliani, who succeeded Michele Marliani as bishop of Tortona (see Appendix 2; and Antonio Marliani to Galeazzo, 8 Sep. 1475, Milan, ASMi, AS, c. 927).

48. Just before his death, Galeazzo decided to keep a book in his Chancery which

would list "the titles of all the benefices" and their value in order that when each was vacated, he would know what it was worth (letter to *iconomi* of all major cities in the dominion, 20 Dec. 1476; ASMi, RM, no. 127, fo. 73v).

49. Galeazzo to G. Giapanno and G. da Castelnovate, 20 May 1471 (Porta Orientale), and to G. Giapanno, 9 June 1471 (Porta Romana) (ASMi, RM, no. 100, fos. 41v–42r and 94r–v). The list for Porta Orientale included two senior bishops and the general of the Umiliati.

50. Galeazzo to dominion's bishops, 12 Nov. 1469 (ASMi, RM, no. 87, fo. 70v).

51. *DBI*, III: 776; Santoro, *Uffici*, 9. Giovanni's wife was a cousin of Galeazzo's *cameriere di camera* Francesco Pietrasanta (G. Sitoni di Scozia, *Theatrum Genealogicum*, 347). Before joining the Privy Council, Giovanni was named to the Council of Justice in 1466. He had requested the episcopal appointment (G. Arcimboldi to Galeazzo, 6 Nov. 1467, ASMi, AS, c. 882).

52. G. Arcimboldi to Galeazzo, 17 May 1473, Pavia (ASMi, AS, c. 913).

53. Galeazzo to bishop of Parma (Giacomo della Torre), to Privy Council, and to G. Simonetta, all 19 May 1473 (ASMi, RM, no. 113, fos. 233v, 234r, and 235r). The bishop's colorful reply is relayed in G. Simonetta to Galeazzo, 20 May 1473, Milan (ASMi, AS, c. 913).

54. This description in Simonetta, *Diari*, 31–32, is followed by the three papal briefs and instructions for conducting the actual ceremony.

55. Simonetta, *Diari*, 50–53, lists Riario's household, with the number of *boche* (69), servants (169), horses (225), and beds needed (129).

56. Galeazzo to Luigi Pietrasanta, 9 Sep. 1473, Galliate (ASMi, AS, c. 914).

57. Simonetta, *Diari*, 48–50.

58. For Bessarion's visit, see Lubkin, "Strategic Hospitality," 184.

59. Some historians have argued that Riario's main purpose was to cement an alliance between Milan and Venice; see F. Catalano in Treccani, *Storia di Milano*, VII: 287–288. At the other extreme, Corio accuses the Venetians of poisoning the cardinal because of Riario's new friendship with Galeazzo (*Storia di Milano*, II: 1393). Corio's account of the visit generally corroborates Cicco's but adds his usual exaggerations.

60. See biographies by Breisach, Pasolini, and Graziani/Venturelli.

61. Treccani, *Storia di Milano*, VII: 276–279; Santoro, *Uffici*, 11.

62. G. da Castelnovate to Galeazzo, 21 Dec. 1468, Milan (ASMi, AS, c. 886) (Christmas lodgings); Galeazzo to G. Giapanno, 9 Feb. 1470 (ASMi, RM, no. 91, fo. 187r (Galeazzo Manfredi); Galeazzo to A. Anguissola, 28 Jan. 1471, Vigevano (ASMi, AS, c. 898) (stipend); Santoro, *Uffici*, 11 (Privy Council); Treccani, *Storia di Milano*, VII: 276–279.

63. Galeazzo to officials in Parma, Piacenza, and Pavia, late Jan. 1472 (ASMi, RM, no. 103, fos. 141v–142v); and list of "Li infrascripti sono che ha venir con lo Ill[ustrissimo] S[igno]re d[omi]no Tadeo" (ASMi, AS, c. 903).

64. Luigi Pietrasanta to Giacomo Alfieri, 1 Feb. 1472, Milan (ASMi, AS, c. 903) (halt of expenses); M. Andreasi to L. Gonzaga, 24 Apr., Milan (ASMa, AG, b. 1624) (San Giorgio); Galeazzo to Gabriele Stampa, 24 Sep. (ASMi, RM, no. 105, 237r) (*gentiluomini*); Galeazzo to G. Simonetta and to Privy Council, 1 Dec. (ASMi, RM, no. 110bis, fo. 77r) (Christmas); Taddeo to Galeazzo, 17 Nov. 1472, Milan (requesting

money); Giovanni Avvocati to Galeazzo, 19 and 20 Nov. 1472, Milan (all in ASMi, AS, c. 909); and Galeazzo to G. Avvocati, 18 Nov. (ASMi, RM, no. 110bis, fo. 24r) (arrival of wife and sisters).

65. See ASMi, AS, c. 903, for Taddeo's letters from February and 909 for his 14 Dec. letter. For the first governor, see Galeazzo to Niccolò Pallavicino di Scipione, 26 Feb. 1472 (ASMi, RM, no. 103, fo. 214r); for the replacement, see Galeazzo to G. Stampa, 19 Mar. 1473 (ASMi, RM, no. 113, fo. 32v).

66. Galeazzo to G. Stampa, 19 Mar. 1473 (ASMi, RM, no. 113, fo. 32v); Galeazzo to G. Simonetta, 5 Apr. 1473 (ASMi, RM, no. 113, fo. 111r) (security precautions); G. Simonetta to Galeazzo, 8 Apr., Milan; ASMi, AS, c. 913 (*camerieri*); G. Avvocati to Galeazzo, 3 Feb., Milan; ASMi, AS, c. 911 (Galeazzo Manfredi's flight).

67. Simonetta, *Diari,* 26. According to Cicco, Galeazzo gave Imola immediately to the city of Florence.

68. Stampa and the four *camerieri* were supplemented with four guards by day and eight at night (Ambrosino da Longhignana to Galeazzo, 17 Sep. 1473, Milan; Ambrosino and Alessandro da Foligno to Galeazzo, 2 Oct., Milan; and Ambrosino and Antonio Meraviglia to Galeazzo, 23 Oct., Milan; all ASMi, AS, c. 914).

69. Galeazzo to G. Avvocati and G. Stampa, 30 Mar. 1474 (ASMi, RM, no. 115, fo. 209r).

70. T. Manfredi to Galeazzo, 11 Feb. and 14 Feb. 1474, Milan (ASMi, AS, c. 922), and 18 Feb. 1475, Milan (ASMi, AS, c. 926). See ASMi, RM, no. 116, fo. 232r, on his investiture in February 1474 with Bosco; he also received Cusago, where the duke sometimes hunted. Castelnuovo was granted to Roberto da Sanseverino on January 9, 1474 (Simonetta, *Diari,* 77; charter in ASMi, AS, c. 1541); Roberto's son Giovanni Francesco came as proxy on January 14 (ASMi, RM, no. 116, fo. 159r).

71. Galeazzo to Taddeo Manfredi, 10 Oct. 1474 (ASMi, RM, no. 118, fos. 246r–v) (Cusago) and 24 Aug. 1476 (ASMi, RM, no. 125, fo. 330v) (condolences).

72. Guidaccio Manfredi to Galeazzo, 24 Feb. 1474, Milan (ASMi, AS, c. 922); Galeazzo to Ambrosino da Longhignana, 25 Feb. (ASMi, RM, no. 115, fo. 136r) (visit from Taddeo's wife); Fiordelisa to Galeazzo, 22 Apr. 1475, Milan (ASMi, AS, c. 928); Galeazzo to Guidaccio, 20, 24, and 24(?) May (ASMi, RM, no. 120, fos. 248r, 256r, and 257r, respectively); Galeazzo to "fictabilis poss. Cusaghi," 1 June (ASMi, RM, no. 120, fo. 300v).

73. Galeazzo to G. Stampa, 10 Aug. 1473 (ASMi, RM, no. 112, fo. 110v) (Jew); Gabriele to Galeazzo, 7 Oct. 1473, Milan (ASMi, AS, c. 914) (dispute).

74. For Gabriele's career and background, see Litta, d. 132, t. 2; and Santoro, *Uffici,* 98, 147, 187, 554. He became a *gentiluomo* by January 1469 (ASMi, RM, no. 89, fo. 51r). For work with ambassadors, see, e.g., Galeazzo to Niccolò Gambaloito and G. Stampa, 20 Sep. 1471 (ASMi, RM, no. 102, fo. 37v); Galeazzo to G. Giapanno and G. da Castelnovate, 6 Apr. 1474 (ASMi, RM, no. 115, fo. 223r); G. da Castelnovate and G. Giapanno to Galeazzo, 9 Dec. 1475, Milan (ASMi, AS, c. 928), and 13 July 1476, Milan (ASMi, AS, c. 1462).

75. Gabriele excused himself from escorting the Venetian envoy because his wife was suffering complications of childbirth. She died within two weeks (G. Giapanno to Galeazzo, 17 Jan.—cited—and 1 Feb. 1472, Milan; ASMi, AS, c. 903).

76. The average of one per week was derived by dividing the 1,183 days covered

by Cicco's diary by the 167 embassies whose presence he notes. The latter figure includes some consultations with resident envoys but does not include all the embassies that met with the duke. Many entries in the diary are blank, and some embassies to Milan were not recorded by Cicco (e.g., an English visit in 1475; Galeazzo to G. Giapanno, 16 Sep., ASMi, RM, no. 122, fos. 104/c v and 130v).

77. Mattingly, *Renaissance Diplomacy,* 61ff. and 83, respectively. Ilardi, *Dispatches,* III: xiii-xxxi, focuses on Milanese resident ambassadors in France. The Sforza archives abound with documents related to Milanese ambassadors; for the expenses of Antonio d'Appiano in Savoy, see list (headed "1465") in ASMi, AS, c. 926.

78. Mattingly, *Renaissance Diplomacy,* 64, defines resident ambassadors. See also the introduction to Ilardi and Kendall, *Dispatches,* I. For another perspective on the ambassadorial system, see Martines, *Lawyers and Statecraft.*

79. Simonetta, *Diari,* 63, 98; Galeazzo to G. da Castelnovate, 9 June 1475 (ASMi, RM, no. 120, fo. 301v); Galeazzo to G. Simonetta, 8 July 1474 and 28 Aug. 1474 (ASMi, RM, no. 118, fos. 49v and 142r); Galeazzo to Antonio Cicinello, 1 Sep. 1474 (ASMi, RM, no. 118, fo. 153v); ASMi, RM, no. 102, fos. 32v–33r; and Franceschini, "Palazzo dei conti di Urbino."

80. See, e.g., Simonetta, *Diari,* 20, 29, 132.

81. Cerioni conflates Antonio with his uncle "Turco" (*Diplomazia Sforzesca,* I: 266). For correspondence between Galeazzo and Antonio, see ASMi, AS, c. 913 and 914, *passim.* For nephew, see Francesco Pietrasanta to Galeazzo, 5 July 1474, Pavia (ASMi, AS, c. 855).

82. Angelo della Stufa to Galeazzo, 11 and 14 [cited] June 1475, Pavia (ASMi, AS, c. 855); see also letter of 1 July, for a mention of his son Pandolfo.

83. Those serving during Galeazzo's reign included Donato Acciaiuoli (ASF, Map, filza xlviii; Galeazzo to Donato, 13 Feb. 1475, ASMi, RM, no. 120, fo. 54r; and *DBI,* I: 80–82); Tommaso Soderini and Luigi Guicciardini (ASF, MAP, filza xvi, no. 212); Francesco Dini (Galeazzo to officials of Piacenza and Parma, 21 Oct. 1470, ASMi, RM, no. 97, fo. 65r); and Angelo della Stufa (n. 82; and Galeazzo to officials of Piacenza and Parma, 5(?) Oct. 1470, ASMi, RM, no. 97, fo. 40r; Cicco to [unknown], 12 Aug. 1470 [postscript], ASMi, AS, c. 894; and Cerioni, *Diplomazia Sforzesca,* I: 237).

84. "Copia unius partis lrarum. d. Jo. Bapte. ad Camillum" (n.d.; ASMi, AS, c. 890). The letter was probably from Giovanni Battista Coppola of Naples to Camillo Barzi of Urbino. Even the duke's closest allies sometimes spoke ill of him; see, e.g., Z. Saggi to L. Gonzaga, 12 Nov. 1468, Milan (ASMa, AG, b. 1623).

85. E.g., the mission of Giulio da Pisa to Milan on behalf of Naples (Simonetta, *Diari,* 199).

86. Galeazzo used the first person singular for himself (rather than the ducal plural) when writing to his parents; see, e.g., Galeazzo to Bianca Maria, 7 Jan. 1468, Pavia (ASMi, AS, c. 883), in which he asks his mother to use the *tu* toward him again, instead of the more distant *voi* she had adopted. For Galeazzo's use of *tu,* see his letter to Giovanni Francesco de Coconate, 21 Sep. 1474 (ASMi, RM, no. 119, fo. 191v), and Galeazzo to Battista Visconti, 27 Apr. 1474, Milan (ASMi, AS, c. 923). Galeazzo used *voi* to captains of the *lanze spezzate* (see letters from Galeazzo to Alessandro Visconti and to each of the three other captains, 2 June 1474, ASMi, RM, no. 115, fo.

349r); his half-brother Tristano (Galeazzo to Tristano, 21 May 1468, Pavia, ASMi, AS, c. 1461); and his full brother Ascanio (Galeazzo to Ascanio, 5 July 1472, Mirabello, ASMi, AS, c. 905).

87. Biblioteca Ambrosiana, *Codex Ducalis Cancelleriae Mediolani 1476,* fos. IIIr and ff. Another ducal titulary was copied into ACM, BT, cod. 1325.

88. See letters of introduction for Tommaso Moroni da Rieti (18 Dec. 1468, Vigevano, ASMi, AS, c. 886).

89. Pietro Rossi to Galeazzo, 8 Sep. 1469, Pavia (ASMi, AS, c. 890) ("servant"); and Filippo Pietrasanta to Galeazzo, 20 July 1473, Milan (ASMi, AS, c. 914) ("dog").

90. E.g., in G. Simonetta to Galeazzo, 21 Feb. 1472, Milan (ASMi, AS, c. 902); Raffaelle da Vimercate to Galeazzo, 2 Sep. 1475, Milan (ASMi, AS, c. 1475); Privy Council to Galeazzo, 3 Oct. 1474, Milan (ASMi, AS, c. 925); and A. Anguissola to Galeazzo, 21 Oct. 1470, Milan (ASMi, AS, c. 896).

91. See Fazio Gallerani to Cicco, 8 Sep. 1469, Milan; Tommaso Tebaldi da Bologna to Cicco, 27 Sep. 1469, Milan; G. Simonetta to Cicco, 28 Sep. 1469, Milan; "Iri de Venegono" to Cicco, 12 Sep. 1469, Milan; Pietro Landriani to A. Anguissola, 15 Sep. 1469, Milan; G. Alfieri to A. Anguissola, 19 Sep. 1469, Milan (all ASMi, AS, c. 890); G. A. Girardi da Pavia to Cicco, 8 Oct. 1475, Milan (ASMi, AS, c. 927).

92. The use of these greetings is described by observers of the various diplomatic visits discussed above and in the following chapters. For Bona, see chap. 2.

93. For invitation list, see ASMi, RM, no. 112, fos. 302r–303r and 332v–334r (reordered). For condottieri, see Galeazzo to Giovanni Conti; to Giovanni Battista Anguillara; and to Roberto da Sanseverino (ASMi, RM, no. 112, fos. 320r–v); and Galeazzo to Pietro dal Verme, 21 Nov. 1473 (ASMi, RM, no. 112, fo. 343r).

94. G. da Castelnovate and G. Giapanno to Galeazzo, 21 June 1468, Milan (ASMi, AS, c. 1463).

95. Simonetta, *Diari,* 65–67.

96. Corio (1978), II: 1393.

97. Galeazzo to G. Giapanno, 21 Oct. 1473, Milan [draft] (ASMi, AS, c. 914). The fifth councillor was Melchiorre Marliani.

98. Note the concern of the ducal administration in Gabriele Paleari to Galeazzo, 26 Nov. 1473, Milan (ASMi, AS, c. 915; numbers not specified). For comparison with earlier totals, see chap. 4.

99. Corio (1978), II: 1393.

100. Of three extant lists of *gentiluomini,* at least two were made by Cicco in late March 1474. One forms the entries for 25–28 Mar. in *Diari,* 101–104. The second (in ASMi, AS, c. 922) is identical but clarifies an ambiguity that led Professor Natale to publish the *Diari* with the names of seven "new gentlemen" (*gentilhomini novi*) under the heading of Bona's "old gentlemen" (*gentilhomini vegi*). The third list, which classifies the *gentiluomini* by cities of origin, is in ASMi, AS, c. 925, with other lists of court personnel.

101. Forty-five of these men were the duke's *gentiluomini,* and 23 the duchess's. Ten of Galeazzo's "old" *gentiluomini* also became supplementary *gentiluomini* to Bona at this time. They may have replaced those on the original list Galeazzo drew up in 1468 (ASMi, RM, no. 81, fo. 133v), although Pietro Maria Malletta appears in both cases.

102. For Gerolamo's background, see chap. 4. Giovanni Andrea was a former

ducal *cameriere* (SSL, RF, cod. 5, fo. 138r), the brother of a trusted civil administrator (Princivalle), and the son of Pietro; he is often confused with two other contemporaries of the same name, a ducal chancellor (son of Maffiolo) and a feudatory/administrator (son of Oldrado). Cerioni conflates the three, an error avoided by Filippo Raffaelli in "Famiglia Lampugnani," 231, t. II. Further clarification of this ambiguity is on the witness list of the pardon for murder granted Giovanni Grande in 1470 (ASMi, AS, c. 1535).

103. Litta, d. 8, t. 1.

104. Galeazzo to podestà and *commissario* of Pontremoli [Alessandro Castiglione], 12 Dec. 1473; to Privy Council, 12 Dec.; and to *commissario* and deputies of Novara, 28 Dec. (ASMi, RM, no. 115, fos. 19r, 20r, and 35r).

105. Declaration dated 30/8/74, Galliate, ASMi, AS, c. 925. In a letter from mid-May, the duke addressed Giovanni Antonio as "vice-podestà of Novara" (ASMi, RM, no. 115, fo. 301r).

106. ASMi, RM, no. 122, fos. 228r and 235r (Galeazzo to Alessandro Castiglione, 20 Dec. 1475); for *cameriere* post, see Appendix 2.

107. Corio (1978), II: 1393.

108. Francesco Birago to Galeazzo, 7 Jan. 1476, Milan (ASMi, AS, c. 929).

109. Galeazzo to *commissari* of Parma, Piacenza, Lodi (and podestà), Como, and Pavia; podestà of Alessandri and Tortona; and lieutenants of Cremona and Novara, 9 Dec. 1473 (ASMi, RM, no. 115, fo. 16r).

110. Simonetta, *Diari,* 61 (Neapolitans' arrival), 104–107 (lists). Most of the twelve Neapolitan youths recruited as *camerieri* in 1473 left the following year (see document headed "Translacione et diminutione. . . ," ASMi, AS, c. 922; and lists of *camerieri* in ASMi, AS, c. 925), but Artusio Pappacoda da Napoli stayed as late as January 1475 (Porro, "Lettere" 1879, 262). For Pietro Minuto's departure, Galeazzo gave him a "license from our official *da le bollette*" and "a letter of passage so that he can return safely to his home" (Galeazzo to G. da Castelnovate, 7 Mar. 1474, ASMi, RM, no. 115, fo. 158v).

111. ASMi, RM, no. 115, fo. 16r (see above). In 1475, Galeazzo asked Giovanni Borromeo to send his eldest son to court. Giovanni had served faithfully on the Privy Council but refused this request. A furious Galeazzo confiscated the count's lands, but Giovanni did not give in, and the duke relented (*DBI,* XIX: 55; Calvi, *Familie Notabili,* II, Borromeo, t. 6; Morbio, *Codice Visconteo-Sforzesco,* 475–477).

112. Corio (1978), II: 1393; "Translacione et diminutione de salarij facti . . . de li camereri"; the document is undated but was composed soon after 23 Mar. 1474 (ASMi, AS, c. 922). The *cameriere* in question was Antonietto Arcelli, and the 80-ducat phrase was lined out and replaced with 150 ducats.

113. Unheaded list; on the reverse: "1474. Liste facte delanno 1474 ma renovate vz. de camereri." The list must have been composed before 6 January.

114. Simonetta, *Diari,* 64.

115. Simonetta, *Diari,* 67–71.

116. Simonetta, *Diari,* 72–74, for the Savoyards' arrival and the festive activities, including the betrothal. Pp. 75–77 have the text of the bishop of Turin's Latin oration to Galeazzo. A draft copy of the betrothal contract (6 Jan. 1474, Porta Giovia Castle) is in ASMI, AS, c. 922.

117. Corio (1978), II: 1394. For repairs to the ceiling, see Bartolomeo Gadio

da Cremona to Galeazzo, 8 and 10 Jan. 1474, Milan (ASMi, Autografi, 88), and Galeazzo to B. Gadio, 22 Jan. 1474 (ASMi, RM, no. 115, fo. 75r).

118. See ASMi, AS, c. 1467 (letters from her governor, Cristoforo da Gallarate); Bona to Giovanni Agostino Olgiati, 8 Apr. 1476, Vigevano; ASMi, AS, c. 931 (wet nurse). After this event, Bianca was generally identified by her presumptive title, "duchess of Savoy."

119. Simonetta, *Diari,* 71 (1474); Crivelli-Visconti, *Nobiltà Lombarda,* 16–18 (1450). See also De'Rosmini, *Istoria di Milano,* IV: 169–172, for GianGaleazzo's ducal investiture in 1478.

120. See, e.g., Appendix 2 and 1475 household list in Porro, "Lettere" (1879): 261–263 (also printed in Morbio, *Codice Visconteo-Sforzesco,* 440–442). The "d." could also indicate an academic degree; see, e.g., lists of ducal singers in Simonetta, *Diari,* 197–198, and Porro, "Lettere" (1878): 255–256.

121. "Lista de li ducali camereri di camera quali vole lo nro. Illmo. Sigre. siano vestiti," 8 Nov. 1472, Galliate (ASMi, AS, c. 909).

122. Barber, *The Knight and Chivalry,* 30.

123. Santoro, *Sforza,* 26.

124. The recipients are listed in Simonetta, *Diari,* 74. For a discussion of mass knighting as a device to draw young nobles together in a court, see Keen, *Chivalry,* 69–70.

125. Besides Giuliano, Giberto, and Carlino, the new knights were Giovanni Francesco Pallavicino di Scipione, Francesco Malaspina di Fosdenovo, Giorgio del Carretto, Galeotto Bevilacqua, Giovanni Francesco Pusterla, Antonio Caracciolo, Marcello Colonna, and a son of Count Manfredo Landi.

126. Galeazzo to Oddo Colonna, 4 Feb. 1474 (ASMi, RM, no. 117, fo. 49r).

127. For the Borromei, see above. For the Pusterla, see chap. 7.

128. Cicco to [unknown], 12 Aug. 1470 [postscript] (ASMi, AS, c. 894).

129. This section has been adapted from a paper given at the American Historical Association annual meeting in 1984.

130. Galeazzo to Bianca Maria, 13 Jan. 1467, Milan (ASMi, AS, c. 879).

131. Galeazzo to podestà of Milan, 30 Sep. 1474 (ASMi, RM, no. 118, fo. 219v). Lorenzo first became a councillor under Duke Francesco (Santoro, *Uffici,* 6); he was appointed auditor-general in 1473, in part because he was a foreigner (from Pesaro), thus free from "all passion" (Galeazzo to Lorenzo, 7 Aug. 1473, ASMi, RM, no. 112, fo. 93v). The position required him to review and act on petitions to the duke.

132. Galeazzo to G. Simonetta, 19 Feb. 1474, Mortara; ASMi, AS, c. 922.

133. G. Simonetta to Galeazzo, 23 Feb., and Luigi Castiglione to Galeazzo, 26 Feb. 1474, both Milan (ASMi, AS, c. 922).

134. Genealogical material on the Castiglioni and Pallavicini derives from Litta, d. 8 and 90, respectively.

135. Galeazzo to G. Simonetta, 19 Mar. 1474 (ASMi, RM, no. 115, fo. 175v).

136. Galeazzo to Maddalena Torelli, 22 Feb. 1474, Vigevano [draft] (ASMi, AS, c. 922).

137. Material on the Malletta has been drawn from various sources, including undated petitions in ASMi, Famiglie, c. 113-Malletta.

138. Giuliano was an "alevo" of Galeazzo (Giovanni Antonio and Francesco Bigli to Galeazzo, 3 Mar. 1476, ASMi, AS, c. 929). For his uncle's name (Bartolomeo

Piccinino da Locarno), see Galeazzo to Luca Crotti, 30 Nov. 1476 (ASMi, RM, no. 126, fo. 55v).

139. Galeazzo to Cristoforo Gioche, 19 Mar. 1475 (ASMi, RM, no. 120, fo. 122v); Giovanni Antonio and Francesco Bigli to Galeazzo, 3 Mar. 1476 (ASMi, AS, c. 929); Galeazzo to Giovanni Antonio and Francesco, 25 May, Pavia [draft] (ASMi, AS, c. 931).

140. Antonio "de Pizonibus" and Caterina "dil fu Johane de Cremona" to Galeazzo, 6 Aug. 1476, Milan (ASMi, AS, c. 931).

141. Galeazzo to G. Giapanno, 23 Nov. 1469 (ASMi, RM, no. 91, fo. 49v).

142. Galeazzo to Privy Council, 17 Feb. 1474; Galeazzo to G. da Castelnovate and G. Giapanno, 19 Feb. and 20 Feb. (ASMi, RM, no. 115, fos. 127v–128r, 129r, and 131v, respectively). Passage cited from Z. Saggi to L. Gonzaga, 22 Feb., Milan (ASMa, AG, b. 1624).

143. For details of entry, see Simonetta, *Diari,* 95–97; and Z. Saggi to L. Gonzaga, 14 and 16 Mar. 1474, Milan (ASMa, AG, b. 1624). For preparations, see Galeazzo to G. Giapanno and/or G. da Castelnovate, 3, 5, 9, 10, and 11 Mar.; Galeazzo to *commissario* of Como, 9 Mar. (ASMi, RM, no. 115, fos. 150v, 154r–v, 165r–169r); G. Giapanno to Galeazzo, 25 Feb., Milan (ASMi, AS, c. 922); Z. da Pisa to L. Gonzaga, 2 and 11 Mar., Milan (ASMa, AG, b.1624).

144. Galeazzo paid for the baldacchino with funds drawn from the clergy.

145. Galeazzo to G. da Castelnovate and G. Giapanno, 19 Feb. and 20 Feb. 1474 (ASMi, RM, no. 115, fos. 129r, and 131v, respectively). Passage cited from Z. Saggi to L. Gonzaga, 14 Mar., Milan (ASMa, AG, b. 1624).

146. Christian's stay is described in Simonetta, *Diari,* 97–100.

147. See Z. Saggi to L. Gonzaga, 16 Mar. 1474, Milan (ASMa, AG, b. 1624). The letters of 13, 14, 16, and 18 March are published in Signorini, "Cristiano I in Italia," 41–45.

7: "With the Greatest Pleasure and Contentment of the Heart"

1. See Simonetta, *Diari,* 100–117, and letters below.

2. Galeazzo's monetary policy remained the Milanese standard, and *testoni* continued to be minted well into the sixteenth century; see Cipolla, *Moneta a Milano.* The term "testone" was used for any coin showing the duke's head; see, e.g., Galeazzo to A. Anguissola, 26 July 1473, Monza (ASMi, AS, c. 914).

3. Galeazzo to Fabrizio Elfiteo, 9 Apr. 1474 (ASMi, RM, no. 115, 231r). Galeazzo felt Filippo Sforza did not need to attend if Tristano did (Galeazzo to Fabrizio, 12 Apr., ASMi, RM, no. 115, 234r). For other ducal preparations, see ASMi, RM, no. 116, fos. 297r, 297v, 339r, and 346v. For the tax in general, see Ghinzoni, "L'inquinto"; in his first will, Galeazzo declared that it should be lifted (18 May 1470, Pavia [draft], ASMi, AS, c. 1461).

4. Zaccaria Saggi da Pisa watched this visit closely, because of its Mantuan connection. He was upset because he thought Galeazzo would not pay Eberhard's expenses or provide him an escort (letter to Ludovico Gonzaga, 20 Mar. 1474, Milan, ASMa, AG, b. 1624. See also letters of 12 and 18 Mar.). For other ambassadors' visits, see ASMi, RM, no. 115, and ASMi, AS, c. 922 and 923. The count had come to Mantua to marry Barbara Gonzaga.

5. For San Giorgio preparations, see Galeazzo to Giovanni Giapanno and Giovanni da Castelnovate, 28 Mar. 1474; to Gottardo Panigarola, 8 Apr.; and to Filippo Corio, 23 Apr. (ASMi, RM, no. 115, fos. 202v, 229r, and 257v–258r).

6. For preparations, see Galeazzo to Tristano Sforza, 14 May 1474; to G. da Castelnovate and G. Giapanno, 16 May (two letters); to Privy Council, 17 May; to *commissario* and castellan of Lodi, and Francesco Olgiati, *cameriere,* 18 May; to Antonio Meraviglia, 20 May; and to *commissario,* podestà, and *referendario* of Como, 22 May (ASMi, RM, nos. 115, fos. 305, 308v–309r, 312r, 315v, 320v, and 324v, respectively); also Galeazzo to A. Meraviglia, 16 and 18 May (ASMi, RM, no. 119, fos. 2r and 6r). For an account of the visit, see Simonetta, *Diari,* 116–117.

7. Galeazzo to Z. Saggi, 26 Mar. 1474 (ASMi, RM, no. 115, fo. 201r).

8. Galeazzo to Carlo Visconti [ducal secretary], 20 Mar. 1474, Pavia (ASMi, AS, c. 573; published in Paganini, "Documentazione fra Milano e l'impero," 37). See also Z. Saggi to L. Gonzaga, 16 Mar. 1474, Milan (ASMa, AG, b. 1624). In another letter to Carlo Visconti (Paganini, 36; 21 Dec. 1473, Milan, ASMi, AS, c. 572), Galeazzo had offered no more than 120,000 ducats.

9. For Burgundian and Venetian efforts, see Paganini, "Documentazione fra Milano e l'impero," 30 and 37. For embassy to emperor, see Galeazzo to Agostino Rossi, 7, 10, and 11(?) May 1474 (ASMi, RM, no. 115, fos. 286r, 292v, and 298r, respectively); and Simonetta, *Diari,* 111. Zaccaria's letter of 16 Mar. describes an earlier version of this plan.

10. See ASMi, RM, no. 116, fos. 217r, 218r, 228v, and 239v; also Simonetta, *Diari,* 170. For a full description, see Giovanni Niccolò Bergonzi, *referendario* of Pavia, to Galeazzo, 1 Mar. (ASMi, AS, c. 855).

11. Ghinzoni, "Galeazzo e regno di Cipro." The effort failed; Venice already occupied Cyprus. For rumored deals with the Riario, see Lee, *Sixtus IV,* 5, and Catalano in Treccani degli Alfieri, *Storia di Milano,* VII: 288, n. 1.

12. ACM, BT, cod. 1329 (by Raffaelle da Vimercate).

13. G. Simonetta to Galeazzo, 12 Nov. 1473, Milan (ASMi, AS, c. 914).

14. Galeazzo to Gerolamo Malletta, 23 May 1473, Pavia (ASMi, AS, c. 913).

15. See copies (headed "Antonius Cincinellus S.R.M.") of two letters from Antonio Cicinello to King Ferrante and to Marino Tomacelli (30 May 1474, Milan; ASMi, AS, c. 923). The imprisoned singers were Antonio Ponzo and Alexander Agricola. For more on Cordier, see chap. 4 and Barblan in Treccani, *Storia di Milano,* IX: 843–846. At Galeazzo's command, Cordier spent a short time at the court of Savoy, so the duke could not be accused of hiring him directly away from Ferrante.

16. See Barblan in Treccani, *Storia di Milano,* IX: 837–840. For Martini, see 825 (photo of Feb. 28, 1474, passport to Mantua) and Galeazzo to L. Gonzaga, 1 Mar. 1474 (ASMi, RM, no. 117, fo. 74v).

17. 13 June 1474 (ASMi, RM, no. 115, fo. 377r). The singers in question were probably Agricola and Ponzo; see n. 15. Lewis Lockwood discussed Galeazzo and Ercole in "Strategies of Patronage," but he did little research on Milan. He appears to have misread a sarcastic letter from Galeazzo to Ercole about a singer who had left Milanese service (24 July 1475, Pavia, ASMo, CDE, CE, Principi, Milano, b. 1).

18. Compare Atlas, *Music at the Court of Naples,* Chap. III.

19. See Noblitt, "Ambrosian Motetti Missales"; Barblan in Treccani, *Storia di Milano,* IX: 827–831; and Ward, "Motetti Missales."

20. Quoted in Treccani, *Storia di Milano,* IX: 823 (facsimile of letter on 824); and Motta, "Musici," 310.

21. Z. Saggi to L. Gonzaga, 5 Feb. 1473 (ASMa, AG, b. 1624).

22. Z. Saggi to L. Gonzaga, 12 and 18 Apr. 1474, Milan (ASMa, AG, b. 1624).

23. See Lorenzo de' Medici, *Lettere,* II: 475–484; and F. Catalano in Treccani, *Storia di Milano,* VII: 288–289. The summer activities are documented in ASMi, RM, no. 118; ASMi, AS, c. 922 and 923; and Simonetta, *Diari.*

24. Francesco Pietrasanta to Galeazzo, 7 July 1474, Milan (ASMi, AS, c. 923).

25. See Lorenzo de' Medici, *Lettere,* II: 485–487.

26. Corio (1978), II: 1409.

27. See, e.g., Galeazzo to vice-podestà and *commissario* of Pavia, 10 Oct. 1469 (two letters) (ASMi, RM, no. 87, fos. 53r and 53v).

28. Z. Saggi to L. Gonzaga, 2 Feb. 1471, Milan (ASMa, AG, b. 1624).

29. "Lista delli dinari del zocho della balla che sonno stati vincti & persi prout infra" (ASMi, AS, c. 1483-*giuoco della palla*).

30. Letter of passage, 22 June 1474, Pavia (ASMi, AS, c. 923).

31. Galeazzo to Carlino Varesino, 22 June 1474 (ASMi, RM, no. 118, fo. 16r; duplicated in ASMi, RM, no. 119, fo. 59r); Galeazzo to Giovanni da Rosate, 22 June (ASMi, AS, c. 923).

32. Galeazzo to Carlino Varesino, 23 June 1474 (ASMi, RM, no. 119, fo. 61r).

33. Galeazzo to Carlino Varesino, 24 and 26 June 1474 (ASMi, RM, no. 119, fos. 67r and 70r).

34. Galeazzo to A. Anguissola, 11 July 1472, Bereguardo (ASMi, AS, c. 905).

35. Draft document headed "20 dicembre 1474" ("12 januari 1475" lined out), ASMi, AS, c. 925.

36. Giacomo Cusani to Galeazzo, 27 Aug. 1475; see also Giovanni Varesino to Galeazzo, 27 Aug. (both Milan, ASMi, AS, c. 927).

37. For 1474, see list headed "1474" (composed before 19 Jan.) of *camerieri di camera* and *di guardacamera,* with incomes and size of households maintained by the duke (ASMi, AS, c. 925). For 1475, see Porro, "Lettere" (1879): 260.

38. Cerioni, *Diplomazia Sforzesca,* I: 209, conflates the two men. For Francesco as *primo cameriere,* see 1 Oct. 1475 letter of passage (ASMi, RM, no. 124, fo. 3r); for his replacement as footman (*staffiere*), see Galeazzo to Antonio Anguissola, 11 Sep. 1472, Pavia [draft] (ASMi, AS, c. 908). For mother's position, see Letter Patent [copy] signed by Cicco Simonetta, 23 Oct. 1470, Milan (ASMi, Famiglie, 143-Pietrasanta).

39. See Porro, "Lettere" (1878): 643 (knighting) and *passim* (gifts). For enfeoffments, see ASMi, RM, no. 120, fos. 106v and 121v (Cantù); and no. 122, fo. 99r (Gambolò). See also Santoro, *Registri delle lettere ducale,* 161.

40. For pilgrimage, see 1 Oct. 1475 letter of passage (ASMi, RM, no. 124, fo. 3r); for household size, see Appendix 2; for marriage, see Sitoni di Scozia, *Theatrum Genealogicum,* 347.

41. Z. Saggi to L. Gonzaga, 22 Dec. 1475, Milan (ASMa, AG, b. 1625).

42. E.g., investitures of Antonio Caracciolo (3 Sep. 1473, Vigevano, ASMi, AS, c. 1540), Battista da Montignana (12 May 1469) and Pietro Birago (2 Dec. 1471; both ASMi, Archivio Notarile, *filza* 1580), and Lucia Marliani (9 Jan. 1475; De'Rosmini, *Istoria di Milano,* IV: 121).

43. See, e.g., Welch, "Frescoes for Castello," 181–183; De'Rosmini, *Istoria di Milano*, IV: 148; Porro, "Preventivo," 131.

44. For jousts, see ASMi, RM, nos. 89, fo. 215r, and 110, fo. 147v.

45. Cerioni, *Diplomazia Sforzesca*, I: 172; Calvi, *Famiglie Notabili*, vol. 2, Cotta, t. 1; *DBI*, XXX: 456–457; Marsilio Andreasi to Barbara H. Gonzaga, 27 June 1466 (ASMa, AG, b. 1623).

46. Galeazzo to G. P. del Bergamino, 23 and 30 Sep. 1468 (ASMi, RM, no. 82, fos. 2v and 34r); Porro, "Lettere" (1878): 265; Argegni, *Condottieri*, I: 146–147; Calvi, *Famiglie Notabili*, Brambilleschi (Carminati), t. 1; *DBI*, XX: 430–433.

47. *DBI*, III: 777.

48. Galeazzo to Guido Antonio, 11 May and 10 July 1471 (ASMi, RM, no. 100, fos. 12r[bis] and 194v); Beltrami, *Castello* (1894): 366 (fresco).

49. E.g., G. Arcimboldi to Galeazzo, 17 Jan. 1471, Milan (ASMi, AS, c. 898).

50. Porro, "Lettere" (1878): 265 (military office); *Diari*, 55 (confiscated fief); Galeazzo to GianGiacomo, 8 Apr. 1469 (ASMi, RM, no. 89, fo. 234r) (dismissal). On GianGiacomo in general, see De'Rosmini, *Vita di GianJacopo Trivulzio*; Litta, d. 4 (Trivulzio), t. 1; Argegni, *Condottieri*, III: 330. He was born in 1441 and died at Chartres in 1518.

51. Motta, "Gian Giacomo Trivulzio in Terra Santa," 870–871.

52. Z. Saggi to L. Gonzaga, 26 Nov. 1475, Milan (ASMa, AG, b. 1625). The marquess responded with the excuse that Mantegna was not good at portraits and would have depicted Galeazzo poorly (L. Gonzaga to Z. Saggi, 30 Nov. 1475, Mantua, ASMa, AG, b. 2894, lib. 80, fo. 39v; Z. Saggi to L. Gonzaga, 4 Dec. 1475, Milan, ASMa, AG, b. 1625. Both are cited in Signorini, "Cristiano I in Italia," 39, nn. 80–82).

53. Z. Saggi to L. Gonzaga, 29 Oct. 1474, Milan (ASMa, AG, b. 1624). More generally, see Lorenzo de' Medici, *Lettere*, II: 485–490. Florence had made the alliance with Venice first.

54. See Appendix 1.

55. Galeazzo to G. da Castelnovate, 21 Oct. [should be Nov.] 1474 (ASMi, RM, no. 118, fo. 327v); G. da Castelnovate and G. Giapanno to Galeazzo, 19 Nov., Milan; and G. da Castelnovate to Galeazzo, 22 Nov., Milan (ASMi, AS, c. 925).

56. Z. Saggi to Barbara H. Gonzaga, 27 Dec. 1474, Milan (ASMa, AG, b. 1624).

57. Lucia's sister Cecilia married Cristoforo Landriani: her sister Veronica married Alessandro da Rho (see document of 21 Nov. 1475, Milan, ASMi, Archivio Notarile, f. 1835-Zunico Antonio; they were already married by December 24, 1474).

58. For confirmation of these offices, see Santoro, *Uffici*, 205 and 239.

59. For later gifts to Bona, see, e.g., Leonardo Botta to Cicco, 15 Apr. 1475, Venice (jewels), and Carlo Visconti to Galeazzo, 18 Aug. 1475, Bologna (veils) (ASMi, AS, c. 1483-gioie, abiti, etc.—Galeazzo). See Porro, "Lettere," for more gifts to Bona, Lucia, and Galeazzo's secret lovers in 1475.

60. Cognasso, *Visconti*, 393.

61. Pietro's will (16 Nov. 1462) left substantial dowries for all of his daughters, designating their mother as tutrix. He left a horse to his brother Michele, bishop of Tortona. A document from 20 Dec. 1462, after Pietro's death, shows Lucia's age as six to seven years (ASMi, Archivio Notarile, *filza* 1218-Sudati Lancillotto). (I am very grateful to Professor Grazioso Sironi for sharing with me these fruits of his long and patient research in this vast section of the Milanese archives.)

62. ASMi, Archivio Notarile, f. 954-Sudati Salomone, has a 10 Feb. 1466 document reflecting the marriage of Angela, the eldest; f. 1221-Sudati Lancillotto, has the February 15, 1470, betrothal agreement for Orsina with Francesco Mantegazza; f. 1831-Zunico Antonio, has April 12 and June 6, 1473, dowry and wedding documents for Lucia and Ambrogio. He became procurator for all of the Marliani women, except Angela and Orsina, by an act of March 28, 1472 (f. 1544-Pecchi Bertola).

63. The charters form ACM, BT, cod. 1333 (printed in De'Rosmini, *Istoria di Milano* IV: 109–134; drafts in ASMi, AS, c. 925). For sexual conditions, see De'Rosmini, IV: 109, 112, and 120.

64. De'Rosmini, *Istoria di Milano,* IV: 110.

65. De'Rosmini, *Istoria di Milano,* IV: 113–122.

66. See Cognasso, *Visconti,* 394.

67. De'Rosmini, *Istoria di Milano,* IV: 124.

68. E.g., Porro, "Lettere," *passim.*

69. Corio (1978), II: 1408.

70. For "secreti," see, e.g., payments dated 21 Sep. and 1 and 6 Oct. [1470] on "Lista de li denari a dare via Johanne da Verona . . ." (ASMi, AS, c. 1483-spese-s.d.) and rich stuffs to be worked by the ducal tailor in January 1475 (Porro, "Lettere" [1878]: 120). For widow's tale, see [?] da Corte to Bona [undated] (ASMi, AS, c. 1461). For Cassano girl, see Galeazzo to preposito of Cassano, 2 Apr. 1475 (ASMi, RM, no. 120, fo. 141r), and to castellan of Cassano, 2 Apr. (ASMi, RM, no. 120, fo. 141v). See also "Laura" to Galeazzo, 6 Dec. 1475, Milan (ASMi, AS, c. 928), requesting the grant of an estate as her dowry.

71. Galeazzo to Giovanni Francesco de Coconate, 21 Sep. 1474 (ASMi, RM, no. 119, fo. 191v). The duke was there on September 12 (Simonetta, *Diari,* 138).

72. Z. Saggi to L. Gonzaga, 15 Apr. 1473, Milan (ASMa, AG, b. 1624).

73. Corio (1978), II: 1408.

74. Testimony of Alessandro da Foligno against Ettore da Vimercate, misdated 1457 [must be 1477] (ASMi, AS, c. 1464).

75. Galeazzo to masters of extraordinary revenues, 22 Feb. 1472 (ASMi, RM, no. 109, fo. 15r).

76. Galeazzo to podestà of Cremona, 22 Feb., 4 Mar., and 29 Apr. 1472 (ASMi, RM, no. 104, fos. 56r, 66v, and 121r, respectively); and Galeazzo to Giacomo da Pontremoli [investigator], 1 Apr. 1472 and subsequent letters (ASMi, RM, no. 104, fos. 98v–99r, etc.).

77. Galeazzo to podestà of Cremona, 24 May 1472 (ASMi, RM, no. 104, 155v). One man was declared innocent on the evidence of the others (Galeazzo to podestà of Cremona, 22 Oct. 1472, ASMi, RM, no. 110, fo. 97r).

78. Galeazzo to masters of extraordinary revenues, 6 July 1472 (ASMi, RM, no. 109, fo. 66v).

79. Galeazzo to captain of justice of Milan, 27 Aug. 1472 (ASMi, RM, no. 105, fo. 155v) (petition); Galeazzo to Deputati sopra biade, 3 Nov. 1472 (ASMi, RM, no. 106, fo. 124v) (permit); Galeazzo to Battista Ponzoni, 13 Jan. 1473 (ASMi, RM, no. 110, fo. 131r) (release); Galeazzo to *commissario,* podestà, and *referendario* of Cremona, 29 Apr. 1473, and to lieutenant, podestà, and *referendario* of Cremona, 30 Apr. (ASMi, RM, no. 114, fos. 36r and 38v) (punishment and permission). Cosme

was evidently a wealthy man with an active business career; see, e.g., ASMi, RM, no. 112, fo. 322v; no. 116, fo. 47r; and no. 117, fos. 167v–168r, 363v.

80. Francesco Maletta to Galeazzo, 19 Oct. 1473, Naples; and Galeazzo to Francesco, 5 Nov., Vigevano (ASMi, AS, c. 925). (I owe the references to Vincent Ilardi.) Bernardino was *cameriere di camera* long enough to be included in the 1474 fresco program (see chap. 8); see also document captioned on reverse: "1474. Liste facte delanno 1474 ma renovate vz. de camereri" (ASMi, AS, c. 925). Carlino had gone to Naples in January 1472, bringing hawks and hounds on Galeazzo's behalf (ASMi, RM, no. 102, fos. 352v–353r).

81. Francesco Maletta to Galeazzo, 1 Nov. 1473, Naples (ASMi, AS, c. 225).

82. *DBI,* XI: 429.

83. See Woods-Marsden, "Pictorial Legitimation."

84. Galeazzo to "D. Sforcie Magno" [Sforza Secondo], 20 Jan. and 10, 15, and 27 July 1470 (ASMi, RM, no. 95, fos. 10r, 103v, 109r, and 111v, respectively). See also letters from 1467 and 1470 in ASMi, AS, c. 1480.

85. Antonio da Correggio served briefly on the Privy Council before his death in 1474 (Santoro, *Uffici,* 12).

86. See correspondence with Galeazzo in ASMi, AS, c. 1475-Beatrice d'Este Sforza. He lifted the ban on Niccolò in the year 1475 (Galeazzo to masters of revenues, 26 Apr.; ASMi, RM, no. 120, fo. 186v). See also Galeazzo to Beatrice and to Niccolò, 11 Oct. 1476 (ASMi, RM, no. 124, fo. 58r).

87. Boschino "d'Angheria" to Galeazzo, 14 and 28 June 1468 (ASMi, AS, c. 884) and 14 Aug. 1468, Milan (ASMi, AS, c. 885).

88. Giovanni Agostino Isimbardi to Galeazzo, 17 Feb. 1474 (no location; ASMi, AS, c. 922). That enemy might have been the cardinal of Pavia; they were still involved in a dispute eighteen months later (see Angelo della Stufa to Galeazzo, 1 July 1475, Pavia, ASMi, AS, c. 855).

89. Francesco Salvatico to Galeazzo, 14 Sep. 1471, Milan (ASMi, AS, c. 901). Earlier that year, Francesco had run into problems while on a hunting errand to England for Galeazzo. The *gentiluomo* was captured in Burgundian territory and an ambassador had to be dispatched to secure his release (see various documents of 23 Mar. to 22 Apr. 1471 in Sestan, *Carteggio Diplomatico,* I: 269–279, including letters to and from Galeazzo and instructions to ambassador Cristoforo da Bollate (16 Apr., Vigevano, ASMi, AS, c. 515).

90. Filippo degli Oddi to Galeazzo, 29 Oct. 1475, Castello Porta Giovia (ASMi, AS, c. 927). For Filippo as *cameriere,* see Galeazzo to Antonio Landriani, 13 Aug. 1474 (ASMi, RM, no. 118, fo. 121r).

91. Galeazzo asked a Milanese diplomat to write Colleoni requesting their return (Galeazzo to Gerardo Colli, 18 July 1466, ASMi, RM, no. 75, fo. 133r).

92. Fioramonte Graziani da Cotignola to Galeazzo, 31 May 1473, Milan (ASMi, AS, c. 913). Francesco also had a dispute with two other courtiers; it was resolved by a local *commissario* (Galeazzo to *commissario* of Gera d'Adda, 14 Dec. 1472, ASMi, RM, no. 110bis, fo. 130v).

93. B. Gadio to Galeazzo, 16 June 1475, and to Cicco, 5 July, Milan [both cited] (ASMi, Autografi, c. 88); see also letters to Cicco, 6 and 13 July.

94. "Comatre" to Bianca Maria, 6 July 1468(?), Milan (ASMi, AS, c. 1460).

95. Galeazzo to Gabriele Balbiani and to Giovanni Balbiani, 16 Nov. 1473 (ASMi, RM, no. 112, fo. 337v).

96. See, e.g., Galeazzo to podestà of Milan, 28 Feb. 1467, Pavia [draft] (ASMi, AS, c. 879), for a dispute between members of the court concerning a mill.

97. See Fubini, "Crisi del ducato," 57.

98. Litta, d. 60, t. 5.

99. For general background, see Santoro, *Uffici,* 113; Cerioni, *Diplomazia Sforzesca,* I: 213; Litta (n. 98); Welch, "Frescoes for Porta Giovia," 177; and De'Rosmini, *Istoria di Milano,* IV: 12. For ranking, see chap. 6.

100. Galeazzo to Bianca Maria, 25 Sep. 1467 (printed in Welch, "Frescoes for Porta Giovia," 177–178; original in Bibliothèque Nationale, Paris).

101. See chap. 2.

102. For suspicions, see, e.g., Tristano to Galeazzo, 14 Feb. 1471, Milan (ASMi, AS, c. 898). For *condotta,* see Tommaso Tebaldi da Bologna and Pietro Pusterla to Galeazzo, 10 Apr. 1470, Mantua (ASMi, AS, c. 395; published in Tissoni Benvenuti, "Un nuovo documento"). For choice of *gentiluomini* and for knighting, see chap. 6.

103. See Welch, "Frescoes for Porta Giovia," 176–178, 182–183. The final version added Pietro da Gallarate and Fioramonte Graziani da Cotignola.

104. Fubini has argued that Galeazzo also victimized Gaspare da Vimercate by taking Valenza from him and giving it to Sforza Maria ("Crisi del ducato," 63). In fact, Gaspare died in October 1467 without male heirs, and Sforza Maria received Valenza in January 1468 (ASMi, RM, no. 81, 61r). Corio claimed that Galeazzo actually favored the Ghibellines ([1978], II: 1409).

105. Fubini, "Crisi del ducato," 61–64. Galeazzo intended originally for Pietro to bear the sword (Galeazzo to Pietro, 11 Mar. 1471, Pietrasanta, ASMi, RM, no. 98, fo. 234r). For Welch, see n. 103. During Cardinal Bessarion's entry, Galeazzo wanted Pietro to "bear the sword continuously in the going and returning" (M. Andreasi to L. Gonzaga, 19 May 1472, Pavia, ASMa, AG, b. 1624).

106. For information on Visconti and Pusterla, see Litta, d. 12, t. 14 and 16, and d. 60, t. 5. Battista's uncle Guido was one of Galeazzo's best administrators, even entrusted with the delicate vice-governorship of Genoa (Litta, d. 12, t. 16, and d. 13, t. 17).

107. See Appendix 2 and Porro, "Lettere" (1879): 261.

108. Galeazzo to Sforza Maria, 30 Mar. 1475 (ASMi, RM, no. 120, fo. 134r). Even Ascanio took time off from his studies to hunt (e.g., Galeazzo to Ascanio, 25 July 1471, ASMi, RM, no. 101, fo. 155r). For the debate on prey, see Galeazzo to Sforza Maria, 25 Aug. 1475 (ASMi, RM, no. 122, fo. 90v); Sforza Maria to Galeazzo, 19 and 22 Aug. 1475, Cassino; and Galeazzo to Sforza Maria, 16 Aug., Cassano (ASMi, AS, c. 928).

109. Motta, "Giuoco della palla," 489–490 (original in ASMi, AS, c. 903).

110. The lion came from a Milanese merchant in Venice (see Galeazzo to Ottaviano, and to Biagio da Gradi, 20 Aug. 1475; ASMi, RM, no. 121, fo. 253r).

111. Porro, "Lettere" (1878): 265–266 (*squadre* at San Giorgio 1475); Visconti, "Ordine dell'esercito ducale," 453–454 (mobilization plans); Beltrami, *Castello* (1894): 365–371 (fresco commission with brothers as commanders). See Filippo Sforza to Galeazzo, 5 Mar. 1474, Milan (ASMi, AS, c. 922) for a heartfelt lament over being stripped of a military command.

112. Sforza Maria went to Ferrara in 1468 (see chap. 2) and Montferrat in 1469 and 1472 (with Ludovico) (see chaps. 3 and 4). Sforza Maria and Ludovico each made state visits to Venice; see ASMi, AS, c. 1469, for Ludovico (Jan. 1471), and n. 113 for Sforza Maria (1474–1475).

113. G. Giapanno to Galeazzo, 22 Nov. 1474, Milan (ASMi, AS, c. 925) (departure); Simonetta, *Diari,* 153 (return on 4 Feb.); Galeazzo to Branda Castiglione, to Sforza Maria, to bishop of Lodi [replaced by Pallavicino Pallavicini], to G. Giapanno, and to eight other nobles and three ducal officers, all 15 Nov. 1474 (ASMi, RM, no. 118, fo. 313r) (retinue). For logistical arrangements, see "Memoriale facto per Zohane Giapano per landata del Ill. Duca de Bari ad Venexia" [undated but filed under "1468"], ASMi, AS, c. 1468. (This document was filed with Ludovico's papers in error; he became duke of Bari after Sforza Maria died.)

114. "Instructio et mandata vobis illustri d[omi]no Ludovico Marie Sfortie Vicecomiti . . . ituro Venetias," 8 Jan. 1471, Monza (ASMi, AS, c. 1469; printed in Dina, "Ludovico il Moro," 761–762).

115. Cristoforo Rangoni to Borso d'Este, 23 Nov. 1469, Milan (ASMo, CE, DA, Milano, b. 1). The warning came from a councillor.

116. See chap. 2. By 1471, Ludovico had been named governor of Genoa, another position without substance (see "Instructio," n. 114).

117. Antonio de Alasia to Galeazzo, 15 Apr. 1469, Pavia (ASMi, AS, c. 847) (complaint); Beltrami, *Castello* (1894): 368 (fresco). Ascanio was expected at Christmas (Ascanio to Galeazzo, 18 Dec. 1469, Pavia, ASMi, AS, c. 847).

118. Santoro, *Uffici,* 13. See ASMi, AS, c. 1465, for letters from 1468–1469 about distractions from schoolwork and problems with household staff.

119. Galeazzo sought support from friendly cardinals for Ascanio's elevation (e.g., 9 Nov. 1476, Galliate [draft], ASMi, AS, c. 1465), but Ascanio did not obtain a red hat until 1484. Ascanio (and Galeazzo) wanted more than the half of Chiaravalle's income that he was initially allotted; see petition from abbey (undated, ASMi, AS, c. 1465) and Pellegrino, "Ascanio Maria Sforza."

120. See Santoro, *Uffici,* 334, 425 (council post); and Giovanni to Galeazzo, 24 Oct. 1473, Milan (news of duke of Burgundy's meeting with emperor). The biography is the focus of Ianziti, *Politics and Propaganda* and "Patronage and Production of History."

121. For early diplomatic missions, see Cerioni, *Diplomazia Sforzesca,* I: 234. When Cicco stayed in Milan once while Galeazzo went hunting, Giovanni Giacomo was their liaison (Giovanni Giacomo to Cicco, 30 Oct. 1476, Galliate, and 31 Oct., Fagnano; ASMi, AS, c. 925).

122. For wedding arrangements, see Francesco da Varese [not the ducal *cameriere* of the same name] to Cicco Simonetta, 29 Oct. 1475, Milan, and lists dated 3 Oct. 1476 of "quilli hano andare a Zibello per condure la spoxa," "de le giornate hano a fare quilli vano a Zibello," and "de homini et done sono invitati ale noze" (all in ASMi, AS, c. 927).

123. Giovanni Antonio Girardi to Cicco, 8 Oct. 1476, Pavia (ASMi, AS, c. 927).

124. G. Simonetta to Galeazzo, 17 Apr. 1467, Milan (ASMi, AS, c. 879).

125. G. Simonetta to Cicco, 22 May 1475, Milan (ASMi, AS, c. 926).

126. G. Simonetta to Cicco, 26 Jan. 1470, Milan (ASMi, AS, c. 892) (Valenza). For benefices, see Francesco Birago to Pietro Birago, 19 Feb. 1474, Milan, and Galeazzo's draft letter in Daniele's favor, 13(?) Feb. 1474, Pavia (both in ASMi, AS, c. 922); and Galeazzo to Daniele, 18 Sep. 1475 (ASMi, RM, no. 122, fo. 122v). Francesco visited Daniele in Rome; see Galeazzo to Sagramoro Sagramori da Rimini; and to cardinal (archbishop) of Milan, 26 Dec. 1474 (ASMi, RM, no. 117, fo. 296r).

127. Gabriele Paleari to Galeazzo, 12 Nov. 1473, Milan; and Galeazzo to Gabriele Paleari, 13 Nov., Vigevano (ASMi, AS, c. 915). For Pietro's links to the Lampugnani, see Litta, d. 127, t. 2; and Raffaelli, "Famiglia Lampugnani," 231, t. II. Pietro married Angela, daughter of Princivalle Lampugnani, a pillar of the Sforza administration.

128. Giovanni Grassi to Galeazzo, 26 Nov. 1468, Pavia (ASMi, AS, c. 846). For brother Luigi's appointment, see ASMi, RM, no. 95, fo. 20v (2 Feb. 1470); he performed poorly (*Deputati sopra biade* to Galeazzo, 9 Jan. 1471, ASMi, AS, c. 898). For brother Gabriele as *cameriere,* see list of "Camereri novi" in ASMi, AS, c. 925, and *Diari,* 106.

129. Giorgio and other brothers held the family fief and attended Christmas court as feudatories (see Appendix 3). For *cameriere* position, see undated letter of seven *camerieri* to Galeazzo (ASMi, AS, c. 1484-camerieri); for promotion, see Simonetta, *Diari,* 105. For relationship to Lucia and Michele, see Lucia to Cicco, 1 Dec. 1476, Milan (ASMi, *Autografi,* 66). For Michele's death, see chaps. 5 and 8.

130. Alessandro da Cotignola ("Goffino") and Daniele da Palude to Galeazzo, 25 Aug. 1476, Milan (ASMi, AS, c. 1462), shows her uncle Giovanni Antonio was also present. That letter and Daniele da Palude to Galeazzo, 16 Oct. 1476, Milan (ASMi, AS, c. 931), show her brother-in-law, Alessandro da Rho, with her.

131. Members of the family usually appear in the records with the surname "d'Angelo" or "del Conte." For identification, see Galeazzo to Elisabetta d'Angelo, 29 Dec. 1469 (ASMi, RM, no. 87, fo. 109r).

132. ASMi, RM, no. 81, fos. 133v–134r (appointments); "Confessio" of "Hector de Lugo" and "Procura" of "Hector de Faffis" (same man) and Daria, 5 Feb. and 19 Mar. 1470, respectively (ASMi, AS, c. 1535) (marriage); Bona to Elisabetta, 7 Oct. 1476, Varese, and 14 Oct., Galliate [drafts] (ASMi, AS, c. 931).

133. For Giov. Antonio, see Galeazzo to count of Urbino, 14 Nov. 1468 (ASMi, RM, no. 82, fo. 187v); to L. Suardi, 20 June 1468 (ASMi, RM, no. 83, fo. 306v); and to Elisabetta d'Angelo, 29 Dec. 1469 (ASMi, RM, no. 87, fo. 109r). For Carlino, see Sforza Maria to Bianca Maria, 13 June 1468, Pavia (ASMi, AS, c. 846); and Galeazzo to Marchino d'Abbiate and Antonio Missaglia, 26 July 1470 (ASMi, RM, no. 95, fo. 152r) (jousting); 1474 list of *camerieri di guardacamera* (ASMi, AS, c. 925); Galeazzo to Filippo Sagramori da Rimini, 1 Oct. 1475 (ASMi, RM, no. 124, fo. 4v) (Florence).

134. Galeazzo to podestà and castellan of Cassano, 13 Jan. 1475; to podestà of Treviglio, 14 Jan.; to podestà of Pioltello, 14 Jan.; to Giovanni Visconti and Antonio Pietro Villano, 16 Jan.; and to castellan of Cassano, 19 Jan. (ASMi, RM, no. 120, fos. 8r, 8v, 9r, 13v–14v, and 17v, respectively).

135. Paganini, "Documentazione fra Milano e l'impero," 37 (Galeazzo to bishop of Forlì, 20 July 1475); Galeazzo to Giovanni Giacomo Simonetta, 29 July 1475, Pavia (ASMi, AS, c. 927).

136. Galeazzo to Sforza Maria, 28 Mar. 1475 (ASMi, RM, no. 120, fo. 131v).

137. See ASMi, RM, no. 118, fos. 324v, 328v, 332r, 332v, and 333r; no. 119, fos. 322r and 326r; no. 120, fos. 8v and 34r–v; G. da Castelnovate, G. Giapanno, and A. Meraviglia to Galeazzo, 28 Nov. and 1 Dec. 1474, Milan (ASMi, AS, c. 925).

138. Vaughan, *Charles the Bold,* 165. These dispatches are among the best sources available on Charles's activities.

139. Vincent Ilardi, Richard Walsh, and Riccardo Fubini are the historians who

have given the most attention recently to relations between Milan and Burgundy. See Bibliography and Lorenzo de' Medici, *Lettere,* II.

140. For background of treaty, see Lorenzo de' Medici, *Lettere,* II: 491–496.

141. Galeazzo to Tristano Sforza, 26 Feb. 1475; to Antonio d'Appiano, 26 Feb.; to G. Giapanno, 28 Jan.; and to Taddeo Ghiringhelli, Milanese citizen, 1 Mar. (ASMi, RM, no. 120, fos. 81v, 82r, 84v, and 86v, respectively).

142. Galeazzo to G. Giapanno and G. da Castelnovate, 10 Mar. 1475, to Ambrosino da Longhignana and Filippo Eustachi, 10 Mar., to Gallassio Gallassi, 10 Mar. (ASMi, RM, no. 120, fos. 97r, 97v, and 98r); Bona to castellan of Abbiategrasso, 12 Mar. (ASMi, RM, no. 120, fo. 101r); Galeazzo to Tristano Sforza, 9 Mar. (ASMi, RM, no. 121, fo. 37v); Tristano to Galeazzo, 10 Mar., Mortara (ASMi, AS, c. 855); Simonetta, *Diari,* 158–159.

143. Galeazzo to G. Giapanno and G. da Castelnovate, 11 Mar. 1475 (ASMi, RM, no. 120, fo. 99v); G. da Castelnovate and G. Giapanno to Galeazzo, 11 and 12 Mar., Milan; B. Gadio to Galeazzo, 17 Feb. and 8(?) Mar., Milan; Galeazzo to B. Gadio, 3 Feb. [Mar.?], Pavia [draft] (ASMi, AS, c. 926).

144. Giovanni Agostino Olgiati to Galeazzo, 13 Mar. 1475, Pavia (ASMi, AS. c. 855).

145. Tristano Sforza to Galeazzo and G. A. Olgiati to Galeazzo, both 15 Mar. 1475, Milan (ASMi, AS, c. 926).

146. Pasquino da Bagnacavallo to Galeazzo, 16 Mar. 1475, Milan (2 letters) (ASMi, AS, c. 926); Galeazzo to G. A. Olgiati, 17 Mar. (ASMi, RM, no. 120, fo. 113v) (reply).

8: "To the Praise and Glory of . . . All the Triumphant Celestial Court"

1. Zaccaria Saggi da Pisa to Ludovico Gonzaga, 26 Mar. 1475, Milan (ASMa, AG, b. 1625).

2. Simonetta, *Diari,* 163. A similar dedication was used when the Italian League was proclaimed in 1468 (copy of proclamation, 1 May 1468, Abbiate, ASMi, AS, c. 884).

3. For St. George as ducal patron saint, see Morbio, *Codice Visconteo-Sforzesco,* 451.

4. Galeazzo to Bianca Maria, 20 Apr. 1467, Piacenza (ASMi, AS, c. 879).

5. Porro, "Lettere" (1878): 255; the following pages (256–259) list the names of the men to be clothed in each category.

6. Porro, "Lettere" (1878): 263–267. Lists in ASMi, AS, c. 925 and 1603, show the captains of ducal squadrons accompanying the standards.

7. Porro, "Lettere" (1878): 267; Galeazzo to Giovanni Agostino Olgiati, 27 Mar. 1475 (ASMi, RM, no. 120, fo. 131r).

8. Porro, "Lettere" (1878): 254.

9. For these preparations, see letters and instructions in ASMi, RM, no. 120, fos. 117v–120r (18 Mar. 1475).

10. Simonetta, *Diari,* 162–163; Galeazzo to Giovanni da Castelnovate, 19 Apr. 1475 (ASMi, RM, no. 120, fo. 178v) (Savoyard and Florentine ambassadors); Marsilio Andreasi to Barbara Hohenzollern Gonzaga, 23 Apr., Milan (ASMa, AG, b. 1625); Galeazzo to officials in the Cremona and Lodi districts, 17 Apr. (ASMi, RM, no. 120, fos. 167v–168r) (Ludovico Gonzaga's visit).

11. Simonetta, *Diari,* 163.

12. M. Andreasi to Barbara H. Gonzaga, 25 Apr. 1475, Milan (ASMa, AG, b. 1625).

13. M. Andreasi to Barbara H. Gonzaga, 25 and 26 Apr. 1475, Milan (ASMa, AG, b. 1625).

14. Galeazzo to Giovanni Giapanno and G. da Castelnovate, 28 Mar. 1474; to Gottardo Panigarola, 8 Apr.; to G. Giapanno, 10 Apr.; and to Filippo Corio (ASMi, RM, no. 115, fos. 202v, 229r, 230v, and 257v–258r); and Gottardo Panigarola to Galeazzo, 1 Mar. 1474, Milan (ASMi, AS, c. 922).

15. Original program in ASMi, Autografi, 96; the last scene is incomplete. Beltrami printed it in *Castello* (1894): 365–371; Welch features it in "Secular Fresco Painting," chap. 5, and mentions it briefly in "Frescoes for Porta Giovia," mainly for its location on the upper floor of Porta Giovia. The Sala della Balla was built and painted in 1474, either in the upstairs Sala Grande or the Sala Verde beneath it (see letters from Bartolomeo Gadio da Cremona to Galeazzo, Jan., Feb., and Aug. 1474, Milan, ASMi, Autografi, 88).

16. Ludovico Suardi to Galeazzo, 18 Feb. 1467, Milan (ASMi, AS, c. cart. 879). See also chap. 2.

17. Galeazzo to Francesco Lampugnani, 27 Mar. 1471; and to Dombello Riccardi, 6 Apr. (ASMi, RM, no. 98, fos. 255v and 266r). For 1469, see chap. 3.

18. For damage, see ASMi, RM, no. 103, fos. 347r ff. For ambassadors, see M. Andreasi to L. Gonzaga, 24 Apr. 1472, Milan (ASMa, AG, b. 1624). For feudatories, see Galeazzo to various officials, 20 Feb. 1472 (ASMi, RM, no. 106, fo. 61v) and 20(?) Mar. 1472 (ASMi, RM, no. 106, fos. 157r–158r).

19. Galeazzo to Domenico Guiscardi, 28 Mar. and 1 Apr. 1473 (ASMi, RM, no. 113, fos. 70r and 93v); Galeazzo to Antonio Anguissola, 31 Mar., Abbiate, and Domenico Guiscardi to Antonio, 22 Apr., Milan (ASMi, AS, c. 913).

20. Galeazzo to D. Guiscardi, 5 Apr. 1476 (ASMi, RM, no. 124, fo. 21v).

21. Sforza and Simonetta planners, unfamiliar with Milanese customs, were surprised that Ambrosian Mass was not celebrated on Lenten Fridays, which affected the fifth anniversary memorial service for Duke Francesco's death (Giovanni Simonetta to Galeazzo, 7 Mar. 1471, Milan, ASMi, AS, c. 898).

22. On archiepiscopal dominance, see Cognasso, *Visconti,* chap. 1, and Treccani, *Storia di Milano,* II–III. On Ottone Visconti and lists, see Cognasso, *Visconti,* chap. 7, and Crivelli Visconti, *Nobiltà Lombarda,* 6–13.

23. *Corpus Nummorum Italicarum,* V: 173 (#97).

24. G. Giapanno to Galeazzo, 26 Feb. 1467, Milan (ASMi, AS, c. 879).

25. G. Simonetta to Galeazzo, 20 May 1473, Milan (ASMi, AS, c. 913). See chap. 5 for this event.

26. Galeazzo to masters of revenues, 9 Dec. 1473 (ASMi, RM, no. 115, fo. 18v); and budget suggestions for 1473 ("Spexa . . . ," 28 Nov. 1472; ASMi, AS, c. 909), which earmarks 170 ducats for "the cloth of the servants of the court and of Milan, at the feast of St. Ambrose."

27. Testament dated 3 Nov. 1471 (ASMi, Notarile, f. 1580; summarized in Giulini, *Memorie spettanti,* VI: 593–596).

28. Simonetta, *Diari,* 165–175; G. da Castelnovate to Galeazzo, 8 June 1475, Milan (ASMi, AS, c. 926); Galeazzo to G. da Castelnovate and G. Giapanno, 21 June (ASMi, RM, no. 120, fo. 331v).

29. Simonetta, *Diari,* 176; G. da Castelnovate and G. Giapanno to Galeazzo, 1 July 1475, Milan; and 22 June list of edible gifts (both ASMi, AS, c. 926).

30. Galeazzo to G. Simonetta, 2 July 1475, Pavia [draft] (ASMi, AS, c. 927).

31. G. Simonetta to Galeazzo, 2 July 1475; G. da Castelnovate and G. Giapanno to Galeazzo, 7 and 8 July; Branda Castiglione to Galeazzo, 8 July (all Milan, ASMi, AS, c. 927).

32. See Porro, "Lettere," *passim,* for commands to Gottardo; the Josquin and chessboard references are (1879): 251 and 256, respectively.

33. Porro, "Lettere" (1879): 260 and 265. The money for pheasants also covered predators such as foxes and wolves, caught dead or alive. Quartarari may have been related to one of the four governors of the *lanze spezzate.*

34. Porro, "Preventivo," 131–134; Porro, "Lettere" (1879): 259 (1477 debt).

35. Galeazzo to Lorenzo de' Medici, 13 May 1475, Pavia (ASMi, AS, c. 1461); and to Francesco Filelfo, 2 and 17 Sep. (ASMi, RM, no. 122, fos. 103v and 122r).

36. Galeazzo to bishop of Piacenza (Michele Marliani); to Giovanni Battista de Cotignola; and to *commissario* of Piacenza, 29 Sep. 1475 (ASMi, RM, no. 124, fo. 2v). Antonio Marliani to Galeazzo, 14 Oct. 1475, Milan (ASMi, AS, c. 927) (identifying Lucia); Giovanni Antonio Marliani to Galeazzo, 9 Oct., Milan (ASMi, Famiglie, no. 113-Marliani) (request); Galeazzo to *commissario* of Piacenza, 13 and 21 Oct. (ASMi, RM, no. 124, fos. 2v and 10r); and 12 Oct. inventory of Michele's possessions (ASMi, AS, c. 927).

37. Galeazzo to Giovanni Botta, 2 Dec. 1476 (ASMi, RM, no. 122, fo. 211v) (money); De'Rosmini, *Istoria di Milano,* IV: 125–134 (property); Galeazzo to masters of revenues, 24 Aug. 1476 (ASMi, RM, no. 125, fo. 327r) (podestà).

38. Galeazzo to Gerardo Colli and *commissario* of Gera d'Adda and to Antonio Secco, 23 Aug. 1475 (ASMi, RM, no. 122, fo. 86r); to Vercellino Visconti, castellan of Trezzo, 23 Aug. (ASMi, RM, no. 122, fo. 88r); and to castellan of Novara, 11 Nov. (ASMi, RM, no. 122, fo. 172v).

39. See chaps. 2 and 4.

40. Z. Saggi to L. Gonzaga, 22 Dec. 1475, Milan (ASMa, AG, b. 1625; printed in Belotti, *Gerolamo Olgiati,* 180–183). See "Reverendi & Mag[nifi]ci d[omi]ni de ducale Consilio Secreto pro anno 1476 alio non aparente" (ASMi, AS, c. 929), for names and salaries.

41. Simonetta, *Diari,* 188; Secco was appointed to the Privy Council on 19 Sep. 1475 (Santoro, *Uffici,* 13); for position with Bona, see chap. 2.

42. However, the Appendix 2 lodging list still shows 20 "ducali regazi."

43. Porro, "Preventivo," 134. Ducal budgets were generally drawn up on the last day of the preceding year; e.g., the budget for 1473 is dated 31 Dec. 1472, although a partial budget had been drawn up by 12 July 1472 (ASMi, AS, c. 1483-bilanci, #195 and #194, respectively).

44. Galeazzo to Lucia Visconti, countess of Melzo, 16 Apr. 1476 (ASMi, RM, no. 125, fo. 48v); Simonetta, *Diari,* 200 (date); De'Rosmini, *Istoria di Milano,* IV: 127 (name).

45. Galeazzo to Ambrogio Raverti, 5 May 1476 (ASMi, RM, no. 125, fo. 79v).

46. See Mintz and Wolf, "Analysis of Ritual Co-Parenthood," which begins with an extensive historical section focusing on medieval Europe.

47. Bossy, "Blood and Baptism."

48. See chap. 3. ASMi, AS, c. 1476-Ermes Maria, includes a document (18 June 1470, Urbino), authorizing ambassador Camillo Barzi to act as Federigo's proxy in holding Ermes at the baptismal font.

49. This letter (dated 19 Apr. 1476, Milan) was printed by C[esare] C[antù] in "Anedotti di Lodovico il Moro," 487. He mistook Galeazzo for Ludovico throughout. An undated draft of the letter is in ASMi, AS, c. 881.

50. Galeazzo to Giovanni Conti, 14 May (ASMi, RM, no. 125, fo. 94v); for Giovanni Battista as *cameriere,* see Appendix 2.

51. ASMi, RM, no. 111, fo. 133r, and no. 117, fo. 42v (Bentivoglio); Galeazzo to Roberto, 12 Feb. 1474 (ASMi, RM, no. 117, fo. 58r). Roberto's *condotta* was worth 30,000 ducats, and the marquess's 36,000 (Porro, "Preventivo," 131).

52. Simonetta, *Diari,* 49.

53. Bossy observed also that "godparenthood was a more important institution at the popular level than among the nobility" ("Blood and Baptism," 135).

54. Galeazzo to Giovanni Simonetta, 3 May 1475 (2 letters) (ASMi, RM, no. 120, fo. 201r); and Giovanni to Galeazzo, 4 and 18 May, Milan (ASMi, AS, c. 926).

55. E.g., Stefano Nardini (archbishop) to Cicco, 8 June 1469, Milan (ASMi, AS, c. 889); Alessandro Spinola (councillor) to Cicco, 6 Aug. 1473, Milan (ASMi, AS, c. 914); Pigello Portinari to Cicco, 13 Sep. 1466, Milan (ASMi, AS, c. 878); Federigo to Cicco, 1 Apr. 1468, Milan (ASMi, AS, c. 883); Tristano Sforza to Cicco, 3 May 1474, Milan (ASMi, AS, c. 923); Ottone Mandelli (feudatory) to Cicco, 2 May 1468, Milan (ASMi, AS, c. 884).

56. Fazio Gallerani to Cicco, 8 Sep. 1469 (ASMi, AS, c. 890). Gallerani's daughter Cecilia later became the mistress of Ludovico "il Moro."

57. Simonetta, *Diari,* 24.

58. Michele Bonicci to Lazzaro Tedaldi, 14 Aug. 1473 (ASMi, AS, c. 914); Giovanni Rusca to Fabrizio Marliani, 9 Jan. 1476 (ASMi, AS, c. 929); Angelo Simonetta to Cicco, 20 Feb. 1472 (ASMi, AS, c. 903); Pietro da Carcano to Gaspar van Weerbeke, 26 July 1476 (ASMi, AS, c. 929) (all from Milan).

59. Giovanni Borromeo to Giacomo Alfieri, 14 Jan. 1472, Milan (ASMi, AS, c. 903). For the first daughter, see Giacomo Alfieri to A. Anguissola, 18 June 1470, Milan (ASMi, AS, c. 894).

60. Anna, widow of Francesco Fossati, "commater," to Galeazzo, 13 June 1468 (ASMi, AS, c. 884). For her family name, see Giovanni Botta to Galeazzo, 14 Dec. 1469 (ASMi, AS, c. 891).

61. Galeazzo to Anna Fossati, 11 Dec. 1469 (ASMi, RM, no. 91, fo. 89v).

62. B. Gadio to Galeazzo, 27 Aug. 1473, Milan (ASMi, AS, c. 914).

63. Galeazzo to Sagramoro Sagramori da Rimini, 14 Sep. 1473, Milan [draft] (ASMi, AS, c. 1463). The letter conveyed thanks to the pope for allowing Bona "to enter into the convents of religious men and women."

64. Bona to Leonardo Botta and to ambassadors in Florence and Bologna, 19 July 1476 [draft] (Pavia, ASMi, AS, c. 931). Anna's name was not specified in those letters, but she is not mentioned in any documents before 1476 (ASMi, AS, c. 1473-Anna). Genealogies in Litta, d. 1; Treccani, *Storia di Milano,* VII, and Santoro, *Sforza,* show her as born in 1473, without evidence.

65. Alessandro Airoldi da Robbiate to Bernardino da Ripa, 24 July 1476, Milan (ASMi, AS, c. 931).

66. On 1 Oct. 1476, e.g., Lucia, Bona, and Galeazzo all spent the night at Gambolò (Simonetta, *Diari,* 211).

67. For Galeazzo's itinerary, see Appendix 1. For Bona's whereabouts, see letters in ASMi, AS, c. 929 and 931, plus Simonetta, *Diari.*

68. Bona to Giuliano da Varese, 6 Nov. 1476, Galliate [draft] (ASMi, AS, c. 932) (stable), and to Gaspare Ambrogio Barzizza, 6 Apr. 1476, Vigevano (ASMi, AS, c. 931) (bedchambers).

69. Bona to Antonio Landriani, "*our* treasurer" [italics mine; he was the ducal treasurer-general], 24 Mar. 1476, Abbiategrasso; Bona to constable of Porta Tosa, 12 Mar., Pavia (both ASMi, AS, c. 929). For more 1476 activity, see ASMi, AS, c. 929 and 931, *passim.* The duchess's household allotment rose from 15,151 ducats for 1469 to a projected 23,500 ducats for 1473 and 38,810 ducats for 1476 (1473 budget in ASMi, AS, c. 1483-bilanci-Galeazzo [#195]; #194, a partial budget for 1473, makes the amount 25,000 ducats; for 1476, see Porro, "Preventivo," 132). However, 1476 instructions to her household treasurer put the actual allotment at 107,420 pounds (27,810 ducats), including payment to her courtiers (Bona to Giovanni da Gallarate, 17 Mar., Vigevano, ASMi, AS, c. 929). In 1471–1472, her *gentiluomini* were paid directly by the treasurer-general (Galeazzo to A. Anguissola, 7 Jan. 1471, Milan; and 1 June 1472, Pavia, ASMi, AS, c. 892 and 905, respectively).

70. Alessandro da Cotignola ("Goffino") and Daniele da Palude to Galeazzo, 25 Aug. 1476, Milan (ASMi, AS, c. 1462), and 26 Aug., Milan (ASMi, AS, c. 931); G. da Castelnovate to Galeazzo, 26 Aug., Milan (ASMi, AS, c. 931). See also similar letters from Daniele da Palude to Galeazzo, 16 Oct., Milan (ASMi, AS, c. 931), and 21 Nov., Milan (ASMi, AS, c. 932).

71. Galeazzo to Lucia, 16 Apr. 1476 (ASMi, RM, no. 125, fo. 48v) (convent); for *cameriere,* see Galeazzo to captain of justice of Milan, 19 Dec. 1475 (ASMi, RM, no. 122, fo. 231r) (with note, "Intercedente Mca. d. Comitissa"); and Giovanni Giacomo Simonetta to Simonetta, 18 Dec., Cusago (ASMi, AS, c. 928), stating that Lucia had requested the favor.

72. Lazzaro Tedaldi to Galeazzo, 1 Dec. 1476, Milan (ASMi, AS, c. 1462). Lazzaro referred to the infant as the "Count of Melzo," although Lucia still held the title at the time.

73. For the children's locations from day to day, the most useful source is letters from GianGaleazzo's governor, Giovanni Agostino Olgiati, to Galeazzo (ASMi, AS, c. 1461, 1462, and 1464, *passim,* for the years 1471–1476; also scattered through ASMi, AS, c. 898–932).

74. Dombello Riccardi to Galeazzo, 17 Apr. 1471, "Romanove" (ASMi, AS, c. 902); Galeazzo to Cristoforo da Soncino, 19 Apr. (ASMi, RM, no. 98, fo. 291r), and to G. A. Olgiati, 25 Sep. 1472 (ASMi, RM, no. 107, fo. 274r).

75. For situation with Bona, see Guido Parati to Galeazzo, 6 Jan. 1470, Milan (2 letters, ASMi, AS, c. 1462 and 1464, respectively); Lancillotto del Maino to Galeazzo, 7 Jan. 1470, Milan (ASMi, AS, c. 892); and Guido Parati, L. del Maino, and Cristoforo da Soncino to Galeazzo, 11 Jan. 1470, Milan (ASMi, AS, c. 892). For Galeazzo's involvement, see letter to "Governesses and governors of our children," 10 Apr. 1474 (ASMi, RM, no. 115, fo. 232[bis]v) (moats), and to G. A. Olgiati, 19 Nov. 1475 (ASMi, RM, no. 121, fo. 340v) (rainy travel).

76. For family together at Pavia, see, e.g., Simonetta, *Diari,* 27; see also chap. 2.

For a modern assertion that Bona was occupied primarily with child rearing, see *DBI,* XI: 428.

77. Simonetta, *Diari,* 211.

78. For the legitimate and illegitimate children together, see G. A. Olgiati to Galeazzo, 22 Nov. 1473, Cassino (ASMi, AS, c. 1462), and list in Beltrami, *Castello* (1894): 267.

79. Pietrina Aliprandi to Galeazzo, 9 Mar. 1476, Milan, and Galeazzo to Taddeo Manfredi, 4 Mar., Pavia [draft] (both ASMi, AS, c. 929); Santoro, *Registri delle lettere ducali,* 138, 166 (midwife); Bona to G. A. Olgiati, 8 Apr., Vigevano [draft] (ASMi, AS, c. 931) (wet nurse).

80. For Margherita's care of Caterina, see Guido Visconti to Galeazzo, 6 Sep. 1470, Milan (ASMi, AS, c. 892); for her work under Duke Francesco, see SSL, Raccolta Formentini, cod. 55, fo. 180r.

81. Carlo Sforza to Galeazzo, 27 Aug. 1472, Milan (ASMi, AS, c. 1476-Carlo) (disrespect); Andreotto del Maino to Galeazzo; Angelo Simonetta to Galeazzo; Francesca (della Scala) Simonetta to Galeazzo; Battista da Cremona to Galeazzo; all 9 May 1470, Milan (ASMi, AS, c. 893) (Simonetta marriage).

82. Francesca Simonetta to Galeazzo, 6 Aug. 1470, Milan (ASMi, AS, c. 894), and 10 Mar. 1475, Milan (ASMi, AS, c. 926); Galeazzo to Lorenzo Terenzi da Pesaro, past auditor, and to Giovanni Antonio Talenti da Firenze, present auditor, 18 Sep. 1476 (ASMi, RM, no. 125, fo. 367v) (advocacy); draft will dated 18 May 1470, Pavia (ASMi, AS, c. 1461); and ACM, BT, cod. 1325, fos. 117–122 (invitations to San Giuseppe and Christmas 1476).

83. The grant was probably made before December 10, 1472, when Galeazzo referred to "the count of Galliate, our son" (to G. Giapanno; ASMi, RM, no. 110bis. fo. 111r), and certainly by May 19, 1473), when Galeazzo referred to "our son Alessandro, count of Galliate" (to *iconomo* of Pavia, ASMi, RM, no. 114, fo. 92r). The duke's draft will of May 18, 1470 (Pavia, ASMi, AS, c. 1461), left Alessandro a substantial income of 4,000 ducats per year.

84. G. da Castelnovate, G. Giapanno, and G. Simonetta to Galeazzo, 17 Mar. 1476, Milan (ASMi, AS, c. 1475-Bosio) (funeral); Alessandro to Galeazzo, 19 Nov. 1474, Milan (ASMi, AS, c. 925) (diplomatic reception); Battista da Cremona to Galeazzo, 3 Oct. 1476, Abbiategrasso (ASMi, AS, c. 929) (request).

85. Carlo's tutor was Gabriele Paveri da Fontana (Galeazzo to Francesca Simonetta, 30 June 1474, and to Gabriele, 16 July; ASMi, RM, no. 118, fos. 33r and 66r). Francesca, Carlo's mother-in-law, chose him. For Galeazzo's threat, see letter to Carlo, 18 Nov. 1473 (ASMi, RM, no. 112, fo. 333v). The ducal library included an oration by Gabriele for Tristano Sforza's wedding and verses written for Gaspare da Vimercate (Mazzatinti, "Inventario," 57–58). After Galeazzo's death, Gabriele published the long poem, *De vita et obitu Galeaz M. Sfortiae Vicecomitis* (Milan, 1477).

86. For Alessandro's preceptor, see Galeazzo to *iconomo* of Pavia, 19 May 1473 (ASMi, RM, no. 114, fo. 92r). For GianGaleazzo's, see G. A. Olgiati to Galeazzo, 5 Mar. 1476, Milan (ASMi, AS, c. 929) (beginning); G. A. Olgiati to Galeazzo, 7 Nov., Abbiategrasso (ASMi, AS, c. 1462); Galeazzo to Mattia and to G. A. Olgiati, 1 Dec. (ASMi, RM, no. 126, fo. 59r) (reading limits). In March 1475, Galeazzo did not want his son reading yet (letter to G. A. Olgiati, ASMi, RM, no. 120, fo. 113v). Mattia may have been Sforza Maria's tutor as of 1468 (Beltrami, *Dame Milanesi,* 20).

87. See letters from G. A. Olgiati to Galeazzo (ASMi, AS, c. 1462, *passim*). Galeazzo gave permission for callers to enter the ducal preserve (Galeazzo to Ambrosino da Longhignana, 12 Nov. 1473, Pavia, ASMi, AS, c. 915).

88. Galeazzo to G. A. Olgiati, 3 Mar. 1475 (ASMi, RM, no. 120. fo. 89r). The commission was to be executed by Giorgio Mantegazza; see also Giovanni Agostino to Galeazzo, 28 Feb., Milan (ASMi, AS, c. 926).

89. Galeazzo to bishop of Parma, 27 Feb. 1468, Vigevano [draft] (ASMi, AS, c. 883).

90. Antonio Guidoboni to Galeazzo, 8 May 1467, Milan (ASMi, AS, c. 880).

91. A transcription of the list constitutes Appendix 2.

92. The 1476 budget allots 22 *camerieri* traveling with the duke an aggregate of 2,094 ducats; that category may not include the more expensive *camerieri di camera* and *di guardacamera.* However, the budget also assigns 20 ducats each to 47 other *camerieri* "who have to stay at home" (Porro, "Preventivo," 132). The number of horses allowed to *camerieri* was roughly twice that supported in January 1475 (see Porro, "Lettere" [1879]: 263–264).

93. Giuliano da Varese and Cosmino da Briosco to Galeazzo, 28 Aug. 1476, Palestro (ASMi, AS, c. 856).

94. Galeazzo to Lucia and to castellan of Monza, 9 Oct. 1476 (ASMi, RM, no. 124, fo. 54r); Daniele da Palude to Galeazzo, 16 Oct., Milan (ASMi, AS, c. 931) (Alessandro). Galeazzo had to command Alessandro to "take your wife home immediately and sleep with her" (23 Aug. 1475, ASMi, RM, no. 122, fo. 85r). For marriage, see chap. 7; she was born between December 20, 1462, and July 20, 1463 (see documents of those dates in ASMi, Notarile, f. 1218-Sudati Lancillotto and f. 1219-Sudati Lancillotto, respectively).

95. Litta, *Famiglie Celebri,* d. 1, t. 1; Santoro, *Sforza,* Chap. L and t. V (general background). Bosio's daughter Costanza married Galeazzo's brother Filippo Maria. For Giovanni and Giacomo da Capua among the *camerieri di camera,* see, e.g., the list in ASMi, AS, c. 925. Griseide herself recommended Giacomo to the duke (Griseide to Galeazzo, 20 Jan. and 6 Mar. 1474, Parma, ASMi, AS, c. 1478-Griseide). Bosio died on March 10; for letters on his will and related matters, see ASMi, AS, c. 1478-Griseide.

96. Galeazzo to *commissario* of Parma, 10 Mar. 1476 (ASMi, RM, no. 123, fo. 108r), and to Griseide (da Capua) Sforza, 10, 15, and 19(?) Mar. (ASMi, RM, no. 123, fos. 108r, 112v, and 121r–v, respectively); also Galeazzo to Griseide, 13 Mar., Vigevano [draft] (ASMi, AS, c. 1475-Bosio). See ASMi, RM, no. 123, for various letters from Galeazzo related to Griseide's efforts to straighten out her late husband's finances. At some point before the funeral, Bosio's body was escorted by a military honor guard (Francesco Malletta to Galeazzo, 16 Mar., Milan; ASMi, AS, c. 1475-Bosio).

97. Galeazzo to G. da Castelnovate, G. Giapanno, and G. Simonetta, 15 Mar. 1476 (ASMi, RM, no. 125, fo. 4v). See also G. Simonetta, G. da Castelnovate, and G. Giapanno to Cicco and G. da Castelnovate and G. Giapanno to Cicco, 13 and 15 Mar., Milan, respectively (ASMi, AS, c. 1475-Bosio). Bosio's mother was Antonia Salimbeni, Muzio Sforza's first wife (Santoro, *Sforza,* t. V).

98. G. da Castelnovate, G. Giapanno, and G. Simonetta to Galeazzo and P. da Bagnacavallo to Galeazzo, 17 Mar. 1476, Milan (ASMi, AS, c. 1475-Bosio).

99. Benedetto Dei, *Cronica,* 67 (fo. 22v).

100. Proclamation of 20 Apr. 1476 (ASMi, RM, no. 125, fo. 56r). For Galeazzo's treatment of his own household in 1475–1476, see, e.g., letters excoriating Gottardo Panigarola (Porro, "Lettere" [1878]: 254 and [1879]: 267).

101. Galeazzo to Giacometto del Maino, 21 Dec. 1476 (ASMi, AS, c. 567). See also Galeazzo to Edward IV, 21 Dec. (ASMi, AS, c. 567) (both translated in *Calendar of State Papers: Milan,* I: 229).

102. For guards, see Ambrosino da Longhignana to Galeazzo, 15 Nov. 1467, Milan (ASMi, AS, c. 887) (Milan); Galeazzo to podestà and *deputati officio provisionum* of Pavia, 11 Mar. 1476 (ASMi, RM, no. 123, fo. 109v); and Galeazzo to Ambrosino da Longhignana, 22 Aug. 1470 (ASMi, RM, no. 95, fo. 177v) (Cassano). For locking wells, see Galeazzo to castellans of Pavia, Monza, Cremona, Pizzighettone, Trezzo, and Cassano; to podestà of Vigevano, Galliate, Gropello, and Gambolò; to castellan and podestà of Abbiate; to "officials" of Villanova and Mirabello; and to Filippo Maria Visconti for Fontaneto; all 28 Dec. 1473 (ASMi, RM, no. 116, fo. 150r). See also Galeazzo to castellan of Vigevano, 31 Oct. 1473 (ASMi, RM, no. 116, fo. 73v).

103. Mazzatinti, "Inventario," 58.

104. Niccolo Roberti to Ercole d'Este, 18 Sep. 1476, Milan (ASMo, CDE, DA, Milano, b. 1). Galeazzo had thought of adding 100 mounted crossbowmen to his guard nine months before, when Filippo of Savoy made a threat against him (Z. Saggi to L. Gonzaga, 28 Feb. 1476, Milan; ASMa, AG, b. 1625).

105. Galeazzo to Borella, 7 Sep. 1476 (ASMi, RM, no. 124, fo. 40r).

106. Undated testimony of Gaspare Trivulzio, Guidetto Cusani, and Filippo Pietrasanta (ASMi, AS, c. 894).

107. On plague in Renaissance Italy generally, see Carmichael, *Plague and the Poor*; for antiplague efforts in Milan, see 111–116 and 120–121.

108. Galeazzo excluded an organ master who had come through a plague zone (letter to *commissario* of Parma, 31 May 1476; ASMi, RM, no. 123, fo. 212v) and refused to see a French envoy who arrived ill (letter to *commissario* of Parma, Sep. 1472; ASMi, RM, no. 107, fo. 259v). One of his favorite kennelmen was delayed in returning from a visit to France because he had to avoid plague outbreaks in Piedmont on the way home (G. Giapanno to Galeazzo, 29 Aug. 1473, Milan; ASMi, AS, c. 914).

109. Privy Council to Galeazzo, 6 Apr. 1468, Milan (ASMi, AS, c. 883). See "Hector Marchesius" to Galeazzo, 3 Apr., Milan (ASMi, AS, c. 883), for a report contributing to their recommendation. For the Melegnano case, see Bianca Maria to Hector, 2 Sep. [draft] (ASMi, AS, c. 885). See also an unsigned letter to Galeazzo (3 Sep. 1468, "ex officio n[ost]ro"; ASMi, AS, c. 885) about sending him a list, "according to custom," of those suffering natural deaths in the city. They stated that no cases of plague had occurred and that the city was healthy. Many diseases were mistakenly diagnosed as "the plague" (Carmichael, *Plague and the Poor,* 2).

110. Galeazzo to "nobilibus d[ominis] deputatis supra facto pestis," 4 May 1468, and to "d[ominis] deputatis sanitati M[edio]l[an]i," 5 May (ASMi, RM, no. 83, fos. 105v and 106v, respectively). The city of Parma could not send ambassadors to the duke's wedding because it was in quarantine (Galeazzo to G. Simonetta, Feb. 1469; ASMi, RM, no. 89, fo. 127v).

111. Galeazzo to castellan of Bereguardo, 4 July 1472 (ASMi, RM, no. 107, fo.

90v). See also three letters in ASMi, RM, no. 83, fos. 347v–348r, about a suspected case of plague in the house of an artisan making equipment for the duke's horses. All the equipment he made was to be burned, and restrictions were placed on all stable boys and footmen.

112. Simonetta, *Diari,* 150–151; Galeazzo to "deputati sopra giubileo," 18 Mar. 1475 (ASMi, RM, no. 120, fo. 120v).

113. See various letters in ASMi, RM, no. 123, e.g., fo. 188r; for Pavia outbreak, see letters in ASMi, RM, no. 127, e.g., fo. 14v.

114. For a general account of this visit and documents related to it, see Ghinzoni, "Ambasciatore del Soldan d'Egitto." The sultan was the Mamluk Qa'it Bai (1468–1496); his figurehead caliph was al-Ashraf Saif al-Din. Milanese sources for this visit called him "the Great Sultan." "The Cairo of the Sultan" was renowned in Milan as a city of legendary greatness (Raffaelle de' Nigri to Galeazzo, 7 Jan. 1474; ASMi, AS, c. 922).

115. Simonetta, *Diari,* 211–212; Galeazzo to Cicco, 13 Oct. 1476, Galliate (ASMi, AS, c. 931).

116. Simonetta, *Diari,* 212–213.

117. Simonetta, *Diari,* 213 (Privy Council) and 216 (departure and refusal of gifts); Galeazzo to Ambrosino da Longhignana and castellan of Porta Giovia, 17 Oct. 1476, and to Cicco (ASMi, RM, no. 124, fos. 66v and 76v, respectively). While the envoy was in Milan, he complained that a Sicilian servant "who had been made a Moor and is circumcised" had run off with money and valuables. Galeazzo commanded that the servant be found and forced to return what he had taken but then that he be "released and put at his liberty" (letter of 17 Oct.; ASMi, RM, no. 127, fo. 10r). A month after the ambassador left, he claimed that "one of his Negroes" had hidden from him to stay and become a Christian. Galeazzo agreed with his request that the slave "pay the price" or be restored to his owner (letter to G. Giapanno, 7 Dec., ASMi, RM, no. 126, fo. 69v).

118. See Lorenzo de' Medici, *Lettere,* II: 491–496.

119. For instructions on their message to Charles the Bold, see Galeazzo to Luca Grimaldi, 14 Jan. 1476 (ASMi, RM, no. 122, fo. 262r).

120. Gerolamo Olgiati to Galeazzo, 15 Jan. 1476, Milan (ASMi, AS, c. 1462) (printed in Belotti, *Gerolamo Olgiati,* 183–184); Galeazzo to Gerolamo, 18 Jan. (ASMi, RM, no. 122, fo. 269r).

121. For a description by the ambassadors of the Burgundian loss at Granson, see Colombo, "Iolanda, duchessa di Savoia," 288–289.

122. General narrative drawn mainly from Lorenzo de' Medici, *Lettere,* II, Excursus IV–V; Catalano in Treccani, *Storia di Milano,* VII: 300–305; and itinerary from Simonetta, *Diari,* 218–228.

123. Orfeo Cenni da Ricavo to Z. Saggi, 27 Nov. 1476, S. Agata Vercellese [Santhià] (ASMa, AG, b. 1625).

124. Simonetta, *Diari,* 224, and Dina, "Ludovico il Moro," 765–766. The argument for fratricidal intentions has been made by Riccardo Fubini, in Lorenzo de' Medici, *Lettere,* II: 523–535, and "Crisi del ducato," 67. However, the supporting evidence comes from sources with ulterior motives. In making a case against her brothers-in-law in June 1477, the regent Bona claimed they had plotted against the duke's life in 1476 ("Crisi del ducato," 67, n. 3). That accusation rested on the confession of a participant in the brothers' revolt (Donato del Conte), whose statement may

have been influenced by his circumstances (Dina, "Ludovico il Moro," 764; Santoro, *Sforza,* 189–190).

125. Galeazzo to *referendario* of Pavia, 23 Dec. 1476 (ASMi, RM, no. 127, fo. 76r) (Pavia prohibition); Galeazzo to Ascanio, 21 Dec. (ASMi, AS, c. 856).

126. The most complete account of Galeazzo's death and events leading to it is in Belotti, *Gerolamo Olgiati.* He printed many documents and assembled the facts, although his comments are often implausible. For the days before and after Christmas, see Chap. VIII. Every history of Milan or the Sforza recounts the story, generally based on Corio's account ([1978] II: 1399–1401). Corio was an eyewitness but embellished events; descriptions by Orfeo da Ricavo and Zaccaria Saggi da Pisa are more credible.

127. Corio claims Galeazzo cried, "O Nostra Donna!" The number of wounds is specified in Z. Saggi to L. Gonzaga, 28 Dec. 1476, Milan (ASMa, AG, b. 1625; quoted and paraphrased in Belotti, *Gerolamo Olgiati,* 110).

128. The narrative that follows is drawn mainly from Belotti, *Gerolamo Olgiati.* Many relevant documents that he published (179–203) are filed in ASMi, AS, c. 1462. Some letters there do not belong, among them several from a homonymous contemporary of Giovanni Andrea (see chap. 6).

129. For Latin tags, see Belotti, *Gerolamo Olgiati,* Chap. IX.

130. Corio prints the confession in (1978), II: 1401–1407; Belotti used it throughout *Gerolamo Olgiati.* Montano actually received much support from Galeazzo. In 1468, the duke recommended him for appointment as a professor of rhetoric in the University of Pavia, resident in Milan. Galeazzo suggested an annual salary of 150 florins—more than the Privy Council wanted to spend. Evidently, the duke did not realize Cola was the teacher who had led Milanese youths to Colleoni in 1467 (Galeazzo to Privy Council, 14 Oct. and 12 Nov. 1468; ASMi, RM, no. 82, fos. 97r and 211v). As of 1474–1475, Cola still held the university post (ASMi, RM, no. 118, fo. 280v). In 1475, Galeazzo supported him in litigation at Cola's native Bologna (ASMi, RM, no. 117, fo. 330r).

131. For Carlo as chancellor, see Galeazzo to Council of Justice, 11 Jan. 1474 (ASMi, RM, no. 115, fo. 54r). He should not be confused with a ducal secretary of the same name, who held other civil offices later (see Santoro, *Uffici,* 32, 54, and 88). As Belotti shows (Chap. X), the conspirators' families suffered from guilt by association, but most were cleared of complicity.

132. Belotti, *Gerolamo Olgiati,* Chaps. V–VII, follows Lampugnani and his dispute, printing some letters. The reference to the previous abbot's "evil life" comes from a letter he missed: Branda Castiglione to Galeazzo, 8 July 1475, Milan (ASMi, AS, c. 927). The letter accuses Councillor Giacomo Cusani and his family of hiding the abbot from the bishop, keeping him from trial. See also Branda Castiglione to Cicco, 1 and 2 July 1475, Milan (ASMi, AS, c. 927), about bringing the matter to the court of Rome.

9: "His Court Was One of the Most Brilliant in the Whole World"

1. 3 Nov. 1471, Pavia (ASMi, Notarile, f. 1580; summarized in Giulini, *Memorie spettanti,* VI: 593–596. The narrative that follows derives mainly from Santoro, *Sforza,* and Treccani, *Storia di Milano,* VII–VIII.

2. Galeazzo Visconti died in 1515. For the two sons, see Santoro, *Sforza,* t. II. For Lucia, see Sitoni di Scozia, *Theatrum Genealogicum,* 373, and petition from Lucia Marliani, "consorte de Messer Ambroxio Raverto," to an unnamed duke (probably Ludovico), about feudal dues from which she claimed to be exempt. The petition is undated, but the calligraphy suggests the 1490s (ASMi, *Famiglie,* 118-Marliani).

3. See Lopez, ed., *Nozze dei Principi Milanesi* and *Festa di Nozze per Ludovico il Moro.*

4. For Caterina, see biographies by Breisach, Pasolini, and Graziani/Venturelli. For Taddeo, see Santoro, *Uffici,* 11. Chiara was later suspected of poisoning Pietro (Argegni, ed., *Condottieri, Capitani, e Tribuni,* I, 225).

5. Reported in many places, including Corio (1978), II: 1410. For reaction around Italy, see also Ilardi, "Assassination of Galeazzo Maria Sforza."

6. Benedetto Dei, *Cronica,* fo. 42v.

7. Rinuccini, *Ricordi storici,* CXXV.

8. Machiavelli, *Florentine Histories,* 312–316.

9. Angelo de Tumulillis, *Notabilia Temporum,* quoted in Belotti, *Gerolamo Olgiati,* 106.

10. *Diario Ferrarese,* 29. The "Lamento del duca Galeazo," a piece of doggerel verse published later in the fifteenth century, called the duke "unfortunate" and the assassin Lampugnani "traitor." The text was published in D'Adda, "Canti storici popolari II," 288–294.

11. Bernardi, *Cronache forlivesi,* 3–9.

12. *Corpus Chronicorum Bononiensum,* 445.

13. Corio (1978), II: 1409.

14. From Philippe de Commynes, *Mémoires,* cited in Trexler, *Public Life in Renaissance Florence,* 399.

15. Galeazzo to Carlo Reguardati, 19(?) Feb. 1469 (ASMi, RM, no. 89, fo. 142r). On another occasion, Galeazzo himself was told that "lords want to be obeyed by their servants" (Giovanni Simonetta to Galeazzo, 8 June 1473, Milan; ASMi, AS, c. 913).

16. E.g., Catalano in Treccani, *Storia di Milano,* VII: 227.

17. Braudel, *Capitalism and Material Life,* 223, refers to Renaissance Italy, "economically so far advanced . . . producing new displays for princely and ostentatious courts." He saw "a completely different framework" appearing, "more solemn and formal, . . . a strange foretaste of the Great Century and of that court life which was to be a sort of parade, a theatrical spectacle." Roy Strong and Stephen Orgel have illuminated the concept of the court as a stage for splendid displays with political significance.

18. Zaccaria Saggi da Pisa to Ludovico Gonzaga, 31 July 1470, Milan (ASMa, AG, b. 1623).

19. Porro, "Preventivo," 132–134.

20. Corio (1978), II: 1409.

21. ASMi, Feudi Camerali, no. 333, doc. 4.

22. Gary Ianziti has argued that the Chancery operated independently of the court and that histories written by Giovanni Simonetta and Lodrisio Crivelli "were not products of courtly culture, cut off, as it were, from the surrounding social and political context" (*Politics and Propaganda,* 7). The implication that such a separate "courtly culture" existed in Milan is misleading.

23. See Elias, *Court Society,* 38, for an acknowledgment of, and departure from, Weber's emphasis on bureaucracy.

24. At its most extreme, the idea of the exemplary microcosm is seen in Clifford Geertz's work on south Bali: "This is the theory that the court-and-capital is . . . a microcosm of the supernatural order. . . . The ritual life of the court, and in fact the life of the court generally, is thus paradigmatic, not merely reflective, of social order" (Geertz, *Negara,* 9). "The *negara adat* [court community] was a stretch of sacred space. . . . All those living in its bounds, and therefore benefiting from its energies, were collectively responsible for meeting the ritual and moral obligations those energies entailed" (ibid., 128–129).

25. ASMi, RM, no. 82, fo. 219r.

26. Castiglione to Giacomo Boschetto of Gonzaga [his brother-in-law], 8 Oct. 1499, Milan (printed in *Lettere del Castiglione,* I: 5; quoted in Ady, *Milan under the Sforza,* 303).

Epilogue

1. The quotation is from Zaccaria Saggi da Pisa's letter of 28 Dec. 1476 to Ludovico Gonzaga (ASMa, AG, b. 1625). Details of Galeazzo's dress and burial were collected by Belotti, *Gerolamo Olgiati,* 110. He drew them from Corio's history, a diary from Parma, and Zaccaria's letter, which Belotti thought was dated 27 Dec.

Bibliography

This bibliography is not exhaustive. It
includes only works that have contributed
substantially to this study.

Sources for Milan and the Sforza

Ady, Cecilia. *A History of Milan under the Sforza.* London, 1907.

Ansani, Michele. "Note sulla politica ecclesiastica degli Sforza." *In* Centre Européen d'Études Bourguignonnes, *Milan et les États bourguignons: Deux ensembles princiers entre Moyen Age et Renaissance.* Publication 28. Brussels, 1988.

———. "La provista dei benefici (1450–1466): Strumenti e limiti dell' intervento ducale." *In* G. Chittolini, ed., *Gli Sforza, la chiesa lombarda, la corte di Roma: Strutture e pratiche beneficiarie nel ducato di Milano.* Naples, 1989. 1–114.

Archivio di Stato, Milan. *Squarci d'Archivio Sforzesco (nostra storica documentata).* Ed. Carlo Paganini. Milan, 1981.

Archivio Storico Civico, Milan. *Milano nell'età di Ludovico il Moro.* Milan, 1983.

———. *Milano e gli Sforza: Francesco e Galeazzo Maria (1450–1476).* Exhibit Catalog. Milan, 1981.

Arici, Zelmira. *Bona di Savoia, Duchessa di Milano.* Turin, 1935.

Barbieri, Gino. *Economia e politica nel ducato di Milano (1386–1535).* Milan, 1938.

———. "Gottardo Panigarola mercante e spenditore sforzesco." *Rivista Italiana di Scienze Economiche* X, no. 7 (July 1938): 535–553. Later version in *Atti e Memorie del Congresso Storico Lombardo,* III (1939): 311–326.

Baroni, C., and S. Samek-Ludovici. *La Pittura Lombarda del Quattrocento.* Messina and Florence, 1952.

Belotti, Bortolo. *Il Dramma di Gerolamo Olgiati.* Milan, 1929 (reprinted in 1950 with its originally intended title, *Storia di una congiura*).

Beltrami, Luca. "L'Annullamento del contratto di matrimonio fra Galeazzo Maria Sforza e Dorotea Gonzaga." *ASL* (1889): 126–132.

———. *Il Castello di Milano sotto il dominio degli Sforza.* Milan, 1885.

———. *Il Castello di Milano (Castrum Porta Jovis) sotto il dominio dei Visconti e degli Sforza.* Milan, 1894.

————. *Dame Milanese invitate alle nozze di Galeazzo Maria Sforza con Bona di Savoia.* Milan, 1920.

————. *Per la storia della navigazione nel territorio Milanese.* Milan, 1888.

Benvenuti, Antonia Tissoni. "Un nuovo documento sulla 'Camera degli Sposi' del Mantegna." *Italia medioevale e umanistica* 24 (1981): 357–360.

Bernardi, Andrea. *Cronache forlivesi di Andrea Bernardi dal 1476 al 1517.* Ed. G. Mazzatinti. Bologna, 1885.

Bignami, Luigi. *I Castelli Lombardi.* Milan, 1932.

————. *Francesco Sforza (1401–1466).* 2 vols. Milan, 1937.

Biscaro, Gerolamo. "Panfilo Castaldi e gli inizi dell'arte della stampa a Milano." *ASL* (1915): 5–14.

Bonello-Uricchio, Caterina. "I Rapporti tra Lorenzo de' Medici e Galeazzo Maria Sforza negli anni 1471–1473." *ASL* (1964–65): 33–49.

Breisach, Ernst, *Caterina Sforza.* Glencoe, Ill., 1963.

Bueno de Mesquita, Daniel M. *Giangaleazzo Visconti.* Cambridge (U.K.), 1941.

————. "Ludovico Sforza and His Vassals." *In Italian Renaissance Studies,* ed. E. F. Jacob. London, 1960, 184–216.

Caffi, Michele. "Bianca Maria Visconte-Sforza, Duchessa di Milano, a Sant' Antonio di Padova." *ASL* (1886): 400–413.

————. "Il Castello di Pavia." *ASL* (1876): 543–559.

————. "Creditori della duchessa Bianca Maria Sforza." *ASL* (1876): 534–542.

Caleffini, Ugo. *Diario.* Biblioteca Comunale Ariostea (Ferrara), Classe I, Ms. 769 (paraphrased by G. Pardi, vol. 1, Ferrara, 1938).

Calvi, Felice. "Il Castello Porta Giovia e sue vicende nella storia di Milano." *ASL* (1886): 229–297.

————. *Famiglie Notabili Milanesi.* 3 vols. Milan, 1875.

————. "Il Patriziato Milanese." *ASL* (1874–75): 101–147, 413–464.

Canetta, Carlo. "Le sponsalie tra casa Sforza e casa d'Aragona." *ASL* (1882): 136–144.

Cantu, Cesare. "Anedotti di Lodovico il Moro." *ASL* (1874–75): 483–487.

————. "Curiosità d'Archivio: Nozze di Bona Sforza, e lettere di Tristano e Galeazzo Maria Sforza." *ASL* (1875): 179–188.

————. "Guiniforte Barzizza, maestro di Galeazzo Maria Sforza." *ASL* (1894): 399–442.

————. "Giovanni e Isacco Argiropulo." *ASL* (1891): 168–173.

Caroselli, Susan. *The Casa Marliani and Palace Building in Late Quattrocento Lombardy.* New York, 1985.

Casanova, Enrico. *Nobiltà Lombarda Genealogie,* ed. G. Bascapè. Milan, 1930.

Cassa di Risparmio di Piacenza e Vigevano. *La Biscia e l'Aquila: Il castello di Vigevano, una lettura storico-artistica.* Piacenza, 1988.

Centre Europèen d'Etudes Bourguignonnes. *Milan et les États bourguignons: Deux ensemblers princiers entre Moyen Age et Renaissance,* no. 28. Brussels, 1988.

Cerioni, Lydia. *La diplomazia sforzesca nella seconda metà del Quattrocento e i suoi cifrari segreti.* 2 vols. Rome, 1970.

Cesari, Anna Maria. "Un'orazione inedita di Ippolita Sforza e alcune lettere di Galeazzo Maria Sforza." *ASL* (1964–65): 50ff.

Cesari, Gaetano. *Musici e musicisti alla corte sforzesca.* Milan, 1923 (vol. 4 of Mala-guzzi Valeri, *Corte di Lodovico il Moro*).

Chittolini, Giorgio, ed. *La crisi degli ordinamenti comunali e le origini dello stato del Rinascimento.* Bologna, 1979.

————. "Entrate e alienazioni di entrate nell'amministrazione sforzesca: Le vendite del 1466–67." Milan, 1979.

————. *La Formazione dello stato regionale e le istituzioni del contado.* Turin, 1979.

————. "Infeudazioni e politica feudale nel ducato visconteo-sforzesco." *Quaderni storici* 19 (1972).

————. "Il particolarismo signorile e feudale in Emilia fra Quattro e Cinquecento." *Il Rinascimento nelle corti padane.* Bari, 1977.

————. ed., *Metamorfosi di un borgo: Vigevano in età visconteo-sforzesco.* Milan, 1992.

————. ed., *Gli Sforza, la chiesa lombarda, la corte di Roma: Strutture e pratiche beneficiarie nel ducato di Milano.* Naples, 1989.

Cipolla, Carlo. *Moneta a Milano nel Quattrocento: Monetazione argentea e svalu-tazione secolare.* Rome, 1988.

Clausse, Gustave. *Les Sforza et les arts en Milanais.* Paris, 1909.

Cognasso, Francesco. *I Visconti.* Milan, 1966.

Colombo, Elia. "Iolanda, duchessa di Savoia." *Miscellanea di Storia Italiana* XXXI (1887): 1–306.

Corio, Bernardino. *Storia di Milano,* ed. A. M. Guerra. 2 vols. Turin, 1978.

————. *Storia di Milano.* Vol. 2. Milan, 1565.

————. *Storia di Milano.* Vol. 3. Milan, 1857.

Corpus Chronicorum Bononiensum (RIS² 18:1, pt. 4). Bologna, 1939.

Corpus Nummorum Italicarum. V. Rome, 1914.

Crivelli Visconti, Umberto. *La Nobiltà Lombarda.* Bologna, 1972.

Crollalanza, GiamBattista. "I Conti Balbiani di Chiavenna." *Giornale Araldico-Genealogico-Diplomatico* VI (1878–79): 37ff.

Cusin, Francesco. "Le aspirazioni stranieri sul ducato di Milano e la investitura impe-riale (1450–1454)." *ASL* (1936): 277–369.

————. "L'impero e la successione degli Sforza ai Visconti." *ASL* (1936): 3–116.

————. "Le relazioni tra l'impero ed il ducato di Milano dalla pace di Lodi alla morte di Francesco Sforza." *ASL* (1938): 3–110.

————. *I rapporti fra la Lombardia e l'Impero dalla morte di Francesco Sforza all'avvento di Lodovico il Moro (1466–1480).* Trieste, 1913.

D'Adda, Gerolamo. "Canti storici popolari italiani II: La morte di Galeazzo Maria Sforza." *ASL* (1875): 284–294.

Decembrio, Pier Candido. *Vita Philippi Mariae Tertij Ligurum Ducis (RIS² XX, pt. 1).* Bari, 1926.

————. *Vita di Filippo Maria Visconti,* ed. Elio Bartolini. Milan, 1983.

Dei, Benedetto. *La Cronica dall'anno 1400 all'anno 1500,* ed. R. Barducci. Florence, 1984.

De Roover, Raymond. *Rise and Decline of the Medici Bank.* Cambridge, 1963.

Diario Ferrarese, ed. Bernardino Zambotti (*RIS²,* 24:7). 2d ed. Bologna, 1934.

Dina, Achille. "Ludovico il Moro prima della sua venuta al governo." *ASL* (1886): 737–776.

Ferorelli, Nicola. "Il Ducato di Bari sotto Sforza Maria e Lodovico il Moro." *ASL* (1914): 389–467.

Ffoulkes, Jocelyn C., and Rodolfo Maiocchi. *Vincenzo Foppa of Brescia.* London, 1909.

Filippi, G. *Il Matrimonio di Galeazzo Maria Sforza e Bona di Savoia.* Turin, 1891.

Forcella, Vincenzo. *Iscrizioni delle chiese e degli altri edifici di Milano.* 12 vols. Milan, 1889–1893.

Formentini, Marco. *Memoria sul rendiconto del ducato di Milano per l'anno 1463.* Milan, 1870.

Fossati, Felice. "Altre spigolature d'archivio." *ASL* (1956): 192–210.

———. "Noterelle viscontee-sforzesche." *ASL* (1953): 218–227.

———. "Per la mensa dei duchi di Milano e della loro corte." *ASL* (1961): 252–284.

———. "Relazioni fra una 'terra' ed i suoi signori." *ASL* (1914): 109–186.

Frati, Lodovico. "Un formulario della cancelleria di Francesco Sforza." *ASL* (1891): 364–391.

Fubini, Riccardo. "Osservazioni e documenti sulla crisi del ducato di Milano nel 1477, e sulla riforma del Consiglio Segreto in ducato di Bona Sforza." *In Essays Presented to Myron Gilmore,* ed. Sergio Bertelli and Gloria Ramakus. Vol. 1. Florence, 1978. 47–103.

Fumi, Luigi. "La Sfida di Galeazzo Maria Sforza a Bartolomeo Colleoni." *ASL* (1912): 357–382.

Ghinzoni, Pietro. "Un ambasciatore del Soldan d'Egitto alla corte milanese nel 1476." *ASL* (1875): 155–178.

———. "Galeazzo Maria Sforza e il regno di Cipro (1473–1474)." *ASL* (1879): 721–745.

———. "L'Inquinto ossia una tassa odiosa del secolo XV." *ASL* (1884): 499ff.

———. "Rettifiche alla storia di Bernardino Corio a proposito di Cristierno re di Danimarca." *ASL* (1891): 60–71.

———. "Spedizione sforzesca in Francia." *ASL* (1890): 314ff.

———. "Usi e costumi nuziali principeschi: Girolamo Riario e Caterina Sforza (1473)." *ASL* (1886): 101–111.

Giampietrino, Daniele. "La pretesa donazione di Filippo Maria Visconti a Francesco Sforza." *ASL* (1876): 639–681.

Giulini, Alessandro. "Filippo Maria Sforza." *ASL* (1913): 376–388.

———. "Polidoro Sforza." *ASL* (1913): 257–270.

Giulini, Giorgio. *Memorie spettanti alla storia della citta e campagna di Milano.* VI. Milan, 1857.

Graziani, Natale, and Gabriella Venturelli. *Caterina Sforza.* Milan, 1987.

Great Britain, Public Record Office. *Calendar of State Papers and Manuscripts: Milan.* I. London, 1912.

Hatfield, Rab. "Some Unknown Descriptions of the Medici Palace in 1459." *Art Bulletin* 52 (1970): 232–249.

Ianziti, Gary. "Patronage and the Production of History: The Case of Quattrocento Milan." *In* F. W. Kent and P. Simons, eds., *Patronage, Art and Society in Renaissance Italy.* Oxford, 1987. 299–311.

———. *Politics and Propaganda in Sforza Milan.* Oxford, 1988.

Ilardi, Vincent. "The Assassination of Galeazzo Maria Sforza and the Reaction of

Italian Diplomacy." *In Violence and Civil Disorder in Italy, 1200–1600*, ed. Lauro Martines. Berkeley and Los Angeles, 1972.

———. "Crosses and Carets: Renaissance Patronage and Coded Letters of Recommendation." *American Historical Review* XXIX, no. 5 (1987): 1127–1149.

———. *Dispatches, with Related Documents, of Milanese Ambassadors in France and Burgundy, 1450–1483*. 3 vols. Vols. I–II ed. and trans. with P. M. Kendall, Athens, Ohio. Vol. III, trans. Frank Fata, DeKalb, Ill., 1970-[1981].

———. "Doni di occhiali alla corte sforzesca." *Ca' de Sass*, no. 113, 52–56.

———. "Eyeglasses and Concave Lenses in Fifteenth-Century Florence and Milan: New Documents." *Renaissance Quarterly* XXIX (1976): 341–360.

———. *Occhiali alla corte di Francesco e Galeazzo Maria Sforza*. Milan, 1978.

———. *Studies in Italian Renaissance Diplomatic History*. London, 1986.

Jahn, Lila. *Bianca Maria, Duchessa di Milano*. Milan, 1941.

Lazzeroni, Enrico. "Il Consiglio segreto o Senato sforzesco." *Atti del congresso della societa storica lombarda* (1938): 95–168.

Leverotti, Franca. "La crisi finanziaria del ducato di Milano alla fine del Quattrocento." *In* Archivio Storico Civico, Milan, *Milano nell'età di Ludovico il Moro*. Milan, 1983. 585–632.

———. "Scritture finanziarie dell'età sforzesca." *Squarci d'archivio sforzesco*, ed. C. Paganini. Milan, 1981. 128–133.

Lee, Egmont. *Sixtus IV and Men of Letters*. Rome, 1978.

Litta, Pompeo. *Famiglie Celebri di Italia*. Milan, 1819–1883.

Lockwood, Lewis. "Strategies of Music Patronage in the Fifteenth Century: The *Cappella* of Ercole I D'Este." *In* I. Fenlon, ed., *Music in Medieval and Early Modern Europe*. Cambridge (U.K.), 1981. 227–245.

Lopez, Guido, ed. *Festa di Nozze per Ludovico il Moro nelle testimonianze di Tristano Calco, Giacomo Trotti, Isabella d'Este, GianGaleazzo Sforza, Beatrice de' Contrari, et altri*. Milan, 1976.

———. *Nozze dei Principi Milanesi ed Estensi, di Tristano Calco milanese*. Milan, 1976.

Lopez, Guido, et al. *Gli Sforza a Milano*. Milan, 1978.

Lowinsky, Edward, and Bonnie Blackburn, eds. *Josquin des Prez*. New York, 1981.

Lubkin, Gregory. "Christmas at the Court of Milan, 1466–76." *In* C. Smyth and G. C. Garfagnini, eds., *Florence and Milan: Comparisons and Relations*, II. Florence, 1989. 257–270.

———. "Strategic Hospitality: Foreign Dignitaries at the Court of Milan, 1466–76." *International History Review* (May 1986): 174–189.

Lubkin, Gregory, and Sabine Eiche. "The Mausoleum Plan of Galeazzo Maria Sforza." *Mitteilungen des Kunsthistorischen Institutes in Florenz* XXXII, no. 3 (1988): 547–553.

Machiavelli, Niccolo. *Florentine Histories*, trans. Laura Banfield and Harvey Mansfield. Princeton, 1988.

———. *History of Florence and the Affairs of Italy*, trans. M. W. Dunne. New York, 1960 (translation first published 1901).

Magenta, Carlo. *I Visconti e gli Sforza nel castello di Pavia e loro attinenza con la Certosa e la storia cittadina*. 2 vols. Milan, 1883.

Magistretti, Pietro. "Galeazzo Maria Sforza prigione nella Novalesa." *ASL* (1889): 777–807.

Malaguzzi Valeri, Francesco. *La Corte di Lodovico il Moro.* 4 vols. Milan, 1913–1923.

———. *Pittori Lombardi del Quattrocento.* Milan, 1902.

———. "Ricamatori e arazzieri a Milano nel Quattrocento." *ASL* (1903): 34–63.

Mandrot, Bernard de, ed., *Dépêches des ambassadeurs milanais en France sous Louis XI et Francois Sforza.* 4 vols. Vols. 1–3, Paris, 1916–1920; vol. 4, ed. Ch. Samaran, Paris, 1923.

Martines, Lauro. *Lawyers and Statecraft in Renaissance Florence.* Princeton, 1968.

Maspes, Adolfo. "Prammatica pel ricevimento degli Ambasciatori inviati alla corte di Galeazzo Maria Sforza, Duca di Milano (1468—10 dicembre)." *ASL* (1890): 146–151.

Massetto, Gian Paolo. "Le fonti del diritto nella Lombardia del Quattrocento." *In* Centre Européen d'Études Bourguignonnes, *Milan et les États bourguignons: Deux ensembles politique princiers entre Moyen Age et Renaissance,* publication no. 28. Brussels, 1988.

Mattingly, Garrett. *Renaissance Diplomacy.* Baltimore, 1955.

Mazzatinti, Giuseppe. "Alcuni codici latini visconteo-sforzeschi della Biblioteca Nazionale di Parigi." *ASL* (1886): 17–58.

———. "Inventario dei codici della biblioteca visconteo-sforzesco, redatto da Ser Facino da Fabriano nel 1459 e 1469." *Giornale Storica della Letterature Italiana* I (1883): 33–59.

de' Medici, Lorenzo. *Lettere,* ed. N. Rubinstein and R. Fubini. Vols. I and II. Florence, 1977.

Morbio, Carlo. *Codice Visconteo-Sforzesco* (Vol. VI of *Storie dei Municipi Italiani*). Milan, 1846.

Motta, Emilio. "Ancora di Elisabetta Sforza e delle altre figlie di Francesco Sforza." *Giornale Araldico-Genealogico-Diplomatico* XIII (1885): 165–171.

———. "Ancora sulla pretesa donazione di Filippo Maria Visconti a Francesco Sforza." *ASL* (1892): 386–391.

———. "Armaioli milanesi nel periodo visconteo-sforzesco." *ASL* (1914): 187–232.

———. "Un Documento per il Lampugnano uccisore di Galeazzo Maria Sforza." *ASL* (1886): 414–418.

———. "Elisabetta Sforza, Marchesa di Monferrato (1469–1472): Rettifica genealogica." *Giornale Araldico-Genealogico-Diplomatico* XII (1884): 111–116.

———. "Gian Giacomo Trivulzio in Terra Santa." *ASL* (1886): 866–878.

———. "Giovanni da Valladolid alle corti di Mantova e Milano (1458–73)." *ASL* (1890): 938–940.

———. *Musici alla corte degli Sforza.* Geneva, 1977 (reprinted from *ASL* [1887]: 29–64, 278–340, 515–561).

———. "Per la storia del giuoco della palla." *ASL* (1903): 489–490.

———. "Per la storia della coltura di riso in Lombardia." *ASL* (1905): 395.

New Grove Dictionary of Music and Musicians, XVII, ed. S. Sadie. London, 1980.

Noblitt, Thomas. "The Ambrosian Motetti Missales Repertory." *Musica Disciplina* XXII (1968): 77–104.

Novati, Francesco. "Due poesie inedite di Girolamo Olgiati." *ASL* (1886): 140–146.

————. "Di un codice sforzesco di falconeria." *ASL* (1888): 88–95.

Orano, Domenico. *I "suggerimenti di buon vivere" dettati da Francesco Sforza pel figliuolo Galeazzo Maria.* Rome, 1910.

Paganini, Carlo. "Divagazioni sulla documentazione fra Milano e l'Impero per l'investitura ducale." *In* Archivio di Stato, Milan, *Squarci d'Archivio Sforzesco.* Milan, 1981.

Paoli, Cesare, with Luigi Rubini and Pietro Stromboli [Nozze Banchi-Brini], eds. *Della venuta in Firenze di Galeazzo Maria Sforza, Duca di Milano, con la Moglie Bona di Savoia nel 1471: Lettere di due senesi alla Signoria di Siena.* Florence, 1878.

Pasolini, P. D. *Caterina Sforza.* 3 vols. Rome, 1893.

Pellegrini, Marco. "Ascanio Maria Sforza: La creazione di un cardinale di famiglia." *In* G. Chittolini, ed., *Gli Sforza, la chiesa lombarda, la corte di Roma: Strutture e pratiche beneficiarie nel ducato di Milano.* Naples, 1989. 215–290.

Pellerin, Elisabeth. *La bibliothèque des Visconti et des Sforza ducs de Milan au XVe siècle.* Paris, 1955.

Pirovano, Carlo. *La Pittura in Lombardia.* Milan, 1973.

Porro-Lambertenghi, Guilio. *Catalogo dei manoscritti della Biblioteca Trivulziana.* Turin, 1894.

————. "Lettere di Galeazzo Maria Sforza, Duca di Milano." *ASL* (1878): 107–129, 254–274, 637–668; (1879): 250–268.

————. "Documenti sulla corte ducale sforzesca." *ASL* (1879): 109–115.

————. "Preventivo per le spese del Ducato di Milano del 1476." *ASL* (1878): 130–134.

Prosdocimi, Luigi. "Il conferimento dei benefici ecclesiastici nello Stato Milanese." *In* Giorgio Chittolini, ed., *La crisi degli ordinamenti comunali e le origini dello stato del Rinascimento.* Bologna, 1979. 197–214.

————. "Lo stato sforzesco di fronte alla Chiesa milanese e al Papato." *In Gli Sforza a Milano e in Lombardia e i loro rapporti con gli stati italiani ed europei.* Milan, 1982. 147–164.

Raffaelli, Filippo. "La Famiglia Lampugnani di Milano." *Giornale Araldico-Genealogico-Diplomatico* I (1873–74): 229–235.

I Registri dell'Ufficio degli Statuti di Milano (Vol. III of *Regesti & Inventari dell'Archivio di Stato, Milano*). Index ed. Francesco Forte. Milan, 1950.

Rinuccini, Filippo. *Ricordi storici di Filippo di Cino Rinuccini . . . colla continuazione di Alamanno e Neri suoi figli.* Florence, 1840.

Robin, Diana. *Filelfo in Milan.* Princeton, 1991.

De'Rosmini, Carlo. *Dell'Istoria intorno alle militari imprese e alla vita di Gian-Jacopo Trivulzio detto il Magno.* Milan, 1815.

————. *Dell'Istoria di Milano.* 4 vols. Milan, 1820.

Santoro, Caterina. "Un codice di Bona di Savoia." *ASL* (1954–55): 267–291.

————. *Registri delle Lettere Ducale.* 1961.

————. *I Registri dell'Ufficio di provvisione di Milano.* Milan, 1929–1932.

————. "Un registro di doti sforzeschi." *ASL* (1953): 133–185.

————. *Gli Offici del Comune di Milano e del Dominio Visconteo-Sforzesco (1216–1515).* Vol. 7 of *Archivio della Fondazione Italiana per la Storia Amministrativa.* Milan, 1958.

————. *Gli Sforza*. Milan, 1968.

————. *Gli Uffici del Dominio Sforzesco (1450–1500)*. Milan, 1948.

Schofield, Richard. "Ludovico il Moro and Vigevano." *Arte Lombarda* 78 (1987): 41–58.

Schofield, Richard, with Janice Shell and Grazioso Sironi. *Giovanni Antonio Amedeo: I Documenti*. Milan, 1989.

Sestan, Ernesto, ed. *Carteggi diplomatici fra Milano sforzesca e la Borgogna*. 2 vols. Rome, 1987.

Signorini, Rodolfo. "Cristiano I in Italia" *Il Veltro* XXV (1981): 23–57.

Simonetta, Cicco. *I diari di Cicco Simonetta*, ed. A. Natale (*Acta Italica, 1*). Milan, 1962 (first published in *ASL* [1949]: 80–114; [1950]: 157–180; [1951–52]: 154–187; [1954–55]: 292–318; [1956]: 58–125).

Simonetta, Giovanni. *Rerum Gestarum Francesci Sphortiae mediolanensis ducis libri XXXI*. Milan, 1486 (modern edition in *RIS²*, ed. G. Soranzo, Vol. XXI, pt. 2).

Simonsohn, Shlomo. *The Jews in the Duchy of Milan*. Vol. 1. Jerusalem, 1982.

Sitoni di Scozia, Giovanni. *Theatrum Genealogicum Illustrium, Nobilium et Civicum Inclyte Urbis Mediolani*. MS in Archivio di Stato, Milan. 1705.

Spencer, John. "Il progetto per il cavallo di bronzo per Francesco Sforza." *Arte Lombarda* (1973): 23–35.

Terni de Gregorij, Winifred. *Bianca Maria Visconti, Duchessa di Milano*. Bergamo, 1940.

Fondazione Treccani degli Alfieri per la Storia di Milano. *Storia di Milano*. 16 vols. Milan, 1953–1962.

Valagussa, Giorgio. "De originis et causis ceremoniarum quae celebrantur in Natalitiis." MS in Biblioteca Ambrosiana, Milan.

Villa i Tatti. *Renaissance Studies in Honor of Craig Hugh Smyth*, ed. A. Morrogh, F. S. Gioffredi, P. Morselli, and E. Borsook. 2 vols. Florence, 1985.

————. *Florence and Milan: Comparisons and Relations*, ed. C. H. Smyth and G. C. Garfagnini. 2 vols. Florence, 1989.

Violini, Cesare. *Galeazzo Maria Sforza, quinto duca di Milano*. Turin, 1943.

Visconti, Alessandro. *Storia di Milano*. 2d ed. Milan, 1967.

Visconti, Carlo Ermes. "Ordine dell'esercito ducale sforzesco nel 1472–1474." *ASL* (1876): 448–514.

Walsh, Richard. "Charles the Bold of Burgundy and Italy." D. Phil. dissertation, University of Hull, 1977.

Ward, Lynn Halpern. "The *Motetti Missales* Repertory Reconsidered." *Journal of American Musicological Society* (Fall 1986): 491–524.

Welch, Evelyn Samuels. "Galeazzo Maria Sforza and the Castello di Pavia, 1469." *Art Bulletin* 71, no. 3 (Sep. 1989): 352–374.

————. "The Image of a Fifteenth-Century Court: Secular Frescoes for the Castello di Porta Giovia, Milan." *Journal of the Warburg and Courtauld Institutes* 53 (1990): 163–184.

————. "The Process of Sforza Patronage." *Renaissance Studies* III, no. 4 (1989): 370–385.

————. "Secular Fresco Painting at the Court of Galeazzo Maria Sforza." D. Phil. dissertation, Warburg Institute, London, 1987.

Wittgens, Fernanda. *Vincenzo Foppa*. Milan, 1949.

Woods-Marsden, Joanna. "Pictorial Legitimation of Territorial Gains in Emilia: The Iconography of the *Camera Peregrina Aurea* in the Castle of Torchiara." *In Renaissance Studies in Honor of Craig Hugh Smyth,* ed. A. Morrogh, F. S. Gioffredi, P. Morselli, and E. Borsook. Florence, 1985. II: 553–568.

Comparative and Ancillary Material

Adams, George Burton. *Court and Council in Anglo-Norman England.* London, 1965 (first published 1926).

Argegni, Corrado, ed. *Condottieri, Capitani, e Tribuni* (Series XIX of *Enciclopedia Biografica & Bibliografica Italiana*). 3 Vols. Milan, 1936–1937.

Atlas, Allan. *Music at the Aragonese Court of Naples.* Cambridge (U.K.), 1985.

Barber, Richard. *The Knight and Chivalry.* New York, 1974.

Beattie, John. *Bunyoro: An African Kingdom.* New York, 1960.

Bertelli, Sergio, et al. *Le corti italiani del rinascimento.* Milan, 1985.

———. *Italian Renaissance Courts,* trans. M. Fitton and G. Culverwell. London, 1986.

Bertelli, Sergio, and Giuliano Crifò. *Rituale, Cerimoniale, Etichetta.* Milan, 1985.

Blackley, F. D., and G. Hermansen, eds. *The Household Book of Queen Isabella of England.* Edmonton, 1971.

Bossy, John. "Blood and Baptism: Kinship, Community and Christianity in Western Europe from the Fourteenth to the Seventeenth Centuries." *In* Derek Baker, ed., *Sanctity and Secularity: The Church and the World. Studies in Church History,* Vol. X. Oxford, 1973.

Braudel, Fernand. *Capitalism and Material Life, 1400–1800.* New York, 1975.

Burckhardt, Jakob. *Civilization of the Renaissance in Italy,* trans. S. G. C. Middlemore. 2. vols. New York, 1958.

Cappelli, Adriano. *Cronologia, cronografia, e calendario perpetuo.* 4th ed. Milan, 1978.

Carmichael, Ann. *Plague and the Poor in Renaissance Florence.* Cambridge (U.K.), 1986.

Cartellieri, Otto. *The Court of Burgundy.* London and New York, 1929.

Carter, Albert T. *A History of the English Courts.* 6th ed. London, 1935.

Castiglione, Baldassare. *Il Libro del Cortegiano,* introd. A. Quondam. Milan, 1982.

———. *Il Libro del Cortegiano* (facsimile of original 1528 printing). Rome, 1986.

———. *The Book of the Courtier,* trans. C. Singleton. New York, 1959.

Coffin, Tristram P. *The Book of Christmas Folklore.* New York, 1973.

Colonna, Egidio. [Giles of Rome]. *De Regimine Principum Libri III.* Aalen, 1967 (reprint of ed. G. Samaritani, Rome, 1607).

Conversini da Ravenna, Giovanni. *Two Court Treatises,* ed. and trans. B. G. Kohl and J. Day. Munich, 1987.

Dawson, William F. *Christmas: Its Origins and Associations.* London, 1902 (reprinted Detroit, 1968).

Dean, Trevor. *Land and Power in Late Medieval Ferrara, 1350–1450.* Cambridge (U.K.), 1988.

———. "Notes on the Ferrarese Court in the Later Middle Ages." *Renaissance Studies* III, no. 4 (1989): 357–369.

De la Marche, Olivier. *L'Estat particulier de la maison du duc Charles le Hardy*. In Claude Petitot, ed., *Collection complète des mémoires relatifs à l'histoire de France*. X: 479–556.

Dickens, A. G. *The Courts of Europe*. New York, 1977.

Dizionario Biografico degli Italiani. Vols. 1–39. Rome, 1960–[1991].

Eiche, Sabine. "La Corte di Pesaro dalle case malatestiane alla residenza roveresca," trans. L. Corti. In Maria Rosaria Vallazzi, ed., *La Corte di Pesaro: Storia di una residenze signorile*. Pesaro, 1986. 13–56.

———. "Towards a Study of the 'Famiglia' of the Sforza court at Pesaro." *Renaissance and Reformation* IX (1985): 79–103.

———. "The Villa Imperiale of Alessandro Sforza at Pesaro." *Mitteilungen des Kunsthistorischen Institutes in Florenz* XXIX, nos. 2/3 (1985): 229–274.

Elias, Norbert. *Die Höfische Gesellschaft*. Neuwied, 1969.

———. *The Court Society*, trans. E. Jephcott. New York, 1984.

Ermini, Giuseppe, ed. *Ordini et offitij alla corte del serenissimo signor duca d'Urbino*. Urbino, 1932.

Eubel, Conrad. *Hierarchia Catholica Medii Evi*. Vol. II. Monasterium, 1913.

Forde, C. D., and P. M. Kaberry, eds. *West African Kingdoms in the Nineteenth Century*. Oxford, 1967.

Frazer, James. *The Golden Bough*. Vol. X. New York, 1955.

Galvani, Luigi. *Galleria Araldica*. No publication data.

Geertz, Clifford. "Centers, Kings, and Charisma." *In Culture and Its Creators: Essays Presented to Edward Shils,* ed. Joseph Ben-David and T. C. Clark. Chicago, 1977. 150–171.

———. *Negara: The Theatre State in South Bali*. Princeton, 1980.

Girouard, Mark. *Life in the English Country House*. New Haven, 1978.

Guillemain, Bernard. *La cour pontificale d'Avignon*. Paris, 1966.

Gundersheimer, Werner. *Ferrara: The Style of a Renaissance Despotism*. Princeton, 1973.

Hatton, Ragnhild. *Louis XIV and His World*. London and New York, 1972.

Kantorowicz, Ernst. *The King's Two Bodies*. Princeton, 1957.

———. "Mysteries of State." *In Selected Studies*. Locust Valley, 1965. 381–398.

Keen, Maurice. *Chivalry*. New Haven, 1984.

Von Kruedener, Jürgen. *Die Rolle des Hofes im Absolutismus*. Stuttgart, 1973.

Larner, John. "Europe of the Courts." *Journal of Modern History* 55 (1983): 669–672.

———. *The Lords of Romagna*. London and New York, 1965.

Leroy Ladurie, Emmanuel. "Les cabales de la cour de France sous Louis XIV, d'apres les *Mémoires* de Saint-Simon." *Annuaire de la Collège de France* (1976): 617–635.

Lewis, Peter. *Later Medieval France*. London, 1968.

Lockwood, Lewis. *Music in Renaissance Ferrara, 1400–1505*. Cambridge, 1984.

Luzio, Alessandro, and Rodolfo Renier. "Buffoni, nani, e schiavi dei Gonzaga ai tempi di Isabella d'Este." *Nuova Antologia* XXXIV (1891): 618–650; XXXV (1891): 112–146.

Lytle, Guy, and Stephen Orgel. *Patronage in the Renaissance*. Princeton, 1981.

Map, Walter. *De Nugis Curialium*, ed. M. R. James. Oxford, 1914.

———. *De Nugis Curialium,* ed. M. R. James, rev. C. N. L. Brooke and R. A. B. Mynors. Oxford, 1983.

———. *Courtiers' Trifles,* trans. Frederick Tupper. New York, 1923.

Mallett, Michael. *Mercenaries and Their Masters.* London, 1974.

Martines, Lauro. *Power and Imagination.* New York, 1979.

Mathew, Gervase. *The Court of Richard II.* London, 1968.

Mintz, Sidney, and Eric Wolf. "An Analysis of Ritual Co-Parenthood (Compadrazgo)." *Southwestern Journal of Anthropology* VI (Winter 1950): 341–368.

Die Musik in Geschichte und Gegenwart, ed. F. Blume. Vol. XII. Basel, 1965.

Myers, Alec, ed. *The Household Book of Edward IV and the Ordinances of 1478.* Manchester, 1959.

Nadel, S. F. *A Black Byzantium: The Kingdom of Nupe in Nigeria.* Oxford, 1961 (first published 1942).

New Grove Dictionary of Music and Musicians, ed. S. Sadie. Vol. XVII. London, 1980.

Orestano, Francesco, ed. *Eroine, Ispiratrici e Donne di Eccezione* (Series VII of *Enciclopedia Biografica & Bibliografica Italiana*). Milan, 1940.

Papagno, Giovanni, and Amedeo Quondam. *La corte e lo spazio: Ferrara estense.* Rome, 1982.

Parravicini, Werner. "Structures et fonctionnement de la cour de Bourgogne." *In* Centre Européen d'Études Bourguignonnes, *Milan et les États bourguignons: Deux ensemblers princiers entre Moyen Age et Renaissance,* publication no. 28. 1988.

Parsons, John Carmi. *The Court and Household of Eleanor of Castile.* Toronto, 1977.

Pillinini, Giovanni. *Il sistema degli stati italiani.* Venice, 1970.

Piponnier, Francoise. *Costume et vie sociale: La cour d'Anjou, XIVe–Xve siècle.* Paris, 1970.

Polichetti, M. L. *Il Palazzo di Federigo da Montefeltro.* Urbino, 1985.

Pontieri, Ernesto. *L'età dell'equilibrio politico in Italia.* Naples, 1962.

Prosperi, Adriano, ed. *La corte e "Il Cortegiano"* II (*Un modello europeo*). Rome, 1979.

Ryder, Alan. *The Kingdom of Naples under Alfonso the Magnanimous.* Oxford, 1976.

Salisbury, John of. *Policraticus: The Statesman's Book,* ed. and abridged M. F. Markland. New York, 1979.

———. *The Statesman's Book,* ed., trans., and abridged J. Dickinson. New York, 1927.

———. *Frivolities of Courtiers and Footprints of Philosophers,* ed., trans., and abridged J. F. Pike. Minneapolis and London, 1938.

Scattergood, V. J., and J. W. Sherborne. *English Court Culture in the Later Middle Ages.* London, 1983.

Serassi, PierAntonio. *Lettere del Conte Baldessar Castiglione.* Vol. I. Padua, 1769.

Swain, Barbara. *Fools and Folly in the Middle Ages and Renaissance.* New York, 1932.

Swain, Elisabeth. "My Excellent and Most Singular Lord: Marriage in a Noble Family of Fifteenth-Century Italy." *Journal of Medieval and Renaissance Studies* 16, no. 2 (1986): 171–195.

Thorndike, Lynn. *A History of Magic and Experimental Science.* Vol. IV. New York, 1934.

Trexler, Richard. *Public Life in Renaissance Florence.* New York, 1980.

Tucoo-Chala, Pierre. *Gaston Fébus et la comté de Foix, 1343–92,* Bordeaux, 1953.

Vaughan, Richard. *Charles the Bold.* London, 1973.

Weiser, Francis X. *Handbook of Christian Customs.* New York, 1958.

Woods-Marsden, Joanna. *The Gonzaga of Mantua and Pisanello's Arthurian Frescoes.* Princeton, 1988.

Index

Abbeys, 52, 64, 81, 241, 350 n. 199. *See also* Chiaravalle Abbey; convents; monasteries; Morimondo Abbey; religious houses

Abbiategrasso [Abbiate], 64, 77, 93, 185, 208, 211, 215, 228, 229, 260–264 passim; castle, 54, 78, 79, 94

Abbots, 162, 224, 241, 265, 361 n. 132. *See also* abbeys; convents; monasteries; monks; prelates

Acciaiuoli, Donato (Florentine ambassador), 339 n. 83

Adda River, 93, 243

Administration, ducal, 5, 12, 26, 27, 34, 36, 43, 88, 99, 113, 121, 122, 146, 159, 162, 169, 170, 174, 194, 217, 222, 224, 242, 324 n. 53, 340 n. 98, 351 n. 127; central, 19–22, 96, 140–144, 148, 152, 215, 225 (*see also* administrators; Council of Justice; councils of state; Privy Chancery; Privy Council); military, 19–20, 144, 145–147, 224 (*see also* Cenni, Orfeo; condottieri; military captains); peripheral, 19, 22, 144–145, 175 (*see also* administrators; *commissari*; *referendari*)

Administrators or bureaucrats, 69, 76, 83, 93, 96, 104, 140, 164, 174, 220, 222, 223, 349 n. 106. *See also* Annone; Besazia; Castel San Pietro; Castiglione; Corio; councillors; fiscal officials; Gallerani; Guidoboni; Lampugnani; *magistrati della corte*; Malletta; Marliani; masters of revenues; de' Nigri; Olgiati; Onate; Pagnani; Porro; Rho; Visconti

Adorno, Prospero (councillor and Genoese noble), 154

Agricola, Alexander (singer), 103, 104, 189, 313 n. 97, 344 nn. 15 and 17

Agriculture, 5, 111

Aigues Mortes, 49, 50, 52

Albanians (*Albanesi*), 107, 170, 270, 274

Alberti, Leon Battista, 106

Alessandria, 145; podestà of, 144

Alessandria and Tortona (district), 5, 101

Alfieri, Giacomo (secretary), 106, 108, 130, 143, 148, 204, 226

Alfonso I ("the Magnanimous"; king of Naples, 1442–1458), 23, 153

Aliprandi: Bonifacio (duchess's courtier), 150; Pietrina (Ermes Sforza's governess), 229, 230

Allowances (*provisioni*), 149. *See also* salaries

Alms, 69, 97, 116, 300 n. 21, 318 n. 179; almoners, 116

Alps, ix, 1, 5, 6, 7, 53, 119, 187, 238

Altars, 107, 116, 119, 183, 217

Amalfi, duchess of, 152

Ambassadors or envoys from Milan to: Bologna, 125, 166, 169, 224; Burgundy, 169, 238, 310 n. 56, 348 n. 89, 360 n. 121; Ferrara, 188; Florence, 169; France, 57, 95, 149, 168, 169, 319 n. 191, 332 n. 166, 339 n. 77; Holy Roman Emperor, 74, 186, 195; Montferrat, 319 n. 191; Naples, 169, 202, 298 n. 197; Rome, 155, 169, 226; Savoy, 152, 169, 319 n. 191, 339 n. 77; Venice,

day courts, x, 66, 69, 73, 154, 155, 172, 217, 239, 240, 254, 271–273, 299 nn. 1 and 10, 300 n. 19, 303 n. 80, 351 n. 129; as officers of Sforza court, 139, 140, 141, 168, 181, 194; participation at court on other occasions, 43, 68, 84, 85, 96, 128, 182, 183, 184, 186, 208, 285 n. 1, 306 n. 111, 330 n. 137, 332 n. 161, 341 n. 102. *See also specific persons*

Fiefs or feudal estates, 6, 7, 16, 17, 72, 143, 162, 192, 221, 232, 243; granted by Duke Galeazzo, 40, 42, 82, 124, 133, 135, 156, 159, 161, 167, 194, 291 n. 79, 326 n. 81

Filelfo, Francesco (humanist), ix, 84, 91, 111, 122, 163, 221, 230

Fioramonte, *see* Graziani (da Cotignola), Fioramonte

Fiscal officials, 20, 43, 50, 76, 132, 174, 196. See also *collaterali*; *magistrati della corte*; masters of revenues; *referendari*; *sindaci fiscali*; *vicari generali*

Florence (city), xv, 5, 22, 23, 32, 51, 106, 120, 144, 149, 169, 193, 209, 302 n. 52, 312 n. 79; Duke Galeazzo's visits to, 26, 39, 90, 98–102, 103, 105, 107, 121, 137, 191, 205, 222, 231, 260, 261, 274, 285 n. 67, 305 n. 98; republic of, 16, 38, 39, 45, 84, 87, 169, 170, 178, 189, 195, 196, 244, 246, 293 n. 116, 306 n. 113, 338 n. 67, 346 n. 53. *See also* de' Medici

Fodder, 99, 310 n. 52

Fogliani (family), 23, 157, 335 n. 19; Corrado (condottiere; half-brother of Francesco Sforza), 52, 152, 157; Gabriella Gonzaga (Corrado's widow), 157–158, 202

Fontaneto, 260, 261, 263, 359 n. 102

Food or foodstuffs, 5, 17, 35, 36, 90, 99, 121, 124, 127, 128, 154 242, 250, 288 n. 36; bread, 36, 125, 154, 219, 288 n. 36; cheese, 219, 288 n. 36; fruit, 36; lard, 36; pork, 288 n. 36; poultry or game birds, 36, 219; sugar, 120, 219, 288 n. 36; sweets, 36, 219; veal, 36, 288 n. 36

Footmen (*staffieri*), 29–30, 83, 138, 215, 217, 223, 231, 235, 276, 286 n. 12, 287 n. 19; Cristoforo da Busti, 276; Gallo Boza ("Gallo Moro"), 270, 276; Giovanni Grande, 276, 341 n. 102. *See also* Pietrasanta, Francesco

Foot-soldiers, *see* soldiers

Foppa, Vincenzo (painter), 109

Forlì, 141, 147, 245, 319 n. 191, 335 n. 11; lord of, *see* Ordelaffi, Pino

Fossati, Anna Scaccabarozzi (widow of Francesco), 226

France, 1, 5, 26, 48, 51, 57, 65, 79, 91, 98, 119, 120, 137, 142, 145, 168, 169, 176, 239, 243, 253, 281 n. 1, 315 n. 117, 333

n. 177, 359 n. 108; court of, x, 46, 47, 49, 95, 149, 310 n. 54; kingdom of, xi, 14, 23, 27, 56, 177, 210–211, 224, 238, 244, 246, 284 n. 47, 293 n. 116, 332 n. 166, 339 n. 77; king of, 71, 103, 187, 244, 247 (*see also* Louis XI; Louis XII); marshall of, 88, 118, 194, 243; royal family of, xiii, 14, 29, 188

Franciscans, 11, 116, 196. *See also* friars

Frascarolo, 192

Frederick I Barbarossa (Holy Roman Emperor, 1152–1190), 12, 74

Frederick III (Holy Roman Emperor, 1452–1493), 4, 23, 65, 74, 177, 186, 187, 195, 210, 213, 238, 350 n. 120

Frescoes, 7, 83, 106, 107, 109, 195, 202, 314 nn. 108 and 114, 315 n. 117. *See also* Camera degli Sposi, Mantua

Fresco programs, designed by or for Duke Galeazzo, 106, 193; for Pavia Castle, 49, 81, 83–84, 110, 286 n. 17, 309 n. 38, 329 n. 132; for Porta Giovia Castle, 106–107, 110, 117, 134, 137, 146, 157, 205, 216–217, 229, 318 n. 174, 325 n. 70, 348 n. 80; religious or sacred, 107, 109

Friars, 116, 117, 151, 196, 234, 318 n. 179. *See also* Dominicans; Franciscans

Funerals, 65, 139, 151–152, 155, 232–234, 257, 319 n. 188, 358 n. 96

Fuori di camera, 99, 127, 133, 137, 147, 176

Fuppo, Antonio (papal nephew), 186

Gabelle (salt tax), *see* taxes

Gadio (da Cremona), Bartolomeo (*commissario* of works), 65, 90, 108, 144, 203, 226, 287 n. 30, 315 n. 128

Galesio, Giorgino di (condottiere), 149, 272

Gallarate, 263

Gallarate, da: Cristoforo (Bianca Sforza's governor), 342 n. 118; Maria (duchess's courtier), 140; Pietro (councillor), 45, 234, 271, 274, 349 n. 103

Gallerani: Cecilia (daughter of Fazio; mistress of Ludovico il Moro), 355 n. 56; Fazio (administrator), 50, 132, 225, 332 n. 167

Galliate, 93, 94, 127, 136, 195, 221, 227, 236, 237, 260, 262, 263, 264; county of, 136, 161, 230, 326 n. 86; people of, 136

Galuppi, 37, 138, 203, 215, 218, 268, 328 n. 106

Gambling, 32, 92, 135, 137, 230

Gambolò, 93, 193, 223, 262, 263, 264, 356 n. 66

Garlasco, 262, 309 n. 47

Garrisons, *see* soldiers

Gate-keepers, 189

Genoa, 36, 43, 49–52 passim, 55, 64, 72, 117,

Designer:	U.C. Press Staff
Compositor:	Prestige Typography
Text:	10/12 Times Roman
Display:	Times Roman
Printer:	Thomson-Shore, Inc.
Binder:	Thomson-Shore, Inc.